# Qualitative Economics

Woodrow W. Clark II • Michael Fast

# Qualitative Economics

The Science of Economics

Woodrow W. Clark II, MA₃, PhD
Managing Director and Qualitative
Economist
Clark Strategic Partners
Beverly Hills, CA, USA

Michael Fast, PhD
Member Research Network ORCA
Aalborg University
Aalborg, Denmark

ISBN 978-3-030-05936-1     ISBN 978-3-030-05937-8   (eBook)
https://doi.org/10.1007/978-3-030-05937-8

© Springer Nature Switzerland AG 2019
This work is subject to copyright. All rights are reserved by the Publisher, whether the whole or part of
the material is concerned, specifically the rights of translation, reprinting, reuse of illustrations, recitation,
broadcasting, reproduction on microfilms or in any other physical way, and transmission or information
storage and retrieval, electronic adaptation, computer software, or by similar or dissimilar methodology
now known or hereafter developed.
The use of general descriptive names, registered names, trademarks, service marks, etc. in this publication
does not imply, even in the absence of a specific statement, that such names are exempt from the relevant
protective laws and regulations and therefore free for general use.
The publisher, the authors, and the editors are safe to assume that the advice and information in this book
are believed to be true and accurate at the date of publication. Neither the publisher nor the authors or the
editors give a warranty, express or implied, with respect to the material contained herein or for any errors
or omissions that may have been made. The publisher remains neutral with regard to jurisdictional claims
in published maps and institutional affiliations.

This Springer imprint is published by the registered company Springer Nature Switzerland AG
The registered company address is: Gewerbestrasse 11, 6330 Cham, Switzerland

"In this thoughtful, innovative second edition, Clark and Fast build on human interactionist approaches with qualitative theory from linguistics, law, and circular economics to advance economics into a science."

Deryck J. van Rensburg, DBA, Dean, *Pepperdine Graziadio Business School (PGBS)*

"Economics has been a religion rather than a science perceived by the neoclassical economics paradigm because it not only describes how the world works but also prescribes how it ought to work. This book strongly intends to 'reconnect' economics with everyday life and business activities. The book makes a great contribution in turning economics into a discipline of science that can be understood qualitatively rather than just quantitatively based on solely by narrow assumption and determination related to rationality, maximization, and preference. Science is both quantitative and qualitative."

Li Xing, PhD, Professor and Director, *Research Center on Development and International Relations*, Editor in Chief, *Journal of China and International Relations, Aalborg University*

# Preface

Economics must become a *science*.

That statement was the key goal of our first book on *Qualitative Economics* (QE) in 2008. This second edition of *QE* provides updated information with cases and additional evidence on how to make "the field of economics" into a science. In July 2009, *The Economist* cover had a picture of the *Bible* melting, titled "Modern Economic Theory Failing," because 9 months earlier, the global recession hit early October 2008. Economics is not a *science* because it failed to predict the global economic collapse of Wall Street in the USA and around the world.

Clark and Fast had been working on the first *QE* book for almost 25 years. If the book had come out earlier than the spring of 2008, perhaps, the economic collapse could have been predicted, assuming that economics needs to be a science. The *QE* idea is to develop a scientific perspective that could have prevented or at least prepared everyone for the economic challenges that the world faced then in the fall of 2008. *QE* was then and is now even more important as a book about how economics needs to become a science through knowledge about and understanding of the complexity, contradictions, and social and personal development in and of society. Economics is all about the understanding of how to connect organizations and people through living with the dynamics of science which combines quantitative numbers, statistics, formals, etc. with their definitions, meanings, hypotheses, actions, and behaviors that must be tested and retested to be understood.

Both authors have had experiences, in the USA and Europe, that social science and in particular economics are "locked" in a philosophical western world tradition that has problems understanding the reality of people, their interactions, and the dynamics of social reality. There are other ways to see and understand economic living and behavior and especially its impact on human daily life at home, work, and play.

Economics needs to be able to understand and handle the essence of data, meaning of numbers, and validation of facts, more so for human beings to be engaged in everyday life. The activities, interpretations, and facts are needed to create the meaning for humans that create an everyday life at home, work, play, sports, exercise and travel plus holidays, vacation and more.

This is why we name our ideas of such a perspective *qualitative economics*, as it focuses upon the economic actions of people, groups, and their networks in everyday life and how they are trying to make sense of the present and construct the future. In order to understand everyday interactions through *QE*, we have written the first and now second *QE* book as we have been getting good advice, research, and discussions about the history of science and its different ideas, actions, and results through the last decade. We think that the historical consciousness is important and that scholars, students, and everyone (since we *all* involved) in economics need to have that consciousness in relation to understand the thinking of economics and of people together.

As the twenty-first century moves into a new global economic era, there is a need to examine the ontological roots of economics as people, organizations, environment, and business in order to understand the local and global economies of today and tomorrow as well as to have the discussion of knowledge and how knowledge can be created. The epistemological discussion has never been more important as the world moves on with contradictions, debates, fake news, and technological developments and, at the same time, the many issues of global warming, environmental problems, and the whole matters of sustainability become more and more critical.

Due to our personal interactions with many people, experts and academics, we have had countless encounters with people and groups that reflect the need for *QE*. This includes our years (now decades) of academic research, teaching, and publishing. There are many cases that each of us has had where *QE* is needed then and now. Consider just a few:

The following is the case of Clark while doing the first book on *QE* with the economic journal from the Western Economic Association International (WEAI) titled the *Special Issue of Contemporary Economic Policy* (CEP): Clark was a member of the WEAI due to his professional and personal relationship with the President of the WEAI (early part of the first decade of the twenty-first century) who was also a professor of Economics at the UCLA, Michael Intriligator (who passed away on June 23, 2014). Clark and Intriligator had been over 4 years working together in the WEAI. Their one goal was to get some papers on *QE* published in a special issue of *CEP*. The WEAI journals are well-known for examining contemporary economic issues and exploring new approaches to them. Clark and Intriligator worked hard on the *CEP Special Issue* with 11 peer-reviewed articles, which were also reviewed by the then *CEP* editor at the time. They were proud of the results. However, now, the *Special Issue* articles were not published in the *CEP* journal and instead were in the book titled *The Next Economics: Global Cases in Energy, Environment, and Climate Change* (Springer Press, 2014). The reason was that the book came out first; and the new journal editor did not have Intriligator's permission slip signed. It was signed by Intriligator who passed away at that time, so the *CEP* did not take action. Meanwhile, Springer Press did, and the book version gained a lot of very positive attention in economics, other social "sciences," and science communities.

# Preface

Since then, Clark had done several books on climate change solutions from both technology and economic perspectives, such as *Sustainable Communities* (Springer Press, 2009) and *Sustainable Communities Design Handbook: Green Engineering, Architecture, and Technology* (Elsevier Press, 2010), with cases about sustainable communities. In the next year, Clark completed a new book on *Global Sustainable Communities Handbook: Green Design Technologies and Economics* (Elsevier Press, 2013) with cases of sustainable communities and how they were designed, developed, and planned with resources, finances, and educated workers. Then in the fall of 2018, Clark published *Climate Preservation in Urban Communities Case Studies* (Elsevier Press, October 2018).

A second case was when Clark was appointed as one of the five energy advisors to Governor Gray Davis of California in 2000, when there was a need to change economics away from the "market forces" that were created in prior state government administrations with deregulation of the energy sector. Governor Davis took office (1999) and was immediately confronted with an energy crisis caused by private companies taking over the public energy sectors in California due to the prior two governors before him. So by early 2000, the theory was that the new energy companies would be competitive and therefore would lower prices for energy to consumers. Just the opposite happened. And without very much oversight in the laws for deregulation, the problem had to be taken on by Governor Davis after he was elected in 1999.

By Spring 2000, California had energy crisis with rolling blackouts and brownouts even though there was plenty of energy supply. Clark had warned Governor Davis' senior staff that this would happen 6 months or more before the brownouts started in San Diego. California deregulation was copied in other states and nations which called it "liberalization or privatization." The national utility-controlled energy systems converted from being public-controlled companies to private businesses. The market forces economic model would create competition and hence reduced energy costs.

The California energy crisis came without warning as the new private energy companies controlled and manipulated prices and services through their control of energy. The economic model failed in California and other nations as well. There was something wrong. Private companies manipulated the "energy market" and caused severe problems throughout the state. The California energy crisis was just the beginning because supply and demand did not work when the State was immersed into brownouts and blackouts that threatened business and individual health needing power for commerce and medical care.

The economists' explanation, issued at one point in a Public Memo to Governor Davis (Spring 2001), argued that "market forces" would prevail and get the State energy needs back on course. In reality, those market forces were "gaming the energy sectors" with illegal and deceptive accounting. These companies were responsible for conducting fraudulent actions. The firms (Enron and many others) and their accounting firms "verified" the economic energy data as valid, when it was not. Clark got the Governor's Office legal team to investigate and took those people and their companies to court, where companies went "bankrupt" and individuals were convicted and sent to jail (Clark 2003; Clark and Demirag 2002, 2006b).

Finally, there needs to be cross-disciplinary areas in order for a fresh look to be given to economics. What we did in the first edition of *QE* book and again now in the second edition is look at the science of linguistics that Noam Chomsky invented at MIT in the 1960–1970s and even today to understand the meaning of statistics and numbers by looking them as surface structures which are defined by deep structures. Linguists and other scientific areas show how they interacted as a starter. Based on past economic models, these areas have been lost or not fitted into modern economic theory. Clearly, economics needs research and to probe these areas, as they are major determinants in the macroeconomics and microeconomics of today and the future. The challenge is to explore and look deeply into economics, in order to turn "the field" into a science. Linguistics is a major key science that works.

## Acknowledgments

As we have been working so many years, there are a lot of people that we are grateful to – most of all our families:

Clark's wife, Andrea Kune-Clark, and son, Paxton, who have both been by his side for this book to be done and out soon and his two older children who have been very supportive for his work too over the last three decades.

Fast's wife, Lisbeth, and children, Pelle and Cecilia, who have always being there and always ready for discussions and good times.

We thank all the students that we have met through all those years, and in many ways, the book is for them, the future generations, and their development of a consciousness and a critical mind.

We thank our many colleges at Aalborg University and Pepperdine University with whom we have had classes and lectures as well as held discussions.

We also thank The Fulbright Foundation; without their support in the mid-1990s, we probably would have never met each other, and the book never been written.

A great thanks to Springer Press for believing in the book and the openness to our ideas.

Beverly Hills, CA, USA
Aalborg, Denmark

Woodrow W. Clark II
Michael Fast

# References

Clark WW II. Point and counter-point: de-regulation in America. Util Policy. 2003. Elsevier.

Clark WW II. Sustainable communities. New York: Springer Press; 2009.

Clark WW II. Sustainable communities design handbook. New York: Elsevier Press; 2010.

Clark WW II. Global sustainable communities design handbook. New York: Elsevier Press; 2013.

Clark WW II, Demirag I. Enron: the failure of corporate governance. J Corp Citizsh. 2002;8:105–22.

Clark WW II. US financial regulatory change: the case of the California energy crisis. Special issue, J Bank Regul. 2006b;7(1/2):75–93.

Clark WW II, Fast M. Qualitative economics: toward a science of economics. London: Coxmoor Press; 2008.

Clark WW II, Intriligator M. Global cases in energy, environment, and climate change: some challenges for the field of economics. Special issue of Contemporary Economic Policy (CEP), Western Association of Economics International. Fullerton: Blackwell Publications; 2012.

# Contents

**1 Overview of Qualitative Economics (QE)** . . . . . . . . . . . . . . . . . . . . . 1
Introduction . . . . . . . . . . . . . . . . . . . . . . . . . . . . . . . . . . . . . . . . . . . 1
The Aim of the Book . . . . . . . . . . . . . . . . . . . . . . . . . . . . . . . . . . . . . 4
The Paradigm Shift: Economics Needs to Be a Science . . . . . . . . . . . . 5
The Book Contents . . . . . . . . . . . . . . . . . . . . . . . . . . . . . . . . . . . . . . 8
Subjectivism Paradigm: Lifeworld Perspective
as Symbolic Interactionism . . . . . . . . . . . . . . . . . . . . . . . . . . . . . . 9
Part I: Philosophy of Science . . . . . . . . . . . . . . . . . . . . . . . . . . . . . 9
Part II: Qualitative Economics – Towards a Science of Economics . . 10

**Part I   Philosophy of Science and the Lifeworld Traditions**

**2 The Case for Rethinking the Foundation of Business Economics** . . . 15
The Business Economic Debate . . . . . . . . . . . . . . . . . . . . . . . . . . . . . 15
The Paradigm Debate . . . . . . . . . . . . . . . . . . . . . . . . . . . . . . . . . . . . 20
Qualitative and Interactionism Research Economics to Be a Science . . . 22
Context of Business Economics and Culture . . . . . . . . . . . . . . . . . . . . 23
Sociological Phenomenology and Organizations . . . . . . . . . . . . . . . . . 25
Symbolic Interactionism . . . . . . . . . . . . . . . . . . . . . . . . . . . . . . . . . . 26

**3 Understanding the Organization of Science** . . . . . . . . . . . . . . . . . . . 29
Science and Philosophy of Science . . . . . . . . . . . . . . . . . . . . . . . . . . . 29
The Development of Science . . . . . . . . . . . . . . . . . . . . . . . . . . . . . . . 30
(Natural) Science . . . . . . . . . . . . . . . . . . . . . . . . . . . . . . . . . . . . . 32
Social Science and Objectivism: Positivism and Rationalism . . . . . . 33
Positivism (A Comte 1798–1857, E Durkheim 1858–1917) . . . . . . . 33
Rationalism (R Descartes 1596–1650; B de Spinoza
1632–1677; G W Leibniz 1646–1716) . . . . . . . . . . . . . . . . . . . . . . 36
Empiricism (T Hobbes 1588–1679; J Locke 1632–1704;
G Berkeley 1658–1753; D Hume 1711–1776; J S Mill 1806–1873:
The English Empiricists) . . . . . . . . . . . . . . . . . . . . . . . . . . . . . . . . 38

| | |
|---|---|
| Positivism | 39 |
| Realism | 39 |
| Another Science | 41 |
| The Science of Subjectivism and Lifeworld | 41 |
| The Paradigm | 46 |
| The Placing of the Concept of Paradigm | 51 |
| Paradigms in Social Science | 54 |
| The Dimension of Philosophy of Science: The Debate of Objectivity vs. Subjectivity | 55 |
| Differences Between an Objective and a Subjective Perspective | 58 |
| The Dimension of Philosophy of Society: Regulation vs. Radical Change | 62 |
| Understanding Ontological Themes and Theories in Social Science: Four Paradigms | 64 |
| Traditions of Objectivism: Rationalism and Positivism | 64 |
| Traditions of Lifeworld: Subjectivism | 67 |
| Discussion of Paradigms | 70 |
| Discussion of Paradigm Analyses | 72 |
| Everyday Business Dynamics Can Be Scientific | 75 |

**4 History of Lifeworld Traditions** ..... 79

| | |
|---|---|
| The Search for Another Philosophy and Theory of Cognition | 80 |
| Immanuel Kant (1724–1804) and the Foundation of Subjectivism | 81 |
| Science and the Lifeworld | 84 |
| Dilthey: The Life (Leben) and Science of Spirit (Geist) | 84 |
| Weber and Sociology as Social Action | 85 |
| Husserl and die Lebenswelt | 87 |
| Schutz and Social Phenomenology | 88 |
| Understanding Interrelation of Ontology and Epistemology | 91 |
| Consciousness and Intentionality | 91 |
| Transcendental Phenomenology and Phenomenology as Methodology | 94 |
| Schutz and the Phenomenological Analysis in Social Science | 98 |
| Science and Understanding: The Lifeworld as Understanding | 101 |
| Understanding | 101 |
| Dilthey and Verstehen | 102 |
| Weber: Verstehen, Action, and Social Relations | 105 |
| Gadamer and Understanding | 107 |
| Gadamer and the Hermeneutic Circle | 107 |
| Understanding | 108 |
| Schutz and Understanding | 112 |
| The Lifeworld: The "I" Being in and to the World | 114 |
| Merleau-Ponty and the Lifeworld | 114 |
| Heidegger and *Dasein* | 117 |
| Schutz: The Lifeworld and Intersubjectivity | 119 |

Contents     xv

Typification . . . . . . . . . . . . . . . . . . . . . . . . . . . . . . . . . . . . . . . . 120
Lifeworld as Multiple Realities. . . . . . . . . . . . . . . . . . . . . . . . . 121
Social Action. . . . . . . . . . . . . . . . . . . . . . . . . . . . . . . . . . . . . . . . . 123
Weber and Social Action. . . . . . . . . . . . . . . . . . . . . . . . . . . . . 123
Schutz and Meaningful Action . . . . . . . . . . . . . . . . . . . . . . . . 124
Linguistics: The Science of Qualitative Research . . . . . . . . . . . . . . 132
Use of Linguistic Theory in Everyday Life . . . . . . . . . . . . . . . 134
Surface Structure. . . . . . . . . . . . . . . . . . . . . . . . . . . . . . . . . . . 134
Deep Structure . . . . . . . . . . . . . . . . . . . . . . . . . . . . . . . . . . . . 135
Transformational Linguistics . . . . . . . . . . . . . . . . . . . . . . . . . 136
Transformational Rules in the Case of Business . . . . . . . . . . . . 138
Conclusion . . . . . . . . . . . . . . . . . . . . . . . . . . . . . . . . . . . . . . . . . 139

**5    Mead and Blumer: Social Theory and Symbolic Interactionism** . . . . 141
Introduction: George Herbert Mead . . . . . . . . . . . . . . . . . . . . . . . . 141
Mind, Self, and Society. . . . . . . . . . . . . . . . . . . . . . . . . . . . . . . . . 145
The Mind. . . . . . . . . . . . . . . . . . . . . . . . . . . . . . . . . . . . . . . . . 146
The Self. . . . . . . . . . . . . . . . . . . . . . . . . . . . . . . . . . . . . . . . . . 148
The Social Act, Gesture, and the Generalized Other . . . . . . . . . . . . . 150
The Social Act. . . . . . . . . . . . . . . . . . . . . . . . . . . . . . . . . . . . . 150
Gesture . . . . . . . . . . . . . . . . . . . . . . . . . . . . . . . . . . . . . . . . . . 150
The Generalized Other . . . . . . . . . . . . . . . . . . . . . . . . . . . . . . . 152
Language. . . . . . . . . . . . . . . . . . . . . . . . . . . . . . . . . . . . . . . . . 152
Meaning . . . . . . . . . . . . . . . . . . . . . . . . . . . . . . . . . . . . . . . . . 154
The Society . . . . . . . . . . . . . . . . . . . . . . . . . . . . . . . . . . . . . . . 156
Methodology and Consciousness . . . . . . . . . . . . . . . . . . . . . . . 157
Herbert Blumer Symbolic Interactionism. . . . . . . . . . . . . . . . . . . . . 158
Symbolic Interactionism. . . . . . . . . . . . . . . . . . . . . . . . . . . . . . 159
Methodological Principles of Empirical Science . . . . . . . . . . . . . . . . 172
In Summary. . . . . . . . . . . . . . . . . . . . . . . . . . . . . . . . . . . . . . . . . 175
Science . . . . . . . . . . . . . . . . . . . . . . . . . . . . . . . . . . . . . . . . . . 176
Weber and Ideal Types . . . . . . . . . . . . . . . . . . . . . . . . . . . . . . 177
Traditions: An Overview. . . . . . . . . . . . . . . . . . . . . . . . . . . . . . 179

**Part II    Science of Economics Through Linguistics**

**6    The Study of Qualitative Economics**. . . . . . . . . . . . . . . . . . . . . . . . 185
Economics Studies: The Case of Business . . . . . . . . . . . . . . . . . . . . 188

**7    The Science of Qualitative Economics** . . . . . . . . . . . . . . . . . . . . . . . 197
Introduction. . . . . . . . . . . . . . . . . . . . . . . . . . . . . . . . . . . . . . . . . 197
Philosophy of Science: Economic Theory in Business. . . . . . . . . . . . 199
Applications of Economics to Business in Everyday Life . . . . . . . . . . 202
Consumer Research . . . . . . . . . . . . . . . . . . . . . . . . . . . . . . . . . 203
Transaction Costs . . . . . . . . . . . . . . . . . . . . . . . . . . . . . . . . . . 204
Marketing and Promotion. . . . . . . . . . . . . . . . . . . . . . . . . . . . . 204
Networks and Relationships . . . . . . . . . . . . . . . . . . . . . . . . . . . 205

Interactionism in Business Economics:
Towards a Theory of a Firm .................................... 206
  Conventional-Structural Objectivist Perspective ................. 209
  Resource-Based Perspective................................. 210
  The Interactionism Perspective.............................. 211
Organizations Part: Social Community
Construction of Interactionism .................................. 211
  Actors' Action and Knowledge: The Constitution of the "Firm".... 212
  Environment as Situational Analyses ......................... 216
  Interaction and Knowledge................................. 217
  Organizing: Fitting Together of Lines of Activities and Actions .... 219
  Organizing: Dynamism of the Firm .......................... 219
  Intersubjectivity and the Organizational Approach............... 220
  The Actors' Experiential Space: Organizational Lifeworld ........ 222
  Constituting of the Organizational Activities and of the "Firm" .... 223
Case in Point: The Actors' Development Capability ............... 225
Summary: The Economics of the Firm (Such as Business,
NGOs, Family, Communities, Government, etc.).................. 226

**8**  **Methodological and Theoretical Constructs.**.................... 229
Introduction.............................................. 229
Action Research Methods: Core Data Gathering for Business Life.... 233
  Basic Philosophical Aspects of Methodology................... 234
  Qualitative Principles ...................................... 237
  Silverman: The Action Frame of Reference ................... 238
Sample Economic Action Research Methodological Protocol........ 240
  Multi-Methods ........................................... 240
  Interviews (Personal and Groups)............................ 241
  Participant Observation..................................... 243
  Situational Analysis ....................................... 245
  Legal Methods and Actions.................................. 246
  Documentation and Write-Up................................ 247
Everyday Business Dynamics Is Scientific....................... 248

**9**  **Linguistics as a Science.**...................................... 249
Introduction: Subjective Interactionism and Linguistic Theory ....... 249
  Interactionism in Everyday Life Such as the Business Firm ....... 251
  Macro- and Microeconomics: Interactionism
  and Situational Events...................................... 252
The Science of Linguistics Applied to Economics................. 255
Scientific Paradigm and Theoretical Change .................... 256
  Surface Structure.......................................... 259
  Deep Structure ........................................... 259
  Transformational Linguistics ................................ 260
Transformational Rules in Business ............................ 263
Internationalization as a Social and Economic Construction ......... 265

Contents                                                                    xvii

Knowledge and Meaning ..................................... 266
  Interaction and Knowledge ................................. 267
Economic Rulemaking in Interactionism Process ................. 268
  Organizing the Business Opportunity ........................ 268
  Constituting the Internationalization
  of the Business Opportunity ............................... 268
  Actors' International Experiential Space ..................... 269
  Management and Organizational Interaction in New Ventures...... 271
Intersubjectivity and Construction: Business Situations Rules........ 272
  Surface Structure Rules.................................... 272
  Deep Structure Rules ..................................... 276
Transformations ........................................... 279
  Personal Trust .......................................... 280
  Organizing Networks ..................................... 280
  Technological Modes of Communication..................... 281
Prediction in Subjectivist Paradigm ............................ 281
  Prediction #1: Build Shared Technological Terminology.......... 282
  Prediction #2: Expansion of Overall Business Consortia Vision .... 283
Summary................................................. 284

**10  Everyday Economic Life** ..................................... 287
Introduction............................................... 287
Scientific Interactionism Process and Perspective ................. 294
Case #1: Market Forces Created and Manipulated
    the California Energy Crisis............................... 295
  Situational Analysis ...................................... 295
  The Enron Case: Private Instead of Public Monopolies ........... 297
Case #2: The Economics and Commercialization
    of an Advanced Storage Technology – The Fuel Cell
    and Now All Solar-Powered Cars ......................... 301
  Fuel Cell Technology: US National Energy
  Research Laboratories...................................... 304
  Technology as an Element in the Creation
  of New Business Venture .................................. 305
Case #3: Economics of Entrepreneurship, SMEs,
    and New Ventures....................................... 307
Methodological Considerations in Theory Building................ 309
Practical Applications in Entrepreneurship and Business
    Development ........................................... 311
  The Organizational Actions and the Actors .................... 311
  Organizations as Social Construction of Interactionism........... 313
Organizational Development as Uncertainty and Change ........... 315
  Operational Concepts ..................................... 315
  Surface Structure Representations .......................... 316
  Deep Structure Representations ............................ 318

xviii

Organizations as Collectivity in Competency Building . . . . . . . . . . . 319
Networks and Changes . . . . . . . . . . . . . . . . . . . . . . . . . . . . . . . . . . . . . 322
Qualitative Scientific Descriptive Analysis. . . . . . . . . . . . . . . . . . . . . . 324
Interactionism for Surface and Deep Representations . . . . . . . . . . . . 325
Transformations . . . . . . . . . . . . . . . . . . . . . . . . . . . . . . . . . . . . . . . . . . 326
Conclusion: Understanding Economic Theory
Building to Be a Science . . . . . . . . . . . . . . . . . . . . . . . . . . . . . . . 327
Current (2018) EV Data and References . . . . . . . . . . . . . . . . . . . . . . . 329
Company Press Releases. . . . . . . . . . . . . . . . . . . . . . . . . . . . . . . . . . . 331

**11  Summary and Conclusions**. . . . . . . . . . . . . . . . . . . . . . . . . . . . . . . . . 333
Introduction. . . . . . . . . . . . . . . . . . . . . . . . . . . . . . . . . . . . . . . . . . . . . . 333
Phenomenology: The Tradition of the Lifeworld Perspective . . . . . . . . 337
Symbolic Interactionism: In the Subjectivist Theoretical Paradigm. . . . 338
Transformational Linguistics: Economic Rules
of Formalism in Economics and Business Practices . . . . . . . . . . 341
In Conclusion: On a Personal Note. . . . . . . . . . . . . . . . . . . . . . . . . . . . 342

**Appendix** . . . . . . . . . . . . . . . . . . . . . . . . . . . . . . . . . . . . . . . . . . . . . . . . . 345

**References** . . . . . . . . . . . . . . . . . . . . . . . . . . . . . . . . . . . . . . . . . . . . . . . . 353

**Author Index** . . . . . . . . . . . . . . . . . . . . . . . . . . . . . . . . . . . . . . . . . . . . . . 373

**Subject Index**. . . . . . . . . . . . . . . . . . . . . . . . . . . . . . . . . . . . . . . . . . . . . . 377

# About the Authors

**Woodrow W. Clark II, MA$_3$, PhD** is an internationally recognized, respected expert, author, lecturer, public speaker, and consultant on global and local solutions to climate change. His core focus is on economics for smart green healthy communities. He is now (2018) research professor in Economics at Pepperdine Graziadio Business School (PGSB), Pepperdine University. From 2000 to 2003, he was advisor, Renewable Energy, Emerging Technologies, and Finance, to California Governor Gray Davis. In 2004, he founded and manages Clark Strategic Partners (CSP), a global environmental and renewable energy consulting firm.

Clark has published over a dozen of books by the end of 2017 and over 70 peer-reviewed articles, which reflect his concern for global sustainable green communities. He has authored and edited books such as *The Next Economics: Global Cases in Energy, Environment, and Climate Change* (Springer, 2012) and *Global Sustainable Communities Handbook: Green Design Technologies and Economics* (Elsevier, 2014). In addition, his latest coauthored books, with Grant Cooke, are the *Green Industrial Revolution: Energy, Engineering and Economics* (Elsevier, 2014), *Green Development Paradigm* (in Mandarin, 2015), and *Smart Green Cities: Toward a Carbon Neutral World* (Routledge, February 2016). In 2017, he had three books published, the second edition of his first book *Agile Energy Systems: Global Lessons from the California Energy Crisis* (Elsevier Press) and the second edition of *Sustainable Communities Design*

*Handbook: Green Engineering, Architecture, and Technology* (Elsevier Press 2017).

Three more books are out in 2018, *Climate Preservation in Urban Communities Case Studies* (Elsevier Press), *Qualitative Economics: The Science of Economics* Second Edition (Springer Press), and, then later in fall of 2018, *Economics as a Science: Qualitative and Quantitative Economics* ($Q^2E$) from Palgrave Press, and one in 2019, *Sustainable Mega Cities* (Elsevier Press).

**Michael Fast, MSc, PhD** has been working in the field of business economics for more than 30 years, with a focus on research and teaching in organizational sociology, leadership philosophy, philosophy of science, methodology, and qualitative methods. He is research group leader of ORCA (Organizational Renewal Creativity Applied), former member of the Study Board Business and Economics, program coordinator of the BSc program in Economics Business and Administration, and former vice head of the Department of Development and Planning, Aalborg University. He had been and is supervising PhD fellows in those fields.

Fast has published articles and book in all the abovementioned areas, which focus on qualitative perspective, such as phenomenology, hermeneutics, symbolic interactionism, and critical theory, that centers on the matter of understanding people and organizations, leadership, being, cognition, and everyday life in business. He had all the time tried to develop the philosophical consciousness in writing and teaching of business economics and the alternatives to mainstream thinking.

# Chapter 1
# Overview of Qualitative Economics (QE)

## The Science of Economics

## Introduction

This book is about qualitative economics (QE) which is how science and knowledge matter in understanding the complexity, contradictions, development, and economics in all communities and societies. It is about the understanding of how we can connect organizations and people's living and the dynamic of economics. Specifically, QE is about building economics into a science that is grounded in the understanding of what is beneath the surface of daily numbers, statistics, data, and behavior. Yes, QE is the deep structure to our understanding of everyday life for the future.

Economics needs to become a science with the concern to formulating theories of ideas and understanding of reality that produce descriptions of how to understand everyday personal and group (e.g., individual, family, community, government, business, plus more) actions, phenomena that create experiences, hypotheses generation, and data which need to be proven or disproven through testing, further analyses, and hence predictions. Today much economics is focused primarily on numbers and statistics trying to explain the correlation between this data but has difficulties to establish descriptions of actual reality.

The "field of economics" lacks theory(s), other than those rooted in the neo-classic paradigm which rarely generates hypotheses that are documented, tested, analyzed, and explained. Moreover, economics today infrequently describes and discusses the definitions, meanings, and forecast of those and other numbers. Economics is problematic and unable to claim that it is a science. Science is measured so that it can formulate a general logic of ontology and epistemology that show the economic life of the human being and understands the dynamics. Economics above all needs to predict tomorrow and the future with verified evidence.

Economics needs to be able to understand, define, and handle the meaning of numbers, statistics, graphics, pictures, and even words, sentences, and text. Above all, economics must be defined so that people, their actions, and group interactions are able to communicate, act, and predict the future. Case in point is the California

---

© Springer Nature Switzerland AG 2019
W. W. Clark II, M. Fast, *Qualitative Economics*,
https://doi.org/10.1007/978-3-030-05937-8_1

energy crisis at the turn of the twenty-first century. The state government enacted "deregulation" then got numbers from companies such as $1 + 1 = 7$ validated by CPA firms. Clark started an investigation into these numbers in early 2001 (Clark and Demirag, 2002, 2005, 2006a) that documented the false numbers that put some of the executives in jail and companies to go "bankrupt."

We need a scientific perspective that can analyze and understand human dynamics. We name one perspective on this *qualitative economics*, as it focuses upon the economic actions of people, groups, and their networks in everyday of life and how they are trying to make sense of the present and construct the future. The science of economics is about the monetary and financial numbers that transpire between people and their organizations.

Economics on the macro level is interaction between people and groups, countries, and regions. Yet, economics on the micro level is another form of interaction. Microeconomics can be seen in business and interpersonal transactions. Economics takes place among people: macro and micro. While we acknowledge and recognize the value of quantitative approaches in such macro- and micro-interactions, there is a significant missing element that if the essence of economics is the human being, the understanding of qualitative interactions of people turns into theory of qualitative economics.

In order to understand everyday interactions as "qualitative economics," we have written this book as a purposeful exercise in order to construct a perspective with roots in the historical philosophical tradition of subjectivism. As a starting point, we use philosophy and philosophy of science to establish the perspective and analysis. The reason for this is that all knowledge and all science have a position and are situated in the world, and within that position there is a certain perspective used in the process of creating knowledge. There is no other way to describe what knowledge is and to understand what and how science is in its essence. So the discussion of what this perspective is ontological and epistemological, and which ground it rest on in line of argument and logic, is the starting point of any discussion of science and knowledge.

As the twenty-first century moves into its second decade that reflects a new economic era, there is a need to examine the ontological roots of economics as people, organizations, environment, and business in order to understand the local and global economies of today and tomorrow. In fact, our forefathers in economics were themselves philosophers before the field became an academic discipline. For example, in Europe for over 200 years now, there is a distinction between act and behave that can be seen in the distinction of understand (*verstehen*) and explain (*erklären*). All of these discussions are between objectivism vs. subjectivism – the difference in ontology which is critical in economics today.

It is in that context, we name the perspective and the tradition from an old philosophical tradition: "Lifeworld" which is rooted in a school of philosophy. Lifeworld comes from the German *die Lebenswelt* and the discussions in the eighteenth-century philosophy of Immanuel Kant and later on, e.g., Husserl, Heidegger, Schutz, and Gadamer. The theoretical development from this philosophical tradition is seen in different schools of contemporary social science thought ranging from phenomenology, hermeneutic, critical theory, ethnomethodology, linguistics, and symbolic interactionism. For us, the Lifeworld tradition and its interactionism are an approach to describing, understanding, and explaining everyday life. In short, the Lifeworld and interactionism represent elements of any science. Below we provide the discussion.

Overall the Lifeworld school of thought is placed in the paradigmatic world of science as the "subjectivist" or ideographic perspective. Lifeworld is on existence and the individual whose thoughts and daily interactions between people and larger groups are essential in understanding social reality, everyday life, and social construction in and with the world. Today in Europe, much of the discussion focuses on phenomenology and "social constructionism" which we view as part of the Lifeworld tradition. Below, we also apply US-based theories (particularly interactionism of Mead and Blumer and Chomsky's linguistics) in the tradition of sociology and philosophy to economics, thus creating the science of qualitative economics. All can be seen in the USA where Mead (early twentieth century) talked about being a "social behaviorist." However, what he actually meant was a critique of behaviorism and the whole stimuli-response model of thinking from theories of Adam Smith. Mead's discussion is about the meanings and interpretations of words, ideas, actions, and interactions.

This book takes up these different perspectives which is QE in order to have a different philosophical perspective that applies them to the creation of a science of economics. We see the parallel in linguistics today with the need to understand the meaning behind the surface, ideas, words, sentences, and meanings through following the scientific method. Linguistics is remarkably similar to economics in its need to become a science. In the end, linguists like any science offer hypothesis testing along with universal rules and formalism in predicting future action and interactions.

In Part I, the philosophical roots of the Lifeworld tradition are primarily European. Lifeworld can be traced in order to set the stage for the interactionism subjectivist theoretical perspective exemplified by Herbert Blumer, the twentieth-century American sociologist at the University of California, Berkeley. Blumer and his mentor George Herbert Mead, the early twentieth-century philosopher at the University of Chicago, are the American roots for a Lifeworld tradition. Blumer was one of the key professors of Clark when he was earning his PhD and learned the concept of "indication" which is to point something out such as a man who constructs things by being engaged which are his actions. Behavior is what we observe, but there is more behind that that perspective which we know explains and accounts for these actions.

Part II of the book explores the application of the Lifeworld tradition to business. We take the subjectivist approach as practiced in interactionism for describing and analyzing business, especially in the USA, and focused around the California energy crisis from 2000 to 2003. The crisis in California, America, and the world continues today in part from some of the data and analyses that are explored (Clark and Bradshaw 2004). What is even more significant, however, is the application of linguists combined with symbolic interactionism and phenomenology. As a science, this perspective provides theory and analytical constructions that are appropriate to the science of economics. When such qualitative data is combined or understood on quantitative economics, a comprehensive science emerges.

In short, the entire volume comprises a landmark in economic theory and practice, because it challenges the roots and paradigm of contemporary economic theory. The book presents another strong set of core philosophical arguments directed towards making economics another science. In short, this volume will lead to further debate and discussion of economics becoming a science.

To get the debate focused, the Lifeworld tradition will be applied initially herein to business economics. And to add some perspective, purpose, and planning to it, the focus primarily is upon the business of energy. This particular perspective reflects one of the authors' area of expertise and recent experiences but also a very contemporary issue that merges both economics and science – energy is viewed as science and engineering. Part II presents qualitative data that provides the specifics for a science of economics. Moreover, the business economics of the energy sector is placed in the context of global warming and climate change.

## The Aim of the Book

What can be seen in society and economics is that we can state that it is organized, but not in any clear way. We will discuss how to understand the very concept of organizations and how organizations are constructed and developed. We need to have an understanding of what people are and what they bring to the organizational economic context by interacting with one another and in groups.

We will also discuss how to understand organizations from a methodological viewpoint. It is no mere coincidence that qualitative methods have been developed within a Lifeworld tradition. This is one of the key issues that we discuss in the book. Furthermore, we will show how to understand this subjective and scientific paradigm along with the theorizing within this tradition that transforms economics into a science along the lines of the natural and physical sciences. The aim of this book is therefore –through the everyday life of philosophical and sociological traditions – to discuss the central issues and basic concepts put forth by Herbert Blumer's symbolic interactionism, phenomenology, and Chomsky's linguistics, in order to understand and develop a qualitative economic perspective.

Today there are many insightful criticisms of the objectivist paradigm and neo-classical economics, which is the mainstream theory in economics. We believe, however, that most of these critiques fall within the same philosophical tradition or objectivist paradigm of economics and hence are really "revisionist." An excellent example which has gained considerable attention is "Freakonomics: a rogue economist explores the hidden side of everything" (Levitt and Dubner 2005). In the book and in several lectures, the authors present qualitative insights but in quantitative methods. In short, they rework neo-classical economics around qualitative ideas. While this is a start at being scientific, it lacks explanation and prediction. Hypotheses must be made, tested, and then retested with the purpose to seek understanding.

This volume presents an entirely different route to understanding economic and business phenomena. As Erik Reinert, the economic historian, puts it, there are three significant issues in addressing economic theory:

> One: how economic growth is "created"; two, the alternative mechanisms through which growth and welfare are "diffused" between and within the nation-states, and to the individual; and three, how this alternative understanding is based on a different philosophical basis. (Reinert 1997: 9)

We follow a historical trend which is today the "new paradigm" for economic theory. In other words, our approach to the science of economics is an entirely different paradigm. Our approach argues that the current conventional neo-classic paradigm including economic revisionism with its focus on perfect information in a balanced equilibrium system is the basis of economic theory today and is fundamentally wrong. Even some of the more popular books on the earth being flat, global, or different ("Freakeonomics") are all predicted upon the conventional neo-classic economic paradigm.

Adam Smith, under the objective paradigm along with his followers to this day, notes that the basis for business is barter and exchange. In fact, they are adamantly opposed to a Lifeworld view of economics. The objectivist's paradigm in a pre-mass production globalized world provides little guidance in terms of uneven economic growth and clearly substantive problems with understanding the needs of developing nations. Instead, it argues that "market forces" and business in general can innovate and hence meet new challenges. Yet that neo-classical economic perspective is part of the problem as it mostly considers supply and demand in quantifiable statistics.

For example, how does "climate change" enter into the conventional economic paradigm? It does not because climate change at the United Nations or the USA and EU international levels requires extensive government involvement, public policy, standards, regulations, and controls that can be set and monitored. Indeed that is the message gaining prominence globally totally as all but three nations (one of which was the USA) signed the Kyoto Accords. What is interesting about this issue is that the conventional neo-classical perspective would rather deny the science of global warming and ignore the economic needs for combating climate change. Until recently, that has been the position of most economists such that their answer is that the "market forces" will correct the problem. The code concept for neo-classic economics is to label the global energy crises as a "perfect storm" (sic) which makes it ironic in the context of global warming and now the climate and weather changes experienced globally. Only since science has almost unanimously confirmed global warming have economists sought other ideas.

## The Paradigm Shift: Economics Needs to Be a Science

Business activities are a part of our everyday world, and the phenomena of business present itself in many ways and shapes. Business is a large part of our everyday life, and business is life itself, often helping to define who we are and what we do. We interact with people not only in daily conversations but also in just living: go to work, drive on a highway, study in school, attend a lecture or movie, and go on a holiday. Life for us as individuals and everyone around us is interaction with others in one form or another.

The Internet, email, and wireless and new technologies heighten our daily interactions as never before, now on 24 hours, on 7 days a week, and on a global basis. Business and economics are interaction and "exchanges" of something (information, knowledge, goods and services, or whatever), and in this everyday of situations, we define and construct meanings and understandings.

The reality of business economics has been investigated and explained in many ways. And the *science of business economics* is, as it has "always" been, central in the social discussion and the different discourses in society. But the discussion of how to understand business research, and how the research is done along with the ontological and epistemological assumptions lying behind the research and its reality in everyday life, is rarely discussed. Business economics and its close cousin economics are not sciences but "art forms," as C.P. Snow (1959) would call it, disguised in the aura of scientism. The problem with the dominant objectivist paradigm in the tradition of neo-classical economics in business and economics today stems from its historical roots and their foundations.

Throughout the last few centuries, many western philosophers, theologians, scientists, and laymen have contributed to the discussion and understanding of reality and science. They have agreed or disagreed about thinking in various traditions about how the broad social sciences have been developed. Some traditions have been dominant for a time and have then been replaced by others. Others have been rediscovered and developed. Yet the basic philosophy of business economic has remained following two particular traditions. Most of what we encounter in the scientific world today is an expression of a certain tradition or another tradition which is not presented as one of many, but as *the only one* giving evidence of reality. A particular tradition, or as Kuhn (1962) noted as a "paradigm," has a long history and, to a great extent, is dominating the social discussion and the organizing of society, including science itself.

The dominant business economic tradition for the last century has come from the objectivist nominalist tradition and manifested itself as *positivism* and *rationalism* as contained in the prevailing schools of thought like structural functionalism or system theory. As Reinert (1994: 80) puts it, "Neo-classical economics is essentially a theory of the exchange of goods already produced, taking no account of the diversity of conditions of production and their influence on pricing behavior. Neo-classical theory is, it seems, a theory which cannot accommodate for the existence of fixed costs, since these create increasing returns."

Discussions of philosophy in science and methodology are important for understanding reality and theorizing on its applications in everyday life. It is precisely these connections among philosophy of science that theorizing and methodologies arise to capture the reality, which must be in the center of any scientific discussion. Furthermore, openness and a specific discussion of an alternative philosophical approach to the established traditional way of seeing science and reality are necessary. Thinking and reflection are critical in the scientific investigation of reality together with and related to the basic philosophical assumptions following the line of pure logic and general logic. It is only in this connection that we can talk about something being true (e.g., correct) or false.

There are economists and business academics that discuss philosophy of science as it relates to business economics, but they are only a rare minority to the extent that they make an impact on the research practice of social science and business or economics in particular. The problem with most methodological discussions and theoretical works is that they only discuss "choice" of methods in the context of methodological considerations, techniques of investigation, analysis, and measurements.

It is difficult to find an explicit discussion on connections between philosophy/ philosophy of science and methodology, especially focusing upon opposing philosophical traditions. In particular, the scholarly discussions lack ontological and epistemological considerations and make assumptions that are underlying the very choice of those methods.

Another problem in traditional social scientific research is a lack of in-depth discussion of the background of the qualitative methods, especially of the Lifeworld ontology and everyday life epistemologies. The current conventional objectivism tradition has established positivist and rationalist theories in the functionalistic paradigm, which lack understanding about why the qualitative methods exist and for which epistemological grounds they are significant in understanding business actors, actions, and situations.

Furthermore, the objectivist fails to understand in which contexts these methods appear and to which contexts they relate or underscore and support quantitative and statistical methods. Finally, the issue is rarely raised in business economics as to how to think qualitative theories and methods in the production of knowledge to which they can contribute in-depth understanding.

To a great extent, most of the problems exist because there is a basic lack of historical consciousness, debate, or concern over the progress of science in relationship to social science (i.e., the theoretical discussions and background of science) and understanding of different traditions of philosophical thinking. Hence, recognition must be made that the meta-theory of social science must be philosophy if it is to have any significance. Some scholars may say that the "quantitative" researchers are not especially conscious of or need to be directed to the history of science and ideas in their work (cf. the discussion in Chap. 3). The argument is made that they do not need to think in terms of philosophical traditions, even though they are part of a particular tradition themselves and reflect its biases, beliefs, and assumptions (see Gadamer 1993, cf. Chap. 4).

Hence, these scholars reflect historical traditions that presuppose and bias their results under the guise of "well-establish" (usually) quantifiable "facts." This book challenges that basic traditional assumption and argues instead for a new perspective and paradigm in the study of business economics based on an old tradition in order to understand, appreciate or critique, and apply the results of business research to understand everyday business activities.

When the conventional paradigm continues to dominate both researchers and students alike, then their study of social science phenomena is "allowed" to prevail as the one and only. In short, this perspective directs their work, influences the results, and skews the applications. An alternative perspective is never thought about or presented as a possibility. To some extent, objectivism is now a restrained and an ambiguous concept which according to many researchers covers not only different but also often conflicting relations. We review these arguments in Chap. 3.

In research there has, however, been a slow shift over the years towards a more "qualitative" approach. Empiricism as reflected in structuralism, logical positivism, or quantification of data has not shown that it can understand business and economics. And while we argue that more qualitative science must be a part of business economics, we fully acknowledge the same concern to probe and ask basic scientific questions about perspectives direction of work and skewed results must apply herein as well.

Today we see more "case studies"[1] (but with widely different approaches and perspectives) and qualitative investigations than we have experienced previously being graduate students and even in more recent years as professors. This social constructionism or so-called softening partly originates from the *anomalies*, which Kuhn (1962) explains and is part of the continuing development of science. Researchers must experience the problems and explanations in the existing frame of theory in order to start looking for alternative paradigms. However, we shall demonstrate how "qualitative" research or ethnography can still be associated with the positivist paradigm and therefore subject to the same basic problems as its quantitative equivalent. The key is to "map or link" the subjectivist tradition with the objectivist techniques (numerical, mathematics, etc.) when appropriate and useful.

## The Book Contents

Our approach has its roots (ontological and epistemological) in the Lifeworld tradition, with the theoretical perspectives reflected in the subjectivism paradigm (see Chap. 4). We will discuss a different philosophical tradition that presents an alternative to the objectivist tradition in social science and business economics. The Lifeworld tradition and subjectivist paradigm reflect the conception of science as reflected in linguistics (see Chap. 10) which is an established science directed to the everyday life reality of human interactionism.

This subjectivist paradigm is not an alternative philosophy of science, as it simply follows a different philosophical heritage than the current dominant paradigm of objectivism. The subjectivism paradigm deals with a different strain of theory from the conventional objectivism philosophy of science in vogue today. Subjectivism discusses reality that combines everyday life in a sociological frame of reference

---

[1] Albeit primarily used as exploitative investigations and often used before "the real investigation is started," i.e., a quantitative questionnaire/survey investigation.

whereby business economics is viewed as the everyday business actions and interactions can be seen, heard, recorded, and communicated. In short, this book represents a different philosophical perspective to understanding everyday business economics and how to understand business reality in another scientific line of arguments.

## Subjectivism Paradigm: Lifeworld Perspective as Symbolic Interactionism

The *Lifeworld* tradition as reflected in subjectivism and everyday life perspectives is described by others as an *interpretive paradigm*, *symbolic interactionism*, *hermeneutic approach*, or *qualitative perspective* (see Chaps. 3 and 4). The tradition provides a different set of ideas, theories, and methodologies within which we picture reality and our conception of science. In short, qualitative economics is a science in the philosophical tradition of the natural and physical sciences because it seeks to create understanding, define terms and assumptions, and use logic and empirical data in order to draw both conclusions and further verifiable hypotheses. That process, as seen in modern linguistics, is the basis of a scientific inquiry.

Our discussion in this volume deals with how everyday reality and economic science are understood. Besides discussing the philosophical assumptions and the history behind the tradition, we also discuss some of the traditions related to our perspective. They are primarily hermeneutics, philosophical hermeneutics, sociological phenomenology, and symbolic interactionism. For this perspective, we have chosen part of some heretofore unpublished lectures from Professor Herbert Blumer, the leader in this field, to further explore and explain qualitative economic as it relates to specific everyday business activities. (Those lectures will later be published separately.)

## Part I: Philosophy of Science

The first part discusses the various philosophical traditions that contribute to the understanding of business everyday reality today: positivist and rationalist traditions, known as part of the objectivist paradigm. We purposely pay attention to philosophical arguments that are counter to the current economic paradigm prevalent in American and European business programs, schools, textbooks, and administrations.

Curiously enough, however, these positivist and rationalist traditions are not underlying Asian and transitional economies nor are the predominant economic paradigms today used in practice in most businesses. Instead, in Asia most of their economic and business traditions are based on a different paradigm and tradition, while actual business practices globally are neither locked into a specific rigid model or follow one set pattern of economic actions. The next part gives some examples of actual business economics and also an overview of how Asian economics works, especially in the People's Republic of China (PRC) today.

In fact, it is this "disconnection" between the everyday life of business activity that inspired us to seek different understandings of the situations that actors experience in their daily business lives. We believe that our discussion in the first part hits directly at the heart or core of what Western industrialized capitalism has become today through an in-depth analysis of the philosophical and historical roots of science.

Our argument is that the objectivism paradigm in science became the dominant one with its theories and arguments for rationalism, empiricism, and ultimately quantification of social phenomena. In short, numbers without any deeper meaning and definition became economics. The objectivist paradigm has prevailed for over a century throughout other social sciences as well. The impact on business economics has led to a reductionist approach in theory and methods that dictate how economic and business analyses are conducted.

This volume and especially Part I present another paradigm in philosophy: *subjectivism*. Through the Lifeworld tradition, this paradigm forms the basis for qualitative economics. Herein emanates the focus on Lifeworld, everyday life, symbolic interactionism and the use of interpretative theories and qualitative methods that are missing today in business economics and business studies. Moreover, as will be demonstrated in Part II, economics becomes a science when qualitative theories, data, and methods are used because actors, events, groups, surroundings, and their interactions can be constructed into hypotheses which are tested, described, explained, and analyzed. The outcome can be laws and rules used for forecast and prediction. In short, economics becomes a science.


## Part II: Qualitative Economics – Towards a Science of Economics

The second part discusses how to apply the *subjectivist* paradigm as reflected in an interactionism perspective to specific concepts in business economics. We want to explore a few areas where some of the concepts in the book might be applicable to everyday business. While our concern is primarily with organizations (organizing) and international business, we do present other basic concepts of business in new theoretical perspectives.

In many ways, this volume is a tribute to Herbert Blumer as he was one of the most important scholars in the twentieth century, especially in the USA. Unfortunately, Blumer did not live to see our book completed. We only wish that he were alive today to see his ideas impact business economics. We know that the thousands of students, faculty, and practitioners worldwide who are his legacy will appreciate this tribute.

Given the demand in business economics for fresh, new theories and methods to describe, but also explain and understand business in everyday life, the book is timely as a significant contribution to the economic life in any society. With Blumer's ideas as the core, the book builds around them an argument for the application of qualitative theory and methods in order to create a science of business economics.

In particular, we take both real business situations and cases as examples of how the science of qualitative economics works. We discuss situations whereby research organizations seek to commercialize their discoveries. And we discuss companies that appear to have exposed conventional economic models and annual reports whereby their statistics and accounting lead to false and criminal acts.

Moreover, we look at the science of economics from the public policy perspective wherein decision-makers have created deregulation or privatization schemes for certain vital infrastructure sectors to the determinant of the general public while enhancing the enormously false profits of their executives. A qualitative economics approach to business exposes such financial schemes.

# Part I
# Philosophy of Science and the Lifeworld Traditions

# Chapter 2
# The Case for Rethinking the Foundation of Business Economics

## The Business Economic Debate

One purpose of this second edition book on QE is to frame the debate in business economics around fundamental philosophical issues of understanding business management and organization. Our premise is that conventional science of business economics has problems because of the roots in arguments from the positivist and rationalist traditions of philosophy (e.g., objectivism). On the other hand, a long ontological and epistemological tradition centered in lifeworld – everyday of life and social interaction of people – can be seen as applicable to business economics as an alternative.

K. Weick (1999) talks about theories that matter as theories that make a difference – theories that move people in their assumptions about reality. In his discussion of Kirkegaard and Heidegger, Weick (ibid., p. 139) ends up with some qualities as possible properties of such moving theories that synthesize backward understanding and forward living:

1. Analysis is focused on what people do.
2. Context of action is preserved, and context-free depiction of elements is minimized.
3. Holistic awareness is attributed to the actor.
4. Emotions are seen to structure and restructure activity.
5. Interruptions are described in detail with careful attention to what people were doing before the interruption, what became salient during the interruption, and what happen during resumption of activity.
6. Activity is treated as the context within which reflection occurs, and reflection is not separate from, behind, and before action.
7. Artifacts and entities are portrayed in terms of their use, meaning, situated character, and embedding in tasks rather than in terms of their measurable properties.

© Springer Nature Switzerland AG 2019
W. W. Clark II, M. Fast, *Qualitative Economics*,
https://doi.org/10.1007/978-3-030-05937-8_2

8. Knowledge is seen to originate from practical activity rather than from detached deductive theorizing or detached inductive empiricism.
9. Time urgency rather than indifference to time is treated as part of the context.
10. The imagery of fusion is commonplace, reflecting that activity takes place prior to conceptualizing and theorizing.
11. Detachment from a problem and resort to general abstract tools to solve it is viewed as a last resort and a derivative means of coping rather than as the first and primary means of coping (whatever else people may be, they are not lay social scientists).

In Wieck's discussion of theorizing and understanding, he points at some important issues in science and theorizing: What is interesting science in terms of saying something meaningful about reality, and what is not. What is important to people in their search for understanding of their reality and to organize their everyday of life, and what is not important.

In relation to the business economic understanding, consider some of the more popular and dominant perspectives emanating from American business economist in the objectivist tradition. An interesting set of arguments attempting to foretell the American economic future is found in Robert Reich's *The Work of Nations: Preparing Ourselves for twenty-first Century Capitalism* (1991) and Peter Drucker's *Post-Capitalist Society* (1993). The books complement one another and have had along with Lester C. Thurow, in *The Future of Capitalism* (1996), an influential impact on American public and economic policies in 1990s. Thurow puts the issue succinctly:

> ... the eternal verities of capitalism – growth, full employment, financial stability, rising real wages – seem to be vanishing just as the enemies of capitalism vanish. Something within capitalism has changed to be causing these results. Something has to be changed to alter these unacceptable results if capitalism is to survive. But what is "it"? And "how" can "it" be changed? (Thurow 1996: 3)

Drucker (1993) argues that the nation-state no longer is a viable concept. What we now see throughout the world is megastates with regions and mini-regions within them. In short, NAFTA created the megastate of the USA, Canada, and Mexico, much like how the European Common Market created the European Union. He predicts that the same pattern will occur in the Far East, either with Japan as the one center or with two or more others, but including several like-minded countries. This perspective corresponds with preliminary reports from the Japanese government and MITI, its science and technology commercialization center. However, within these megastates are regions and fractions thereof. For example, the EU has several smaller regions (including and excluding EU members like the Baltic States centered in large part around Denmark and Sweden). Or within NAFTA and even the USA itself, for example, there is the West Coast including Western portions of Mexico and Canada as opposed to the east and Gulf States.

Yet Drucker cautions that there is also "tribalism" (what anthropologist would call "ethnic groups"), which further reduces the geographical size of a region into, often, conflictual language, religion, and cultural areas. In Europe, the conflict in the

The Business Economic Debate

1990s within former Yugoslavia illustrates that phenomena; but others can be found as in the French-German-British rivalries that continue today in the form of the EU, ended up with Brexit.

These issues are not a reversal to traditional and older ways but a reality of the new world in which people live, work, and survive across political boundaries. Drucker notes that the basis of the change in the world is with people. As the world becomes smaller, the economic well-being of any community depends increasingly on its creation of knowledge and handling of information. In short, the new economic strength of any community, region, or mini-region depends on a more global and international perspective. However, more economic internationalism is precisely what makes local people feel less and less in control of their own futures and that of their families. The problem with the new economic internationalism is an existential one; it is one that lacks any "theory" on the order of Adam Smith, Karl Marx, or John Maynard Keynes.

In essence, Reich's study makes some similar points with a series of remarkable analytical points about the world today and the beginning of a new role for America to play in it. In brief, Reich argues that America has changed dramatically as it heads into the next century. The old economic system of "high volume productivity," so prevalent for the last 50 years, has now changed into a "high value system." This new economic system values knowledge and international economic prowess more than the old economic business of mass production followed by marketing and sales.

Within this new business economic system, there are three new categories of workers: routine producers (what were once known as the blue collar and production workers), in-person service providers (the service industries such as insurance, banking, medical staffs, and retail stores), and the symbolic analysts (the professional people from lawyers to business executives). Reich presents a compelling set of arguments and statistics that show how the "core corporations" in America have already begun to make extensive economic changes. These core corporations have recognized the importance of global economic conditions and have therefore already established and transformed themselves.

Reich calls these new economic relationships "global webs" and feels that they are distinctly American. More on that assumption later, suffice is to say now that Reich has documented the global changes for American core corporations and provided convenient and useful labels. Through the use of statistics and documentation, he has described what has happened over the last decade (1980s) to American core corporations. The basic question is what happens next and, perhaps more importantly, what will America's role be in the global economies?

In short, Reich (1991: 311–) argues that America has three choices, which go far beyond economic analysts based on narrow nationalist concepts; either Americans can become:

1. "Zero sum nationalism" who fears everything "foreign" – "jingoism." These people are often the routine producers and in-service providers.
2. "Laissez-faire cosmopolitans" who are usually the symbolic analysis "arguing that the government should simply stay out."

3. "Positive economic nationalists" where "each nation's citizens take primary responsibility for enhancing the capacities of their countrymen for full and productive lives, but who also work with their nations to ensure that these improvements do not come at others expense."

Reich feels that the positive economic nationalists must rise above their own self-interest and provide more "direct investment" by the government into the people and the infrastructure of the nation (any nation). As Drucker would put it, there is a need for renewed "citizenship." Reich feels that the symbolic analysis is in the best position to become positive economic nationalists and therefore help the routine producers and in-person service providers change into internationalists as well. For the vast majority of workers to survive, they must change according to the global economic conditions.

Thurow answers Drucker's call for an economic theory when he argues "the causes (in the worldwide change of the economic structures) are to be found in the *interactions* of new technologies and new ideologies. There are the forces driving the economic system in new directions. Together they are producing a new economic game with new *rules* requiring new strategies to win" (*emphasis ours*, Thurow 1996: 3). He then argues that biological theories can provide the best model for business economics, since they view the world systematically and fit data into organized units and components.

The problem with the Drucker, Reich, and Thurow positions is a simple and straightforward one: they are posited upon a particular philosophical tradition that argues for economics to be ordered into quantifiable structural and functional components and logic. For example, American capitalism is different from Japanese and European version capitalism. The definition of markets, in other words, has developed along national economic policies and programs. In anthropology, the transference of concepts from one culture to another in order to provide direction to policy-makers is known as "modernity of tradition." The Japanese have successfully utilized the concept as they maintain their traditions and customs from centuries ago and adopted Western technologies over the last 100 years.

McNeill and Freiberger provide a refreshing review of literature and debate within philosophy and mathematics which provides the context criticizing the conventional paradigm and presenting a new perspective when they write:

> Complexity reaches its apex with life and society. Biological and social systems can be marbled with subsystems and sub-subsystems and sub-sub-subsystems, all of unthinkable intricacy. For instance, the economy is a complex system. It reacts to politics, weather, new technology, government decisions, pure emotions like panic, and much else besides. (McNeill and Freiberger 1993: 16)

The essential problem is how can anyone define with any precision notions of objects or things when our language actually expresses everything in vagueness and uncertainty. Even precise words attached to objects, like a "chair," have different meanings depending on who, which chair, and in what situation (see Chap. 4 and the discussion of intentionality). A chair is also linked to cultures since one society may consider a chair one thing while another culture may not even have a concept of a chair. For example, McNeill and Freiberger borrow from H.G. Wells:

The Business Economic Debate    19

> Think of arm chairs and reading chairs and dining-room chairs, and kitchen chairs, chairs that pass into benches, chairs that cross the boundary and become settees, dentist's chairs, thrones, opera stalls, seats of all sorts, those miraculous fungoid growths that cumber the floor of arts and crafts exhibitions, and you will perceive what a lax bundle in fact is this simple straightforward term. In cooperation with an intelligent joiner I would undertake to defeat any definition of chair or chairishness that you gave me. (McNeill and Freiberger 1993: 82)

One of the most obvious and well-documented linguistic examples of definitional problems with object is in the different cultural definitions of "snow" where it is simply one word in most of the USA and has 44 different meanings in Greenland. As McNeill and Freiberger put it: "Objects are objects to degrees" (ibid., p. 12). Further, the conventional business economic perspective has defined and forced business concepts into very structured, mechanistic, and artificial constraints that bare little connection to what one experiences in everyday of life. As McNeill and Freiberger note, "Traditional logic, set theory, and philosophy have compelled sharp distinctions. They have forced us to draw lines in the sand" (ibid., p. 12).

Business economy theory needs a challenge from a new paradigm rooted in an entirely different set of ontological and epistemological traditions (Fast 1992a, b; Clark 1994a, b, 1996; Clark and Sørensen 1994b). What Reich offers is a "snapshot" of change in America based upon the notion that changes in the components of rigidly defined economic structures will bring about wider societal change. The American government must invest in "people and infrastructure," he argues. The picture that one gets of America is a society that is stuck in time and space. People and infrastructures are defined by statistics and numbers. While pictures may be "worth a thousand words," they do little to help understanding and then activity pursuing change. Society is not a snapshot but a moving un-edited picture that today is even enhanced and exacerbated because it is on digital video subject to rapid change and uncertainty.

Drucker offers even vaguer notions of "citizenship." He argues that people must rethink and re-establish economic control over their lives. His "existential" view is that people must change themselves. Society will change thereafter. Economic change is dependent on people constrained in their economic roles. So we have set the stage for the need for economic change. The authors have taken and develop vivid portraits of America in need of dramatic change. However, they fall into the traditional traps of the past – each advocates a version of the standard and failed economic structural theories. Reich takes a chapter from Keynes in arguing that all government needs to do is pour money (investments) into people and public works. Drucker falls into the neo-Adam Smith economic theory (with a modern humanistic twist from psychology) that people can do for themselves best; *the invisible hand* will take care of society. Government should stay out of the way.[1]

What is needed, however, is a "moving picture" of business economics. Business economics is dynamic because of people and their interactions. Business economies are uncertain, changing, and full of contradictions. A more accurate portrayal of an

---

[1] See Florida and Smith (1994) for the most recent view of this issue as applied to venture capital funds in economic development.

economy would be to view it as a moving picture that is not viewed or even observed by an audience: instead every person is an actor in the moving picture. Everyone acts daily in a wide variety of economic areas. While this may be viewed by some as microeconomics, in theoretical terms, the microeconomic and macroeconomic are interlinked and must fall within any theory of economics in order to have any validity or predictable usefulness.

The human mind reduces the flood of information down to a trickle. We round off; we take shortcuts; we summarize. "We perceive the precise in a fuzzy way" (McNeill and Freiberger 1993: 44). Zadeh (1965) called this human capacity, "one of the most important that we possess, and noted that it marks off living intelligence distinctly from that of machines" (McNeill and Freiberger 1993: 44). This explains the fuzziness of words like "chair" which "distills an array of objects into one notion. Furniture summarizes even more broadly. Words centralize concepts that may have blurredbounds" (ibid., p. 44).

A new business economic theory is needed. A paradigmatic change is needed. Current analogies and comparisons of economics and business to sports and games are not valid, let alone useful. Each of these popular attempts to formulate business economics into a structural-functional perspective loses a basic tenant in human nature to create, innovate, and change. In short, people interact and as such challenge, change, and create new rules. Thurow, Reich, and Drucker, among many others, are clearly on the right track to question the conventional paradigm. The remainder of the book builds an argument for a new perspective deeply rooted in a different philosophical tradition.

## The Paradigm Debate

Theoretical debates in the social sciences often turn to qualitative versus quantitative perspectives and methods. The positions with ontological and epistemological assumptions have been adequately outlined by others (e.g., Burrell and Morgan 1980; Polkinghorne 1983; Giddens 1979; see Chap. 3). Morgan and Smircich (1980) summarize the arguments along a "continuum" from objective (quantitative) to subjective (qualitative) approaches. They present a table of "Assumptions about Ontology and Human Nature," delineating the spectrum of approaches from the "subjective" approach with "reality as a projection of human imagination" which sees human beings as transcendental beings through phenomenological research on the one hand. And on the other hand, the "objective" approach with "reality as a concrete structure" sees humans as "responding mechanisms as in the research work of behaviorists and social learning theory" (ibid., p. 498).

They argue that the quantitative view of the world attempts to objectify "knowledge that specifies the precise nature of laws, regularities, and relationships among phenomena measured in terms of social 'fact'" (ibid., p. 493),[2] while qualitative

---

[2] This can be tracked to the discussion of Comte and Durkheim and the very establishing of social science (see Chap. 3).

methods are subjective since "reality (is) a projection of individual imagination in favor of an epistemology that emphasizes the importance of understanding the processes through human beings concretize their relationship to their world" (ibid., p. 493). This can indeed be seen in relation to the philosophical discussion by Immanuel Kant (see Chap. 4).

This is an old debate in philosophy and science between on one hand the discussions and assumptions from *the objective idea*, namely, rationalism, positivism, realism, dunctionalism (including structural functionalism, system theory, behaviorism), Marxism, Solipsism, and so on. And on the other hand, *the idea of subjectivity or "Lifeworld"* which is a focus in our book developed from a variety of shared philosophical perspectives including idealism, phenomenology, hermeneutic, critical theory, existentialism, symbolic interactionism, ethnomethodology, and so on. There are differences between the different traditions and perspectives, but their fundamental ontological assumptions can be drawn back to the philosophical debate of an objective-structural versus a subjective-intersubjective approach to reality.

Science, in short, is a "metaphor." Science itself depends upon the worldview of the researcher – it is always *the I* conducting the research – within and from her or his ontological and epistemological position. Also in the natural and physical sciences, the science is conducted by researchers who have certain preconceived truths and beliefs about the world – the matter of position and perspective. In fact, most natural and physical scientists will readily admit, if not advance the theory, that there work is primarily generated and driven by subjective notions and concepts (see Capra 1975). For most, these are turned into "hunches" and "hypotheses" from which to derive later "quantitative" work. By extension to the social sciences, there is no such thing as objective and neutral study of society and social reality.

One of the central philosophers in connection with the development of a subjectivistic and alternative approach is Immanuel Kant (1724–1804). He is one of those philosophers giving inspiration to another philosophic tradition and scientific conception. Kant thought that the inner activities of man as conceptualized in the minds of human beings must be brought into focus. Our thoughts are not turned towards the objects, as they are represented or defined in themselves, independent of human intersubjectivity. Science has only understood the world in so far as we have shaped it ourselves by forming ideas of it. If therefore the sciences shall have at least an element of truth in their analyses, pronouncements, and validity, they must build on the relative necessity,[3] which is maintained by the intersubjective everyday life reality experienced by man.

> one attempts to establish a science unless he has an idea upon which to base it. But in the working out of the science the schema, nay even the definition which, at the start, he first gave of the science, is very seldom adequate to his idea….. For we shall then find that its founder, and often even his latest successors, are grouping for an idea which they have never succeeded in making clear to themselves, and that consequently they have not been in a position to determine the proper content, the articulation (systematic unity), and limits of the science. (Kant 1787/1929: 654–655)

---

[3] That is, the general understanding of man; see Chap. 4.

The sciences do not constitute a reference system standing above, abstracted and removed from the world to justify the validity of everyday life. The scientific conceptualization rests on preconditions, which man places into science himself, by being a participant in the experience world of everyday life. It is not necessary that the single scientist knows everything about the organizing of experience. Therefore he does not necessarily see the viewpoint presupposed by science or the basis of which he works himself. Kant's view of the relation between science and everyday life throws light on science as a human endeavor in which we are responsible ourselves for its outcomes.

Schutz (1973b: 22) underlines this from a phenomenological perspective of the social scientist's facts, events, and data as something with a total different structure than in the objective approach. As we will discuss later in more detail, Schutz observes the field as a social world, which is not structureless in its nature. The world has a special meaning and structure of relevance to those people that live, think, and act in it. Human beings have pre-chosen and pre-interpreted this world through a set of commonsense constructions of everyday life reality.

Such a construct of the world outlines those topics of thoughts that determine individual's actions, define the aim for their actions and the means to achieve them, and are accessible to reach them. This perspective helps people to orient themselves in their natural and sociocultural milieu and to become comfortable with in it. The topics of thoughts that are constructed by the social scientist refer to and are founded upon the topic of thoughts that are constructed by an individual's commonsense thinking as they live their everyday among other people. The constructions, therefore, that the scientist uses are thereby constructions of a second order, namely, constructions that are performed by the actors on the social scene. Then the scientist observes these actions and seeks to understand them in relationship with his scientific procedure rules.

## Qualitative and Interactionism Research Economics to Be a Science

Given that assumption about science itself, then the basic issue for any presentation of theory, method, and empirical research rests with where the researcher starts. Economics in business can be seen as a catalyst to change, since it emanates from the subjective approach since it comes from human imagination. When reality is seen as a social construction through interactionism and symbolic discourse, the researcher can understand how business actors create their realities as social actors. The subjective approach focuses upon understanding of the dynamics of human change within society – the actions related to meanings. Interaction and qualitative methods, therefore, become crucial for describing and understanding as well as explaining the human condition.

In a paper Susman and Evered (1978: 587–) outline "action research" and its historical roots. Without repeating their arguments for action research, they do take the subjective approach with its focus on qualitative methods. For example, they quote Rapoport's 1970 definition: "Action research aims to contribute both to the practical concerns of people in an immediate problematic situation and to the goals of social science by joint collaboration within a mutually acceptable ethical framework." They add to the definition the notion to "develop the self-help competencies of people facing problems." Action research contains a number of elements which correct the deficiencies of positivist science: (1) future-oriented; (2) collaboration; (3) system development; (4) generates theory grounded in action; (5) agnostic; (6) situational.

In summary, the action research approach basically admits that all science is subjective rather than denies it. Therefore, and there is no other way, for any understanding of any society, we have to acknowledge the researcher's position and perspective. From that point, decisions and policies can be asserted and developed.

An example of this subjective perspective can be seen in the works of Alfred Schutz, whom we will discuss in Chap. 4. Suffice it to say, at this point a few points from his perspective need to be made. Schutz thought that the aim of social science was the understanding of social reality that he defined as the everyday Lifeworld. In the natural attitude, the understanding of reality is something which man takes for granted and which is not problematized in the everyday of life. The primary goal of the social sciences is seen as to obtain organized knowledge of social reality. By social reality, Schutz understands the sum total of objects and occurrences within the social cultural world *as experienced by the commonsense thinking of men* living their daily lives among their fellow men, connected with them in manifold relations of interaction. It is a world of cultural objects and social institutions in which we are born, in which we have to find our bearings, and with which we have to come to terms. Seen from outside, we experience the world we live in as a world which is both in nature and of culture, not as a private world, but as an intersubjective world. It is a world common to all of us, either actually given or potentially accessible to everyone; and this involves intercommunication and languages since they are part of an intersubjective world. It is in this world that action shall be understood (Schutz 1970: 5). The social reality is both my reality and my Lifeworld, and the reality is social – it is a cultural reality.

## Context of Business Economics and Culture

Edward Hall (1959) noted that "culture is communication" and, conversely, "communication is culture." Human beings are unique in that they form cultures based upon symbol systems – language. People communicate due to their particular culture. They then learn the culture's meanings of rules, values, and norms. The study of cultures has traditionally been done by anthropologists and later other social sciences such as linguists (see Chomsky's various works). Business economists have used the term "culture" as in "corporate culture" and "organizational culture" or "cultural context" or "cultural variables."[4] In most of these studies, culture is examined from the functionalism perspective.

For example, Hofstede (1980a) argues for the use of "cultural" factors in examining business relationships to the point where he posits a psychological matrix for examining businesses across all cultures. While respecting the differences between cultures, the matrix constructs a new series of "cultural stereotypes." Consider Gullestrup (1992, 1997), who examines business economics on two dimensions with the use of structural-functional explanations. While his perspective is a refreshing contribution to understanding the multidimensionally of businesses, it is derived from the functionalistic paradigm. Kuada (1984) correctly demonstrates that the "Western management" perspective fails in Africa, for example, due to the cultural differences between Western and African cultures. However, he then argues for a structural-functionalist paradigm in examining African societies. In short, he uses the same Western cultural determinist paradigm for justifying African economic cultures that were used to promote Western managerial perspectives and styles in Africa.

Berger (1991) presents a different perspective for understanding culture through the "interpretative" perspective. "Culture," as defined in Berger, "encompasses the totality of life of distinct groups of people, their interpersonal relations and attitudes as well as their values, beliefs, norms, and cognitive styles" (ibid., p. 5). Culture is an "ideal-type" concept and "rarely exists in pure form in social reality" (ibid., p. 6). In other words, culture for any group of people represents their values and beliefs through interpersonal relations. In short, Berger applies an interpretative paradigm to the understanding of entrepreneurship, thereby setting the stage for further inquiry into business economics in general. Her argument is the most compelling one for the use of culture as a concept, but clearly the culture takes on an entirely different meaning with her work. Unfortunately the other contributions to her book are not as compelling.

For the most part, theorists who use anthropological concepts such as culture have traditionally been deterministic logical positivists, who see the culture as divided into measurable functions and structures (see Barth 1962). Without reviewing the epistemological basis for the center field, anthropologists and those who use their concepts (field and site visits, in-depth interviews, participant observation, etc.) as part of their research contribute methodologically to the understanding of businesses. The qualitative methods developed from anthropology, rather its theoretical assumptions, are the most important contribution from this academic specialty.

The interactions between actors within situation must be the focus of empirical research if science is to understand everyday life and be able to "explain" and "predict" human actions. The basic methodology for understanding the business actor rests within the discipline of sociology and anthropology; the theoretical framework is drawn from interactionism, linguistics, and phenomenology.

---

[4] See Hofstede (1980a), Berger (1991), Gullestrup (1992), Kuada (1992), etc.

## Sociological Phenomenology and Organizations

From a sociological-phenomenological perspective, the organization is defined by the present and past actions and interactions of people within situations. As Fast (1993) argues, the very definition of an organization or firm is the sum of all its past, present, and future actions interpreted by the actors and attached meanings. Consequently, understanding a company can be seen in the actions and interactions among the people that comprise it. To understand how organizations operate in a region, nation, or international context, it is critical to analyze its interactions with other organizations and the creation of meanings by those people involved.

An organization can be understood through the actors who by their actions and knowledge create meanings of the firm in their everyday of life. The actions exist in a context that is created by the actor through his actions. The action is related to the concrete understanding of the situation and the actor's context of meanings (see Blumer; Schutz 1972; Mead 1962; Brown 1978; Jehenson 1978).

The actor has motives and definitions of the situation that makes that his social world has an inner logic. Knowledge can be understood as moving pictures of reality: experiences and information are produced through actions and transformed (by interpretation and retrospection) to the knowledge that the actors experiences as useful and relevant. The world with which the actor is confronted is composed of experiences, which the process of consciousness will develop or simplify towards different paths (or structures) and transformed into actions (again). Knowledge is thereby a construction by the actors in their everyday of life and "environment."

Precisely because knowledge is a relation to and an orientation towards the "environment" through action, the environment should be understood in relation to time and space. This can be seen in the conscious human being in "the natural attitude" first of all is interested in that part of his everyday of life world that is in his reach and that in time and space are centered around him (see also Schutz 1973b: 73–). The place where the body occupies the world, the actual Here, is the point from which one orients oneself in the space. In relation to this, one organizes elements in the environment.

Similarly, the actual Now is the origin of all the time perspectives under which one organizes events in the world as before and after, and so on. The actors construct their reality (in the sense of meanings), individually and collectively, but they do not experience it in this way. Moreover, they see reality as if they live in an external world independent of themselves. Through the language and typifications, we understand things as being natural and that society is something "out there" that we cannot change. The reason for this stability is that from our knowledge, we "know" the world and that others' actions confirm us in a given understanding of the world (see also Hennestad 1986; Silverman 1983) (see Chap. 7 for the further discussion).

## Symbolic Interactionism

The primary mode for understanding organizational or collective actions is through the symbols (and meaning of) involved in the interaction. Symbolic interactionism is the study of collective action between groups or organizations. For this discussion, the analysis of organizational actions must be seen within the context. The context helps to define the interactions. However, each context has a history of events that frame it. And the interactions themselves redefine and create a new set of circumstances from which the organization operates. Contextual analysis, therefore, can be limited and static since they reflect the status quo and on-dimensional perspective of the past. In order to understand the present actions of an organization, and even attempt to predict its future actions, specific situations must be studied.

George Herbert Mead (1962, originally 1932) at the turn of the twentieth century from the University of Chicago formulated the philosophical basis for symbolic interactionist theory upon which Herbert Blumer (1969) expounded. The symbolic interactionist theory discusses how human beings act and interact. Mead, with his student and subsequent chief proponent, Blumer, laid the groundwork for much of the theory behind "qualitative theory" today in American sociology. Mead drew upon elements in both European and Eastern philosophy to counteract the empiricist and positivist determinists who dominate the development of the social sciences.

Mead and Blumer argued that individuals are actors who alone or in a group interact in a variety of situations. Since human beings are thinking and reflecting, these interactions and the study of them are the basis of all human behavior. Language is used between actors as they interact. The ability of humans to create symbols (language and gestures, etc.) distinguishes the species from all others. Understanding and then explaining human action, however, is an extension of human interactions.

Blumer refined Mead's theories into a practical and simple approach to understanding how people act and interact. He assumed that since humans think, then they must reflect before they act. In short, humans create and take action in situation through the thinking process based upon their reflective ideas and thoughts. In order to theorize as to how this is done, Blumer used Mead's concept of the "generalized other" or the fact that people think and reflect to themselves before they take action.

Human behavior is unpredictable, full of uncertainty, and therefore chaotic. When scientists study and theorize about normative behavior, they have focused on some set of elements that compose human behavior. Because people are human beings, their everyday lives are made up of uncertainties and chaos. Human beings have an infinite set of behaviors and possible patterns to follow. Everyday life may be composed of set and regular routines, but these are neither normal nor indicative of the creative potential of individual actors. They simply signify what people follow for convenience or expediency sake. They certainly are not the situations from which to draw significant conclusions about actors, situations, groups, or collective behavior. In short, human interaction is by definition "abnormal." The essence of abnormal behavior, however, is that it constitutes its own processes and orderliness for individual actors and groups. The understanding of "abnormal" behavior is really the knowledge of what is "normal" for actors and can best be seen in conflictual situation where actors will display underlying emotions, feelings, and thoughts.

So the questions to ask are what science is and what science can.

# Chapter 3
# Understanding the Organization of Science

## Science and Philosophy of Science

The questions to ask to science are the following: What is the spirit of science? What are the assumptions and beliefs in science? What is the essence of science? Are all sciences alike? What is science in relation to humans, society, and everyday life? What is good science? To raise those questions means that we enter the discussions of philosophy and philosophy of science, e.g., the discussions of ontology and epistemology. First of all what should science do and what is the meaning of science? Kjørup (1987: 35) thinks that initially, one may say that the tasks of science are:

(a) To create new knowledge of which a part may be subjected to technical and administrative utilization.
(b) To maintain and pass on "old" knowledge and factual and ideological traditions, through continuous new interpretations, through which science is consequently ideology producing itself.
(c) To educate candidates of which some will continue the work with solving the tasks outlined here, while others get a series of – in the broadest sense – disseminating and administrative tasks in society.
(d) We will add a fourth task: that the task of science also is to *criticize* itself as science, to criticize social matters, and to contribute with constructive proposals to changes in society, i.e., to reflect on itself and its context.

These tasks are in no way clear and unambiguous. There does not exist a solid agreement on them in the academic research workers and their communities. In other words, there is a sharp and hard disagreement about what science is and what good science should be – provided that there is a discussion of ontology and epistemology in the specific science at all (i.e., of basis of understanding and cognition).

© Springer Nature Switzerland AG 2019
W. W. Clark II, M. Fast, *Qualitative Economics*,
https://doi.org/10.1007/978-3-030-05937-8_3

Science must essentially be understood as human activity, intellectual and action-oriented. Further science is something that a human being does and in a context constituted by other human beings. There is thus nothing mysterious about the activity or that it is something that lies beyond everyday life. In principle, it is an activity that everybody can do or understand. Science is in everyday life and is about our reality, how we understand it, how we see problems and solutions, and how we find our bearings in realities.

Many people talk about social problems and about what real science is. In connection with a technical competition for young amateur inventors, a professor from the Technical University of Denmark in Copenhagen stated:

> We are engulfed with astrology, fandangle medicine and many other things. The thing needed by the Danish industry is real science – natural sciences. (Professor Thor A. Bak, Denmark Radio, Television News 3/6 1994, *our translation*)

We will not discuss whether T.A. Bak might not mean what he says or whether he is expressing himself a little dotty. However, in this short statement, he is guilty of two serious cognitive fallacies:

1. First, he assumes that his definition of "real science" can be used as standard to define and judge all other sciences, and if not, it is not a science that can produce knowledge and solutions.
2. Secondly, which is probably more tragic, he derives his view from natural science, that the problems which may exist in the Danish industry can (only) be solved through his science: that the problems that the Danish industry might have are of a technical and natural scientific nature. How can we be sure about that?

What T. A. Bak is saying here is just one example out of many dealing with science, knowledge, problem understanding, and solutions. We may go as far as saying that this is the standard in many of the trends of science today, possibly especially in the more classically, natural scientifically oriented fields, but indeed also in business economics.

There seems to be a lack of problem-orientation and interdisciplinarity in the discussion and of understanding of reality and thus of the limits and possibilities of the science. It is taken for granted that the science one has is the real one (the only one) and that it can solve (all) the problems. People hang on to their science and its frame of references, and *not* on a discussion of cognition of *how* the problem "is," and how it could be understood. The essence of all knowledge and every perspective on reality is that it is always an *"I"* that is looking upon the phenomenon of reality and is seeking an understanding and in interaction with other. T.A. Bak's statement is based on a tradition that we can trace back in time.

## The Development of Science

In the history of science, there have been many opinions about what science and real science is, what knowledge is, and what should be regarded as unscientific. Von Wright (1991) discusses some of this in his understanding of the development of science. He distinguishes between *magic and science*. Magic is the conception of connections and explanations of the Middle Ages, what Von Wright calls "purpose rationality" in the understanding of reality. Science is the modern natural scientific conception, which we today call the classical natural science, the one from the 1600s and the 1700s (e.g., Kepler *Mysterium Cosmographicum* 1621; Newton *Principia* 1687).

Von Wright thinks that the view existing on the most essential differences between magic and science is that first magic builds on obviously wrong ideas of the legalities of nature and consequently is an inferior, less perfect form of rationality than science. But this is an unjust judgment, as the world of conceptions underlying the magic is not a collection of doubtful hypotheses which can be tested and added to the experiences, but, on the contrary, that to us it is a quite different and promoting *way of thinking* (ibid., p. 41).

In his thoughts about logic, language, and truth, Wittgenstein (1993: 84) arrives at the conclusion that we cannot join the events of the future based on the present events. The belief in chains of events is superstition. Logic, he says, is not a science but a (understood as mine) reflected image of the world (ibid., p. 118). Logic is transcendental – the limits of my language mean the limits of my world. Logic fills the world; the limits of the world are also the limits of logic. In the logic we thus cannot say *this and that* exist in the world, but *the other* does not exist. That would imply that we exclude certain possibilities that cannot be the case, as logic should then exceed the limits of the world, if it could also consider these limits from the other side. What we cannot think, we cannot think; and therefore we cannot *say* what we cannot think. That the world is *my* world is proved by the fact that the limits of the language (the only language that I understand) mean the limits of *my* world (ibid., p. 107).

Therefore, you may ask yourself (if magic and superstition are the same) whether the magic of the Middle Ages was replaced by another kind of magic. Wittgenstein is of the opinion that the entire worldview is based on the illusion that the so-called natural laws are explanations of natural phenomena (ibid., p. 125). Thus they stopped at the natural laws as something unassailable, just like they previously stopped at God and fate. And both parties were right and wrong. The old one was actually clearer, as they recognized a clear conclusion, while in the new system, it shall look as if everything is explained. Nietzsche has a comment on this and says:

> Do you really believe that the sciences had risen and grown big, if the sorcerers, alchemists, astrologers and witches had not been their forerunners and those who – with their prophecies and prospects – first had to create the thirst and the hunger after hidden and forbidden powers and the delight they cause. (Nietzsche 1987: 197; *our translation*)

This discussion of science as ways of thinking is central in the understanding of science and its development. It is exactly about different ways of thinking, and besides, there are different opinions of what reality is. We will return to this later and discuss different ways of thinking and understanding reality in social science.

## *(Natural) Science*

Science, and the new way of thinking, was formulated in the 1600s and the 1700s. Francis Bacon's (1561–1626), Galileo Galilei's (1564–1642), René Descartes's (1595–1650), etc. efforts were of great importance to the appearance of this new scientific way of seeing and explaining reality. The fundamental features in this can be understood in the following ways (see Von Wright, op cit., p. 45):

One feature has to do with a new view of the relationship between *man and nature*: nature is the object, man the subject. Man faces the nature, partly as an observer, partly as a manipulator. The objectification or reification of nature also leads to a clear-cut distinction between facts and values, between to describe and to explain. Values belong to the reality of the subject. They cannot be found by studying the natural order. The natural laws are "iron" and "inflexible," and they give no clues for the good and the right way of living. That values do not exist in nature does not necessarily mean that values are the incidental idea of man.

There is another possibility too that they are an expression of the will of God or otherwise have a "supernatural" source – "an invisible hand." A trait in the understanding of the nature of science is the nature as a lawful order. Combined with the objectivating view, this conception becomes strictly deterministic and mechanical. That this form of determinism is also mechanical means that all events in nature can, in the last resort, be traced back to movements of bodies, i.e., the field of physics.

Another feature in the way of thinking has to do with the relationship between *the whole and its parts* (ibid., p. 48). Both the material bodies and events in nature can be analyzed, divided into elementary components, where their properties and mode of operation determine the whole. The whole is to be understood from the parts. The division into components is analysis: the whole's construction of the parts synthesis. This conception is called *meristic*[1] and *atomistic* (cf. Structure functionalism). As opposed to the meristic methodology, there is the *holistic*.[2] To have a holistic view on the whole (a system, a totality) is to understand its properties and modes of operation on the basis of laws applying to the whole. This means that the whole stands before the parts, and the whole is more than the parts (cf. System theory).

A third feature in the rationality of this view of science is the part that the *experiment*, the deliberate intervention, plays in the attempt to explain nature. In an experiment one studies a piece of "artificial nature." The object under study is isolated from the surroundings and is secured against disturbing influence. One simplifies a situation to be able to get a comprehensive view of it and, if possible, to control and vary the elements, which are supposed to influence the result of the experiment. The scientific method in this science is also named inductive, to go from the single case to the general, and often creates the legal case. The causal relations are in focus.

---

[1] From Greek *meros*, part.

[2] From Greek *holos*, whole.

The Development of Science

A last feature is the *openness or access* of science to the public, here understood as openness to society and ordinary human beings. Science was not available to everyone without more ado. It was necessary to learn to understand the language of science and use its methods to achieve knowledge. This means that science was removed from everyday life reality and developed by certain self-selected persons (the scholars/the researcher) in certain environments (the universities). In this context the new students of science were then admitted and introduced to the universe of science.

## Social Science and Objectivism: Positivism and Rationalism

At the time when the social science was established (i.e., in the 1800s), attention was directed to find a scientific foundation. The conception of science existing at that time therefore influenced the very establishment dominantly. Social science would try to replicate or emulate the established natural science and its roots in objectivism. The existing conception of science was just that of natural science and the positivistic (and empiricist) and rationalistic philosophy of science.

## Positivism (A Comte 1798–1857, E Durkheim 1858–1917)

The tradition of positivism can partly be seen as a designation of a philosophic system and partly as a scientific way of thinking. An understanding and characterization of the scientific positivism is the belief that science is neutral to metaphysical matters, that scientific knowledge must be limited to the field of experience (the senses), and that the ideal form of knowledge is of a natural scientific character. As human knowledge is limited to that which is experienced, then science – cleared of metaphysical preconditions – must be concentrated (reduced) to discovering reliable correlation's within these experiences.

On this basis future events can thus be explained. Explanation of a phenomenon therefore means to demonstrate it as an example of one or more laws, and such a law is understood as "a well-confirmed, generally descriptive assertion about uniform states which have been observed previously" (cf. Flato 1985: 28). The characteristic feature of the approach can thus be seen in the following statements[3]:

1. A rejection of metaphysics (i.e., the speculative, philosophical, ideological) as being nonscientific.
2. What can immediately be observed is the object of science (empiricism).
3. Scientific work should, dependent on its object, have effects according to one and the same method (the idea of a unitary science).

---

[3] cf. Arbnor and Bjerke (1981, 1997: 52–); Cuff and Payne (1982: 190).

4. The explanations to be produced about the social reality should be of the same type as the natural scientific. This means that assertions about legalities should be expressed in the form "A causes B."
5. To the greatest possible extent, the same types of methods should be used as in natural science to construct and test these explanations. An important consequence of this is that you have to formulate your procedure from the logic underlying the most distinguished instrument of natural science, i.e., the experimental method.

Above all, the positivist approach to science was quantifiable, from the ontological argument that the world and thereby reality were mathematical in its structure. Observation of this reality could be counted. They could be segmented into variables that could then be verified by deriving probabilistic statements from the statistical counting of discrete elements within each variable. Related to the above, we may also say that the positivistic tradition can also be called a single-method tradition. Its primary themes can be summed up in three statements (Polkinghorne 1983: 18):

1) All metaphysics should be rejected and knowledge confined to what has been experienced or can be experienced. Thus science should restrict itself to discovering reliable correlation within experience.
2) The adequacy of knowledge increases as it approximates the forms of explanation, which have been achieved by the most advanced sciences.
3) Scientific explanations are limited to only functional and directional laws or to only mathematically functional laws.

The very concept of positivism originates from A Comte who viewed the science of sociology as studying society and man (cf. Comte 1844: Korpen 1991: 25). Comte had some fixed ideas of the part of science in society and what it should be. In this discussion Comte introduced *the positive* and incorporated the following five issues of the concept (ibid., p. 37; cf. Kjørup 1987: 93):

1) The positive is the *real*, in contrast to the fictive or imagined. Positivism does not deal with loose speculations, but with the world of reality within the reach of common sense.
2) The positive is the *useful*, in contrast to the harmful or useless. A positivist must tackle subjects with relevance to humanity and improve our conditions and solve problems that can improve its situation. This, instead of trying to satisfy an unfruitful curiosity.
3) The positive is the *secure*, in contrast to the insecure and debatable. It is about arranging a logical harmony, both inside the individual and inside the intellectual fellowship of the entire mankind, instead of diffuse doubt and endless discussions.
4) The positive is the *precise*, in contrast to the vague and unclear, which was characteristic of the thinking of that time. It is about achieving an extent of precision which is compatible with the nature of events and which is in accordance with our actual needs (of discipline).
5) The positive is just *positive*, in contrast to the negative. It is about building up and organizing, not destroying.

There was a particular reason for Comte to formulate the foundation of science around the positive, which is connected with his view and criticism of the thinking and lack of (scientific) rationality in society and history. Comte was of the opinion that the development of science will pass three stages: "the primitive theological state, the transient metaphysical, and the final positive state" (Comte 1965: 1332). In the final, the positive state, the mind has given over the vain search after absolute

The Development of Science                                                          35

notions, the origin and destination of the universe, and the causes of phenomena and applies itself to the study of laws, i.e., their invariable relations of succession and resemblance. Reasoning and observation duly combined are the means of this knowledge (Burrell and Morgan 1980: 41).

These three stages in social development and in cognition are understood as *the theological state*, in which man takes his bearings on the basis of religious conceptions and the phenomena and events of nature are explained through the intervention of gods. *The metaphysical state*, in which these conceptions slowly are undermined, but without an establishment of a new sustainable basis of orientation. The phenomena are explained through impersonal and abstract ideas and forces. In society unrest and egoism are prevailing; the royal power is replaced by the rule of the people and the military machinery of power by the legal (cf. Fink 1973: 9). *The positive* is characterized by a sustained scientific attitude to all fields of the existence, and no superior reality behind the world of experiences was recognized. The notion in this is that science must be used to free man from irrationality: science should become a philosophy of life so that any decision on action can be rationally founded. Comte goes so far that he calls the part of science in society *the positive regime*: "… it is only at this stage, the only entirely normal that the human common sense gets it's in all senses final regulation" (Comte 1844: Korpen 1991: 9).

Thus Comte thought that knowledge and society were in a process of evolutionary alteration and that the function of sociology was to understand the necessary, absolute, and clear causes in history, in a way that contributes to the realization of a new social order. The vision was a world in which scientific rationality was the superior and basic feature in a regulating social order in the society. This means that science is able to predict (and rule) the future by uncovering history – on the basis of objective criteria – and through the evolutionary manifestation.

The natural scientific methods should play a decisive part in uncovering the social world, observation techniques, and supervision being pointed out as means for this. Sociology should be based on the methods and models used by natural science. The laws explaining the relations between different parts of the society should be discovered: the *social statics* (the structure) and in which way they changed over time and by which this is controlled, the *social dynamics* (the process – the evolutionary).[4] Comte thought that the core of science lies in *the laws* of the events, while the facts we find do never offer anything but a valuable material (Comte 1844: Korpen 1991: 19). The true positive thought, according to Comte, before all consists in watching to be able to predict, to study things, as they are to be able to derive the future, in unity with the thesis on the constancy of the natural laws. Comte made much of stressing the connection between biology and social science. Biology was to him a dividing line between organic and nonorganic, in the way that it was the living totality, which was sought and explained (Comte 1965: 125–).

It was thus an objectivistic tradition, which sprang up, characterized by an image of an objective world in itself (an autonomic reality external of the individual human being), lawfulness, and distance as well as facts and strictness (technical and

---

[4] Comte (1965: 125); cf. Burrell and Morgan (1980: 42), Cuff and Payne (1982: 36).

mathematical/quantitative) in the research approach and in the research practice. Even if it is the positivism that is described here, there are different traditions and perspectives in this period, within which there was great disagreement between supporters of either of them. Superiorly these objectivistic traditions are the following:

## Rationalism[5] (R Descartes 1596–1650; B de Spinoza 1632–1677; G W Leibniz 1646–1716)

Rationalism is the other main tradition influencing social science and business economics, and it can be seen as a critique of the epistemology of empiricism and positivism, even though they shared the ontology of a reality in itself. According to rationalism cognition rests on insight into the logical connections of the reality. These are understood and proved logically by means of reason – thinking. The senses – the empirical experiences – may inspire us, but they cannot give us certain knowledge of universal laws. We cannot through sensory observations find out what is right and what is wrong. The method of proof implies buildup of a formal system using formal logical (pure logic) procedures of proof, especially mathematical models (a technical symbol language). The thought is that common sense can release man where the impersonal and the deductive production form is a mathematical ideal of cognition, at the same time being an expression of the rationalistic thought that the order of common sense is identical with the natural order (Spinoza, in Lübcke 1994a: 406).

R. Descartes' central purpose was to establish an overall philosophical system of thoughts, where the foundation should be a united science based on mathematic. The two most widely known of Descartes' philosophical ideas are those of a method of hyperbolic (or exaggerated) doubt and the argument that, though he may doubt, he cannot doubt that he exists: "I think, therefore I am" ("Cogito, ergo sum"), followed by – "I am a being of consciousness" ("Sum res cogitans") – and with a soul. The existence of everything else – physical things, the past, other human beings, my body, God, etc. – must if possible be explained from what is given, my own existence, and consciousness. The attribution of thought to the soul is the starting point of his ontological distinction. That distinction is between thinking substance (res cogitans) and extended substance (res extensa). The two substances are mutually exclusive. A thinking substance is nonphysical or spiritual in nature, and an extended substance is physical, but not capable of consciousness or thought. For Descartes, a thinking thing is a thing which doubts, understands, (conceives), affirms, denies, wills, refuses, which also imagines and feels.

The method of doubt comprises a key aspect of Descartes' philosophical method. He refused to accept the authority of previous philosophers – but he also refused to accept the obviousness of his own senses. In the search for a foundation for philosophy, whatever could be doubted must be rejected. He resolves to trust only that

---

[5] From Latin *ratio* – reason. See also Leibniz G W (1646–1716) Rationalism.

The Development of Science

which is clearly and distinctly seen to be beyond any doubt. In this manner, Descartes peels away the layers of beliefs and opinions that clouded his view of the truth. But, very little remains: only the simple fact of doubting itself and the inescapable inference that something exists doubting, namely, Descartes himself. So the Cartesian method consists of a belief in the certainties of the "clear and distinctive perceptions" of the solitary individual contemplating an external reality. Everything else is to be treated with skepticism (see also Delanty 2005)

Descartes next task was to reconstruct our knowledge piece by piece, such that at no stage is the possibility of doubt allowed creeping back. In this manner, Descartes proves that he himself must have the basic characteristic of thinking and that this thinking thing (mind) is quite distinct from his body, the existence of a God, the existence and nature of the external world, and so on. What is important in this for Descartes is, first, that he is showing that knowledge is genuinely possible (and thus that skeptics must be mistaken) and, second, that, more particularly, a mathematically based scientific knowledge of the material world is possible.

Descartes meant, that the human being was more able to see through machines and therefore as far as possible should seek to explain all movements in the world as if the whole world was a machine.[6] But the security of mathematics was not enough to legitimate science, and his argument for natural science ends up in a metaphysics, where its primal function is to give balance in and fundamental worldview in natural science, that the human being has to create in its own picture.[7] Balance and a fundamental view are for him the same as absolute security. Science cannot be argued from *the I* in the subjective soul but demands as its fundament the metaphysical I, which existence is proved by the cogito-sentence.

The scientific procedure is founded in a complex of analyses, whereby the problem – the complex topic – is broken down in its intuitively recognized smallest parts and syntheses, whereby the topic is reconstructed from its smallest part by logical operations (deduction). Used in the proper way, this will secure the correct results in all topics that can be treated rational.

Descartes notes that when he contemplates the certainty of his existence, he knows the truth of his existence clearly and distinctly. He proposes a general rule: everything he perceives clearly and distinctly is true. This rule has in effect been in operation throughout the previous discussions. Descartes would like to use this general rule in order to move beyond the "I think, I exist," for example, to show both the existence of external objects and the truth of mathematics. Unfortunately, knowledge of external objects does not rise to the level of clarity and distinctness. Sensory judgments about particular things in the external world at first seemed vivid and immediate but later proved to be questionable. By contrast, mathematical judgments are perceived in a manner that appears to be clear and distinct. Such judgments were thus able to pass unscathed through most of the tests in the procedure of hyperbolic doubt. However, he believed that a more condensed and universal list of methodological rules was better than a lengthy and varied list.

---

[6] Næss (1991a: 456).

[7] Nerheim and Rossvær (1990: 99).

The first was never to accept anything as true if I did not have evident knowledge of its truth, that is, carefully to avoid precipitate conclusions and preconceptions and to include nothing more in my judgments than what presented itself to my mind so clearly and distinctly that I had no occasion to doubt it. The second, to divide each of the difficulties I examined into as many parts as possible and as may be required in order to resolve them better. The third, to direct my thoughts in an orderly manner, by beginning with the simplest and most easily known objects in order to ascend little by little, step-by-step, to knowledge of the most complex, and by supposing some order even among objects that have no natural order of precedence. And the last, throughout to make enumerations so complete, and reviews so comprehensive, that I could be sure of leaving nothing out (Burnham and Fieser 2001).

## Empiricism (T Hobbes 1588–1679; J Locke 1632–1704; G Berkeley 1658–1753; D Hume 1711–1776; J S Mill 1806–1873: The English Empiricists)

The empiricism perspective is that all knowledge on reality originates from the sensory experience. The core is the two theses which both contradict the basic theses in rationalism:

1. All concepts are derived from the sensory experience. That is, an expression is only meaningful if the rules of the language either directly or indirectly (through other expressions) are linked to something given in the experience. The thesis excludes the existence of a priori concepts understood as concepts, which have valid application at the experience but which exist in the consciousness (the language) and are independent of it. The basic thing is to show that declared a priori concepts can either be analyzed into more simple concepts derived from experience or they are simply empty.
2. Any statement expressing knowledge of actual facts is based on the sensory experience. The statement itself is either a description of something given by experience or it has logical relations to such a description. In the latter case, there are two possibilities: that the statement is a logical consequence of descriptions of experiences or that logically it results in descriptions of experiences so that the truth of those inductively issues the statement probability or security. The thesis excludes the existence of (so-called synthetic a priori) truths that at the same time are informative about reality and logically independent of the experience. Any truth, which stands firm independently of experience and in that sense is necessary, is analytical. This means that a definitional truth like "all bachelors are unmarried" is only a consequence of randomly fixed relations between the meanings of words and tells nothing about reality (i.e., is a tautology – a meaningless statement). The formal truths of mathematics and logic are thus analytical. Our knowledge of reality is identical with our empirical knowledge that

The Development of Science 39

materializes through observance, remembrance, and inductive conclusion. The two first mentioned deliver the given basis of cognition, and the third permits the transgression of it, as it justifies statements about what was once, what will be, or always is the case.

## Positivism

In relation to tradition of empiricism and positivism, the following can be added: *J. Bentham* (1748–1832) utilitarianism, moral theory according to which the correct action, from a moral point of view, is the one which – as compared with other possibilities – produces the quantity of positive (nonethical) values. The moral value of the action depends on its ability to increase the quantity of positive values of nonethical nature, for example, happiness, richness, good health, beauty, insight, etc. *H. Spencer* (1820–1903) structural functionalism, *R. Avenarius* (1843–1896) empirical criticism, epistemological movements within positivism trying to find the basis for cognition in the pure sensations, and *E. Mach* (1838–1916, empirical criticism). *Logical positivism* (the Wiener circle, around 1923 in Vienna) was based on a confrontation with the view that philosophy a priori, i.e., only through thinking can become aware of the nature of the world. The supporters thought that all sciences aim at finding legalities between observable phenomena and that there is no decisive logical or methodological difference between the sciences. It is therefore possible to coordinate the different sciences within one unitary science.

## Realism

Realism is in the conception where the reality exists independent of whether it is experienced or can be experienced. This means that the surrounding world, the space-time reality, exists independent of human consciousness. It contains an epistemological conception that with our sensory experiences, we have access to a reality independent of consciousness. This can take three forms: (a) Our sensory experiences give a direct and safe access to reality (naive realism). (b) Our sensory experiences originate in the physical reality but can never give us certain cognition. What we experience directly is always representations of reality, for example, in the shape of sensory data, and we never have the possibility of comparing them with reality itself (representative realism). (c) Our sensory experiences only give us indirect access to reality, and it is possible to go behind our sensory experiences to a well-founded conception of the physical reality.

The impression is thus that reality is bipartite: *the visible* that which can be sensed and which can produce relevant data and *the invisible*, where the laws/mechanisms for reality exist (Fig. 3.1).

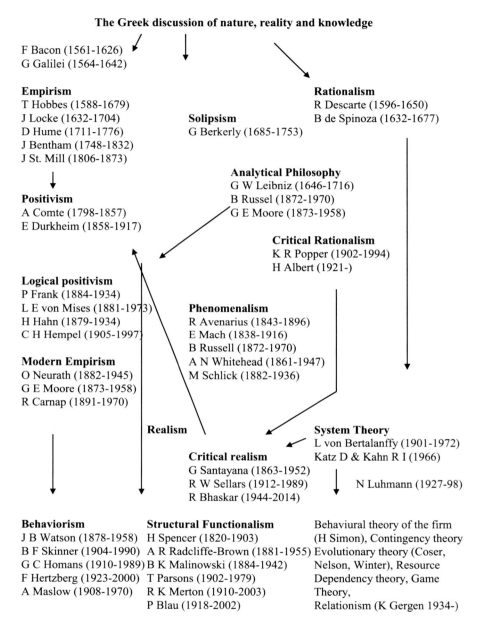

Fig. 3.1 A chart over objectivistic traditions and persons – some examples of thinking and movements of thoughts

Positivism is described in many ways, but the perhaps most adequate is Nietzsche's description of positivism, "as the science stopping at phenomena" (and says): "there are only facts." To which Nietzsche quickly replies: "No, facts are exactly what does not exist – there are only interpretations."[8]

Today positivism as philosophical thinking could be discussed if it is dead and gone. Few would think of calling himself a positivist, and there has been a tendency the last decade to state that one is a critical realist. But this seems to be an attempt to state that one has a scientific perspective, and in general it looks like system theory. The weakness of critical realism seems to be the lack of a line of arguments from ontology, epistemology, and the concrete empirical study. In everyday life the positivistic and critical realist thoughts are natural to all of us, and it is difficult to maintain a consequent non-positivistic way of thinking. This is the case not just in science, but the discussion of truth and objectivity is also natural theoretical attitudes for people in general. The above appears clearly, when – for example – we think of the statements of politicians and experts on connections, causes, and effects in society. The simple positivism lives on in everyday logic and in conceptions of connections: cause – effect, true – false. We find the logic of positivism in the language and the usage, which reflects our conceptions of reality, e.g., in system, structure, organism analogy, behavior, stimuli – response, explanation, time concept (that time could be explained of the movement from one point to another), numeral concepts (e.g., marking scales), knowledge concepts (as a sum that accumulates), etc. In other words, people attempt to quantify and objectivate various qualitative phenomena that we experience in our social context, without reflecting: is it possible to do that?

## Another Science

### *The Science of Subjectivism and Lifeworld*

There are, of course, many alternative ways of thinking, which can be traced through history, all the way back to the old Greeks. Parallel with the strong influence from a positivistic-rationalistic philosophy in the development of social science, a subjectivist philosophy and scientific tradition have existed and been developed. Andersson (1992: 110) thinks that this always has been the case, in all cultures, because it is the natural way to acquire knowledge. He calls the tradition the hermeneutic research method. The keywords in this are empathy ("sympathetic insight"), engagement, and understanding and can be seen in relation to what it means to exist as a human being – it is the way in which we live our lives. It should therefore also be a natural consequence that the social science formulates its epistemology and methodology on this basis, too. This is the central point in the tradition: It is about us and our lives and how to investigate it – the everyday of life reality and the matter of nearness.

---

[8] See, for example, Alvesson and Sköldberg (1994: 25).

The philosophical assumption and discussion of the concepts of Lifeworld and reality can, in short, be understood in the following way.[9] In general it is through discussions that describes and seeks understandings of everyday of life, people's life situations, life and reality as it appears and is unfold for people.[10] The Lifeworld can, in short, be understood as the immediate experienced world, as it appears before it is made an object for scientific investigation and as the historical reality as human beings immediately orientate themselves out of. It is the reality we are in and confronted with.

Reality can be understood as what W. James (in Schutz 1973b: 60) proclaims: "reality simply means the relation to our sensitive and active life. The origin of reality is subjective; everything that stimulates our interest is real. To name a thing real means that this thing is in a certain relationship to us." The word "reality" is briefly a frame.

This is the broad understanding of Lifeworld as the reality, especially in relation to hermeneutic and phenomenology (see Heidegger, Gadamer, Schutz, and Merleau-Ponty). It is this Lifeworld we have to relate ourselves towards and understand every human activities upon and that all scientific and philosophical understanding must be based upon. The argument for this in which way is however different between the traditions.

For example, Gadamer (1993: 247) means that the concept of Lifeworld is the antithesis of all objectivism. That it is an essentially historical concept, which does not refer to a universe of being ("Dasein" – see Heidegger in Chap. 4), to an "existent world." In fact, not even the infinite idea of a true world can be meaningfully created out of the infinite progress of human historical worlds in historical experience (*Erfahrung*). It is something quite different from what the natural science could even ideally achieve. The Lifeworld means something else, namely, that in which we live as historical creatures. And here we cannot avoid the consequence that, given the historicity of experience implied in it, the idea of a universe of possible historical Lifeworld simply does not make sense. It is clear that the Lifeworld is always at the same time a communal world that involves being with other people as well. It is a world of persons, and in the natural attitude, the validity of this personal world is always assumed.

Schutz and Luckmann (1974: 3) talk about the reality as "the everyday Lifeworld." This is the province of reality which man continuously participates in ways that are at once inevitable and patterned. It is the region of reality in which man can engage himself and which he can change while he operates in it by means of his animate organism. At the same time, the objectives and events that are already

---

[9] In Chap. 4 we will develop this discussion by looking at the history of the assumptions and the basic concepts of the Lifeworld tradition.

[10] This is typical sociology and anthropology in a broad sense. The most well known in general social science are Goffman (1959), Berger and Luckmann (1966), Garfinkel (1967), and of course Blumer (1969/1986). With those as the theoretical background, scholars have made several different empirical investigations, and one can identify different methodological discussions as arising from the everyday of life thought (e.g., qualitative methods in general, action research).

found in this realm (including the acts and the results of actions of others) limit his free possibilities of action. They place him up against obstacles that can be surmounted, as well as barriers that are insurmountable. Furthermore, only within this realm can he be understood by his fellow men, and only in it can he work together with them. Only in the world of everyday life can a common, communicative, surrounding world be constituted. The world of everyday life is consequently man's fundamental and paramount reality.

The everyday Lifeworld is to be understood as province of reality that the wide-awake and normal adult simply takes for granted in the attitude of common sense. By this taken for grantedness, we designate everything that we experience as unquestionable; every state of affairs is for us unproblematic until further notice. The circumstance that what has up until now been taken for granted can be brought into question and is a point with which, of course, we still have to deal with. In the natural attitude, I always find myself in a world that is for me taken for granted and self-evidently "real." I was born into it and I assume that it existed before me. I simply take it for granted that other men also exist in this world and indeed not only in a bodily manner like and among objects but rather as endowed with a consciousness that is essentially the same as mine. Thus from the outset, my Lifeworld is not my private world but, rather, is intersubjective; the fundamental structure of its reality is that it is shared by us.

Merleau-Ponty (1994: 327) discusses this in relation to the understanding of the human being and the human beings' self-understanding and the natural world: Human behavior opens upon a world (*Welt*) and upon an object (*Gegenstand*) beyond the tools which it makes for itself, and one may even treat one's own body as an object. Human life is defined in terms of this power, which it has of denying itself in objective thought, a power that stems from its primordial attachment to the world itself. Human life "understands" not only a certain definite environment but also an infinite number of possible environments, and it understands itself because it is thrown into a natural world.

The discussion at the level of philosophy of science and on the methodological level within a subjectivistic approach is critical towards the science conception of positivism and rationalism. It was a general view that the objectivistic development within social science made the science ahistorical and psychologically unconscious. The exaggerated assumption of the views of natural science, the use of a reifying descriptive language (e.g., the statistical/mathematical), and the objective of viewing the social systems as mechanical or biological analogies were criticized. Bengtsson (1993: 45) writes, for example, about the mathematical and logical objectivism (understood as positivism): It replaces the tangible Lifeworld with the total of the facts, where the most distinctive characteristic feature is that they can be replaced by any other facts, as neither mathematics nor logic cares for individual attributes and differences. $1 + 1 = 2$, no matter whether it is a human being and a nuclear bomb which is multiplied. The study of human beings thus means that they are reduced to objects, unlike subjects, whose individual lives and characteristic features are disregarded. In such a science, the contact to the Lifeworld has been interrupted completely – it is a study of a reality in which it is not possible to live.

One of the philosophers with an interest in the connection with the development of an alternative approach of thinking in the everyday of life is Immanuel Kant (1724–1804) (1787/1929). He may be considered as central and one of those giving inspiration to an alternative philosophic tradition and science conception. Kant thought that the own activities of man as a conceptualized being must be in focus. Our thoughts are not turned to the objects, as they are in themselves, independent of human intersubjectivity. Our sciences only understand the world insofar as we have shaped it ourselves by forming ideas of it. If therefore the sciences shall have a safe basis, they must build on the relative necessity,[11] which is maintained by virtue of the intersubjective everyday life reality of man:

> No one attempts to establish a science unless he has an idea upon which to base it. But in the working out of the science the schema, nay even the definition which, at the start, he first gave of the science, is very seldom adequate to his idea… For we shall then find that its founder, and often even his latest successors, are grouping for an idea which they have never succeeded in making clear to themselves, and that consequently they have not been in a position to determine the proper content, the articulation (systematic unity), and limits of the science. (Kant 1787/1929: 655–)

The sciences do not constitute a reference system standing above and which can justify the safety of everyday life. The scientific conceptualization rests on preconditions, which man draws into science himself by being a participant in the experienced world of everyday life.

It is not necessary that the single scientist knows anything about this organizing of experience, and therefore he does not necessarily see the viewpoint presupposed by science and on the basis of which he works himself. Kant's view of the relation between science and everyday life throws light on sciences as a human project – it is something for which we are responsible ourselves.

Kant's criticism of the natural scientific, mechanical conception has also another aspect. In his view the tendency in the natural scientific progress since the Renaissance, which shall make man master of nature and the existence meaningful to everybody, may also result in a dehumanization of our own life. The everyday human community that constitutes the proper link, not only between man and nature but also between men, is fixed through a mechanical causation. Thus the natural sciences seem – by virtue of their mechanistic reality conception – to threaten the freedom of man. If everything is causally determined, how can any action then be free, so that man can be held responsible for his actions?

It is in this context that Kant discusses morals. He attaches an experience concept to morals, which is not fixed by the mechanistic concept of causation, which makes the philosophy of morals its own ontology parallel with the theoretical philosophy: We have both a theoretical and a practical reason. The theoretical reason controls the knowledge of reality, which can be perceived by the senses, while the practical reason controls the life of the moral will of man.

Kant's epistemological philosophy has been a source of inspiration, not just as a criticism of the positivistic and rationalistic conceptions but also through the

---

[11] That is, the general understanding of man, see Chap. 4.

establishment of a new foundation for knowledge and understanding reality. There are of course many philosophers throughout history who shall be given the "credit" of the "new thoughts" and the establishment of other traditions. Kant is one of them and is central. We shall return to Kant in Chap. 4 but also to some of the other philosophers who have a central position and who base on this discussion but who also criticize some of the conceptions of, for example, Kant.

A historic understanding of the alternative science goes primarily back to the last century and the German idealism and subjectivism as well as the time around the turn of the last century (the period 1880–1920, especially in German, based on the thoughts of I Kant and J F Fichte (1762–1814)).[12] Flato (1985: 61) thinks that in the period around the turn of the century, the European consciousness passed through a fundamental crisis. A number of the intellectuals of the period realized that human knowledge is limited and that all cognition of both human and social connections is subjective. The common approach was "the (re-)discovery" of the subjective nature of man and thus the need to study the fullness of human experience, including values and meaning in addition to perception (cf. Polkinghorne 1983: 20). This discovery can be regarded both as a liberation of consciousness, through an epistemological approach in the scientific work, and a formulation of a criticism of the positivistic, natural scientific research approach, as an ideal to understand phenomena within social science, too.

The objectivistic, positivistic position was considered with growing discontent and was problematic: Within *natural sciences (Naturwissenschaften)*, it became clear that human values intruded upon the process of scientific inquiry. It was evident that scientific methods could not be regarded as value-free: the frame of reference of the scientific observer was increasingly seen as an active force which determined the way in which scientific knowledge was acquired.

Within the realm of the *cultural sciences (Geisteswissenschaften)*, another set of difficulties was also arising, since its essentially spiritual character distinguished their subject matter. It was realized that man could not be studied as an actor through the methods of the natural sciences, with their concern for establishing general laws through the classification of structures and functions. Criticism was primarily levelled against the unit scientific ideal hidden in positivism, i.e., the thought that the many different types of science were species of the same and that the real type of scientific spirit was the one to be found in the natural sciences.

The humanistic sciences and the social science had to have their own methods and ideals.[13] This discussion can partly be summed up in the controversy in

---

[12] But in many ways also back to the Greek philosophers, with statements and concepts like Socrates (470–399 B.C.) "I know that I know nothing"; "Know yourself" (to determine your own fate), his development of rhetoric and the dialogue as investigation approach; Plato (428–348 B.C.): that truth is something that we cannot once and for all determine and pass on in a lecturing form. Plato thought that truth is something that the single man must reach, disregarding his narrow and selfish view of things (cf. Lübcke 1994a: 338) and, partly, (the "father" of natural science) Aristoteles (384–322 B.C.), with discussion of knowledge, especially phronêsis ("practical ethical understanding" or practical rationality).

[13] cf. Burrell and Morgan (1980: 228); Kjørup (1987: 95).

philosophy of science and in methodological approach containing the explanatory method of natural science (*erklären*) and the understanding method of social science (*Verstehen*).

*Erklären* shall be seen as a methodological approach in connection with the positivistic analytical and rationalism system of theoretical research methodology. We shall discuss Verstehen – understanding – ontologically and epistemologically in Chap. 4 and in relation to various theoretical perspectives and traditions within the Lifeworld tradition and later in relation to qualitative methodology.

## The Paradigm

Science tries to make sense of reality, create knowledge, and say something useful of the past, present, and future. Science is organized in schools of thought belonging to different traditions, meaning that we do not have one science but several different and competing ideas of reality and knowledge, e.g., what reality ontological is and what the theory of cognition should be.

First of all, we are always having a position and a perspective in the world. All of our knowledge and understanding of the reality we experience build on theories or theoretical perspectives. Our way of thinking and the interpretations we make of the reality that we meet take place in a certain way and are organized in a certain way. In all research work, certain preconditions are included, implicitly or explicitly. This means that in theories and empirical investigation, conceptions exist on how reality and human beings are. These conceptions exist in the mind of every single researcher before entering a theoretical discussion and the actual work, e.g., the conceptions themselves become preconditions in the theoretical work. If therefore, through the theories, a phenomenon or a problem is discussed without discussing or acknowledging first their underlying conceptions or preconditions, then that knowledge of the phenomenon and the understanding of the theories are reduced to those preconditions. It is not realized which ideas are implicitly lying in the theories on reality, nor are reflections made on from where they come, why they exist (in which connections they are included), which limitations they have, and what the consequences are, when used.

In the understanding of science, the understanding of paradigm is therefore important, not only to the understanding of science and its development but also to concrete investigations and theorizing of reality: acknowledgment on how a phenomenon is understood, why we problematized it in a certain way, which conclusions we reach, and which solutions we point out and their consequences.

The very concept paradigm, in the discussion of science and conceptions, is understood in numerous ways. The concept comes from Greek *paradeigma*, "pattern, example, sample" from the verb *paradeiknumi*, "exhibit, represent, expose," and from *para*, "beside, beyond," and *deiknumi*, "to show, to point out." So in its etymological sense, it mean something of showing the pattern that lies beyond the surface.

The Paradigm

In 1938 H. Reichenbach introduced the terms *context of discovery* and *context of justification* to mark a distinction between the process in which a scientific result is achieved (discovery) and the process by means of which the result is presented, justified, and defended before the scientific community (justification) (Polkinghorne 1983: 112). At this time the scientific notion was a focus on the result and the relevance of the formulated hypotheses and to a less extent on the process of cognition and the scientific activity as an activity:

> ... a small number of writers expressed the opinion that to understand the nature of science, and thus how one comes to *epistêmê*, the focus had to be changed to the history of the ongoing social enterprise which is the actual practice of science. (Polkinghorne 1983: 112)

Scientific activity has to be understood as human activity directed to the production and acquirement of knowledge and insight, and this is within a frame of reference. In other words, what matters, which influence discovery, development, and acceptance of scientific theories, is related to a conceptual frame, in which the scientific work is carried out – a worldview.

The first significant academic discussion of this topic came about through Toulmin's analysis in 1953. As Polkinghorne reported 30 years later:

> Toulmin maintained that the function of science is to build up systems of ideas about nature which have some legitimate claim to "reality". These ideas provide an intellectual framework of thought – or *Weltanschauung* – which determines the questions scientists ask and the assumptions underlying their theorizing. Their theories are neither true nor false; they are ways of looking at phenomena which work or do not work, which are fruitful or are not fruitful. Theories are merely instruments; they are not correct descriptions of reality. (Polkinghorne 1983: 113)

One of the most outstanding persons in this discussion (to whom everybody refers) is the late physicist T. Kuhn (1970, first ed. 1962). Kuhn's problem can be formulated as "What is science, and how is scientific cognition produced?" He thought, based on natural science, that scientific activities take place within the frames of a generally (but mainly unconsciously) acknowledged paradigm which consists of four different elements: (1) natural law-like symbolic generalizations, (2) metaphysical convictions of the structure of reality, (3) standards of the scientific activity, and (4) exemplars.

Ritzer (1977: 13) thinks that originally, Kuhn used the concept paradigm about the whole constellation of ideas, values, and techniques, common to the members of a given scientific community. However, Kuhn himself expressed that the use of the concept paradigm is inappropriate in this sense and prefers to define the phenomenon as a professional matrix. Kuhn (1970: 182) says that a paradigm can only be used as an exemplar and defines this as a certain element in this constellation (the metaphysical paradigm), the specific mystery solutions which – when used as models and examples – can replace explicit rules as basis for the solution of mysteries left in normal science. In this also other fundamental assumptions and concepts are underlying research than those which have become a symbolic, generalized form: the metaphysical convictions. An example that "everything has a cause" has not been found out through empirical research. It is a basic conception of a fundamental feature of the structure of reality that lies before research, for example, before a search for causes of events (cf. Kant in Chap. 4).

The paradigm also contains certain standards for the scientific activity, in the same way as certain professions and disciplines are using certain methods. We can also say that a paradigm indicates a *space of cognition* in which we are locked up together with our colleagues. In practice the paradigm turns out to be a group of research workers, a scientific community accepting the same models of explanation and cherishing the same scientific standards. The contents and requirements of the paradigm are only in exceptional cases formulated explicitly anywhere. We cannot find a book about, for example, "*the paradigm* in modern business economics." This must be learned in practice, through exemplars and examples. This practice both consists in participation under guidance in specific research processes (in the educational course) and reading of books and articles, not *about* science but *in* theories within scientific field. It is in other words through exemplars and examples that the contents of the paradigm are disseminated and maintained. This is indeed implicit.

To Kuhn it is not accumulation of knowledge that has created decisive changes in science but the revolutions within science. Accumulation plays a large part in the development of science, in normal science, but the decisive changes arise as a result of what Kuhn termed *anomalies* that turn in to "scientific revolutions." As such paradigmatic revolutions themselves are subject to other revolutions and so on.

Mainstream or normal science is research within a given paradigm. This is a piecewise activity in which a certain "frame" is slowly "filled out" – without necessarily understanding that there is a frame. One of the ways to realize the existence of the frames is if you make observations that do not fall within the frame or conflict with them. Scientific revolutions can be understood as a situation and process in science, in which observations and inconsequence are accumulating, so that you (i.e., some: the young research workers within science) start calling the assumptions and frames of science in question. This Kuhn calls *anomalies*. Gradually this criticism (or crisis) will turn into a revolution, and new assumptions and frames for the scientific work are formulated. The idea that "the great jumps" in science take place in revolution periods and not in the long periods of normal science is the very foundation in Kuhn's model:

$$\text{Paradigm}\,1 \rightarrow \text{Normal} \quad \text{scientific period} \rightarrow \text{Irregularities}\,(\textit{anomalies}\,) \rightarrow$$
$$\text{Crisis} \rightarrow \text{Revolution} \rightarrow \text{Paradigm}\,2\,(\text{a new normal} \quad \text{scientific period}\,) \rightarrow$$
$$\text{Repeat Process}$$

The purpose of the prevailing paradigm is according to Ritzer (1977: 17) that it puts the research worker in a position to accept the basic assumptions of the field indisputably. Then the paradigm allows the researcher to have the freedom to investigate even the smallest detail thoroughly but framed by the paradigm. The researcher can work in the protected environment of the indisputable paradigm without being burdened with the demand to defend any basic assumptions. A few researchers will probably reveal matters that do not agree with the prevailing paradigm. On this background Ritzer asks whether there are good objective reasons for researchers to work as they do, or do we only say they are good, because they get acceptance from

The Paradigm

49

the dominant scholarly members of a certain scientific community? He thinks that it points in the direction of the latter interpretation. This can also be seen in the measuring system of publication in certain journals and publishers that have an impact on the founding of universities all over the world. In other words, the growth and fall of paradigms take place as a result of subjective and not objective relations.

Ritter's paradigm of understanding of phenomena is based on a synthesis by Masterman's (1970) trichotomy of the concept:

> A paradigm is the basic conceptions of a science of what its subject is. On this basis it is defined, what is to be studied, which questions are to be raised, how they shall be raised and which rules shall be observed when interpreting the obtained answers. The paradigm is the most comprehensive unit about which there is agreement within a science branch and which serves to separate a scientific community (or subcommunity) from another. It arranges, defines and connects the exemplars, theories, methods and instruments of a given science. (Ritzer 1977: 14)

Burrell and Morgan (1980: 23) regard paradigms as being defined by very basic meta-theoretical assumptions, which underwrite *the frame of reference*, modes of theorizing, and *modus operandi* of the social theorists who operate within them (e.g., the methodology used in investigations and theorizing). Paradigms shall be seen as those which indicate intellectual fellowship and which link together the work of a group of theorists in a way that shows that they can understand each other within the limits of the same problems. They think that their definition does not implicate a complete agreement of thoughts (ibid., p. 24). It allows the existence of discussions between scholars with different viewpoints within the frames of a given paradigm. The paradigm has, however, an underlying agreement in the given ideas, which separates one group of researchers in a fundamental way from others placed in other paradigms.[14]

Brown thinks that the paradigm discussion can be seen in relation to two complementary ways: to Marx's discussion of "ruling ideas" ("the political economy of consciousness") and Kuhn's paradigm understanding as well as a pragmatic institutional approach which goes beyond being cognitive. Brown's paradigm understanding is thus:

> …those sets of assumptions, usually implicit, about what sorts of things make up the world, how they act, how they hang together, and how they may be known. In actual practice, such paradigms function as a means of imposing control as well as a resource that dissident may use in organizing their awareness and action. That is, we view paradigms as practical as well as cognitive, and as a resource as well as a constraint. (Brown 1978: 373)

Brown (1978: 378) discusses paradigms in this way, because of the interest in what he calls "a political phenomenology of organizations." He regards organizational change as being analogous with Kuhn's thoughts about scientific revolutions. In organizations, paradigms can be seen as both practical and formal knowledge. This is apparent in both formal rules in thinking, rhetoric and practical use. In Brown's organizational and social understanding, it can be seen by the

---

[14]We shall later return to Burrell and Morgan and elaborate their discussion of the paradigm concept and of different paradigms in social science.

phenomenological and paradigmatic approach: Organizational realities are not external to human consciousness, out there waiting to be recorded. Instead, the world as humans know it is constituted intersubjectively. The facts (facta) of this world are things made. They are neither subjective nor objective in the usual sense. Instead, people through a process of symbolic interaction construct facts, that is, the relationships or exchanges between people, objects, things, and institutions.[15]

A revision of our symbolic structures, of our shared forms of perception and expression, is thus an auditing of the world. This symbolic interaction is no more true for the artist or the scientist than it is for the citizen or manager or bureaucratic politician. All such actors can be seen to share a basic affinity: they create and use paradigms through which experience acquires significance. By stressing the world-view, creating aspects of conceptual innovation, such a perspective also provides a bridge between theoretical and organizational praxis, as well as between what experts do and what workers do in their workaday lives. We all create worlds. The more we are able to create worlds that are morally cogent and politically viable, the more we are able, as workers and citizens, to manage or to resist.

The discussion in Scandinavia of the concept of paradigm primarily originates from Tørnebohm (1974, 1977) and Bärmark (1976). Their discussion is, for example, reflected in Arbnor and Bjerke (1981/1977, 1997), Ingebrigtsen and Pettersson (1979), and H. Andersen (1990a), where it contains the following:

**Worldview** (reality conception) – ontology – is the general presumptions and conceptions, as well as hypotheses, which the researcher has about a greater part of reality than the one under investigation in the specific project. It is the basic ideas that prevail as regards human and social images. The worldview means, for example, that problems are put forward and generated in a certain way within a field and how the very limit of the field is imagined.

**The science conception** contains the assessment of the researcher of his own science and in relation to other sciences and possibly also his view on other schools of thought and traditions, including how methods, hypothetic statements, and problem identifications deviate or are identical. This means what is science and how does it constitute itself in relation to other forms of knowledge?

**The science ideal** is the normative assumptions on how science should be developed. It is also the ideas and standards one has as to which properties shall be present to call something a good science. The desire be within normal science and follow "an exemplar" in the footsteps of the master or to strike out a path for oneself, with a possible scientific revolution as the result.

**Ethics** concern the role of the researcher within the field. It may contain one role conception in which the research worker must execute a series of tasks, and to execute these, one must be in possession of certain intellectual abilities. But also ethical matters come into play. Ethics can be seen as containing two dimensions: internal and external ethics. It is about standards for the social interplay. The internal ethics concern intra scientific honesty (honesty around originators,

---

[15] See Chap. 5 on Blumer for a more detailed discussion.

quotations, etc.), while the external ethics concern the social responsibility of the research worker (e.g., the consequences of research results) on the local community and society in general.

**Aesthetics** concerns the attitude of the researcher to the form of appearance of scientific work. How to present your work, for example, in a literary style, is often used in contrast to mathematical/statistical style.

The discussion throughout the years of paradigms and the organizing of science can to a certain extent be understood as building on three theses: (1) Observations are theory-burdened; (2) meanings (explanations) are theory-dependent; and (3) facts are theory-burdened. In spite of the fact that research workers are different and come from different sciences and different traditions, the discussion of the concept of paradigm shows what its essence is:

> **A paradigm** is the basic assumptions of the reality and at the same time a frame of reference and an example, one applies to "measure" in what sense and when the research is "**good**". In other words, it contains a general logic that one believes in and is accepted – taken-for-granted. The paradigm has therefore both an "**optical**" and a "**social**" side; It implies certain "glasses" that the individual scholar wears when s/he carries on investigations and is theorizing about reality. Science is also a social phenomenon: science is tradition and organized into societies of scholars – science is at the same time, an individual as well a collective phenomenon.

The discussion of the concept of paradigm thus stresses that science both deals with human thoughts and human interrelations. Science, as everyday life reality, is brought into being by creating it socially to ourselves, through our experience of it, and, together, through the interaction with others, where we confirm each other or mark disagreements. Science as such does thus *not* differ fundamentally from other human activities.

It is important to stick to the concepts inherent in a paradigm as the superior and fundamental features in scientific activities and thus separate it from perspectives/schools/approaches, etc. within the social scientific community. This separation will be discussed in the following.

## *The Placing of the Concept of Paradigm*

In the attempt to understand alternative conceptions of reality, it is important to realize the ideas on which our own paradigm is based. This implies among other things that we become conscious of the relations that constitute our views of reality. The theories are related so that we also acquire knowledge of other paradigms and their understanding of reality. In other words, we must be able to understand other people's perspectives and view of reality. In this way, we enhance our own paradigm. Not until we achieve this can we retrospectively comprehend and fully understand the precise nature of our own basis and logic and what this means to our theoretical work and understanding of something. In an attempt to understand orthodoxy in theories, it is necessary to understand the relations between specific ways of theorizing and investigating and in which way they reflect conceptions of reality and different views.

Morgan (1980: 606), in line with Kuhn, thinks that three broad interpretations can be derived from the concept of paradigm: (1) as a complete view of reality or way of seeing paradigms as alternatives realities, (2) as relating to the social organization of science in terms of schools of thought connected with particular kinds of scientific achievements – metaphors basis of schools of thoughts – and (3) as relating to the concrete use of specific kinds of tools and texts for the process of scientific puzzle solving.

A comment to this is that in social scientific research, i.e., the theoretical work or in empirical investigations, we rarely see deeper discussions of the paradigmatic foundation or a cognitive reflection of the preconditions and assumptions, which the person in question uses as one perspective alternative among many. We typically see a discussion of the next: the theoretical frame to which is referred, as well as the specific activities and theories drawn on in the research, i.e., how well it agrees with the works and results of others (i.e., a discussion of reliability). The discussion here illustrates that it is important to reflect on the concept of paradigm, both in relation to aspects of consciousness and cognition and in relation to a specific theoretical work and for the understanding of empirical phenomena.

Morgan (1980: 607) thinks that one of the most important implications of Kuhn's work is the identification of paradigms as alternative realities. A random or uncritical use of the concept of paradigm in other ways tends to camouflage this insight. He therefore uses the concept paradigm in a meta-theoretical, philosophical sense to indicate an implicit or explicit point of view of reality. Any adequate analysis of the role of paradigms in social theory must uncover the core assumptions that characterize and define any given worldview. This, to make it possible to grasp what is common to the perspectives of theorists, whose work may otherwise, at a more superficial level, appears diverse and wide-ranging.

Each paradigm includes different schools of thought often with different fields but which at an ontological level relate to and understand reality from a common worldview. The different perspectives in the paradigm may have very different approaches (e.g., transaction cost theory, network approach, institutionalism, contingency theory). These approaches put forward certain questions and try to answer some specific questions, but they are limited to their frame of theory – their space of cognition – i.e., to their concepts and the ideas they give implicitly of connections. They may disagree at the surface and in analyses on how to look at and study phenomena, but in the basic (paradigmatic) conception, they agree and can thus be placed within the same paradigm. This can also be seen from the fact that the more specific the theories and analyses are, the greater divergence and criticism there is concerning the conclusions produced by the theories. This can also be expressed differently; the fact that they "bother" to quarrel indicates that they understand each other but disagree about the "correct point of view." If they did not "bother," the natural attitude would be not to relate to the others or to reject the theories of the others completely with arguments like "unscientific," "ideological mess," "fantasies," "placed within another science which has nothing to do with our (economic) science," etc.

# The Paradigm

At the puzzle solving level, it is possible to identify several activities in which it is attempted to operationalize the implications of detail produced by the metaphor level. At this level many specific theories, models, and tools of analysis are competing for the attention of the researchers. Scientific knowledge is shaped by the way in which researchers try to concretize the basic assumptions that underwrite their work. Images of a social phenomenon, usually expressed in terms of a favored metaphor, provide a means of structuring scientific inquiry, guiding attention in certain ways. The image favors a particular epistemological stance in suggesting that certain kinds of insight, understanding, and explanation may be more appropriate than others (Morgan 1983: 21).[16]

Arbnor and Bjerke (1981, 1997) discuss the placing of the paradigm in the research process in a similar, but not quite identical way. They try to place the paradigm in relation to methodology. Their discussion primarily deals with methodology and the three method views: the analytical approach and the system approach, which can be found in objective traditions, and the actor approach that is based upon subjective traditions. They draw a line between philosophy of science and methodology, where the discussion of presumptions and paradigm belongs to the first and the discussion of operative paradigm, methods, and the study field to the last.

The relation between philosophical assumptions and the methodological approach is the discussion with which the philosophy of science deals with. One cannot, therefore, discuss methods and research without indicating how it is related to the superior assumptions. This relation is the paradigm, which can be understood as a tool of description and analysis.

The methodological approach/perspective thus has a double relation, as it comprises some philosophical assumptions and preconditions, at the same time giving the forms of a more specific procedure, i.e., the form of the development of the operative paradigm.

The operative paradigm is the relation between methodological view and field of investigation, which is the methodological discussion or what Arbnor and Bjerke discuss as methodology. The operative paradigm contains methodical procedure and methodic. This means that the relation between methodological approach and a topical field of investigation will be determined by the effected methodical procedures and that used by the methodic. The starting point in the methodological discussion is therefore to show and argue for how the methodological view, the problem formulation, investigation plans, methods, techniques, and the field of investigation harmonize and relate to each other in the specific project.

The methodical procedure is the research worker's way to integrate, develop, and/or modify a pre-given technique (e.g., data collection techniques) from particular methodological viewpoint. A technique will not become a method, until – through a *consciously* methodical procedure – it is argued in relation to the chosen view and the character of the field of investigation.

---

[16] Morgan's interpretation shall here be seen in relation to his interest in metaphors and their meaning to an understanding of theories and theorizing, cf. Morgan (1986).

The methodic is the way in which one, in the plan of investigation, relates to and integrates the methods and the way in which one carries through the investigation specifically. To adapt a technique to a method view is thus a methodical procedure, while the adjustment of this adaptation is the methodic. The use of theories, previous results, and techniques should therefore always be discussed within the frame of the development of the operative paradigm. Methodology thus rather deals with the research worker's personal development of insight and understanding than with learning of special knowledge and skills.

In the following we shall discuss different paradigms within social science, which is related to theorizing within business economics.

## Paradigms in Social Science

Within social science there are many ways to theorize and to view reality. The question is how to identify paradigms and how to understand their basic assumptions and aspects of knowledge. Principally, they are innumerable and dependent on how the concept of paradigm is used. This is, however, an abstraction from the research practice of today. As it appears in the practice of social science, the thoughts and the theoretical work are not so diverging and colorful that one could think but rather the opposite. Today, there is an astonishing uniformity in thinking and theorizing.[17] As we have described, the theorizing in social science still can be understood as building on an objectivistic ontology and epistemology (e.g., rationalism or positivism) or less upon a subjectivistic ontology and epistemology (e.g., Lifeworld tradition and phenomenology, symbolic interactionism, hermeneutic, and so forth).

There are many possibilities on how to explore, determine, and characterize these discussions of theoretical science and how to understand theories and paradigms. Others have had similar discussions, looking in to different perspectives or schools in which patterns of explanation are stressed or specific phenomena are discussed and how different directions of theory understand them.[18]

If we maintain our previous understanding of the concept of paradigm, then Burrell and Morgan (1980) have a discussion related to this. They have tried to analyze different theories and recapitulate many of the discussions in and of science, of different traditions and perspectives within social science, especially in relation to business economics, sociology, and organization theory. The work of Burrell and Morgan's consists of two things: a classification of theories and thoughts in relation to each other, as well as a study and description of these

---

[17] cf. the introduction to this chapter.

[18] For another classification of paradigms and perspectives, see, for example, Parsons et al. (1965), Eisenstadt and Curelaru (1976), Ingebrigtsen and Pettersson (1979), Van de Ven and Joyce (1981), Scott (1981, 1987), Cuff and Payne (1982), Pfeffer (1982), Astley and Van de Ven (1983), Silverman (1983), Habermas (1984), Reed (1985), Morgan (1986), Bradley (1987), Andersen (1990a), Knudsen (1991), and Reed and Hughes (eds.) (1992).

# Paradigms in Social Science

different theories and schools that show which complex nature there is in paradigms and in the network of ideas they reflect. Their basis in this work can be deduced from the first sentence:

> Central to our thesis is the ideas that all theories of organisation are based upon a philosophy of science and a theory of society. (Burrell and Morgan 1980: 1)

Based on this thesis, they discuss how to understand and place the different theories, which in the first instance seem to differ in a paradigm. In their analysis of theories, they work on the basis of two dimensions: a philosophy of science dimension and a philosophy of society dimension.

## The Dimension of Philosophy of Science: The Debate of Objectivity vs. Subjectivity

The *philosophy of science dimension* is a discussion between a *subjective* and an *objective* dichotomy in theories and thinking. This debate originates in a discussion which has existed for the last 200 years, as this appeared from the above. The discussion concerns an argument and a defense for objectivity based on the classical positivism and rationalism and the newer traditions: logical positivism/neopositivism/logical empiricism (the Wiener circle), sociological positivism/scientific empiricism, structure functionalism, and system theory.[19] On the other hand, there is a subjectivistic criticism of positivistic and rationalistic understanding of what reality is, of epistemology and theory of cognition, and of research and theory building.

This criticism and alternative is based on the German idealism/subjectivism and Neo-Kantianism, with traditions like phenomenology, hermeneutics, symbolic interactionism, and critical theory (and the Frankfurter School). The essence of this discussion is very much in line with the thoughts of Kant (see Chap. 4) and his discussion of cognition where he states the matter of das Ding an Sich vs. das Ding für Uns. The question is if we can look upon the reality in itself (objectivism) or if reality is a question of the observer (subjectivism).

*The objectivistic approach* is based on an epistemology that tries to describe, explain, and predict social events and phenomena by looking for regularity and causal relations between different factors. One assumes that growth in knowledge takes place cumulatively, i.e., that new knowledge is acquired through the use of an exact scientific method and is added to the already existing knowledge. Cognition of the nature of reality is achieved through preconceived scientific methods (the quantitative), which are regarded as objective (e.g., that they thereby can produce objective true knowledge). It is assumed within this approach that the behavior of man is largely determined by factors in situation and environment.

This can be seen in the following way: the scientific endeavor is likely to focus upon an analysis of relationships and regularities between the various elements that

---

[19] See, for example, Kjørup (1987), Nørreklit (1984), Flor (1982), Arbnor and Bjerke (1981).

it comprises. The concern, therefore, is with the identification and definition of these elements and with the discovery of ways in which these relationships can be expressed quantitatively. The methodological issues of importance are thus the concepts themselves, their measurement, and the identification of generalized underlying themes. This perspective expresses itself most forcefully in a search for universal laws, which explain and govern the reality being observed (Burrell and Morgan 1980: 3).

The discussion of what objectivity is in scientific work can be summarized in a classification of objectivity in several areas (see also Andersen and Gamdrup: in H Andersen (ed.) 1990a, vol. 1: 32, Delanty and Strydom 2003: 13) As an ideal and standardized contemporary approach, this research perspective may be understood in the following ways:

1. **Unified science**. Based on a series of assumptions, i.e., that the universe is a causally ordered, homogeneous, one-layer world, that there is a basic unity to human experience, and that we are therefore able to gain knowledge of reality and indeed construct a knowledge system about it. It is claimed that it is possible to produce a unified scientific language for all scientific disciplines, including the social sciences.

2. **Freedom of value**. The researcher has to make his values explicit and keep them outside the scientific work. This can also be understood in relation to the distance concept that he must keep at a distance the object he is investigating. It is also understood as an ideal of a science, exclusively consisting of descriptions and explanations and which desists from all explicit and implicit assessments. This ideal requires a clear boundary between facts and values. It is also possible to distinguish between internal and external freedom of value in the discussion. A theory is internally value-free, if it is impossible syntactically (the system of rules of the language) or semantically (the meaning aspects of linguistic expressions) to derive assessments from the theory. A theory is externally value-free, if it does not serve certain interests (of a moral, political, religious, economic, etc. nature).

3. **Unconditionally**. This means that the researcher shall not implicate (personal) preconditions but try to explain the nature of the object on its own premises, i.e., describe and explain the object as it is in itself, free from other influences and constrains. The approach assumes that the object can be defined and even isolated unto itself. In other words, objects are one-dimensional and devoid of history, meaning, and substance.

4. **Consciousness and openness**. This is connected with the two first points, where one must be conscious in the scientific work: know what one does and seek a complete uncovering of the object. Consciousness and openness both concern the consciousness of the research worker and his methodology and are especially central in the Lifeworld discussion (cf. Chap. 4). This discussion, however, concerns validity and reliability: security that the results of the research are optimum and true, through a complete uncovering of the object so that the reality of the whole object is mapped and explained.

5. **Many-sidedness (or plurality)**. The researcher must work from different bases so that the explanation of the phenomenon is verified. Many-sidedness means generally through discussions of method pluralism/triangulation, where one imagines that a description about the whole reality can be uncovered. It is only a question of methods and the number of angles one puts on the object. In short, the object must be seen from different angles or through the use of multi-methods.
6. **Impartiality**. (cf. distance to the object and freedom of value). The researcher shall not take a position morally nor ethically in the research work, i.e., what is good or bad, what is right and wrong, etc. The researcher must keep to the truth. This criterion is related to the documentation of truth, which should be seen in relation to the demands and rules of the science.
7. **Intersubjectivity**. It is stressed that it must be possible for any other observer to make the same scientific observation (the discussion of reliability and verification) to considered it valid. Intersubjectivity will be a kind of guarantee that the observation is unblemished by other factors than those common to all observers. The concept of intersubjectivity is therefore not the same as within a subjectivistic orientation. In the natural and physical sciences, this is often the question of "replication," whereby the researcher can run countless other experiments and come out with the same results.
8. **Instrumentalism**. An orientation towards the manipulation of the world rather than understanding it and, closely related, an instrumental view of theory as consisting of nothing but observations and being nothing more than a tool of prediction.
9. **Technism**. The tendency to value techniques or methods more than results or the development of knowledge, even to the point of essentializing the former.

A social science, on the other hand, based on a *subjectivistic* orientation, sees the social world as constructed by human beings – it focuses on an everyday life reality and tries to describe and understand it from the point of view of them living in it. This world can thus only be understood with basis in a position, where one participates and is involved in the activities that are studied. Science therefore becomes a subjective occupation, as involvement and nearness will become essential and where objective and neutral knowledge are not possible.

It is the understanding of this social world that is in focus, how man is, and how people are together.[20] The approach stresses voluntarism – being and the acting – in the nature of man and prefers research methods which make an analysis of the subjective ideas and views of the subject possible, as well as experiences in connection with psychological and social phenomena.[21] The principal concern is with an understanding of the way in which he or she finds himself.

The emphasis in some cases tends to be placed upon the understanding of what is unique and particular to the individual rather than of what is general and universal.

---

[20] See an amplifying discussion of this in Chap. 4.

[21] cf. the discussion of methodology in Part II.

This approach questions whether there exists an external reality worthy of study. In methodological terms, it is an approach which emphasizes the relativistic nature of the social world to such an extent that it may be perceived as "anti-scientific" by reference to the ground rules commonly applied in the natural sciences.

## Differences Between an Objective and a Subjective Perspective

In this introduction to the objective versus the subjective discussion, some distinct differences in the reality conceptions and in the research approach appeared. We shall return to this in the discussion but shall in the following illustrate the main features of the differences, and later (in Chap. 4) we shall vary this picture.

Andersen (in H. Andersen (ed.) 1990a, vol. 1) discusses some of the differences between objective and subjective in relation to the reality conceptions of our everyday life. On one hand he calls it the human and social sphere (subjective – knowledge of interpretation) and on the other the physical-natural (objective – empirical-analytical theory of science). He continues pointing out the most important differences in the preconditions between subjective (which is called the interpretive-scientific paradigm) and objective (which is called the positivistic paradigm). Comparisons between subjective (e.g., social sphere) and objective (e.g., natural sphere) approaches and the differences between the interpretive and positivistic paradigms can be presented in the following way.

The understanding and amplification of Andersen's discussion can be deduced from Burrell and Morgan's (1980: 3) way of looking at these differences between objective and subjective. They build up a methodical scheme according to coherent ideas of objectivity – subjectivity – which is related to ontology, epistemology, human nature, and methodology.

*Ontology* is conceptions dealing with the very essence of the phenomenon in the investigation (its being). Social researchers, for example, are confronted with the basic ontological question: What is reality? Reality is: (a) wish to investigate external in relation to the individual (forces itself upon the consciousness of the individual from outside); (b) focus on a product of individual consciousness; (c) be an objective nature and or a product of individual cognition; and (d) given out in the world or a product of your consciousness (e.g., the subject's interpretations of objects and events).

*Epistemology* is conceptions of the background of knowledge – how one can start understanding the world and communicate this as knowledge to fellow human beings. It is epistemological problems that are discussed. These conceptions contain, for example, ideas of the form of knowledge that can be acquired and how to sort that out, which is considered as truth, from that which is considered as false. Burrell and Morgan (ibid., p. 1) mean that this dichotomy of "true" and "false" itself indeed presupposes a certain epistemological stance. It is predicated upon a view of the nature of knowledge itself.

Paradigms in Social Science

Whether, for example, it is possible to identify and communicate the nature of knowledge as being hard, real, and capable of being transmitted in tangible form or whether knowledge is of a softer, more subjective, spiritual, or even transcendental kind based on experience and insight of a unique and essentially personal nature, the epistemological conceptions in this sense are extreme points in the attitude to knowledge: whether knowledge can be acquired or whether it must be experienced personally.

Conceptions of the *human nature*, especially relations between human beings and the relation of human beings to their environment, are central, because the human life is the essential subject and object in social science. Burrell and Morgan (ibid., p. 2) think that theories of social science can be identified that contains an image of human beings as responding in a mechanical or deterministic way in the situation they meet in their external world (Fig. 3.2).

This process tends towards viewing human beings and their experiences as products of the surroundings. This can be seen in contrast to an attitude, which ascribes a more creative part to man and in which the "free will" is in the center; man is seen as "creator" of the surroundings, i.e., he who controls instead of him who is controlled. These points of view identify the philosophic discussion between the supporters of determinism on one side and voluntarism on the other.

| | **The social sphere** | **The natural sphere** |
|---|---|---|
| **Subject** | Actions, Subjects, Objects | Occurrences |
| **Basic attitude** | Subjectivated, Objectivated Appreciated | Neutral |
| **Knowledge type** | Interpretations | Explanations |
| **Connections** | Actions as expression for subjective conditions | Occurrences as manifestations of mechanical laws |
| **Action orientation** | Communicative, normative orientation | Instrumental, control- orientated |
| **Illustrative Concepts** | Language, intention, feelings, will, obligations, responsibility | Causes, effects, lawfulness |
| | **Interpretive Paradigm** | **Positivistic paradigm** |
| **Ideal of Science** | Interpretation of the contents of subjective meanings | Empirical test of theories of causal connections |
| **World view** | Actions as subjective, meaningful expressions | Behavior as manifestations of universal regularities |
| **Scientific ethics according to knowledge** | Interpretation as part of overcoming barriers of understanding and subversion of prejudice | Knowledge about regularities as basic for use of "social engineering" |

**Fig. 3.2** The social and the natural sphere and some differences between interpretation knowledge and positivism. (Andersen; in H. Andersen (ed.) 1990a, vol. I: 153 and 159 (*our translation*))

*Methodology* is a direct implication of the preceding conceptions, where the different conceptions influence the very choice of method. This means that if you have an objective conception of the world, then you regard it as material and real. Therefore methods are used which can measure, identify, and express this search for the universal laws which are supposed to explain and control the reality one observes, what we can broadly describe as quantitative, statistically orientated methods.

And vice versa, if you have a subjective conception, you understand the reality as unique and individualistic, where man constructs reality. Therefore, methods are used which can catch the conceptions and actions of the individual. These methods can broadly be called the qualitative methods. They cover a wide range of different approaches, for example, the actor's point of view, action research, and qualitative interviews.

These four conceptions give a characterization of the discussion that Burrell and Morgan find in different theories and in an analysis of conceptions of social scientific nature. The discussion of objective-subjective dimension is drawn up in the following way (Fig. 3.3):

Their use and classification of concepts require amplification as they have an understanding which is somewhat different from the general one but which in this context can be understood in the following ways:

*Realism* postulates that the social world external to the individual cognition is a real world, made up of hard, tangible, and relatively immutable structures. Whether or not we label and perceive these structures, the realist maintains that they still exist as empirical entities. To the realist, the social world exists independently of an individual's appreciation of it. The individual is seen as being born into and living within a social world which has a reality of its own. It is not something that the individual creates – it exists "out there." Ontologically, it is prior to the existence and consciousness of any single human being.

The *nominalist* position revolves around the assumption that the social world external to individual cognition is made up of nothing more than names, concepts, and labels that are used to structure reality. The nominalist does not admit the existence of any "real" structure to the world, which these concepts are used to describe.

| The Subjective approach to Social Science | | | The Objectivist approach to Social Science |
| --- | --- | --- | --- |
| Nominalist | - | Ontology | - | Realism |
| Anti-positivism | - | Epistemology | - | Positivism |
| Voluntarism | - | Human Nature | - | Determinism |
| Idiographic | - | Methodology | - | Nomothetic |

**Fig. 3.3** The subjective-objective dimension. (Burrell and Morgan 1980: 3)

The "names" used are regarded as artificial creations whose utility is based upon their convenience as tools for describing, making sense of, and negotiating the external world – it is the individual's way of handling experiences and situations.

*Positivism* reflects an epistemology that seeks to explain and predict what happens in the social world when searching for regularities and causal relationships between its constituent elements. It is in essence based upon the traditional approaches that dominate the natural sciences.

*Anti-positivism* may take various forms but is firmly set against the utility of a search for laws or underlying regularities in the world of social affairs. To the anti-positivist, the social world is essentially relativistic (e.g., socially constructed) and can only be understood from the points of view of the individuals who are directly involved in the activities which are to be studied. He rejects the standpoint of the "observer," and one can only "understand" by occupying the frame of reference of the participant in action – understanding from inside rather than the outside. One tends to reject the notion that social science can generate objective knowledge of any kind.

The *nomothetic*[22] approach lays emphasis on the importance of basing research upon systematic protocol and technique. It is epitomized in the approach and methods employed in the natural sciences, which focus upon the process of testing hypotheses in accordance with the canons of scientific rigueur. It is preoccupied with the construction of scientific tests, experimentation, and the use of quantitative techniques for the analysis of data. Surveys, questionnaires, personality tests, and standardized research instruments of all kinds are prominent among the tools that comprise nomothetic methodology. One deals with classes of objects and is looking for legal, variable connections in those.

The *idiographic*[23] approach is based on the view that one can only understand the social world by obtaining firsthand knowledge of the subject under investigation. It is stressed to get close to the subject and explore its detailed background and life history. The emphasis is on the analysis of the subjective accounts which one generates by "getting inside" situations and involving oneself in the everyday flow of life – the detailed analysis of the insights revealed in impressionistic accounts found in diaries, biographies, and journalistic records.

The methodologies of *participant observation* and *in-depth interview* or *focus groups* stress the importance of letting one's subject unfold its nature and characteristic during the process of investigation. The discussion of nomothetic versus idiographic was discussed by the neo-Kantian Windelband (1894). He had the distinction between natural science and science of history in that the natural science approach aims at the construction of physical causality and "explanation" (Droysen's *erklären*) of events by identifying them as instance of a general law. The historical science approach, by contrast, is individualizing; it concentrates on the uniqueness of the event and attempts to identify its meaning and specific characteristics (Polkinghorne 1983: 23).

---

[22] Nomothetic from Greek *nomos* – "law".

[23] Idiographic from Greek: *idio* – "personal," "special," or "particular".

## The Dimension of Philosophy of Society: Regulation vs. Radical Change

Burrell and Morgan's second dimension is characterized by two basically different attitudes to society and the matter of research. It deals with the point of view and attitude of a single researcher to society as phenomenon: Which normative view the researcher has on the use of the research and which problems one thinks shall be put forward and investigated.[24]

Burrell and Morgan (ibid., p. 17) call the first attitude the "*sociology of regulation*." This refers to theories that are primarily concentrated on producing explanations about the society in terms that indicate an underlying agreement and accordance in the society. It is a science that is essentially interested in the need of the regulation of human activities. The fundamental question asked tends to focus on an explanation of why the society is kept as a whole and why it hangs together.

The other attitude is called the "*sociology of radical change*" and stands in contrast to the sociology of regulation. It is primarily interested in finding explanations to process and radical changes, deep conflicts, states of domineering, discrepancy, and conflicting interests between social groups and classes. The theorists see this as being characteristic of the society, and therefore it must also be the basis of science and the object of one's efforts. Burrell and Morgan think that it is a sociology (or social scientific approach) that is essentially concerned with man's emancipation from the structures that limit and stunt his potential for development. The basic questions that it asks focus upon the deprivation of man, both material and physical. It is often visionary and Utopian, in that it looks towards potentiality as much as actuality; it is concerned with what is possible rather than with what is, with alternatives rather than with acceptance of the status quo (ibid.). Formulation in this dimension is expressed in the following way (Fig. 3.4):

*Consensus* means, according to Burrell and Morgan, voluntary and "spontaneous" agreement of opinion, i.e., a broad and general agreement in the views of people. *Solidarity* stands for the conception that community between individuals and groups is primary. *Emancipation* makes a point of the significance of the fact that some individuals and groups may have an interest in freeing themselves of existing social and hierarchical relations of dominance. The term "need satisfaction" is used to refer to the focus upon satisfaction of individual or system "needs," e.g., that the society/system primarily reflects these needs. *Deprivation* marks the notion that the social system prevents human fulfillment indeed that "deprivation" is created as the result of the status quo.

Burrell and Morgan use the two dimensions, the nature of science (subjective-objective) and social orientation (regulation change) in a collocation that emanates into four paradigms, which in turn each defines four fundamentally different approaches to the analysis of social phenomena (Fig. 3.5).

---

[24] This dimension is somewhat problematic, which we will be discussed and criticized in section "Discussion of Paradigms".

# Paradigms in Social Science

| The sociology of "REGULATION" is concerned with: | The sociology of "RADICAL CHANGE" is concerned with: |
|---|---|
| a) The status quo | a) Radical change |
| b) Social order | b) Structural conflict |
| c) Consensus | c) Modes of domination |
| d) Social integration and cohesion | d) Contradiction |
| e) Solidarity | e) Emancipation |
| f) Need satisfaction | f) Deprivation |
| g) Actuality (the existing) | g) Potentiality (the obtainable) |

**Fig. 3.4** The regulation-radical change dimension. (Burrell and Morgan 1980: 18)

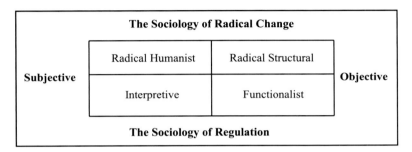

**Fig. 3.5** Four paradigms for the analysis of social theory. (Burrell and Morgan 1980: 22)

These four paradigms represent fundamentally oppositional ways of analysis and have fundamentally different implications for studies of social phenomena. The paradigms are therefore mutually exclusive. They contribute with alternative points of view on social reality, and a comprehension of their nature is an understanding of four fundamentally different points of view on society – they represent different ways of viewing reality. A synthesis of them is therefore not possible, as in their pure form, they are contradictions which are based on oppositional, meta-theoretical (ontological) ideas. They are alternatives in the sense that one can work within them over time, i.e., intellectually one can understand them and therefore also craftsman like meeting the demands that they make individually on good research.

However, they are mutually exclusive in the sense that one cannot work in more than one paradigm at a given time, i.e., if the preconditions in one paradigm are accepted, then the ideas in all the rest are rejected at the same time. Intellectually, of course, one can shift between the paradigms over time, writing on one topic in one paradigm and the year after another topic in another paradigm. But the heart and the mind are always belonging to a specific belief of ontology and epistemology, related to one paradigm.

# Understanding Ontological Themes and Theories in Social Science: Four Paradigms

The four paradigms appearing through the discussion can be described in the following ways:

## *Traditions of Objectivism: Rationalism and Positivism*

### 1. The Functionalist Paradigm

This paradigm is based on the idea that society has a specific, real existence which has a systematic character and which is orientated towards producing an established order (status quo) through a regulated stage of events. It encourages an approach that focuses on explaining the role in society of the human being. Behavior is considered as being contextually linked to a real world of specific and tangible social relations. The ontological idea encourages a belief in the possibility of an epistemology that can be objective and value-free science. In this paradigm the researcher has a distance to the object that is analyzed, through strict methodological techniques. The paradigm is primarily regulating and pragmatic in its basic orientation and interested in explaining society in a way that generates applicable empirical knowledge.

Ritzer (1977) discusses some of this, in what he calls the *social facts paradigm*. The exemplar in the paradigm is E. Durkheim who thought that the basic subject of sociology is social relations. He developed the concept of "a social fact" in order to distinguish the emerging field of sociology from competing disciplines like psychology and philosophy. A social fact should, according to Durkheim, be treated as a thing standing outside man and which uses force against man. But Durkheim did not mean to give all social facts the same ontological ranking as real phenomena. Most social facts shall only be treated as "things." They are not necessarily real material units that have an own existence independent of human consciousness. Some social facts have material existence (laws), but the most important of them are rather passing currents that exist within and between consciousnesses (ibid., p. 196).

P. Blau thinks that there are two kinds of social facts: the common values and norms embodied in a culture or subculture and the networks of social relations in which processes of social interaction become organized and through which social positions of individuals and subgroups become differentiated (Blau 1960: 178). Ritzer (ibid., p. 34) calls them "social structures" and "social institutions" and thinks that sociologists, who define one of or maybe both these types as basic for sociology, are tied to the social facts paradigm. They assume that these social relations must be treated as "real" things. Some of these scholars go as far as to maintain that they are real things, and Ritzer thinks the supporters of the social facts paradigm of today are inclined to overlook these ambiguities in Durkheim's works.

Understanding Ontological Themes and Theories in Social Science: Four Paradigms 65

They think that social facts must not only be treated as things but that they are also things. Furthermore, they maintain that groups are real and by a logical inference that social facts are just as real (ibid., p. 196).

A social relation may be a "real" structure (e.g., a group, a bureaucracy) or a "real" institution (e.g., family and religion). Within the paradigm one is often interested in the character of these structures and institutions, their interrelation, and their compulsion against the single human being. In other words, the group or family takes on the characteristics of the individual as if it has feelings, emotions, and values.

There are more perspectives in the paradigm, which comprise both structure functionalism, conflict theory, system theory, and macro-sociology. Ritzer (ibid., p. 196) thinks that structural functionalism and conflict theory are the most important and that they differ only in their conceptualization on the relation between social facts. Structure functionalism regards the society as being in a state of equilibrium, which is gradually developing. The conflict theorists experience social facts as being in some extent of conflict. If society is in some state of equilibrium, it is because the persons who control it are powerful.

Another paradigm of Ritzer, which can entirely be placed in Burrell and Morgan's functionalist paradigm, is *the social behavior paradigm*. It has its most important exemplar in the work of Watson and B.F. Skinner (behaviorism). The social behaviorist considers the topic of sociology as being behavior within conditions of intensification (as in the response of the actor). Bushell and Burgess (1969) express the opinion that the social behaviorist focuses on the behavior of individuals who work within their environment in such a way that it implies consequences or changes in it, which then again modifies the succeeding behavior (in Ritzer op cit., p. 200). This approach differs from the idea of the two other paradigms as regards the topic of sociology.

The social behaviorist denies the idea of the social definition that a voluntaristic consciousness exists. He is inclined to take the position that an attitude just as negative to the facts paradigm by its stressing of the importance of structures and institutions. In other words, it is only the behavior that counts, and concepts like consciousness, social structures, and social institutions exclusively serve to draw attention away from the essence of the phenomenon itself.

Within the behavior paradigm, there are two important theoretical perspectives: The first one is the behavior sociology, which is an attempt to translate psychological principles of behavior directly to sociological questions. The other perspective is the exchange or interchange theory closely connected to G. Homans who is strongly influenced by Skinner.[25] These theorists argue that economic systems, for example, work simply on the input of isolated variables or objects yielding predictable outcomes of objects. No discussion or analysis of what goes on with the "black box" (e.g., human behavior, consciousness, or events) is given.

---

[25] Examples of research workers and their theories which can be placed within this paradigm are Blau (1960), Thompson (1971), Child (1972), Williamson (1975), Pfeffer and Salancik (1978), Hofstede (1980a, b), Cavusgil (1982), Arndt (1983), French and Bell (1984), Cheng (1984), Dunning (1985), Winter (1986), Scott (1987), Johansson and Mattsson (1988), and Daft (1989).

## 2. The Radical Structural Paradigm

The radical structuralist paradigm is, like the radical humanist paradigm, based on a point of view that society is a potentially dominating force. But it is tied to a materialistic conception of the social world, in which this is defined through hard, specific, ontologically real structures. Reality is regarded as independently existing and as independent of man's way of understanding it through the everyday life activities. Reality is characterized through tensions coming from within and contrasts between factors which are in opposition and which randomly lead to radical changes in the system as a whole. The radical structuralist is interested in explaining these inner tensions and explaining in which way powerful people in the society try to maintain control through various ways of domineering. The main stress is laid on the importance of practice, as a means to transcend this domineering. Some of the concepts and notions, which can be viewed as being central in the paradigm and in research, are (Burrell and Morgan, op cit., p. 358):

**Totality** All theories within the paradigm address themselves to the understanding of total social formations.

**Structure** The focus, in contrast to that of the radical humanist paradigm, is upon the configurations of social relationships which characterize different totalities and which exist independently of men's consciousness of them. Structure is treated as hard and concrete facilities, which are relatively persistent and enduring. Social reality for the radical structuralist is not necessarily created and recreated in everyday action. Reality exists independently of any reaffirmation that takes place in everyday life.

**Contradiction** Structure, while seen as persistent and relatively enduring, is also seen as posed in contradictory and antagonistic relationships one to another. The notion of contradiction, like that of alienation within the radical humanist paradigm, has both a symbolic and a substantive aspect. It is symbolic in the sense that it stands for the radical structuralism's hope and belief that capitalist social formations contain within them the seeds of their own decay. In substantive terms, the notion of contradiction varies in definition and use within the context of this overall symbolic umbrella.

Some of the fundamental contradictions, which have been recognized, are those between the relations of production and the means of production: between exchange value and surplus value; between the increasing socialization of the forces of production and the narrowing basis of their ownership; between capital and labor; and between the increasing anarchy of market and centralization of production. Different theorists tend to select and emphasize different contradictions and with varying degrees of explicitness. (The concept of development in the paradigm can partly be seen as having its origin in contradictions and their changes.)

**Crisis** All theories within the paradigm view change as a process involving structural dislocation of an extreme form. The typical pattern is that in which contradictions within a given totality reach a point at which they can no longer be contained. The ensuing crisis, political, economic, and the like, is viewed as the point of transformation from one totality to another, in which one set of structures is replaced by another of a fundamentally different kind.

The notable researchers and their traditions as central in the paradigm are K. Marx ("the old"), Russian social theory (with reference to F. Engels), sections of M. Weber's work ("radical Weberianism"), L. Althusser's sociology, anarchist communism (cf. P. Kropotkin), and conflict theory.[26]

## Traditions of Lifeworld: Subjectivism

### 3. The Interpretive Paradigm: The Lifeworld Tradition

This paradigm is based on the point of view that the social world has a special ontological status: that which appears as a social reality does not exist in a specific sense but is a product of the subjective and intersubjective experience and consciousness of individuals. The society is understood from a participation in actions rather than from the attitude of an observer. The interpretive theorist tries to understand the process through which common multiple realities rise and are maintained and changed. Science is viewed as a network of "language games"[27] based on a set of subjective, determining concepts and rules that the agents of science develop and follow in the study. The state of knowledge of science may be regarded as being problematizing "the commonsense" knowledge in everyday life.

This approach can be seen in Ritzer's *social definition paradigm*. The exemplar, Ritzer thinks, is Weber's writings on social action and his interest in the subjective importance that man attaches to his actions. Weber regarded the subjective and intersubjective state in consciousness as the one that characterizes social action. The social definition process of the actor and the resulting action and interaction is to Weber the topic of sociology. To be able to investigate such phenomena, Weber invites to use an understanding based on interpretation – Verstehen (see Chap. 4).

To the interpretive supporters, the human being is in some respects an active creator of his own social reality. Consequently, social facts are not viewed as static or compulsory. This leads to an interest in the social definitions of man or its reality created by society. The center of interest is the social processes originating in the social definitions of man, and one must observe social processes to be able to find and draw conclusions on the largely invisible and intersubjective state of the participants (Ritzer op cit., p. 198). This also implies that one rejects the behavioristic attitude. Behavior is not a matter of a single stimuli-response phenomenon but a result of a process of assessment, made by the individual in a particular situation or event.

---

[26] See, for example, Heydebrand (1977), Bravermann (1978), and Baran and Sweezy (1966).

[27] Understood as conceptual development in connection with the specific research project.

The most important theoretical perspectives in this paradigm according to Ritzer are action theory, symbolic interactionism, and sociological phenomenology.[28]

### 4. The Radical Humanist Paradigm

This paradigm stresses, like the interpretive paradigm, how reality is socially constructed and socially maintained. It criticizes the objective approach in science. This criticism is due to the fact that this paradigm has common philosophic roots with the interpretive paradigm. But the analysis is tied to an interest which can be called "the pathology of consciousness," through which the existence of man is limited within the boundaries of reality that he has created and maintains himself. This is based on the point of view that the creation process of reality will be influenced by psychological and social processes. These processes canalize, force, and control the thoughts of man in a way that makes them promoting to the potentials lying in the nature of man.

The radical humanist criticism focuses on the aspects of alienation in connection with different ways of thinking and acting which characterize life in the industrial society. Capitalism, for example, is regarded as essentially totalitarian, the idea that a capital accumulation forms the nature of work, technology, rationality, logic, science, roles, and mystifying ideological concepts like scarcity, spare time, etc. These concepts, which the functionalistic theorist regards as bricks in the social order and the human freedom, are to the radical humanist ideological ways of dominance. The radical humanist is interested in discovering how human beings can link thoughts and action (practice) as a mean to transcend their alienation.

Below some of the concepts that can be regarded as central in the paradigm and especially related to critical theory are stated (Burrell and Morgan 1980: 298):

**Totality** The notion that any understanding of society must embrace in its entirety the objective and subjective worlds, which characterize a given epoch. Totality embraces everything; it has no boundary. An understanding of this totality must precede an understanding of its elements, since the whole dominates the parts in an all-embracing sense.

**Consciousness** The force that ultimately creates and sustains the social world. Consciousness is internally generated but influenced by the forms, which it assumes through the process of objectification and the dialectic between subjective and objective worlds.

**Alienation** The state in which, in certain totalities, a cognitive wedge is driven between man's consciousness and the objectified world, so that man sees what are essentially the creations of his own consciousness in the form of a hard, dominating, external reality. This wedge is the wedge of alienation, which divorces man from his true self and hinders the fulfillment of his potentialities as a human being.

---

[28] Examples here are Hedberg et al. (1976), Brown (1978), Weick (1979a), Silverman (1983), Bartunek (1984), Hennestad (1986), and Kallinikos (1989).

**Criticism** In their criticism of contemporary society, critical theorists focus upon the forms and sources of alienation, which they see as inhibiting the possibilities of true human fulfillment. The various exponents of this perspective approach it in somewhat different ways, at varying levels of generality: Lukács focuses upon the concept of reification, which provided the socio-philosophical solution to the epistemological and practical problems facing Marxism in the 1920s. Gramsci focuses upon the notion of ideological hegemony as reflecting a belief system among the proletariat fostered by the ruling class. In his view, the belief system stressed the importance of order, authority, and discipline and was propagated through institutions such as the family, school, and workplace.

Marcuse through his notion of one-dimensional man focuses attention upon the alienating characteristics, which he sees as being embedded in the growth of purposive rationality within advanced industrial societies. In particular, he emphasizes the alienating role of technology, science, and logic. These supplement other forces identified in his earlier work relating to the excessive repression of libido and the maintenance of a happy workforce through the creation of affluence and false needs. Habermas focuses upon the role which language plays as an alienating force in all aspects of social life. His theory of communicative competence seeks the common denominator in human interaction, whether verbal, sexual, productive, or whatever, and seeks to show how in contemporary western societies there is an element of communicative distortion which lies at the heart and most basic level of mans' alienation.

The notable researchers and their traditions which Burrell and Morgan view as central in the paradigm are besides the abovementioned: J. G. Fichte, W. F. Hegel, K. Marx ("the young"), J. P. Sartre, M. Stirner, critical theory, and the Frankfurter School (e.g., M. Horkheimer, T. W. Adorno, E. Fromm).

Ritzer has no counterpart to the radical humanist paradigm. He points at critical theory and the Frankfurter School as a possible fourth paradigm, as they differ from the other theories and paradigms. Ritzer (ibid., p. 231) believes that they are a combination of social facts and social definitions, with a strong emphasis on the importance of social criticism. Ritzer thinks that this approach has an evident connection to Marx and refers to Schroyer (1970, ibid., p. 231) who is of the opinion that such critical science has three basic principles: (1) a notion of man as being both actively and historically limited, which is in line with Marx's dialectic view on the relation between social facts and social definitions; (2) a work to succeed in finding the forms of authority, exploitation, alienation, and repression, which are not socially necessary; and (3) an attempt to reflect on "the necessity" of the conditions that produces the apparent legalities in society and history.

Critical theory places Burrell and Morgan in the radical humanistic paradigm. This could also be a solution for Ritzer to his difficulties with a paradigmatic placing of critical theory.[29]

---

[29] Examples here are Benson (1977a), Imershein (1977), Zeitz (1980), Alvesson (1983a, b), Heydebrand (1983), Kallinikos (1986), Neimark and Tinker (1987), Harste (1988), and McGuire (1988).

## Discussion of Paradigms

In general, this discussion of theories and perspectives can be seen as covering a large part of social science. It describes different central assumptions and theoretical perspectives that one can find in the development of social science. In relation to the descriptions of Burrell and Morgan versus Ritzer, there are certain important matters on which they agree. However, Ritzer has not included the radical humanist paradigm. Otherwise his three paradigms can to a great extent be placed in Burrell and Morgan's three other paradigms.

There are, however, some differences between Ritzer and Burrell and Morgan: the social definition paradigm can largely form part of the interpretive paradigm, apart from action theory which Burrell and Morgan place in the left half of the functionalist paradigm. The social behavior paradigm suits excellently into the functionalist paradigm, where it is placed in the right half. The social facts paradigm can be divided into the functionalist and the radical structuralist paradigms. Ritzer has here schools like structure functionalism, conflict theory, and system theory which Burrell and Morgan place in the functionalist paradigm. Macro-sociology and parts of Marx, Weber, and Durkheim's writings are also placed in social facts. Burrell and Morgan place these, independent of the specific theory, in the radical structuralist and in the functionalist paradigms.

Some of the theories and perspectives, which Ritzer are placing in his facts paradigm, Burrell and Morgan place in the radical structuralist paradigm. Ritzer believes, for example, that Marx and conflict theory should be placed in the facts paradigm, while Burrell and Morgan think that they should lie in the radical structuralist paradigm in relation to the radical change dimension and perspective.

The difference in the classification could be equalized, if in his political conflict discussion Ritzer introduced Burrell and Morgan's philosophy of society dimension. This would result in Ritzer being placed even closer to the two. At the same time, it appears that Ritzer (ibid., p. 71) thinks that Marx "is one the few remarkable sociologists who have been able to build a bridge between different paradigms." Marx's "bridge building" shall be seen in relation to the fact that the Marxist theory and the radical structuralist paradigm concur with the functionalist paradigm in the objective dimension. But the supporters of the two paradigms fundamentally disagree as regards a philosophy of society dimension or, more correctly, discussion. This means that they have different ideological understandings and objectives of the science. Marx can also be understood in relation to two periods appearing from the two latter paradigm descriptions: "the young Marx" and "the old Marx." "The young Marx" was inspired by Hegel and what we might call the interpretive and critically theoretical aspects. The "old" was the Marx who wrote *Das Kapital* and *Grundrisse* which bases his theoretical attention on a structural notion of reality and society.

The paradigm discussion shows that a conception of reality and of science is in no way unambiguous. There is not one reality or one correct answer, and therefore research workers and their works may be seen as (multiple) subjective realities and as intersubjective reality, as the research worker is part of a scientific community. Our attitude to knowledge and understanding of the world is that human beings do not acquire this through external events but that it appears through man's attempt to objectivate the world. This is an essential, subjective process and as Morgan says:

> Words, names, concepts, ideas, facts, observation, etc., do not so much denote external "things", as conceptions of things activated in the mind by a selective and meaningful form of noticing the world, which may be shared with others. They are not to be seen as a representation of a reality "out there", but as tools for capturing and dealing with what is perceived to be "out there." (Morgan 1980: 610)

The researcher is a human being, and therefore he cannot fence his work from the social construction in which he participates and which he creates. This implies that theories have to be seen in relation to an understanding of the researcher and his notion of reality as well as his scientific community, i.e., the research worker's conception of his scientific tradition which also involves a discussion of use of theory and theory relations.

The very categorizing of theories in paradigms may be seen as kind of standardizing the aim of which is to create a basis for a discussion of reality understanding and a basis for cognition. They do not think that the very classification of paradigms, as Burrell and Morgan and Ritzer advance and understand them, shall be seen as a sharp boundary; they can be understood as ideal types in a Weberian sense in relation to the practice of the research (see Weber in Chap. 4).

One can find theories which are difficult to place unambiguously within a single paradigm and which seem to be in the borderland between two paradigms. This means that it is open to discussion whether there is a gentle transition between the paradigms. But on the other hand, one has to find the essence in theories to be able to understand them. This essence must be understood as the notion of the ontology and epistemology. This creates two different discussions, where the first deals with a placing of theories in different paradigms. The other is the problem concerning theories, which seem to lie on the borderline between two different paradigms.

There is a third aspect in this which is important to stress: research is also a craft (some might say, it is an art), and like in all other fields, there are good and less good craftsmen with their finished works. A theory therefore also has to be understood in relation to the fact of how good and stringent the logic of it is – will it hold or is it just an attempt to mix two different paradigms without taking into account and discussing the ontological and epistemological ideas and preconditions?

If the paradigm concept shall make sense and be used in an ontological and epistemological discussion of theories and research, it is necessary to use it with a sharp division between paradigms, where one paradigm excludes the other. In other words, it is not possible to work with theories placed in two paradigms at the same time, as a manifestation and understanding of the same reality – the same phenomenon in which one is interested.

This discussion is a reflection of the philosophy of science and philosophical discussion taken place concurrently with the development of humanity. As a social scientific research worker, one cannot disregard this, if one is serious about the work as a knowledge-producing activity and with cognition as a central point. A historical understanding is therefore central, as we all base on a tradition when performing our activities. We have different conceptions of reality that must be maintained. Besides historical consciousness and cognition, it is also about self-criticism and development of the scientific activities.

The thought of paradigm-exceeding theories, or the theories that seem to lie on the "borderline," does not hold, if we stick to the discussed paradigm understanding and to the historical discussion. The theories one understands as "inter-paradigmatic" have typical preconditions and concepts which have exclusively been taken from another paradigm, but one uses these on the premises of the own paradigm (the own notion of this). This means that the preconditions and logic of the paradigm are maintained and the concepts are defined and used on the basis of the requirements on good research of this paradigm.

The other discussion related to the above and to the discussion of good workmanship is whether the theory is logically consistent. This means whether the preconditions put forward also appear in the argumentation and discussion in the very object field of the theory or whether they are "forgotten"/reformulated in the theory. Thus the discussion is not inter-paradigmatic but paradigmatic, where one "borrows/is inspired/steals" concepts from other paradigms to explain anomalies in the own science but with a transformation of them within the own paradigm.

## *Discussion of Paradigm Analyses*

Burrell and Morgan's notion of reality and their paradigmatic discussion reflect that they have their basis within their own radical humanist paradigm (cf. Morgan 1980). This basis, as well as the philosophy of science point of view, which they take on the theories, implies that they get a discussion to which not everybody agree but which has a historical background which is important to understand. Individuals have to take a stand on their approach, because at the same time it concerns the way of thinking and theorizing of the research worker. This is important, to be able to assess scientific work but also in relation to reflection and self-criticism, which is always necessary from a purely developmental point of view. Their subjective-objective dimension is both reasonable and relevant, being the core in the criticism that resulted in the birth of alternatives to the positivistic and rationalistic inspired, functionalist paradigm.

The philosophy of society dimension is debatable and should be regarded as a reflection of their view on reality and science conception and as an attempt to emphasize their paradigm as good research, which is human in itself. Burrell and Morgan have a subjective conception with roots in critical theory and think that theories must be used to change things, especially the society. But at the same time, this implies that they partly move away from the subjective understanding of human beings and relation to reality: Their work is based on what human beings are, through predefinitions and definitions on what society should be. This appears especially from the following statement by Morgan:

# Discussion of Paradigms

> The radical humanist and radical structuralist paradigms offer a similar kind of challenge, which draws attention to the political and exploitative aspect of organizational life. From the perspective of these paradigms, both functionalist and interpretive theory fail to understand that the apparent order in social life is not so much the result of an adaptive process or a free act of social construction, as the consequence of a process of social domination. Organizations from this point of view oppress and exploit, and embody a logic which sets a basis for their eventual destruction. The order which interpretive theory seeks to enhance, is from the radical humanist and radical structuralist perspectives, a superficial order making fundamental contradictions. (Morgan 1980: 619)

As a description, their radical humanist paradigm can be accepted, but Burrell and Morgan fall into the trap against which they warn themselves not to deify paradigms and reality notions. Social dominance "exists," but to go out and investigate this is to leave out a stage: men's understanding of *their* own reality and the acts that *they* perform in this reality – *not the one* defined by the researcher in advance.

Burrell and Morgan's criticism of the interpretive paradigm based on their dimension regulation-radical change is self-contradictory and a misinterpretation. Considering the interpretive paradigm from a defensive angle can elucidate our criticism here:

To maintain that the interpretive paradigm focuses on status quo is rather a postulate, the basic notion in science being to understand human beings in their social situation. We are working on development of concepts and consciousness, with the objective of increasing the consciousness both of the human beings involved and the research worker himself. It is the consciousness and action that constitutes reality. The very status quo conception falls to the ground with this objective.

The social order, which Burrell and Morgan maintain, is imagined by the interpretive paradigm and fits badly into what they regard as a characteristic feature of the paradigm that reality is a product of the subjective and intersubjective consciousness and of the experience of individuals. In this no "underlying pattern" can be found; at a given time, a common (intersubjective) understanding may exist in a group of people which implies that they function together through the expectations that they have to each other. But they all have their own consciousness. This is therefore not the same as to say that an underlying pattern exists which the researcher will "uncover."

Consensus, social integration, and cohesion are concepts not used within the paradigm, but they are very characteristic and central for many theories within the functionalist paradigm.

One may be surprised that they want to place the solidarity concept in an understanding of the interpretive paradigm, as they refer to Durkheim's concepts mechanical and organic solidarity in connection with the functionalist paradigm (op. cit. p. 45). To place solidarity as a common denominator shows the problems they have in linking the two paradigms within a discussion of social orientation.

It is probably not necessary to comment on need satisfaction, as it is a purely functionalist phenomenon with roots in behaviorism. In the interpretive paradigm, consciousness and motives are referred to in connection with acts, and not stimuli-response.

Actuality is acceptable, because the interpretive paradigm is largely based on human beings and situations, and it is therefore a distinctive mark. But also the biography of human beings, experiences, and a historical understanding are central, and therefore history (understanding of the preceding) gets an important placing to understand the present. At the same time, hermeneutics, for example, has its roots in textual analysis: for example, of the Bible and the antique and Greek philosophers (cf. the introduction and Chap. 4).

Burrell and Morgan's concepts should therefore rather be seen as characteristic of the functionalist paradigm, in contrast to the radical humanist and the radical structuralist paradigms, and not as characteristic of the interpretive paradigm. Their attempt to link together the two paradigms, through a legitimization of the philosophy of society dimension, creates problems. The problem rises from their attempt to classify the four paradigms in four "boxes," where the dimensions shall be identical for all the paradigms – understood as a continuous scale. When linking together the two dimensions – subjective-objective and regulation change – they mix up concepts and understanding. The problem rises, when they try to find and maintain common preconditions for the interpretive and the functionalist paradigms as well as for the radical humanist and the radical structuralist paradigms.

If we consider the development of the sciences from a historical point of view, the interpretive paradigm raised as a criticism of the functionalist paradigm and the radical humanist paradigm as a criticism of the radical structuralist paradigm. In this criticism both the interpretive and the radical humanist paradigms have common philosophic roots in the German idealism/subjectivism and thus common preconditions. In the same way, both the functionalist and the radical structuralist paradigms have roots within an objectivistic and a positivistic-rationalistic science tradition and conception.

In short, the distinctive mark of science and paradigms should to a great extent be seen as a discussion of whether science is *objectively founded, e.g., nomothetic* or *subjectively orientated or idiographic*. Therefore, there is a belief in "autonomic structures and laws in the world" or the basis in "the man and subjective processes" in a discussion of consciousness and intersubjectivity. Objective and subjective must be understood in a broad discussion which we have partly shown in the historical understanding and through the paradigm discussion and which we shall discuss further in Chaps. 4 and 5. The fact is that they are only superior assembly concepts in which there are a complex discussion of conceptions and of different traditions of man and the social world and how this can be investigated.

Ritzer does not fall into the same methodological problems in his paradigm discussion. But he gets into some other problems, making the paradigms too "broad" (understood as simplified and uniform) and placing perspectives, which have widely different ambitions within the same paradigm (cf. Marx's discussion and the philosophy of society discussion). Ritzer comes to focus on a descriptive discussion of theories, which make him forget some of the philosophy of science, cognitive discussions. Ritzer also forgets to look at the objective in the methods and how this is linked to an ontological and epistemological discussion. An example is when he emphasizes observation as the preferred method in the social definition paradigm.

Within this it is held that understanding *cannot* be created by observing behavior. To obtain *understanding*, one must *interact* with the actors and through a *dialogue* create an understanding of why they act as they do and what they think about it. It is about how people think in their acts and interactions and in their construction of their Lifeworld.

One of the aims of Ritzer was to show the political conflicts that exist because of the mutual competition of the three paradigms and to demonstrate the discrepancies that exist within science and which thus, according to Ritzer, result in the fact that three paradigms can be put forward. Ritzer himself says that there does not exist a science that is a completely rational enterprise. Irrational factors are constantly getting into the picture. The fight between the supporters of the different paradigms is often political, and we often see that less importance is ascribed to the scientific or intellectual value of a paradigm than to the relative power which the supporters of the competing paradigms can win (op cit., p. 195). He (ibid., p. 217) thinks that the fight between the paradigms is founded on misunderstandings and is destructive. According to Ritzer it is a matter of fact that the different aspects of the social reality cannot be explained adequately without using knowledge and insight from all the paradigms. With this, Ritzer means that the ideal would be to combine the three paradigms so that we could work from one paradigm.

This is Utopian, which Ritzer realizes himself, but he forgets or avoids discussing why science is not objective, as Ritzer would like to conclude, and the "true" objective science on reality does not exist, being an impossibility: Research workers and their work are and must be understood as subjective. Ideology and political issues are parts of science, in the same way as they are part of man's everyday reality in other respects. Ritzer forgets this in his visions, and he tends to reify paradigms in spite of the fact that he warns against it himself. Human beings (and also research workers) are different, think differently, and have different reality conceptions. What else can social science do but to take a stand on this – how should science be able to rise above man, when science is the research worker and when the knowledge of reality is produced by the research worker as a man?

Even if it is attempted to deify the research process and the production of knowledge through the use of analytical tools, it cannot be severed from a thinking subject – the researcher. We can therefore in no way avoid neither the subject nor the Lifeworld, neither in the research nor in the everyday of life reality.

# Everyday Business Dynamics Can Be Scientific

Our thoughts of an interactionist perspective and the Lifeworld traditions have led us to consider symbolic interaction, phenomenology, and transformational linguistics as a foundation for our discussion. We think that if economics is to become science, then the field must operate with a ground in a clear ontology and epistemology, with a focus on general logic and pure logic. Reliance upon statistics and quantification are not in itself science, e.g., it is not enough to measure "things." They may be tools and even part of various approaches to discovery, but they are not what pure scientists would call science. We have examined transformational linguistics and found that it is a field close to being a pure science, in, for example, producing rules and representations for language interaction that are parallel to those in business economics.

At this point, we must return to the field of economics and attempt to compare our work with others. Since we have started with the supposition from Schumpeter that industrial research and development are the "heart of the capitalist engine," we concur with Nelson when he states that Schumpeter's basic premise is correct but he fails to take it much further. Our acceptance of Schumpeter's hypothesis is even more basic. Indeed, research and development are the cornerstones to any economy (not just a capitalist one). However, we do not feel that Schumpeter or his successors (Nelson 1990: 199) have developed an adequate theory of innovation, commercialization, and understanding of the organization.

We are convinced of this assertion on three levels. First, economics has failed to prove itself to be a science. Instead, as a field it continues to be an art form, performed by many creative people. There is no science. Or to paraphrase Gertrude Stein when speaking of a city, "there is no there, there." Second, there are few instances in economics where everyday business situations have been documented, leaving the field to speculate or quantity phenomena. Finally, while historical economists like Heilbroner (1989) clearly describe the impact of innovation and research in industrialized countries, the data lacks any understanding and explanatory power.

In this volume, we present in detail the Lifeworld philosophical tradition in order to lay the groundwork for the subjectivism paradigm. Once the perspective is established, it is easy to see why symbolic interactionism and phenomenology are so significant. When adapting the transformational linguistics approach to economics, we have constructed a powerful theoretical framework.

What our case studies in Part II do is consider the commercialization of an innovation into the business world. Significantly, we approached this from the interactionist perspective such that we were able to apply our action research and qualitative methods to the actual point of commercialization. The resultant set of rules needs to be examined by others and explored for universality. Suffice it to say, however, that we have started our own interactive dialogue with other scholars in the field. This exchange we hope will prove useful to the field of business economics.

One recognition in this discussion of paradigms and different conceptions of reality is that knowledge production and thus theories are a discussion of subjective preconditions and conceptions of reality but also in an intersubjective context. The different conceptions and traditions existing bring about theories with widely different results and conclusions, even though they treat the "same" object field. The logic in these originates in their preconditions. Therefore we cannot criticize the logic without having an understanding of the preconditions of the theories and their basic conceptions. It is here criticism of philosophy of science shall be placed, i.e., whether there is coherence in the logic between preconditions and statements. Criticism of preconditions is a *question of belief*, an ontological discussion, and an epistemological discussion of how we acquire knowledge of the reality in which we are interested. Therefore the linking between an ontological and an epistemological discussion and the methodology in the knowledge production is what is important.

From a subjectivistic and everyday of life point of view, it must be maintained that the paradigms are only labels on different perspectives, logics, and their preconditions. They are not real in the sense that they exist autonomously from people – they are thoughts and actions made by *someone*. Theories are products originating in actions, reflecting the conception and interpretation of reality of the researcher.

Some labels may, however, be more adequate than others. We shall therefore below dissociate ourselves from Burrell and Morgan as well as Ritzer and call the interpretive paradigm/social definition paradigm *the subjectivist paradigm*. The subjectivism refers to the fact that it is about an attitude – a being, in the research work, to the everyday life reality of man – the world in which they live their lives, how it is from their standpoint, and how they create it. The approach to understand this Lifeworld can be regarded as interpretive. To interpret has thus something to do with the methodological discussion within the subjectivist paradigm. The discussion of the Lifeworld tradition and the subjectivism paradigm and the methodology in relation to the ontology and epistemology will be tackled in Chaps. 4 and 5 and Part II). It is within this perspective that the discussion of interaction provides us with an approach and methodological perspective for the research worker to describe, understand, and attempt to explain phenomenon in everyday life.

# Chapter 4
# History of Lifeworld Traditions

The old tradition and philosophy of science of Lifeworld and subjectivism are an alternative to the foundations forming the basis of much of the theory developed in business economics and also social science in general. The discussion in this chapter will involve several multidisciplinary fields: ontological and epistemological thoughts, methodological attitudes and implications, as well as consequences and connections between them. The focus is especially on the understanding of the basic discussions and thinking in the tradition, what has been and is being thought of reality, science, the human being, and creation of knowledge.

The discussion of subjectivism and Lifeworld is an alternative to the understanding of reality and the logic that lies in objectivism, positivism, and rationalism and in the functionalistic paradigm. In a number of ontological and epistemological respects, it can be said to take the opposite point of view. This is, however, a somewhat simple and crude statement, as the ideas and the logic are more complex than to distinguish between a subjective versus an objective conception of reality and of the human being. A comprehensive discussion is hidden behind this, which in many ways abolishes the distinction between subjective and objective. But it should still be understood in relation to distinctions between an objective tradition: "the world in itself" versus a subjective tradition, the world as social and individual constructions, and "the world is nothing unless the world-has-meaning."

In 1935, Husserl criticized a natural science approach in social science, being of the opinion that science had lost its soul. (Social) Science had to a great extent been studying the culture at the terms of nature. That is, natural science had determined the trend of science, also in cultural science and social science. But man has a soul, a life, and a history, which disappear completely, if it is studied on the premises of natural science. Husserl was of the opinion that man has to seek his roots to understand the meaning of his life (Bjurwill 1995: 37). His phenomenology is the study of consciousness, and he rejects the notion that consciousness or its contents can be fully investigated from a "theoretical attitude" using the philosophical assumptions, conceptual categories, and quantitative methods of science. Instead, the study of

---

© Springer Nature Switzerland AG 2019
W. W. Clark II, M. Fast, *Qualitative Economics*,
https://doi.org/10.1007/978-3-030-05937-8_4

79

consciousness should start from the *natural attitude*: the relationship of consciousness to the Lifeworld – the world of ordinary, everyday experience. Only from the "natural standpoint" can we do justice to the exploration of consciousness and human experience (see White 1990: 78).

The crux of the paradigm and the Lifeworld traditions can thus preliminarily be seen as "The idea of man being an active creator of his own social reality, and an interest in the creating process taking place in the mind, as well as an interest in the social process" (Ritzer 1977: 96). "To talk about actors is in itself an important attitude, as it points at an interest in man as man, i.e. to understand man as acting and creating, and not as determined by external elements" (Arbnor and Bjerke 1981: 124). This implies that the subjectivistic ontology and science do not ask for the general or the common. The person asking for the meaning of something must of course have an idea what the expression meaning does at all comprise. One can only ask a question if there is coverage for the words and the language used, i.e., if one wants other answers than those held in advance (cf. Wind 1987: 13). The ontology seeks to account for the logic and meanings of everyday language and an understanding of these constructions of everyday of life.

The philosophical attitude towards this and towards the tradition is captured well by Merleau-Ponty (1994: XIV), who thinks that the philosopher is a perceptual beginner, which means that he takes for granted nothing that men learned or, otherwise, believe they know. It means also that philosophy itself must not take itself for granted, in so far as it may have managed to say something true; that it is an ever-renewed experiment in making its own beginning; that it consists wholly in the description of this beginning; and, finally, that radical reflection amounts to a consciousness of its own dependence on an unreflective life which is its initial situation, unchanging, given once and for all. Philosophy is not the reflection of a pre-existing truth, but, like art, the act of bringing truth into being is as actual or real like the world of which it is a part (ibid., p. XX).

It is, in other words, a discussion of cognition and understanding of man and man's being in the world – in to the Lifeworld. It is a discussion of how to understand social reality and the human being.

## The Search for Another Philosophy and Theory of Cognition

There are many persons that have left their marks on the discussion through history and on a foundation of an alternative to the positivistic and rationalistic philosophy lying behind the functionalistic paradigm and mainstream theory. One philosopher who is central in the establishment of this and difficult to ignore is Immanuel Kant and his theory of cognition.

## Immanuel Kant (1724–1804) and the Foundation of Subjectivism

Kant thought that the problem with all classical objective metaphysics was that it forgot to investigate the meaning and cognitive reach and boundaries of its own concepts (cf. Wind 1976: 17). He did not reject any form of metaphysics (e.g., his discussion of religious belief as grounded in a metaphysic discussion and idea; see Gadamer 1993: 54). But Kant stressed that the metaphysician should be self-critical and investigate the limits for the possibilities of cognition of man, before he engages in metaphysical speculations on the arrangement of the world. Kant thus on one hand turns towards the dogmatic confidence in reason of the rationalists, and on the other he has no doubt that we have scientific cognition, and he therefore turns to the radical empiricist skepticism.

Kant's first attempt, in creating an understanding of the relation between man and reality, was to establish a synthesis of two ways of thinking which were mutually contradictory: the Cartesian dualism between soul and body, as well as Hume's resolution of self-conceit. That is, *Descartes's* distinction between thought and extension: thinking has its own principles of movement, and the thing follows other principles. And *Hume's* view that the relationship of man to the world is based on natural belief and faith – a practical relationship that cannot be explained theoretically as cognition and through the ego.

Kant was of the opinion that all cognition starts with the experience of something and that knowledge must be a synthesis of experiences and concepts: without sensing we cannot be aware of any objects (the empirical cognition); without understanding we cannot form an opinion of the object (the a priori cognition):

> There can be no doubt that all our knowledge begins with experience. For how should our faculty of knowledge be awakened into action did not objects affecting our senses partly of themselves produce representations, partly arouse the activity of our understanding to compare these representations, and, by combining or separating them, work up the raw material of the sensible impressions into that knowledge of objects which is entitled experience? In the order of time, therefore, we have no knowledge antecedent to experience, and with experience all our knowledge begins. (Kant 1929/1787: 41)

But though all our knowledge begins with experience, it does not follow that it all arises out of experience. For it may well be that even our empirical knowledge is made up of what we receive through impression and of what our own faculty of knowledge (sensible impression serving merely as the occasion) supplies from itself (ibid., p. 41). So the process in which knowledge is acquired is composed of sensation, powers of conception, and understanding.

Firstly, we have all had *space* and *time* given as pure *a priori forms of intuition*.[1] This form of intuition is absolute, and it is independent of and precedes the sense

---

[1] Knowledge a priori is knowledge exclusively originating from rational thinking and which precedes and is independent of experience. Actually should "forms of intuition" be more exact if it were translated to "forms of perception," which should be more in line with Kant's thoughts. But in the first three translations of Kant, the first one was used and still is. The German expression is *"Formen der Anschauung."*

impressions. Secondly, thought has *(reason) categories* structuring the way in which we understand reality. It is a fundamental conceptual apparatus giving meaning to the world that we experience.

However, there are limits to knowledge. Kant distinguishes between the phenomena (the world of phenomena) and reality (the noumenal world): we cannot apprehend the mysterious substance of the thing, what he called "das Ding an Sich" ("the thing in itself"). If we try to go outside the world of phenomena, i.e., if we wish to use the concepts outside the limits of the comprehensible world, it will lead to paradoxes, fallacies, and pure self-contradictions. Kant argued that the traditional metaphysical arguments about the soul, immortality, God, and the free will all exceed the limits of reason. Reason can only be used legitimately in the practical sphere, i.e., if we try to acquire knowledge of the world. If we cannot reach das Ding an sich, then we must be satisfied with "das Ding für Uns" ("the-things-as-they-presents-themselves-to-us"[2]).

Kant thought that all cognition starts with the experience, but, even so, cognition does not anyhow fully result from experience. The conditions that make the sensuous and subjective consciousness of man a consciousness of objective objects are the same conditions that give the concept of causation status of a law governing the interrelation of these objects. This fact reduces the validity of the principle of causation for the sensuous experience. Its necessity is relative in relation to man. This does, however, not imply that the principle of causation gets status of an empirical truth. Its relativity does not abolish its necessity (Nerheim and Rossvær 1990: 141). Or in other words, principles of causation belong to reason; it is a way in which we think.

The realization that reality is relative to man implies that it is no longer tempting to assume that the order existing in reality is only resulting from certain habits and expectations. Neither is it a question of an objective mathematical structure applying to the very things, independent of the viewpoint of man. Kant thought that the objective order in the experience results from a general comprehension which man himself brings into the world, as soon as he begins to experience the world. This general comprehension is a network of concepts arising concurrently with the experience, even though they do not originate in the experience. By virtue of his intersubjective concepts, man persists in a point of view or a certain general perspective, and he creates this perspective through his shaping of everyday reality. In this way, necessity arises in the relative necessity created by man, at the same time creating intersubjective, empirical concepts.

Kant claims, for example, that the space is the form of our sensory faculty. This makes the space a kind of a passive registration of facts, and thus all the things that we sense get space dimensions. This explains that the space is valid to all our sensory experience (but not to the things themselves) and explains what it means that our sciences can only be considered as valid in relation to our sensory experience. But more significantly, Kant says that the space depends on the way in which we make the world comprehensible or, to be more precise, on our conception of the

---

[2] cf. also Husserl's concept of intentionality.

world from substance and causation categories. In other words, our space view depends on our conception of the physical reality as consisting of three-dimensional objects which can be moved around in time and space.

This perspective reveals a connection between time and space (the forms of intuition) and the categories (the forms of reason) – they are interdependent. As time and space are primarily linked to the sensory faculty, while the categories are linked to the intellect, Kant's argumentation is based on maintaining the balance between these two forms of reality contact. It is at this point where both forms act as agents to each other, that the necessary relations and structures of the world are lying. Therefore, we preserve the world, by preserving our own forms of understanding reality.

Kant's transcendental main argument is therefore: I am conscious of a number of conceptions that are adjusted in time. But I can only be conscious of them, if I can ascribe them to myself. And this is only possible, if I can distinguish between myself and my conditions and on the other hand with what is not myself. This means that I must be able to distinguish between subjective and objective as which is a condition of having conceptions at all. I can, however, only make this distinction, if I can avail myself of objectively valid concepts, which again implies that the world shows the minimum of order and regularity that are sufficient to support such an objective use of concepts. I can thus only be conscious of conceptions if I have at my disposal a number of concepts (e.g., "thing" or "cause") by means of which I can describe an objective world showing a certain lawfulness and which is independent of whether I sense it or not. Hence, the forms cannot be private, because if they were, I would not be able to distinguish between the private and the objective. Therefore, my synthetic a priori[3] statements about these forms express valid cognition (Lübcke 1994a: 230–).

To Kant, there is nothing immediately given in our sensation of the world, but on the other hand, certainly an existing material world which through experience presents sensed things, i.e., everyday phenomena, to our consciousness (see Tonboe 1993: 72). These phenomena then make out the disseminating material which reason can work up (abstractly or theoretically) through the consciousness, rubricate in a priori ideally given categories and concepts (e.g., time and space), relate to each other in theories, etc.

Kant was of the opinion that before we can talk of scientific experiences, we must have some preceding organized ideas into which we can arrange them. We must know the limits of our acquired experiences so that our knowledge does not only create an aggregate but a system. In a system, the whole comes before the parts, whereas in an aggregate it is conversely. The world is in this way (only) a substratum (foundation) for our cognition and our practical experiences. When we have such limits, we can, with our intellect and reason, exceed or transcend the sensed surrounding world. Kant has thus turned the interest of philosophy from the very thing to the human consciousness that can apprehend the thing.

---

[3] Synthetic a priori cognition means judgments that will not be self-contradictory to deny but where we can all the same determine a priori whether they are true or false.

Kant has inspired many "subjectivists" after him, for example, through the neo-Kantianism dominating philosophy and history in Germany at the turn of the century. He has in many ways influenced the philosophic viewpoint on how an alternative science could be understood and formulated, based on the human consciousness. But here the agreement stops, and as it will appear from the following, the different traditions have different views of the human consciousness and everyday life and how science can be formulated.

## Science and the Lifeworld

Some of those, in Europe, who can be regarded as central in a foundation, not only of a Lifeworld philosophy but also of a science oriented to the Lifeworld, are Wilhelm Dilthey (1833–1911), Edmund Husserl (1859–1938), Max Weber (1864–1920), Martin Heidegger (1889–1976), and later on Alfred Schutz (1899–1959) and Hans-George Gadamer (1900–2002).

### *Dilthey: The Life (Leben) and Science of Spirit (Geist)*

Dilthey was interested in a new foundation of social science – a science of spirit *(geist)* – and he did not think that the foundation established in natural science and its methods could be used at phenomena created by man. He was interested in life – "Leben," the inner life of man and historical consciousness. Historical consciousness is consciousness of the fact that with its standards and institutions, the given society is not natural but a product of the thoughts and actions of man. The given facts in history and society are produced by man, and exactly therefore it is possible for the individual to understand them.

Dilthey started from the varied nature of the objects of cognition within natural science and humanities, respectively.[4] Nature and history are two different regions, which require two different forms of cognition and theory of knowledge. We apprehend the nature through a causal-analytical explanation. Historically, however, we apprehend through a psychological, empathizing understanding. The spiritual history ("Geistesgeschichte") requires its own theory of science different from the cognition theory of natural science, and it is hermeneutic, as Dilthey understands it, which is to deliver such a theory of knowledge.

Dilthey maintained that the distinction was one of content. For this reason, he insisted on using the term *Geisteswissenschaften*. History, economics, and jurisprudence study man's mind *(Geist)* in contrast to physics and chemistry, which study external processes. Of course it is man's mind as objective *(objektiver Geist)*, in other words, as a system of cultural products and institutions, together with the meanings they bear, that is the object of these "sciences of mind." But the important

---

[4] cf. Habermas (1972: 141 and 145), Schutz (1972: XV), Herva (1988), Wind (1987).

Science and the Lifeworld

thing from his point of view is that the mind is central. In turn, what is most important in the mind is *Erlebnis* – lived experience or immediate experience. This intimate inner life achieves an outward expression (*Ausdruck*), as in art. By interpreting this outward expression in terms of what lies behind it, we come to understand (*Verstehen*) others. We do this by reconstituting our own inner experience "in" the other person by "reading" him. Understanding is thus a "rediscovery of the I in the Thou." This insight is therefore the knowledge that is proper to the social sciences (Schutz 1972: XV–).

Dilthey's explication of a methodology for the human sciences must be viewed within the context of his philosophy of life. Life cannot be understood as a machine. Neither can it be explained merely as an organic system shared with other life forms, because human life is something far more than organic metabolism and mechanical movement. For Dilthey, life is what we experience in our activities and reflections as we live out our personal histories (Polkinghorne 1983: 25). Dilthey was of the opinion (with inspiration from Kant's criticism of pure reason, directed to the empiricists and the rationalists) that science of history must be supplemented with a criticism of the historical reason – an elaboration of a historical consciousness.

Consciousness should precisely be consciousness with a view to clearness of method in the sciences that did not have the nature but the history and the social reality as fields. He thought that understanding of a historical event could not consist in arranging it in a given lawfulness but that historical cognition is cognition of single events. Therefore, historical experiences consist, among others things, of an insight into the fact that – for example, being researchers – we are part of history ourselves. It is the homogeneity of subject and object, of the research worker and the research object, which makes history and spiritual science possible (cf. Gadamer 1993: 219; Wind 1987: 35).

What constitutes Dilthey's special importance and distinguishes him from the neo-Kantians, who tried to involve the human sciences in the renewal of critical philosophy, is that Dilthey did not forget that this instance experience is something quite different from what it is in the investigation of nature. What we call experience is a living historical process; and its paradigm is not the discovery of facts but the peculiar fusion of memory and expectation into a whole (cf. Gadamer 1993: 221).

## *Weber and Sociology as Social Action*

Following Dilthey, Weber was interested in a type of social science that was an empirical science of concrete reality (*Wirklichkeitswissenschaft*). The aim was the understanding of the unique characteristics of the reality in which we move. He wished, on the one hand, to understand the relationships and the cultural significance of individual events in their contemporary manifestations and on the other to understand the historical reasons of their being historically so and not otherwise (Weber 1948: 72, 1977: 119). Weber states (in relation to the debate on the editorial line of the journal, *Archiv fur Sozialwissenschaft und Sozialpolitik*):

> Liberated as we are from the antiquated notion that all cultural phenomena can be *deduced,* as a product or function of the constellation of "material" interests, we believe nevertheless that the analysis of social and cultural phenomena with special reference to their economic conditioning and ramifications was a scientific principle of creative fruitfulness and with careful application and freedom from dogmatic restrictions, will remain such for a very long time to come. The so-called "materialistic conception of history" as a *Weltanschaung (worldview)* or as a formula for the causal explanation of historical reality is to be rejected most emphatically. The advancement of the economic interpretation of history is one of the most important aims of our journal. (Weber 1948: 68)

This discussion of science, causal explanation, analysis, and objectivity is central in the understanding of Weber. His discussion largely deals with what is the crux of science and what scientific work is. Central to him is the striving towards creating knowledge about the phenomena of life in their cultural *importance.* This importance of a cultural phenomenon and the cause of this importance cannot be deduced, motivated, or made comprehensible from a system of laws, irrespective of the perfection of this system, because this importance assumes that the cultural phenomena are related to conceptions of value. The concept of culture is a concept of value, and the empirical reality of "culture" comprises the elements of reality, which become important for us through the fact that the relation has a value, and exclusively these elements – the elements and relations – are important to us being researchers in social science (Weber 1977: 124).

Weber thought that the sighting points in research must be the meaningful actions of individuals and understanding of these. It is only the individual who can produce meaningful actions – not groups or communes. Still he thought that in some cases it might be necessary to treat social groups or aggregations "as if" they were individuals but that this was only a theoretical "fiction." Social groups are a result and way of organizing the individual actions of persons (see Parkin 1982: 17).

Organizations cannot think, feel, and experience; only individuals can. These individuals have motives for their actions, and their behavior is derived from subjective views, where they have their own ideas and interpretations of how they behave and why. Weber (1964: 88) therefore defined sociology as the study of *social action*: sociology is a science seeking the interpretative understanding of social action, to reach a "causal explanation" of the cause and effects of the action.

In his discussion of scientific validity and objectivity, Weber (1977: 104) distinguishes between what something "is" and what something "should be" and between "knowledge" and "values." He thought that the ability to distinguish between knowledge and values, to fulfill the scientific duty and to accept the truth of a fact, as the practical duty to fight for own ideal, is what you should strive for. But it can never be the task of an empirical science to fix binding standards and ideals, in order to derive practical recipes from them.

As Weber (1948: 58) states, there is and always will be an unbridgeable distinction among (1) those arguments which appeal to our capacity to become enthusiastic about and our feeling for concrete practical aims or cultural forms or values; (2) those arguments in which, once it is a question of the validity of ethical norms, the appeal is directed to our conscience; and (3) those arguments which appeal to our

Science and the Lifeworld

capacity and need for analytically ordering empirical reality in a manner which claim to be valid as empirical truth.

This proposition remains correct, despite, as we shall see, the fact that those highest "values" underlying the practical interest are and always will be decisively significant in determining the focus of attention of analytical activity in the sphere of the cultural sciences. It has been and remains true that a systematically correct scientific proof in the social sciences, if it is to achieve its purpose, must be acknowledged as correct by everyone. Or, more precisely stated, it must constantly strive to attain this goal, which perhaps may not be completely due to faulty empirical material.

Furthermore, the successful logical analysis of the content of an ideal and its ultimate axioms and the discovery of the consequences that arise from pursuing it, logically and practically, must also be valid for everyone. At the same time, those one can lack a "sense" for our ethical imperative and he can certainly often will to deny the ideal itself and the concrete value judgment derived from it. Neither of these two latter attitudes can have any effect on the scientific value of the analysis in any way.

Science can help the acting human being to become conscious of the fact that all actions – also the actions not performed – have consequences that imply an attitude to certain values. This normally also implies that an attitude towards other values is taken. To make the choice is the sole matter of the actor (Weber 1977: 99). An empirical science has no ability to teach someone what he *should*, only do what he *can* and – in some cases – what he *wants*.

Weber (ibid., p. 128) stated that it is meaningless to try to treat cultural events in an "objective" way. He was of the opinion that the ideal goal of research should be to reduce that, which is empirically given, to "laws," not because cultural or psychological phenomena happen in a (from an "objective" angle) less lawful way but because (1) knowledge of social laws is not knowledge of the social reality but exclusively one of the means that our thoughts need to acquire such knowledge and (2) knowledge of cultural phenomena is only conceivable to us on the background of the significance of the obstinate, individual reality. For which purpose and in which respect this is the case, no "law" can reveal to us what we experience in everyday life, but it is determined by the conceptions of value from which we see culture in each single case.

## *Husserl and die Lebenswelt*

Husserl is central in understanding the development of a Lifeworld-based science, as he took departure in Kant's das Ding für Uns. Husserl's[5] conviction was that none of the so-called rigorous sciences, which use mathematical language with such efficiency, could lead towards an understanding of our experiences of the world: a world the existence of which they uncritically presupposed and which they pretend to measure by yardsticks and pointers on the scale of their instruments. All empiri-

---

[5] Husserl was professor in mathematic.

cal sciences refer to the world as pre-given; but they and their instruments are themselves elements of this world (see Schutz 1973a: 100).

Husserl tried to link the philosophy of phenomenology and science by discussing reality through the concept *die Lebenswelt* – the Lifeworld. His transcendental phenomenological philosophy is based on the world that we daily live in, experience, talk about, and take for granted in all our activities (Bengtsson 1993: 43–). But at the same time, this everyday of life approach to the world is *naive*, as in the natural attitude, we are ignorant of the possibility conditions for our existence. In the daily experiences, man takes naturally naively the whole reality for granted, as a substance existing in itself, and is unconscious of himself and thus also of the role that he plays himself in the experience. Husserl therefore thought that the task of the transcendental phenomenology, in a philosophic reflecting attitude, was to investigate the possibility conditions of the natural existence. It is this existence that Husserl describes as the Lifeworld.

The complexity in this is that the Lifeworld is a condition of all empirical theories and of all scientific activity. It is from the Lifeworld that science gets its experience material; it is to the extreme of this world that the theories must be related, and it is in this same world that science is carried on. The Lifeworld is thus not only pre-reflexive, but also prescientific; it goes on and is assumed by both philosophy and science. Science thus depends on the Lifeworld, but it is not identical with it. Science consists of attempts, with theories, to define reality systematically. Thus, it consists necessarily of an idealization of the specifically lived reality – it loses in the concretization but wins at a higher, intellectual level. But the purpose of science must be maintained: to understand reality, not to control it.

Like Gadamer (1993: 259) commented on Husserl's work, by noting that his analysis of the Lifeworld and of the anonymous creation of meanings that forms the ground of all experience, gave the question of objectivity in the human science a completely new background. He did that by making the concept of objectivity to appear to be a special case, *science is anything but fact from which to start*. Rather, the constitution of the scientific world presents a special task, namely, of clarifying the idealization that is endemic to science. But this is not the most fundamental task. When we go back to "productive life," the antithesis between nature and spirit does not prove to be of ultimate validity. Both the human and the natural sciences are to be understood as achievements of the intentionality of universal life – i.e., of absolute historicity. Only this kind of understanding satisfies the self-reflection of philosophy.

## *Schutz and Social Phenomenology*

Schutz (1973b: 22) took his start in Husserl's phenomenology and was of the opinion that the facts, events, and data of the social scientist have quite another structure than in the natural science. The observation field of the scientist, the social world, is *not* structure less in its essence. This world has a special meaning and structure of relevance to the people living, thinking, and acting in it. They had pre-chosen and pre-interpreted this world in advance through a series of common-sense constructions of everyday life. It is those objects of thought which determine their actions and define the goal of their actions, the means which are available to achieve them – in short, which help them to find their bearings in their natural and sociocultural environment and to feel at home in it.

The world understood as "the commonsense world," "world of daily life," and "everyday world," which are variant expressions for the intersubjective world experienced by man within what Husserl terms "the natural attitude." This world exists before our birth, has its history, and is given to us in an organized fashion. It is primarily the scene of our actions and the locus of resistance to action: we act not only within but upon the world. And our initial purpose is not much the interpretation or understanding of the world but the effecting of changes within it; we seek to dominate before we endeavor to comprehend. The commonsense world, then, is the arena of social action; within it men come into relationship with each other and try to come in terms with each other as well as with themselves.

All of this, however, is typically taken for granted, and this means that these structures of daily life are not themselves recognized or appreciated formally by common sense. Rather, common sense sees the world, acts in the world, and interprets the world through these implicit typifications. That there is a social world, that there are fellow men, that we can communicate meaningfully with others, and that there are very broad and general principles true for daily life – these prime facts are in woven in the texture of the natural attitude (see Schutz 1990a: XXVII).

The objects of thought, which are structured by the scientist, therefore refer to and are founded on the objects of thought structured through the commonsense thinking of the man who is living his everyday life among his fellow men. The structures used by the scientist are thus structures of the second degree, i.e., structures of the structures that have been made by the actors at the social stage whose acting he observes and tries to understand according to the procedural rules of his science.

In this, Schutz think that the aim of social science is understanding of social reality – the everyday Lifeworld and the natural attitude to life of the wide-awake human being. The understanding of reality as something which man takes for granted and not problematized in everyday life. The primary goal of the social sciences is to obtain organized knowledge of social reality. Social reality he understands as the sum total of objects and occurrences within the social cultural world *as experienced by the "commonsense" thinking of men* living their daily lives among their fellow men, connected with them in manifold relations of interaction (Schutz 1970: 5).

It is a world of cultural objects and social institutions in which we are born, in which we have to find our bearings and to come to terms with. Seen from outside, we experience the world we live in as a world which is both nature and of culture, not as a private world but as an *intersubjective world*. This means that it is a world common to all of us, either actually given or potentially accessible to everyone; and this involves intercommunication and languages. It is in this intersubjective world that action shall be understood.

In this everyday Lifeworld, the actors use "common sense knowledge," as kind of knowledge held by all socialized people. The concept refers to the knowledge on the social reality held by the actors in consequence of the fact that they live in and is part of this reality. The reality experienced by the actors as a "given" reality; i.e., it is experienced as an organized reality "out there." It has an independent existence, taking place independently of the individual. However, at the same time, this reality has to be interpreted and made meaningful by each individual through his experiences – we experience reality through our commonsense knowledge, and this knowledge is a practical knowledge of how we conduct our everyday lives.

First of all, Schutz devotes himself to understand the orientation of man in this reality through social action. Social is understood as relations in behavior between two or more persons. Therefore, social action is understood in the light of the meaning that the action has to the actor (and to the Other). Schutz considers the subjective interpretation of meaning as a typification in the world of everyday life. To understand the social world is to understand the way in which human beings define the different social situations, and the very definition is a process and an action, and that interpreting the world is acting in the world. A social action is therefore an action oriented towards the past, present, or future behavior of another person or persons, where the specific mode of orientating is its subjective meaning (Schutz 1972: XVII).

All our knowledge about the world involves *constructions*, i.e., a set of abstractions, generalizations, formalisms, and idealizations which are specific for the organizational level of thoughts in question (Schutz 1973b: 21). Such things as pure and simple facts do not exist. From the beginning, all facts are facts chosen by the activities of our consciousness from a universal context. Facts are consequently always interpreted facts, either facts seen separately from their context through an artificial abstraction or facts considered in their special surroundings. This applies both to the social reality of everyday life and to research.

Schutz is interested in replacing the objective analysis of the things in the world by a subjective analysis of the things in the consciousness. He does this in a distinction between "the act of thinking" and "the object of thought" (Schutz 1973a: 102). Schutz attached great importance to a phenomenological analysis of meaning and searched for the underlying elements in that which he called "the stream of consciousness." This is decisive for his analysis, as it introduces the temporal dimension supporting the concept "reflexivity." *Consciousness* is fundamentally an unbroken stream of lived-through experiences (*Erlebnisse*) which have no meaning in themselves.

The meaning depends on reflexivity – the process of turning to oneself and which reflects on the experience of the act. Meaning is connected with actions in a retrospective way. This process of giving meanings reflexively depends on the actor's identification of the aim or the goal that he or she tries to reach. (This discussion will be elaborated in Chap. 4.3.)

Accordingly, it is another reality that we are imagining and which therefore requires another approach to understanding everyday life. Hence, this discussion of philosophers of the Lifeworld tradition presents an entirely different foundation for social science and understanding of reality than the philosophy and science of objectivism.

# Understanding Interrelation of Ontology and Epistemology

The alternative conception of reality and science raised some problems on what to deal with as a social scientist and which scientific demands that should be made in this field. It was necessary to formulate ontological and cognitive grounds in the philosophy of Lifeworld and of science and how to understand the process of knowledge.

## *Consciousness and Intentionality*

The phenomenological formulation of the concept of *intentionality* created one philosophic foundation that could support the criticism of the positivistic philosophy and create an alternative approach to social science (see Husserl 1962; Heidegger 1992; Merleau-Ponty 1994/1962; Schutz 1978a, b).

This radically different conception did make that the consciousness of identity no longer appears as an explicandum but, on the contrary, was made the defining property of the mind. That essential property without which the mind could not be what it is. For that reason, it is insufficient, though true and valid as a first approximation, to define intentionality as directedness. In saying, that in experiencing an act of consciousness, we find ourselves directed to something. For example, in perceiving we are directed to the thing perceived, in remembering we are directed to the event recalled, in loving or hating we are directed to the person loved or hated, etc. (cf. Gurwitsch 1982: 60; Moustakas 1994: 50). There is no act of thinking without an object that is thought, no will without the willingness of something, no act of judgment without something being judged, and so on. The concept of intentionality therefore involves a change in the understanding of reality and in the cognition of reality, as here we understand it as the *relation* of the man to the reality; it is our consciousness that creates the impressions of our mind and not vice versa.

This means that intentionality is the structure and the force in consciousness giving meaning to the experience. In the intentionality, a subject and an object are connected: the consciousness of man is directed to something else than itself, and this is why neither experiences nor acts and their goals can be separately analyzed. This means that we think of something and we are aware of it in a certain way. This makes man an active creator of the object of the surroundings, intentionality being the processes through which the logic and reality picture of the actor are created. Therefore, intentionality is not the same as intentions but a dimension lying behind in the consciousness. What is meant is that the very objects are shaped according to the way in which we understand them – *the objects do not exist in themselves*, i.e., they do not exist with meaning in themselves.

This philosophic foundation created a conception, where the consciousness and subjectivity of man were the essential elements in the understanding of reality. One of Husserl's first comments was that in itself, (all) science was characterized by intentionality.[6] Despite the fact that the results of science were always approximate and imperfect, the scientist was guided by the intention of absolute objectivity. It was this aim of science, this idea of science rather than its results, that was important in distinguishing it as a discipline worthy of its name (Burrell and Morgan 1980: 241). Husserl therefore encouraged the philosophers to return "to the facts in themselves." In this, he stressed that we can in no way acquire knowledge about the objects as they are as such (in themselves). We must instead devote ourselves to the objects, as they appear to *the experience*, in favor of which Kant argued – "das Ding für Uns." It is thus a criticism of "das Ding an Sich," as Husserl understands reality as all which *can* be made available in the immediate and evident experience. If we insist on a reality which exists in itself, will this not only be a groundless doubling of reality but also a metaphysical explanatory foundation just like the God of the Middle Ages or other mysterious powers (cf. Bengtsson 1993: 29). Hence, he criticized the naturalistic empiricism for treating the objects existing in nature as if, by means of the senses, it was possible to acquire an objective knowledge about them (as they exist as such):

> How can the experience by way of the consciousness describe or get in contact with the object? How can the experiences mutually legitimate and correct each other instead of just replacing each other or confirm each other subjectively? How can the stream of consciousness, whose logic is of an empirical nature, pass objective, valid sentences, valid for things existing in and for themselves? Why is that what we might call the rules of game of consciousness not irrelevant, when they concern objects? How can natural science be understandable in every single case to such an extent that at any time it claims to have knowledge of and be able to produce a nature, which exists in itself – in itself contrary to the subjective stream of consciousness? (Husserl, in Ritzer 1977: 118)

Intentionality is constituted of a *noema* and *noesis*, and both refer to meanings. The *noema* is not the real object but the phenomenon and not the thing but the appearance of the thing. The object that appears in perception varies in terms of when it is perceived, from what angle, with what background of experience, etc. From whatever angle as one views an object, the synthesis of perceptions means that the thing will continue to present itself as the same real thing. The thing is out there present in time and space, while the perception of the thing is in consciousness. Regardless of when or how and regardless of which components or what perception, memory, wish, or judgment, the synthesis of noemata (perceived meanings) enables the experiencing person to see the thing as just this thing and no other.

*Noesis* constitutes the mind and the spirit and awakens us the meaning or sense of whatever is in perception. *Noesis* brings into being the consciousness of something and refers to the act of perceiving, thinking, and feeling – all of which are embedded with meanings that are concealed and hidden from consciousness.

---

[6] Husserl distinguished between intentionality of the act, which is that of our judgments and of those occasions when we voluntarily take up a position. And operative intentionality, that which produces the natural and anti-predicative unity of the world and of our life, being apparent in our desires, our evaluations, and in the landscape we see (c.f. Merleau-Ponty 1994: xviii). It is the concept of operative intentionality that it is referred to in this discussion.

Understanding Interrelation of Ontology and Epistemology 93

The meanings must be reorganized and drawn out (see later on *Epoché*). Every intentional experience is also noetic; "it is its essential nature to harbour in itself a "meaning" of some sort, it may be many meanings" (Husserl 1962: 257 in Moustakas 1994: 29). In considering the noema-noesis correlate is that the thing "perceived as such" is the noema; the "perfect self-evidence" is the noesis. Their relationship constitutes the intentionality of consciousness:

> For every noema there is a noesis; for every noesis there is a noema. On the noematic side is the uncovering and explication, the unfolding and becoming distinct, the clearing of what is actually presented in consciousness. On the noetic side is an explication of the intentional processes themselves (Husserl 1989: 46). What is meant noematically is continually changing in perception; the something meant is more, more than what is originally meant explicitly. The something meant achieves a synthesis through a continual perceiving of the whole throughout its angular visions and perceptions. (Moustakas 1994: 30)

The working out of the *noema-noesis* relationship, the textural (noematic) and structural (noetic) dimensions of phenomena, and the derivation of meanings are an essential function of intentionality. Moustakas (1994: 31) summarizes the challenges of intentionality in the following processes: (a) explicating the sense in which our experiences are directed; (b) discerning the features of consciousness that are essential for the individuation of objects (real or imaginary) that are before us in consciousness (*noema*); (c) explicating how beliefs about such objects may be acquired, how it is that we are experiencing what we are experiencing (*noesis*); and (d) integrating the noematic and noetic correlates of intentionality into meanings and essences of experience.

Merleau-Ponty demonstrates his view on intentionality in other, but not quite diverging, manners, sticking to the original characteristics of Husserl's concept of intentionality[7] – the operative intentionality...:

> or that which produces the natural and antepredicative unity of the world and of our life, being apparent in our desires, our evaluations and in the landscape we see, more clearly than in objective knowledge, and furnishing the text which our knowledge tries to translate into precise language. Our relationship to the world, as it is untiringly enunciated within us, is not a thing which can be any further clarified by analysis; philosophy can only place it once more before our eyes and present it for our ratification. (Merleau-Ponty 1994: xviii)

Merleau-Ponty thinks that this original intentionality must be seen together with the Lifeworld. The conscious or distinct intentionality is not the original; ahead of the conscious act of thought, we "intend" something. When, for example, I reach out my hand to something, I aim at it, not as an imagined or thought thing but as this particular object with which I "associate": it may be a brush that I need to paint a window.

The consciousness of this object does not have to be declared. My action is "intentional." I do not expressly think that this is a brush that must be cleaned in order that I can paint the window. This deeper intentionality means that, originally, consciousness is not an "I think that" but an "I can." The conscious reflection or analysis builds upon a richness of preceding unexpressed intentions. The reflection is just the reflection on something that precedes it.

---

[7] See Merleau-Ponty (1994), Grøn, in Lübcke (ed.) (1994b: 33).

Sight and movement are specific ways of entering into relationship with objects. And if, through all these experiences, some unique function finds its expression, it is the momentum of existence which does not cancel out the radical diversity of contents, because it links them to each other, not by placing them all under the control of an "I think" but by guiding them towards the intersensory unity of a "world." Movement is not thought about movement, and bodily space is not thought of or represented. Each voluntary movement takes place in a setting, against a background determined by the movement itself. We perform our movements in a space which is not "empty" or unrelated to them but which, on the contrary, bears a highly determinate relation to them: movement and background are, in fact, only artificially separated states of a unique totality. In the action of the hand which is raised towards an object is contained a reference to the object, not as an object represented but as that highly specific thing towards which we project ourselves, near which we are, in anticipation, and which we haunt. Consciousness is being-towards-the-thing through the intermediary of the body (Merleau-Ponty 1994: 137–).

When viewing intentionality and Lifeworld in this way, there is a clear connection in the way of thinking of Merleau-Ponty and Schutz, to Heidegger and Gadamer, and also to symbolic interactionism with the focus up on interaction and meaning between human beings (see later in this chapter about the discussion of the Lifeworld and in part II).

## *Transcendental Phenomenology and Phenomenology as Methodology*

In the question about investigation and of objectivity in science, Husserl tried to open up a new way to see things, the phenomenology, which seeks to investigate experienced data as they appear to the consciousness, by means of the theoretical tool of philosophy.

Husserl's phenomenology was not a dogmatic science but was a method from the beginning. The basic principle was: "We will return to the very things "(*"Zu den Sachen selbst"*) and "At the beginning there is the pure and so to say dumb experience, the own meaning of which we must now give expression in the first place."[8] With this, Husserl means a return to the phenomena, as they appear to consciousness – the essence of the phenomena (*"das Wesen"*). By phenomena he means: "That which, having been subjected to the phenomenological reduction, is purified from the reality attributed to it by naive consciousness"[9] (which Heidegger understands as that which appears through itself, the obvious – *"das-Sich-an-ihm-selbst-zeigende, das Offenbare"*[10]). It is a question relating to the objects as real and treating them as they are thought and experienced and as they appear.

---

[8] cf. Bengtsson (1993: 25), Merleau-Ponty (1994: viii).

[9] Heap and Roth (1973: 357).

[10] cf. Lübcke (ed.) (1994b: 121).

Understanding Interrelation of Ontology and Epistemology 95

This understanding of phenomenology is thus closely connected with the concept of intentionality and the understanding of reality. In phenomenology, one must not take scientific theories, the common sense, and other attributes for granted. It is instead a question of giving justification in full to the objects that are in focus of the investigation: mathematical or logical objects, feelings, physical things, culture objects, social institutions, etc. These are the very things, and our approach to them is the experience. It is in the experience that they appear, and it is thus on the basis of the experience that the thing must be investigated and made clear. In the same way, the experience is a "dumb" beginning, as all theories, concepts, attitudes, etc. originate in the experience. They constitute an attempt to control the experienced realities intellectually and linguistically.

Phenomenology thus aims, in one sense, at getting hold of the things as they appear in the experience – to define them, but not do violence to them. Therefore, openness and sensibility are required, unlike the summarizing and classification in fixed categories of functionalism. Husserl's phenomenology was thus not a method in a traditional sense, understood as principles to be followed. Thévenaz views practicing phenomenology:

> Phenomenology is never an investigation of external or internal facts. On the contrary, it silences experience provisionally, leaves the question of objective reality or of real content asides in order to turn its attention solely and simply on the reality in consciousness, on the objects insofar as they are intended by and in consciousness, in short on what Husserl calls ideal essences. By this we must not understand mere subjective representations (which would leave us on the plane of psychology) nor ideal realities (which would "reify" or hypostasize unduly the data of consciousness and would put us on the level of metaphysics) but precisely the "phenomena"… The phenomenon here is that which manifests itself immediately in consciousness: it is grasped in an invitation that precedes any reflection or any judgement. It has only to be allowed to show itself, to manifest itself; the phenomenon is that which gives itself (*Selbstgebung*). The phenomenological method then, faced with the object and the contents of knowledge, consists in neglecting what alone counts for philosophers and scientists, namely their value, their reality or unreality. It consists in describing them such as they give themselves, as pure and simple intentions (*visées*) of consciousness, as meanings, to render them visible and manifest as such. In this Wesenschau, the essence (*Wesen*) is neither ideal reality nor psychological reality, but ideal intention (*visée*), intentional object of consciousness, immanent to consciousness. (Thévenaz 1962, in Burrell and Morgan 1980: 241)

In this quotation, we see Husserl's transcendental phenomenology in his attempt to reach the absolute possibility conditions of knowledge. This is to be understood from his clear-cut distinction between *essentia* and *existentia* and between what something "is" and "that" it is.[11] In the investigation of essentia, he introduces the concept of *epoché*.[12]

As a philosophic method, epoché has the purpose of separating the existence of the object and its contents: to put the existence in brackets and not use it. What is left outside the initial reduction are the complete contents of the experienced objects as pure (ideal) phenomena – as intentional objects through the intentional act (cf.

---

[11] See the discussion of Lifeworld about Heidegger's understanding of this distinction.

[12] Epoché can also partly be named "the phenomenological reduction" and "putting the world in brackets."

Bengtsson 1993: 36; Heap and Roth 1973: 356). A condition is that existence is regarded as a performance of consciousness, i.e., that it is the consciousness that constitutes the experienced as real. In the natural attitude, we hold knowledge judgmentally; we presupposed that what we perceive in nature is actually there and remains there as we perceive it. In contrast, epoché requires a new way of looking at things, a way that requires that we learn *to see* what stand before our eyes and what we can distinguish and describe (Moustakas 1994: 33).

In another way, the "reduction" involves a consciousness ignoring of one's prejudices about the world and focusing on the essential aspects of ones object or subject of study. The epoché requires the suspension of commonly held beliefs about one's objects of study. By suspending our beliefs, we open ourselves to new experiences; we allow our object of experience to present itself to us in new forms. Finally, our experience needs to be "bracketed" in much the same way that a portion of a mathematical equation is bracketed for special treatment while the rest of the equation is ignored. Taken together, these three metaphors describe the phenomenological attitude, as Husserl put it, "to the things themselves" (White 1990: 79).

Husserl himself was very well aware of the problematic in this process of epoché. What he meant was that in order to see the world and to grasp it as paradoxical, we must break with our familiar acceptance of the world and, also, from the fact that from this break we can learn nothing but the unmotivated upsurge of the world. The most important lesson, which the reduction teaches us, is the impossibility of a complete reduction. This is why Husserl is constantly reexamining the possibility of the reduction. If we were absolute mind, the reduction would present no problem. But since, on the contrary, we are in the world, indeed our reflections are carried out in the temporal flux on to which we are trying to size (since they *sich einströmmen*, as Husserl says); there is no thought which embraces all our thought (Merleau-Ponty 1994: xiv). It is, however, not only the existence of the object that is put in brackets. An example of how to understand Husserl's point:

If we want to understand Director Jensen, we must focus on him. Not on what a director is, or what a man is in general or what management theories says, or what we think and mean as subjects: we must put this in brackets and instead take a stand on that which is our object: Director Jensen himself.

Phenomenology exclusively turns its attention to the reality in the consciousness, at the objects, as they are experienced by and in consciousness. With this perspective, we shall precisely understand "phenomena." That is what immediately manifests itself in the consciousness: it is caught in an immediate understanding that precedes any reflection or judgment. The phenomenon is what is given – *that* which makes the phenomenon precisely *this* phenomenon. An example:

> That which makes Director Smith Director Smith and not Director Andersen (an entirely different matter would be if our object investigation was to investigate the phenomenon director).

Another example with a materialistic thing, such as the essence of "ball":

> There are many different balls: basketballs, footballs, tennis balls, golf balls. They vary in many ways, but the essence in them is that they are all "round" – to me they present them-

selves as round – and round in a certain way. Not round like a wheel or the sun or a pipe, but as *ball-round*.

The essentia and existentia of the phenomena consequently mean that the essence is the unchangeable in the phenomenon that which makes the phenomenon what it is, the being of the thing, and in contrast to this the changeable, the specific of the phenomenon. Husserl wants to stress the general in this discussion; he ignores the specific. An example with a chair:

> A chair has a certain shape and a certain color, a certain material, etc. These are all specific things that can be changed without the chair stopping being a chair. But what is it that we cannot take away from the chair, if it is still to be considered as a chair? That is the essence of the chair, its being. In this case the thing must have a seat and a number of legs, maybe of a certain length so that they are adapted to the angle in the hips and the knees, or another type of under frame for the seat, and it must have a back of some kind. This is the general of the chair. If it does not have these general characteristics, we stop calling it a chair, and instead we may call it a stool, a pedestal, etc. (Bjurwill 1995: 18; *our translation*)

The phenomenological method of Husserl means a confrontation with objects, where the content of knowledge consists in ignoring their value and their reality or unreality. It consists in describing them as they give themselves pure and simple "intentions" (*visées*) in the consciousness, as meanings, and in reproducing them as being visible and manifest. In this, the essence (*Wesen*) is ideal intention (*visée*), an intentional object in the consciousness. This means that the point is the relation between consciousness and reality, where Husserl distinguishes between "the object as it is understood" (*noema*), i.e., the purpose of my thoughts. And "to understand the object" (*noesis*) – the intentional act of consciousness – the very process of consciousness makes me direct my thought to the object.[13]

A phenomenological investigation, in this sense, does not seek to develop theories. Instead, its focus is investigation and then a description of the phenomenon (or the essences) as they appear: the commitment is to examine all phenomena carefully and to take none of them as familiar or understood until each has been carefully explicated and described. Phenomenology is held to be not only descriptive but also presupposition-less. The claim of presupposition-lessness expresses, instead, a resolution to eschew all unexamined assumptions. Phenomenology attempts to examine all premises, including its own, so as to permit the phenomena to show themselves in their essential structures (Polkinghorne 1983: 43).

Merleau-Ponty meant that the understanding of Husserl's discussion of investigation of essence is that the essence is a mean and not the end: seeking the essence of consciousness will therefore not consist in developing the *Wortbedeutung*[14] of consciousness and escaping from existence into the universe of things said. It will consist in rediscovering my actual presence to myself, the fact of my consciousness, which is in the last resort what the world and the concept of consciousness mean. Looking for the world's essence is not looking for what it is as an idea once it has

---

[13] Here intention must not be mistaken for purpose, as this is connected with judgment and action, i.e., the actor's purpose of the action, cf. the discussion between Weber and Schutz in Chap. 4.4.

[14] "The connection of meanings".

been reduced to a theme of discourse; it is looking for what it is as a fact for us, before any thematization (Merleau-Ponty 1994: xv). To seek the essence of perception is to declare that perception is not presumed true but defined as access to truth (ibid., p. xvi).

## Schutz and the Phenomenological Analysis in Social Science

According to Schutz (1973b: 47), social science must deal with the behavior of man and commonsense interpretation in the social reality, based on an analysis of the entire system of projects and motives and of relevance and structures. Such an analysis refers necessarily to the subjective viewpoint, i.e., to interpretation of the action and its surroundings from the viewpoint of the actor. Any social science that wishes to understand "social reality" must adopt this principle. This means that you always **can** and for certain purposes *must* refer to the activities of the subjects in the social world and their interpretation through the actors in project systems, available means, motives, relevance, etc.

To be able to understand the social reality and handle the subjective views, science must construct its own objects of thought, which replace the objects of commonsense thinking. This approach allows for an understanding of research work on models of parts of the social world, where typical and classified events are dealt within the specific field in which the research worker is interested. The model consists of viewing the typical interactions between human beings and analyzing this typical pattern of interaction as regards its meaning to the character types of the actors who presumably created them. The social research worker must develop methodological procedures to acquire objective and verifiable knowledge about a subjective structure of meaning.

In the sphere of theoretical thinking, the research worker "puts in brackets" his physical existence and thus also his body and its system of orientation, of which his body is the center and the source (Schutz 1973b: 96). The research worker is interested in problems and solutions, which in themselves are valid, to anybody, everywhere, at any time, anywhere, and whenever certain conditions, from which he starts, are present. The "jump" in theoretical thinking involves the decision of the individual to suspend his subjective viewpoint. And this very fact shows that it is not the undivided self but only a partial self, a role player, a "Me," i.e., the theorist, who acts in scientific thinking. The features of the epoché, which is special for the scientific attitude, can be summarized through the following: (a) the thinking subjectivity as man among fellow men, including his bodily existence as psychophysical human being in the world; (b) the system of orientation through which the everyday Lifeworld is grouped in zones within actual, restorable, achievable reach, etc.; and (c) the fundamental anxiety and the system of practical relevance, which originate from it (ibid., p. 97).

The system of relevance, reigning within the province of scientific contemplation, arises in the random act of the research worker, when he chooses the object of his further exploration, i.e., through the formulation of the existing problem. Thus, the more or less anticipated solution to this problem becomes the summit of the scientific activity. On the other hand, the mere formulations of the problem, the sections, or the elements of the world, which are topical or may be connected to it as relevant concerning the present case, are determined at once. After that, this limitation of the relevant field will pilot the investigation.

The difference between commonsense structures and scientific structures of patterns of interaction is small.

*Commonsense* structures are created on the basis of a "Here" in the world. The wide-awake human being in the natural attitude is first of all interested in the sector of his everyday Lifeworld, which is within his reach, and which in time and space is centered around him. The place that my body occupies in the world, my topical Here, is the basis from which I orient in the space. In a similar way, my topical *"Now"* is the origin of all the time perspectives under which I organize events in the world, like before and after, past and future, presence and order, etc. (ibid., p. 73). I always have a Here and a Now from which I orient and which determines the reciprocity of the assumed perspectives and which takes a stock of socially derived and socially recognized knowledge for granted.

The participant in the pattern of interaction, led by the idealization of the reciprocity of the motives, assumes that his own motives are joined with those of his partner, while only the manifest fragments of the actions of the actors are available to the observer. But both of them, the participant and the observer, create their commonsense structures in relation to their biographic situation.

The researcher has no Here in the social world which he is interested in investigating. He therefore does not organize this world around himself as a center. He can never participate as one of the acting actors in a pattern of interaction with one of the actors at the social stage without, at least for some time, to leave his scientific attitude. His contact is determined by his system of relevance, which serves as schemes for his selection and interpretation of the scientific attitude which is temporarily given up to be resumed later. The researcher observes, assuming the scientific attitude, the pattern of interaction of human beings or their results, in so far as they are available to become observations and open to his interpretation. But he must interpret these patterns of interaction in their own subjective structure of meaning, unless he gives up any hope of understanding "social reality" on its own merits and within its own situational context.

The problematic that Schutz brings up here and the understanding that one may reach of the subjective knowledge of another person can be expressed in the following way: the whole stock of my experience (*Erfahrungsvorrat*) of another from within the natural attitude consists of my own lived experiences (*Erlebnisse*) of his body, of his behavior, of the course of his action, and of the artifacts he has produced. My lived experiences of another's acts consist in my perceptions of his body in motion. However, as I am always interpreting these perceptions as "body of another," I am always interpreting them as something having an implicit reference to "consciousness of another."

Thus, the bodily movements are perceived not only as physical events but also as a sign that the other person is having certain lived experiences, which he is expressing through those movements. My intentional gaze is directed right through my perceptions of his bodily movements to his lived experiences lying behind them and signified by them. The signitive relation is essential to this mode of apprehending another's lived experiences. Of course, he himself may be aware of these experiences, single them out, and give them his own intended meaning. His observed bodily movements become then for me, not only a sign of his lived experiences as such but of those to which he attaches an intended meaning. The signitive experience (*Erfahrung*) of the world, like all other experience in the Here and Now, is coherently organized and is thus "ready at hand" (Schutz 1972: 100–).

The point is how two "streams of consciousness" get in touch with each other and how they understand each other. Schutz expresses it quite simply, when he talks about the connection, as the phenomenon to "grow old together," to understand the inner time (*durée*) of each other. In fact, we can each understand all others by imagining the intentional acts of the other, when they happen. For example, when someone talks to me, I am aware – not only of the words but also of the voice. I interpret these acts of communication in the same way as I always interpret my own lived experiences. But my eyes go directly through external symptoms to the internal man of the person talking. No matter which context of meaning I throw light on, when I experience these exterior indications, its validity is linked with a corresponding context of meaning in the mind of the other person. The last context must be where his present, lived experiences are constructed step by step (Schutz 1972: 104).

The simultaneousness of our two streams of consciousness does not necessarily mean that we understand the same experiences in identical ways. My lived experiences of you are, like the surroundings that I describe to you, marked by my own subjective Here and Now and not by yours. But I assume that we both refer to the same object that thus transcends the subjective experiences of both of us. But at the same time, not all your lived experiences are open to me. Your stream of lived experiences is also a continuum, but where I can catch detached segments of it. If I could become aware of all your experiences, you and I would be the same person. Hence, the very nature of human beings is that they do not have exactly the same interpretation of experiences and therefore are different. It is precisely this human diversity that distinguishes humans from other life forms yet creates conflict and turmoil within societies and between them.

We also differ in other ways; how much of the lived experiences of the other we are aware of; and that I, when I become aware of the lived experiences of the other, arrange that which I see within my own meaning-context. And in the meantime, the other has arranged them in his way. But one thing is clear: this is that everything I know about your conscious life is really based on my knowledge of my own lived experiences. My lived experiences of you are constituted in simultaneity or quasi-simultaneity with your lived experiences, to which they are intentionally related. It is only because of this that, when I look backwards, I am able to synchronize my past experiences of you with your past experiences (ibid., p. 106).

My own stream of consciousness is given to me continuously and in all its perfection, but that of the other person is given to me in discontinuous segments and never in its perfection and exclusively in "interpreted perspectives." This also means that our knowledge about the consciousness of other persons can always be exposed to doubt, while our own knowledge about our own consciousness, based as it is on immanent acts, is in principle always indubitable. In the natural attitude, we understand the world by interpreting our own lived experiences of it. The concept of understanding the Other is therefore the concept: "Our interpretation of our lived experiences of our fellow human beings as such." The fact that the You confront me as a fellow human being and not a shadow on a screen – in other words that the Other's duration and consciousness – is something that I discover through interpretation of my own lived experiences of him. In this way, the very cognition of a "You" also means that we enter into the field of intersubjectivity and that the world is experienced by the individual as a social world.

# Science and Understanding: The Lifeworld as Understanding

## *Understanding*

Understanding is regarded as the crux of the matter, both in the ontological and the epistemological discussion. Understanding becomes essential in relation to establishing a science and in the methodological discussion, and it is central in relation to man in his creation of meaning in every day of life.

In his discussion, Heidegger focuses on the universal aspect by emphasizing that all science and methodical cognition is secondary in relation to the understanding on the basis of which man finds his bearings in his everyday life and world of practice (Wind 1987: 13). This universality view originates in Husserl's phenomenology as the science of the sciences – and that the precondition of all scientific knowledge is the knowledge experienced in the prescientific Lifeworld. The concept of universality should be understood in two ways: a going back to the history of the individual, i.e., to its possibilities of conceiving the life as a whole, and partly by basing on the phenomenological description of the things as objects for everyday use – they therefore have a meaning to the individual.

In the scientific and empirical contexts, to understand is *to seek understanding*. This has no underlying positivistic ideal of seeking for natural laws and rules, nor of explaining or predicting. It is an understanding of the phenomenon based on investigation through a description and/or an interpretation of the description. Jensen (1991: 14) does not think that understanding is to study the individual horizon of another person in the form of re-experience or empathy. There is no such method. Understanding, Jensen thinks – and refers to Gadamer – *is something that overtakes you or happens to you*, when being open and impressionable. In that sense understanding is to make experiences.

As Gadamer (1986: 109–) says, first of all, understanding, like action, always remains a risk and never leaves room for the simple application of a general knowledge of rules to the statements or texts to be understood. Furthermore, where it is successful, understanding means a growth in inner awareness, which as a new experience enters into the texture of our own mental experience. Understanding is an adventure and, like any other adventure, is dangerous. Understanding is not satisfied with simply wanting to register what is there or said there but goes back to our guiding interests and questions; one has to concede that the hermeneutical experience has a far less degree of certainty than that attained by the methods of the natural sciences. But when one realizes that understanding is an adventure, this implies that it affords unique opportunities as well. It is capable of contributing in a special way to the broadening of our human experiences, our self-knowledge, and our horizon, for everything understanding mediates is mediated along with ourselves.

Gadamer's discussion builds on the conception that our situation as human beings is that we are historical beings – we are always standing in the middle of history. The phenomenon that we wish to understand and the I, who want to understand, are both related to a *context of traditions*. The aim of understanding is not only to understand the other but also always understanding of oneself. Understanding is something penetrating all our experiences, because understanding is not a method but a way of existing as a human being (cf. Jensen 1991: 9). And all understanding is ultimately self-understanding (*Sichverstehen*) (Gadamer 1993: 260). During our whole life, we continue to interpret and reinterpret our experiences in life. The very memory is a continuously repeating act of interpretation. As we remember the preceding, we reconstruct it in accordance with our present attitudes to what is important and what is not (Berger 1980: 55).

## Dilthey and Verstehen

Dilthey was of the opinion that the solution to the problems of social science and formulation of an alternative foundation – hermeneutic – to the social scientific research could be found in *Verstehen* (Understanding). Verstehen could be seen as a method through which the research worker could try to understand human beings, their internal mind and their feelings, and in which way this was expressed in the external action and performances of man. The external manifestations of human life needed interpretation and connection with the internal experiences: "The notion of Verstehen provides a means of studying the world of human affairs by reliving or re-enacting the experience of others" (Burrell and Morgan 1980: 230).

Dilthey thought that there was a great difference between cognition of nature and understanding of history. He motivated this distinction in a scientific discussion of the concept *Verstehen* that he comprehends as understanding or empathy. Dilthey took the concept from the German historian Droysen (1858) who made a division between *erklären* (explain) as a description of the methodology of the natural sciences and *Verstehen* as a description of the methodology of the social sciences.

# Science and Understanding: The Lifeworld as Understanding

Dilthey believed that it was not possible to explain the human societies legally. Research, through the method (the hermeneutic), had to start from the researcher himself, from his empathizing understanding, where interrelationships are experienced and re-understood. Knowledge is thus acquired through an internal, an "interior," process – the things are experienced "from within" through re-experience and understanding (cf. Flato 1985: 62):

> Verstehen... was the means by which we comprehended the meaning of a historical or social situation or cultural artefact. It was a method of understanding based upon re-enactment. In order to be comprehended, the subject of study needed to be relived in the subjective life of the observer... One of the main avenues for verstehen was through the study of empirical life assertions – institutions, historical situations, language, etc – which reflected the inner life of their creators. The study of these social creations was seen as the main avenue to an understanding of the world of objective mind. (Burrell and Morgan 1980: 236)

Dilthey thought that we did not only see and apprehend physical objects, but we also apprehend meanings. When people communicate with us, for example, through texts, we experience more than the visual – the ink-written letters – we catch the meaning of the words used and the message of the writer. He expressed that any social phenomenon should be analyzed in detail and be interpreted as texts, in order to realize its essential meaning. At this point, the hermeneutic reflection of understanding emphasizes what actually happens when we understand a text; in other words, we turn our eyes not only towards the text but also towards the reader.

A precondition is that the subject does not leave the meeting with the text unaffected. The experience emerging from this meeting is an experience which affects both the text and the reader. If such an experience succeeds, a turn, a change may take place in the meeting between the reader and the text. The turn and the change are that where at the beginning it was the reader, who addressed and asked the text, it later becomes the text, which asks questions to the reader and the own self-understanding which he has brought along. The text becomes living, not because the reader puts something into it but because the text itself starts asking questions directed to the pre-understanding of the reader (Wind 1976: 24–). Thus, Dilthey (Polkinghorne 1983: 30) describes three relations that make it possible to understand the meanings of others:

1. One needs to be familiar with the mental process, through which meaning is experienced and conveyed. Since each person is involved in trying to communicate meaning to others, everyone is familiar with these processes to some extent, but researchers can enlarge this familiarity through the study of biographies and descriptive psychology.
2. One needs knowledge of the particular concrete context in which an expression is made. A word is understood in the context of its sentence; an action is understood in the context of its situation.
3. One needs knowledge of the social and cultural systems that provide the meaning for most expressions. To understand a sentence, we need to know the language; to understand a chess move, we need to know the rules of chess.

## The Hermeneutic Circle

Dilthey claims that it does not suffice to explain the knowledge we have of human phenomena – our understanding of life and other persons, as this understanding is expressed in conversations and poetry and in our informal "philosophy of life" (ibid., p. 220). Unlike stable natural scientific laws, he thinks that the organizing pattern in the human field is historical; it changes and develops. This can be seen in relation to Dilthey's understanding of the hermeneutic circle, where the social whole cannot be understood independent of its parts and vice versa (i.e., a criticism of both the meristic and the holistic approach). Like in a text, coherence in life is understood as a relationship between the whole and the parts. Each part expresses some of the wholes of the life – has significance for the whole, just like the part has its significance dependent on the whole in which it is part.

Dilthey wished to formulate methodical rules of interpretation, and through his conception of part-whole, there also was recognition of that there was no absolute basis. There is nothing that is evident for certain and on which we can build, because we are always in the middle of a complex situation, which we try to manage by constructing provisional ideas, which we revise later. In this way, the methodological rules are regarded as a circle movement, which repeatedly increases the understanding. Dilthey was interested in hermeneutic knowledge that he regarded to be that which could reveal the meaning of the human expressions. The hermeneutic knowledge focuses on structures of interactive powers that should be seen in relation to the hermeneutic circle and in a discussion of context.

Dilthey was trying to explain "how ones inner life is woven into continuity" (*Zusammenhang*) in a way that is different from explaining the knowledge of nature by appeal to the categories. He used the concept of structure to distinguish the experiential character of psychological continuity from the causal continuity of natural processes. Logically, "structure" is distinguished by its referring to a totality of relationships that do not depend on a temporal, causal succession but on intrinsic connections. The decisive step for his epistemological grounding of the human science is the transition from the structure of coherence in an individual's experience to historical coherence, which is not experienced by any individual at all (Gadamer 1993: 223–).

Dilthey talks about "logical subjects" instead of "real subjects," because of the way in which individuals *belong to each other* (like in solidarity within a generation or nation – that one has something in common). It represents a spiritual reality that must be comprehended as such because it is not possible to get behind it and explain it. Dilthey apprehended that "full" knowledge of the human world can never be acquired, because it is both historical and in a continuous process, and that the tools to acquire knowledge were also part of this changed and developed world (cf. Polkinghorne 1983: 221). He emphasizes that the greater distance between that which is to be understood and the person who understands, the greater is the uncertainty of the acquired knowledge. Here he especially thinks of understanding as understanding in a historical sense. At this point, Gadamer, for example, has quite another view that we will discuss below.

Science and Understanding: The Lifeworld as Understanding          105

## *Weber: Verstehen, Action, and Social Relations*

Weber follows Dilthey, and his concept of *Verstehen* is linked with the concept of action[15] and understanding of the organizing of society and social relations. He uses social relations to denote the behavior of a plurality of actors in so far as in its meaningful content the action of each takes account of that of the others and is oriented in these terms. The social relationship thus *consists* entirely and exclusively in the existence of a probability that there will be, in some meaningfully understandable sense, a course of social action (Weber 1964: 118). His understanding of social relations is the behavior of (many) people, where the way of acting is meaningful and each action considers the actions of other actors and adapts to them.

The method to investigate social action builds on his idea of *Verstehen*. On the basis of interpretation, it is attempted to understand the behavior of the investigated person and the subjective meaning behind by identifying with the "psychical" processes (cf. Weber 1948, 1977: 121; Herva 1988). By this Weber means that the researcher should attempt to comprehend social action through a kind of empathetic liaison with the actor. The strategy is to try to identify with the actor and his motives and to view the course of conduct through the actor's eyes rather than his own.

Weber did not regard Verstehen merely as a way of sounding out a person's own account and evaluation of his conduct by way of interview and the like (Parkin 1982: 19). It implies that we must understand the motives of the actor (the purpose of the action) – the meaning behind the action. He saw two ways of understanding motives: through empathy and by re-experiencing the experiences of the person. Weber (1964: 89) thinks that meaning can be understood in two ways: it may refer to an actual, existing meaning in a specific action of a specific actor, or it may refer to the average or "approximate" meaning in a given group of actors. Or it may refer to a theoretical conception of "pure types" of subjective meanings, which are ascribed to a hypothetical actor or actors in a given type of action. He stresses that it does in no way refer to an objective, "correct" meaning or to a meaning that is "true":

> Access to the meaning of actions is different in kind from access to the mere presence of actions. Ordinary perceptions provides the data base for the investigation of action as a mere physical occurrence. And in order to provide greater surety to ones own knowledge of an action, to support of others´ perceptions can be called on. However, the meaning of actions is not directly present in ordinary perception. The awareness of what an action or speech act means, requires another kind of "perception" that allows meaning to be known. This second kind of "perception" has been called "Understanding" or Verstehen. The human realm is primarily the realm of meaning, and meaning fills human experience. (Polkinghorne 1983: 215)

Verstehen refers here to a technical meaning in the method used in the investigation and can be seen in two, but not independent, ways: the two senses of understanding, the commonplace and the technical, can be distinguished from each other but not entirely divorced. The term understanding (without a capital letter) is used to mean any type of comprehension, including the comprehension of physical relationships

---

[15] See Weber's concept of action.

("I understand why the ball falls") and the mathematical relationships ("I understand that two and two make four").

The term *understanding* (with a capital letter) does not have this broad connotation in the human sciences. It refers to a specific type of understanding, the comprehension of meaning ("Do you understand what she meant by that?") (ibid., p. 217). Weber (1964, 90–) called the first understanding the *Aktuelles Verstehen*, which refers to a direct, observable understanding, and the second the *Erklärendes Verstehen*, an explanatory understanding. In the latter, we try to catch the motives and the subjective meanings behind various actions. The question "why?", which represents the search for "explanatory understanding," is naturally tantamount to referring the action back to the motives, i.e., the "adequate ground" of action in the form of a subjectively adaptable purpose. This is an explanatory understanding. It goes beyond what we actually and "currently" see and experience; it is an intellectual operation, which requires bringing together bits of knowledge obtained and other times and occasions than the reading of the text or the observation of the act (Bauman 1978: 83).

In Weber's apprehension of research, there is no total rejection of statistical methods, and he could see them as a way to control the general validity in notions. But the fact that two variables show a great extent of correlation is not enough in itself to establish a causal relation between them. If this shall be the case, it must be proven that the relation between the variables is *intuitively meaningful*. And it is the cultural meaning to human beings that must be in focus and be understood. Weber (1977: 126) thought that in causal explanations, it was not only impracticable to give an exhaustive description of causal chains in any phenomenon in its full reality, which is also meaningless.

We exclusively choose the causes related to the elements of events that we see as essential in each single case. When it is about the individuality of the phenomenon, the causal problem is not a question of laws but of specific causal connections. It is not a question under which formula the phenomenon shall be arranged but a question which individual constellation it results from – it is a question of relating in relation to something else. In all the places where a causal explanation applies for a "cultural phenomenon," knowledge of laws cannot be the goal of the investigation, but exclusively a mean. Like Parkin (1982: 21) expresses Weber's attitude, if adequacy in respect to meaning is lacking, then no matter how high the degree of uniformity and how precisely its probability can be numerically determined, it is still a comprehensible statistical probability. Statistical information constitutes understandable types of action and thus constitutes sociological generalizations, only when they can be regarded as manifestations of the understandable subjective meaning of a course of social action.

## Gadamer and Understanding

Gadamer is described by some as a philosophic or existential hermeneutic, but as a previous student of Heidegger, Gadamer comes closer to his thoughts of phenomenology than to Weber and Dilthey – and classical hermeneutics. Directly and indirectly we may also regard Gadamer as a renewal and updating of Plato's and Aristotle's thinking (cf. Wind 1987: 7). Gadamer (cf. Lübcke 1994b: 163) thinks that philosophy cannot be carried on, if the way to the systematic points does not pass through a historical study of the tradition. The interpretation of the historical tradition is not only a philosophic-historical activity side by side with the systematical philosophizing. The relation to the tradition is part of the very philosophy.

Gadamer considers philosophical hermeneutics to be a view on man: as an attempt to identify and emphasize the characteristics which are part of being a human being – and understanding is just such a feature of human life. Life is *not* something that we face but something that *we are in the middle of.*

## Gadamer and the Hermeneutic Circle

Gadamer argues that the hermeneutic circle of understanding is not a methodological circle but describes an ontological, structural element in understanding. We cannot relate, for example, to a historical tradition, as if it exists as an objective part separated from us, as there is interplay between the development in the tradition and the interpreter of that tradition.[16] In his discussion, Gadamer starts from Heidegger's discussion of an understanding of the hermeneutic circle and interpreting tradition. Heidegger writes:

> It is not to be reduced to the level of a vicious circle, or even of a circle which is merely tolerated. In the circle is hidden a positive possibility of the most primordial kind of knowing, and we genuinely grasp this possibility only when we have understood that our first, last, and constant task in interpreting is never to allow our fore-having, fore-sight, and fore-conception to be presented to us by fancies and popular conceptions, but rather to make the scientific theme secure by working out these fore-structures in terms of the things themselves" (*Being and Time:* 153). What Heidegger is working out here is not primarily a prescription for the practice of understanding, but a description of the way interpretive understanding is achieved. The point of Heidegger's hermeneutical reflection is not so much to prove that there is a circle as to show that this circle possesses an ontologically positive significance. (Gadamer 1993: 266)

Gadamer (1993: 267) therefore states that a person who tries to understand a text always projects onto that text. He projects a meaning for the text as a whole as soon as some initial meanings emerge from the text. The initial meanings emerge, because he reads the text with certain expectations in relation to a certain meaning: working

---

[16] See below; cf. Gadamer (1986: 100–, 1993: 293), Burrell and Morgan (1980: 237), O'Neill (1978).

out this fore projection, which is constantly revised in terms of what emerges as he penetrates into the meaning, is understanding what is there.

In an attempt to understand social and cultural phenomena, the observer must therefore enter a dialogue with the subject he is studying. This can be understood from Gidden's discussion of Gadamer's hermeneutic conception (cf. Gadamer 1986): in Gadamer's words, the understanding of a language "does not comprise a procedure of interpretation." To understand a language is to be able to "live in it." The hermeneutic problem is therefore not a problem of the accurate mastery of a language but of the correct understanding of the things that are accomplished (*geschieht*) through the medium of language (Giddens 1976a: 55). Gadamer therefore denies that understanding may consist in "reconstruction" of another person – the foreign physic – through "empathy" in a foreign life of consciousness, the way Dilthey and Weber comprehend the aim of understanding.

When, for example, we wish to understand a text, we do not try to make ourselves acquainted with the mental life of the writer. When, everything considered, it shall make sense to talk about "making ourselves acquainted with something" (*Sichversetzen*), then we must say that we make ourselves acquainted with the writer's *meaning* of the matter that he talks about. This implies that we try to let the things said be heard with their claims to saying something true (*Wahrheitsanspruch*) (cf. Lübcke 1994b: 167–).

Therefore, Gadamer talks about a "fore-understanding" (and a prejudice; see below), which we drag in when we wish to understand something. We therefore cannot talk about an understanding that relates neutrally to that which we wish to understand. To understand a text or a practice. we must look through these areas fore-understanding or forming an opinion of the whole area that we meet.

It is not a full meaning that lies in the text or in practice but an anticipation of the fore-understanding of what may be meant by a perfect text. Only on the basis of this anticipation of what can meaningfully be said to hang together is it possible for us to meet the text and interpret it in the light of the ideal of the perfect text. The fore-understanding of the interpreter is therefore part of the hermeneutic circle, as this can be determined as the mutual conditional relationship between what the text says and the full meaning, on the background of which the interpreter assesses the text, when he construes it (cf. Gadamer 1993: 269).

## *Understanding*

This discussion of the dialectical circle movement in understanding of hermeneutics is central in Gadamer's discussion, where his objective is to discuss the universal conditions of understanding and being, through a *description of what happens in understanding* and in the being in the world of man. Central concepts in this discussion are prejudice, fore-conception of completeness, temporal distance, history of effect (*Wirkungsgeschichte*), historically effected consciousness (*wirkungsgeschichteliches Bewusstsein*), situation, horizon, fusions of horizons, experience (*Erfahrung*), and application (cf. Gadamer 1993; Wind 1987; Jensen 1991).

# Science and Understanding: The Lifeworld as Understanding

*Prejudice* is something inevitable and indispensable – it is part of the being of man. Prejudice is the specific manifestation of the historical existence of man, because history does not belong to us, but we belong to history – as a part of the tradition. Before we understand ourselves through retrospection, we understand ourselves in a natural way in family and in the context of society. This belonging to history means that prejudice, far more than our own judgments, is the reality of our being. That is, we meet the world as children, and upbringing and socialization are just to have layer after layer of a prejudice laid on top of each other.

> The recognition that all understanding inevitably involves some prejudice gives the hermeneutical problem real thrust. In the light of this insight it appears that *historicism, despite its critique of rationalism and of natural law philosophy, is based on the modern Enlightenment and unwittingly shares its prejudices.* And there is one prejudice of the Enlightenment that defines its essence: the fundamental prejudice of the Enlightenment is the prejudice against prejudice itself, which denies tradition its power. (Gadamer 1993: 270)

Prejudices are indispensable, because mutual understanding rests on prejudices we also use in interaction: (a) in the situation, where we have common prejudices in respect of a problem or a phenomenon. These prejudices thus create no problems, as we can immediately understand another person or come to terms with him. (b) In the situation where we are confronted with something new and unfamiliar. When we wonder, we do this by virtue of our prejudices. This is new to us, just because we have no prejudices against it. In this situation a process of understanding can thus be started, with the aim of understanding the new things.

Prejudices are thus opening and confirming to understanding, i.e., the precondition of all knowledge and cognition is the preconceived and preliminary meaning of the question. Prejudices have a treble character of time: (a) they have come to us from tradition and history (before); (b) they are constituent for what we are now and are about to be (now); and (c) they are expectant, being open to future testing and change (future). The epistemologically fundamental question is thus not about how we get rid of our prejudices, in order to find a safe foundation of cognition, but it is about on which we can base our prejudices and how to distinguish fruitful prejudices from unfruitful.

In this Gadamer opens the discussion of objectivity and subjectivity, by stressing the meaning of the subject in all understanding and cognition. Cognition does not become subjective, in the meaning private, because we must make two suppositions to get into the process of understanding. First we must have two previous expectations, which Gadamer calls *fore-conception of completeness.* We must expect coherence and truth. An example: when we receive a letter, we both expect that the letter is a whole – complete, and thus understandable, and that the letter speaks the truth about its content. We must thus decide that it is possible to understand the other person.

A process of interpretation must emanate from a "preconception on completeness," as a formal condition of all understanding. So when we read a text, we assume its completeness, and only when this turns out to be wrong (i.e., that the text is not understandable), we begin to suspect the text and try to discover how to attack it. Secondly, understanding is first of all, always understanding of a case, and in the case there are criteria for what it means to have understood. Pure and simple understanding does not exist. Understanding is always understanding of something.

Gadamer sees *temporal distance* as a productive possibility, because tradition is unbroken up till ourselves and is filled with the interpretations of the own situation of other generations and epochs. We can relate to these, and we can make new interpretations. In our historical situation with its special interests and problems, new questions crop up. This opens us to new questions we can ask to old texts in which we can thus find new insight. The time interval is that which permits true cognition. To distance things improves the possibility of estimating the proportions and meaning of events, because error sources (i.e., own interests) are excluded and because the continuous interpretations of events illustrate new aspects of them. The context in which I am, and therefore, I with my experiences can ask other questions and find other perspectives than those which I or others could do previously. For example: the Women's Rights Movements (through the @MeToo movement today) questions the historical role of the women and what is happening to them today. However, it must also explore and expose the historiography of women with also a focus on the historical importance of man (i.e., the powerful kings, noblemen, and the church) and their dominance.

The subject itself lives in history with its new situations and requirements for action. As man himself must create the history by forming it, he is referred to the past and to an interpretation of it. A human being who today experiences a situation as a revolutionary situation at the same time stands in a new relationship of interpretation to the revolutions about which history tells (cf. Wind 1987: 65). In this way Gadamer regards the time interval as something fruitful, in contrast to Dilthey who thought that there were problems in this related to a correct interpretation of historical events.

The above can be summed up under the concept *history of effect*: history is previous to man and we are thrown into existence. In our understanding of history, history is already operative by virtue of the prejudices with which history has supplied us. This means that our understanding is always bound by the situation, and this breaks through in all processes of understanding whether we are conscious of it or not. That is exactly what we must require from the research worker (and all others) – that he is conscious of this. We can never disregard our own historicism.

We are *all* part of history and are doomed to start a dialogue with the past, if we shall understand it. Therefore Gadamer maintains that we can never understand the events of the past in full, if they are reduced to being mere facts. They must be understood as manifestations with claim for truth and for being accepted or rejected as such. History is always more than an objective, presents and finished past. History is also tradition and as such binding, as it affects us. When we are part of history ourselves, it also means that we are standing in the middle of the effect history of the writings and stories handed down and thus depend on tradition, both when we revolt against it and when we try to remain neutral.

That we are bound by the situation and that this requires consciousness, Gadamer calls to achieve *historically effected consciousness*. This involves a claim in the process of understanding always to reflect on what it means to understanding/cognition/research that we always are standing in and are bound by a situation, in other words, that consciousness is deeply rooted in self-consciousness. In the self-consciousness, consciousness is reflexive – consciousness can withdraw from that of which it is conscious and the context to which it is immediately attached and thus focus on itself in its difference from all other beings.

Gadamer (ibid., pp. 284) states that the value and importance of research cannot be measured by a criterion based in the subject matter. Rather, subject matter appears truly significant only when it is properly portrayed for us. Thus we are certainly interested in the subject matter, but it acquires its life only from the light in which it is presented to us. We accept the fact that the subject presents different aspects of itself at different times or from different standpoints. We accept the fact that these aspects do not simply cancel one another out as research proceeds but are like mutually exclusive conditions that exist by themselves and combine only in us. Our historical consciousness is always filled with a variety of voices in which the echo of the past is heard. Only in the multi-furiousness of such voices does it exist: this constitutes the nature of the tradition in which we want to share and have a part. Modern historical research itself is not only research but also the handing down of tradition. We do not see it only in terms of progress and verified results; in it we have, as it was, a new experience of history whenever the past resounds in a new voice.

To be conscious of *the situation* is difficult, because the situation is not something we face but something we are *in*. We cannot get it at a distance. It cannot be determined by analytical conditions. We can only maintain the situation as it rules in any understanding: as that which has barriers. A situation has a horizon.

A *horizon* is the range of vision that includes everything that can be seen from a particular vantage point. Gadamer's view and use of horizons shall in the situation of understanding be understood in a certain way, applied to the thinking mind. For example, we can speak of narrowness of horizon, of the possible expansion of horizon, of the opening up of new horizons, and so forth (cf. Gadamer 1993: 302). The horizon is thus a series of inevitable, implied concepts, theories, and experiences which color our interpretation of life and the world in which we live. The horizon is in constant movement and construction through a process in which we continuously test our prejudices and reinterpret them. Horizon thus is to be understood as if consciousness has a horizon. It always appears in a context, i.e., a consciousness of the context in which the single phenomenon is standing. In the Lifeworld this shall be understood in the way that the single object of our consciousness does never stand alone but in relation to others. It has a horizon to us. We have a relation to it, and this means that we see certain connections and relations. In short, we all have some prejudices.

Understanding can thus be seen as *fusions of horizon* (ibid., p. 307). It is not to leave the own horizon and make yourself acquainted with that of another person and try to reconstruct it but to take an open and receptive attitude in order to acquire experiences, the situation considered. We draw our historicism into the understanding and in relation to the historicism of the other person. The other person talks from his horizon of meanings, prejudices, and questions, and we do the same. We must continuously alternate between penetrating the horizon of the other person and linking this back to our own horizon. Understanding thus has a dialectic character in the interaction between the person who interprets and the meaning formed. In other words, through this fusion of horizons, the other person and I will reach a common horizon – and at the same time I apprehend the other person in his own peculiarity. Here we therefore cannot talk about a correct interpretation or meaning, it is about openness and change in understanding, as everyone has his own horizon and perspective in the understanding. The process of experience may thus be understood as change that we change (through self-cognition, etc.) and that the phenomenon gets another interpretation and meaning.

Gadamer thus considers philosophical hermeneutics to be a view of man: an attempt to identify and emphasize the features that are part of being a human being. Understanding is exactly such a feature of human life. Gadamer's work deals with possible conditions to understand each other in common and texts in particular with the truth process of which our understanding is part, with transcendental inevitableness. Given this way of viewing existence – as something that we are *not facing* but are *standing in* – Gadamer's concept of understanding can be seen in relation to the Lifeworld concept, in the way that Husserl, but especially Merleau-Ponty and Schutz, understands it. (This will appear from the next, especially Schutz's understanding of intersubjectivity, and in Chap. 4.3.)

## *Schutz and Understanding*

Schutz does not think that it is possible, in the understanding of another subject, to catch the whole unique context. What he was aiming at was an understanding of the common characteristics in human beings. This is seen in his conception of science – "the science of essences" – and the study of subjective meanings, where social phenomena shall be related to the human activities which have created them, i.e., the human actions. Schutz accept the existence of the social world as it appears in the natural attitude (the Lifeworld and the world taken for granted). But in an analysis and in understanding, it is important to ignore your knowledge, notions, and own personal experiences and person in the understanding of the subject, i.e., to be conscious of your pre-understanding (or prejudice) everyday life in the form of situations, events, actions, and phenomenon:

The phenomenologist does not deny the existence of the outer world, but for his analytical purpose, he makes up his mind to suspend belief in its existence. That is, to refrain intentionally and systematically from all judgments related directly or indirectly to the existence of the outer world. Borrowing terms from mathematical technique, Husserl called this procedure "putting the world in brackets" or "performing the phenomenological reduction." There is nothing mysterious in these notions, which are merely names for the technical device of phenomenology for radicalizing the Cartesian method of philosophical doubt, in order to go beyond the natural attitude of man living within the world he accepts, be it reality or mere appearance (Schutz 1973a: 104).

Schutz's approach to the practice of sociology, which can also be seen as one of the differences between him and Husserl (and the transcendental phenomenology),

# Science and Understanding: The Lifeworld as Understanding

is that a sociologist bent on understanding, and not just describing, social phenomena. He faces two possibilities only: he can take his human objects preoccupations to his heart and try to assist them in their constant testing and retesting the consistency and coherence of their images of reality. Or, alternatively, he can tell them that what they take for "objectively," "truth," etc. derives all the sense it may possess from their own activities. Therefore the only sensible way of approaching it is to illuminate the socially organized setting in which it is produced and kept alive (Bauman 1978: 188).

What Schutz (1972: 98–) thinks is that we can never understand in full the intention of another person. This will imply that we will have to develop the lived experiences of the other person in the same way as he does himself. Schutz's phenomenological sociology therefore is based upon this distinction between the actor's self-developing understanding and the research worker's interpretation of the experience of the other person. Referring to Husserl, Schutz (1972: 100) says the listener notices that the speaker is expressing certain subjective experiences of his and in that sense may be said to notice them; but he himself does not live through these experiences – his perception is "external" rather than "internal." This kind of perception, which is significant in character, should not be confused with that in which an object directly appears to us. I apprehend the lived experiences of another only through signitive-symbolic[17] representation, regarding either his body or some cultural artifact he has produced as a "field of expression" for those experiences.

Schutz's discussion of understanding – *Verstehen* – is the subjective interpretation of meaning as well as the whole problem of interpretive understanding. This involves three related but different issues (Schutz 1990a: XXIV): *Verstehen* (1) as the experiential form of commonsense knowledge of human affairs, (2) as an epistemological problem, and (3) as a method peculiar to the social science. As the experiential form of commonsense knowledge of human affairs, *Verstehen* means simply that men in daily life interpret their world from the outset as a meaningful one.

The philosophical problem involved here, however, transcends the scope of the commonsense world and constitutes the second meaning of *Verstehen* as an epistemological issue. Schutz argues that *Verstehen* is rooted in the Lifeworld that encompasses the rich totality of commonsense experience lived through by the individual in his concrete existence. It is the Lifeworld that also is the ground for understanding the meaning of *Verstehen* as a method peculiar to the social science. The objects investigated by the methods of the natural sciences are first-order constructs; they are however complex merely objects within the world of the observer. The social scientist, on the other hand, must face a qualitatively different situation. His objects are not only objects for his observation; they are beings who have their own pre-interpreted world and who do their own observing; they are fellow men caught up in social reality. These "objects," then, are second-order constructs, and the method of *Verstehen* is employed in the social sciences in order to come to terms with the full subjective reality of the human beings they seek to comprehend.

---

[17] Signitive and signitive acts are Husserl's concepts synonymous with act of meaning. Signitive can also be understood as symbolic.

Understanding thus implies that you apprehend reality. The reality exists, but it is not autonomous in relation to man. It has no independent size, with its own logic and lawfulness, unlike what is argued in positivism and in the functionalist paradigm. It is of another nature.

## The Lifeworld: The "I" Being in and to the World

The Lifeworld can shortly be understood as the immediately experienced world, as it appears before it is subjected to a scientific investigation and thus also to the historical reality from which man immediately takes his bearings. It is the reality we live in every day and can be understood as that which W. James maintains: reality simply means relation to our emotional and active life. The origin of all reality is subjective – all that titillates and stimulates our interest is real. To call a thing real, mean that this thing stands in a certain relation to us. The word "reality" is in short a frame (Schutz 1973b: 60).

Gadamer thinks that the concept *Lifeworld* is the antithesis of all objectivism. It is an essential historical concept that does not refer to a universe of being, to an "existing world." Nor can the infinite idea of a true world be meaningful, when created out of the infinite progress of a human historical world in historical experience. It is not this conception of the world that natural science tries to imagine or to acquire knowledge of. The Lifeworld means something else, namely, the whole in which we live as historical creatures. And here we cannot avoid the consequence that, given the historicity of experience implied in it, the idea of a universe of possible historical Lifeworlds simply does not make sense. It is clear that the Lifeworld is always at the same time a communal world that involves being with other people as well. It is a world of persons, and in the natural attitude, the validity of this personal world is always assumed (Gadamer 1993: 247). It is into this Lifeworld that one must relate and understand all human activities and on which scientific and philosophic understanding have to be based. The argumentation is, however, different in the various philosophical traditions.

## *Merleau-Ponty and the Lifeworld*

Merleau-Ponty (c.f. Bengtsson 1993: 65) argued for the nature of reality through the Lifeworld. He takes the concept from Husserl (but also agrees with Heidegger about the being – *Dasein*). However, he thought that Lifeworld could not be founded on Husserl's discussion of pure consciousness. Instead Merleau-Ponty takes his part of origin in that: that the world is therefore before all analyses.

A skeptic may say that we can doubt the existence of the world. But his very doubt implies that which he will be doubtful about. In short, the argument is an erroneous circular conclusion. A condition of his doubt is, as a matter of fact, the

The Lifeworld: The "I" Being in and to the World                                    115

existence of the world; otherwise it would be senseless to doubt it. Thus, we can never escape the world.

The whole universe of science is built upon the world as directly experienced. If we want to subject science itself to rigorous scrutiny and arrive at a precise assessment of its meaning and scope, we must begin by reawakening the basic experience of the world of which science is the second-order expression. Science has not and never will have, by its nature, the same significance *qua* forms of being as the world which we perceive, for the simple reason that it is a rationale or explanation of that world. I am not a "living creature," nor even a "man," nor again even "a consciousness." I am the absolute source. My existence does not stem from my antecedents, from my physical and social environment. My existence moves out towards them and sustains them. For I alone bring into being for myself (and therefore into being in the only sense that the word can have for me) tradition which I elect to carry one. Or the horizon whose distance from me would be abolished – since that distance is not one of its properties – if I were not there to scan it with my gaze (Merleau-Ponty 1994: VIII–).

To Merleau-Ponty the Lifeworld is the world that is "livingly" present in our experiences and which is therefore indissoluble bound to the experiencing subject of man in the world. It is in the world that we know ourselves. The world is not what I think but what I live through. I am open to the world, I have no doubt that I am in communication with it, but I do not possess it; it is inexhaustible. "There is a world," or rather "There is the world"; I can never completely account for this ever-reiterated assertion in my life. This facticity of the world is what constitutes the *Weltlichkeit der Welt*, what causes the world to be the world; just as the facticity of the *cogito* is not an imperfection in itself but rather what assures me of my existence (Merleau-Ponty 1994: XVI–).

Inversely it is also a fact that the world is indissoluble bound to a subject. The only world we know of is the world that is available to us as experiencing subjects. The Lifeworld consequently turns out to be both pre-objective and pre-subjective. It is exclusively from abstractions from the Lifeworld that we can talk of a pure nature and a pure subject, respectively. With that Merleau-Ponty means that the Lifeworld represents a third dimension as agent between naturalism (objectivism) and subjectivism by building a bridge between contrasts. The reason is that on one side, the Lifeworld is a world that transcends the subject but which at the same time is an experienced world, i.e., a world connected to a subject. There is a circular dialectical relation between the world and the subject: the subject is marked by the world, and the subject marks the world.[18]

---

[18] This conception of Merleau-Ponty originates in his early inspiration by dialectics (from a Marxist conception) and a configuration of contrasts: for example, individual-society and nature-culture. This dialectic conception is also seen in the work of Berger and Luckmann (1966), Arbnor and Bjerke (1981), Silverman (1983), etc. A dialectic conception is generally incorporated in hermeneutics in relation to interpretation and understanding. For example, understanding in Dilthey's hermeneutic circle: the whole-part movement in interpretation. We can also find it in phenomenology like here with Merleau-Ponty, and in Simmer's discussion of dialectic of the subjectivity of the experience and the continuity of the object, i.e., ultimately psychologically (Gadamer 1993: 224). There are, however, different conceptions of dialectics in the different traditions.

The experience of the Lifeworld is never an opening to a number of incoherent feelings, without proving always to be more and something different than purely particular feelings – the experience is both historical, cultural, and social (Bengtsson 1993: 68). The importance that the experienced have to us always appears against the background of the previous experiences made by the experiencing subject in the world. On the other hand, the Lifeworld is no conceptual world either. It must not be identified with concepts or theories that we formulate or with the statements we make on it. The world that we know from our experiences is not covered by ideas, theories, etc.

We can, of course, always interpret the world from theories, but our life in the world can never be reduced to a permanent summarization through fixed concepts or theories. Experience is not free of intellectual influence either, always acting on the background of our previous experiences, including also intellectual experiences. However the meaning, which is active in the experience, is not a regular adaptation of concepts and theories. Neither is it our free choice to choose the experiences that shall be actualized in the specific situation of experience. And the importance of the specific experience to us is not completely determined by the previous experiences either.

That which happens in a specific situation of experience is instead that a new specific meaning rises in interplay with previous experiences. The rising meaning is then capable of changing the meaning of the previous experiences. Merleau-Ponty therefore thinks that if we start from the world that we experience in specific situations and investigate that which turns up in its own existence and fullness, something quite different from universal meanings and particular feelings will appear (cf. Bengtsson 1993: 69). The Lifeworld is both ordinary, in that it has a meaning, and particular. In other words, it is both spiritual and situated. From the individual point of view, it is thus ambiguous, in a fundamental way.

Merleau-Ponty also starts from Heidegger's *Dasein*.[19,20] However, Merleau-Ponty emphasizes that above all, the subject is the own living body. It is a psychophysical notion, where man is both consciousness and physical.[21] One's own body is not a thing we move around in space in the same way as with chairs and tables. It is the subject that moves the thing and is the subject of all action. As subject, the physical being, does not exist in space and time, like trees and bushes and tables or chairs, but it *occupies* the space and the time. To one's own body, a lived space and

---

[19] Heidegger (1992), cf. Bengtsson (1993: 71), Wind (1987: 54). See below.

[20] Merleau-Ponty (cf. 1994: VII) will not accept the general opinion of Husserl and Heidegger being so in contradiction that they could not be seen in the same tradition. He thinks especially on Husserl's thoughts on a "constructive phenomenology" and the Lifeworld and on Heidegger's discussion of *Dasein* – being in the Lifeworld and his entire work *Sein und Zeit* (being and time) that springs from an indication of on Lifeworld.

[21] As Merleau-Ponty (1994: XIX) says, when he discuss the necessity of *not* look upon the world from different isolated views, referring to Marx statement on historical development: "It is true, as Marx says, that history does not walk on its head, but it is also true that it does not think with its feet. Or one should say rather that it is neither "head" or "feet" that we have to worry about, but its body."

The Lifeworld: The "I" Being in and to the World 117

a lived time arise through its being in the world and through its interaction and communication with the world (cf. Merleau-Ponty 1994: 243–; Bengtsson 1993: 74). Space and time manifest themselves to us in our activities. The geometrical space and the chronological time thus do not constitute the foundation of the lived space and the lived time. They constitute an attempt to imagine the lived space and the lived time, respectively, and to control them by means of mathematical constructions. Merleau-Ponty therefore says that: "I am not in the space and the time, I do not think the space and the time; *I am to* the space and the time. My body embraces them." (cf. Bengtsson 1993: 74).

In the same way, as through his body, man is to the world; he is also to other human beings. And in the same way as we have a fundamental belief in the world, we also have a fundamental faith in other people. This spontaneous belief and faith do, however, not necessarily justify anything, as its justifications as well as all other rational activity always presuppose both the world and other people. This does, however, not make the world and intersubjectivity a solid foundation. It is rather a sensitive foundation.

Normally, we understand other people spontaneously, but now and then problems of understanding arise. When this happens, the normal-functioning, practical behavior is replaced by a theoretical behavior, where we try to enter into the spirit of the intentions of the other person. In this way we can understand the conditions of communication and interaction. The communication materializes, when I let my own understanding of the to-the-world-being to the other person express itself in my own to-the-world-being. In other words, I take over and carry on the bodily meaning indicated by the action of the other person. In this way a dialogue may develop – as a spontaneously functioning interaction, where I confirm the other person and the other person to me, where I correct the other person and the other person to me, especially where both agreement and disagreement may arise.

Understanding is, however, never definitive, because it is never frozen in the moment. Through a continuous action, one may change the first understanding or modify it. In this way Merleau-Ponty considers the Lifeworld as intersubjective. We live and interact with other people, and we experience the world, as intersubjective and social affairs are consequently neither a notion, a thing, or the sums of things. It is instead a dimension of existence that we can never escape, above which we can never rise and at the outside of which we can never stand.

## *Heidegger and* Dasein

Heidegger's conception of the Lifeworld appears, as he abolishes the "I" and introduces *Dasein* (being) in the understanding of the subject and of existence: "Dasein always understands itself of its existence – in terms of a possibility of itself: to be itself or not itself." (Heidegger 1992: 33) Any being, which is similar to man, relates to its own being (existence), as it is aimed (intended) at the surrounding being on the background of an understanding of the world, in which this being exists, and this being on the background of which the being can be interpreted. In other words, *Dasein* as a human form of existence is different from anything else that exists in the world.

According to Heidegger (Wind 1987: 54), it does not suffice to say that this difference is due to consciousness. It is meaningless to maintain that man excels above everything else in the world, including the animals, by having sense and cognition. Heidegger goes the other way round in his argumentation: everything that is for the world has an objective; it is from a utility function of a given thing that we understand what the thing is and not from its essential or accidental properties. It is at this point, in the distinction between essentia and existensia, Heidegger and Husserl disagree and at which Heidegger formulates his *Dasein* (the subject as a worldly, the subject as being, as existence, as situated in the world and as agent – as acting in the world).

When we discuss "what" something is and "that" it is, we discuss that which "is." What does this "is" mean here? Heidegger expresses it: on which kind of general concept of being are we basing, when we distinguish between "what" a being "is" and "that" the being "is"? That a distinction is made is certain, but why this distinction is made, and whether it has always been the same, and whether it bases on a fundamentally wrong concept of the being. That is exactly the problem. Is the distinction between "what" something is and "that" it is analogous with the distinction between dogs and cats – or if not, how are we then to understand the distinction? This question of being is to Heidegger the most important – and most neglected – in philosophy (Lübcke 1994b: 125).

If we now implicate the being of man under this point of view and if we ask the question purely phenomenologically, we shall arrive at the conception that the human being itself does not "exist" with a view to something definite. Negatively expressed, man does not exist for any purpose. Put positively, man, unlike other beings, exists with a view too also existing tomorrow. It is life (*Leben*) as self-affirmation or self-preservation. When Heidegger therefore discusses being in the world, he does not understand the world, as it is understood traditionally in objectivism: as a physical space and as structured. Instead Heidegger understands it as situated, as existential.

"World," in the sense of this existential, would be found in the self-reflective consciousness even of a rather primitive awareness, for which the limits of the world may well be the limits of a village or country. It is, in this sense, the most general concepts about existence: the place in which one is. As the analysis then grows more specific and particular, Heidegger is shifting from the various ways and modes in which "world" has meaning: such as "to be of use" – to the more internal and personal modes of self-existence, such as fear, fateful existence, and the awareness of possibilities (Gelven 1989: 57).

Dasein, being in the world, Heidegger just understands as being *in* the world, as a feeling, through experience, of the world as familiar. In other words, the world is something that we know and feel safe about and which constitutes our "home." To be in the world is the ultimate presupposition of knowledge (this puts ontology prior to epistemology – a move that incurs the wrath of all Neo-Kantians and positivists.)

The bases of epistemology are the knower and the known. But prior to the distinction between knower and known (or subject and object) is the fact that the subject can relate to a known, which means that the presupposition of the very subject-object distinction is grounded in an already admitted basis of relationship, i.e., that the subject has a world in which the object can occur. Knowledge does not occur in isolation from one's worlds of concern and environment (Gelven 1989: 60).

## Schutz: The Lifeworld and Intersubjectivity

Schutz (1973b: 26, 1978a, b, c, d: 121) focuses especially on intersubjectivity and how we achieve and construct understanding of each other. He is interested in illustrating the way in which we know other peoples lived experiences, once we have postulated and taken for granted the general thesis of the alter ego. In understanding of intersubjectivity, this is linked with the private world and with the world as an intersubjective cultural world, i.e., Schutz's discussion of the concept of Lifeworld.

Among the elements of my experience of the outer world are physical objects and fellow men, *alter egos*. Encountering the body of another human being is qualitatively different from the experience of inert bodies, bodies as things. First of all, the body of a fellow man is experienced as part of a psychophysical unity. This mean coeval with the recognition of the body is the awareness and appreciation of the ego that possesses, in addition to a body, a world of cognitive and cognitive awareness similar in general to mine.

Taken my body as the center point for the coordinates which map my world, I may say that the position of my body constitutes my Here in relationship to which the body of a fellow man is There. I find that it is possible to alter my position and move from Here to There. Having moved, the There becomes a Here. But the body of my fellow man remains There for me as it remains still a Here for him. Although I cannot in fact stand directly in the perspective of the other's Here, I can as subjectively attribute to him a reciprocity of perspectives. Thus the objects and events of the world are common to both of us because I can perceive from There the same things I perceive from Here, despite the change in perspective. Within the common-sense world, it is simply taken for granted that the reciprocity of perspectives holds and that the objects and events of human experience are intersubjectively available and more or less the same for all "normal" perceivers. The concept of normalcy itself, it might be suggested, is derivative from the implicit assumptions common sense makes about the structure of sensory perception. The interchangeability of Here and There between two egos is the necessary condition for a shared reality (see Schutz 1990a, b, c, d: XXXII).

Schutz's (1973b: 23) thought is that even if the everyday social reality is experienced through the own consciousness of each individual, it is not a question of a private reality, especially for every single individual. Reality is experienced by the actors as a common reality – intersubjectivity is taken for granted as an obvious quality of our world. The world is intersubjective, because we live in it as human beings among other human beings, connected with them through common influence and work, understanding others, and being understood by them. It is a cultural world, because from the beginning, the everyday Lifeworld is a universe of meaning to us. In other words, it is a structure of meaning that we must interpret to orient in it and to agree with it. This world exists before our birth and was experienced and interpreted by others, our ancestors, as an organized world. Now it is given to our experiences and interpretations. All interpretation of this world is based on a stock of previous experiences consisting of our own or those which have been handed down to us by others; these experiences in the form of available knowledge ("stock of knowledge") function as a scheme of reference.

This structure of meaning arises in and is institutionalized through the action of human beings, our own and those of our fellow men, and those of our contemporaries and our predecessors. All objects of culture (tools, symbols, language systems, social institutions, etc.) point back, through their origin and meaning, to the activities of human subjects. Intersubjectivity, therefore, can be seen as a common subjective state or as a dimension of consciousness that is common to a certain social group who mutually affects each other. The social connections are rendered possible through the intersubjectivity such as through a mutual understanding of common rules that are, however, experienced subjectively. Intersubjectivity refers to the fact that different groups may interpret and experience the world in the same way that is necessary at a certain level and in some contexts out of regard for collective tasks.

In this connection, Schutz is interested in structures of consciousness, which are necessary in order that such common activities and common understanding can arise. Human behavior is part of a social relationship, when people connect a meaning to the behavior, and other people apprehend it as meaningful. Subjective meanings are essential to the interaction, both to the acting person who has a purpose with his action and to others who shall interpret that action and react in correspondence with the interpretation (cf. Ritzer 1977: 120). The basis for intersubjectivity is the social origin of knowledge or the social inheritance in which the acting persons are socialized to collectively typify repeated social events as external, objective events (which shall be seen in relation to structures of meaning). However, in consciousness such a typification is experienced as subjective reality.

# Typification

In the discussion of intersubjective consciousness, Schutz uses the concept of typification as the ability of arranging a situation or an object in such a way that it becomes part of a socially important category of situations and objects. Acting persons having common typifications are thus enabled to structure their worlds of experiences so that they are alike, through the common meanings that they lay down on the essential fields of experience (cf. Ritzer 1977: 121). The process of understanding the behavior of others may be understood as a process of typification, where the actor uses interpretive structures, like "ideal types," to understand the

Typification   121

object of the actions of other people. These structures come from the experiences of everyday life that Schutz understands as "the stock of knowledge" or the "commonsense" understanding laying in the natural attitude of life. It is through the use of typification that we classify and organize our everyday life reality.

Typification can be understood as a two-pronged process; on one hand, it solidifies some aspects of reality into an incorrigible, self-evident field of "un-problems"; on the other hand, it draws the line that renders everything left on the other side potentially problematic. That is to say, the process of typification determines, by the same token, what is to be determined and what is to remain indeterminate. The stock of knowledge includes the information that other people like us exist in the world and that their conduct has the same structure which we "know" from the experience of our own behavior. This knowledge renders other people potential partners in communication when viewed as a "trade in meanings," and as a mutual effort to grasp the message conveyed by words, gestures, facial expressions, etc. Other people (again defining a piece of knowledge as being an indispensable part of natural attitude towards life) differ from all other types and from inanimate objects in particular. In short, people's conduct is to be interpreted as a basic voluntary and purpose-oriented action (Bauman 1978: 184).

## *Lifeworld as Multiple Realities*

Schutz sees commonsense knowledge as the way in which we typify the actions of others and to understand the world around us varying from context to context. In other words, we live in a world full of multiple realities and where each of them is defined through "finite provinces of meaning" (i.e., context-dependent meanings as William James' concept of sub-universe). Schutz talks about provinces of meaning (and not sub-universes) because it is the meaning of our experiences and not the ontological structure of the objects that constitutes reality. Each province has its own cognitive style with respect to which experiences within each world are inter-consistent. And each of the finite provinces of meaning may receive the "accent of reality" and may be attended to as real. Not only are the images of reality of each individual different but also that when the actor changes the social context, there are other basic rules for the individual, dependent on whether he is at work or at home. To make these changes (which Schutz call "leap of consciousness") makes it possible for actors to overcome differences between different worlds.

The core social relation is directed towards the "We-relationship," and all other notions of social forms that are applied by actors in their everyday social life are derived from this. In any face-to-face encounter, the actor brings to the relationship a stock of "knowledge in hand," or "commonsense understandings." Thus the actor typifies the other actors, is able to calculate the probable response of the other to his actions, and sustains communication with him. An actor's "stock of knowledge" is taken for granted as "adequate until further notice." It is totality composed of "self-evidences" changing from situation to situation and being set in to relief at any given time by a background of indeterminacy (cf. Giddens 1976a: 29). If we consider the everyday working Lifeworld, it is a "finite province of meaning" among many others, though it is emphasized as the extreme and all-important reality.

Schutz (1973b: 81) summarizes the basic characteristics which constitute its specific cognitive style in the following:

1. A certain tension of consciousness, i.e., the states of being wide awaken which arises in full attention towards the life
2. A certain epoché, i.e., suspension of doubt
3. A prevailing form of spontaneity, i.e., work (a meaningful spontaneity based on a project and characterized by the intention of producing the state of the projecting things through bodily movement interfering in the external world)
4. A certain kind of experience of yourself (the working self as a total self)
5. A certain kind of sociality (the common intersubjective world of communication and the social act)
6. A certain time perspective (the standard time arising in the crossing between *durée* and cosmic time as the universal time structure of the intersubjective world)

As long as our experiences of the world fall under this cognitive style (or framework), we may consider this province of meaning to be real and may ascribe the accent of reality to it. In respect to the reality of everyday life, we are, in the natural attitude, made to do it because our practical experiences prove that the unity and congruity of the labor (work) worlds are valid and that the hypothesis on its reality is irrefutable. This reality seems natural to us. Furthermore, we are not ready to leave our natural attitude towards it without having experienced a certain shock that forced us to break through the boundaries of this finite province of meaning and change the accent of reality to another.

These experiences of shock are often made in the middle of everyday life. They are part of its reality themselves. They show that in the standard time, the labor (work) world is not the only finite province of meaning but only one of many which are available to my intentional life. We have the same world of directly experienced social reality in common: the world that surrounds my Here and Now corresponds with that which surrounds the Here and Now of other people. My Here and Now include that of the other person, together with his attention to my world, in the same way as the content of me and my consciousness belongs to the world of the other in his Here and Now. However, this domain of directly experienced social realities is only one of many social fields. My actual perception is only a fragment of the world of all my experiences, and hence this is only a fragment of the entire world of possible experiences. Seen in this way, I directly experience the social world in fragments, as I live from moment to moment (Schutz 1972: 142).

Schutz therefore divides the social world into different realities: my contemporary fellows are both "fellow men" (*Mitmenschen*), (1) those I am with and interact within everyday life and whose subjective experiences I know of, and "contemporaries" (*Nebenmenschen*), (2) those who live in the world with me but where I do not know their subjective experiences. In addition to these two worlds, I also apprehend that a social world has existed before me which is in no way overlapping my own life. This can be divided into the social world of predecessors (*Vorwelt*) or history to which I can only be an observer and not an actor. I also know that there will be a world after me, a social world of successors (*Folgewelt*) of which I have no knowledge and of which I can never get any experience.

In using the term "world" for these domains or realms, Schutz means only that different people are consociates, contemporaries, predecessors, or successors to one another and that they accordingly experience one another and act upon one another in the different ways in question. All these considerations merely serve to outline the vast theoretical field of the social world, the methodological exploration of which is the field of the social sciences. We shall have to ascertain how our knowledge of each of these regions draws its original claim from the general thesis of the other self, in other words, from the simultaneity or quasi-simultaneity of the other self's consciousness with my own (Schutz 1972: 143).

## Social Action

The concept of action is in focus in the essence of the Lifeworld and in a science that is oriented towards understanding the everyday life of human being. Especially Weber and Schutz were particularly interested in the concept of action in relation to the establishment of a science of everyday life. However, they disagreed on several important points and on the certain philosophical assumptions. Weber can be seen as a sociology derived from the "traditional hermeneutic" and Schutz as representing the perspective from the sociological phenomenology.

### *Weber and Social Action*

Weber (1964: 112) defines social action as all kinds of human behavior, when and to the extent that the acting individual connects a subjective meaning to it and is oriented towards the previous, present, or future actions of others (known or unknown). Action may in this sense be turned out, exclusively turned in or subjective. It may consist of direct intervention in a situation, of a voluntary intervention to renounce such an intervention or of a passive type to come to terms with the situation. Action is social in so far as it considers the action of others by virtue of the importance attached to it by the acting individual and original. Social action has other characteristics, too: it can be oriented to the behavior of others, as it is just now, but it can also be oriented to their previous or future behavior. The "other," to whom the actor adapts his action, may moreover be an individual or a social group. It is not a social action, if the action is directed to dead things (like to throw a stone over the water), or if two cyclists collide unintentionally, i.e., actions which are not in a meaningful way are directed to other people.

Weber (1964: 115) thought that not all forms of social action were identical and grouped social actions in four types, partly on the basis of their extent of accessibility for understanding predicated upon interpretation as well as through the orientation of the action.

1. A rational orientation to a system of discrete individual ends (*zweckrational*). That is, through expectations as to the behavior of objects in the external situation and of other human individuals, making use of these expectations as "conditions" or "means" for the successful attainment of the actor's own rationally chosen ends.
2. Rational orientation to an absolute value (*wertrational*), involving a conscious belief in the absolute value of some ethical, aesthetic, religious, or other form of behavior, entirely for its own sake and independently of any prospects of external success.
3. Effectual orientation, especially emotional, determined by the specific effects and states of feeling by the actor.
4. Traditionally oriented, through the habituation of long practice. Weber (1964: 117) thinks that these types of action must be seen as conceptual, pure types, and that it would be very unusual to find specific cases with these social actions.

Ritzer (1977: 94) interprets Weber's social types of action in the following ways: (1) in *zweckrational* action the actor does not only assess which means is best suited to reach the goal but also fixes the value of the goal in itself. The goal of a zweckrational action is thus not absolute and may be a means to reach a new goal. (2) In a *wertrational action*, the actor cannot assess if the means he chooses is the most expedient, and neither is it possible for the goal to be a means of a new goal. It must be considered as a goal in itself. In the case of a *wertrational* action, it may be difficult to keep a part goal and means. The action is, however, still rational, because the choice of means is assumed to lead to the desired goal. The two latter forms of action may be objecting too through our understanding. To a limited extent, the actors do not, in a meaningful way, adapt to each other. (3) Affective acts are dominated by the feelings, moods, and passions of the actor. (4) A traditional act is dominated by a habitual performance of something which has been done innumerable times in the past. Often, traditional actions and affective actions are only automatic answers to external stimuli (which could be seen as the social action of another person), and therefore they do not contain a meaningful action orientation. Other times these two types of action may be oriented in a meaningful way and thus become available to understanding.

## *Schutz and Meaningful Action*

A central issue in a sociological phenomenology to understanding social life is action. Schutz's starting point is that action cannot be understood unless referred to the actor's object of it. His criticism of Weber's concept of action and understanding

Social Action 125

of its purpose appears from the following. Especially, he criticizes Weber's lack of interest to amplify the ontological preconditions of his primary concepts.[22] As Schutz (1972: 7–) notes: it is at this point that the theoretical limitations of Weber become evident. As noted above, the current contemporary @MeToo movement for women is a case pointed for everyone to learn and change today. Modern technology in the twenty-first century has started and supported that change.

Schutz's opinion is that Weber breaks off his analysis of the social world when he arrives at what he assumes to be the basic and irreducible elements of social phenomena. Schutz argues that Weber is wrong in this assumption. Weber's concept of the meaningful act of the individual, which is the key idea of interpretive sociology, by no means defines a primitive, as Weber thinks it does. It is on the contrary, a mere label for a highly complex and ramified area that calls for much further study. Weber does not make any distinction between the action, considered as something in progress and the complete act: (a) between the meaning of the produced, (b) between the meaning of my own action and the meaning of another's action, (c) between the meaning of my own experience and that of someone else, and (d) between my self-understanding and my understanding of another person.

Weber does not ask how the actor's meaning is constituted or what modifications this meaning undergoes for his partners in the social world or for a nonparticipating observer. He does not try to identify the unique and fundamental relation existing between the self and the other self. In other words, we must know about that relation whose clarification is essential to a precise understanding of what it is to know another person. To be sure, Weber distinguishes between the subjectively intended meaning of an action and its objectively knowable meaning. But he recognizes no further distinctions along this line and pays as little attention to the ways in which an interpreter modifies meaning as he does to the conceptual perspectives in which our fellow human beings are given to us.

The understanding of this criticism of Weber's concept of action, and Schutz idea of understanding and interpretation of the meaning behind social actions, can be exemplified: if through "direct observation" (Weber's methodological concept) we name the purpose of a person's action – for example, when we see a man performing such an act as chopping wood, we name it "wood chopping." Consequently, we have named his activity as "wood chopping" and thus already interpreted it.[23] We have already interpreted and understood the act, but how can we be sure that the purpose of the act was just chopping wood and nothing else (to get rid of aggressions, physical training, etc.)?

The observation of a person's behavior does not suffice to understand the act and the subjective meaning of the action. Schutz therefore makes a central distinction in relation to the greater meaning-context in which the behavior shall be understood: he distinguishes between to observe the behavior of a person and to name the behavior. In other words, to place the behavior in an objective context of meaning is not

---

[22] See Schutz (1972) for the amplifying criticism of Weber.

[23] See Schutz (1972: 26– and 110–), Giddens (1976a: 28).

126                                                                                                    4   History of Lifeworld Traditions

identical with the actor's own meaning-context in his mind – the actor's subjective context of meaning (Schutz 1972: 27).

Besides, Schutz is of the opinion that Weber's discussion of meaningful action does not consider the fact that action is *episodic*. When we consider the actor from a subjective angle, this mean that it is a "*lived-through*" experience. Because Weber is unaware of this, he does not see the ambivalence in the expression, action, which may refer either to the subjective experience in itself or to the completed act. It is therefore a misunderstanding to take for granted that we can connect meaning with an action that is lived through, as we are involved in the very action.

To connect meaning with experiences, in the sense of a reflexive consideration of the act by the actor or others, is something that can only be carried out retrospectively to the concluded act. It is also misleading to say that experiences are naturally meaningful: only that which has already *been experienced* is meaningful, not that which will be experienced. The reflexive categorizing of action therefore depends on identification of the aim or the project the actor tried to carry through.

There is a difference between action and project (*Entwurf*) which is essential to understand. The expression *action* describes the behavior of human beings, formed in advance by the actor, i.e., behavior based on a preconceived project. The expression *act* describes the result of this ongoing process, as the completed action. Action may be hidden (e.g., the attempt to solve a scientific problem mentally) or openly intervening in the external world; it may happen through completion or omission, as premeditated abstention from an action is an action in itself (Schutz 1973b: 34).

All projecting consists in an anticipation of future behavior by means of fantasizing (i.e., what Schutz also calls to "think in the future"). It is, however, not the process of action taking place but the fantasized act, *as if* it were completed, which starts all projecting: what is projected is the act which is the goal of the action and which is brought into being by the action. The project is thus a complex of meaning or context of meaning (S*innzusammenhang*) within which anyone phase of the ongoing action finds its significance (Schutz 1972: xx).

There is a difference between the project in an action (its orientation towards future fulfillment) and its "in-order-to motives" (*um-zu-Motive*). Projects or "because motives" (*weil-Motive*) have no explanatory significance in themselves. Schutz explains this, referring to the action of opening an umbrella, when it rains, as follows: the project to open the umbrella is not caused by the action but by an imagined anticipation.

On the other hand, the action does neither "fulfill" nor "fail to fulfill" the project. In contrast to this situation, the very perception of the rain is no project. It has no "connection" with the judgment. For example, "If I expose myself to the rain, my clothes will become wet; this is not the wish; therefore I must do something to prevent it."[24] The connection or link which is constructed arises through an intentional

---

[24] Consider when an actor is given an umbrella and does not know what to do with it because he has had no prior experience with one (a person from a part of the world that does not use umbrellas). That actor cannot act upon the umbrella. And will either discard it as useless or seek help in understanding it. The actor cannot project onto the umbrella. Observers of this actor would the wonder if the person intentionally got wet, was unable to operate the umbrella, or was stupid.

Social Action 127

act by me, where I turn towards the total complex of my previous experiences (see Schutz 1972: XXI and 92–; Giddens 1976a: 28). To understand an actor's act, we therefore have to know about his past and future (experiences and projects) and which motives he relates his actions to in order to understand the meaning-context of the actor.

By calling the motive "a complex which seems to the actor a meaningful ground for his conduct," Schutz (1972: 28) means two different things: first there appears to me, as the meaningful ground of my behavior, a series of future events whose occurrence I propose to bring about. I am orienting my behavior to this end. But there is a second sense in which I sometimes speak of the meaningful ground of my behavior. Here I refer to those past experiences of mine which have led me to behave as I do. In the first case, I regard my behavior as the means of accomplishing some desired goal. If I am trying to find my motive in this sense, I ask myself the following question: "Which of all the future events I expect to happen are distinguished from the rest by the fact that my expectation of their occurrence constitutes or jointly constitutes the meaning of my behavior?" In the second case, I regard my present behavior as the result of past experiences, as the effect of preceding "causes." If I am searching for my motive in this sense, then I ask myself a different question: "Which of all my past experiences are distinguished from the rest by the fact that they constitute or jointly constitute the meaning of my behavior?" In both cases the motive being sought after lies outside the time span of the actual behavior.

## Meaning-Context

Another important question here and in understanding of action is whether the actor's intention of his action is identical with his motives. In other words, what is the meaning complex that he considers being a meaningful (or significant) background for his actions? In other words, the motive is not the same as the intended meaning of the act since motives give no amplifying expression to the whole structure of "intended meaning" of the actor.

On the contrary, the actor takes for granted the meaning of his action: it is self-evident to him in the proper sense of the term. If he asks himself what his motives were, he takes this self-evident meaning as his point of departure and then looks for past experiences which were relevant to his action or for future events towards which his action is conducive. It can, therefore, be said that the actor must already know the intended meaning of his action before he can inquire about its motive (Schutz 1972: 29).

We cannot thus understand the action and its motive, if we do not know the actor's purpose of the action. There is, however, an epistemological point in this underlying the distinction between observational and motivational understanding. In everyday life we experience the acts of others directly. We interpret these external events as the acts of others, as indications of a "stream of consciousness" lying outside our own. As far as we do this, we can "understand" these events, what they indicate when they happen, and be direct witness of the action or at least witnesses it in the mode of actuality (Schutz 1972: 30). Observational understanding is then focused on the action as it takes place. The observer, living alongside the actor and sharing his present, participates in an experiencing way in the completion of his action occurred.

The essence of this is therefore that observance or direct understanding is quite simply the understanding that we practice in everyday life in our direct relations to other people. Precisely for that reason, however, the inference from the overt behavior to the intended meaning behind it is anything but a cut-and-dried matter. Motivational understanding, on the other hand, is not tied to the world by directly experienced social reality (*Umwelt*). It may take any action as its object, as this understanding does not take as its starting point an *ongoing* action. Its object is rather the accomplished act. This process may be considered as something already completed in the past or as something whose future complete form is now being envisaged. It may be considered to be motive in the form of origin or goal (cf. above). Schutz argues that this form of understanding starts out on the basis of an established objective meaning as merely an indication of the existence of a subjective meaning. This is all the more reason why a higher degree of scientific clarity and exactitude is attainable in motivational understanding.

Schutz concludes that the "interpretive understanding" which is definitive of interpretive sociology cannot be observational understanding. Rather, the scientific method of establishing subjective meaning is motivational understanding. Whereas on the other hand, the kind of understanding proper to everyday life is observational in character basing on a starting point. Objective understandings of meanings form the basis defining meanings that are not lying in the mind of an actor.

The intended meaning eludes the grasp not only of the everyday act of "getting the meaning" but also of the two kinds of understanding as well. Further, that external behavior is merely an "indication" of the existence of subjective meaning and that all meaning-contexts are given to us only objectively. Schutz uses the term "objective meaning" in two senses: (a) in a merely negative sense that refer to a meaning *other* than the subjective one in the mind of the actor and (b) meaning constituted as an intersubjective phenomenon, and as that we intend to attribute objective meaning also to certain ideal objectivities (*idealen Gegenständlichkeiten*), such as signs and expressions (cf. Schutz 1972: 31–). For instance, the expression "$2 \times 2 = 4$" has an objective meaning regardless of what is in the minds of any or all of its users. Only insofar as an expression can be considered in terms of what it means (*Bedeutung*) can it be regarded as truly objective. In this context, Schutz means that Husserl taught us to distinguish between "meaning" (*Bedeuten*) as an act and "that which is meant" (*Bedeutung*).

The latter is an ideal unity in contrast to the multiplicity of all possible acts of meaning. Husserl's distinction between "essentially subjective and occasional" expressions, on the one hand, and "objective" expressions, on the other, is only a special case of this general and fundamental insight. An expression is objective if it binds its meaning merely by its appearance to the content of sound and can be understood without regard to the person uttering it or the circumstances of its utterance. On the other hand, an expression is essentially subjective and occasional when

Social Action                                                                                     129

it is "such that its occasional and actual meaning must be oriented with respect to the seeking person and his condition" (Schutz 1972: 33).


## Signs

A third problem field, in the understanding of others, is the signs the actor uses in his/her communications. Schutz regards a sign to be artifacts or act objects which are interpreted not according to those interpretive schemes which are adequate to them as objects of the external world but according to schemes not adequate to them and belonging rather to other objects. Furthermore, it should be said that the connection between a sign and its corresponding non-adequate scheme depends on the past experience of the interpreter or the applicability of the scheme of that which is signified to the sign is itself an interpretive scheme based on experience. This last concept is called the "sign system." A sign system is a meaning-context which is a configuration formed by interpretive schemes; the sign-user or the sign-interpreter places the sign within this context of meaning (Schutz 1972: 120). The following applies in the problematic about signs and understanding (ibid., p. 131):

1. In the first place, when I make use of a sign, those lived experiences signified by that sign stand for me in a meaning-context. These experiences have already been constituted into a synthesis, and I look upon them as a unit.
2. For me the sign must already be part of a sign system, or I will not be able to use it. A sign must be interpreted, before it can be used. But the understanding of a sign is a complicated synthesis of lived experience, which results in a special form of meaning-context. This meaning-context is a configuration involving two elements: the sign as an object in itself and a *signatum*.[25] Any of these involve separate meaning-contexts in their own rights. The entirely new meaning-context embracing both of them, which Schutz calls the "coordinating scheme" of the sign.
3. The act of selecting and using the sign is a special meaning-context for the user of the sign, as any use of a sign is an expressive action. Any action comprises a meaning-context, by virtue of the fact that the actor visualizes all the successive lived experiences of that action as one unified act. Therefore, any expressive action is therefore a meaning-context. This does not necessarily imply that any use of signs is *ipso facto*[26] a case of communication. A person may, for example, when he talks to himself use a sign as an exclusive act of self-expression, without any intention of communicating to others.
4. The meaning-context "sign-using as an act" can serve as the basis for a superimposed meaning-context "sign-using as a communicating act" without in any way accounting the particular person addressed.
5. However, this superimposed meaning-context may become part of a superior and broader meaning-context in which the addressee is taken into account. In this

---

[25] Understood as the specific mark or characteristic of this sign

[26] "High-handed by the very action".

130      4 History of Lifeworld Traditions

case the communicating act has the goal not only that someone takes cognizance of it but that its message shall motivate the cognition of the person for a certain attitude or specific behavior.

6. The fact that this particular person has been communicated with here and now implies that it can be placed in a still broader meaning-context by finding the in-order-to motives of the communicated act. All these meaning-contexts are in principle open to the interpreter, and he can uncover them systematically. Which of them he will try to investigate will depend on his interest in the sign.

The statement that all these meaning-contexts in principle lie open to interpretation requires some modification. As Schutz have said repeatedly, the structure of the social world is by no means homogeneous. Our fellow men and the signs they use can be given to us in different ways. There are different approaches to the sign and to the subjective experience it expresses. Indeed, we do not even need a sign in order to gain access to another person's mind; a mere indication can offer us the opening. This is what happens, for instance, when we draw inferences from artifacts concerning the experiences of people who lived in the past (Schutz 1972: 132).

## Social Interaction

Any kind of social interaction is founded on the structures that are developed socially through the experiences by the actor, in understanding the *Other* and the pattern of actions in common. An example is the interaction between actors involved in questions and answers. When I project my question, I anticipate that the *Other* will understand my action as a question and that his understanding will lead him to act in such a way that I can understand his action as an adequate answer. (I: "Where is the salt?" –.

The *Other* points at the table.) The in-order-to motive of my action is to acquire adequate information. In this particular situation, it implies that the understanding of my in-order-to motive becomes the because motive of the *Other*, in-order-to furnish me with this information – provided that he is able and willing to do it, which I presume that he is. I anticipate that he understands me linguistically and in the context that I am asking. I anticipate that he lets himself lead by the same type of motives which I have myself, and many before me, according to my available stock of knowledge, let myself lead by in similar circumstances.

This example shows that even the simplest interaction in everyday life implies a number of commonsense structures which are all based on the idealization that the in-order-to motives of the actor become the because motives of his partner or vice versa. Schutz (1973b: 38) calls this idealization: *the idealization of the reciprocity of the motives.*

This idealization depends on the general thesis on the reciprocity of the perspectives, as it implicates that the motives ascribed to the *Other* are typically the same as my available pure or socially derived knowledge. A genuine understanding of the Other, however, is only possible for me only because I have previously had similar

# Social Action

experiences as the *Other*, whom I try to understand, either in external manifestations or in imaginations (Schutz 1972: 117).

In the social world, where the actor lives his everyday life, this is experienced as built around his place in it, as open to his interpretation and actions, but always referring to his actual biographically determined situation. In the social relations, and only in relation to the actor, a certain kind of the relations to the actor and to others obtains the specific meaning which may be designated with the word "We."

Furthermore, only in relation to "Us," whose center I am, do others appear as "You." In relation to "You," which refers to "Me," the third party appears as "They." In this community the actor shares space and time with his cohabitants which means that a certain sector of the surrounding world is within the equal reach of any of the actors and contains objects of common interest and relevance. To any actor the *Other* is immediately observable, not only as surrounding things or events but also in their physiognomic importance, i.e., as symptoms of the thought of the *Other*.

To share a community in time, not only in external (chronological) time but also in internal time (*durée*), Schutz implies that any actor participates in the progressing life of the *Other* can catch the thoughts of the Other in a living presence, as they are built up step by step. They must thus share the anticipations of the future with each other as plans, hopes, or anxieties. In short, they are mutually involved in the biography of each other. They live in a pure We-relation.

Apart from the pure We-relations between contemporaries, we can never catch the individual uniqueness of another fellow man in his unique, biographic situation. In the structures of the commonsense thinking, the *Other* appears, at best, as a partial Self, and he even forms part of pure We-relations with only part of his personality. If I enter into interaction with a person, my structure of the *Other* as being a partial Self, as performer of typical roles or functions, has a correlate in the self-classification process taking place, if I enter into interaction with him. I am not involved in such a relationship with my entire personality but only with certain layers of it. By defining the role of the *Other*, I undertake a role. By typifying the behavior of the *Other*, I typify my own which is connected to his and convert myself to a student, a passenger, a consumer, a tax payer, etc. (c.f. Schutz 1973b: 31–).

The commonsense structures used for typological classification of the Other and of the actor is socially derived to a considerable extent and socially recognized. The greater part of character types and sequence of event types are taken for granted within the in-group (until they are proved wrong) as a set of rules and recipes which have stood the test and are expected to do so in the future. The pattern of typical structures is even often institutionalized as a standard of behavior, secured by traditional and habitual customs and at times by specific means for so-called social control, like the law.

It is thus obvious that the meaning of an action is different to (a) the acting actor, (b) the partner involved with him in the interaction and who thus has a set of relevances and aims common with him, and (c) the observer who is not involved in such a relationship. This fact leads to two essential consequences: in the commonsense thinking, we have only a chance of understanding the action of the Other sufficiently for our immediate purpose; and, secondly, in order to increase this chance – we must look for the meaning which the action has to the actor.

132                                                          4   History of Lifeworld Traditions

The demand for "the subjective interpretation of meaning" is a principle for structure of sequence of event types in the commonsense experience. Therefore, according to Schutz (1973b: 39), there is nothing specially unique at Weber's sociology or at the methodology of social science in common. However, subjective interpretation of meaning is only possible, if the meaning and motives are revealed which determine the given sequence of an action.

## Linguistics: The Science of Qualitative Research

We review many of the Lifeworld perspectives but concentrate primarily upon the symbolic interactionist perspective and phenomenology. Here we see a link both theoretical and methodological with transformational or generative linguistics as espoused by Noam Chomsky. In the late 1950s, Chomsky, forced to publish his revolutionary work in Europe since no American publisher would accept it then, caused a paradigmatic revolution in linguistics.

Essentially he defined the field of linguistics for three decades, including those who would challenge his paradigm and build further upon his basic concepts. Chomsky drew much of his work from the same subjectivist philosophers discussed in this chapter. Our purpose is to link the theoretical constructions provided by linguistics to symbolic interactionism and phenomenology to business economics.

Consider first that the study of human beings and their activities in business as well as the larger society as parallel to the natural sciences, physics, biology, etc. Chomsky asks the basic question: "what is the "science-forming capacity" that enables us to recognize certain proposed explanatory theories as intelligible and natural, while rejecting or simply not considering vast array of others that are no less compatible with evidence?" (Chomsky 1980: 250).

Basically, science must be able to describe, explain, and predict phenomenon. Linguistic theory led by Chomsky has been able to do just that in a nonphysical and natural science environment. The key is to push the construction of a theory beyond the descriptive phase and into an explanatory and hopefully predictive phase.

Chomsky theorizes in language usage much the same as Mead (1934/1962) and Blumer (1969/1986) did in their study of social and cultural phenomenon.[27] Linguistic theory allows us to probe "the human mind (since it) is endowed with some set of principles that can be put to work when certain questions are posed, a certain level of understanding has been achieved, and certain evidence is available, to select a narrow class of possible theories" (1980: 250).

Chomsky (1975: 28) cites Weinberg on the theoretical relationships, "In the natural sciences, it is common to adopt what has sometimes been called "the Galilean style" – that is, to construct "abstract mathematical models of the universe to which at least the physicists give a higher degree of reality than they accord the ordinary world of sensations""(ibid., p. 218).

---

[27] See next Chap. 5 and the discussion of Mead and Blumer.

Language is then seen as "A comparable approach (which) is particularly appropriate in the study of an organism whose behavior, we have every reason to believe, is determined by the interaction of numerous internal systems operating under conditions of great variety and complexity" (ibid.). In terms of paradigm changes and the impact on theory, Chomsky argues that "Progress in such an inquiry is unlikely unless we are willing to entertain radical idealization, to construct abstract systems and to study their special properties, hoping to account for observed phenomena indirectly in terms of properties of the systems postulated and their interaction" (ibid.).

For Chomsky, the critical question and even the most controversial was how to proceed? If one assumes, as Chomsky that the "creative aspect of language is a characteristic species property of humans" (ibid., p. 222). In short, what makes human beings unique is their communications system of language: "Language serves as an instrument for free expression of thought, unbounded in scope, uncontrolled by stimulus conditions though appropriate to situations, available for use in whatever contingencies our thought processes can comprehend" (ibid.). Mead and Blumer applied this property of language use as a criterion for the existence of "other minds" in the study of human beings and society.

Language distinguishes human beings from all other species in that "We construct new sentences freely and use them on appropriate occasions, just as we comprehend the new sentences that we hear in novel circumstances, generally bringing much more than our knowledge of language to the performance of creative acts" (ibid.). Human beings are infinitely able to create and innovate. That gives them the ability to manage and control their environment.

The scientific approach to the study of language means that to the linguist, grammar (as distinct from speaker-hearer's grammar) is "a scientific theory, correct insofar as it corresponds to the internally represented grammar" (ibid., p. 220). "The grammar of the language determines the properties of each of the sentences of the language. For each sentence, the grammar determines aspects of its phonetic form, its meaning, and perhaps more" (ibid.). In other words, "The language is the set of sentences that are described by the grammar," and the "grammar "generates" the sentence it describes and their structural description..." (ibid.). Thus a "generative grammar" is "sufficiently explicit to determine how sentences of the language are in fact characterized by the grammar" (ibid.).

A number of basic principles then follow that compose the theoretical basis of linguistics:

1. The language generated by the grammar is infinite (ibid., p. 220).
2. The grammar itself is finite (ibid., p. 221).
3. Thus, the rules of grammar must iterate in some manner to generate an infinite number of sentences, each with its specific sound, structure, and meaning (ibid., p. 221).
4. This process of applying finite grammar to form infinite language is the "recursive property" of grammar (ibid., p. 222).
5. Finally, it is what allows humans to construct new sentences (ideas) freely in all situations.

For example, structure is seen in linguistic theory as "generated by a system of rules and principles that enter into complex mental computations to determine the form and meaning of sentences. These rules and principles are in large measure unconscious and beyond the reach of potential consciousness" (ibid., p. 231).

The studies of language structure leads to linguistic universals which are "principles that hold of language quite generally as matter of biological (not logical) necessity" (ibid., p. 232). "To determine these principles is the deepest problem of contemporary linguistic study" (ibid., p. 232). That is, "highly restrictive universal principles must exist determining the general framework of each human language and perhaps much of its specific structure as well" (ibid.).

Therefore, structurally, "human language is a system with recursive structure-dependent rules, operating on sequences in a hierarchy of phrases to generate a countable infinity of sentences" (ibid., p. 239). "These basic properties are, so far as we know, unique to human language, and the same is true, a fortiori, of more complex principles of universal grammar that characterize human language" (ibid., p. 240). However there is little known now on (c) physical basis, (d) development of the individual, and (e) evolutionary development in language and the study of the mind (ibid., p. 240).

## Use of Linguistic Theory in Everyday Life

Chomsky (1975) outlines his theory of languages such that natural language is common "to discover "the semantic and syntactic rules or conventions (that determine) the meanings of the sentences of a language", and more important, to discover the principles of universal grammar (UG) that lie beyond particular rules or conventions" (Chomsky 1975: 78–). Chomsky's "primary purpose is to give some idea of the kinds of principles and the degree of complexity of structure that it seems plausible to assign to the language faculty as a species-specific, genetically determined property" (ibid., p. 79). He does this by distinguishing between "surface" and "deep" structures.

## Surface Structure

Chomsky describes the surface structure as the basic everyday words and sentences we use to communicate. On the surface, we understand each other, or think that we do, and proceed to communicate and behave based on those sets of assumptions. At the surface level, we can form "various components of the base interact to general initial phrase markers, and the transformational component converts an initial phrase marker, step by step, into a phonologically represented sentence with its phrase marker" (ibid., p. 81). In short, we can take everyday discussions and mark the sentences into a theoretical form for further detail and analysis. This process leads to the transformational derivation which is "The sequence of phrase markers generated in this way..." to form sentences (ibid.). From this process we have the syntax of a language.

## *Deep Structure*

The terms basic structure and deep structure as referring "to non-superficial aspects of surface structure, the rules that generate surface structures, the abstract level of initial phrase markers, the principles that govern the organization of grammar and that relate surface structure to semantic representations, and so on" (ibid., p. 86). The deep structures are the semantics that give meanings to the sentence and words of the surface structures. Chart I illustrates the relationship between surface and deep structures. Transformational relations or rules connect the two structures.

"We use language against a background of shared beliefs about things, and within the framework of a system of social institutions" (Chomsky 1980: 247). Transformations are rules (shows the occurrence of a word corresponding to a yes-no question), which "map phrase markers into (other) phrase markers" (Chomsky 1975: 80). Transformation component is "One component of the syntax of a language consists of such transformations with whatever structure (say, ordering) is imposed on this set" (ibid.). For the transformation component to function in generating sentence structures, must have "initial phrase markers" (ibid.).

More details will come in Chap. 9 on Linguistics. For now the concept of universal grammar indicates that all languages contain the components in Chart 4.1. In other words, the transformational theory can apply to all languages. "The study of language use must be concerned with the place of language in a system of cognitive structures embodying pragmatic competence, as well as structures that relate to

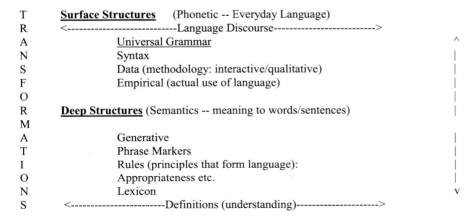

**Chart 4.1** Linguistic transformation theory. (N. Chomsky 1975)

matters of fact and belief" (Chomsky 1980: 247–). What Chomsky did was construct a theoretical paradigm that is universal for all languages. From hundreds and thousands of studies in almost all languages, the theory has proven correct in its ability to describe, explain, and predict everyday language usage.

## *Transformational Linguistics*

A number of useful concepts can be borrowed from linguistic theory for the understanding of business and economics. The application of linguistic theory to economics and businesses can be done with a focus in four areas.

First, as noted, language distinguishes human beings from all other forms of life. While some researchers posit that animals and even bees and dolphins have language or communications systems, the evidence is inconclusive. Humans do have complicated language and therefore communication systems that allow them to send messages, symbolize, create, and build on a body of knowledge. Human language is composed of complicated sets of symbols that when used interactively allow messages to be transmitted. No other creature on earth has that capacity. This point is often taken as the philosophical basis for the rationalists and determinists to argue how to study and explain human behavior.

Second, linguistic theory argues that language is divided into two components: surface and deep structures. The surface structures are those symbols that people use in their everyday life to speak and write. The surface structures are the part of the grammar that cultures devise in order to record their history, communicate, and transact business. The deep structures are an entirely different phenomenon. Language has meaning attached to words and combinations of words (sentences) that are not expressed in the communication act itself. Furthermore, many of the deep structures are not defined in dictionaries or other guides to the language. In short, deep structures constitute the real core and understanding of any language and therefore of any culture and people's actions.

Third, individuals learn surface structures (speaking and dialogue of a language) throughout their lives. Some of aspects of language can be taught. However, empirical studies show people understand or learn the deep structures (grammar and syntax) at an early age. Research consistently demonstrates that babies must learn vocabulary, for example, but need little training in the deep structure of their native language. Children put sentences together and derive meanings from their creation without any formal training or educational process.

Fourth, linguistic theory has been applied to social systems – individual and group behavior by sociologists and psychologists, especially throughout the 1970s and 1980s after Chomsky's paradigm had been well established. What many of the researchers attempted to do is use linguistic theories to explain social and individual behavior. The most successful applications have been in psychological studies of cognition. Here empirical research has shown that the mind does process and operate within the linguistic theoretical paradigm.

The sociological and anthropological applications of linguistic theory have been more problematic however. While a number of theorists have posited that societal behavior, for example, can be seen as interactions between surface structures, the empirical data is lacking. For the most part, these studies break a society down into structural and functional components in an attempt to describe them. Additionally rigid separations between theorists and researchers usually lead to difficult results with inadequate descriptions and nonexistent explanations. When the theorist tries to incorporate the research work, there is usually a forced mix of ideas that result in both muddled data and strained theories.

The purpose here is not a review of the entire research and theoretical literature on the application of linguistic theory (see Chomsky 1975, for a good overview). Instead, the purpose is to apply these theoretical perspectives drawn from organizational sociology and internationalization of the firm and linguistics in order to provide an understanding and perhaps explanatory theory of entrepreneurship. A useful point of departure for both theories can be seen within phenomenological perspective and through the use of qualitative methods.

Consider now Chomsky's linguistic paradigm in more detail as it could apply to business economics. If the linguists' sentence-dependence principle is correct, "then the rules of grammar apply to strings of words analyzed into abstract phrases" that is in the technical literature "to structures that are called 'phrase markers'" (Chomsky 1975: 79). In a business concept, a basic universal grammar of economics exists which can generate rules, which apply deep structure meanings to surface structure interactions. The action of actors can thus be explanatory and predicable. Linguists call these rules transformations (shows the occurrence of a word corresponding to a yes-no question), which "map phrase markers into (other) phrase markers." Chart 4.2 illustrates Transformational rules.

More details will come in Chap. 9. The transformational component of language is "one component of the syntax of a language consists of such transformations with whatever structure (say, ordering) is imposed on this set." For the transformation component to function in generating sentence structures, there must first exist some class of "initial phrase markers" (ibid., p. 80). The present state of the field of economics provides such descriptive classes. Since the economic corpus of terms and concepts (especially since the end of the Cold War) are international, they constitute a "universal grammar" to which "transformational rules" can apply.

* **Appropriateness**
   Qualitative method as empirical data in discourse and sentence usage.
* **Phrase Markers**
   Terms applied to parts of speech in order to
* **Generative Grammar**
   Use of the transformational rules
* **Defining Characteristics and Terms**
   Definitions in Lexicon and terms with meaning in everyday life

**Chart 4.2** Transformational rules

Syntax contains a "'base component' that generates a class of 'initial phrase markers'." The initial phrase marker class must be finite, thus "assigning to the base component the recursive property" which is central of any grammar. In order for rules to be useful, they must reoccur and be applicable to numerous situations. The base component itself consists of two sub components: "a 'categorical component' and a lexicon. The categorical component presents the basic abstract structures by means of 'rewriting rules' that state how a syntactical category can be analyzed into a sequence of such categories" (ibid.).

By way of example, consider a typical linguistic situation. A sentence (S) contains a noun phrase (NP) followed by a verb phrase (VP) or in symbols (NP VP --- > S) where "among the categories that figure in the categorical component are the lexical categories," Noun (N), Verb (V), Adjective (A), and others (ibid.). The representation of the parts of the sentence into symbols allows the surface structure to be broken down into components. The arrow denotes the transformation (--->) from the deep structure (NP VP) into the surface structure sentence (S). In business applications, consider how the arrow or transformation provides an explanation of interactions when deep structure meanings are seen in everyday business interactions and relationships:

> The lexicon consists of the lexical items that belong to the lexical categories, each with its phonological, semantic, and syntactic properties." The lexicon also contains rules of "word formation" that delimit the class of lexical items and express their general properties." ""Lexical transformations" insert items from the lexicon into the abstract phrase markers generated by the categorical component, giving the initial phase makers". The use of lexical transformations are abstract and through their phonological use with other grammatical transformation and rules, "they become sequences of words that count as sentences of the language." (ibid., p. 81)

## *Transformational Rules in the Case of Business*

Consider the overall use of transformation rules in understanding and explaining economic and business interactions. The businessperson is one of many actors in a situation. The researcher must observe the entrepreneurial interactions and determine if they are "appropriate." In linguistics, this would mean simply does the language act conform to common sense and everyday usage? If appropriateness is observed and recorded, then the question is to identify the specific phrase markers attributable to the defining characteristics of the entrepreneur.

Finally, the generative grammar theory allows the researcher to make the connections around situations in terms of the actors, interactions, and symbols thereto described. When transformational rules are applied, the explanations for entrepreneurial actions become apparent and predictable. Extending this theoretical framework to businesses in general and to economics itself will be left for another time. At this point, however, entrepreneurship can be explained and better understood.

With these theoretical concepts in place, the actual transformation rule making process can be seen. That is, the entrepreneur becomes successful or unsuccessful

Conclusion

because she/he draws upon the defining characteristics in the deep structures of the new business creation interactive process (surface structure) and applies the proper rules. The rule making process is often intuitive and based upon common sense.

For example, there are transformational rules between the entrepreneur and the inventor of a product. The interactions of the deep and surface structures allow the product to be sold or marketed or made into an entire company. These rules demonstrate how the entrepreneur must secure the "legal" ownership in order to have control. If the entrepreneur does not follow that basic transformational rule, then the entire new venture may fail, if not soon, then later. The surface structure is seen as success but purposely left undefined. Clearly, success for an entrepreneur can be many things: money, status, ego gratification, family values, non-monetary rewards, etc. While business entrepreneurs may want success in terms of profit or wealth, that is not the only criteria. Application of other transformational rules may define success in a variety of other ways. When those transformations are "mapped" over other transformations, then a much clearer picture emerges as to the explanations for the surface structure results of entrepreneurial interaction.

In conclusion, the basic defining characteristics of an entrepreneur are (1) ability to visualize; (2) need for control; (3) legal ownership over core product, innovation, or technology; (4) formation of a team; (5) find and manage the finances; (6) experience several failures; (7) form relations and networks; and (8) promote various alliances. These defining characteristics form the lexicon for the generative grammar of business entrepreneurs. From the interrelations of the defining characteristics, deep structure meanings can be seen as "phrase markers" as concepts are structured. The interconnectedness of these concepts depends in large part on their transformation by rules to surface structures or everyday business interaction.

## Conclusion

A number of useful concepts can be borrowed from linguistic theory for the understanding of business economics and organizations. Much of the theory is based on the seminal works of Chomsky in the late 1950s and first published by The Hague Press because no American press would publish his works. His theories produced a major paradigm change in both linguistics and later (1970s) in the social sciences, especially psychology. While Chomsky today has his own set of theoretical challenges, the most useful theories from his works are the earliest and are the basis of all contemporary theoretical modifications within the field. The application of linguistic theory to business theory and specifically to entrepreneurship in the international firm can be seen in four areas.

First language is what distinguishes human beings from all other forms of life. While some researchers posit that animals and even bees have language systems, the evidence is inconclusive. However, humans do have complicated language systems that allow them to communicate, create, and build on a body of knowledge.

Human language is composed of complicated sets of symbols that when used interactively allow messages to be transmitted.

Second, linguistic theory argues that language is divided into two structural components: surface and deep structures. The surface structures are those symbols that people use in their everyday life to speak and write. The surface structures are the part of the grammar that cultures devise in order to record their history, communicate, and transact business. The deep structures are an entirely different phenomenon. Language has meaning attached to words and combinations of words (sentences) that are not expressed in the communication act itself. Furthermore, many of the deep structures are not defined in dictionaries or other guides to the language. In short, deep structures constitute the real core and understanding of any language and therefore of any culture and its behavior.

Third, individuals learn surface structures (speaking and dialogue of a language) at an early age. However, empirical studies show that people understand deep structures (grammar and syntax) at an early age. Research consistently demonstrates that babies must learn vocabulary, for example, but need little training in the deep structure of their native language. Children put sentences together and derive meanings from their creation.

Fourth, linguistic theory has been applied to social systems – individual and group behavior by sociologists and psychologists throughout the 1970s and 1980s. What many of the researchers attempt to do is use linguistic theories to explain social and individual behavior. The most successful applications have been in psychological cognitive studies. Here empirical studies have shown that the mind does process and operate along linguistic theory perimeters.

The sociological and anthropological applications of linguistic theory have been more problematic however. While a number of theorists have posited that how societal behavior, for example, can be seen as interactions between deep and surface structures, the empirical data is lacking. For the most part, there are too often rigid separations between the theorists and the researchers. When one tries to incorporate the work of the other, there is usually a forced mix of ideas, which result in both muddled data and models.

The purpose here is not review the entire research and theoretical literature on the application of linguistic theory. In fact, the paradigm revolution started by Chomsky has since the early 1970s been challenged and revised by other linguists. Today there are the three theoretical perspectives within his paradigm: "standard theory," "extended standard theory," and "generative semantics" (Chomsky 1975: 238). Chomsky sees himself as an "extended standard theorists" for reasons not appropriate for this discussion. The purpose here is to use the general "transformational grammar" theory in linguistics and explore how to apply it to organizational sociology and internationalization of the firm in order to understand and perhaps explain entrepreneurship. A useful construct can be derived from the phenomenology.

# Chapter 5
# Mead and Blumer: Social Theory and Symbolic Interactionism

## Introduction: George Herbert Mead

The discussion of Lifeworld as an alternative in the previous chapter rises in a European context, but late in the nineteenth century, an alternative discussion as well was brought to being at the American universities, especially at the University of Chicago.

George Herbert Mead (1863–1931) was central at the department of sociology and is important in order to understand the philosophical base of symbolic interactionism and Blumer's work and thoughts. Mead worked and taught at the Department of Social Science and Anthropology, University of Chicago, in the years 1894–1931. His thoughts and discussion of social theory has to be regarded as one of the beginnings of alternative traditions to the dominating functionalistic sociology and structure functionalism in North America, mostly inspired today by Parsons and Merton (see Chap. 3).

This alternative perspective arouses from a critique of objectivism and structure thinking, especially of Watson and later on Skinner's behaviorism. The general focus in the criticism of the structural-functional model was its presumed presentation of man as a "role-player." Furthermore, the assumption is made that the human and social essence was exhausted by performance of social roles. Finally, the criticism focused upon the organizational and systemic aspect of social life as being the constitutive element of social reality.

Even though the tradition of Mead and of symbolic interactionism is American with inspiration from the American pragmatism,[1] one can find some of the roots in

---

[1] Pragmatism can be seen as "truth" understood as a question of capability to practical use. In Mead's discussion of a theory of value, the value is the character of an object in its capacity of satisfying an interest – it resides neither in the object alone nor in an emotional state of the subject. Stated in ethical terms, in the moral act the motive for action is the impulse itself as directed to a social end. A social self has social impulses that demand expression as imperatively as any other impulses. Moral ends are social ends, because in the first place, the only standard for impulse that

---

© Springer Nature Switzerland AG 2019
W. W. Clark II, M. Fast, *Qualitative Economics*,
https://doi.org/10.1007/978-3-030-05937-8_5

the European traditions[2]: Neo-Kantianism, with the weight upon an idiographic research, the German historicism, with a qualitative discussion and methodology focused on understanding. The European thinking should both be seen as a basis of inspiration and understood out from a criticism of European thoughts, especially the criticism of "pure" subjectivism.[3] Some of the central people in Mead's work from the European traditions are Georg Simmel (*Wechselwirkung* – interaction), Henri Bergson (social act), Immanuel Kant (philosophy of moral, ethical theory and science, of thinking and the relation between the human being and his environment[4]), and partly some of the ideas from Max Weber (1968).

When comparing the American tradition to the European, we can see the different focuses with other discussions, questions, and phenomenon, as well as in the use of language and concepts. Mead's point of origin is not as in the classical European discussion and distinction between understanding vs. explanation and action vs. behavior. Therefore, he talks about explanations, behavior/conduct, mechanisms, stimuli-response, the organism, and so forth. The emphasis is not on the philosophical discussion as evidenced among the European thinkers about the above distinctions. Neither can Mead be related to the ontological and epistemological tradition in European philosophy and philosophy of science. Certainly Mead draws from such traditions but stands out as uniquely American.

One understanding of this situation can be grounded in the American context at that era, where the dominant scientific approaches were behaviorism and structure functionalism. This totally dominated sociology[5] and psychology but also in the general way of thinking in society – as grounded in the pragmatic approach both in life in general, in philosophy, and in science. The European discussions and traditions were simply geographically too far away. And in general, Americans did not have the tradition to discuss European philosophers, theory of knowledge, and problems of recognition in the concrete work in social science.

Mead looked upon himself as a social behaviorist and underlines *social* and *society* as the main area of interest. It was social psychology that he was interested in, which he meant was especially focused on the effect that the social group has in the

---

impulse makes possible resides in the answer as to whether the impulse in question feeds or dies on its own satisfaction and whether it expands and harmonizes, or narrow and defeats, other impulses and second, because the self, as a social being, must be concerned within and without a social harmony of impulses. Moral action is socially directed actions in which one acts with the interest of others as well as one's self in mind. What principally characterizes pragmatism is its emphasis on human beings as agents and their practical relations to the world (see also Delanty and Strydom 2003: 277–).

[2] See Tonboe (1993: 215 and 218); Joas:94, in Giddens and Turner (eds.) (1990).

[3] Both Mead and Blumer are strongly critical towards Husserl's thoughts of "pure consciousness," which they mean cannot be connected to a social context where people interact and develop a self. Because of this they refuse (a transcendental) phenomenology as a sociological basis for understanding people.

[4] See Mead (1962: 379–); Blumer (1986: 168).

[5] Ritzer (1977: 99) thinks that especially the sociology in the USA, before the depression, was inspired by Comte, Spencer, Gumplowicz, Ratzenhofer, and Tarde.

Introduction: George Herbert Mead 143

determination of the experience and conduct of the individual member. The individuals, with minds and selves, are essentially social products, products or phenomena of the social side of human experience. Today, we would not refer to Mead as a social behaviorist, due to other connotations for that label, but as "social cognitivist."

Mead did consider his task to distance himself from the behaviorism, which dominated sociology and social psychology, of that era. Behaviorism accordingly meant for Mead, not the denial of the private mental thoughts, nor the neglect of consciousness, but the approach to all experience in terms of conduct. Mead's (and Dewey's) use of the term "behaviorism" to suggest the approach to experience – reflective and non-reflective – in terms of conduct simply signalizes with an appropriate name the direction implicit in the evolutionary approach of pragmatism. A direction established long before Watson appeared on the scene with his stresses upon the correlatively of stimulus and response in order to be scientific (Mead 1962: xvii).

Mead's philosophical foundation could be seen in the work of John Dewey. Mead was a close friend of Dewey at the University of Michigan and later on at the University of Chicago. William James had also a certain influence upon Mead's thinking, especially in relation to consciousness and experience. At the same time, Mead had a point of departure in the scientific assumption and debate of that time: the focus on behaviorism.

In *Mind, Self and Society* Mead used much space discussing J. B. Watson and W. Wundt. A large part of Mead's work can thereby be seen as a "reinterpretation" of their works. For instance, he discussed Wundt's concept and understanding of gesture, which is a central concept in Mead's discussion of social interaction and understanding of communication between people (see Mead 1962: 42–). His criticism of behaviorism arouses from a different and oppositional understanding of the human being and the human being's capability to think and reflect. This can be seen as the basis to what later on was named symbolic interactionism by Blumer.[6] The connection to the Lifeworld tradition and the European traditions is seen in Mead's point of view on the individual and society:

> The individual is no thrall of society. He constitutes society as genuinely as society constitutes the individual." (p. xxv)... "Human society as we know it could not exist without minds and selves, since all its most characteristic features presuppose the possession of minds and selves by its individual members; but its members would not possess minds and selves if these had not arisen within or emerged out of the human social process in its lower stages of development – those stages at which it was merely a resultant of, and wholly dependent upon, the physiological differentiations and demands of the individual organisms implicated in it. (Mead 1962: 227)

Mead's social theory and as it is expressed in Blumer's view of symbolic interactionism shall therefore still be seen as understanding reality and action in everyday life. Understanding is grounded and connected to comprehension from the actor's view upon oneself and to the actor's interpretation of the environment and objects and in social interaction.

---

[6] See, e.g., Mead (1962: 33–41 and p. 42–51). See Blumer (1986: 1).

Mead is primarily a social psychologist thinker of the society. He did not develop a methodological framework or methods that took into consideration his approach. In essence this is what Blumer did with his focus upon symbolic interaction as an applied approach to understanding society through Mead's social theory and philosophy of science.

The central concepts in Mead's understanding of social reality are, as in the European traditions, understanding, action, interpretation, meaning, and experience. The concept of consciousness that is central in the European discussion of thinking and acting is due in a large amount used by Mead as "to be consciousness about something" – as "being aware." The discussion of consciousness and intentionality in European traditions (especially phenomenology) is not discussed; instead the discussion is of the mind. The mind is understood as a process, as thinking:

> The mind reflects the human capacity to *conceive* what the organism *perceives*, define situations, evaluate phenomena, convert gestures into symbols, and exhibit pragmatically and goals directed behaviour. (Singelmann 1972: 416)

*Mind and self* in Mead's discussion should be understood as generated in a social process, and the questions how they arise in the process of conduct are answered by him in a biosocial term. Mead (1962: xv) tried to avoid an extreme position, by appealing to an ongoing social process of interacting biological organisms; within those processes, through the internalization of the gestures (in the form of vocal gesture), mind and selves arise. The transformation of the biological individual to the minded self takes place through the agency of language, while language in turn presupposes the existence of a certain kind of society and certain physiological capacities in the individual organism. The minimal society must be composed of individuals participating in a social act and using the early stages of each other's actions and gestures, that is, as guides to the completion of the act. The concept of consciousness is used in an ambivalent way, both as being aware of something and to perceive something, and that the individual is conscious of what he is about, and also as creative construction of the objects in the environment and in social interaction.

> Our constructive selection of our environment is what we term "consciousness," in the first sense of the term. The organism does not project sensuous qualities – colours, for example – into the environment to which it responds; but it endows this environment with such qualities, in a sense similar to that in which an ox endows grass with the quality of being food, or in which – speaking more generally – the relation between biological organisms and certain environmental contents give rise to food objects. If there were no organisms with particular sense organs there would be no environment, in the proper or usual sense of the term. An organism constructs (in the selective sense) its environment; and consciousness often refers to the character of the environment in so far it is determined or constructively selected by our human organisms, and depends upon the relationship between the former (as thus selected or constructed) and the latter. (Mead 1962: 165, footnote)

The environment or the society cannot be considered as something "objectively there" but (subjectively) defined in terms of action problems to be solved by the actor. What does and does not constitute the "environment" of an individual varies according to the problems at hand and can, strictly speaking, be determined only ex post facto, since it is functionally defined as that which is being acted upon (Mead, in Singelmann 1972: 420).

This environment is defined through the interpretations and the meanings the individual puts on the objects confronting him. All objects in the environment are thereby seen as social products, in that they are formed and transformed through the process of definition that happens in the process of social interaction. Meanings are formed through the way others refer to the objects or act in relation to them, which appear in the interaction. The environment becomes changed by human action, thus giving rise to new problems of definition and action and constituting a new "social world" for the individual who, in turn, must now redefine himself as a social object and solve new action problems. Individual and environment thus mutually determine one another, and the very nature of the relationships between the two is a constant source of change in these relationships.

## Mind, Self, and Society

Mead, in contradiction to many of the European thinkers in the Lifeworld tradition, starts with an objective social process. Out from this, he works inwards through the importation of the social process of communication into the individual by the medium of the vocal gesture. The focus is upon the social experience in a social psychological approach, where Mead defines social psychology as an interest in the social groups' effects upon the individual member's experience and conduct. It is an approach that both looks on the external circumstances or events and the inner experience of the individual:

> The point of view I wish to suggest is that of dealing with experience from the standpoint of society, at least from the standpoint of communication as essential to the social order. Social psychology, on this view, presupposes an approach to experience from the standpoint of the individual, but undertakes to determine in particular that which belongs to his experience because the individual himself belongs to this social structure, a social order. (Mead 1962: 1)

Mead's (1962: 75) point of departure is particularly with intelligence on the human level, that is, with the adjustment to one another of the acts of different human individuals within the human social process and with an adjustment that takes place through communication: by gestures on the lower lever planes of human evolution and by significant symbols (gestures that possess meanings and are hence more than mere substitute stimuli) on the higher planes of human evolution. The central factor in such adjustment is "meaning." To understand the work of Mead, some central concepts and discussions are important to focus upon. They are primarily the mind, the self, the social act, the gesture, the generalized other, language, and society.

## The Mind

The mind is the presence of significant symbols in behavior. It is the internalization within the individual of the social process of communication in which meaning emerges. It is the ability to indicate to oneself the response (and implicated objects) that the gesture indicates to others and to control the response itself in these terms. Mead (1962: 308) understands the *mind* as constructive or reflexive or problem-solving thinking. It is socially acquired means or mechanism whereby the human individual solves the various problems of environmental adjustments which arise to confront him in the course of his experience and which prevent his conduct from proceeding harmoniously on its way, until they have thus had been dealt with. The mind or thinking is also the means or mechanism whereby social reconstruction is effected or accomplished by the individuals. For it is the possession of minds or powers of thinking which enables human individuals to turn back critically upon the organized social structures of the society to which they belong and to reorganize, reconstruct, or modify these social structures to a greater or less degree.

Nature – the external world – is objectively there, in opposition to our experience of it or in opposition to the individual thinker himself. Although external objects are there independent of the experiencing individual, nevertheless they possess certain characteristics by virtue of their relations to his experiencing or to his mind, which they would not possess otherwise or apart from those relations. These characteristics are their meanings for him, or in general, for us. The distinction between physical objects or physical reality and the mental or self-conscious experience of those objects or that reality – the distinction between external and internal experience – lies in the fact that the latter is concerned with or constituted by meanings. Experienced objects have definite meanings to individuals thinking about them (Mead 1962: 131, footnote).

Thinking is action where the reflections arise, but this demands self-consciousness. Mead means that self-consciousness is grounded in the human being's ability to take the same attitude towards oneself as another human being has towards himself. Only in the terms of gestures which are significant symbols is the existence of mind or intelligence possible; for only in terms of gestures can thinking – which is simply an internalized or implicit conversation of the individual with himself by means of such gestures – take place. The internalization in our experience of the external conversation of gestures, which we carry on with other individuals in the social process, is the essence of thinking. And the gestures thus internalized are significant symbols because they have the same meanings for all individual members of the given society or social group. That is, they respectively arouse the same attitudes in the individuals making them that they arouse in the individuals responding to them: otherwise the individual could not internalize them or be conscious of them and their meanings (Mead 1962: 47). Thinking is thereby an ongoing inner conversation of gestures and as in its completeness means expression of what one is thinking to others.

Thinking takes place in terms of universals, and a universal is an entity that is distinguishable from the object by means of which we think: when we think of a

Mind, Self, and Society 147

spade, we are not confined in our thought to any particular spade. In thinking the universal spade, there must be something that we think about, and that is confusedly not given in the particular occurrence which is the occasion of the thought. The thought transcends all the occurrences.[7] What Mead also understands in relation to the object and thinking is, in line with Dewey, that the meaning is not lodged in the word (e.g., the spade) itself. The meaning resides in the spade as a character that has arisen through the social nature of thinking – the meaning has emerged in social experience.

The human being is distinguished by that power of analysis of the field of stimulation which enables him to pick out one stimulus rather than another and so to hold on to the response that belongs to that stimulus, picking it out from others and recombining it with others. Man can combine not only the responses already there, but he can also get into his activities and break them up, giving attention to specific elements, holding the responses that answer to these particular stimuli, and then combining them to build up another act. This is what Mead means by learning. One can say to a person "Look at this, just see this thing," and he can fasten his attention on the specific object. He can direct attention and so isolate the particular response that answers to it. That is the way in which we break up our complex activities and thereby make learning possible. What takes place is an analysis of the process by giving attention to the specific that call out a particular act, and this analysis makes possibly a reconstruction of the act (Mead 1962: 95).

The mind is in this way understood as characterized by reflexive intelligence, which can adapt an attitude towards the present, the past, and the future, in form of ideas. It is through the reflexivity that the whole social process becomes experience and makes it possible to the individual to have attitudes towards others and relate himself to this process. Experience must start with some whole. It must involve some whole in order that we may get the element we are after. The mind involves relations to objects external itself, and as demands response, but also, those relations and objects are in a certain way that involves meaning. Man's ability to reflect and relate himself to his environment also means a special development of the human being – a development of a self – the mind arises through reflexivity in the social process.

One can also recognize in a general attitude towards an object an attitude that represents alternative responses, such as those involved when Mead talks about our ideas of an object:

> A person who is familiar with a horse approach it as one who is going to ride it. He moves towards the proper side and is ready to swing himself into the saddle. His approach determines the success of the whole process. But the horse is not simply something that must be ridden. It is an animal that must eat, that belongs to somebody. It has certain values. The individual is ready to do a whole series of things with reference to the horse, and that readiness is involved in any one of the many phases of the various acts. It is a horse that he is going to mount; it is a biological animal; it is an economic animal. Those characters are involved in the ideas of the horse. (Mead 1962: 11–)

---

[7] Mead (1962: 88). Compare this to Husserl's discussion of the essence of the object.

148 5 Mead and Blumer: Social Theory and Symbolic Interactionism

There are whole sets of connections, which are of such character that we are able to act in a number of ways, and these possible actions have their effect on the way in which we do act.

## *The Self*

Mead's approach builds upon the assumption that there are differences between the reaction of an animal and the human being's actions. An animal can learn through trial and error, but the human being's action implies a consciousness, and the consciousness is something specific to the human being. The body is not a self, as such; it becomes a self only when it has developed a mind, within the context of social experience. The self is developed; it is not there from the beginning by birth but arises in the process of social experience and activity. It is a development inside the single individual as a result of his relations to the whole process and relations to the other individuals in this process.

Mead meant that the *I* is specific in that the human being is the only creator that can be both a subject and an object. For example, the human being can both experience phenomena and be aware of this experience.[8] The self is primarily a process where the individual reflects upon himself as an object. This is a reflexive process and not structure. The complete self is being both "I" and "Me." The "I" is the principle of action and of impulse, and in its action it changes the social structure. The I and the Me are different phases of the self: the "me" answering to the organized attitudes of the others which we definitely assume and which determine consequently our own conduct so far as it is of a self-conscious character. Now the "me" may be regarded as giving the form of the "I." The novelty comes into the action of the "I," but the structure, the form of the self, is one that is conventional (Mead 1962: 209).

The totality of the acting self is in the I, and the carried out acts partly selves are "me's." The I appears first in the experience after the carrying out of the act and there becomes and appears a part of me. For example, the Me shows itself in our experience in the memory.[9] The I is the response upon others' attitudes, and the Me is the organized set of attitudes as one imagines others – the Me is a social me. Me and I are in the process of thinking and are mutually dependent to each other and dependent on the situation. The self reflects the connections and the structure of the social process as a whole. The I is his action against that social situation within his own conduct, and it gets into his experience only after he has carried out the act.[10] Then he is aware of it. He had to do such a thing and he did it. He fulfills his duty, and he may look with a pride at the throw that he made. The Me arises to do that duty – that is the way in which it arises in his experience. He had in him all the attitudes of others, calling for a certain response; that was the Me of that situation, and his response is the I (Mead 1962: 175–).

---

[8] See Kant's discussion of theory of knowledge and recognition.

[9] See Mead (1962: 175); see also the discussion of the "I" in Schutz (1973b: 68).

[10] See Schutz's concept of action, in Chap. 4.4.2.

Mind, Self, and Society                                                    149

So the reason for Mead to introduce the I and Me into his discussion is to account for the possibility of reflection, planning, and anticipation, and me has a central place in these processes. The Me is the image through which the I can imaginatively project itself into future events and to which it can invest its hopes, ambitions, etc. It is also the reflexive looping of I and Me which allows the subject to engage in dialogue with itself and thus to decide, with a fair degree of conscious awareness, what it wishes to do (see also Crossley 1996: 55).

Different to animals that react (automatically) upon stimuli, there is no fixed connection between the individual action and an event – there is flexibility in the human being's acting that the action has a unique character (see Blumer 1986; Cuff and Payne 1982: 112). Actions can variate over time and situations, in that man acts out from expectations of what can happen. Afterwards he can judge his actions from what actually has happened and from this adjust his expectations and future actions on the basis of those experiences. The human being has a capability to anticipate the future, to plan his actions, and to reflect on earlier actions. When this is the case, the human being must also have the ability to reflect upon itself – to see upon itself in the same way as man sees upon other objects. The self-consciousness and reflection are therefore central in understanding the self:

> The apparatus of reason would not be complete unless it swept itself into its own analysis of the field of experience; or unless the individual brought himself into the same experiential field as that of the other individual selves in relation to whom he acts in any given social situation. Reason cannot become impersonal unless it takes an objective, non-affective attitude towards itself; otherwise we have just consciousness, not *self*-consciousness. And it is necessary to rational conduct that the individual should thus take an objective, impersonal attitude towards himself, that he should become an object to himself. For the individual organism is obviously an essential and important fact or a constituent element of the empirical situation in which it acts; and without taking objective account of itself as such, it cannot act intelligently, or rationally. (Mead 1962: 138)

The human being is not only aware about other objects (including other people) in the environment but has also a consciousness of himself as an object in this environment. Self-consciousness as grounded in the human being's ability to take the same attitude towards himself, as other people have towards themselves, means that our self-concept variates, dependent on which social structures we are involved in. Mead (1962: 142) talks therefore about "multiples selves" or multiple personalities as something normal to the human being.[11]

The organizing of the self is organizing of the individual of a set of attitudes towards his social environments, and towards himself. Self-consciousness is an attention of oneself of the sets of attitudes one awakes in others, especially when it is an important set of response that creates the member of this society. Self-consciousness arises not in groups or because the individual is influenced by others, but it arises *in* the individual, through experience as a self by virtue of the actions one directs towards others. Of course we are more or less unconsciously seeing ourselves as others see us. We are unconsciously addressing ourselves as others address us; in the same way as a sparrow takes up the note of the canary, we pick up

---

[11] See also Schutz and "finite provinces of meaning."

the dialects about us. We are calling out in the other person something we are calling out in ourselves, so that unconsciously we take over these attitudes. We are unconsciously putting ourselves in the place of others and acting as other act.

## The Social Act, Gesture, and the Generalized Other

### *The Social Act*

To understand what Mead meant by development of a self and interaction, the social act is important to understand. Mead understands a social act as something that can be defined as one in which the occasion or stimulus which sets free an impulse is found in the character or conduct of a living form that belongs to the proper environment of the living form whose impulse it is and in which, however, the social act is restricted to the class of acts which involve the cooperation of more than one individual and whose objects as defined by the act are a social object. It means that by a social object one that answers to all the parts of the complex act, though these parts are found in the conduct of different individuals. The objective of the acts is then found in the life process of the group, not in those of the separate individuals alone (Mead 1962: 7, footnote).

The social act must be taken as a dynamic whole – as something going on – no part of which can be considered or understood by itself, a complex organic process implied by each individual stimulus and response involved in it. The individual notes the possibilities for the act and the action and relates them, as symbolic means, to each other to reach the final action. He has a tendency to go in a certain direction, and what he attempts to do is already there in his attitudes towards the act. Those symbols are ways of pointing out the stimuli so that the various responses can organize themselves into a form of action. The reflexive act consists in a reconstruction of the perceptual field so that it becomes possible for impulses that were in conflict to inhibit action no longer (Mead 1962: 123 and footnote). The act is a part of a complex context, both dependent on the group life process and the individual making a reflexive act and pointing out which stimuli and which response. It is this freedom of reconstruction, then, that is the prerequisite of reflection, and it is our social self-conduct that gives this freedom to human individuals in their group life.

### *Gesture*

Gesture in this shall be understood as that phase of the individual act to which adjustment takes place on the part of other individuals in the social process of behavior. The vocal gesture becomes a significant symbol (unimportant, as such, on the merely affective side of experience) when it has the same effect on the individual

The Social Act, Gesture, and the Generalized Other 151

making it and on the individual to whom it is addressed or who explicitly responds to it and thus involves a reference to the self of the individual making it (Mead 1962: 46). The function of the gesture is to make adjustment possible among the individuals implicated in any given social act with reference to the object or objects with which that act is concerned. The significant gestures or significant symbols make the individual aware of the attitudes (or meanings) the objects have for others, and he adjusts his/her behavior according to these actions.[12]

Gestures become significant symbols, when they explicitly arouse in an individual making them do the same responses which they explicitly arouse or are supposed to arouse, in other individuals, the individuals to whom they are addressed. And in all conversation of gestures within the social process, whether external (between different individuals) or internal (between a given individual and himself), the individual's consciousness of the content and flow of meaning involved depends on him thus taking the attitude of the other towards his own gestures.

In this way every gesture comes within a given social group to stand for a particular act or response, namely, the act which it calls forth explicitly in the individual to whom it is addressed and implicitly in the individual who makes it; and this particular act for which it stands is its meaning as a significant symbol. Only in terms of gestures as significant symbols is the existence of mind or intelligence possible; for only in terms of gesture can thinking – which is an internalized conversation of the individual with himself by means of such gestures – take place. The internalization in our experience of the external conversation of gestures, which we carry on with other individuals in the social process, is the essence of thinking.

And the gestures thus internalized are significant symbols because they have the same meanings for all individual members of a given society or social group. That is, they respectively arouse the same attitudes in the individuals making them and in the individuals responding to them: otherwise the individual could not internalize them or be conscious of them and their meanings.

> the same procedure which is responsible for the genesis and existence of mind or consciousness – namely, the taking of the attitude of the other towards ones self, or towards ones own behaviour – also necessarily involves the genesis and existence at the same time of significant symbols, or significant gestures. (Mead 1962: 47–)

The significant gesture or symbol always presupposes for its significance the social process of experience and behavior in which it arises. Or a universe of discourse is always implied as the context in terms of which, or as the field within which, significant gestures or symbols do in fact have significance. This universe of discourse is constituted by a group of individuals carrying on and participating in a common social process of experience and behavior, within which these gestures or symbols have the same or common meanings for all members of that group, whether they make them or address them to other individuals or whether they overtly respond to them as made or addressed to them by other individuals (Mead 1962: 89).

---

[12] See Schutz's typifications.

## The Generalized Other

From the perspective of other individuals, one's self is an object in their environment. To look upon oneself as an object is to look upon oneself in the same way as perceived by other individuals. This is what Mead (1962: 154) names as the "the generalized other."

The generalized other – or role-taking – is necessary to all social activity, because on behalf of this view, the human being can interact through the conceptions of and the expectations one has to each other. It is thereby an attitude towards the whole society one is a part of and towards the common organized activities in this society. It is also in this role-taking that the organized personalities are developed (ibid., pp. 158). For example, the self becomes a self in interaction with others and through that I look upon myself – man develops himself in social interaction. Thereby interaction shall not only be understood as interaction between two subjects but also in the self, as interaction between the I and the Me.

This ability to put oneself in others' views, attitudes, and roles is only possible if we have common significant symbols – e.g., that we can involve ourselves in meaningful communication with each other through the language. It is through interaction – dialogue – with others that the individual becomes aware of the others' attitudes and point of views. Through this reciprocal action, the individual can learn those patterns of action that the others demand of him and create the self-consciousness that is crucial for coordinating of the collective life.

The relation between the idea and the symbol itself, in the conversation of gestures, is not given in the immediate response. In the conversation the relation could be that, but one form of an act gives rise to another different form of an act. In the conversations of gestures, there are some preparations of the whole social processes that involve different forms of actions, and the gestures as a part of this act function as to stimulate the other forms. They give rise to acts different from themselves: while they may call out acts which are alike, as a rule the response is different from the stimulus itself; the cry of a child calls out the response of the care of the mother; the one is fear and the other protection, solicitude. The response is not in any sense identical with the other act (Mead 1962: 54).

## Language

Language is a part of social behavior, a part of a cooperative process. The transformation of the biological individual to the minded self takes place through the agency of language, while language in turn presupposes the existence of a certain kind of society and certain physiological capacities in the individual organism. Mead sees the language as a carrier of a set of symbols answering to certain content that is measurably identical in the experience of the different individuals. The symbols of the language are significant or consciousness gestures.

The symbols used by the individuals in communication have to have the same meaning and mean the same thing to all the individuals involved. But the conversation of gestures does not carry with it a symbol that has a universal significance or meaning to all the different individuals. It is not essential that the individuals should give an identical meaning to a symbol because, in interaction, people adjust themselves to others they meet. The critical importance of the language in the development of human experience lies in that the stimulus is one that can react upon the speaking individual as it reacts upon the other:

> Conditioned reflexes plus consciousness of the attitudes and meanings they involve are what constitutes language, and hence lay the basis, or comprise the mechanism for, thought and intelligent conduct. Language is the means whereby individuals can indicate to one another what their responses to objects will be, and hence that the meanings of objects are; it is not a mere system of conditioned reflexes. Rational conduct always involves a reflexive reference to self, that is an indication to the individual of the significance which his actions or gestures have for other individuals. (Mead 1962: 122, footnote)

The language has a social context, where all vocal expressions are elements in an elaborate social process and carry with them the value of those social processes. Language is a process of indication of specific stimuli and change of the response of them. The languages as a social process make it possible for us to point out responses and internalize them, so they are there in relation to what we indicate.

Conscious communication – conscious conversation of gestures – arises when gestures become signs, that is, when they come to carry for the individual making them and the individuals responding to them definite meanings or significations in terms of the subsequent behavior of the individuals responding to them and of the subsequent behavior of the individuals making them. By serving as prior indications, to the individuals responding to them, of the subsequent behavior of the individuals making them, they make possible the mutual adjustment of the various individual components of the social act to one another. And also, by calling forth in the individuals making them the same responses implicitly that they call forth explicitly in the individuals to whom they are made, they render possibly the rise of self-consciousness in connection with this mutual adjustment (Mead 1962: 69 footnote).

It is the relationship of the symbol, the vocal gesture as a set of responses in the individual himself as well as in the other that makes of that vocal gesture what Mead (ibid., p. 71) calls a significant symbol. A symbol does tend to call out in the individual a group of reactions such as it calls out in the other. But there is something further that is involved in its being a significant symbol: this response within oneself to such a word as "chair" or "dog" is one which is a stimulus to the individual as well as a response. This is what is involved in what Mead terms the meaning of a thing or its significance.

So language is a means by which thought is achieved, and it is equally a means by which thoughts are made apparent to the thinker. When we speak, we can hear ourselves thinking, and this initiates for us a relationship to ourselves. We can both speak and listen to ourselves.

Mead breaks this discussion into four points (see Crossley 1996: 58):

First: speech, whilst it is clearly an action, can equally be regarded as a shortening of action, something which falls short of action whilst communicating the intent of an action. Second, that verbal thought can therefore mediate our relationship to our environment, presenting our possibilities for action to us before we act upon them. Third, this thought represents possibilities to subjects. Subjects speak, hear themselves and respond. Finally, the internal dialogue, because it relies upon significant symbols whose meanings are ubiquitous throughout the linguistic community, involves subjects taking the attitude of the other towards their thoughts; that is, in replaying to their own suggestions, subjects play the role of the other in relation to themselves. They respond to themselves as they would to another speaker and thus become an-other to themselves. Speech in this sense, effects the reflective and reflexive process that is constitutive of self.

## *Meaning*

Central in this adjustment between individuals is meaning. Meaning as such, i.e., the object of thought, arises in experience through the individual stimulating himself to take the attitude of the other in his reaction towards the object. Meaning is that which can be indicated to others while it is by the same process indicated to the indicating individual. Meaning arouses and lies within the field of relation between the gesture given by an individual and the subsequent behavior of this individual as indicated to another human being by that gesture. If that gesture does so indicate to another individual the subsequent (or resultant) behavior of the given individual, then it has meaning. In other words, the relation between a gesture and the later phases of the social act of which it is an early phase constitutes the field within which meaning originates and exists. Meaning is thus development of something objectively there as a relation of certain phases of the social act; it is not a physical addition to that act and it is not an "idea."

A gesture by one organism, the resultant of the social act in which the gesture is an early phase, and the response of another organism to the gesture, are related in a triple or threefold relationship of gesture to first organism, of gesture to second organism, and of gesture to subsequent phases of the given social act; and this threefold relationship constitutes the matrix within which meaning arises, or which develops into the field of meaning. (Mead 1962: 76)

The gesture stands for a certain resultant of the social act, a resultant to which there is a definite response on the part of the individuals involved therein, so that the meaning is given or stated in terms of response. Meaning is implicit – if not always explicit – in the relationship among the various phases of the social act to which it refers, and out of which it develops. The understanding of meaning is that it always is aroused out from a social process. In the same way as the social process is responsible for the existence of objects (understood as meanings), it is in a sense also responsible for the appearance of new objects in the field of experience of the individual human being implicated in that process. The social process constitutes the objects.

That is to say, objects are constituted in terms of meanings within the social process of experience and behavior through the mutual adjustment to one another of the responses or actions of the various individuals involved in that process. It is an adjustment made possibly by means of a communication which takes the form of a conversation of gestures in the earlier evolutionary stages of that process and of language in its later stages.

Mead understands meaning not as a stage in the consciousness but as aroused in interaction in the field or context of meaning. Meanings are thus not to be conceived as a state of consciousness or as a set of organized relations existing or subsisting mentally outside the field of experience into which they enter. It should be conceived objectively, as having its existence entirely within this field itself:

> Awareness or consciousness is not necessary to the presence of meaning in the process of social experience... The mechanism of meaning is thus present in the social before the emergence of consciousness or awareness of meaning occurs. The act or adjusted response of the second organism gives to the gesture of the first organism the meaning which it has. (Mead 1962: 77–)

But it is in the self-consciousness that a gesture becomes a significant symbol, and where the interpretation of gestures is not, basically, a process going on in the mind as such; it is an external, overt, physical, or physiological process going on in the actual field of social experience. Meaning can be described in terms of symbols or language at its highest and most complex stage of development, but language simply lifts out a social process, a situation that is logically or implicitly there already. The language symbol is simply a significant or conscious gesture (ibid. p. 79).

Mead makes two main points on this: (1) The social process, through the communication, which it makes possible among the individuals implicated in it, is responsible for the appearance of a whole set of new objects in nature, which exists in relation to it (objects, namely, of "common sense"). (2) The gestures of one individual and the adjustive response of another individual to that gesture, within any given social act, bring out the relationship that exists between the gesture as the beginning of the given act and the completion or resultant of the given act to which the gesture refers.

Here Mead draws upon Dewey's thought and says that meanings arise through communication. It is the content to which the social process gives rise that this statement refers, not to bare ideas or printed words as such but to the social process which has been so largely responsible for the objects constituting the everyday life environment in which we live: a process in which communication plays the main part.

The logical structure of meaning is to be found in the threefold relationship of gesture to adjustive response and to the resultant of the given social act. Response on the part of the second individual to the gesture of the first is the interpretation – and brings out the meaning – of that gesture, as indicating the resultant of the social act which it initiates and in which both individuals are thus involved. This threefold relationship between gesture, adjustive response, and resultant of the social act which the gesture initiates is the basis of meaning. For the existence of meaning depends upon the fact that the adjustive response of the second individual is directed towards the resultant of the given social act as initiated and indicated by the gesture of the first individual (ibid. p. 80).

There are two characters that belong to the concept of meaning: participation and communicability. Meaning can arise only in so far as some phase of the act that the individual is arousing in the other can be aroused in himself. There is always to this extent participation. And the result of this participation is communicability, i.e., the individual can indicate to himself what he indicates to the other. The meanings of objects are actual inherent properties or qualities of them; the locus of any given meaning is in the thing which, as Mead says, "has it."

The processes that go to make up our objects must be present in the objects themselves, which have not the use of language. It is the language that gives us control over the organization of the act.[13] We refer to the meaning of a thing when we make use of the symbol. Symbols stand for the meanings of those objects that have meanings. They are given portions of experience which point to, indicate, or represent other portions of experience not directly present or given at the time when, and in the situation in which, any one of them is thus present (or is immediately experienced) (ibid. 122, footnote).

It is the agency of language that makes possible the appearance of the self. Indeed, the self, mind, "consciousness of," and the significant symbols are in a sense precipitated together. Mead finds the distinguishing trait of selfhood to reside in the capacity of the minded individual to be an object to himself. The mechanism by which this is possible is found in the role-taking that is involved in the language symbol. In so far as one can take the rôle of the other, he can, as it was, look back at himself from that perspective and so become an object to himself. Thus again, it is only in a social process that arise people – selves as beings that become conscious of themselves.

## *The Society*

The minimal society must be composed of biological individuals participating in a social act and using the early stages of each other's actions as gestures. Not merely is the self as a social being developed on the basis of the biological organism, but society itself, as an organic whole of complex order, cannot be put into opposition with its distinguishable and recognizable components – biological individuals at the simpler social levels and selves at the higher.

The recognition of the biological individual (the "I" over against the "me") and that the selves presuppose a prior social process make possible the organization of a distinctively human society. Through society the impulsive animal becomes a rational animal, a man (ibid. p. xxv). In virtue of the internalization of the social

---

[13] See Mead (1962: 13); also compare this to Husserl's discussion of the essence; there is a similarity of understanding between those two, although Mead refuses Husserl's phenomenology.

The Social Act, Gesture, and the Generalized Other    157

process of communication, the individual gains the mechanism of reflective thought, acquires the ability to make himself an object to himself and to live in a common moral and scientific world, and becomes a moral individual with impulsive ends transformed into the conscious pursuit of ends-in-view.

Because of the emergence of such an individual, society is in turn transformed. It receives through the reflective social self the organization distinctive of human society; the individual regulates his part in the social act through having within himself the roles of the others implicated in the common activity, only because we have this internalized control function, that is, because we take the attitudes and views of others and of the community as a whole into account before we act. In addition to controlling action, moreover, this process equally coordinates it. Individuals anticipate each other's responses to events and actions and are able to accommodate them on this basis. This, for Mead, is quite fundamental to the possibility of social life in itself (see Crossley 1996: 56).

## *Methodology and Consciousness*

Mead was occupied of the study of mind and consciousness, where the central philosophical issue and question were of the relationship between the consciousness and the nature. The discussion here is connected to the separation and distinction between natural science method (*erklären*) and social human science method (*verstehen*). Mead did not think it was necessary to draw the sharp boundary, for example, as Dilthey and Weber did. He meant that the consciousness is a part of the nature and is likewise a "natural" part of it, as everything else that the evolutionary process has created. For example, mastery of language, which is decisive for the rise of the consciousness, depends upon the physiological development of the organism of the human being, i.e., the development of the speech organ. It arises, in other words, a possibility for the human consciousness, through its physiological development. And this is a phenomenon that separates the human being from other living creators. But the study of man cannot be satisfied with describing and explaining the human being's physiology and organic qualities, but the other way around; that is, it is essential to study thoughts, the consciousness, and experiences to understand the human being and the social (collective) life:

> As it is in this physical world that we attain our most perfect controls, the tendency towards placing the individual, as a mechanism, in this physical world is very strong. Just in so far as we present ourselves as biological mechanisms are we better able to control a correspondingly greater field of conditions which determine conduct. On the other hand, this statement in mechanical terms abstracts from all purpose and all ends of conduct. If these appear in the statement of the individual, they must be placed in mind, as an expression of the self – placed, in other words, in a world of selves, that is, in a social world… This immediate experience which is reality, and which is the final test of the reality of scientific hypotheses as well as the test of the truth of all our ideas and suppositions, is the experience of what in have called the "biological individual". The term refers to the individual in an attitude and at a moment in which the impulses sustain an unfractured relation with the

objects around him... What is sought is a coincidence of an anticipated result with the actual event. I have termed it "biological" because the term lies on the living reality which may be distinguished from reflection. A later reflection turns back upon it and endeavours to present the complete interrelationship between the world and the individual in terms of physical stimuli and biological mechanism; the actual experience did not take place in this form but in the form of unsophisticated reality. (Mead 1962: 351–)

Mead means that the method to investigate this lived reality has to be built upon observations of the social activities of the everyday of life, on common available and observable facts, as those any one of us can catch sight of and discover in our life.

## Herbert Blumer Symbolic Interactionism

Herbert Blumer (1900–1989) inspired, trained, mentored, and encouraged generations of sociologists to look at society from the perspective of human interaction. His particular theoretical view became known as "symbolic interactionism" through his only published book by the same name in 1969. Blumer was a teacher first of all. While he had a few other articles published, he believed that students needed to be taught and devoted his life to that goal. As a giant intellect and scholar in the field of sociology, he was one of the most unassuming and least pretentious. He stood above other scholars in his field.[14]

Blumer's mark upon the social sciences was enormous; his achievements too extensive to measure. His influence upon students, scholars, and practitioners is legendary. In fact, he would not have wanted these accomplishments quantified. Yet, Blumer is credited with establishing and being the first departmental chair for the Department of Sociology at the University of California, Berkeley. He made the department into an internationally recognized group of professors and students constantly grappling with societal interaction and change. His life work was devoted to creating and enhancing "qualitative theory and methods." Blumer felt that the greatest published works on sociology came from his own mentor, the social philosopher, George Herbert Mead. In fact, it was their relationship at the University of Chicago in the early 1900s that certainly inspired Blumer himself to spend his lifetime career devoted to teaching others. Not content with accepting institutional retirement, required by the University of California, or needing the money, Blumer actively taught at other universities well into his mid-80s. He accepted new teaching positions and traveled weekly to other campuses throughout California. On more than one occasion, he would leave his Berkeley office to catch a plane to San Diego, where he was scheduled to teach later in the evening of the same day. Tirelessly, Blumer taught and inspired others until his death.[15]

---

[14]A little known fact about Blumer was his height of 6 feet 4 inches, which came in handy as a graduate student. In order to pay for his tuition and way through the University of Chicago, Blumer played professional American football as a lineman for the Chicago Bears.

[15]Clark was a student of Blumer's at the University of California, Berkeley, in the mid-1970s. As

# Symbolic Interactionism[16]

Symbolic interactionism could also be named the Chicago School. It was at the Department of Social Science and Anthropology, University of Chicago, that the approach was developed in the three first decades of this century and from there further developed by different scholars.[17] The point of origin in symbolic interactionism is in the two concepts: *interactionism*, an interest in understanding people's interaction and larger social formations, the collective, and *symbolic*, a discussion and understanding of how people interact and communicate, how this is possible. It could be understood as a dialectical interdependence between the human being and his natural and social environment (Singelmann 1972: 415):

> The term "symbolic interactionism" has come into use as a label for a relatively distinctive approach to the study of human group life and human conduct... The term "symbolic interaction" refers, of course, to the peculiar and distinctive character of interaction as it takes place between human beings. The peculiarity consists in the fact that human beings interpret or "define" each other's actions instead of merely reacting to each other's action. Their "response" is not made directly to the actions of one another but instead is based on the

---

part of Clark's doctoral work in anthropology, linguistics, economics, and education (now as Cross-Disciplinary Studies) at Berkeley, he took classes from Blumer in sociology. Critical of his own field (anthropology) for its support of the status quo paradigms and mired in determinism and structuralism, Clark found Blumer's ideas stimulating and well-founded upon an entirely different philosophical line of thought that Clark had not been exposed heretofore. What also occurred to Clark, who was (and is today) a research associate at the Center for the Study of Social Change (CSSC), University of California, Berkeley, was the need to communicate Blumer's ideas to a broader academic audience. Scholarly publications in the mid-1970s were primary composed of scholars communicating to one another and to students worldwide. The academic community was aware that there were very few materials published by Blumer. Most considered this a real tragedy, since it meant that only Blumer's students would benefit from his teaching. In that context, Clark initiated a publication project. He approached the CSSC to support the recording and transcribing of Blumer's classroom lectures. Blumer agreed and the project continued for one semester. A series of six papers from Blumer's lectures was transcribed and edited. After the first semester, Blumer (a member of the CSSC himself) agreed to participate in a special seminar for senior faculty and invited graduate students to discuss the ideas presented in his lectures the prior semester. Afterwards, Clark edited the lectures. Later he sought publication for the Blumer lectures and seminar in the late 1970s, especially with the University of California Press. While the press was interested, the concern then was that some of the materials had already been presented by Blumer in his book (*Symbolic Interactionism – Perspective and Method*, University of California Press, 1969, reissued 1986). There was "nothing new." In short, the reaction was that there was not enough "new" material to warrant a separately published book on Blumer's ideas. Clark left academics to pursue entrepreneurial business opportunities throughout the 1980s. He dropped the project, until his Fullbright to Aalborg University in the Winter of 1994–1995. Those lectures will later on be published in a separate volume. Stay tuned now in 2018.

[16] The term "symbolic interactionism" is what Blumer calls a "somewhat barbaric neologism" that he coined in an offhand way in an article written in "Man and Society" (Schmidt E P (ed.) N.Y., Prentice-Hall, 1937). The term somehow caught on and is now in general use.

[17] See Fig. 5.1 in the end of this chapter. Blumer (1986: 1) and Rose (1962: 3) mention G H Mead, J Eder, W I Thomas, R E Park, W James, C H Cooley, F Znaniecki, J M Baldwin, R Regfield, and L Wirth as some of the prominent scholars who have used the approach in their work.

meaning which they attach to such actions. Thus, human interaction is mediated by the use of symbols, by interpretation, or by ascertaining the meaning of one another's actions. (Blumer 1986: 1 and 78)

The basic assumptions and ideas can shortly be summarized as:

- Human group life consists of the fitting to each other of the lines of action of the participants.
- Such aligning of actions takes place predominantly by the participants indicating to one another what to do and in turn interpreting such indications made by others.
- Out of such interaction, people form the objects that constitute their worlds.
- People are prepared to act towards their objects on the basis of the meaning these objects have for them.
- Human beings face their world as organisms with selves, thus allowing each to make indications to himself.
- Human action is constructed by the actor on the basis of what he notes, interprets, and assesses.
- And the interlinking of such ongoing action constitutes organizations, institutions, and vast complexes of interdependent relations (Blumer 1986: 49).

A deeper understanding of this basic concept can be seen in five assumptions Rose finds among symbolic interactionists (Rose 1962: 5–): (1) Man (as in mankind) lives in a symbolic environment as well as a physical environment. (2) Through symbols, man has the capacity to stimulate others in ways other than those in which he is himself stimulated. (3) Through communication of symbols, man can learn huge number of meanings and values – and hence ways of acting – from other men. (4) The symbols – and the meanings and values to which they refer – do not occur only in isolated bits, but often in clusters, sometimes large and complex. (5) Thinking is the process by which possible symbolic solutions and other future course of action are examined, assessed for their relative advantages and disadvantages in terms of the values of the individual and one of them chosen for action.

As a former student of Mead, Blumer starts with his discussion of social theory and consider the philosophical ground of symbolic interactionism as based upon Mead's and John Dewey's works and as strongly humanistic (see Blumer 1986: 1 and 21). Blumer focused especially upon understanding of the human being, the human condition, and science and therefore on the methodological discussion of how to investigate empirical reality.[18] It was his conviction that an empirical science necessarily has to respect the nature of the empirical world that is its objects of study. In his judgment symbolic interactionism shows that respect for the nature of human group life and conduct. But the respect necessitates, in turn, the development of a methodological perspective congruent with the nature of the empirical world of study (op. cit., p. VII).

---

[18] Blumer's PhD thesis has the title "Method in Social Psychology."

Blumer did see symbolic interactionism not as a philosophical doctrine but as a perspective in empirical social science – as an approach designed to yield verifiable knowledge of human group life and human conduct (op. cit., p. 21). And he considered symbolic interactionism as a down-to-earth approach to the scientific study of human group life and human conduct. Its empirical world is the natural world of such group life and conduct. It lodges its problems in this world, conducts its studies in it, and derives its interpretations from such naturalistic studies. If it wishes to study religious cult behavior, it will go to actual religious cults and observe them carefully as they carry on their lives (op. cit., p. 47).

Blumer is strongly critical to what he saw as the structural and natural scientific approach in social science and of a philosophy of realism. In his opinion this widely held and deeply entrenched the social and psychological sciences (ibid., p. 4; c.f. Chap. 3 on Realism); especially he criticizes "variable analyses," analyses that seek to define and specify the relationship between two or more "variables": the conventional procedure here is to identify something which is presumed to operate on group life and treat it as an independent variable and then to select some form of group activity as the dependent variable. The independent variable is put at the beginning part of the process of interpretation and the dependent variable at the terminal part of the process. The intervening process is ignored or, what amounts to the same thing, taken for granted as something that need not be considered (see ibid. p. 133).

This form of investigation gives us results there are empty of content and meanings, stripped bare of the complex of things that sustain it in a "here and now" context. It gives us no picture of people as human beings in their particular world. We do not know the run of their experience, which induced an organization of their sentiments and views, nor do we know what this organization is. We do not know the social atmosphere or code in their social circles. We do not know the reinforcement and rationalizations that come from their fellows. We do not know the pressures, the incidents, and the models that came from their niches in the social structure, and we do not know how their ethical sensitivities are organized and so what they would tolerate (ibid. p. 131).

Blumer means that the dominant prevailing view is that the human being is a complex organism whose behavior is a response to factors playing on the organization of the organism. Schools of thought in the social science and psychological sciences differ enormously in which of such factors they regard as significant. This is shown in such a diverse array behavior theories on topics covering areas such as stimuli, organic drives, need-dispositions, conscious motives, unconscious motives, emotions, attitudes, ideas, cultural prescriptions, norms, values, status demands, social roles, and institutional pressure (ibid. p. 14).

Various positivists and rationalists schools of thought differ also in how they view the organization of the human being, whether as a kind of biological organization, a kind of psychological organization, or a kind of imported societal organization incorporated from the social structure of one's group. However, they are all very much alike in seeing the human being as a responding organism, with its behavior being a product of the factors playing on its organization or an expression of the interplay of parts of its organization. The human being is "social" only in sense of either being a member of social species, of responding to others (social stimuli), or of having incorporated within it the organization of his group.

The view of the human being and social life held in symbolic interactionism is fundamentally different. Blumer (ibid. p. 2) sees symbolic interactionism rests in three simple premises:

1. Human beings act towards things on the basis of the *meanings* that the things have for them. Such things include everything that the human being may note in his world. Symbolic interactionism sees the meanings that things have for human beings are central in their own right. To ignore the meaning of the things towards which people act is seen as falsifying the behavior under study and is to neglect the role of meaning in the formation of behavior.
2. The meaning of such things is derived from, or arises out of, the *social interaction* that one has with one's fellows. The source of meaning arises in the process of interaction between people in a social context. The meaning of a thing for a person grows out of the ways in which other persons act towards the person with regard to the thing. Their actions operate to define the thing for the person. Thus, symbolic interactionism sees meanings as social products, as creations that are formed in and through the defining activities of people as they interact (ibid. pp. 4).
3. These meanings are handled in, and modified through, an *interpretative process* used by the person in dealing with the things he encounters. The use of meanings by a person in his action involves an interpretive process. This process has two distinct steps (op. cit., p. 5): (a) The actor indicates to himself the things towards which he is acting; he has to point out to himself the things that have meaning. The making of such indications is an internalized social process in that the actor is interacting with himself. (b) By virtue of this process of communicating with himself, interpretation becomes a matter of handling meanings. The actor selects, checks, suspends, regroups, and transform the meanings in the light of the situation in which he is placed and the direction of his action. Accordingly, interpretation should not be regarded as a mere automatic application of established meanings but as a formative process in which meanings are used and revised as instrument for the guidance and formation of action.

### "Root Images or Basic Ideas"

Symbolic interactionism is grounded in what Blumer calls "root images" or basic ideas. These refer to and depict the nature of the following matters: human groups or societies, social interaction, objects, the human being as an actor, human actions, and the interconnection of the lines of action. These root images represent the way in which symbolic interactionism views human society and conduct. They constitute the framework of study and analysis.

## The Nature of Human Society or Human Group Life

Human groups are seen as consisting of human beings who are engaged in action. The action consists of the multitudinous activities that the individuals perform in their life as they encounter one another and as they deal with the succession of the situations confronting them. The individuals may act singly, they may act collectively, and they may act on behalf of, or as representatives of, some organization or groups of others. The activities belong to the acting individuals and are carried on by them always with regard to the situations in which they have to act. The import of this simple and essentially redundant characterization is that fundamentally human groups or society exists in action and must be seen in terms of action. This picture of human society as action must be the starting point (and the point of return) for any scheme that purports to treat and analyze human society empirically (ibid. p. 6). The life of any human society, organization, or group consists necessarily of an ongoing process of fitting together the activities of its members.

A society or group would never exist, expand, or continue except for *interaction* among its members. That is what makes a society; a group by definition is interaction that takes place between the members. What one does affects others, and one in turn may be affected by others. If we speak in a purely hypothetical sense, that is, if human beings were simply physiological organisms, each going his or her own way, each capable of acting, surviving, and living independently of all the others, and with none of their actions being called forth by or involving the actions of one another, then there would be no society. There would be no human group life. All that one would have would be an aggregate of independently acting individuals.

Parenthetically, any scheme to study human society which uses as its population group an aggregate of independently or separately independent units, as in the case of a statistical array, should be viewed with a great deal of skepticism. Arrays or surveys are simply a data collection point in time and fail to account for the interaction between members of a group. This scheme is not what a society is, nor could be.

Instead a society or a group (in the sense of human group life) necessarily signifies that the members therein are interacting. A group signifies that its members are in association with one another through a variety of symbols such as language, traditions, shared values, and the like. They are not in association with one another, as reflected in some statistical table. Groups are in association with one another by one another's very presence or proximity. They address each other; they respond to one another; they talk with one another; they get scared and are frightened by one another; or they get interested in one another. They have to take each other into account as they carry on their respective activities. An interlinkage exists between members of a group.

The simplest way of expressing this idea would be to declare that the very essence of a human society consists of the fitting together of lines of activity. That is what one has in a society. That is what one has in the activities of a group. People mixing, sharing, competing, and cooperating are parts of the interactive processes that define groups. Blumer illustrates this significant aspect of human group life in his own classroom teaching:

> Human group life is represented by and can be illustrated right here in this classroom. What are its characteristics? What makes us a group here? Human group life makes us a miniature society. We are fitting our lines of activity towards one another. I talk, and you listen. I perceive that you are listening as I talk. I have some appreciation of what you are in here for. I have some realization of what I am supposed to do in relationship to you; you do similarly. So we fit our lines of action towards one another. If there were no lines of action, we would have pandemonium in here even though this is a small group. For example, one of you could decide to go to sleep and two of you might decide to go over in a corner and play games. Another one of you could want to get over in a corner and do your thing, or another individual could decide to roll up spit balls and throw them. Those are just a few of the commonest kinds of actions that could happen. If they did happen we would not have a group, a functioning group. We would not have a society. (Blumer 1976c)

What happens is that they fit their behavior towards one another and that is what makes that a society. This society is constituted by the fitting together, the interlinking of lines of action. It is not an aggregate. Society is not an aggregate of separate individuals, each acting independently and going his own way. The very essence of society and group life presupposes interaction. One cannot have any society without interaction. One can have an aggregate without having interaction.

## The Nature of Social Interaction

That brings out what is involved in interaction. It is a matter of interpretation, of understanding what is anticipated and what is expected. Response is not automatic. Group life necessarily presupposes interaction between the group members. The activities of the members occur predominantly in response to one another or in relation to one another. Social interaction is interaction between the actors (and not between factors forcing upon the human beings). Social interaction is a process that forms human conduct; people interacting with one another have to take account of what each other is doing or is about to do; they are forced to direct their own conduct or to handle their situations in terms of what they take into account.

Thus, the activities of others enter as positive factors in the formation of their own conduct; in the face of the actions of others, one may abandon an intention or purpose, revise it, check or suspend it, intensify it, or replace it. The actions of others enter to set what one plans to do, may oppose or prevent such plans, may require a revision of such plans, and may demand a very different set of such plans. One has to fit one's own line of activity in some manner to the actions of others. The actions of others have to be taken into account and cannot be regarded as merely an arena for the expression of what one is disposed to do or sets out to do (1986: 8).

In understanding different forms of or levels of social interaction, Blumer refers to Mead[19] and makes a separation between "non-symbolic interaction" and "symbolic interaction." The first one takes place when one responds directly to the action

---

[19] Mead (1962) calls the two "the conversation of gestures" and "the use of significant symbols."

of another without interpreting that action – reflex responses. Symbolic interaction is related to Mead's discussion of *gestures*: as a presentation of gestures and a response to the meaning of those gestures. A gesture is any part or aspect of an ongoing action that signifies the larger act of which it is a part, for example, the shaking of the fist as an indication of an attack or the declaration of war by a nation as an indication of a posture and a line of action of that nation.

> the meaning of gesture flows out along three lines (Mead's triadic nature of meaning): It signifies what the person to whom it is directed is to do; it signifies what the person who is making the gesture plans to do; and it signifies the joint action that is to arise by the articulation of the acts of both… If there is confusion or misunderstanding along any one of these three lines of meaning, communication is impeded, and the formation of joint action is blocked. (Blumer 1986: 9)

We think of interactionism as consisting of the following steps (Blumer 1976c):

1. The first step consists of making indications to another, pointing out to another to do this or do that, or approaching another with the expectation that he is going to act in a certain way. In the interaction between people on the symbolic level, we note that they are making indications to one another to do something, either orally or by gesture. There are also indications by physical gesture, indications for a person to get out, to get away, to shout to him to get away, and so forth. Hence, we have designation.
2. In the second step, interpretation is made of that designation by the person to whom the gesture is directed. The other aspect of interaction is the ability of the other person to interpret a designation.
3. The third step is the response of the other person who interprets the gesture. The response of the other person who interprets the gesture becomes based upon more than just the interpretation of the gesture, because he has to take into account the situation. He takes other things into account from the gesture that is presented to him.

If we go back to the example of opening the window, I ask you to get up and open that window. You understand perfectly well what I want you to do, but you take other things into account. You may take into account the way in which I have addressed that request to you. You find that there is a taint of an insult and disrespect in it. So you may decide that you are not going to open the window. Or it may be that you do not feel well; you do not want to move. There may be a rip in your plants, let us say, or something like that. You take that into account and, consequently, you decide not to do it.

In interaction, it is not adequate to say that one merely interprets the action of the other. One has to add to that what the individual interprets or takes into account of the situation in which he is lodged. Next, before the individual, who now has interpreted the gesture of the other and interpreted the situation responds, he maps out his response. One maps out what one is going to do before one does it. One carves out the line of action. One decides, "Well, I will get up and open the window," or decides, "I'm not going to open the window," or decides for some reason known only to oneself that one is going to ask someone sitting next to one, "Won't you go open the window?" One constructs, in other words, a mode of response before one acts and then one responds.

People are interacting with each other, both individually and collectively, in terms of the things that are being presented to them. That portion of their acts or utterances is gestures. They are different declarations or activities which people are engaged in. Individuals must interpret these things as a means of getting a line to try out their own actions. Interaction is an ongoing process in which people are approaching each other by using gestures. Everyone engaged in an interaction must handle those gestures.

## The Nature of Objects

For human beings, nothing exists except in the form of objects. It must be something to which they can refer. By definition, of course, they are incapable of pointing out anything which does not exist for them. That same thing is true for anyone else. As far as people are concerned, their world consists solely of and is confined to the objects that they can indicate. In order to be perfectly clear, Blumer says that everything and anything can be an object. They do not have to be tough, resistant, or material things (Blumer 1976c). The position here is that the "world" that exists for human beings and for their groups is composed of "objects" and that these objects are the product of symbolic interaction. An object is anything that can be indicated, anything that is pointed to or referred to a cloud, a book, a banker, a religious doctrine, a ghost, and so forth. In an attempt of classify objects, Blumer points at three categories: (a) physical objects (such as chairs, trees, and cars), (b) social objects (such as students, politicians, managers, a mother, or a friend), (c) abstract objects (such as moral principles, philosophical doctrines, or ideas such as justice exploitation, or compassion).

The nature of an object consists of the meaning that it has for the person for whom it is an object. This meaning sets the way in which he sees the object, the way in which he is prepared to act towards it, and the way in which he is ready to talk about it. An object may therefore have a different meaning for different individuals. The meaning of objects for a person arises fundamentally out of the way they are defined to him by others with whom he interacts.

The consequences from this are: First, it gives us a different picture of the environment or milieu of human beings. From their standpoint the environment consists only of the objects that the given human beings recognize and know. The nature of this environment is set by the meanings that the objects composing have for those human beings. Second, objects (in the sense of their meaning) must be seen as social creations – as being formed in and arising out of the process of definition and interpretation as this process takes place in the interaction of people. The meaning of anything and everything has to be formed, learned, and transmitted through a process of indication – a process that is necessarily a social process (Blumer 1986: 11–). Human group life is a process in which objects are being created, affirmed, transformed, and cast aside. The life and action of people necessarily change in line with the changes taking place in their world of objects.

As a summary proposition, anything that can be indicated by human beings is an object. An object exists in terms of the meaning which it has. It is the meaning that constitutes the object. The meaning is something that is not indigenous to the object in the sense of being impermeable incorporated in the object. Meaning is not something that is fixed and which just reflects itself back to someone who is observing the object. Instead the meaning of an object is brought to the object by the individuals for whom it is an object. The meaning, accordingly, resides in a relationship, not in terms of something that is intrinsic to the makeup of the object.

The next proposition is that the meaning of objects arises inside a context of interaction between people (Blumer 1976c). Since meanings are connected with the indications by representing what is indicated, they are necessarily something that emerges out of a social process. To understand that, consider this: the process of indication is the process of designating something or pointing to something; it is inevitably a social process. If one stops to think about it, one will perceive that it necessarily involves someone; some person is making the indication; it always necessarily involves someone to whom the indication is being made.

Blumer is interested in stressing that to point out something, to indicate it, and to designate it mean that one has a relationship, which necessarily involves the person who is making the indications. The person to whom the indication is being made and the thing that is being designated, by virtue of having a self, gets into the position of being able to make an indication to himself. It is a social relationship. An indication is noting something to someone. It is this social relationship that is represented. An individual is making an indication to someone by having to take the role or position of the person to whom the indication is being made.

Objects are defined differently by different people. Objects are products of interaction since they exist as indications. Accordingly, the processes of interaction take place in each case differently. The production of the objects varies. One has different groups of people coming to develop different worlds of objects through the process of the interactions taking place among them. These people live in different worlds. If there is anything that is a truer characteristic of human group life, it is that (Blumer 1976c).

There is an interesting commentary that can be attached to the discussion here. Science and the natural sciences particularly are dedicated to trying to discover the nature of things in their empirical domain. These sciences study things. The more they study them, the more questions they ask, and the more questions they ask, the more they are disposed to approach them in different ways. The more they find out, the more they then approach them in new ways to find out even more. Given things that they are studying are constantly changing. So we have what seems to be an anomaly. It actually is not, but it seems to be an anomaly in that things studied most continuously, astutely, and most earnestly are certain to undergo changes. It is true with reference to many other kinds of objects which one wishes to think of studying. We see things as very different kinds of objects today than they were thought of a century ago (Blumer 1976c).

## The Human Being as an Acting Organism

The human being must have a makeup that fits the nature of social interaction. The human being is seen as an organism that not only responds to others on the non-symbolic level but as one that makes indications to others and interprets their indications. He can do only this by virtue of possessing a self – he can be an object of his own action; recognize himself, for instance, as being a man, a student, a police-man, and so on; and act on the basis of the kind of object he is to himself. To become an object to himself, a person has to see himself from the outside – by placing himself in the position of others and viewing himself or acting towards himself from that position.

The roles the person takes range from that of discrete individuals (Mead's "play stage") through that of discrete organized groups (the "game stage") to that of the abstract community (the "generalized other"). In taking such roles, the person is in a position to address or approach himself – as in the case of a young girl who in "playing mother" talks to herself as her mother would do. We form objects of ourselves through such a process of role-taking. It follows that we see ourselves through the way in which others see or define us – or, more precisely, we see ourselves by taking one of the three types of roles of others that have been mentioned (Blumer 1986: 13).

If one is ready to engage in some kind of action which calls for the participation by another person in a given way and if that person does not respond and does not carry out the line of action which one's own line of action presupposes, one cannot account for what is going on by going back to motives or made-up social structures. Nor can one account for it by referring to the motives or whatever on the part of the other person, particularly as these people who are acting have to work out a relationship with each other.

In working out a relationship, people emerge with a mode of behavior that neither of them knew anything about before; knew nothing about to begin with; and had no idea about at all. It is something, in other words, that emerges as they interpret each other's behavior.

Consider participants who put themselves in the role of each other. Each is putting in the role of the other. That is quite true on the level of symbolic interaction. That has to take place. However, two things should be noted here in this matter of role-taking. First of all, the person may put himself in the role of the other person on a very shallow basis and to a limited extent.

For example, the superintendent of a factory tells a worker that he is laid off. The only extent to which he may take the role of that worker is in the form of receiving an order. This factory worker is going to pick up his check and not report to work the next day. On the other hand, the superintendent might, in telling that worker that he is laid off, form an image of what the effect of that layoff is going to have on that worker. He might, as I stated, think about the fact that that worker has got to go home and report to his wife that their income is severed. So the superintendent might, in a sense, take the role of that worker on a much more profound and a much more extended way.

This is the first point when one talks about "role-taking" which is when a person is taking the role of the other so that she/he is taking the role of the other usually in only the carrying out of his/her own act. Consequently, she/he need not be profound or extensive at all, and this provides the basis for so much of the ethical criticism that happens in group life. Take, for example, the labor reformer decrying this superintendent for his callousness in discharging people without giving any thought to the fact that that layoff is going to be adverse on the family life. Role-taking does make a difference. This varies enormously in terms of the levels or the depths of the roles that are taken by the participants in their association with one another. This can have a great deal of effect upon how they consequently act towards one another and respond to one another.

The second point about role-taking is that one can take the role of another but misinterpret that other person. Or one takes their role but makes a mistake in what he attributes to the other. That is really where the most difficulty lies, of course; namely, people, in attributing intentions to one another and in foreseeing the other's engaging in a given line of action, may go greatly astray. So, taking the role of the other should not be misunderstood in signifying that one takes the role of the other perfectly or profoundly. Indeed, if one look at our modern life, we encounter each other as strangers. We meet each other in ways that do not give us an opportunity (Blumer 1976c).

An even more important matter that stems from the fact that the human being has a self is that this enables him to interact with himself. This interaction is social – a form of communication, with the person addressing himself as a person and responding thereto. This self-interaction exists fundamentally as a process of making indications to oneself, a process that is in play continuously during one's waking life, as one notes and considers one or another matter.

Or observes or is aware of anything is equivalent to his indicating the thing to himself – he is identifying it as a given kind of object and considering its relevance or importance to his line of action. The human being interacts with itself through a social process of making indication to itself and responding upon those indications. The human being gets through this social process in a profound sense; the human being has to deal with what he notes and make an object of what he notes, give it a meaning, and use this meaning as the basis for directing his actions.

**The Nature of Human Actions**

The capacity of the human being to make indications to himself gives a distinctive character to human action. It means that the human individual confronts a world that he must interpret in order to act. He has to cope with the situations in which he is called on to act, ascertaining the meaning of the actions of others and mapping out his own line of action in the light of such interpretations. Fundamentally, action on the part of a human being consists of taking account of various things that he notes and forging a line of conduct on the basis of how he interprets them. The things taken into account cover such matters as his wishes and wants, his objectives, the available means for their achievement, the actions and anticipated actions of others, his image of himself, and the likely result of a given line of action. His conduct is formed and guided through such a process of indication and interpretation (Blumer 1986: 15–).

To the extent that the human being makes an object of something, he puts himself in the position of developing or controlling his action towards it. The very fact that he notes it is itself a suspension of the immediate response to it, and having noted it, he can then entertain the possibility of different ways of acting towards it.

If one observes water, one might ask oneself, "Shall I drink it or shall I not? Shall I use it to put into a balloon and throw water on people, test it in a laboratory?" Instead of water being an object, which the individual can designate to himself, it is rather something to which he responds, like the medium of air; we do not even make a notation of it. It is just more a matter of being responsive. We do not do anything about it. As soon as one notes it, one changes one's posture to it. It is that feature that Blumer brings out here.

There is a fundamental difference between, on one hand, an organism whose behavior is in the nature of a response to stimuli and, on the other hand, an organism pointing out objects and acting on the basis of the meaning of those objects. The fundamental difference is that in the latter case, the organism is putting himself in the position of acting differently towards the object, whereas in the former case, he just responds. The organism is automatically bound up in a definitive response that is set off by the stimulus. The very logic of the concept of stimulus-response is the effect that given the organism which is sensitized to respond in a certain way, the application of the given stimulus will just automatically call forth a given type of response. That is the logic of this scheme. The stimulus coerces the response based on the fact that the organism has an organization and is sensitized to respond in a certain way.

When one has an object, one also has a different relationship. When confronted with an object which the organism knows, it has put itself in the position of not just having a given action called forth but also having an object call forth the decision of what to do when:

> you get thirsty and you note you are thirsty. There may be water there at the water cooler, at the water tap. It does not mean that by getting thirsty you just go ahead and drink. In making an object of your thirst, you take things into account. You may decide to just wait awhile because it is not appropriate to drink; you are going to test yourself to see what kinds of heroic and stoic qualities you have; see how long you can control yourself before giving in. You can play with yourself this way. So what kind of an object will you make of a thing? You are very thirsty; there is water over there in the water cooler; you have been reading recently about the fact that the people who have been supplying water for water coolers have not been subjecting it to proper kinds of sterilization, so it is full of bacteria; therefore, you are not going to satisfy your thirst by drinking it. (Blumer 1976c)

There are all these kinds of designations and indications that one can make to oneself. There is a basic fundamental difference in the relationship as it exists between an organism and a stimulus on one hand and an object on the other hand. With an object one can do different things which means that one builds up one's conduct

Herbert Blumer Symbolic Interactionism

towards the objects. One can have human beings who are developing inanimate objects or what we might think of, from our point of view, as being quite imaginary objects. Yet they may be a form of significance in the life of those people as certain concrete things.

For example, the devil was an exceedingly important object to people living in Western Europe during the Middle Ages; it was an important object. But today, most people would say, "Oh, it's an imaginary creation." We have the same case in Rome. For people in that same period, the deity, God, was an object of the greatest kind of significance. If we polled the multitudes of people living in our current day and time, we would say the gods are quite a different kind of object. The important thing in the study of human behavior is to understand the nature of objects in the world of people. How do they see their objects? Those are the kind of objects one wants to get at. Their behavior is organized with regard to what they can designate (Blumer 1976c).

This view on human action applies equally to joint or collective action in which numbers of individual are implicated. This is what Blumer means as constituting the domain of sociological concern, as exemplified in the behavior of groups, institutions, organizations, and social class. Such instances of social behavior, whatever they may be, consist of individuals fitting their lines of action to one another.

## Interlinkage of Action

Human group life exists in the fitting of lines of action to each other by the members of the group. Such articulation of lines of action gives rise to and constitutes "joint action" – a societal organization of conduct of different acts of diverse participants. A joint action, while made up of diverse component acts that enter into its formation, is different from any one of them and from their mere aggregation. Joint action has a distinctive character in its own right, a character that lies in the articulation or linkage as apart from what may be articulated or linked. This is what we do when we speak of such things as marriage, a trading transaction, war, a parliamentary discussion, or a church service (1986: 17).

Similarly, we can speak of the collectivity that engages in joint action without having to identify the individual members of that collectivity, as we do in speaking of a family, a business corporation, a church, a university, a nation. But the understanding of collectivity and joint actions must be seen in relation to the single individual interlinked separate acts. Joint actions always have to undergo a process of formation; even though it may be a well-established and repetitive form of social action, each instance of it has to be formed anew. The participants still have to guide their respective acts by forming and using meanings.

Consequently, thinking of the act as something that is developed by him, Blumer (1976d) points out that an individual can have collectivities acting and they do act. It is very important to realize this. A group of people act together, as a group of individuals or family may decide to go to a motion picture show. They make indications to one another, guiding themselves collectively in that direction. A boy's gang can act as a group, business partners directing a firm can act as a group, and so on down the line. To make the picture even still clearer, we may have individuals who are essentially delegated to map out the lines of action of a huge collectivity, so, let us say an individual has a general staff in a major army preparing to combat an opposing army; the action is all mapped out in advance.

Collectivities, in other words, can be actors, and the formation of the acts of individuals can also apply to the acts of collectivities. They also have careers. They also are developed and worked out. They also are fashioned on the basis of things that are taken into account; they also may be stupid or intelligent because the actors may not size up correctly the situation in which they are; they do not take the right things into account. They fail to take given things into account and so forth.

Blumer's symbolic interactionism sees a human society as people engaged in living. Such living is a process of ongoing activity in which participants are developing lines of action in the multitudinous situations they are encountering. They are caught up in a vast process of interaction in which they have to fit their developing actions to one another. This process of interaction consists in making indications to others of what to do and in interpreting the indications as made by others. They live in a world of objects and are guided in their orientation and action by the meaning of these objects. They accordingly approach each other differently, live in different worlds, and guide themselves by different sets of meanings. Nevertheless, whether one is dealing with a family, a boy's gang, an industrial corporation, or a political party, one must see the activities of the collectivity as being formed through a process of designation and interpretation (1986: 20–).

## Methodological Principles of Empirical Science

The research approach demands a "naturalistic" method of investigation, to study the phenomenon of social life as they appear in their natural environment – in their everyday of life. The empirical social world is the world of everyday experience, the top layers of which we see in our lives and recognize in the lives of others. The researcher should strive to see the reality in the same way as the actors he is studying. To achieve this understanding, it could be necessary to live together with those people, participate in their daily routines, and expose oneself to the same experiences as those common in their life. The researcher should strive towards an "understanding of recognition" of their general view of the world – to get inside of the defining process of the actors in order to understand their actions.

Blumer sees collective or joint action as constituting the domain of sociological concern. To study larger social formations can be done by viewing these as joint actions and as peoples trying to fit their lines of actions to one another. It is both proper and possible to view and study such behavior in its joint or collective character instead of its individual components. Such joint behavior does not lose its character of being constructed through an interpretive process in meeting the situations in which the collectivity is called to act. Whatever the collectivity is an army

# Methodological Principles of Empirical Science

engaged in a campaign, a corporation seeking to expand its operations, or a nation trying to correct an unfavorable balance of trade, it needs to construct its action through an interpretation of what is happening in its area of operation. The interpretative process takes place by participants making indications to one another, not merely each to himself. Joint or collective action is an outcome of such a process of interpretative interaction (ibid. p. 16).

These large societal organizations or moral units are arrangements of people who are interlinked in their respective actions. The organization and interdependency are between such actions of people stationed at different points. At any point the participants are confronted by the organized activities of other people into which they have to fit their own acts. The concatenation of such actions taking place at the different points constitutes the organization of the given moral unit or large-scale area. A skeletonized description of this organization would be the same for symbolic interactionism as for the other approaches. However, in seeing the organization as an organization of actions, symbolic interactionism takes a different approach. Instead of accounting for the activity of the organization and its parts in terms of organizational principles or system principles, it seeks explanation in the way in which the participants define, interpret, and meet the situations at their respective points. The linking together of this knowledge of the concatenated actions yields a picture of the organized complex (ibid. p. 58).

An empirical science must presume the existence of an empirical world: that such a world is available to observation, studies, and analyses. The empirical world must be the point of origin in the study: that place of departure and that place where one always returns. It is upon this one has to make all the tests of the declarations one has on the empirical world. The "reality" to the empirical science only exists in the empirical world, can only be found here, and can only be verified there. The proper picture of empirical science is that of a collective quest for answers to questions directed to the resistant character of the given empirical world under study. One has to respect the obdurate character of that empirical world – this is indeed the cardinal principle of empirical science (ibid. p. 23).

Blumer (1976c) thinks that the definition of laws is important. If we define them in the same sense as they are spoken of in the case of physical sciences and biological sciences, then we have one sort of definition. There are two kinds of generalizations that are present in the instance of the physical and biological sciences.

One type of generalization would be the quantum mechanical law such as the law of falling bodies. It does not matter what the body is that is falling or the prescribed conditions present, such as the elimination of all air interference in a vacuum tube. One knows the story of a feather, which will fall just as rapidly or at the same rate of speed as will a lead ball. When one speaks of a law, it is not a proposition, which applies equally well to each and every member of the class to which the proposition is being indicated.

The other generalization, which tends to become increasingly more common in the case of the biological and physical sciences, is a statistical generalization. It is quite different in character because a statistical generalization does not apply equally well to every member in the array. The "class" that a statistical generalization refers to is what one calls an array. It is, by definition, a set, an assembly; actually an aggregate is a better term. It is an aggregate of individual instances. By definition they vary so that the statistical generalization applies or represents only the central tendency in the case of the array. It represents, in other words, a kind of relationship to something else. In that relationship, one has a central tendency of the array, which means that again, by definition, one has a great deal of variation of the instances in the array away from the central tendency. That is why a measure of certain standard deviation has been produced to give some idea of the nature of the spread of one's array.

In other words, in the case of a statistical generalization, it is not possible. It is just not possible to extend a generalization that one has for that array. All one can do is to extend it to the random instances of the array. Logically, what this means is that just to the extent to which one finds out more about any instance in the array, it ceases to be random. To this extent, the generalization does not apply. Or to out the matter another way, the generalization applies in the case of statistical generalization; it applies to those instances, which are of the point of central tendency. One cannot use that to cover the instances, which deviate from that central tendency. One may ask, is that a law? Is a statistical proposition a law? One can call it a law. It is not a law at all in a way that is true of the first kind of generalization. It is the kind of generalization that we associate with physical mechanics.

As to having a law or laws in sociology, Blumer's only disposition would be to state that aside from a mere uttering of platitudes, there are no laws. He would say there is *primary knowledge* in the social sciences. Regrettably, this is not sufficiently appreciated, as it comes in the form of *principles*. There is a difference here. The principle is an assertion, which represents a logical relation, which need not, however, be found in the individual empirical cases with which one may be concerned. Consequently, to make a statement such as "people who recognize that they are being insulted develop resentment or feel resentment" would be a principle. A lot of individuals who would be insulted would never disclose or would never show any resentment. Others, who are insulted, as they reflect upon the insult, may be led to define it in such a way. Think of the person who is acting irrationally and therefore should not be taken seriously.

One can have a principle; from that principle, one can even presuppose something of the nature of a uniform and consistent type of action. That principle is probably the major form which knowledge takes in the case of the discipline. One can have statistical generalizations there. Statistical generalizations are almost inevitably relationships, which are peculiar to a given time and to a given place. Consequently, one does not have the possibilities of extension and application of these, as is true in the case of principles.

In the field, for example, in the employment of the statistical procedure in quantitative or statistical research, one will note that what is actually being gotten at is an effort to establish a relationship between two or more variables. But these two or more variables are imbedded in a particular kind of time-space phenomenon. Any relationship that one comes up with can be invalid by the time the next situation arises.

If one declares, for example, that inflation is an independent variable, which is accompanied by divorce as a dependent variable in the USA during a period from 1960 to 1975, then one can work out a statistical relationship. The data that one has is verified and validated. What one comes up with is a correlation between two time series. But that is a statement that one would not be in a position to project outward to a situation where one has a society that is heavily imbedded in a type of religion, which frowns upon or discourages divorce. One would not do it.

One's statistical generalization is essentially bound by time and space. They apply to a restricted sort of domain. This does not invalidate them as applied to that domain. But students in the field ought not to deceive themselves into thinking that in undertaking quantitative studies of this sort, their endeavors to establish a statistical relationship of three and one in so-called independent or dependent variables or a series of either with regard to the other are arriving at something that approximates a condition of law.

Inflation can be seen as an example of a principle. It is a discouraging influence in family life. One treats this fact as a principle. In other words, one is making a declaration that inflation is a disorganizing influence in family life. As a principle, one would expect that the principle would work in any society in which inflation is operating without presupposing the degree of destructiveness that would be involved or the forms that it would take. It is the principle. Principles can be exceedingly valuable if they are true and if they are sustained. A principle is the type of knowledge, which probably comes closest to representing what is genuine scientific knowledge. A principle is an approximation of general and scientific knowledge in the field. It comes closer to an approximation than what is represented by statistical propositions. It certainly is much closer than what is represented by mechanical laws because we have no mechanical laws in the social sciences.

## In Summary

We shall try to summarize some of the ontological and epistemological characteristics of the Lifeworld tradition and of science. In other words, what is the reality we are talking of, when we try to understand social science phenomena from this; how do we get it; and what to do with the results? We will outline the main features and show the basic relations and some of the consequences.

The history of the Lifeworld and subjectivism go long time back in the history of philosophy, but in relation to social science, it starts with I. Kant and his discussion of consciousness and the subject's experience of reality. The different traditions from here all have common roots in a subjectivistic ontology and epistemology, and they all in some way start from the Lifeworld. They are, however, different and in some points disagree on how to understand man and reality. They have a commonality that they deal with and start from man's construction of everyday life reality. They agree on the criticism of positivistic and rationalistic sciences, ontology, and epistemology. The common feature (especially in phenomenology) is the thought

176      5 Mead and Blumer: Social Theory and Symbolic Interactionism

that you cannot distinguish between the consciousness and that which conscious-ness is about, subject and object. This is due to the active, spontaneous, and inten-tional character of consciousness. They have been developed for different traditions, as regards the choice of perspectives, which phenomena they deal with, as well as development of methods.

## *Science*

In the subjectivism paradigm, there is a common fundamental attitude to the focus-ing and linking of science: philosophy, the ontological assumptions and understand-ings that all human activity is based upon; philosophy of science, the epistemological recognition and discussion that everyone must do in understanding reality and the phenomena in focus, that is, leaving the natural attitude and entering the scientific reflection; methodology, as qualitative understanding and recognition of subjects and phenomena in focus; and the Lifeworld, as an empirical reality is one that is interested in, as lived everyday reality.

There is a fundamental conception of how to theorize. Empirical discussions have to be understood in relation to an ontological and epistemological discussion as a reflection on life for being, understanding, and self-understanding. The subjec-tivistic discussion thus starts from and discusses the concepts of intentionality (the consciousness discussion of the subject-object relation), understanding (to being in everyday life and scientific cognition), intersubjectivity (the subject-subject rela-tion), the Lifeworld (everyday life and being), and methodology (understanding qualitative investigation of meaning and being). Schutz's (1973b: 56 and 126) dis-cussion of demands on the structure of models and understanding of the social real-ity can be seen as relevant to understanding the Lifeworld in science. He categorizes this in three basic principles or demands:

(a) **The demand for logical consistency**. The system of typical structures drawn up by the research worker must be established with the largest extent of clear-ness and precision in the frame of concepts implicated and must be fully com-patible with the principles of formal logic. The fulfillment of this demand guarantees the objective validity of the objects of thought constructed by the research worker. Their strictly logical character is one of the most essential features with which scientific objects of thought differ from the objects of thought constructed by common sense thinking in everyday life which they are to replace. In other words, a logically connected system implies that the means-goal relations together with the system of constant motives and the system of life plans must be constructed in such a way that (a) it is and remains uncontra-dicted by the principles of formal logic; (b) all its elements are drafted in full clearness and precision; and (c) it only contains scientifically verifiable assump-tions which must be totally uncontradicted by all our scientific knowledge.

In Summary                                                                                          177

(b) **The demand for subjective interpretation**. The research worker must, to explain human action, ask which model can be constructed by an individual consciousness and which typical content must be ascribed to it in order to explain the observed facts as a result of such an activity of consciousness in an understandable relation. The acceptances of this demand guarantee the possibility of referring all kinds of human action or its result to the subjective meaning that such an action or its result has to the actor.

(c) **The demand for adequacy**. Any expression in a scientific model referring to human action must be constructed in such a way that a human act carried out in the Lifeworld by an individual actor in the way which is indicated by the typical structure is rational and understandable to the actor himself, as well as to his fellow men in the common sense interpretation of everyday life. This demand is of the greatest importance to social scientific methodology since it makes possibly for social science to refer to events in the Lifeworld. The methodological interpretation of the research worker of any human act must correspond with that of the actor or his partner. Accordance with this principle therefore guarantees the consistency of the structures of the research worker with structures in the common sense experience of social reality.

The structure of the social world is before all not the random act of the scientist, which he can perform at discretion. This occurs because (1) there are historical limits to his fields of science which any research worker has inherited from his ancestors as a stock of recognized statements (cf. the discussion of paradigm, Chap. 3). (2) The demand for adequacy requires that the typical structure is no more contradicted by the totality of our everyday life experiences than by our scientific experiences. It is therefore a misunderstanding of the essential character of science to think that it deals with reality, if we consider the everyday Lifeworld to be the pattern of reality. Neither the world of the natural scientist nor that of the social research worker is more or less real than the worlds of thinking can be in common. But it is the real home for these important events and performances which, at all times, humanity has called culture (Schutz 1973b: 129).

## *Weber and Ideal Types*

One example of how to theorize is Weber's discussion of what an empirical cultural science can do, and how it can get status as science, and shall be seen in his discussion of treating communes or social groups as individuals. That is through Weber's (1948, 1977: 139) discussion of the ideal type. Ideal types can, for example, be seen in relation to the investigation of institutions and how they influence social actions. Weber's starting point in this is a criticism of the positivistic search for lawfulness. He writes (in 1904):

> The "abstract"-theoretical method even today shows unmediated and ostensibly irreconcilable cleavage from empirical-historical research. The proponents of this method recognize

in a thoroughly correct way the methodological impossibility of supplanting the historical knowledge of reality by the formulation of laws, or vice versa, of constructing "laws" in the rigorous sense through the mere juxtaposition of historical observations. Now in order to arrive at these laws – for they are certain that science should be directed towards these as its highest goal – they take it to be a fact that we always have a direct awareness of the structure of human actions in all their reality. Hence – so they think – science can make human behavior directly intelligible with axiomatic evidentness and accordingly reveal its laws. The only exact form of knowledge – the formulation of immediately and intuitively *evident* laws – is however at the same time the one which offers access to events which have not been directly observed. Hence, at least as regards the fundamental phenomena of economic life, the construction of a system of abstract and therefore purely formal propositions analogous to those of the exact natural sciences, is the only means of analyzing and intellectually mastering the complexity of social life. In spite of the fundamental methodological distinction between historical knowledge and the knowledge of "laws" which the creator of the theory drew as the *first* and *only* one, he now claims empirical *validity*, in the sense of the *deducibility* of reality from "laws", for the propositions of abstract theory. (Weber 1948: 87)

Weber (1977: 138, 1948: 89–) thinks that the abstract economic theory can only give us an example of the syntheses which are named "ideas" of historical phenomena. It offers us an ideal picture of events on the commodity-market under conditions of a society organized on the principles of an exchange economy, free competition, and rigorously rational conduct. This conceptual pattern brings together certain relationships and events of historical life into a complex, which is conceived as an internally consistent system.

Substantively, this construct in itself is like a utopia that has been arrived at by the analytical accentuation of certain elements of reality. Its relationship to the empirical data consists solely in the fact that where market-conditioned relationships of the type refereed to by the abstract construct are discovered or suspected to exist in reality to some extent, we can make the characteristic features of this relationship pragmatically clear and understandable by reference to an ideal type. When focusing on superior features like institutions (e.g., capitalism, religion, bureaucracy), the use of ideal types is a way to bring a conceptual order into that which Weber called "the chaos of reality."

Ideal types are conceptual abstractions, the pure core or the central feature, which we use in the attempt to understand the complexity in the social world. They do not exist in their pure form in the social world, and they can only be regarded as a description of and basis for an investigation, and certainly not as understanding of social actions and subjective meanings.

Weber suggests that ideal type is to be used as a kind of yardstick against which to compare ends evaluate empirical cases. The discrepancies between the ideal type and the factual forms of the institution or behavior pattern being investigated thus become the object of theoretical interest. The aim is to show the nature and extent of variation between our ideal type and particular cases of these phenomena (Parkin 1982: 29).

Ideal types thus have a heuristic value, as they render visible and make us understand the phenomena in reality. To research, Weber (1977: 139) thinks, this implies the ideal typical concept, a development of the ability of thoughtfulness: the ideal type is no hypothesis but indicates the direction of advancement of hypotheses; it is no presentation of reality but gives unique means of expression to the presentation.

The task in research is to determine how close or how far away from this ideal picture is reality lying, but it is not a picture that has an empiric parallel. Ideal types are subjective constructions. They are (necessary) research tools where they are both an abstraction from reality and at the same time help us to understand it. Ideal types are not goals in themselves but a means.

With this Weber (1948: 72) says that all knowledge about reality is always knowledge from a special perspective and that no absolute "objective" scientific analysis exists which is independent of special and "one-sided" viewpoints according to which – expressly or tacitly, consciously or unconsciously – they are selected, analyzed, and organized for expository purposes. Ideal types and ideas, in the meaning associations, thus are to be seen as illustrations of reality, dependent on the perspective and the aim. That, which Weber maintains as the goal of research, is knowledge about the cultural meanings of specific historical connections as the one and only goal, also to the conceptualizing and concept critical research. Weber's conception that social science shall be value-free must be seen on this background.

Weber proclaims that the social sciences must abstain from value judgments. He took up the battle against those political and moral ideologies which all too easily influence the judgment of the social scientist, whether this influence is conscious or not. In the same vein, he defined the task of sociology not as metaphysical speculation but as the simple and accurate description of life in society. To him sociology is no longer the philosophy of human existence. It is the particular science of human behavior and its consequences (Schutz 1972: 5).

## Traditions: An Overview

We shall outline here persons who in some way are inspired by each other. This can be seen as an overview of part of the tradition, and it shows that this science tradition is not new but has existed for many years, however not within business economics. During the latest 10–20 years published work has appeared which in some way discusses science as interpretation with business economics. But not in any ontological and epistemological perspective are these notions related to the Lifeworld discussed (Fig. 5.1).

The Lifeworld tradition in science is of course not so limited and simple as this outline indicates, and the lines and arrows indicate only ideas and discussions over time, and not a direct influence in thinking and writings. The outline is in no way fully adequate and only contains some of the prominent persons to whom we attach great importance. These persons have also written works which can be placed differently (e.g., Weber, Simmel, Heidegger, Gadamer), or they may have other names (e.g., Schutz is named as an existential phenomenologist or sociological phenomenologist). Other traditions of cognition and thinking have of course inspired than those outlined here. This is, for example, reflected in Kant's thinking and background of thoughts, in Hegel's dialectics, in (young) Marx's dialectics and praxis, as well as in the pragmatic American philosophers Dewey, James, and Colley.

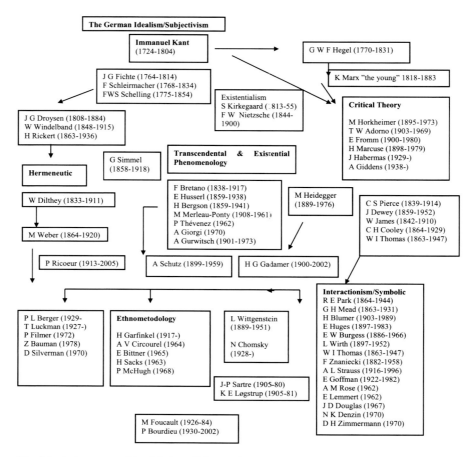

**Fig. 5.1** A chart over subjectivistic traditions and persons – some examples of Lifeworld thinking and movement (lifetime/year for central contributions)

In most cases people do not discuss a tradition as such, but a phenomenon, where they base commentary and develop theory upon a criticism or partly in continuation of others' earlier works. They seldom name themselves as being one thing or the others. Often scholars have an extremely complex body of works so that it is difficult both to interpret these works and to find a common philosophic line. In the outline there are both "pure" philosophers, i.e., those who exclusively dealt with the thinking and ontological and epistemological questions, for example, Kant, Husserl, and Heidegger. Most of them both discuss ontological and epistemological questions related to a specific empirical Lifeworld, for example, Schutz, Gadamer, Berger, and Luckman. There are others who can clearly be connected to one tradition or a school, for example, the Frankfurter School and critical theory (Horkheimer, Adorno, Fromm, Habermas), the Chicago School and symbolic interactionism (Park, Mead, Blumer), and ethnomethodology (Garfinkel, Cicourel, Bittner, McHugh).

In Summary 181

What makes us consider those scholars' thinking and work for a subjectivistic tradition called the subjectivism paradigm is that, to a great extent, they draw on the same persons and thoughts: especially on Kant, Dilthey, Weber, Husserl, Heidegger, and later on Mead and Blumer, Schutz, and Gadamer. Each starts from the central and general philosophical tradition, with an everyday life as reality. But they also criticize the objectivistic ontology and the notion of science, placing themselves very much in agreement as to the nature of the problems. Heidegger, for example, pictures the being of man as a being in the world, as a being out close to the things. Philosophical hermeneutics link directly to this notion, especially analyzing what it is saying the being of man is a historical being (cf. Wind 1976: 180).

Some of those that we will link also with the criticism of the positivistic and objectivistic tradition but espouse the formulation of hermeneutics are Dilthey and Weber, and later Gadamer. However, Gadamer cannot be seen in direct continuation of Dilthey and Weber, having a different and more existential interpretation of the issues of hermeneutics. He can rather be seen in continuation of Heidegger and in relation to the sociological phenomenology of Merleau-Ponty and Schutz. However, Gadamer is still a hermeneutic in the sense that he is interested in some of the same questions as Dilthey and Weber. For example, Gadamer is interested in understanding everyday life and historical understanding, but with focus on *the being* of man and understanding that. This may be seen as a manifestation of the turn that takes place within hermeneutics with Gadamer, away from historical understanding to a philosophically existential approach to *the being* and to social science.

The task of hermeneutics is traditionally understanding and interpretation, especially historical understanding of phenomena and events. But through the criticism contributing to the foundation of hermeneutics in a social scientific context, we must also have a discussion of science and methodology. This can be seen in Dilthey and Weber's formulation that man must be studied as a man and that social science must inevitably be a social human science. Dilthey calls it "a Science of Geist (spirit)" (*Geisteswissenschaften*) (cf. Lübcke 1994a: 27) and Weber (1948: 67) "a cultural science," and through Gadamer's formulation of man as a "historical being," with understanding and experience as the central issues. Hermeneutics shall be understood as being philosophical, among others, through the universality concepts of Gadamer, who tries to discuss the more general view that is not philosophy as system thinking and universal.

The principal interest and discussion in phenomenology is that phenomenology is the study of essences; and according to it, all problems amount to finding definitions of essences: the essence of perception, or the essence of consciousness, for example. But phenomenology is also a philosophy that puts essences back to existence, and does not expect to arrive at an understanding of man and the world from any starting point other that of their "facticity." It is a transcendental philosophy that places in abeyance the assertions arising out of the natural attitude, the better to understand them. But it is also a philosophy for which the world is always "already there" before reflection begins – as an inalienable presence; and all its efforts are concentrated upon re-achieving a direct and primitive contact with the world and endowing that contact with a philosophical status. It is the search for a philosophy which shall be a "rigorous science," but it also offers an account of space, time, and the world as we "live" them (Merleau-Ponty 1994: vii).

A person who is counted among the sociological phenomenologists is Alfred Schutz, as he tried to develop an everyday life sociology based on a transcendental phenomenology. Schutz (cf. 1973a, b, 1978a) considered himself to be a phenomenologist, with philosophical background inspired by Husserl. In the first place he was a sociologist and tried to develop Husserl's philosophical ideas and use them for a scientific study of social life with his theories on the phenomenology of social life and an interpretive sociology. At the same time Schutz derived from Weber's work about social action and understanding of social reality, both in relation to a criticism and to a further development of some of Weber's ideas and problems.

Schutz's criticism was primarily directed towards Weber's lack of ontological discussion of understanding (*Verstehen*), action (*Handeln*), and subjective meaning (*gemeinter Sinn*). He also noted Weber's failure to see social life in being understood as a reality that is both an intersubjective reality and a multiple reality. Other sources of inspiration to Schutz were Henri Bergson, Aron Gurwitsch, and Dorian Cairns (phenomenologists, from Schutz's period in the USA) but also George H. Mead and social psychology. Schutz can, however, also be seen in relation to the discussions and conceptions of Merleau-Ponty and Gadamer on everyday life reality and the Lifeworld and on a social science as a science aiming at understanding the experiences and actions in this world of human beings. But he can also be seen in relation to Mead and his discussion of interaction and the concept of the generalized other.

Our world is an interactionistic everyday life sociology.

# Part II
# Science of Economics Through Linguistics

# Chapter 6
# The Study of Qualitative Economics

Students, academics, and practitioners of economics are often exposed to and then taught to learn theories and methods that have little or no resemblance to everyday life. Nevertheless, for a variety of reasons (as discussed in Chap. 3 in the understanding of philosophy of science and paradigms), economics from neo-classical roots through to the current "supply-side" macro- and microeconomic applications have been steadfast for several decades.

This updated second edition book from a decade ago (2008) challenges the western nation, historical, and conventional core of the philosophical basis for economics into how it has evolved today. In short, this book creates a new perspective for economics that is based on a different paradigm and nothing short of an intellectual revolution for the "field of economics" itself. The evidence of this in Green Development Paradigm (Mandarin) from Clark and Cooke with two Chinese PhD co-authors (2014) and another book by just Clark and Cooke titled Green Industrial Revolution (2015).

Now 2018, there is also the concept that has been enacted in the EU and will be soon in China, called *circular economics* which will be discussed in other chapters and is in the Appendix as a paper by Clark with a co-author from Milan, Italy. QE is considered a significant factor in all of the areas that are part of CE.

Our basic arguments rest in the philosophical roots of economics. Historically, while the neo-classical approach to economics followed the objectivist philosophical tradition, another paradigm existed but was ignored. This volume revealed in Part I another philosophical tradition (subjectivism) which was ignored for decades. In the subjectivist roots, we find another, revealing, deeper understanding of economics. In Part II, we explore these philosophical roots with specific details and case study data from economics and its application in business, politics, and everyday life.

One of the few, and very refreshing, early contemporary perspectives on economics that recognizes the inherent "comatose nature" of the discipline as the "dismal science" was Buchholz (1989) who examines "new ideas from dead economists." Buchholz, trained as an attorney, was a professor at the Kennedy School at Harvard

© Springer Nature Switzerland AG 2019
W. W. Clark II, M. Fast, *Qualitative Economics*,
https://doi.org/10.1007/978-3-030-05937-8_6

185

and became a policy advisor to President George Bush (1989–1991) and now in private practice in San Diego, CA. Buchholz reviews some contemporary books in economics through the mid-1990s (Economist, July 19, 1997a). There he pointed out how scholars were finding new concepts and trends in economics' history. However, Buchholz finds specific kernels of concepts from economics' past intellectual philosophical founders that are useful for today's field of qualitative economics.

In other words, upon close historical and philosophical examination, a number of good ideas over the last three decades in economic historical literature can be derived from past economic scholars and philosophers, which can be applied to the world today, as Clark did in 2013 and then with *The Next Economics* (2014) book. And then Fast and Clark continued with other publications in peer-reviewed journals on qualitative economics (2012, 2014). Both authors teamed up with other scholars and researchers for more papers and book chapters on the application of QE such as Clark and Li in book chapter about "The Political-Economics of the Green Industrial Revolution: Renewable Energy as the Key to National Sustainable Communities" (2009) and "The Political-Economics of the Green Industrial Revolution: Renewable Energy as the Key to National Sustainable Communities" (2013).

Buchholz argued that not enough emphasis is paid to the ideas and insights from these philosophical and historical scholars. Instead, they are overlooked because too much attention is spent on economic pressures and special business or political interests today for statistical measurement and quantitative variables that support one point of view or another. In short, economic data, analyses, and conclusions have become the tools and support for particular political agendas and business objectives. Statistics can be manipulated and reported to justify predetermined end goals.

In modern times and especially since the end of World War II, two opposing approaches to economics have emerged from the fields historical and philosophical roots: one is rooted in the objectivistic tradition of social sciences which was explored in Part I, *Positivism/Empiricism*, as the physical approach to reality, and *Rationalism*, as the mental approach to reality. This volume presents a different perspective: Lifeworld whose basis is presented in concrete and specific terms that form the basis of economics becoming a science. Each chapter then explores how a science of economics works in terms of examples, cases, and scientific inquiry.

While all economic paradigmatic models are not reviewed in this volume, the intent here is to explore the details of how the subjectivist historical philosophical tradition influenced phenomenology, symbolic interactionism, and linguistics and thus would create the foundation for a new economic perspective and paradigm today. In short, having covered the traditional and conventional roots for the dominant neo-classical objectivist paradigm in economics today, this volume argues for a different Lifeworld perspective. It is in this other paradigm that interactionism fits and hence is the basis for creating a science of economics as seen in the parallel field of theoretical linguistics.

Consider first, however, a standard conventional definition of economics from Heilbroner:

# 6 The Study of Qualitative Economics

> Economics is essentially the study of a process we find in all human societies – "the" economic problem is simply *the process of providing for the material well-being of society*. In its simplest terms, economics is the study of how mankind earns its daily bread. (1989: 1, emphasis in original)

The founder of modern objectivist economics, Adam Smith (republished 1937), in the sense that his theories established the field itself, reflects the same perspective. It was Smith, after all, who set the standard to which almost all discussions start, noted in *The Wealth of Nations* that:

> A certain propensity in human nature... the propensity to truck, barter, and enhance one thing for another.

In other words, to Smith and his contemporaries today, economics depends on countable or quantifiable things (good and services). However, Heilbroner (1989: 17) points out that Smith's real insight concerns the notion of the "exchange act" as the central part of economic life. Transaction cost analysis begins to examine the economic exchange process, as we will explore in subsequent chapters, but fails to capture the everyday life of business interaction.

Exchange, however, when viewed as symbolic interaction, becomes a central focal point of our perspective. While Smith never defined exchange as interaction between people, the symbolic interaction perspective does. As such, economics can be better described, understood, and even predictable. Unfortunately, most economists in the USA, the UK, and other western industrialized nations do define exchange as only quantifiable.

Heilbroner outlines three approaches that economists use in trying to understand society: (1) tradition economy in which society operates as it had since the beginning of its recorded history; (2) command economy whereby a single authority would dictate all activity; and (3) market economy from which modern industrial states arouse. While Heilbroner notes that both traditional and command aspects of an economy are present in today's industrialized western states, his basic premise is that the modern industrial state, as historically developed by Adam Smith and others, rests only the market economy approach.

There is no argument with the premise of the "market." However, there is an important distinction with the "market" being the only factor in economics. What is being challenged in this volume is the underlying historical and philosophical assumptions which lead to *only* the market as being *the* approach and perspective of economics. The subjectivist paradigm argues that this market economy approach is made to the detriment of any other approaches that might give a different theoretical meaning to the exchange act as interaction. In short, the notion of a market economy or by extension the free market is either not defined or ill-defined as to be meaningless (Jones et al. 1998).

One of the basic reasons discussed in Part I, for using subjectivism or interactionism in economics, is the exploration of what a market is and how it operates. In short, there is a need to define it. Such an investigation leads directly into socioeconomic approaches to business. In that context, scholars and practitioners alike can explore new business development and the role of networks in terms of people and organizations among other areas connected to economics. Even more significantly, economics if it is to be science cannot be just objective with the focus upon structures and variables. Reality is not that way. Subjectivism is first in the form of theory, hypotheses, and analyses. Then experiments and trail runs become the objective measurement or proof of the theories and hypotheses. And from the beginning, science requires that terms, words, and numbers are defined. How else can they make sense and result in analysis, further tests, and predictions?

## Economics Studies: The Case of Business

Several economic trends and areas focus upon business, especially with Porter (1980, 1990), which argues that companies and nations have competitive advantages, if they follow certain linear "objective" courses of action. Porter identifies five forces that constitute the two competitive advantages for firms. Some business development practitioners then apply Porter's notion of "business clusters," where firms co-locate due to common business interests and to economic and urban planning (Dalum 1995; Hinton et al. 1997).

Later, Porter and van der Linde (1995) note that governmental environment regulations can result in an industry being even more competitive in the global marketplace. Other scholars, especially Saxenian (1994), argue that competitive advantage can be seen regionally, as she compared the high-tech areas of Silicon Valley in California to Route #128 around Boston. Her work identified a number of elements (e.g., from lifestyle to venture capital) that distinguished Silicon Valley from Boston's Route #128 and hence made it far more competitive and ultimately successful than the Boston area.

By identifying the characteristics of a region, economic analysts try to build models and economic programs for any region. This was the emphasis in California for its economic development as a result of "defense conversion" (Clark 1995a, b, c, d) during the early 1990s and the purpose of designing a State Economic Strategic Plan first issued in 1996 and revised every 2 years. Unfortunately, most of the analyses and policy recommendations take the "business cluster model" and apply it in all industrial cases at one point in time. The value of the "industrial cluster" concepts tends to be overemphasized and are purported to be predetermined and systematically installed in select communities.

Business networks that evolve over time (Håkansson 1994; Håkansson and Snehota 1994; Sorensen 1993; Sørensen and Nedergaard 1993; Jones et al. 1997), for example, are far more likely to result in business development. The empirical evidence is beginning to arise on networks in both Silicon Valley and Boston. A study by Boston Bank (1997) traced the affiliation or networks from MIT faculty and students on business development in general (beyond the Boston region). Clark et al. (2004b) had proposed a more targeted and detailed study of engineering graduates and faculty from the University of California system on regional economic development.

Ironically, as Silicon Valley in the San Francisco Bay Area became the global center for the IT economic and business revolution, the "dot.com" growth in businesses in the late 1990s, also evolved into the "dot.bombs" only a few years later in the early part of the twenty-first century. Silicon Valley has now started another global rebirth in a technological area that it barely recognized until Al Gore's film "An Inconvenient Truth" won an Academy Award (2007) and worldwide attention again as he was awarded the Nobel Prize along with the 2000+ scientists who produced the Intergovernmental Panel on Climate Change Reports (IPCC∗).[1]

While public awareness is now enhanced and spread globally by Gore's film and others, such as Leonardo DiCaprio's "The 11th Hour" (2007), these films do not provide solutions. Advocates of "clean technology" do try to do that and now is the current buzzword position with venture capital companies who see this new "space" or investment sector as both extremely profitable and a solution to global warming and climate change. The endorsers for Clark's second edition of his first book on *Agile Energy Systems* (Clark 2004a, b, c, d, 2017a) that only focused on the nation-state of California are key people in California and globally who are directly involved in how to have both on-site power distributed (via solar, wind and geothermal systems) and central grid energy (use of wind farms on land and in the ocean, solar farms, run of river, and hydropower dams) systems.

It is exactly here that qualitative economics emerges. Case in point is Silicon Valley entrepreneurial successes and the growth of venture capital, social networks, and relationships, mostly surrounding Stanford University and the University of California, Berkeley, but also State Universities like San Jose and San Francisco, where former students met one another and faculty continued to be "mentors" in the new businesses. Moreover, the issues historically and today with the growth of "clean technologies" also need definition. Later there will be more in-depth discussion on this issue, but there is a vast difference between "clean" and "green" technologies (Clark et al. 2006). Today, Silicon Valley does not see or understand that. Hence there is Silicon Beach in Southern California just south of the city of Santa Monica.

In short, there is a need to understand and define what causes global warming and then the solutions to it. In those discussions, there then emerges the definition and meaning of clean vs. green. Clean technologies are usually defined (and funded from VC funds and the US federal government) as natural gas, clean coal, and even nuclear power. None of these are environmental friendly and benign. All are continuing the global dependency on fossil fuels and other dangerous energy materials that continue to harm the planet and threaten humankind.

Green technologies are based on renewable energy generation such as solar, wind, ocean waves, geothermal, "run of the river," and biomass among others. While the economics of these green technologies are not yet comparable with the fossil and nuclear fuels, they are getting there fast. Now in 2018, these green technologies are often far less expensive than fossil fuels and nuclear power. But even more

---

[1] Co-author Clark was one of the 1000+ scientists where for the Third UNIPPC, he was co-author of Chapter 3 (Financial Structures) and co-editor for Chapter 4 (Legal and Business Structures).

significantly, when green technologies are compared to so-called clean technologies, the cost of fuel is zero, externalities such as impact on health and the environment are zero, and the stranded costs for plants, systems, and equipment are far less than clean technologies. The new potential "clean tech bomb culture" in Silicon Valley and Silicon Beach is based upon this lack of qualitative economic analyses.

Thus the "green tech culture" as in Silicon Valley has become a now oft-used concept for many business professionals in economics. While there is a vast literature on the concept of culture as it applies to economics, consider one current that has gained considerable acceptance both within the field of economics and among business people. A special issue of *Organization Science* (1995) was devoted to "culture industries." In this usage of the term culture, the editors applied the concept to those creative industries such as the arts, music, and film. Jones and Hesterly (1995) examine the film industry in that light. Some of that data will be referenced in the chapters below since one of the authors had been involved in the entertainment industry.

Jones and now others argue that the "culture industries" are really like any growing SME (small medium-sized enterprise) or entrepreneurial dynamic industry such as computers, telecommunications, and semiconductors, among others. However, the use of culture industries is clearly a misnomer, since the concern of culture has more to do with history and is not usually with any new industries, which are based on creativity and innovation. Silicon Valley has emerged, and other regions throughout the world attempt to copy it, as creating its own unique "innovative culture." In that sense and meaning, "culture industries" have meaning. Saxenian (1994) verified that premise in her classic study contrasting Silicon Valley to Route #128 around Boston. Since then, she and other scholars have documented the same phenomenon globally.

From another perspective on culture, Hofstede argues in two books (1980a, 1991) that countries or regions must be seen and understood in terms of their "inherent cultures" (1991: 4). People have constructed "mental programs" which are "patterns of thinking, feeling, and acting" that are learned from one's environment. When people are in a group, they form a culture or "collective phenomenon," wherein groups of people are distinguished from other groups due to their learned patterns (ibid., p. 5). He models that idea on computer programs and even uses the computer jargon in the title, "software of the mind."

Hofstede in the functional objectivist tradition follows the conventional understanding of culture that most social scientists do as well, when he argues that there are both characteristics of culture and attributes for entire countries that can be measured quantitatively. In short, he reduces culture to a series of quantifiable input variables. Culture, while operating on multi-levels, is simply a black box in which measurable variables are inputted with expected outputs at the results. The problem is that culture is not simply learned, but is also inherited and also a matter of interpretation and situation. While we will not engage in this larger genetic debate, the issue is that the individual and his or her culture are not a *tabula rasa*.

Gullestrup (1994) presents a theory of human interaction within cultures that operate as if a culture is a concentrate circle on a vertical plain. In other words, culture appears to be defined within one plain within certain boundaries. Aside from the theoretical constraints and considerations for this view of culture, the fact that human group life does interact within certain perimeters is a useful notion. Nevertheless, it should not be limited by this more functional approach to culture. Soderberg (1996) argues that when firms are acquired across national boundaries, the particular national cultures will clash. She attempts to understand why. Her analyses target "relations" within the cultural circles described by Gullestrup.

The problem inherent in these studies and attempts to conceptualize microeconomics data to macroeconomics theory is in basic definitions and meanings of concepts. In short, the knowledge base of concepts is not well defined. Consider the notion of "relations" from Soderberg. The concept is nowhere defined in her paper, and when queried, she had difficulty defining the concept. While this is typical problem with scholarly papers, the need to define "relations" was not meant to diminish the work but only to enhance it. The reason is clear. The concept of relations within defined cultural settings such as the firm from Soderberg is parallel, if not further differential, than that of interactions between actors.

If relations, instead, can be seen within multilayers of culturally bounded circles, then the concept has specific and dynamic meaning. For example, the relational interaction between the CEO of a firm being acquired by another from another nation is very revealing. One could imagine that the CEO and the new owners must define the meanings of their new relationship, roles, and responsibilities. However, one can also imagine that relations between the new owners and that of the other employees who work for the acquired company must be examined.

In other words, there are at least two concentric cultural circles operating within the workplace described by Soderberg. Equally important there are a number of cultural concentric circles operating outside the workplace that further complicate and define relations. These cultural circles include the family, community, and other firms, among many others that intersect. All these cultural circles further compose the actor's arena of interactivity towards any situation or event. What concerns us here is the elaboration on these interactions and how they impact the innovative process for new businesses. None of these concepts appear in Soderberg or the literature.

Again the problem with such analyses is that they are projected and perpetrated on businesses causing severe problems and misunderstandings. Hofstede even speculates that there may be more to culture than his functionalistic model when he notes that superficial manifestations of culture (e.g., fashion, entertainment, leaders, values, etc.) are sometimes mistakes since they are overlooked in "the deeper, underlying level of values, which moreover determine the meaning of people for their practices" (Hofstede 1991: 181).

Hofstede and others only conduct quantitative research into these underlying values and thus indeed miss this important point. Meanings in an actor's everyday life are derived from their situations and interactions, which cannot be quantified, as they are qualitative, by their very nature. It is precisely the point of this book to explore these deeper meanings of everyday business interactions. In order to understand everyday business life, basic fundamental concepts, situations and events, and the symbolic interaction between actors must be described, analyzed, and explained.

Another economic development approach is advocated by Castells and Hall (1994), after considerable study of successful high-tech areas or geographical regions in Europe. The authors conclude that the success of these high-tech areas or "technopoles" rests on their combined and linked dedication to research and educational and industrial development in one geographical location.

Among others, they cite the success of Sophia Antipolis (known locally as CERAM GROUPE) near Nice in Southern France. Indeed Sophia Antipolis is a technology complex or "technopole" (Clark visited the complex), which is an integral part of the region's business development, since it combines a variety of resources in the area while attracting others from national and international areas. Nevertheless, the creation or expansion of business activity fails to be explained solely on research work. If new technology is the impetus for new business, then its commercialization is never addressed.

Economics is dominated today by combinations or assortments of these theories. However now there is the concern for climate change and what the costs and economics will be. The key is have QE in order to get the accurate current costs of the use of fossil fuels as compared to "green" (e.g., wind, solar wave, run of river power, etc.) for reversing climate change (Clark et al. 2006; Clark 2009, 2010a) and more current such as Climate Preservation (2018). The technologies, cases, and costs all have in common the same functionalistic and deterministic roots in western philosophy. While some of the leading economists might argue that they are concerned with everyday business life or with the dynamic of change or even the macroeconomic interaction among companies and countries, the reality is that they *do not* consider these issues in-depth. Furthermore, the students of these scholars also do have even an exposure to a different way in understanding economics.

The problem is that aside from being a narrow perspective on economics, the world has dramatically changed since the early 1990s. The overwhelming global movement toward free and open markets has prompted the need to understand economics in the subjective format Lifeworld and interactionist perspective. In order for companies or countries to exchange goods and services, they need to understand one another. The dominant economic model is a more collaborative one of consortia and alliances (Mowery et al. 1997). Competitive advantage, for example, does not make sense in the twenty-first-century world of business. Cooperation and collaborative alliances do make sense in a shrinking business world.

Entrepreneurial and growing companies need new technology(s) to advance and compete. Thus on a microeconomic level, business creation must be linked to macroeconomic policies, plans, and programs. "Industrial symbiosis" as implemented in Kalundborg, Denmark, or the NOVI Science Park in Aalborg, Denmark, are good examples of business development that linked directly into environmental and advanced technology research due to government funding policy support and cooperation for new business creation. Worldwide, science parks have taken root that combine technology, finance, and commercialism from either existing or newly created entrepreneurial businesses (Clark 2001, 2002a, b, c, d, 2007a, b; Clark and Cooke 2011; Clark and Li 2013).

Singapore, on a massive and urban city-state level, is perhaps the best example. And now in China, there are over 30 science parks which are all connected to universities in order that professors and students can work together on creating new technologies, businesses, and systems that start companies due to the funding from Angel Investors, local and state governments (Clark 2014). This does not happen in the USA, since there are *no* science parks anywhere in America.

In the USA, at the end of the Cold War, the American Congress has passed federal legislation (Bayh-Dole Act) in 1980 and expanded throughout the 1980s when the Supreme Court confirmed it, thus enabling the national laboratories (funded by tax payers) to transfer their technologies to the private sector. Heretofore, the American government to conduct nuclear, weapons, defense, and military research had heavily funded these laboratories. Their inventions and technologies were highly classified. Most of the research and development was never patented.

By the early 1990s, the attitude within the American government had changed. It was time to "sell" or license the technologies developed by taxpayer moneys so that the possibility existed for some return on the research and development investment. In a matter of a few years, technology transfer organizations were created within the laboratories and on most university campuses throughout the USA. Now in the USA, inventions and research results became valuable intellectual property(s) that have commercial value. For the US federal government, the operational legal mechanism to create new technology became "Cooperative Research and Development Agreements" (CRADAs).

Clark was appointed the first Manager of Energy Technology Transfer at 1 of the 12 national-funded laboratories, Lawrence Livermore National Laboratory (LLNL) in mid-1994. While there until 1999, he created a Certificate Program in Technology Transfer through the University of California, Berkeley, where 72 people earned certificates over 1 year.

Federal agencies would fund the National Laboratories to conduct the research matched by the private sector. Until 1994, the federal government adequately funded this activity. However, after that point, given the election of a new more conservative Congress, continued funding levels for technology creation and transfer decreased substantially by the federal government as is currently (2018) the situation with the US President and Congress. Then and now, the prior government actions were considered "corporate welfare." The result after the twenty-first century, however, demonstrated that Asian and EU nations were correct, while the USA was not since they have all now "leaped frogged" the USA in economic development (Clark and Isherwood 2007, 2009; Clark et al. 2010; Clark 2009, 2012, 2014).

In other industrial countries, the private and public sectors have historically had a close relationship. Even the USA has had corporate welfare in the form of 50 years of a massive defense and military budget, which supported industry and a considerable amount of university research and development (Clark 1994a, b). While some universities had been involved in technology transfer practices for decades (e.g., Stanford, University of California System and its campuses, and especially MIT), they too had never been enfranchised or encouraged to create and then transfer technologies developed from federal research funding to the private sector. This was clearly a new mission for the American research community. The problem was (is) that no one knew how to transfer technologies.

Without fully reviewing the field of technology transfer here (see Clark 1995a, b, c, d; Clark and Decker-Ward 1995), the basic problem, as the field evolved, concerned its (1) lack of definition; (2) basic approach of "technology push"; (3) reliance on legal or licensing mechanisms; and (4) little or no marketing and sales. Briefly, the technology transfer field was created and established upon the patented technologies within an organization. Therefore, it assumed that the transfer of the institutional technologies should be primarily through licensing.

The entire technology transfer process in the USA tends to be oriented towards legal mechanisms, rather than basic business deal making. The description of some technologies developed within American national research laboratories that follow in Chaps. 9, 10 and Appendices that give current cases which need to be examined and followed, with a different perspective of the technology push model that currently attempts to commercialize technologies. Nevertheless, the basic issue to be established is the concern over the parameters under which successful technological commercialization can be judged, assessed, or evaluated.

As a case study of business innovation and technology commercialization, we are able to demonstrate the use of our Lifeworld and symbolic interactionism perspective in an everyday economic life for a new commercial venture. For scholars and students, the case study of technology innovation, economics, and commercialization provides an understanding of everyday business activities. It also provides in-depth description and explanation of the interaction between business and research. When applying formalism from linguistics, we are able to create predictive rules that apply to other economic situations. Future policy and legislative indications for decision-makers also are clear from this case since issues such as the cost of commercializing technology are worth the governmental investment.

Without engaging in the political debate over the role in government in business (Clark and Jensen 1995; Clark et al. 1997 and especially Clark 2004a, b, c, d, 2017a), the basic issue often focuses upon the justification of federal or state funds for research, development, and technology commercialization in terms of "job creation." Aside from the political popularity of job creation, further analysis reveals that this is not the best and certainly not the sole metric for success (cf. Lundvall 1987).

The ultimate goal as the book documents and presents is to build a theoretical framework from the interactionism perspective and Lifeworld tradition which is applied in economic situations. In that context, we need to reflect for a moment on some considerations from economics on theory building towards a new economics perspective.

For example, Teece's (1996) comment that "there is no theory of the firm" in the economic literature. Shortly after that, he begins to outline what such a theory might look like. The process itself was interesting (he asked question in a seminar and then proceeded to summarize the points made with some guidance from a book) since he was using interactionism to solicit the ideas of the students and colleagues. However, it was the actual notion of what constituted a theory, which proved even more enlightening. With the theory constructed, a firm could develop its strategic plans or better understand its transaction costs and the various factors of production.

Yet a decade later, the theory (s) of the firm are still not defined in part to the changes in "corporate cultures," terrorism, war, and political confrontations. By the later part of the first decade in the new twenty-first century, corporations are being to be far more rigid in accounting and financial matters. And with the advent of awareness about climate changed, corporations large and small globally are seeking to be far more "socially responsible." Whether or not if they have yet to be determined on a case-by-case basis. But the corporate culture is certainly mindful of the environmental and social concerns impacting the planet.

Clearly, from the conventional economist point of view, the theory of any firm is to help better inform and guide management and employees. However, such a "theory of the firm" is not a theory in the same sense as the natural or physical sciences. It is instead a set of concepts that may be informative and interesting but nevertheless lack explanatory or predictive power. Hence, the field of economics can explain and predict phenomena through a new economic paradigm that gives meaning and depth to a theory of a firm. Theory is used herein along with the same context as in the natural and physical sciences, as applied by Chomsky and others in modern linguistics. When science-based theories are used for understanding a firm or a business, they provide insight and guidance which are strategic, ethical, viable, and far more accurate.

The following chapters apply the subjectivist perspective of the Lifeworld philosophical tradition into the economic business cases for technology innovation, new ventures, and governance of businesses. While not much historical or quantitative data can be provided with the advanced technology case, the detailed examination of how the theory on interactionism with actors, organizations, social construction, and knowledge constitute everyday business life.

Additional case material, related data are also added from the environment and energy industries. In order to provide a comparative perspective, published materials from other works by Clark (1998–2018) are used such as his being participant-observation during the California energy crisis. As a result, a science of economics is constructed that satisfies the theoretical science perimeters of description, explanation, understanding, analysis, and prediction.

To get started, consider what science is and is not. Chapter 7 does that!

Society continues to promote the conventional theoretical economic paradigm and its empirical data or cases, rather than the debate, and investigate the basic scientific paradigm to economic problems. This ideological bias needs to be changed. Few scholars challenge the conventional economic paradigm that argues for the balance between supply and demand. Least of all, there are examples of those who are anxious to proclaim the scientific nature of economics.

Instead, the implicate assumption is that economics is scientific.

Economists have claimed that economics is the most scientific of the social sciences. This might be due to the fact that there are Nobel Prizes in Economics. Hence economics is science by virtue of the companies and universities that support economics in the Nobel Laureate community. In any case, it is wrong.

There is an inherent problem in economics and its offspring, business, those scholars and practitioners alike do not understand. They need to know what constitutes a scientific paradigm, namely, to:

1. Carefully systematize and describe all observed facts.
2. Create and frame hypotheses from these facts.
3. Lead into the prediction of fresh conclusions on the basis of these hypotheses.
4. Finally, test and repeat the conclusions against further observed facts and experiments (Colin Clark 1940).

# Chapter 7
# The Science of Qualitative Economics

## Introduction

Little has changed in economics over the last 50 years and even longer since the mid-nineteenth century with Adam Smith. A brief summary of economics over the decades starts before the twentieth century with the field being in the domain of philosophy. Aside from the political extremes that grew before and after WWI, global economics were dominated by few individuals from either the political right or left. Then in the 1930s, scholars and politicians began to focus more and more on numbers, since the global depreciation meant that countries needed to invest in themselves. Numbers had to be created both to account for the investments and to manage them.

The debates became even more intense after WWII with the financial need for restoring the Western world. Economic development became the norm for decades until the late 1960s when the "supply-side" economics of Milton Friedman gained "control" and dominated the field. Then into the first two decades of the twenty-first century came the dot.com and wifi industries. Some economics reflected Adam Smith such as Thomas Friedman with his book in 2005, *The World Is Flat*. That book reflected the Adam Smith ideology of economics. Even more so is that the government has an *invisible hand*. Now of this was and is true as many academics (mostly *not* in economics) disputed the ideology and students searched for new ways to express and implement economics.

Many of the American most prestigious universities such as University of Chicago, Stanford University, and Ivy League like Yale, Harvard, Dartmouth, Cornell, Penn, Columbia, Brown, and Princeton had generations of scholars trained in the economics of Adam Smith who then "spread" the theory that economics was a science of quantifiable supply vs. demand. However, while economics is included in the Nobel Prize Awards as an area of science, it is not a science, like chemistry, physics, or engineering. The "field of economics" as *The Economist* labeled it in July 16, 2009, after the global economic collapse 9 months before in October 2008,

---

© Springer Nature Switzerland AG 2019  
W. W. Clark II, M. Fast, *Qualitative Economics*,  
https://doi.org/10.1007/978-3-030-05937-8_7

197

still today suffers from its own internal problems, issues, and inability to understand the present and predict the future.

This book makes economics into a science. Historically, the field of economics has been unable to theoretically predict economic events. Economics is limited today. In fact, Heilbroner (1989: xiii), the noted economist, said "the ability of economists to forecast the emergence of new problems is very poor." As Reinert and Daastol (1997) note by the late 1990s: "In the 1990s there is a growing awareness among economists of the inadequacy of our understanding of economic growth" (1997: 8).

Even *The Economist* admitted the need in 1992, "True enough: economists are interested in growth. The trouble is that, even by their standards, they have been terribly ignorant about it. The depth of that ignorance has long been their best-kept secret" (1992: 9), or as Heilbroner generalizes, "the wisest thing to expect in the economy is the unexpected" (op cit., ix). Then in July 2009, *The Economist* noted that economics was not a science as it failed to predict the global economic collapse in October 2018.

In the hard cover printed issue of *The Economist*, it noted that economics as a "field of study." Several major American academic institutions got very upset with that so *The Economist* took out that phrase in its online version. In other words, economics is not in the same class of science as the physical or natural sciences. As C.P. Snow would call the distinction: economics is an "art" (as all of the social sciences) rather than a "science." Reinert (1998) in a brilliant analysis of economic theory examines it in the context of history. He concludes that economic theory has "physics envy" and moved into "biology envy" as it paradigms and went from describing the mind to understanding matter.

In today's economic theory, we find this tension reflected in the movement of economic theory from "physics envy" towards "biology envy" and in the increasing importance of innovations – the creativity of man's mind – added to the physical matter of the products being exchanged" (ibid., p. 285). In other words, the field of economics has tried to model itself after the hard sciences, like physics (see Chomsky 1957 and McNeill and Freiberger 1993 for a critique of how the social sciences try to emulate the hard sciences and constructive approaches to making social science more scientific).

Economics as a science is discussed in more detail below with the works of Schumpeter (1934, 1942) and some of his contemporary proponents. For example, see various works from Freeman and Perez, among many others for biological or evolutionary approaches to economic theory that has developed from another viewpoint. Above all note the work that we quote from Noam Chomsky, Professor of Linguistics at MIT. From these perspectives, a number of important concepts have emerged including the notion of entrepreneurship, dynamic economic development, and now "circular economics" (CE) created by the Ellen MacArthur Foundation (2007) and implemented in the European Union about a decade later (Clark and Bonato 2015). Qualitative economics plays an important role in CE as can be seen and later in the book and Appendix).

# Philosophy of Science: Economic Theory in Business

The basic issue is where one starts with understanding any field of study. We argue that the philosophical and historical roots must be examined of economics. Based on that, contemporary economic theories can be better understood. Reinert noted that there are three significant issues in addressing economic theory: "one: how economic growth is 'created', two, the alternative mechanisms through which growth and welfare are 'diffused' between and within the nation-states, and to the individual, and three, how this alternative understanding is based on a different philosophical basis" (1997: 9).

In an earlier work, Reinert argues that the core problem with economics is its own internal struggle over its roots in philosophy. Hence, for example, the neo-classical economist struggles unsuccessfully with the theory of the firm and the larger context of economic development because of "unrealistic assumptions. The neo-classical economic paradigm which today rules the world cannot – because of its core assumptions – produce any insights into the study of uneven growth" (Reinert 1994: 75).

From an entirely different philosophical tradition, Schumpeterian "or evolutionary economics better explains industrialized country growth which contains insights... used in order to study how to generate more growth in the industrialized countries..." (ibid., p. 75), but not applied to the developing nations. Schumpeter's work has become, for example, the basis for OECD analysis, most EU program, and country-by-country economic programs in Europe (see various works from Lundvall, Freeman, Perez). This is not the case in the USA and England, however.

The Anglo-Saxon rooted or neo-classical view by Adam Smith, which traces its philosophical base from Locke and Hobbes, among others, dominates American and British economics today. And "is primarily a theory of exchange whereas German economic theory (such as the Schumpeter tradition), differs in circumstances of production which translate into differences in wealth" (ibid., p. 77). Nevertheless, the history of philosophy is linked between American economics and German in the nineteenth century in a number of ways. Friedrich List (a German national), for example, was the most significant intellectual linkage when in the mid-nineteenth century he taught in the USA and advised the American government on economic policy. He was then appointed by the American government to represent the USA in Germany (Prussia at the time). Reinert does an excellent job of tracing these and other roots in economic theory between the USA and Germany (Reinert 1994, 1997).

Two assumptions from neo-classical economics must be explored. The first is "perfect information and the absence of increasing returns. It is the inclusion of these two assumptions – both counterfactual – which has created the *blind spot* of neo-classical economics: the inability to account for the extremely different levels of development between the nations of the world" (Reinert 1994: 79, emphasis ours). The key difference between the Anglo-Saxon and German traditions rests with their views of the world and especially economics. In the Anglo-Saxon worldview, there are the "assumptions of perfect information and constant return to scale in place, any theory of economic growth automatically becomes a theory of 'even' growth. These assumptions seem to remove the reasons for a Smithan "division of labor": difference in human knowledge and fixed costs in specialized machinery" (ibid., p. 79).

Schumpeter, on the other hand, views economics as a dynamic system which he drew from within the German tradition and outlines in two basic assumptions: "(1) the uneven advances of the 'technological frontier'" which most economists see as orderly; "technological change looks more like a scatter diagram than an orderly frontier" (ibid., p. 83); and "in a system with perfect information and constant returns to scale, the sequence of technological change makes no difference to the distribution of wealth." On the other hand, "in a system with increasing and diminishing returns and imperfect competition, 'choosing economic activity' becomes a crucial strategic decision" (ibid., p. 84) as with technological waves. (2) "The two alternative ways in which the benefits from technical change spread. Under perfect competition, the advances from technical changes will spread in the economic in the form of lowered prices to the end user" (ibid.).

As seen in the classical forms for distribution with Smith and David Richardo "To the customers buying the product in the form of lowered prices and/or better quality" (ibid.). But the other approach is a "Collusive form of distribution for the gains from technical change, because the forces of the producing country (e.g. capital, labour, and government) in practice – although not as a conspiracy – 'collude' to appropriate these gains." Or put another way, collude is "to the owners and workers in the producing firm, and the later to the government of the producing country in the form of higher taxable income" (ibid.). Collusive is principally collaborative and cooperative economics, rather the "competitive" and "zero-sum" economics (Porter 1980, 1990). As Reinert notes (1995) "Competitiveness' management buzzwords invade economic theory." And in a Footnote states "A recent article in *Financial Times* (1994: 10) suggests the term (competitiveness) 'corporate graffiti' – or 'management graffiti' – to describe the unthinking use of buzz-words. Management language is 'opaque, ugly, and cliché-ridden', the FT claims. 'Management graffiti' is intended as the catch-phase to end all catch-phases" (1995: 24).

"Most technical changes contain an element of both classical and collusive distribution of the benefits from technical change," concludes Reinert (1994: 85). The collusive mode of technical change "is accompanies by the creation of higher barriers to entry, more imperfect competition, and it normally affects the minimum efficient size of an operation" (ibid.). The classical mode allows movement through the firm of new technologies so that the end results are "lower prices of the end product." And then, "Typically an invention initially creates a temporary monopoly which allows for 'collusive' spread of benefits, but as the technique in question becomes common-place, its benefits will spread more and more as lower prices, not as higher wages and profits" (ibid.). We will see this process described in Chaps. 9 and 10 herein.

What Schumpeter demonstrated was that economic growth and business development should be seen from a fundamentally different philosophical tradition than that of the prevailing neo-classical paradigm. In the first place, economic growth is the core of economic theory since it reflects a dynamic view of any society. Without growth and hence change, a society will fail and self-destruct. Evidence of this can be seen in any analysis of civilization.

The questions are: What is growth? What are dynamic and changes? How can we understand them? More significantly is that the process in which society grows is through the creativity of its people. This "knowledge" base is the primary ingredient of economic change. We ascribe to these basic concepts here, especially with how creativity and knowledge become the basic building blocks to the creation of new businesses. This fundamental concept of "entrepreneurism" stands as an important insight into the development of new businesses and the firm (Clark and Sørensen 1994a, b).

Here, we are taking the concept of economic growth (macro) and business development (micro) further. Like Reinert's observations at the micro level, we agree that firms are in competition with each other. In terms of competitiveness, however, macro level competition is not properly defined by Porter who says "the only meaningful concept of competitiveness at the national level is national productivity" (1990: 6).

This is not useful as an operational definition in terms of absolute level of productivity and national wealth. Competitiveness can only be achieved in the "neo-classical law of factor-price equalization." Instead competitiveness must be separated from productivity and efficiency. The core of the argument is that micro level competitiveness of the firm "simultaneously increases the national standard of living" (Reinert 1994: 40). At the micro level, competition is being re-examined by most business scholars since it can better be seen as the formation of "networks" (see especially, Hagedoorn and Schakenraad 1990, 1992; also Håkansson and Snehota 1994; Håkansson 1994; Håkansson and Johanson 1993) as we shall discuss below.

We start with the examination of the micro level development of the firm through advanced technology, which is turned into a new business venture. Yet, we argue that this micro level entrepreneurial development of a firm is an integral part of macro level theory when considered within the Lifeworld perspective. Our presentation of this micro level analysis for a firm is linked directly through the interactionism theories of Blumer to macroeconomic theory. We demonstrate that process through the innovative use of linguistic theories into practices from Chomsky (see also Clark and Sørensen 1994b; Clark 1996).

Like most conventional economists today, Heilbroner defines the field of economics as "the study of a process we find in all human societies" or as he puts it in simple everyday survival terms, "economics is the study of how mankind earns its daily bread" (op. cit., p. 1). He does not examine the philosophical roots of the theories and thus misses some important distinctions and problems with his approach to economics.

We differ with Heilbroner's definition, for example, since the ability to earn ones daily bread is often defined by neo-classical economics as exchanging one thing for another (e.g., use of money to buy bread). While this exchange is a part of everyday life, it ignores the creation of not only the bread (recipe, ingredients, and right baking) as well as the creativity of the person using money or barter to buy the bread. There is, and certainly never discussed in conventional economics, the entire issue of the use of the bread (e.g., as breakfast food, for lunch or dinner and then with what other foods, etc.).

Heilbroner and others fail to understand how knowledge and creativity are a significant part of an economic theory and everyday business life. Instead, the conventional economist in following the neo-classical tradition wants to "atomize" and reduce everyday life to simple transactions. It is with these measurable transactions that they can apply quantitative methods in both micro and macro analyses. Without going into details here (see Clark and Paolucci 1997b; Clark et al. 1997), the quantification of economic activity and everyday life is usually based on models and statistics, which follow a certain linear logic. All of which cannot be called either science or practical.

The neo-classical approach to economics rests entirely upon the basis of exchange of goods and services. Reinert in a series of articles dismantles the neo-classical (Anglo-Saxon) view of economics by contrasting it with the German tradition whereby manufacturing or creating products is the key to economic analyses and everyday life. We concur with that perspective and will present below the subjectivist paradigm, which provides an entirely different approach to economics through the use of interactionism in everyday life. Therefore, economics, in our terms, is *about* everyday life and is *in* everyday life.

Like Reinert and Daastol (1997), among others, we can construct two categories or worldviews ("weltanschauungen"): one mechanical and static, centered around 'matter' and 'sein' (being), and one dynamic and organize, centered around 'thought' (logos) and 'werden' (becoming) (ibid., p. 2). It is this "werden" or becoming which reflects the dynamic and changing perspectives as the basis for knowledge and creativity within any form of economic growth and business development. When seen in economic terms, the two are "the mechanical world view is centered around barter, accumulation, physical metaphors, equilibrium, and optimality. In this mechanical view, a fundamental characteristic of Man is his propensity to barter. The organic view in economics is centered around inventions, production, evolution, biological metaphors, and disequilibrium" (ibid.).

## Applications of Economics to Business in Everyday Life

Consider a few related issues within business economics where some concepts from the subjectivism paradigm in interactionism have been applied.

## Consumer Research

A discussion today of the subjectivist and interaction perspective in understanding the consumer has taken shape as a debate in the "postmodern" philosophical tradition. A number of books have been written on the subject, and the debate over material and mental determinism continues. Citing Hirschman and Holbrook (1992) who want to end the "war" between the opposing factions on consumer research, a middle ground of compromise appears to be emerging: interactionism. The issue concerns the point of departure for the researcher: is it a subjectivist or objectivist point of view. In other words, can qualitative and quantitative analysis, theories, and methods coexist?

Phenomenology, in the subjectivist tradition, looks at the intentionality of objects. The individual construction of reality is psychological, according to Hirschman and Holbrook, and not group, subcultural or cultural so that it is mental determinism. "Phenomenology holds that, after being co-constituted by the interaction between an individual's consciousness and the social world, individual construction of reality resides primarily in the mind" (ibid., p. 38). The argument is that if a subjectivist perspective is taken, then the results are:

socialization (from Berger and Luckmann 1966) "every individual is born into an objective social structure within which he encounters the significant others who are in charge of his socialization so that 'their' definition of his situation is posited for him as objective reality..." (ibid., p. 53) The problem is that this is a static view and not correct one of Berger and Luckmann's overall perspective and work.

texts "is knowledge system as common sense, ideology, false consciousness but also in academics are theories, paradigms, schools of thought." And "Each refers, in one way or another, to an integrated system of beliefs about the nature of reality" (ibid., p. 55), thus, "text refers to knowledge structure as diverse as human actions". Text becomes the focal point of their work and the area in which they see measurement and validity in the objectivist tradition of:

vocality is derived from linguistics and literature since it "refers to number of meanings a text may have" (ibid., p. 57). Everyday language has meanings of two types: univocal or single meaning, and multi-vocal or multiple meanings depending on the situation.

interpretation is "process by which a researcher decides what meaning to associate with a given text that involves interpretation." (ibid., p. 58)

Therefore, Hirschman and Holbrook define "subjectivism" as the "construction of the text" which includes phenomenology, existentialism, and psychoanalysis. In keeping with the conventional economist tradition, they even argue to replace McCarthy's view in 1971 of the 4 P's of product, price, place, and promotion with commentary and criticism in consumer research as purpose, philosophy of science, perspective, and personality (ibid., p. 115).

Finally, Hirschman and Holbrook note that the "Interpretative task is not to remove such preconceptions, but rather to test them critically during the course of analysis" which leads to "validity of interpretations" (ibid., p. 33). In short, they misunderstand science and the purpose of research. In the end, they use concepts, such as "validity" and "measurement" thinking that quantification is a substitute for understanding, explanation, and prediction.

## Transaction Costs

As noted in Grabher (1993), the Adam Smith neo-classicist paradigm, whereby human economic interaction is "atomized" in a form of a quantitative analysis, is found in the "new institutional economics" (e.g., transaction cost analysis). Transaction cost analyses are economic functions performed within the boundaries of hierarchical firms rather than by market processes that cross these boundaries. Organizational forms that prevail are those that deal efficiently with cost of economic transactions.

Hence transactions are moved from the market into hierarchies: (1) are "bounded rationality" or "the inability of economic actors to write contracts that cover all possible contingencies." When all transactions are internalized, then the firm's governance structure and bureaucracy handle them. (2) "Opportunism" or "the rational pursuit by economic actors of their own advantage, by every means at their disposal, including guile and deceit" (ibid., p. 3). These are the basic arguments underlying "competitive advantage" from Porter (1980, 1990) and others. Therefore, Grabher notes that "'Embeddedness' refers to the fact that economic action and outcomes, like all social action and outcomes, are affected by actors' dyadic relations and by the structure of the overall network of relations" (ibid., p. 4). He is careful of dyadic reductionism that takes activity as if it is structured by norms and interests entailed by buyers and seller (ibid.). Or temporal reductionism that isolates transactions in time with no history but as if foreshadow of future (ibid.).

Instead, Grabher (and others in the volume) argues that the "relational view" of transactions "is focused on the relation between the exchange partners. In ongoing relations, exchange partners do not start from scratch each day but rather from some set of previously attained common understandings" (ibid., p. 5).

Economic actors neither behave as atomized individuals outside a social context nor adhere slavishly to unchangeable habits or norms. Consequently, opportunism, bounded rationality, and uncertainty – basic elements in Williamson's approach – are not treated simply as exogenous determinants of economic behavior. Rather, they are seen "as emerging in the course of exchange processes" (ibid., p. 5).

Lundvall (1993) notes the limitations of the transaction cost model in economics as lacking "interactive learning (which) involves both the learning of substance (technical learning), learning of communication (communicative learning), and learning of proper behavior (social learning). Organized markets present themselves as sets of stable and selective social and economic user-producer relations that adapt only slowly to new technical opportunities" (ibid., p. 62). However, he does not provide direction for how to understand everyday life in business interaction.

## Marketing and Promotion

Popova and Sørensen (1996) review three approaches to marketing: planning, network, and action-experience in an attempt to apply the "social construction perspective" to which they mean an "emphasis on the social processes" (1996: 5). They

Applications of Economics to Business in Everyday Life

contrast the planning and network approaches as being opposites in the understanding of everyday business life. However, "the two approaches, representing two different lived worlds, may be present in the same company, the one being the everyday life of top management, the other being the everyday life from the employees in daily interaction with customers and competitors" (ibid., p. 28).

Popova and Sørensen conclude that the everyday world of the employees in the firm is important to understand. And while not stated directly, they see the "action-experience" approach to research as the best way to understand the everyday life of a business. In this perspective, they consider marketing from a qualitative methodological point of view. Therefore, "a company needs (market) research related to the uniqueness of its social construction as well as research which search for what is termed temporary and context bound laws guiding everyday life" (ibid., p. 29).

Below we consider networks in more depth. However, the marketing area appears to be significant in any consideration of a subjectivist paradigm with the symbolic interactionism perspective. Aside from the methodological considerations in action-experience research, there are the useful concerns for understanding everyday life. Such insights provide the firm with new and useful approaches for new products, distribution, and creative problem-solving.

## *Networks and Relationships*

Grabher notes that networks have become of increasing interest to researchers. Håkansson and Johanson (1993) point out that "there is an important difference between these social networks and the industrial networks of interest... Social networks are dominated by actors and their social exchange relations" (ibid., p. 35). Håkansson and Johnson argue that "activities and resources in interaction are the more significant factors" in networks (ibid.).

Some of the network theories fit in to a social constructionist framework and within an interaction perspective for an understanding of everyday business life. Nevertheless, many scholars in the field find themselves rapidly moving into the objectivist paradigm because it offers structures that provide pre-defined and convenient explanations of the business activities. Thus a few years later, Håkansson and Snehota argue:

> We are convinced that adopting the relationship perspective and the network approach has rather far-reaching theoretical as well as managerial implications. It seems to open up a quite new and different theoretical world compared to the traditional way of conceptualizing companies within markets. It offers new perspectives on some broad traditional problems of business management and yields some novel and perhaps unexpected *normative* implications for business management. (Håkansson and Snehota 1994: 1:4, emphasis ours)

Therefore, "Relationships between companies are a complex knitting of episodes and interactions. The various episodes and processes that form business relationships are often initiated and triggered by circumstances beyond the control of people in companies. They are however never completely random, they form patterns" (ibid., Chapter 1: 15). In order for the authors to understand a network, they revert to "structural characteristics, such as 'continuity,' 'complexity,' 'symmetry,' and 'informality'" (ibid.).

Process characteristics are considered next: "adaptations," "cooperation and conflict," "social interaction," and "routinization" (ibid.). With these standard and very typical perspectives on business, networks become something other than everyday business activities. They quickly are reduced to a quantifiable and often statistical issue (not Håkansson et al. view however) of validity and measurability. All notions of interactions, situations, and understanding everyday business life are lost.

## Interactionism in Business Economics: Towards a Theory of a Firm

The interactionism perspective within the Lifeworld tradition provides a theoretical and methodological approach when combined with formal linguistics and allows the economist to understand and possibly predict actual events and phenomena. Economics fails to measure up to the physical or natural sciences. In fact, no less a proponent of classical economics, *The Economist*, queried rhetorically a decade ago, "The puzzling failure of economics" (Aug. 23, 1997b: 11).

Consider how a physicist would describe his field and how that definition measures against economics: physics or physics envy is often described as the fundamental science as it seeks to understand the "rules" or "laws" by which the universe operates. It is interesting to speculate if we will ever fully understand these "rules" and why they operate in the first place. The latter question is, however, today the domain of the philosopher and the theologian.

Furthermore, physics is typically defined as the study of the properties of matter and energy and their interaction. This simple description covers nearly all of the basic areas of physics including classical mechanics which deals with things as diverse as the motion of your clothes in the washing machine and the motion of galaxies in the universe; quantum mechanics which deals with atoms and light; electricity and magnetism which describes, for example, ball lightning and electric guitars; relativity which deals both with things traveling near the speed of light and gravitation; and particle physics which deals with nuclei, the constituents of nuclei, and, interestingly enough, cosmology and the birth of the universe!

Finally, physics is a science. That is the test of its validity is experiment and the experiences of observations. Thus, our understanding of the "rules" of physics comes from knowledge confirmed by reasoning and experience. The word "science" comes from the Latin *scientia*, "to know".

There are a number of important points to be made in this description of physics, but the most significant are three issues related to economics: scientific theories are derived from broad and universal concepts and ideas; scientific methods consist of observations and repeatable experiments for validity; and the scientific results are expressed in terms of "rules." Since economics can only attempt to describe, barely explain, and not predict phenomenon (Chomsky 1957), let alone provide any understanding of everyday business life. While economists might argue that the discipline can analyze and explain, the field has been woefully inadequate in those areas too. The best that modern economics appears to be able to do is count.

What we will do in later chapters is provide a case study analysis of a new advanced technology in business, and we construct scientific formalist for understanding Lifeworld in everyday business life through the use of "rules" derived from linguistic theory. It is our fundamental argument that economics can be scientific when it acts like a science, such as physics, living up to the general logic (the line of arguments in ontology-epistemology-methodology) and the pure logic (the validity of stamen and premises). The result of the natural, biological, and physical sciences are "rules," "principals," or "laws." Economics should have the same aspirations if it is to be scientific. Instead, as *The Economist* clearly demonstrates time and again, economics has only one definition. It is based in a "Western European" tradition with theoretical biases and methodologies that lead to ethnocentric definitions, understandings, and results of businesses and their economic systems. The best example can be seen in the neo-classical (Adam Smith, *Wealth of Nations*) argument for separately the public and private sector.

When *The Economist* editorial declares that "economics failed" (Aug. 23, 1997b: 11), it only means in not conveying strong enough that the "market economy is a marvel" (ibid.). Citing the failure of command and control economics, the position is that the "market" should be the only consideration in any economic system. Thus, "the biggest economic-policy mistake of the past 50 years, in rich and poor countries alike, has been and still is to expect too much of government" (ibid.), blaming this policy in large part on liberal economists like Paul Samuelson. Or in another issue, we are all capitalists now, are we not? These days the victory of market over state is quite taken for granted (Sept. 20, 1997c: 17).

And again, "What is surprising is the nearly unanimous support for the idea that government has in fact been in retreat" (ibid.). And that is not the end of the philosophical bias and misguided perspective. Later in the same issue and constantly, *The Economist* attacks the "Nordic" countries (Aug. 23, 1997b: 37–39) for having too much government involved in their economies (code word is "welfare-state pampering"). In fact, the magazine argues that economic recovery in the Nordic countries is a result of less government welfare and more neo-classical economic reforms. Nothing could be further from the truth.

Without going into a detailed debate, the problem, as will be discussed later, is that *The Economist* only considers "surface" economic phenomenon; it ignores the fundamental "deep structural" changes in each of the countries that have provided strong economic recovery with government and industry in strong collaborations.

What becomes troubling in these analyses, aside from their influence on the policy makers and the general public, is that they reflect the objectivist philosophical tradition that promotes one paradigmatic view of the world. This particular viewpoint, while even internally contradictory and inconsistent (e.g., Western economies such as France and Germany have a considerable amount of government involvement in their "markets"), relies upon statistical methods and probably theory (derived from objectivism) to justify their philosophical (and politicized) position. It is exactly the distinction that Reinert was conveying in his analyses of Anglo-Saxon neo-classical versus German-American Renaissance historical roots in economics (Reinert 1996, 1997, 1998).

Quantitative models and simulations have not been very successful. Economics is a field dominated by statistical manipulations of numbers. It is not a field that uses mathematical models or more subjectivistic traditions. As McNeill and Freiberger (1993: 96) note in economics, "the mathematical and linguistic realms stand quite apart." Since economics is seen as concerning money and money is viewed as numerical, then mathematics brings powerful tools to the field of economics. Yet the precision of math leads to overly crisp estimates and idealized models that seem to describe a society of robots. "Hence, economics also employs verbal concepts like recession. Language handles real-life questions better and treats details more subtly, but it also narrows the scope of models and shortens chains of reasoning" (ibid.). The application of linguistic theory(s) is a central theme of this volume (see Chap. 10) in that we exploit in terms of linguistic theories as applied to describing, understanding, and predicting economic and business activities in everyday life.

Despite the interest and Nobel Prize Award recognition of "game theory" being applied to economics, it too falls far short of providing predictability. For example, economics and its tool of statistics rely heavily upon "probability" which obeys the twin laws. "A flipped coin can't be both heads and tails, and it must be either heads or tails. A card can't be both the king of diamonds and not the king, and must be one of them" (ibid., p. 57). Furthermore, "probability treats yes/no occurrences, requires ignorance, and is inherently statistical. Other perspectives deal with degrees, do not require ignorance, and ... are completely nonstatistical" (ibid.). Probability fails when there is more information. McNeill and Freiberger argue that other philosophical traditions when examined at their logical core (ontological roots) produce other perspectives that rely upon "possibility" which is "the degree of ease with which an event may occur. Possibility is whether it can happen, probability is whether it will" (ibid., p. 70).

Professor Lofti Zadeh, the well-known Hungarian logician, at the University of California, Berkeley, says that "Possibility is a distinct theory from fuzziness (logic)... though possibility distribution is basically the same as membership function" (ibid.). In other words, the possibility of events or expectations that something will or could happen. Zadeh noted that while reducing the possibility of an event normally reduces it probability, the reverse does not hold. Thus, if an event is impossible, it will have zero probability. However, if an event is improbable, it could be 100 percent possible (ibid., p. 71). This perspective has been a central argument in the development of "uncertainty" in systems, codes, and models being used today to understand problems as wide ranging as global climate change to the manufacturing of automobiles to reduce their use of fossil fuels and thus prevent climate change.

## Conventional-Structural Objectivist Perspective

A variety of economic perspectives are used today to characterize the deployment of innovations and new technologies in the firm. An example is seen in Porter's approach to economics in which he uses a structural analysis of the firm in order to understand its competitive advantages and plot strategies against other firms (see Porter 1980, 1990). In order to accomplish the analysis of the firm, Porter created what he calls the "five forces" framework: that is, entry barriers, substitutes, buyers' and suppliers' bargaining power, and intraindustrial rivalry. Each force needs to be carefully analyzed in order that the firm becomes competitive. However, as Mowery et al. (1997: 2) note, "The primary determinants of success thus are external to the firm, resting on characteristics of industry structure, rather than on the firm's internal managerial, technical, marketing, and other resources" (ibid., p. 2). Instead, they argue that a "resource-based framework" must be employed to analyze the firm, its behavior, and competitive strategy (ibid., p. 1).

Relying on the competitive advantage perspective further limits the "firm's ability to enter new markets or lines of business" (ibid., p. 2). In other words, the conventional perspective ignores innovation, research, or other internal significant resources of the firm – they ignore the context and the situation of the firm. One of those resources is corporate management in the context of risks, incentives, and rewards and the logic of the minds. All, nevertheless, follow the conventional-structural functionalist perspective albeit with a new or novel twist to the analysis.

The study of organizations has been guided by functionalist theories and by positivist/rationalist epistemology and methodology. These efforts have proceeded on the basis of an uncritical acceptance of the concepts for organizational structure. The distinction between divisions, departments, occupations, levels, goals, strategies, recruitment and reward policies, and so forth, through which actors in organizations arrange their activities, has become scientific categories (see Benson 1977b and his dialectical critique). Hence, enter the notion of "corporate culture" which is popular in the business economics literature because it neatly labels and places business problems and solutions into a predetermined set of categories.

Furthermore, the conventional perspective, as represented by Porter's work, emphasizes competition to the determinant of collaboration and alliances. Mowery and Oxley (1995) argue that there has been a "dramatic growth" in the founding of international joint ventures and strategic alliances over the last 15 years. These new ventures involve everything from manufacture of goods for global markets to joint new product development in domestic markets (Hagedoorn and Schakenraad 1990). Even though Mowery and Oxley analyze the firm from the same philosophical tradition as Porter, they can begin to see that the narrow confines of structural functionalism are too limiting for understanding how business works in the real world. Data collected by Hagedoorn and Schakenraad (1990, 1992) in the early 1990s support this trend for interfirm alliances with the addition of biotechnology, new materials, and information technology.

The interactionist tradition takes a very different perspective than the conventional-structural-functionalist perspective. Rather than placing the actors in a firm within preconceived roles and norms, it focuses attention on the actors within the firm as they interact among themselves and others outside the firm. This focus upon interactions among actors provides a very different perspective of the firm. Yet as Zadeh and others note, the analysis of situations does not preclude the use of logic and mathematics. What it does accomplish, however, is taking a different perspective of everyday business activities. From that perspective, new understandings, descriptions, analyses, and predictions can be made of economic phenomenon.

## *Resource-Based Perspective*

The resource-based perspective, in contrast to the conventional perspective, argues that "a business enterprise is best viewed as a collection of sticky and difficult-to-imitate resources and capabilities" (McNeill and Freiberger 1993: 3). The presentation of a corporate financial managers' survey analysis (see Clark et al. 1998a) supports and assumes a resource-based framework for data gathering. The focus upon resources is limited; except now this time, it is limited to the internal structures and functions of a firm. This perspective argues that the firm must understand and analyze itself as having capabilities or resources (people, capital, equipment, distribution, supply, etc.). In most cases, these capabilities cover a wide range of areas.

Teece et al. (1994a, b) note that in the short run, firms have to live within their current capacities: First, business development is viewed as an extremely complex process. Quite simply, firms lack the organizational capacity to develop new competencies quickly. Second, some assets are simply not readily tradable, for example, tacit know-how and reputation. Thus resource endowments cannot equilibrate through factor input prices. Finally, even when an asset can be purchased, firms may stand to gain little by doing so (ibid., p. 10).

While a resource-based perspective concerns issues like management, knowledge, process, and design manufacturing, among others, Teece, like other economists, talks about theory(s) as abstract concepts vaguely describing a firm (in this case). This form of neo-classical analysis lacks theory and hence insight among other things. Further, it falls short for only noting that classical theorists discuss labor, capital, and property (as in land, facilities and equipment). Teece also destroys Smith basic notion that a firm must produce one product by pointing out that the firm must be diverse in order to survive in the global economy. Elsewhere Teece has written about "complementary assets" as a useful concept in understanding the diverse and multiplicity of resources, often overlooked or ignored, available to a firm. Yet a theory of the firm has eluded him (which he readily admits) only to be seen in the popular press in terms of business "fad gurus."

Yet, a theory of the firm is needed. Teece begins to construct one, which contained such "salient" concepts such as "adaptability" or how the firm must use its resources (e.g., human, financial, etc.). Should the firm have "slack" or excess capacity (such as people and inventory)? It needs to contract or scale down its scope. Other salient points are described, such as "information processed and exchanged", "learned and performance attribution" and others. Several of these salient needed further work, and most had little available literature in them. In short, the theory was providing new research areas for further study. On another level of theory building, "resources" needed to be identified. The resources of a firm in such a theory included its "capability" to redefine or redirect or transform itself. Another resource would be the "competence" of the firm seen in terms of workers' skill levels and executive management expertise. Once the salient points and resources were completed, the theory provided a framework for analysis in a business context.

## *The Interactionism Perspective*

As discussed in Part I, the traditional scientific approach (objectivism, positivism, and rationalism) can be characterized as (1) reductionistic, by narrowing or reducing phenomena to operational definitions; (2) deterministic, in that all phenomena are believed to have courses which can be duplicated; (3) predictive, in that the goal is to predict behavior; (4) observer independent, in that the researcher tries not to influence the data; (5) empirical, in that only observable data are to examined; (6) repeatable, so that the research can be replicated by other investigators; and (7) quantitative, in that the phenomena should be described in measurable terms (see Giorgi 1971: 7). Giorgi posits that the essential question for the human sciences is not "How do we measure phenomena?" but rather, "What do the phenomena mean?" (ibid., p. 21).

Consequently, the interaction perspective and the Lifeworld tradition focuses attention on the intersubjective contextual meanings assigned by organizational members in the constitution of "organizational life" with the purpose of understanding "organizational reality" as experienced and produced by its members. This seems to be a far more useful and applicable to business innovation and creation.

What Teece and others are missing is a different paradigm and philosophical perspective from which they could construct theories and provide empirical studies. An interactionist allows the researcher as well as the practitioner (businessperson) an extremely realistic and vibrant understanding of everyday business life. Such a perspective allows greater understanding of how economic exchange occurs and sets in motion a broader understand of how economic events work.

## Organizations Part: Social Community Construction of Interactionism

When the functionalist economic theory fails to understand business life, the root to the problem is in the lack of a conceptual ontological discussion on the very understanding and meaning of business activities within the firm. This section focuses on interaction and the firm as a social construction and upon understanding the process of change and development of the firm. The purpose is to discuss a conceptual understanding of the firm as a subjective, interactionistic, and processual phenomenon. The discussion focuses upon the way in which actors in their *every day of life* create an understanding of business reality and through their actions and interactions construct and change the firm.

The discussion starts with how to understand the constitution of what we call the "firm." The firm should be understood as the actions and meaning knowledge of the individual actor and of the actors' collective actions over time. These actions and interactions have some consequences: i.e., the organizing of activities and creation of meanings and knowledge. In this organizing, intersubjective moving pictures of what the firm and the environment are will be created among the actors and create a view of seeing, both on themselves and of the context. The firm and its development come from interpretation and understanding of the situation by those actors who are involved in their organizational actions.

Changes in the firm can therefore be understood as situations in the organizing that can be characterized as changes of assumptions and action interactions in the actors' context. This is a dialectical process, involving both the dialectic of the mind in cognition and the dialectics of the movements in the context and the search of creating meanings in the organization.

## *Actors' Action and Knowledge: The Constitution of the "Firm"*

All business is conducted by individuals communicating in an interactive or face-to-face manner, where the relations consist of concrete meetings between members in the firm and the relations content are the interpretations and meanings construction of each other and the situations. So to improve our understanding of the firm, we have to start with an understanding of what constitutes the "firm": What is a firm, or rather what is a business organization?

> The word organization is a noun, and also a myth. If you look for an organization you won't find it. What you will find is that there are events, linked together, that transpire within concrete walls and these sequences, their pathways, and their timing are the forms we erroneously make into substance when we talk about an organization. (Weick 1979b: 88)

> When we look at organizations, especially the larger, older, famous ones, they seem *solid*, they seem *permanent*, they seem *orderly*. This is, after all, why we call them organization. Images of organizations as solid, permanent, orderly entities run through many textbooks. But, in our view, they only tell half the story. They obscure the other half: the chaos which looms behind the order, surfacing from time to time, such as when computer systems break down, when products are sent to the wrong destination or when bookings are made for the wrong dates. They also obscure the immense human efforts and energies which go into keeping organizations solid and orderly. (Sims et al. 1993: 1)

> the most taken-for-granted factors of organizational life are the products of considerable intersubjective works. By reinterpreting such micro sociologists of consciousness as studies of formal organization, it becomes clear that formal organizations are essentially processes of organizing enacted by persons. (Brown 1978: 371)

The word "organization" is (only) a concept, which we use to describe a phenomenon. It is a conceptualization of what we believe and do and what we orient our actions towards. Organization is a concept in the same way as the concepts of family, class in school, a football team, an union, etc. In other words, organization is a phenomenon that we experience when and where we see more than one person involved in activities over time.

Thus, organization becomes a collective arrangement where people try to give the situation and the activities meanings. In line with Blumer (1986/1969, and in Part I of this volume), organizations consist of *the fitting together of lines of activity – the interlinking of lines of action*. Actors mixing, sharing, competing, and cooperating are parts of the interactive process that define groups and organization. And that is why most organizations, by definition, change and move dynamically in space and time.

By fitting together the lines (what we will call later the "rule") of action and interaction as logically prior in organization, we are discouraged from mistakenly regarding organizations as "things" or simply "solid entities" such as a building or structure. Some scholars argue that organizations are "living things" akin to the biological sciences and refer to organizations as "evolving" with "life cycle" attributes (Graedel and Allenby 1995).

Organizations are not concrete, immutable, or even life-like objects that, somehow independent of our conscious intentions or unconscious motives, shape and determine what we do. The philosophical term for this kind of cognitive error is "reification," an unconscious tendency to forget or be obvious to the role of human agency in creating, sustaining, and transforming social relations (see Hummel 1990: 12). We actively construct our social reality through language, through a process of symbolization by forming words and sentence to describe our experiences as well as our wants and desires. We create our organizational existence.

The language we share and use constitutes our relationships and the way we look upon it (see White 1990: 82). An organization should therefore be understood through the actors who by their actions and knowledge create the firm in their everyday pursuit of life. The focus and start of understanding organizations are the members or the actors within the organizational life. In this the relation between action and knowledge is the central issue of interaction.

The very concept of action can be understood as formulated by Weber (1964):

> Action included all human behavior when and in so far as the acting individual attaches a subjective meaning to it. Action in this sense may be either overt or purely inwards or subjective; it may consist of positive intervention in a situation or of deliberately refraining from such intervention or passively acquiescing in the situation. Action is social in so far as, by virtue of the subjective meaning attached to it by the acting individual (or individuals), it takes account and is thereby oriented in its course (1964: 112).

Yet as Schutz (1973b: 34, 1972: 57) points out, this is not enough for an understanding of action. Instead, an understanding of action is dependent upon identification of the project that the actor seeks to improve. It is essential to understand the separation of action and project. First of all, every action is a spontaneous activity oriented towards the future. This orientation is a property of all primary constituting processes whether they arise from spontaneous activity or not. Each such process contains within itself intentionalities of lived experiences that are directed towards the future. Action is therefore the execution of a projected act.

Action expresses the behavior of people, expressed in advance by the actor whose behavior is then based upon an anticipated project. The expression "the act" expresses the result of the ongoing process or the fulfilled action. Action could be hidden or open intervening into the outer world. All projection consists of an anticipation of future behavior with help of "fantasy" (*thinking in future*) or as Blumer puts it, acting in relation to "the generalized other." But it is not the ongoing action process but the fantasized act, *as it* was fulfilled, that starts all the projection.

The actions exist in a context that is created by the actor through his/her actions. The action is related to the actor's interpretation and understanding of the situation in the context of meanings imparted in the interaction of the phenomenon (see Blumer 1986/1969; Schutz 1972; Mead 1962; Brown 1978; Jehenson 1978). The actor has motives and definitions of the situation that makes the social world into an inner logic, which have rules and lines of action derived from the situation itself. Actions also happen in connection with expectations. When the actors are involved in the society, they expect suitable actions from themselves and from others: They are capable of understanding meanings of action by others and make their own point of view on themselves based on the response of other actors. They associate meanings to situations and to other actor's actions and act in relation to their interpretations of these meanings. This can be understood in relation to typifications, formed by the earlier experiences of the actor, which define his/her "*thinking in future*" of others' possible reaction to his/her actions.

The typifications on what the actor uses in a situation are dependent on his/her knowledge in everyday life ("the stock of knowledge" *and* "the generalized other"). The typifications give the individual a frame of reference that the actor can use to create actions and make sense of others' actions (see Blumer's notion of "reflections"). Typifications are thereby expectations to others actions containing symbols in relation to community and collective interpretations.

This social reality is pre-defined in the language by which we are socialized. The language gives us categories that both define and emphasize our experiences. The language spoken and dialogue among actors within an organization can be seen as communication of meanings and actions. But such language usage is also a means to create a new understanding, changes in meanings, and a new worldview. Language is the baseline from which we understand and can interpret knowledge.

Thus, knowledge, as expressed in language usage, can thereby be understood as moving pictures of reality: experiences and information are produced through actions and transformed (by interpretation and retrospection) to the knowledge that the actor's experiences are useful and relevant.

The world with which the actor is confronted is composed of experiences which the process of consciousness will develop or simplify towards different paths (or structures) and then transformed into actions (again). In Chaps. 9 and 10, herein, we present concrete examples from the knowledge and creative development of new technologies into actual businesses through this interactive process. In the examples, the actor uses and develops a scheme for interpretation to connect episodes of social action in a sensible way.

A "scheme" should be understood as active information seeking pictures that accept information and orient actions continuously (Weick 1979b; Bartunek 1984). The action-knowledge process gives an understanding of the way in which people think, act, reflect, and interact. Simultaneously it shows that the actors engage their environment by means of interpretation and orientation with one another.

This knowledge is developed and can be illustrated in the figure below which shows both the formation and organization of interactionism (Fig. 7.1).

The interpretation by the actor therefore transforms information into knowledge and experiences, which are in turn transformed into knowledge through retrospection or reflection. Knowledge is organized in a certain way. Behind knowledge (or in the very knowledge-thought production), there are processes connected to the development of knowledge acquisition. There are processes of thinking in which we do not have full control and which, for some parts, are unconscious or are unreflected.

Knowledge and experiences are dependent on the actor's concrete understanding of the situation. Experiences that he creates through actions are organized and related towards the knowledge that he or she possesses. Knowledge is thereby what the actor defines as his/her knowledge from experiences in various situations. People's views of reality are influenced by conscious and unconscious social constructions associated with language, history, culture, gender experience, etc.

The focus in the understanding of the organization is upon the way organizational members interpret their own organizational world, which is nothing else than a special sphere of the individual's Lifeworld. As we discussed in Part I, the concept

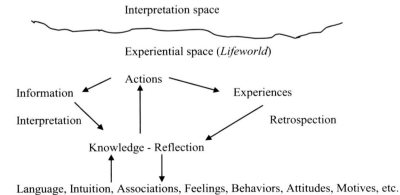

**Fig. 7.1** The process of knowledge development

of Lifeworld refers to the fact that in any real-life experience, there is something that is given in advance or something that exits in advance and thus, taken for granted. This taken-for-granted world includes our everyday life and whatever prejudices and typical interpretations we may derive from it. Acting as a member of an organization, therefore, does not differ essentially from acting as an individual, for "whether we happen to act alone or, cooperating with others, engage in common pursuits, the things and objects with which we are confronted as well as our plans and designs, finally the world as a whole, appears to us in the light of beliefs, opinions, conceptions, certainties, etc., that prevail in the community to which we belong" (Gurwitsch, in Jehenson 1978: 220).

The important characteristic of this experience in any organization becomes the typical form of everyday life. Or as described by Schutz (1990a: 7), "The individuals commonsense knowledge of the world is a system of constructs of its typicality." In social interaction, the role of typification is important and can be expected to vary according to the nature of the relationship.

## *Environment as Situational Analyses*

The actors in their "environment" construct reality and knowledge. These areas constitute situations and need to be analyzed as such. Suchman (1987, 1994) and others have done so when examining and understanding large technological businesses, such as Xerox, among others. It is precisely because knowledge is a relation to and has an orientation towards the "environment" through action that the environment itself can be seen and defined as *the experiential space* and as *the interpretation space*.

The experiential space is what is close and concrete, where, for example, the actors travel and interact. This can be seen in the consciousness of human beings in "the natural attitude" first of all being interested in that part of the actor's every day of life world that is in his reach and that in time and space are centered around him/her (see Schutz 1973b: 73). The place where the body occupies the world, the actual here, is the point from which one orients oneself in the space. In relation to this place, one organizes elements in the environment.

Similarly, the actual now is the origin of all the time perspectives under which one organizes events in the world as before and after and so on. This experiential space is experienced by the actor as the core of reality, as the world within his reach. It is the reality in which we are all engaged.

The interpretation space can be seen as the reality beyond the actor's knowledge (e.g., through stories, tales) where something which the actor relates to, but which is not centered around his or her every day of life, e.g., not in time.

In relation to this, we can see the distinction that Weick (1999: 2) talks about when he says that humans live in two worlds – the world of events and things (or the territory) and the world of *words* about events and things (or the map). In this, the process of abstraction is the process that enables people to symbolize (see Blumer,

1969 and Part I of this volume) and is described as "the continuous activity of selecting, omitting, and organizing, the details of reality so that we experience the world as patterned and coherent." This process becomes necessary but inherently is inaccurate, because the world changes continuously and no two events are the same. The world becomes stable only as people ignore differences and attend to similarities. In a social constructed world, the map creates the territory. Labels of the territory prefigure self-confirming perspectives and action.

This perspective also means that the development of knowledge has its start in the actor's existing knowledge. Or as Weick (ibid., p. 5) put it: "it takes a map to make a map because one points out differences that are mapped into the other one. To find a difference, one needs a comparison and it is map like artifacts which provide such comparisons."

The development can be seen in relation to the actor's everyday experiences with his attempt to orient and to solve problems. When the actors act in their experiential space, they thus widen their understanding of reality by interpreting and relating themselves to the result of the actions. Development of knowledge involves interpretation and retrospection whereby the actors create their experiential space: Reality is what one sees; hence it changes every time the actor constructs a new concept or a picture of connections. Development of knowledge thus demands that the actor reflects and relates to an understanding of the situation and the experiential space.

The essence is in the idea that we all develop knowledge through actions and that actions are the means by which we engage ourselves in the reality; our actions construct and keep us in touch with the world (Garfinkel 1967; Morgan and Ramirez 1984). The action-knowledge discussion is built upon the assumption that we only have a reality in force of that we are engaged in it: reality as meanings is constructed. This does not imply that people are in full control over the process of constructing the reality or that they have possibilities to change it basically, because they do not act alone and because it is an ongoing process. It is necessary now to take the discussion of actors, actions, and knowledge and develop an understanding of the way in which people are oriented towards each other and in which way the organizational reality actually becomes a reality.

## *Interaction and Knowledge*

As we have seen in Blumer's discussion above, interaction is symbolic in the sense that actors respond to the actions of others, not for some inherent quality in them, but for the significance and meanings imputed to them by the actors. Meanings shared in this way, in an intersubjective way, form the basis for human social organization (Singelmann 1972: 415). People learn symbols through communication (interaction) with other people, and therefore most symbols can be thought of as common or shared meanings and values (Rose 1962: 5).

This mutually shared character of the meanings gives them intersubjectivity and stresses that it is interaction and intersubjectivity that constitute the firm as a reality for the actors. Interaction in this relation should be understood as a complete sequence of interaction, as a process of interaction (see also Mangham 1978). The central point in this is the time perspective and the dependency of the context and the acts: it is the actions by the actor and the process of interaction that give and make the firm over time. The "firm" therefore both has a past (the experiences of the actors) and a present (the actors interpretations and pictures) and a future in relation to the actors fantasies of the future and orientations. The processes related to interaction are presented in the figure below.

Figure 7.2 outlines interaction between the actors in the firm. It is a process of knowledge development, which occurs through the process of interpretations and interaction in an experiential space. Organizational knowledge is thereby a result of the interaction – the construction of meanings. It is intersubjective and can be seen as a moving picture that defines what the actors' experience as important and real. Thus, knowledge has an impact on future actions and is central for an understanding of the actors' orientation and the organizational actions.

The actors' act in relation to the picture and definition they have of the experiential space and the situation. Each action means possibilities for experiences and information and for strengths or weaknesses in interpretation of connections in the situation. In every situation there is the possibility of several different interpretations. This means that changes in the experiential space create ambiguity and the actors are tempted to use previous successful actions and interpretations – the existing picture of reality.

Knowledge is enlarged, and in the same time, it becomes obsolete when the experienced reality changes. Understanding therefore involves both development of new knowledge and discarding obsolete and misleading knowledge (Hedberg 1981).

Development of knowledge is thereby a change of knowledge that can occur in many ways. The actors construct through the processes of interaction, some results that have consequences for their organizational situation.

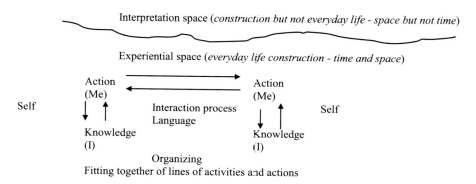

**Fig. 7.2** Knowledge and interaction

## Organizing: Fitting Together of Lines of Activities and Actions

Through the processes of interaction, the actors construct some results: the interaction means organizing and creation of the firm, and the actors create a moving picture of and a relation to the experiential space. The actors create intersubjective moving pictures of the reality, which is an organizational paradigm.

## Organizing: Dynamism of the Firm

The actors create over time something they define and name the "firm." The processes that occur can be understood as organizing, which not only focuses upon action and interaction but also on moving pictures of reality and intersubjectivity. Essentially, the firm can be understood as overlapping interactions. The actors create the firm through interactions, but "it" has also an influence upon them through their interpretation of "it." This dialectical perspective appears from the view that the firm only exists through the interactions between the actors and thus is viewed as a corollary of these interactions and their content meanings and definitions.

Simultaneously, the organization is historically to the individual member: the individual enters into an already existing organizational every day of life, which sets the institutional parameters for his self-development. The self and organization thus develop together because of each other in a dialectical process of mutual transformation (Singelmann 1972: 415; see also Mead 1962; Berger and Luckmann 1966; Benson 1977a, b; Arbnor and Bjerke 1981/1997).

The actors have to live with and exist with uncertainty and ambiguity. In other words, the way in which the actors handle themselves is in itself uncertain and exposed to many different interpretations and understandings. To reach security, the actors attempt to organize their activities.

Organizing means assembling the actions and should be seen in relation to interpretation and understanding by the actors. The actors form their actions so as obtain information and experiences that give meanings to the organizational world. This is organized by the actors in an attempt to construct an understanding. In the organizing the dependent actions are oriented towards removing contradictions and uncertainty: the actors seek to define and make sense in their situation, and thus they both create the firm and the experiential space. Organizing is to be seen as a social, meaning-making process where order and disorder are in constant tension with one another and where unpredictability is shaped and "managed." The raw materials of organizing are people, their beliefs, actions, and their shared meanings that are in constant motion (see Sims et al. 1993: 9).

There is a similarity between the phenomenological meanings of the practical activity of organizing and theorizing – the act of sense-making is in fact the central feature of both. Theorizing is most fundamentally an activity of making systematic as well as simplified sense of complex phenomena that often defy understanding by everyday, commonsense means. Theorizing might also be seen as a means by which people in organizations make their own and other's actions intelligible by reflective observations of organizing processes; through these processes, novel meanings are created, and possibilities for action are revealed.

Theorizing becomes an act of organizing, first, when it is a cooperative activity shared in by several or even all of the actors in an organizational setting and, second, when its purpose is to reveal hidden or novel possibilities for acting cooperatively. Organizing is cooperative theorizing and vice versa (see Hummel 1990: 11). In short, the firm is a social construction and a collective phenomenon.

This discussion of organizing can be seen as a beginning of an understanding of changes and innovation in the "firm."

## *Intersubjectivity and the Organizational Approach*

The actors act and develop knowledge, and in the same time, they create a moving picture of the firm and what the experiential space is, which over time, through interaction processes, becomes the actors' intersubjective moving picture of reality (or paradigm). In this reality there are experiences of specific actions (routines, traditions, procedures, politics, myths, etc.), mental maps of the experiential space, norms, and values (as symbols). This is related to the actors' interpretations and expectations of each other in the organization or firm. In Chaps. 9 and 10, we present concrete examples. At this point, consider the theoretical conceptualization of the firm.

In the social subsystem constituted by a formal organization, the assignment of meanings is not left to the discretion of the members alone. The organization presents the individual member with a number of anonymous, functional typifying schemes that will help him orient his behavior towards the incumbents of other positions, especially hierarchical positions. These types are furnished to the newcomer in the organizational chart or the nomenclature of organizational titles. They underlie job descriptions, exposes of rights and duties attached to each organizational position, rules of conduct, customs, etc.

By such standardization of the scheme of typifications, the organization attempts to establish a congruency between the typified scheme used by each actor as a scheme of orientation and that of his organizational fellow men as a scheme of interpretation. This standardization is supposed to promote the smooth flow of authority relationships required for the efficient functioning of the organization (see Jehenson 1978: 226; Benson 1977a, b).

Silverman's (1983) understanding of action and development can be seen in relation to the discussion of organizing and the organizational paradigm. His understanding of the organizational connections is that the path in interactions and in related meanings is built up over time. This reflects the consequences of the actions of the different actors and their knowledge. There are institutionalized expectations of possible actions by others – the foundation for social life – "the rules of the game." In the group there is an acceptance of this, because the actors do not themselves feel that they can change "the rules," and at the same time, stabile group relations give some advantages and security.

The organizing should be seen in relation to the extent of the actors' involvement in a more or less involvement to keep or to change the rules. Organizational changes are the actors' change of the rules, or they change their attitudes towards them. The actors solve problems with developed definitions and take actions in relation to the dominant views of reality. They act rationally and logically according to their understanding and interpretation.

Rationality should therefore be understood as a social construction in itself and as a social product rather than action guiding rules for organizational life. It is a symbolic product, constructed by actions dependent of the actors' moving picture of reality and interaction. That is, the structuring of organizational interactions requires members to rely upon shared but largely tacit background knowledge that is embodied in an organizational paradigm (Brown 1978: 374; Garfinkel 1967). Rationality and the definition of "problems," "situation," "leadership," and so on are afforded by the dominant moving picture of reality.

Interaction between actors in a situation allows for many different interpretations whereby the actors are facing multiple realities. The interaction between different opinions means that new conceptions may arise. The reality is seen differently which produces changes. Brown states that the organizational change could be seen as an analogy with scientific change (see also Imershein 1977):

> most of what goes on in organizations, involves practical as well as formal knowledge. That is, the relevant knowledge is often a matter of application, such as how to employ the official procedures and when to invoke the formal description of those procedures, rather than abstract knowledge of the formal procedures themselves. Paradigms, in other words, may be understood not only as formal rules of thought, but also as rhetoric and practices in use. (Brown 1978: 373)

Bartunek (1984: 355) talks about an organizational paradigm as interpretive schemes (with references to Schutz and Giddens), which describes the cognitive schemata that map our experience of the world through identifying both its relevant aspects and how we are to understand them. Interpretive schemes operate as shared, fundamental (though often implicit) assumptions about why events happen as they do and how people are to act in different situations.

Essence of all this is that the meaning people create in their everyday reality gives the understanding of why people are like they are which can be seen in their interaction and intersubjectivity, including their common interpretations, expectations, and typifications. As long as organizational actors act as typical members, they tend to take the official system of typification for granted as well as the accompanying set of recipes that help them define their situation in an organizationally approved way. The emergence of other, non-organizationally defined typifying schemes results from the breaking down of the taken-for-granted world when the actors enter into face-to-face relationships.

## The Actors' Experiential Space: Organizational Lifeworld

The actors construct their reality, individually and collectively, but they do not experience it in this way. Moreover, they see reality as if they live in an external world independent of themselves. Through the language and typifications, we understand things as being natural and that society is something "out there" that we cannot change. The reason for this stability is that from our knowledge we "know" the world and that actions confirm us in a given understanding of the world (see Hennestad 1986; Silverman 1983).

However, the experiential space is not something that exists independent of the actors, and, as it is argued, it is through the action-knowledge process that the actors create their organizational activities and the experiential space. Therefore it is problematic to talk about borders between the firm and the environment:

> While the categories external/internal or outside/inside exist logically, they do not exist empirically. The "outside" and "external" world cannot be known. There is no methodological process by which one can confirm the existence of an object independent of the confirmatory process involving oneself. The outside is a void, there is only the inside. A person's world, the inside or internal view is all that can be known. The rest can only be the object of speculation. (Weick 1977: 273)

The experiential space exists "inside the firm": The experiential space is the actor's moving picture as constituted by the interaction and knowledge processes. On the other hand, the actors are confronted with circumstances in the experiential space that one cannot claim that they have invented and that they cannot disregard: the actors exist in a society outside which they cannot place themselves.

But the firm cannot be seen as a reaction on things that happen "out there": What is "out there" is still an item for a subjective and an intersubjective interpretation and understanding (see the discussion of Kant and Husserl in Chap. 4). In other words, the organizational actions will influence and change the experiential space directly. The central point is not only the product, marketing, or economy but everything what the actors see and talk about: it is the way in which they talk about it and the way in which this talking creates a situation, actions, and moving pictures of reality.

The actors have to understand how they create their experiential space and how they can act sensibly. So actors who are conscious about that they create their experiential space will be less oriented towards what is true or false and more oriented towards what is sensible in the situation. Therefore nothing represents true or false but only versions that are more or less commonsensible and exhibit their own logic.

Through interaction the actors have constructed a moving picture of the experiential space. This contains not only their orientation towards and relation to well-known actors (customers, suppliers, agents, competitors) but also moving pictures of less known actors (other firms, other competitors, public authorities, and institutions). There are happenings in the world that are not directly connected with the actors but which they may notice and relate themselves to their interpretation space and with which they may be confronted in an interaction (such as the reconstruction of USSR, the Golf War, the situation in the former Yugoslavia, among others).

The experiential space that one has chosen and formed does not directly influence actions and senses. But when the experiential space exists, it works as a possible guide for actions and interpretations. Thus, a newly created experiential space is a historical document, formed as knowledge. An important characteristic is therefore that the experiential space is a social construction. It is through interpretation that the actors create a moving picture of the experiential space and from this act and interact.

The above discussion is the basis for understanding organizational changes and activities. Through the discussion of action, knowledge and interaction, and its consequences (i.e., organizing, the organizational paradigm, and experiential space), we can begin to understand all about what is the "firm" and how it changes.

## *Constituting of the Organizational Activities and of the "Firm"*

If we relate this to organizing and intersubjectivity, the following figure can be presented. The idea is to illustrate that the actors' knowledge and actions should be seen in relation to interaction and intersubjectivity in their every day of life as seen below in the chart about organizational context and organizational activities developed and then interacting (Fig. 7.3):

The experiential space is dialectical and is what the actors interpret as their situation, market, and surroundings and understood in the situations where the actors interact as a member of the organization. But the experiential space is also the social situations and the relations that the actor has with other actors "from outside the firm." This is a broad spectrum of relations and is the actors' involvement in interaction connected with knowledge and understanding of reality such as friendship, family, etc. or seeing reality as a "multiple reality." In other words, the actors do not only create their understanding of reality at work between nine and five. They have a being, a history, and a life beside their involvement in the firm.

The organizational context is the actors and their perceptions and meanings. Their organizing and intersubjectivity are the organizational paradigm or their orga-

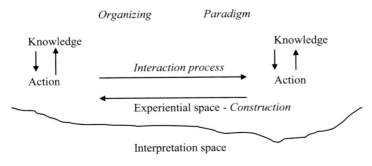

**Fig. 7.3** The organizational context in organizational activities and development

nizational identity. This includes the circumstances that involve the actors, their situation, problems, and possible solutions. Interpretations and understanding in this context influence the way in which the actors construct the experiential space and interact but also the way in which the development of knowledge occurs and to what extent it influences actions. It is the actors who interpret and have influence on the organizational development through their knowledge and experiences from different situations. The actors interpret others' actions in the experiential space or changes in it and construct an understanding, a moving picture of the connections between them and the experiential space.

In the process actions and knowledge are seen in the actors' attempt to improve their capability to act in the experiential space: in other words, in the actors' construction and extension of the experiential space. This is constituted in the organizing and in the actors' attempt to thinking in future. The attempt to implement the thoughts depends on the action and interaction processes, and "success" in the situation is seen in the organizational actions or as an attempt to act in relation to new situations and moving pictures of reality. The background for this is in the actors' intentions with the actions and the development of the actor's knowledge. Success should also be understood as the actors' motives and expectations and in their experiences of the results of the actions. The important issue in the actors' attempt to improve their situation is therefore the connection between the organizing and thinking in future and the foundation for development: the connection between knowledge and action. Thinking in future should be understood in relation to processes of interaction and to intersubjectivity and as a formulation of the project and the future actions.

Therefore, e.g., internationalization can be seen as a construction and an extension of the experiential space and development of knowledge in the experiential space. The differences between the actors' interaction on the home market and interaction on the international market are exactly the confrontation of different moving pictures of reality and typifications between the actors involved. The actor's knowledge, typifications, and scheme to interpretation are confronted with foreign actors with another moving picture of reality deriving from the fact that they have a different context and every day of life and thus having developed their understanding and interpretations. This is, for instance, what some regard as differences in culture (Bate 1984; Meyerson and Martin 1987; Gullestrup 1992) and what others discuss in relation to international communication as an important dimension in internationalization.

When the actors interact with the foreign actors, they have to interpret and form an understanding of those actors' moving pictures of reality and their way of interpreting reality. They have to construct intersubjectivity, which is the foundation for a further interaction, as they are the strangers. Their approach is comparative to researchers approach quite in accordance with hermeneutic and qualitative methodology. The approach of in which way we understand others actions and the meaning of those actions.[1]

---

[1] See Weber (1948, 1972), Goffman (1959), Garfinkel (1967), Schutz (1978b, 1982), Morgan (1983).

When the actors act and interpret the situation, they try to be sensible. There is logic in their attempt to be sensible, and they use earlier interpretations that have worked. When a new uncertainty is confronted with those earlier enactments, not everything is noticed, and others are noticed as well-known, in line what we talked about in Gadamer's discussion of prejudgments. In the same time, the actors experience that the world as changing and as unpredictable and therefore that it is something more than what they already know. The actors try to reach out for those changes through interaction and enactment and act in such a way that those changes could be recognized and that they could be able to relate themselves towards them.

The understanding of action and knowledge processes can be discussed into a frame of reference based on three areas: the actor's development capability, organizing and the organizational paradigm, and the actor's extension of the experiential space.

## Case in Point: The Actors' Development Capability

The actors' development capability should be understood as a process and as a result of the actions. The development is connected with processes of interaction but where the state of development is dependent of the interpretations and the actors' creation of interaction. The actors, with their specific qualifications, experiences, and personality, are not passive participants in a prefabricated reality; they are contributors and creators of meanings (Allaire and Firsirotu 1984).

Interaction and development are results and process: a situation and an involvement of something (not necessary a product) in a situation. But the process of development does not start with the situation or the involvement but with a combination of both, based on the actors' interpretation and understanding of experiences used in future activities and in processes of interaction. The firm's development can thereby be understood as the actors' development and readjustment capability to change moving pictures of reality and interpretations and new actions. This can be seen as capability to develop knowledge and transform this to actions, realized through the process of interaction in the organizing and with actors in the experiential space.

**Organizing and the organizational paradigm** can be seen in the actors' understanding of formal structures, goals, politics, management processes, and resources and is all in all a result of the organizational reality and the way of functioning in the every day of life. It contains a living dimension in a connection of shared and meaningful symbols manifested in interactions, interpretations, myths, ideology, values, and in multiples cultural forms of expressions as the result of interaction processes and interpretations. An important part of this every day of life is the business area which is based upon previous actions oriented towards what to produce, which resources and technology one should use, and an understanding of the existing knowledge and needs for knowledge development in relation to the business area. This could also be understood as what Diamond (1990: 34) named as "the organizational identity."

Organizational identity is the product of the group's intersubjective organization of experiences at a given point of time: the "story" they share about what is real to them. It is a picture of the meaning, purpose, and intention, collectively and unconsciously assigned to common experience and behavior of organizational members especially during critical incidents, or what Benson (1977a, b) calls "organizational morphology," which refers to the officially enforced and conventionally accepted view of the organization. It refers to the organization as abstracted from its concrete, intricate relations with other aspects of social life. This is the administrators' vision of the organization, the form that they try to impose upon events. Since they are partly successful, the morphology may also be somewhat accurate as a description of the organization.

It is the connection between the actors' knowledge, their understanding of the business area, and their organizational actions that create the orientation towards and the mode of handling organizational activities. This should be seen in the light of the actors' attitudes of and intentions with the activities. The actors' development capability is constituted through the interaction process and by the actors' interpretation and knowledge of the business area. The actors' change of moving reality picture is therefore important in a situation where a contradiction exists between the business area and the experiential space. This can be seen in situations where one shifts to new technology, new products, entering new market, changing services, etc. or an extension of the experiential space. In each of the situations, there is a need to change the knowledge; therefore recognition among the actors of the problem, new actions, or actions in a new way is important.

Through the interaction process and interpretation *the actors' experiential space* influences the organizing and the development capability. There is a confrontation with other actors' external firm, but the organizing and the development of knowledge are to a less extent activated when the actors experience the experiential space as stabile. This experience means less possibility for changes in the actors' organizing and development capability due to intersubjectivity, and the interaction is satisfied.

On the other hand, activation in the interaction is more probable when the experiential space is experienced as uncertainty or ambiguous. In other words, it is the experiences in the interaction with other actors and the way in which the actors interpret and act accordingly what is crucial to their development. The foundation for experiences and interpretation of the experiential space, for knowledge development, and for changes of organizational activities are the actors' interaction and involvement. In situations with changes, the central issue is the actors' knowledge and change of interpretations that can be related to and transformed into actions.

## Summary: The Economics of the Firm (Such as Business, NGOs, Family, Communities, Government, etc.)

In our discussion of the "firm" and its constant organizational changes, it is important to have an understanding of both the organizing and the experiential space as a subjective and intersubjective phenomenon. Organizational change should be understood as a situation in organizing that can be characterized as changing assumptions with a picture of reality and changing actions in the actors' context of everyday life. The process of organizational activities and actions comes from interpretation and understanding of the situation by those actors involved in the actions. It is thereby a discussion of interaction processes and the way in which the actors interpret the processes and how the interpretations effect changes in the organizational development of the firm.

The collective actions constitute the firm, but it is understood in relation to interpretation and intersubjectivity. The constitution is formed by the actors, but at the same time, it is a restriction for the actors through the picture of reality that they have built and act in relation to. This is central, because the relation between the development of knowledge and the actions is the foundation for the process of interaction.

All this is about how to understand every day of life processes in the actors' construction of the firm. Brown expresses this in the following way:

> Organizational realities are not external to human consciousness, out there waiting to be recorded. Instead, the world as humans know it is constituted intersubjectively. The facts (facta) of this world are things made. They are neither subjective nor objective in the usual sense. Instead, they are constructed through a process of symbolic interaction. A revision of our symbolic structures, of our shared forms of perception and expression, is thus a revisioning of the world. This is no more true for the artist or the scientist than it is for the citizen or manager or bureaucratic politician. All such actors can be seen to share a basic affinity: they create and use paradigms through which experience acquires significance. By stressing the world-creating aspects of conceptual innovation, such a perspective also provides a bridge between theoretical and organizational praxis, as well as between what experts do and what workers do in their workaday lives. We all create worlds. The more we are able to create worlds that are morally cogent and politically viable, the more we are able, as workers and citizens, to manage or to resist. (Brown 1978: 378)

The development of the firm is a complex phenomenon but also an every day of life reality for people and thus very simple on another level of understanding. It is not something one experiences as abstract. Individuals are engaged in and related to the firm and are thinking about it in very concrete ways.

Firms are unique phenomena, because people are unique. To understand a firm – an organization – we have to treat it as subjective and qualitative phenomena, as lived every day of life. In this, the central issue in understanding is an understanding of the actors' subjectivity and intersubjectivity with their motives and intentions in their everyday business life. People understand themselves retrospectively and act accordingly, but additionally they are thinking in future: What are the projects they are thinking upon? In which way do they try to realize them? How do the projects change through the process of action and interaction?

People construct their organizational reality through actions in everyday life, and they build paradigms in order to orient themselves to their own reality. We have to relate ourselves to this discussion if it is the empirical reality and not the theoretical "reality" in which we are interested. In other words, understanding of the social construction of people's organizational life and activities is the context of their everyday business life within the firm.

When considering a Lifeworld perspective today in an international context where the economic power and models of the industrial world are being "explored" to other countries, the contrast between the two opposite views of economics (neo-classical and Lifeworld) the issues of economic growth and the role of the firm and business development become even more apparent. In terms of international policy, the USA and some other industrial nations claim to have neo-classical economics in exporting to other nations but operate internally in "heavy-handed protection of national industry at home" (Reinert 1994: 82). Today this is "managed free trade." Most industrialized countries have used some form of the German model for economic growth: "combine competition and protection" (ibid., p. 82), yet preach and advocate free trade. The reality of Western industrialized economic growth has always been one of "protect and promote" (see Reinert for a thorough analysis, 1998).

Within this political (philosophical) economic context, the basic issue for most actors in firms is how to make the company survive and grow during any particular point in time. They must be free to move in the marketplace but also be secretive enough to protect its privacy. In America, these issues are reflected in the American Constitution. For example, under Article #8, individuals are guaranteed protection of their ideas and inventions. This section is the basis for the patent, copyright, and trademark office of the national government whose responsibility is to file, store, and protect the intellectual property of all Americans. While patents, copyrights, and trademarks make up a thriving industry for the attorneys, the concern to protect intellectual property is the core for almost all business activity.

How does a company get control and ownership over technology? Is technological innovation gained through development, research or acquisition, mergers, and takeovers? In other words, how does the firm act in order to be both competitive and profitable? Consider first how to look at innovation and corporate growth in America. We suggest further exploration of the commercialization of a new technology(s) and applying this case study to other everyday business examples. More empirical examples are needed of how an interaction perspective would construct a topic, methodologically approach it, and theoretically describe, understand, expand, and perhaps even predict how innovations can occur within a firm. Finally, we outline how this formalism from linguistics provides theoretical power for converting economics from an art form into a science.

# Chapter 8
# Methodological and Theoretical Constructs

## Introduction

The purpose in this chapter is not to discuss all issues of qualitative methodology or to show the different interpretations of what qualitative is and does. The purpose is more to highlight some of the central arguments in our discussion of ontology and epistemology in Part I in relation to methodology and theoretical construction and to raise some of the critical aspects in understanding reality and economic life.

For this chapter, the case of innovation in research, as a catalyst to change, is seen as emanating from the interactionistic perspective in that it comes from human imagination and interaction. As we have been discussing, the whole idea in the perspective is interactionism combined with Chomsky and phenomenology. This is in relations to the understanding of everyday business life and as the fundament for the methodology of interactionism. When reality is constructed socially through interaction and symbolic discourse, the researcher can better be able to understand how business people create their own realities as social actors, if he creates knowledge in the same way: through interaction with the purpose to create meaning.

So to create this knowledge, we need concepts of method and methodology: method comes from *meta* "from or after" and *hodos* "journey," and so method means "a going after" or "pursuit." Methodology add *logos*, so it is a question of principle of reason in acquire knowledge. Together they stand with the discussion of how to plan the journey and how to travel. As we discussed in part I, the creation of knowledge is a journey of understanding meaning and making experiences, not so much in relation to a fixed goal that we pursuit but more an expansion of horizon. The matter is nearness and how to get close the people. The brief description in all of the traditions that we draw upon is that they talk about participation, conversions, dialogue, how to be conscious about ones prejudgments, and how to be open.

© Springer Nature Switzerland AG 2019
W. W. Clark II, M. Fast, *Qualitative Economics*,
https://doi.org/10.1007/978-3-030-05937-8_8

The key to collecting experiences or data on actors, situations, groups, and collective behavior are the methods and methodology employed. Here the qualitative methods[1] from anthropology and sociology play a significant role. The exemplar of data collection is face-to-face interview or conversation. Written documents, artifacts, and other forms of expression are species of the interaction between the researcher and the actor, but there is a difference between the situation in a face-to-face situation and the situation that exist between a text and a reader. The face-to-face encounter provides the richest data source for the researcher seeking to understand economic life.

For decades, anthropologists and sociologists have conducted research studies using qualitative methods. The results of these studies are often case studies, which describe the "static state" of a culture or group of people. One of the basic methods used is "participant-observation."

The qualitative studies require that the researcher must get close to the phenomenon under investigation; some studies even require that one must live and work in a particular environment in order to understand the people's everyday life. In addition to the traditional anthropological methods, other related qualitative methods are used. Collection of prior data is always a method used by a qualitative researcher before going into the "field." In the context of business, this method would be called "market assessment" whereby the researcher/business person would want to know what information is already available about the culture and how to understand them and evaluate what are missing.

However, the researcher needs to be critical about these materials since previous studies may be biased in different ways and are collected from a certain perspective. As outlined later, field or site visits are used to gather data, analyze it, and then draw conclusions. What remains critical in the qualitative perspective are the interactive methods utilized in the actual data collection process along with the interpretation itself. The "site or field visit" is the single most important method in qualitative research. Here the researcher/business person must actually go and see what the culture looks like. The researcher/business person must live in another place and experience the culture and people. It is not enough to visit or tour to get the deeper understanding of economic life.

There are a number of subtle, but often critical facts learned from such visits. Among others is the local infrastructure (transportation, communications, housing, and commerce) which may influence the market in a particular way. However, observation is not enough. And in many cases, observations can be wrong – we are imprisoned in our tradition of seeing.

Interaction and in-depth interviews/conversations are necessary from a variety of people. Usually, anthropologist identifies a "key informer" or someone whose information is consistently "correct" and "objective." These people are not always the leaders of the culture, but they have rare insights into how the culture operates. Such people can verify and correct observations with their meanings and definitions. More importantly, through interactions with them, a deeper understanding of the phenomenon, situation, event, and market can be made.

---

[1] Field work, participant-observation, action research, interaction, dialogue analyses, text analyses, etc.

Introduction                                                                                          231

Research results are "analyses – checking of results and verification" in order to provide useful written descriptions. This entire process resembles what Blumer (1986/1969) describes as the "symbolic interactionist perspective." The basic assumption for the symbolic interaction is that actors interact with one another and form relationship with others and meanings. However, each actor also interacts with him/herself. In short, the actor reflects and contemplates his/her actions. Blumer calls this thinking process, the "generalized other," because actors do this all the time: they think, reflect, think again, act, think, and continue to move ahead. In other words, Blumer provides a theoretical framework for understanding intuition when seen as part of an actor interaction with others. This is what we want to grasp in using qualitative methods and make sense of reality.

For the business actor, the result of qualitative research can be a plan of action. Even though the anthropologists rarely do anything with the data regarding a plan of action or implement changes, the business actor can. In particular, the anthropologists never forecast or explain situations and cultures. They try not to influence the local culture in any way. This non-action model has come under considerable criticism but is considered by most anthropologists as following the natural scientific method: objectivity.

A business person would develop an "action plan" and move on it immediately. The person would want to see the problems solved and the needs of the culture fulfilled. In many cases, the person has the vision of a concept for the future economic development of the culture and will act upon it. Typically, the person will "carry through" or "follow up" on their analysis of the culture because they see a business opportunity.

The entire qualitative approach is the process of interaction at work. It also sets the stage for understand how actors interact and create universal concepts which can be applied in a variety of situations. The underlying rules that explain the action of the actors can then follow the linguistic perspective outlined by Chomsky (1980) so that the explanation of interaction is seen in the formation of rules. Linguistics uses a qualitative methodology in order to identify sources of data such as native speakers/hearers of a language.

Sentences are created and repeatedly tested against that of native speakers. Underlying the transformational grammar approach to linguistics is the assumption that languages have universal characteristics. The task of the linguistics is to identify and derive the grammar for a language. Data is collected and comparisons are made to other languages. However, linguistics (and now psychologists) has found that native speakers/hearers do not know rules and representations of their own language. Instead, they know what sounds right and correct.

> Some evidence may bear on process models that incorporate a characterization of grammatical competence, while other evidence seems to bear on competence more directly, in abstraction from conditions of language use. (Chomsky 1980: 201)

In order words, qualitative methods for language usage are the basic data collection procedure for linguists. They use discovery and description of everyday language as the basic core for their analyses and theories. These methods can readily be applied to business economics for a variety of purposes. Some are, in fact, in wide use already as with "interviews" and the more formalized concept which is derived from interviews and put into a collection of people, focus groups.

Morgan and Smircich present a table of "Assumptions about Ontology and Human Nature," delineating the spectrum of approaches from the subjective approach with "reality as a projection of human imagination" which sees human beings as transcendental beings through phenomenological research to the objective approach with "reality as a concrete structure" which sees "humans as responding mechanisms in the research of behaviorists and social learning theory" (1980: 498).

However, Morgan and Smircich caution the researcher from depending upon qualitative methods alone. For one thing, they argue correctly that qualitative methods can certainly be used to describe and explain objective approaches. In fact, the one social scientific method (e.g., participant observation) most recognized for using qualitative methods is derived from anthropology, which has a long and distinguished tradition of coming to such "objective" conclusions about cultures as being static, concrete, and mechanistic.

> Participation observation in the hands of a positivist may be used to document the number and length of interactions within a setting, but in the hands of an action theorist the technique may be used to explore the realms of subjective meaning of those interactions. (Morgan & Smircich 1980: 498)

As distinguished from participant observation, action research places the researcher in the business situation. Instead of being only an observer who participates in limited or self-imposed constraints ways in business, the action researcher is a part of everyday business activity. For example, action research means that the researcher would be involved in the ongoing business. If decisions are made or strategies followed, the role of the action researcher is to participate and even initiate and carry out those business decisions. Nonetheless, Morgan and Smircich fail to describe "action research" and provide examples.

Moustakas (1994: 21), in discussing qualitative methods, talks about the common qualities and bonds of human science research as being:

1. Recognizing the value of qualitative designs and methodologies and studies of human experiences that are not approachable through quantitative approaches
2. Focusing on the wholeness of experience rather than solely on its objects or parts
3. Searching for meanings and essences of experience rather than measurements and explanations
4. Obtaining descriptions of experience through first-person accounts in informal and formal conversations and interviews
5. Regarding the data of experience as imperative in understanding human behavior and as evidence for scientific investigations
6. Formulating questions and problems that reflect the interest, involvement, and personal commitment of the researcher
7. Viewing experience and behavior as an integrated and inseparable relationship of subject and object and of parts and whole

The interactionistic perspective focuses on understanding of the dynamics of human change within society. Qualitative methods therefore become crucial for describing, understanding, and perhaps predicting the human condition. Case in point is Clark's PhD thesis done in the late 1970s which was updated in 2017 into a book and published as *Violence in Schools, Colleges and Universities* (NOVA Press) that enacts these qualitative methods. On the other hand, quantitative methods do not provide an adequate framework or even set of tools to understand the creativity of innovation and its adaptation in everyday business life.

The interactionistic perspective is strongly humanistic, with focus upon the understanding of the human being, the human condition, and of science. An empirical science has to respect the nature of the empirical world, that is, its objects of study, and the empirical world is understood as the natural world created by group life and conduct. To study it is to involve and interact with the actual group of actors, to understand how they carry on in their lives – social life appears in their natural environment – in their everyday of life.

Blumer's method in study larger social formations is that it can be done by viewing these as joint actions and as people trying to fitting their lines of action to one another. Such joint action does not lose its character of being constructed through an interpretive process in meeting the situations in which the collectivity is called to act: a firm seeking to expand its international operations or develop a new product or reorganize its organization needs to construct its action through an interpretation of what is happening in its area of operation. The interpretive process takes place by participants making indications to one another, not merely each to himself. Joint action is an outcome of such process of interpretive interaction.

Organizations are arrangements of people who are interlinking their respective actions. The organization and interdependency are between such actions of people stationed at different points. At any point the actors are confronted by the organized activities of other people into which they have to fit their own acts. The concatenation of such actions taking place at the different points and over time constitutes the organization. In seeing the organization as an organization of actions, interactionism seeks to understand the way in which the actors define, interpret, and meet the situations at their respective here and now. The linking together of this knowledge of the concatenated actions yields a picture of the organized complex.

# Action Research Methods: Core Data Gathering for Business Life

Construction of scientific knowledge should in principal follow the same principles as the everyday of life construction: for example, central in this construction is subjectivity, meaning, action, intersubjectivity, interaction, and language. Economic life is construction, and science is about understanding of business everyday of life activity.

## Basic Philosophical Aspects of Methodology

Susman and Evered (1978) establish action research as scientific, within a subjective and interpretative philosophical tenant, which differs dramatically from the methodology used by positivist and rationalist science. The basic philosophical aspects underpinning action research as a core qualitative method can be drawn from the four areas that they discuss and argued furthermore and which should be seen in relation to our discussion of phenomenology, symbolic interactionism, and Chomsky.

First is "praxis" which originates with Aristotle as "the art of acting upon the conditions one faces in order to change them" (ibid., p. 594) and connected with his discussion of *Phronesis*.[2] Karl Marx made praxis the core of his early theories of "alienation, economics, and society" (ibid.; Clark 1977) by empowering people and noting how they changed in the process itself. Benson (1977b: 16) in his dialectical discussion argues that praxis attends to the interplay between practical interest and scholarship. Furthermore theories must reflect the social context as socially constructed, dependent of human beings' action and interaction.

Therefore the importance of how theories are used is central to understand everyday business life. The analysis of business situations should be concerned with conditions under which people may reconstruct organizations and establish social formations in which continuous reconstruction is possible. A commitment to praxis or the free and creative reconstruction of social arrangement is a description that is both about people as active agents reconstructing their own social relations and the ethical commitment that social sciences should contribute to the process of reconstruction in the everyday business world.

The second aspect concerns *hermeneutics*, which referred to the interpretation of texts (Susman & Evered, ibid., p. 595) and creation of meanings. Today the field sets the stage for modern linguistics and culture by "attempting an initial holistic understanding of a social system and then using this understanding as a basis for interpreting the parts of the system" (ibid.). Methodologically, "knowledge is gained dialectically by proceeding from the whole to its parts and then back again." This is Dilthey's understanding and discussion of the hermeneutic circle and *Verstehen* (understanding) of a concrete reality. In other words, to have any situation that involves action, there must be interaction between actors.

Dilthey describes three relations, which make it possible to understand (*Verstehen*) the meanings of others (Polkinghorne 1983: 30). The researcher needs:

1. To be familiar with the mental process, through which meaning is experienced and conveyed. Since each person is involved in trying to communicate meaning to others, everyone is familiar with these processes to some extent, but researchers can enlarge this familiarity through the study of biographies as well as descriptive and cognitive psychology.

---

[22] "practical ethical understanding" or "practical rationality" related to the Lifeworld.

2. To obtain knowledge of the particular concrete context in which an expression is made. A word is understood in the context of its sentence; an action is understood in the context of its situation. This is precisely the same point made by linguistics like Chomsky for understanding language which is the basis for the theoretical and methodological transition to business situations.
3. To have an understanding of the social and cultural systems that provides the meaning for most expressions. To understand a sentence, we need to know the language; to understand a chess move, we need to know the rules of chess. To understand everyday business life, we need to know the rules derived from the situation.

Susman and Evered (ibid., p. 596) note that action research is similar to existentialism since they both are a reaction to the limitations of rationalistic science. However, that does not appear to be enough to argue for existentialism to be a basic philosophical element in this area. A better philosophical tenant (thirdly) exists in their argument for *pragmatism* where science is seen as another actor in society and therefore would make statements, challenge them, and revise them in order to derive some concept of truth. Blumer notes that this "reflective" nature of interaction is precisely what defines human behavior from that of animals or machines. People reflect on their actions. The reflective thought processes of humans allow for learning, adaptation, and change. It is the underlining dynamics of everyday business life.

A fourth and more contemporary approach to action research using qualitative methods has been the "legal system." As some anthropologists have argued for decades, understanding the legal system in any society is important in terms of conflict resolution and characterizing societal values. More recently and especially as seen in the American legal system, *court cases* are a new and significant source for data, facts, and either implementing or verifying institutional behavior. This has become even more apparent in the USA due to the corporate scandals in early part of the twenty-first century, especially related to the de-regulation and subsequent energy crises in California and other parts (counties, cities, states, etc.) in the USA.

While new corporate rules and standards have been installed for monitoring business actor behavior for operating companies, it is the court room where the actual data is collected and verified. Later we will describe this deference as between the surface (legal standards and rules) and deep structures (actual everyday business actions). Suffice for now to consider just the data collection methods used for legal actions. Aside from actual courtroom testimony (under oath so as to assure truth), there are depositions (also under oath but not taken in court), records, files emails (now often referred to as "eEvidence,") tracking of telephone and electronic actions, and observations of individuals and groups.

The legal system has also become more scientific in its evidentiary process from the identification of clothing to the DNA from human hair and body fluids. Laboratories are available and equipped as well with new computer-generated visual aids and potential scenario building for a variety of potential predictive opportunities or actions. These same methods are now being applied to businesses as well as actors.

Finally, there is a sociological *phenomenology* aspect of *action* research. The argument is that any future ends desired by an individual, groups, and events in society have no objective reality that can be measured. Instead, any understanding of "ends, values, and norms have a phenomenological reality from the perspective of the person or groups taking action…" (ibid., p. 596). The key is to understand those actions and interactions in order to understand how human beings create or enact their world, individually or/and collectively. Action is the means through which we engage in our everyday reality.

The phenomenological methodology is well summarized by Moustakas (1994: 58–), and as an extract from his discussion, we can state that the essences of the phenomenology are that[3]:

1. Phenomenology focuses on the appearance of things, a return to things just as they are given and removed from everyday routines and biases, from what we are told is true in nature and in the natural world of everyday living.
2. Phenomenology is concerned with wholeness, with examining entities from many sides, angles, and perspectives until a unified vision of the essences of a phenomenon or experience is achieved.
3. Phenomenology seeks meaning from appearances and arrives at essences through intuition and reflection on conscious acts of experience, leading to ideas, concepts, judgments, and understandings.
4. Phenomenology is committed to descriptions of experiences, not explanations or analyses. Descriptions retain, as close as possible, the original texture of things, their phenomenal qualities, and material properties. Descriptions keep a phenomenon alive, illuminate its presence, accentuate its underlying meanings, enable the phenomenon to linger, and retain its spirit, as near to its actual nature as possible.
5. Phenomenology is rooted in questions that give a direction and focus to meaning and, in themes that sustain an inquiry, awaken further interest and concern and account for our passionate involvement with whatever is being experienced.
6. Subject and object are integrated – what I see is interwoven with how I see it, with whom I see it, and with whom I am.
7. At all points in an investigation that intersubjective reality is part of the process, yet every perception begins with my own sense of what an issue, object, or experience is and means.
8. The data of experience, my own thinking, intuiting, reflecting, and judging, are regarded as the primary evidences of scientific investigation.
9. The research question that is the focus of and guides an investigation must be carefully constructed, every word deliberately chosen, and ordered in such a way that the primary words appear immediately, capture my attention, and guide and direct me in the phenomenological process of seeing, reflecting, and knowing. Every method relates back to the question, is developed solely to illuminate the question, and provides a portrayal of the phenomenon that is vital, rich, and layered in its textures and meanings.

---

[3] See also A Giorgi different writings of a phenomenological method.

## Qualitative Principles

In a qualitative approach, some general demands to scientific constructions are needed. The discussion of science and its demands on the structure of models for the understanding of the social or business reality can be categorized in four principles (see Schutz 1973b: 56, 126):

1. **The demand for logical consistency**. The system of typical structures drawn up by the research worker must be established with the largest extent of clearness and precision in the frame of concepts implicated and must be fully compatible with the principles of formal logic. The fulfillment of this demand guarantees the objective validity of the objects of thought constructed by the research worker, and their strictly logical character is one of the most essential features with which scientific objects of thought differ from the objects of thought constructed by common sense thinking in everyday life which they are to replace. In other words, a logically connected system implies that the means–goal relations together with the system of constant motives and the system of life plans must be constructed in such a way that (a) it is and remains accepted by the principles of formal logic; (b) all its elements are drafted in full clearness and precision; and (c) it only contains scientifically verifiable assumptions which must be totally accepted by all our scientific knowledge.

2. **The demand for subjective interpretation**. The action researcher must, to explain human action, ask which model can be constructed by an individual consciousness and which typical content must be ascribed to it, in order to explain the observed facts as a result of such an activity of consciousness in an understandable relation. The acceptance of this demand guarantees the possibility of referring all kind of human action or its result to the subjective meaning that such an action or its result has to the actor.

3. **The demand for adequacy**. Any expression in a scientific model referring to human action must be constructed in such a way that a human act carried out in the Lifeworld by an individual actor in the way which is indicated by the typical structure is rational and understandable to the actor himself as well as to his fellow men in the common sense interpretation of everyday life. The demand for adequacy is of the greatest importance to social scientific methodology. Adequacy makes it possible for social science to refer to events in the Lifeworld at all. The interpretation of the researcher of any human act and situation could be the same as that of the actor or his partner. Accordance with this principle therefore guarantees the consistency of the data of the researcher with data in the common sense experience of everyday business reality.

4. **The demand for ethics**. Ethics must be applied to research in everyday business life. Because the interaction between the researcher and the subjects is intense and often revealing, it is important that the results of the work reflect the concerns and well-being of those who provided the data. Dire consequences could come to people if certain business secrets (as in the case presented in Chaps. 9 and 10 below regarding intellectual property of commercialized inventions) or

strategies are revealed. Everyday business life has numerous hazards attached to it; the work of the researcher should not be one of them. In the end, the researcher should be able to contribute and enhance the well-being of the everyday business activity under study. And this is precisely the purpose of action research: to contribute to the business situation through interaction.

The structure of the social world is not the random act of the scientist which can be performed at detached discretion because: (1) There are historical limits to the fields of science which any research worker has inherited from the historical ancestors as a stock of recognized statements (see Schutz, Gadamer).[4] (2) The demand for adequacy requires that the typical structure is no more contradicted by the totality of our everyday life experiences than by our scientific experiences.

## Silverman: The Action Frame of Reference

One classical example of the attempt to formulate an organizational action research is Silverman's *action frame of reference* (1970/1983). In the understanding of organizations, he build upon Weber's concepts of *Verstehen* (as observation and theoretical interpretation of the individuals subjectivity) and ideal types.[5] For Silverman this is about understanding the actor's definition of the situation and his objectives in it and to illustrate in which way the actor's actions are related to objectives and where the actions should be seen in relation to the actor's background (biography) and interpretation of the environment. The action approach shall thereby be understood as a method to analyze social relations in an organization. The starting point for this is understood as seven propositions (Silverman 1983: 126–):

1. "The social sciences and the natural sciences deal with entirely different orders of subject-matter. While the canons of rigour and skepticism apply to both, one should not expect their perspective to be the same."
2. "Sociology is concerned with understanding action than with observing behaviour. Action arises out of meanings which defines social reality."
3. "Meanings are given to men by their society. Shared orientations become institutionalised and are experienced by later generations as social facts."
4. "While society defines man, man in turn defines society. Particular constellations of meaning are only sustained by continual reaffirmation in everyday actions."
5. "Through their interaction men also modify, change and transform social meanings."
6. "It follows that explanations of human actions must take account of the meanings which those concerned assign to their acts; the manner in which the everyday world is socially constructed yet perceived as real and routine becomes a crucial concern of sociological analysis."

---

[4] cf. the paradigm discussion in Chap. 3.

[5] Some of the inspiration for Silverman is Schutz, Berger and Luckmann, and Cicourel and Garfinkel.

Action Research Methods: Core Data Gathering for Business Life

7. "Positivistic explanations, which assert that action is determined by external and constraining social or non-social forces, are inadmissible."

In those propositions we can recognize the thoughts from the Lifeworld traditions[6] as presented in Chap. 4. Silverman talks about emphasized explanations in terms of meanings as the purpose of the analyses and with a dialectical understanding of development. The main features of the action approach as a method of organizational analyses can be seen as three problems: (a) understanding of the origin of organizations, (b) actions in organizations and (c) organizational change.

Silverman's suggestion to the path along which an action-analyses of organizations might proceed is summarized as six interrelated areas[7]:

1. The nature of the role system and pattern of interaction that has been built up in the organization, in particular the way in which it has historically developed and the extent to which it represents the shared values of all or some or none of the actors
2. The nature of involvement of ideal typical actors (e.g., moral, alterative, instrumental) and the characteristic hierarchy of ends which they pursue (work satisfaction, material rewards, security). The way in which these derive from their biographies outside the organizations (job history, family commitments, social background) and from their experience of the organization itself
3. The actor's present definitions of their situation within the organization and their expectations of the likely behavior of others with particular reference to the strategic resources of others (degree of coercive power or moral authority; belief in individual opportunity)
4. The typical actions of different actors and the meaning which they attach to their action
5. The nature and the source of the intended and unintended consequences of action, with special reference to its effects on the involvement of the various actors and on the institutionalization of expectations in the role system within which they interact
6. Changes in the involvement and ends of the actors and in the role system and their source both in the outcome of the interaction of the actors and in the changing stock of knowledge outside the organization (e.g., political or legal changes; the varied experiences and expectations of different generations)

The action approach involves meta-theoretical assumptions in line with what we discuss in Chaps. 4 and 5 and should be seen more as a method of analyis rather than a theory of organization.[8] The organizational sociologist is concerned not with restating social meanings but with placing them in the context of the logic of an academic discipline. That is to say, he reinterprets the meanings of common sense in terms of the meanings of Sociology. While normally one reflects very little on the taken-for-granted meanings associated with each act, the sociologist seeks to under-

---

[6] Especially in relation to Schutz and Berger and Luckmann.

[7] Silverman, op cit. p. 154.

[8] Silverman, op cit. p. 222.

stand the nature and implications of the common sense world. While the individual often believes that his actions are entirely unique to him as a person, the sociologist is concerned with interpreting the typical acts of typical individuals by the use of ideal types which take account of subjective meaning. Sociology is thus specifically devoted to "unmasking" (to use Berger's term) the assumptions upon which social life are based.

# Sample Economic Action Research Methodological Protocol

## *Multi-Methods*

We advocate a qualitative multi-method approach in understanding everyday business life. By that we mean the use of any combination of the methods discussed below. The choice of the methods is up to the action researcher, following the principles above, but more significantly appropriate to the particular situation. A pluralistic attitude, usually totally quantitatively oriented, is a combination of various methods, often cited as triangulation. This pluralistic methodological perspective is fundamental different from qualitative multi-methods. For one thing, triangulation is derived from engineering and assumes that each method is independently scientific. The result of using triangulated methods is to produce the "greatest truth." An example of the combination conception in the methodological discussion is reflected in the following:

> This perspective aims in short at combining a qualitative procedure, depending on the goal of the investigation. This available method book joins the attempt of such an integration between the two procedures. The mentioned methodical combination perspective, which in short aims at using more than one method for investigating the same phenomenon (Kruuse 1989), has several designations like convergent methodology, multi methods (Campbell & Fisker 1959), convergent validation or method triangulation (Webb et al. 1966). The expression triangulation is taken from land surveying, where two different bases are used to determine a third… Our main point of view is that it is primarily the aim, object field and the problems of the investigation which are to be decisive for the choice of methodical procedures. (In Andersen (ed.) 1990a: 15–; *our translation*)

There are a myriad of problems in this discussion and in this quotation. Consider only a few. (1) Who raises the questions and formulates the investigation and where? (i.e., who is the subject and what is the context); (2) what is the starting point? (i.e., the ontological assumptions and background that we all have when we look upon reality); (3) how do we determine which method is the "best"? Issue such as problems, investigations, and solutions are not self-evident, so someone needs a subject to check and settle them.

Some of the consequences of this approach will be a lack of in-depth cognition in the investigation and the theorizing about the phenomenon under study, as well as a tremendous confusion about the following set of issues: (4) What is methodology, philosophy of science, theory, reality, etc.? (5) Why do we have to deal with it? (6) What is the result or impact of the research? While this last issue could be seen as an ethical one, our concern is primarily to what use is the research result being put. Most importantly, (7) will the results benefit society as a whole, people, and the environment?

In summary three components are embedded within interactionism: (1) Action research methods fit well into business practices. (2) Qualitative methods are rooted in certain philosophical principles. (3) Business dynamics (at the micro- and macro-economic levels) can be scientific following the subjectivism paradigm and interactionistic perspective. While these methods are not definite, they are well known and tested. We use many of them in our case examples. Finally, qualitative methodologies have also expanded as new forms of communication become viable today, so we present some methods from the use of the "Internet" and "digital information data."

In line with those arguments, the process of research has to start with and handles the following topics:

1. *Purpose* of the study or exercise must be established. Often this is a simple declaration of a "Problem Statement," followed by a discussion of how to understand it and from which perspective.
2. *Formulating the question (the qualitative working hypothesis(es) or ideas)* needs to be postulated. A series of questions should be examined in advance of the actual study. Sources (next section) should be reviewed for information and details that can be part of the inquiry. Often the questions are disproved as part of the actual fieldwork.
3. *Target population* (the customer, if a marketing study) should be identified. For example, it is impossible to get a qualitative sampling (although quantitative researchers claim sampling validity by +/− percentage points) for the inquiry; efforts should be made to gather divergent viewpoints and perspectives.
4. *Data sources* include many things. Prior to the inquiry, some sources might include: documents, statistical data, research or market studies, reports, and public records, among others.
5. *Field work* is the crucial demarcation between qualitative and quantitative inquiries. For the quantitative researcher, data collected by surveys, published reports, or statistical methods is adequate. For the qualitative research direct experience in the field can be the only valid method for data collection (including the other data sources).

Since the qualitative methodology argues for scientific inquiry that includes as its base line, description of phenomena, fieldwork is the only valid approach. Within fieldwork are two fundamental means of inquiry:

## *Interviews (Personal and Groups)*

A qualitative methodological approach often creates a simple yet comprehensive protocol for the inquiry and analysis of any event, situation, market, or phenomena under study which might be constructed as follows. The key to good qualitative methods is the interview or series of them. Today, with the use of smartphones, texts, internet, online, and teleconferencing along with especially email, Twitter, Facebook, and more to come, these areas are all immediate and constant in the interaction between actors and more possible than ever before. The following are some basic interview guidelines that can be used on a one-to-one basis or over the new electronic media:

## Structure

Provide a list of questions/topics in advance for the researcher to use. The questions can be noted in the form of short phrases or bullets for easy recognition during the actual interview. For example, most interviews should start with the researcher asking questions about the history and background of the situation. Once the interview starts, personal questions (how she/he got the present position and what are her/his future plans, etc.) are good for analytical reasons but also to establish rapport for further interaction.

## Content

As indicated above, the beginning of the interview should gather information to construct the background of the situation. However, the interview should try to be focused upon the purpose of the inquiry. The interviewee will most likely give freely of time, often want to talk further, and certainly provide additional documentation. Nevertheless, the interview itself needs to be directed and pointed.

## Collection

Notes should be taken. Most interviewees feel complemented when the interviewer takes down notes of what she/he is saying. The notes consist of keywords jotted and phrases that can be quoted later. Some researchers advocate the use of audio and video equipment since it gives the appearance of being more "objective" or "full" in both present data collection and later analyses.

However, there are some basic facilities with this line of thinking (not to be reviewed here), but more importantly, such equipment is very "obtrusive" in the interview itself. More recently some researchers use portable computers to take notes. This is most effective in group meetings rather than individual interviews but could be attempted.

## Analyses: Interpretation and Explanation

Trying to understand and interpret the interview is the hardest task. There is no set approach or easy formula. The key to analysis is the link to the original working perspective for the study. If the interview data works (follows or reflects the logic of

Sample Economic Action Research Methodological Protocol

the situation and the actors' interaction studied) with the perspectives, even as they have changed as a result of the research, then the analyses are productive.

## Prediction

As in linguistics, once actions and situations are described and analyzed, they can be characterized in generating formalistic sets of rules. We will demonstrate with our case study how these rules might work for understanding everyday business reality. The most important consequence of rulemaking is the ability to predict future business actions. Our rules allow that yet nevertheless need to be field tested in other everyday business situations.

## *Participant Observation*

We have described and commented on participation observation already, as well as the basic methodological perspective of action research. Suffice it to say that we would now want to outline some of the actual methods used by the action researcher in the field.

### Cast of Actors

Within any business situation, there are a number of people with whom the researcher interacts. The basic issue is that not everyone can be interviewed and constantly part of the business situation. Even more significantly, not all the actors provide both reliable and accurate information. For a variety of reasons, actors may be not forthcoming with truth data. Therefore, the action researcher must constantly check and double check information to actually get a deeper understanding of the story.

In most research situation, furthermore, the action researcher will identify and befriend at least one actor with whom the data and information appear insightful and adequate. There is no set procedure for identifying the key actor. However, one notion to follow in the field is that usually the first actors to become friendly and close to the researcher is not usually the best for adequate and accurate data.

### Groups (Meetings, Focus, and Ad Hoc)

Business situations involve meetings and groups discussions. In fact, most businesses have a preponderance of group activities. While often time-consuming and appearing unproductive by the action researcher, much can be learned from participating in these meetings. For example, most groups will attempt to discuss and resolve some business matter. While a few meetings follow an agenda, most are usually intended to resolve issues and make plans. The action researcher can understand much about everyday business life within the firm by participating in these sessions.

## Reports

As noted earlier, the use of electronic devises in interviews of actors or of groups or meetings can be disruptive, if not totally inhibiting. The best method is still the use of notes written and collected for future use and study. Some researchers have attempted to either take notes on a hand held or laptop computer. Others have even had handmade notes keyed into a computer later by a secretary. Both approaches while laudable are often too expensive and wasteful in terms of cost and time. Note-taking is far more unobtrusive as well. However, great attention must be given to accuracy: (1) of direct quotations in the sense of exactly what was said, (2) getting permission or understanding that such note-taking was acknowledged, and (3) checking with other actors for comprehension of what was said and why and what was the consequences.

## Digital Information Data

We need to turn to a new growing area of qualitative research methods that deserve special attention. While we want to present these methods here, we acknowledge that much more careful consideration must be done in examining these methods. Nardi (1993, 1996a, b) begins to make a case for some of these methods especially in looking at the computer industry.

The authors have seen a growing and pervasive use of electronic data exchange in the work of graduate students studying businesses all over the world. The availability of the "Internet" means that people and firms have instant ability to communicate with one another. We need to spend some time discussing these new methodologies in qualitative action research:

Email (or Electronic Mail)

Preceded in the early 1990s, data and information were electronically transmitted by fax (see studies by Alan Firth 1996 and unpublished 1997). With the dawn of the twenty-first century, email has become a worldwide dominant form of communication. Clark and Fienberg (2002) on The Next California Economy which was (and is now) wireless and eGovenment argued that email can be seen as a qualitative method when consider as interaction between different actors. In fact, as noted above, often email is used to set the agenda for meetings as well as record the results. Research using the collection of email (when given permission) is very valuable and insightful data. However, email must be supplemented or part of personal interaction. It cannot be a substitute for the action researcher becoming engaged with the actors.

http//:www (or World Wide Web)

A large and an increasing number of firms (and even individuals with their own "home page") are using the www to display information about their company and its activities. This is a good source for basic data on a firm but must be viewed with skepticism as to its accuracy and adequacy. A firm will provide in-depth and revealing information. Here, the action researcher will be able to get a portrait of the firm but must dig deeper with further interaction among the actors and in specific situations.

Film/Video/Photographic

Qualitative researchers have increasingly used visual media for studies over the last two decades. However, today there is such a plethora of visual data that it is difficult to comprehend and let alone organize it into a comprehensive study. Visual data allows the researcher to communicate to others what the firm looks like in terms of its building, location, internal rooms, and activities. Often visual media is helpful to picture the actors in the study. Again, visual media should not be substituted for direct and constant interaction with the actors in the business situation.

Teleconferencing/Video Phone

An area not much utilized today but with increasing potential, especially as firms appear to use the means of video communications, teleconferencing rather than having meetings in person are extremely good sources of data. With the advent of new computer software, a number of actors are interacting over long distances. Sometimes this means of communicating is referred to "virtual" connectiveness since the actors might be talking to each over the computer internet terminals.

*Wifi, Cell/Text, Facebook, LinkedIn, WeChat, Albaba, Twitter* and many more from Google, Apple, and Microsoft and many other international companies around the world.

## *Situational Analysis*

Throughout our discussion on methodology and theory, we have made reference to everyday business situations.

We draw from Lucy Suchman (a colleague and former Blumer student with Clark) whose work over the last 15 years at Xerox Corporation has concentrated primarily on how to improve the "interface" (e.g., a computer science term meaning how humans interact with computers)[9] between copying machines and people. Suchman's research (1987) has extensively applied qualitative methods to understanding and explaining how people use copying machines. Without repeating this work and subsequent publications, she has been an action researcher (trained anthropologist in symbolic interaction) able to contact studies and implement results within the engineering of Xerox machines. Her methods include some combination of the multi-methods described here.

Even more significant is that Suchman and also Nardi (also an action researcher at Apple Computer) are able to be action researchers by using qualitative methods for discovering and understanding issues in the copying and computer businesses, respectively. Once they understand the needs within specific situations, they are able to recommend to the various corporate units to make changes or follow courses of further action.

## *Legal Methods and Actions*

One of the most dramatic and verifiable forms of data collection today that is clearly qualitative are legal proceedings. Most are the result of legal actions taken against firms for issues ranging from fraud to accounting. In general, the adjudication situation in the US came about in the early 2001 due to the California energy crisis. It was caused initially by Enron corporation who by early 2002 declared bankruptcy. Then over the last 5–6 years, many more prominent American corporations went bankrupt as well, except in different sectors ranging from telecommunications to airlines. As a result the US Congress passed the Sarbanes-Oxley Law which placed national regulatory rules on all corporations including the need for accountability and holding liable corporate officers and Board members (Clark and Demirag 2006b).

While many companies and their officers have been under legal investigation and been punished, that is not to say that all companies in bankruptcy have been corrupt. However, as the Methodology Appendix documents, there is considerable quantitative evidence against Enron and its role in the California energy crisis. A number of senior officials in the company have been convicted and sent to jail. In Chaps. 9 and 10, the outcomes are discussed in more detail as they apply to the science of economics.

The issue is that law and its methods including testimony, depositions, and jury trial take qualitative methods as described above as verifiable facts. Hence, the use

---

[9] Clark taught a course in "Human-Computer Interface" in the College of Engineering, Department of Applied Sciences, University of California, Davis. And now teaches at the University of California, Los Angeles and Riverside, Heckmann Center for International Entrepreneurship.

of email is a well-documented legal trail of evidence. In fact, within the legal profession, lawyers refer to "email" as "evidence mail." The same is true of recording from voice messages and conversations. Such methods also are documented facts that have been accepted by judges, juries, and the courts. Hence, qualitative methods are considered facts which are *not* often the case for qualitative methods and numbers.

## *Documentation and Write-Up*

Descriptions of the phenomenon have to be interpreted to give a meaning, and the qualitative interpretation and understanding of qualitative interviews and studies can be seen in six "continuous" steps (Kvale 1990a: 226, in Andersen (ed.)):

1. The actor describes him/herself, without any special interpretations.
2. The actor discovers on his own new connection, without any direct affection.
3. The interviewer interprets and seeks comments from the actor in the dialogue situation.
4. The interviewer interprets on his one finished interview. This approach can be seen on three levels:

    (a) Summing up and formulate what the actor himself understand as the meaning with what he describes.
    (b) The interviewer interprets "between the lines," a more critical commonsense interpretation.
    (c) Draw more theoretical interpretations into the interpretation.

5. A new interview, with the actor comments to the first interpretations.
6. Describe and understand also the actions in the actor's everyday world.

The result of a qualitative perspective and its methods to understanding phenomenon, situations, events, markets, or even products is an analysis that is descriptive and interpretive. Some researchers might even see the end results as predictive. This is an understanding of the concrete actor situation and of what they put into it. But the result can also be a general understanding of the phenomena, in relation to, for example, a characteristic of ideal types in a discussion of the phenomena. Knowing well that those ideal types do not exist in the reality in their pure form but exactly are theoretical constructions which generalize the phenomena – that is, draw attention towards some certain characteristics (see Weber 1948: 90).

If the researcher/business person is to better understand others, then the use of Lifeworld traditions and the qualitative methodology is the only place to start. The use of additional data to support the study(s) and even content is important, but the basic approach must be one that attempts to understand others using concepts from qualitative theories and methods. The end result will be a far more "market- or consumer-"oriented understanding of the human condition.

## Everyday Business Dynamics Is Scientific

Our use of interactionist perspective and the Lifeworld paradigm has lead us directly to consider the combination to transformational linguistics as the closest social science to being pure science available today. We feel that if economics is to become science, then the field must operate in the same way that the natural and physical sciences do. Reliance upon statistics and quantification are not enough. They may be tools and even part of various approaches to discovery, but they are not science in themselves.

Transformational linguistics is a field very close to being science. The results of linguistic inquiry, for example, produce rules and representations for language interaction that are parallel to those in business economics. Linguists may debate among themselves about heroes in the various areas, but at least they have a theoretical perspective from which to start. Heretofore, economists have not had the luxury of a theory that produces tangible, verifiable, and significant results.

At this point, returning to the field of economics is useful in comparing this volume's work with others. Since starting with the supposition from Schumpeter that industrial research and development is the "heart of the capitalist engine," it is possible to concur with Nelson when he states that Schumpeter's basic premise is correct, but he fails to take it much further. Our acceptance of Schumpeter's hypothesis is even more basic. Indeed, research and development are the cornerstones to any economy (not just a capitalist one). However, we do not feel that Schumpeter or his successors (Nelson, 1990: 199) have developed an adequate theory of innovation and commercialization.

This assertion is valid on three levels. First, economics has failed to prove itself to be a science. Instead, as a field it continues to be an art form, performed by many creative people. There is no science. Or to paraphrase Gertrude Stein when speaking of the city of Oakland, California, "there is no there, there." Second, there are few instances in economics were everyday business situations have been documented, leaving the field to speculate or quantity phenomena. Finally, while historical economists like Heilbroner (1989) clearly describe the impact of innovation and research in industrialized countries, the data lacks any understanding and explanatory power.

In this volume, we have presented in detail the subjectivist philosophical tradition in order to lay the groundwork for the Lifeworld paradigm. Once the perspective is established, it is easy to see why phenomenology and symbolic interactionism is so significant on human and group interaction. When adapting the transformational linguistics approach to economics, we have constructed a powerful theoretical framework.

What our case study in Chaps. 9 and 10 does is to consider the commercialization of an innovation into the business world. Significantly, we approached the entire case from the interactionist perspective such that we were able to apply our action research and qualitative methods to the actual point of commercialization. The resultant set of rules need to be examined by others and explored for universality. Suffice it to say, however, that we have started our own interactive dialogue with other scholars in the field. This exchange we hope will prove useful to the field of economics.

# Chapter 9
# Linguistics as a Science

## Introduction: Subjective Interactionism and Linguistic Theory

Blumer describes interactionism as the essence of being human. People interact with themselves through the generalized other; they reflect; they think about their actions for themselves and with others. In short, humans talk to themselves and to others too. Interaction is what defines human beings from other species. Fast and Clark (2008; Fast et al. 2014) have published also how interaction of the human minds is a key factor making economics into a science. For decades, Chomsky led linguistics into understanding the same argument for human behavior due to the uniqueness of language – the ability of human beings to communicate endlessly.

The use of language is what makes humans different from animals, insects, and other forms of life. Language allows people to communicate – to interact. Language is the symbolic form of interactionism. The argument was made in the last chapter that the use of formalism from linguistics may not only describe and understand human interactionism but also provide a formalism in which everyday business life can be explained and predicted. Formalism is using the basis of the scientific method applied to the social sciences like linguistics and economics. This chapter demonstrates that the data from the case studies earlier provides good examples on how linguistic theory and interactionism can provide a new approach to economics.

At this point, it is important to acknowledge and review some of the history within linguistics that led to a "paradigmatic revolution." Chomsky caused one in the early 1960s when he literally established linguistics a "science" by arguing for formalism through the creation of theories in "transformational grammar."

This chapter makes the argument for the application of linguistic theory and application into business and economics. In short, modern linguistic theory provides the framework for a paradigm revolution in business and economics. Chomsky is the place to start, since he himself started a paradigm revolution in linguistics in

---

© Springer Nature Switzerland AG 2019
W. W. Clark II, M. Fast, *Qualitative Economics*,
https://doi.org/10.1007/978-3-030-05937-8_9

249

the 1960s. Economics needs to learn, follow, and apply linguistics into what it needs as a new philosophical paradigm that is a science.

Most of modern linguistic theory is based on the seminal works of Chomsky from the late 1950s and early 1960s. Chomsky's first book 1957 was on linguistics, Syntactic Structures published by The Hague Press in Holland because no American Press would publish his articles and this book at that time. His theories produced a major paradigm change in both linguistics and later (1970s) in psychology. By the early 1970s, however, some of his former students and others staged their own paradigmatic revolution. The difference in the two approaches to language studies rests primarily in what Chomsky initially defined as "competence" and "performance." For Chomsky originally, competence or the mental processes in which the language user structured (surface and deep structures) the use of words, sentence, and thoughts were the key to linguistics. Performance or the meaning of those words, sentences, and thoughts was less important. Because of this difference, competence research turned into a new academic field of study: cognitive sciences.

During the last 40+ years (1970s into decades of the twenty-first century), linguists like George Lakoff (1970a, b, 1971), Paul Kay, and Charles Fillmore, among others, who agreed with Chomsky, objected strongly to the focus on competence. For them competence was the "meaning" in linguistics which they saw as the most important part of language. So they developed a new field in linguistics known as "cognitive science" which has grown substantially in the 1990s and twenty-first century. Some scholars would argue that ethnomethodology (which has its inspiration from phenomenology) itself represented the performance paradigm within linguistics since it focused upon the content or meaning of action. Without meaning, language competence and its formal structures made no sense.

Language competence was nontemporal, linear, and isolated from everyday life went the argument. Various sub-theories grew around this paradigm such as discourse analysis, speech act theories, and pragmatics. By the late 1980s and early 1990s, however, Chomsky had incorporated performance and meaning into his theories. Or to put it another way, he stated that meaning had always been part of his paradigm ("government binding").

This book does not debate the challenges within linguistics. Clearly the distinctions between competence and performance are significant. The basic paradigm remains the same and is now globally well established. Critical to this discussion is the basic notion instead that meaning cannot be separate from structure. However, the discussion below is not aimed to review or enter into the current linguistic debate over these issues. Instead, the business cases of advanced technologies demonstrate that meaning and structure must be combined within a linguistic theoretical framework. An argument is presented that uses linguistic formalism for describing and understanding the actions of actors in everyday business life. Linguistic formalism allows scholars and observes to see relationships in the context of micro and then macro theories. Indeed for that reason alone, transformational linguistic grammar theory is a very powerful theoretical paradigm.

Linguistic theory provides the framework for combining meaning and structure in human interaction. In short, linguistic theory allows the study of business

Introduction: Subjective Interactionism and Linguistic Theory

economics to be scientific. Above all, the importance of performance is paramount and acknowledged as a key element in everyday business life. It is the basis of what Blumer argues makes humans human – human beings reflect through the "generalized other" on their actions and those of others. In short, actors think; they do not just react to stimuli or events. Thus Blumer and phenomenology established the basis of understanding how and why actors interact with one another. The approach today would be called nonlinear and parallel processing of actions rather than a simplistic linear or causal sequence of activities and events. What Chomsky's linguistic transformational grammar does is formalizes the micro and situational analysis level to a universal and macro scientific level.

The everyday business activities of actors and hence firms must be seen in their present situations which include a past, meaning, and other actors. Through interactionism, everyday business life transpires. It is constantly changing and moving. The conventional paradigm and neo-classical theorists would describe and quantify only one moment or snapshot in time of a business activity. Such a rigid perspective of business is clearly not realistic and certainly limited in any scientific sense. Statistics do not provide scientific understanding, certainly are not explanatory, and are never predictive. Linguistic formalism, derived from an entirely different set of philosophical roots and when combined with the same philosophical thought from interactionism, transforms business economics into a scientific discipline. Below, such a paradigmatic revolution is demonstrated in business economic.

## *Interactionism in Everyday Life Such as the Business Firm*

Since interaction between actors is universal in all human groups, it is equally critical in the formation and daily activities of all organizations, firms, and institutions of any size. In fact, the core definition of entrepreneurship and any new venture rests on a team or group interaction as noted in Chap. 9. The ability of any group to operationalize teams and focus upon concepts, ideas, and events provides them with an inherent ability to change. It is change that characterizes organizations. Human groups only survive if they not only handle new conditions but also grow or innovate in new ways. Such change is not restricted to technological innovation. The dynamics of change are part of any group. The task of the action researcher or scientist is to describe, understand, and explain the business everyday life or economic reality of a group or firm. As seen earlier, there are a number of economic studies about the dynamic nature of companies. Some use metaphors from other fields.

Thurow (1996) presents an economic model drawn from evolution, much along the lines of Schumpeter's (1934) original notion that innovation allows some firms to replace older ones over time. In other words, firms change as in evolution of humankind. Schumpeter used that idea as well as his basic concern was with the how economics patterns are disrupted with new innovations. Teece et al. (1994a) argue that behavioral factors limit decision-making in the firm: bounded rationality within cognitive frames and inconsistent risk aversion.

Graedel and Allenby (1995) use a biological or "life cycle" model in order to explain industrial ecology, which places map industrial production into a life cycle model. The neo-classic approach simply states either supply or demand rooted in the market (technology push or pull approach), which both is badly defined or undefined. None of these economic models and theories presupposes the uniqueness of human beings and their ability to construct their own social and economic realities. Instead, the conventional functionalist paradigm and its many manifestations in behaviorism, systems theory, neo-classic economics, and structural functionalism present a fixed or stagnant approach to understanding economics which are modified with metaphors and models.

Earlier, neo-classical economics was reviewed due to their mistake on not understanding what science is and how science works. At this point, consider how groups become firms and internationalized. However, a fundamental question must be asked of economics: What is the theory of the firm? As noted earlier, Economics Professor David Teece asked this rhetorical question repeatedly of his graduate students and other scholars. As he repeated through a series of graduate-level seminars, the answer is rhetorical in that "there is no theory of the firm." Yet even positing the question represents a fundamental need and fallacy within economics: lack of theory building, especially for practical business applications.

Other social sciences have contributed to the literature of economics. While most anthropologists view economics on a micro level (see Barth 1962, e.g.), a number of studies have broader and meta-theoretical applications. Economists such as Reich (1992, 1994), Tyson (1992), Nelson (various articles, as well as 1990), and Teece (various citations, especially 1994 and 1996) note that macroeconomics need not be only statistics, historical econometrics, M1 flows, interest rate calculations, computational models, and mathematical formulas.

## Macro- and Microeconomics: Interactionism and Situational Events

Few macroeconomists venture into the area of microeconomic analyses in order to articulate macroeconomic theories. Can microeconomic studies lead to macroeconomic theories? In other words, can macroeconomic theory building be constructed on microeconomic theories of the firm? Qualitative economics thinks so. Therefore, it is important to construct a scientific theory of the firm. Theoretical power of linguistics has successfully examined both macro and micro levels of analysis with considerable success.

The key is often how the social sciences "structure" actions, situations, and events. Along with Suchman (1987) and Boden (1994), structure can be seen as not preceding or ordering interaction, but instead is derived, from it. "All social life is, first and finally, episodic. The essence of humanness is contained and communicated through verbal interaction, face-to-face or, at stage and places removed, telephonic and even electronic" (ibid., p. 6).

Language is the medium of communication among human beings. While linguistic analysis of action is used (e.g., discourse analysis, cognitive science, speech act, pragmatics, etc.) in qualitative economic theory building, the basic notions and assumptions within linguistics place an emphasis on micro data gathering (methodologies) for descriptive and understanding phenomena, situations, and events for describing the interactions in macro theories which can then be explanatory and predictive. In other words, the theoretical value of the insights by scholars like Chomsky is to see that everyday life as expressed in language both as universal human phenomena and as a particular interaction among people.

The competence of human beings for language usage is interactive with their performance of language actions on a daily basis. Blumer, built upon Mead and a philosophical tradition that articulated this interaction among actors. Hence transformational linguistics becomes a formalism derived from everyday interaction to better understand business activities, the firm, and how they fit and influence larger and more universal events in society. It is the chore element in this chapter to articulate and merge these various parallel and connected perspectives into a new approach to business economics.

Barth, for example, from anthropology, is one scholar who attempts to postulate macro theories from micro field work studies. However, he too follows the neo-classical economic paradigm into a focus only upon barter and exchange of goods and services at the community (micro) level. Consider his concept of "profit" or what he calls the "common sense" concept of profit, such that profit "take(s) the form of power, rank, or experience and skills…" (1962).

Profit is not simply the monetary or material gains often assumed in the economics literature. Such a common sense definition of profit derived from microeconomic studies in various community studies allows a more comprehensive and complete understanding for building macroeconomic theories, but it rests clearly in a predetermined organizational structure. "Costs" (the other side of the business ledger on a balance sheet) for most business economics are also viewed from a microeconomic level to derive macroeconomic theory.

Again Barth (1962) considers not only the monetary and material costs for a new business venture but also the "social costs" for the entrepreneurial venture within the community. When an entrepreneurial business fails, the social costs in the community are high in terms of failure to perform, conflict among family members, not delivering on a promise or deal, or violating the trust of people. Often when a business venture works not work, there are investors, suppliers, and creditors who also loss. This is the conventional cause-effect economic model for business economic activity. Entrepreneurship, therefore, encompasses the individuals starting business but also an array of chain events or casual factors. The entrepreneurial venture must constantly "balance" the monetary and human profits and losses.

For this book, the consideration of the firm, and particularly the commercialization of an innovation, allows any observer to understand the building of macroeconomic theory from the Lifeworld tradition for everyday business life. Interactionism is the cornerstone for moving from the microeconomics or case study perspective to the larger more "universal" macroeconomic one. In that context, there is a need to understand the case about technological innovation in light of business economics. The further definition of economics as exchange and therefore as engagement allows us to understand economic phenomena, events, or situations as drawing from a knowledge base in order to construct an economic reality of everyday life. Since actions among actors is predicated upon their knowledge and understanding of others, consider a description of the case in such terms.

Academic disciplines discover each other, only after one field cannot explain what it is doing to itself and others, or arrive at the end of long endless theoretical debates, or find phenomena impossible to describe or explain. The philosophical underpinnings of most scientific fields are rooted in inquiry, debate, and usually insights if not direct theoretical application from other fields. This is true with the physical sciences as must as it is for the social sciences and their sub-fields.

Thomas Kuhn (1962) captured the process perfectly in what he labeled "paradigms." His basic argument was that core scientific changes occur dramatically and permanently, until the next paradigm change comes along. At each juncture of paradigm change, a new set of assumptions, theories, and proposals are made. Kuhn, however, failed to identify where and how these paradigms change happens in social science. Furthermore, he fails to link the practical applications of paradigms to the real world. Neither of these concerns was important for Kuhn. Nor should they have been. As a physicist turned philosopher, he achieved much in just stating that paradigms existed only to be changed, reformed, or totally thrown out for other paradigms. Kuhn left the more dynamic and applied issues for others to contemplate.

If paradigms exist and change, then theories and explanations of society and its in situations must do likewise. This chapter answers both issues left by Kuhn: where or how paradigms change and their application to the real world. In discussing the where and how paradigms change, the chapter examines the interactionism perspective in a Lifeworld tradition of qualitative research and theory building, since this field concerns actors, action, and interaction which provide the basis for a dynamic explanation of human behavior and by extension societies engaged in economic and business activities. In short, people and their everyday lives provide the basic data for linguistics, much the same as they should in any new theory of economics.

The second area of concern is to link the theories to the real world of business. Here the chapter applies these theories to the real world of business. In any culture, communities act and interact due to the economic realities of everyday life. While the world economies are changing dramatically, local communities and groups continue to do business as usual. Business activity impacts work, individuals, their families, other businesses, and the quality of life in a region. Much of this business activity can be seen through entrepreneurship, as either originating the enterprise or creating the economic opportunities.

Elsewhere (Clark 1994a, b), the argument is made that the world economic changes have changed the way in which traditional economic theories are applied to business activities, or not applicable at all. The end of the Cold War has brought about new concepts and definitions of business. More significantly, the need for new theories has never been greater.

As new nations are formed and economics emerge rapidly, the conventional macroeconomic models, derived from Western industrial experiences, become irrelevant to emerging and developing countries. Even among the industrialized world, there is little agreement on basic economic issues such as a "free market," market economy, profit, or the role of government in business development. New theories and perspectives must be created. Linguistic theory appears to provide many useful and applicable concepts within the interactionism perspective.

## The Science of Linguistics Applied to Economics

A number of useful concepts can be borrowed from linguistic theory for the understanding of entrepreneurship and economics in general. The application of linguistic theory to business theory and specifically to entrepreneurship in the international firm can be seen in four areas. The subjectivist paradigm sets a new and different stage for economics because it is part of the science method. Each of these areas fits into the interactionism perspective and Lifeworld tradition to form a science of economics. Consider the arguments:

First language is what distinguishes human beings from all other forms of life. While some researchers posit that animals and even bees have language systems, the evidence is inconclusive. However, humans do have complicated language systems that allow them to communicate, create, and build on a body of knowledge. Human language is composed of complicated sets of symbols that when used interactively allow messages to be transmitted.

Second, linguistic theory argues that language is divided into two structural components: surface and deep structures. The surface structures are those symbols that people use in their everyday life to speak and write. The surface structures are the part of the grammar that cultures devise in order to record their history, communicate, and transact business. Surface structures, in other words, are those things that can be objectified, since actors can see, feel, or touch them. They are business events and situations in any understanding of everyday life.

The deep structures are an entirely different phenomenon. Language has meaning attached to words and combinations of words (sentences) that are not expressed in the communication act itself. Furthermore, the deep structures are not defined in dictionaries or other guides to the language. In short, deep structures constitute the real core and understanding of any language and therefore of any culture and of people's actions and interactions. Meanings are attached to situations, events, and surface structure business phenomena.

Third, individuals learn surface structures (speaking and dialogue of a language) at an early age. However, empirical studies show people understand deep structures (grammar and syntax) at an early age. Research consistently demonstrates that babies must learn vocabulary, for example, but need little training in the deep structure of their native language. Children put sentences together and derive meanings from their creation.

Finally, linguistic theory has been applied to social systems – individual and group behavior by sociologists and psychologists throughout the 1970s and 1980s. What many of the researchers attempt to do is use linguistic theories to explain social and individual behavior. The most successful applications have been in psychological cognitive studies. Here empirical studies have shown that the mind does process and operate along linguistic theory perimeters.

The sociological and anthropological applications of linguistic theory have been more problematic however. Until now, there has been no application of linguistic theory to business economics. While a number of theorists have posited that how societal behavior, for example, can be seen as interactions between deep and surface structures, the empirical data is lacking. For the most part, there are too often rigid functional separations. When one tries to incorporate the work of other fields, there is usually a forced mix of ideas, which result in both muddled data and models.

The purpose here is not to review the entire social science research and theoretical literature on the application of linguistic theory. As noted above, in linguistics itself, the paradigm revolution started by Chomsky has since the 1970s been challenged and revised by other linguists. Today there are, acknowledged by Chomsky himself, three theoretical perspectives within his transformational paradigm: "standard theory," "extended standard theory," and "generative semantics" (Chomsky 1975: 238). Chomsky sees himself as an "extended standard theorists" for reasons not useful for this discussion. The purpose here is to use the general "transformational grammar" theory in linguistics and explore how to apply it to build a theory in order to understand and perhaps explain new enterprises in business economics.

## Scientific Paradigm and Theoretical Change[1]

The study of human beings, their activities in business, and the larger society is parallel to natural science study of physics, biology, etc. Chomsky asks the basic question:

> what is the 'science-forming capacity' that enables us to recognize certain proposed explanatory theories as intelligible and natural, while rejecting or simply not considering the vast array of others that are no less compatible with evidence? (Chomsky 1980: 250)

Basically, science must be able to describe, explain, and predict phenomenon. Linguistic theory led by Chomsky has been able to do just that in a nonphysical and natural science environment. The key is to extend the construction of a theory beyond the descriptive phase and into an explanatory and hopefully predictive phase.

Chomsky theorizes in language usage much the same as Mead (1932) and Blumer (1969) did in their study of social and cultural phenomena. Linguistic theory allows us to probe "the human mind (since it) is endowed with some set of principles that can be put to work when certain questions are posed, a certain level

---

[1] Some of this section was developed with Olav Jull Sørensen; see Clark and Sørensen (1994a, b).

Scientific Paradigm and Theoretical Change 257

of understanding has been achieved, and certain evidence is available, to select a narrow class of possible theories" (ibid., p. 250). Chomsky cites Weinberg (1976: 28) on the theoretical relationships, "In the natural sciences, it is common to adopt what has sometimes been called 'the Galilean style' – that is, to construct 'abstract mathematical models' of the universe to which at least the physicists give a higher degree of reality than they accord the ordinary world of sensations" (ibid., p. 218).

Language can be seen then as "A comparable approach (which) is particularly appropriate in the study of an organism whose behavior is determined by the interaction of numerous internal systems operating under conditions of great variety and complexity" (ibid.). In terms of paradigm changes and the impact on theory, Chomsky argues that "Progress in such an inquiry is unlikely unless we are willing to entertain radical idealization, to construct abstract systems and to study their special properties, hoping to account for observed phenomena indirectly in terms of properties of the systems postulated and their interaction" (ibid.).

For Chomsky, the critical question and even the most controversial was how to proceed? If one assumes, as Chomsky has that the "creative aspect of language is a characteristic species property of humans" (ibid., p. 222). In short, what makes human beings unique is their communications system of language. Conducting business in everyday life is an extension of that concept. "Language serves as an instrument for free expression of thought, unbounded in scope, uncontrolled by stimulus conditions though appropriate to situations, available for use in whatever contingencies our thought processes can comprehend" (ibid.).

Language distinguishes human beings from all other species in that "we construct new sentences freely and use them on appropriate occasions, just as we comprehend the new sentences that we hear in novel circumstances, generally bringing much more than the knowledge of language to the performance of creative acts" (ibid.). Human beings are infinitely able to create and innovate. That gives them the ability to manage and control their environment.

The scientific approach to the study of language means that to the linguist, grammar (as distinct from speaker-hearer's grammar) is "a scientific theory, correct insofar as it corresponds to the internally represented grammar" (ibid., p. 220). "The grammar of the language determines the properties of each of the sentences of the language. For each sentence, the grammar determines aspects of its phonetic form, its meaning, and perhaps more" (ibid.). In other words, "The language is the set of sentences that are described by the grammar." and the "grammar 'generates' the sentence it describes and their structural description…" (ibid.). Thus a "generative grammar" is "sufficiently explicit to determine how sentences of the language are in fact characterized by the grammar" (ibid.).

A number of basic principles then follow that compose the theoretical basis of linguistics:

1. "The language generated by the grammar is infinite" (ibid., p. 220).
2. "The grammar itself is finite" (ibid., p. 221).
3. "Thus, the rules of grammar must iterate in some manner to generate an infinite number of sentences, each with its specific sound, structure, and meaning" (ibid., p. 221).
4. "This process of applying finite grammar to form infinite language is the "recursive property" of grammar" (ibid., p. 222).

5. Finally, language is what allows humans to construct new sentences (ideas) freely in all situations.

Consider the parallel study in the natural sciences, for example, of the human being, as applied to social organizations: (a) function, (b) structure, (c) physical basis, (d) development of the individual, and (e) evolutionary development.

As demonstrated earlier, the use of function and structure in linguistics is very different than that used in behaviorism and the conventional deterministic paradigm. Think of "function" as purpose: then "functions of language are various" including but limited to expression of thought and communication. Both rather empty since no formulations can be made "from which any substantive proposals follow" (ibid., p. 230).

Therefore from a functional point of view: "human language is a system for free expression of thought, essentially independent of stimulus control, need-satisfaction, or instrumental purpose, hence, qualitatively different from the symbolic systems taught to apes" (ibid., p. 239). Or consider "structure": then structure is seen in language "generated by a system of rules and principles that enter into complex mental computations to determine the form and meaning of sentences" (op.cit.).

These rules and principles are in large measure "unconscious and beyond the reach of potential consciousness" (ibid., p. 231). The studies of various language structures lead to linguistic universals which are "principles that hold of language quite generally as matter of biological (not logical) necessity" (ibid., p. 232).

When the social construction of everyday business life is considered, then people are essentially following the same logical process. "To determine these principles is the deepest problem of contemporary linguistic study" (ibid., p. 232). That is, "highly restrictive universal principles must exist determining the general framework of each human language and perhaps much of its specific structure as well" (ibid.). Therefore, structurally, "human language is a system with recursive structure-dependent rules, operating on sequences in a hierarchy of phrases to generate a countable infinity of sentences" (ibid., p. 239).

The research challenge is to find, describe, and explain these recursive rules as they are embedded in the deep economic structure and transformed into action at the surface business structure. From one point of view, everyday business life of actors rests in different situations.

With enough studies and data, qualitative economics can form basic or universal rules that will have predictive power. "These basic properties (meanings and structures) are unique to human language, and the same is true, a fortiori, of more complex principles of universal grammar that characterize human language" (ibid., p. 240). However there is little known now from the list above on areas of (c) physical basis, (d) development of the individual, and (e) evolutionary development in language and the study of the mind (ibid., pp. 240–247).

Chomsky (1975) outlines his theory of languages such that natural languages are common "to discover 'the semantic and syntactic rules or conventions (that determine) the meanings of the sentences of a language', and more important, to discover the principles of universal grammar (UG) that lie beyond particular rules or conventions" (ibid., p. 78).

Chomsky's "primary purpose is to give some definitions of the kinds of principles and the degree of complexity of structure that it seems plausible to assign to the language faculty as a species-specific, genetically determined property" (ibid., p. 79). He does this by distinguishing between surface and deep structures. While definitions are outlined of surface and deep structures in Chap. 4 in order to orient the reader and illustrate their explanatory utility for the EV and ZAFC cases, it is best to define the concepts as derived from linguistic theory.

## *Surface Structure*

Surface structure is the basic everyday words and sentences that humans use to communicate. On the surface, actors understand each other, or think that they do, and proceed to communicate based on those sets of assumptions. At the surface level, actors can form "various components of the base interact to general initial phrase markers, and the transformational component converts an initial phrase marker, step by step, into a phonologically represented sentence with its phrase marker" (ibid., p. 81).

In short, human beings can take everyday discussions and mark the sentences into a theoretical form for further detail and analysis. This process leads to the transformational derivation, which is "The sequence of phrase markers generated in this way…" (ibid.) to form sentences. From this process a syntax of a language can be derived with universal sets and rules.

## *Deep Structure*

The terms basic structure and deep structure as referring "to non-superficial aspects of surface structure, the rules that generate surface structures, the abstract level of initial phrase markers, the principles that govern the organization of grammar and that relate surface structure to semantic representations, and so on" (ibid., p. 86). The deep structures are the semantics, which give meanings to the sentence and words of the surface structures.

"We use language against a background of shared beliefs about things and within the framework of a system of social institutions" (Chomsky 1980: 247). Transformations are rules, which "map phrase markers into (other) phrase markers" (Chomsky 1975: 80).

The transformation component is "One component of the syntax of a language consists of such transformations with whatever structure (that is, as in ordering) is imposed on this set" (ibid.). For the transformation component to function in generating sentence structures must have some class of "initial phrase markers" (ibid.).

Chart 9.1 illustrates the relationship between surface and deep structures. Transformational relations or rules connect the two structures.

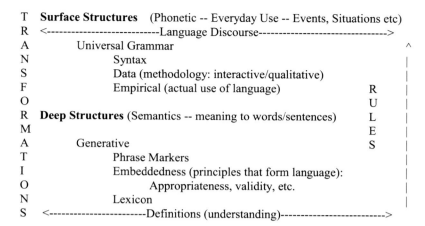

**Chart 9.1** Linguistic transformation theory. (Source: From: Noam Chomsky: "Reflections on Language." NYC: Pantheon Books, 1975)

The concept of universal grammar indicates that all languages contain the components in Chart 9.1. In other words, the transformational theory can apply to all languages. "The study of language use must be concerned with the place of language in a system of cognitive structures embodying pragmatic competence, as well as structures that relate to matters of fact and belief" (Chomsky 1980: 247–). What Chomsky did was construct a theoretical paradigm that is universal for all languages. From hundreds and thousands of studies in almost all languages, the theory has proven correct in its ability to describe, explain, and predict everyday language usage.

## *Transformational Linguistics*

A number of useful concepts can be borrowed from linguistic theory for the understanding of business and economics. The application of linguistic theory to economics and businesses focuses on four areas.

First, as noted, language distinguishes human beings from all other forms of life. Human language is composed of complicated sets of symbols that when used interactively allow messages to be transmitted. No other creature on earth has that capacity. This point is often mistaken as the philosophical basis for the rationalists and determinists to argue how to study quantitatively and explain human behavior.

Second, linguistic theory argues that language is divided into surface and deep structures. The surface structures are those symbols that people use in their everyday life to speak and write. The deep structures are entirely different since it attaches meaning to words and combinations of words (phrases and sentences) that are not

Scientific Paradigm and Theoretical Change

expressed in the surface interaction itself. In other words, deep structures constitute the real core and understanding of any language and therefore of people's actions.

Third, actors experience surface structures (events and situations) throughout their lives. Some of aspects of language can be taught, but children acquire the deep structure grammar or linkage of meanings at an early age. Research consistently demonstrates that babies must learn vocabulary, for example, but need little training in the grammar of their native language. There is a universal process at work that connects meaning to sentence structure and usage.

Fourth, linguistic theory has been applied by psychologists to cognitive studies. What many of the researchers attempt to do is use linguistic theories to explain individual behavior. Here empirical research has shown that the mind does process and operate within the linguistic theoretical paradigm. The goal or purpose here is to apply the linguistic theoretical to the interactionism perspective within the Lifeworld tradition.

The purpose here is not a review of the entire research and theoretical literature on the application of linguistic theory (see Chomsky 1975 for a good overview). Instead, the purpose is to apply these theoretical perspectives drawn from linguistics in order to provide an understanding and perhaps explanatory theory of business economics.

Consider now Chomsky's linguistic paradigm in more detail as it could apply to business economics. If the linguists' sentence-dependence principle is correct, "then the rules of grammar apply to strings of words analyzed into abstract phrases" that is in the technical literature "to structures that are called 'phrase markers'" (Chomsky 1975: 79). In a business context, a basic universal grammar of economics exists which can generate rules, which apply deep structure meanings to surface structure interactions. The action of actors can thus be explanatory and predictive. Linguists call these rules transformations, which map phrase markers into other phrase markers. Chart 9.2 illustrates the boundary considerations for transformational rules.

The transformational component of language is again "One component of the syntax of a language consists of such transformations with whatever structure is imposed on this set. For the transformation component to function in generating sentence structures there must first exist some class of "initial phrase markers" (ibid., p. 80). The present state of the field of economics provides such descriptive

* **Appropriateness**
   Qualitative method as empirical data in discourse and sentence usage.
* **Phrase Markers**
   Terms applied to parts of speech in order to
* **Generative Grammar**
   Use of the transformational rules
* **Defining Characteristics and Terms**
   Definitions in Lexicon and terms with meaning in everyday life.

**Chart 9.2** Transformational rulemaking considerations

classes. Since the economic corpus of terms and concepts (especially since the end of the Cold War) are international, they constitute a "universal grammar" to which "transformational rules" can apply under the assumption of changing global conditions and the subsequent deep structure meanings of words and phrases.

Syntax contains a "'base component' that generates a class of 'initial phrase markers'." The initial phrase marker class must be finite, thus "assigning to the base component the recursive property" which is central to any grammar. In order for rules to be useful, they must reoccur and be applicable to numerous everyday business situations. The base component itself consists of two subcomponents: "a 'categorical component' and a lexicon. The categorical component presents the basic abstract structures by means of 'rewriting rules' that state how a syntactical category can be analyzed into a sequence of such categories" (ibid.).

By way of example, consider a typical linguistic situation. A sentence (S) contains a noun phrase (NP) followed by a verb phrase (VP) or in symbols (NP VP → S) where "among the categories that figure in the categorical component are the 'lexical categories,' Noun (N), Verb (V), Adjective (A), and others" (ibid.). The representation of the parts of the sentence into symbols allows the surface structure to be broken down into components. The arrow denotes the transformation (→) from the deep structure (NP VP) into the surface structure sentence (S). In business applications, consider how the arrow or transformation provides an explanation of interactions when deep structure meanings are seen in everyday business interactions and relationships.

"The lexicon consists of the lexical items that belong to the lexical categories, each with its phonological, semantic, and syntactic properties" (ibid.). The lexicon also contains rules of 'word formation' that delimit the class of lexical items and express their general properties. "Lexical transformations insert items from the lexicon into the abstract phrase markers generated by the categorical component, giving the initial phase makers" (ibid., p. 81). The uses of lexical transformations are abstract, and through their phonological use with other grammatical transformation and rules, "they become sequences of words that count as sentences of the language" (ibid.).

Formalism Basic Structures

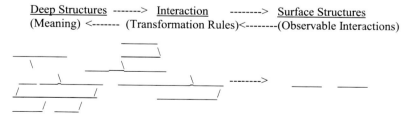

**Chart 9.3** Transformational linguistic formation

## Application of Interactionism within Formalism

**Chart 9.4** Transformational formation in business applications

Chart 9.3 illustrates transformational linguistics, while Chart 9.4 formulates the transformational application to some business concepts and terms used in the ZAFC case from Chap. 9.

## Transformational Rules in Business

The interactions among the actors in the ZAFC case form the lexicon for the generative grammar of a new business. On the surface structure level, various events and situations can be seen which need to be understood from the transformations generated in the deep structures where meanings can be seen as "phrase markers" or concepts that are discussed and put into actions. The interconnectedness of these concepts operates in large part on the transformational rules back and forth (interactionism) between the surface structures or everyday business interactions and the deep structure definitions and meanings.

Consider now the overall use of transformation rules in understanding and explaining economic and business interactions. The businessperson is one of many actors in a situation. The researcher must observe the entrepreneurial interactions of the actors and decide if they are "appropriate" in understanding explaining the everyday business actions. In linguistics, this would mean simply does the language act conform to common sense and everyday usage? If appropriateness is observed and recorded, then the question is to identify the specific phrase markers attributable to the defining characteristics of the business activity(s).

Finally, the generative grammar theory allows the researcher to make the connections around situations in terms of the actors, interactions, and symbols. When transformational rules are applied, the explanations for business actions become apparent and predictable. Extending this theoretical framework to other business areas will be left for another time. At this point, however, the ZAFC case as an entrepreneurial new business venture can be explained and better understood.

With these theoretical concepts in place, the actual transformation rulemaking process can be seen. That is the entrepreneurial experience becomes successful or unsuccessful because the team draws upon the defining characteristics in the deep structures of the new business creation interactive process (surface structure) and applies the appropriate rules. The rulemaking process is often intuitive, based upon common sense, and is situational. That is one reason why "teaching" and "learning" entrepreneurship are so difficult. All too often, the entrepreneurial venture is forced into the context of traditional business practices.

The use of a "business plan" is seen, for example, as the process that all entrepreneurs must go through in order to create, manage, and succeed in their business ventures. The problem is that business plans violate the transformational rules for entrepreneurs and new business creation. Business plans assume a linear approach to new ventures when the process itself is nonlinear and totally interactive. New firms are not created on a one-dimensional plane with prescribed steps to follow. New companies are formed from a constant iterative process among many actors.

While a complete "business grammar" cannot be presented at this time, one example of the transformational rules will illustrate how the theory could work. Chart 9.4 illustrates the application of the linguistic model into the ZAFC entrepreneurial experience. Later in the chapter, formal transformational rules for business interactions from the ZAFC case are presented.

The entrepreneurial team interacts with other actors as they define words and concepts in the lexicon of the deep structure. The actual surface structure can be seen as the set of interactions observed between actors (the entrepreneur and others necessary in conducting the new business). For example, there are transformational rules between the entrepreneur and the inventor of a product to form a business relationship as a team. The interactions in the deep and surface structures allow the product to be sold, marketed, or made into a new company.

These rules demonstrate how the entrepreneurial team must secure the "legal" ownership or status in order to have control over the technology (legal agreement). Through much discussion and dialogue, the team actors must be able to transform the process into a workable business deal (event and situation). If the entrepreneurial team does not follow that basic transformational rule, then the entire new venture may fail, if not soon, then later. The surface structure is seen as the actual situations such as the documents, organizations, and their everyday life business activities.

# Internationalization as a Social and Economic Construction

The ZAFC case discussed how a new technology is commercialized. In that discussion, empirical data was presented which illustrated how commercialization in this case depended on an international consortium, in part due to global environmental regulations which in turn were driving the need for new technologies to come into the marketplace. Here the discuss focused on how the internationalization of the firm is due to the interaction of the actors, the construction of their economic reality based upon mutually understood representations and definitions, and the directions or decisions that lead these actors and their businesses into the future.

In the first place, the symbolic interactionist perspective presents an approach to understand human group behavior and by inference the behavior of many institutions. What is clear is that actors behave within groups and across groups and that the interaction differs depending on the situation and events occurring at the moment. Human group life is, in other words, interacting at many different levels at one time.

Now consider the ZAFC case again for a moment. Here the actors have been interacting in different parts of the world. While English is the common language and native tongue of most of the actors, there are others who have English as second language. In today's international business world, English is the standard for almost every country. Great emphasis is placed upon the learning and use of English. However, contrary to some cultural anthropologists and linguists (Hofstede 1980a, b is the classic example), the English language is not bounded by national borders. Interaction among actors must create common "representations" of words and concepts. The concentrate cultural circles have no geographical or other boundary.

Even for English-speaking countries among themselves, there are enormous differences in the exact meaning of many English ideas, concepts, and events. This was extremely self-evident in the Australian-American business discussions. For example, the entire definition of intellectual property became a major hurdle for the actors. While easily defined in terms of the actual patents involved in the ZAFC, the business deal surrounding it was steeped in language difficulties. Attorneys were summoned for both sides, but even then the difficulty in defining "exclusive rights," areas or regions of the world, and particularly what was an "American company" which is a US legal requirement for any technology commercialized from a national laboratory became extraordinarily difficult.

Within the English-speaking world, the UK and the USA, for example, there are regional differences in language usage as well. The issue is not the differences but the need to seek the similarities within English. To derive the mental representations of words requires constant interaction at the deep structure level between actors and the groups in which they associate.

Common understanding and therefore collaborative international business relationships are only accomplished when the meanings of ideas are clarified, understood by everyone, and communicated through further interaction to other or larger groups by the actors. Across national boundaries, constant interaction among actors between firms allows for change and growth. All of this interaction, however, is predicted upon the shared knowledge based in representations formed over a period of time.

Soderberg (1996) further reports, for example, that one area of conflict between the British CEO of a company acquiring a Danish company concerns "unions." The foreign management did not understand the Danish unions. However, the analysis stopped only at the point of identifying and describing the issue of conflict over unions with a judgment analysis blaming the Danish union for the failure of the acquisition. That is not substantive enough since there is no understanding or explanation for the situation.

Upon reflection from an interaction perspective, the problem that the companies had in the acquisition rested in the nationalistic definition of unions themselves. For the British CEO, he had one concept of unions and what their role was in a company. Unions for him represented the blue-collar workers. However, the Danish have an entirely different definition of unions. Their unions comprise management and labor together, or when separate, each level has its own union. Furthermore, many Danish unions participate in the decision-making of the firm itself. Without this knowledge base to define the representations, the British CEO encountered considerable misunderstanding, which provoked unwanted employee conflict. Again, the basic knowledge must be well defined in the deep structure in order for constructive surface structure business interaction to occur, transform, and allow a firm to progress.

## Knowledge and Meaning

Knowledge, built upon representations, plays a fundamental role in business. The ZAFC case provides some interesting perspectives. Aside from the governmental environment legislation for zero-emission vehicles, there is an inherent economic demand from industry for a high-energy storage device, especially in the power and utility sectors. Commercial interest in the ZAFC is in part a response to its commercial staying power when compared against the advances in batteries and fuel cells. In the longer term, hydrogen can be used as an anodic reactant in the electrochemical recovery of zinc from alkaline electrolytes using proven technologies.

The voltage required drops from 1.8 to 0.5 V if a hydrogen anode is used. This decreases the electricity used by a factor of 3.6. The total energy conversion efficiency is nearly 30% Y about the same as a fuel cell. With the lower initial cost of the zinc-air fuel cell technology, the zinc-air solution has the long-term advantage over other fuel cells for energy storage as well as a transportation fuel.

In other words, when the knowledge base of the ZAFC technology was shared among other circles of businesses, the technology appeared to have applications to power, utility, and electric companies. ZAFC with its recovery unit could be used as standby and backup energy storage for communities. Some considerations could be made to use ZAFC to other energy-generating technologies that are environmentally

Knowledge and Meaning 267

benign. This link occurred because the actors defined terms and made representations of technical concepts about fuel cells that were then shared among themselves and with others. Because of that deep structure interaction, surface structure planned situations are under way in several areas to create and build ZAFC facilities that service both mass transit buses and utility power stations under one roof.

## *Interaction and Knowledge*

Parallel to the period of time when businesses were sought for commercialization of ZAFC, the interactionist perspective worked on another level and signaled what appears to be the successful commercialization path. One growing principle of American industry today is that an increasing amount of business production and manufacturing comes from international and global corporations. Foreign industry is often more innovative and willing to take risks that the American marketplace is unwilling to do. Some economists would agree that one of the reasons is due the market size: the American market is simply too big to experiment with, while the Scandinavian, Dutch, or French markets are smaller and therefore more likely to provide production viability.

Not surprising, the laboratory's announcement in the "Commercial Business Daily" attracted worldwide attention. A potential commercial market arouse through the manager of the Committee for the Australian Olympics for the year 2000. Without the public and widespread announcement (a frequent occurrence now with the Internet), the actors would never have linked up. None of the key actors ever met one another throughout the first 18 months of the process for formalizing a business demonstration project.

What become crucial for the international consortia partners that formed concerned the actual costing for the final stages of the ZAFC and ZRU for their adaptation to buses. The Australian power-utility company and the local Australian cities needed to get cost per bus low while for the research, development, and implementers (power company, the laboratory, bus company and its suppliers) needed the buses to be ready in time for the Olympics. It was one thing to have successful laboratory experiments, but quite another for reliable and consist usage on the people movers for the Olympics.

Hence the cost for ZAFC on the buses would be a further demonstration of the technology and be more costly that a standard commercialized technology already mass produced and manufactured. A considerable amount of discussion needed to take place in which technical details were shared in order to pinpoint the actual costs for the research/demonstration as amortized over the price per bus.

This discussion and interaction between all the actors resulted in seeing the additional linkage to the power and utility infrastructure for application of ZAFCs. In other words, the constant search for research and economic solutions netted a creative new and compatible application of the technology itself. Now not only had the pathway to commercialization been identified, but it was also considerably shortened. Funds for the dual purpose of power utility and transportation infrastructures could be combined. Plans and designs were made, therefore, for the establishment of a power substation in which ZAFC and the ZRU technologies could serve as both a power storage for electricity and zinc fuel refueling site for the people movers (buses).

## Economic Rulemaking in Interactionism Process

### *Organizing the Business Opportunity*

Turning to the ZAFC case study data, a pivotal event occurred in Europe in December 1995 with the "International Electric Vehicle Conference" sponsored by the State of California, US Government, and the Federal Republic of Germany. The laboratory sent two key technical scientists to present a paper on ZAFC, tour Germany, and visit automakers, as well as hold private meetings with bus manufacturers and battery makers, previously identified by the Australian power-utility company. After 2 years, the power company was replaced by the new entrepreneurial venture in Australian and with an American manufacturing partner. Most of the following analysis covers the consortia period of business operations and the initial entrepreneurial venture created after the key executive in the power company left to form a new company to commercialize the ZAFC and related technologies.

The result of the German Electric Vehicle Conference was the formation of an informal international consortium of private companies and public governmental organizations who will provide the final research and development funding for the ZAFC and ZRU technological demonstration. The common goal was to create a prototype in order to show the world that ZAFC can power zero-emission vehicles for the Olympics. However, the longer-term goal was to commercialize the revolutionary ZAFC innovation on buses throughout the Pacific Rim and eventually Europe and North America. The final marketplace would be worldwide, but major industrialized and newly industrialized nations would be targeted immediately.

The interactionism perspective provides both a macro- and microeconomic perspective for implementing technical advances into any society. When a region, state, or nation is seen in its totality, it represents a governmental unit, often driven by competing needs, demands, and powerful sectors.

### *Constituting the Internationalization of the Business Opportunity*

A detailed proposal (with different modifications for various consortia members) was written with exact tasks, costs, and timelines outlined for external funding. The entire consortia would build on the core ZAFC technology into exploring other

Economic Rulemaking in Interactionism Process 269

technologies for zero-emission vehicles. And in fact, the laboratory had another potential breakthrough energy storage device technology (a flywheel) that heretofore was not considered by the power-utility company or the consortia.

However, once the ZAFC was clearly defined, a technical gap existed in the zero-emission bus system (power peaking) that could be solved with the laboratory's flywheel. While the solution was known to the laboratory staff, they did not pressure or push the technology on the new international consortia. Instead, the consortia requested it. Again this is an example of the dynamics of interactive rules when actors are engaged in discussions about technical and business ventures.

The facilitation and operation of the consortia itself are another significant parts in constituting a firm or organization dedicated to demonstration of the ZAFC. The power-utility company was the driving force here both in terms of the macroeconomic identification of the year 2000 Olympics. It was also uniquely situated to see the market potential in Asia and implement its network of bus manufacturers and zinc producers. Furthermore, due to the Australian government designation of ZEV requirements as well as dozens of Australian cities pre-buying the people movers for use after the Games, the power company saw a new line of business developing. Unfortunately this situation changed after the Australian national elections and the power company became less aggressive in pursuing the ZAFC, terminating its development and the consortia's most active participant.

Finally, the constant interaction between the two organizations (the power-utility company and the laboratory) provided a strong and technologically competent relationship to market and then secured the participation of other groups. Along the pathway to commercialization, trust was built between the actors, even though the principles had not met in person. Conference calls, faxes, and documents established a constant dialogue. From the power company came the key executive who formed the new venture to commercialize the ZAFC. It was this actor who also went to the USA in early 1997 and spent 8 months of that year at the laboratory.

The building of an organization, in this case around a specific technology for commercialization, requires the establishment of a common base of knowledge with well-defined technical as well as business concepts. Once these relations are set, they change with the dynamic interaction of the actors in the group. The new company organizes in several concentrate cultural circles through a network of actors, thus making it subject to even more change.

## *Actors' International Experiential Space*

The key to the formation of an organization for conducting research and product development is the experiential characteristics that the actors bring to the business situation(s). When actors are seen in specific surface structure situations or isolated by events, misunderstandings can follow between the parties engaged in the business activities. Some of these misunderstandings arise from not understanding one another.

For example, a technical actor may state a figure that one of the marketing or business actors misconstrues. Aside from misquoting the technical expert, the two actors might become suspicious of one another. Trust via business networks and understanding via interaction are the keys to commercialization of a new product or invention.

The basic distrust that arises between organizations often starts with such deep structure interaction between different actors. There is no easy solution or suggestion to make for resolving this common problem. Some interpersonal and communications experts might argue that there are a few steps to follow to correct the problem. Others would wrongly attribute the problem to cultural attributes or characteristics (Hofstede 1980a, b).

The interactionist would view the entire issue differently. Miscommunication between actors can be attributed to problems in understanding each other's actions, both verbal and nonverbal. Often this is the case when the actors are from different communities, regions, or nations.

None of the conflictual situations can be attributed to a stereotypical concept of a culture. Nor can the conflicts be associated with historical background or variables. Instead, conflicts between actors over problems arising from misunderstandings are found in the lack of defining the meaning of ideas and concepts. There is little or no effort on reflection and clear thinking about one another's actions.

This is both a theoretical and methodological problem. On the theoretical side, the actions of the actors are not understood by other actors because they fail to understand the meaning behind the actions in a given situation.

When transformational linguistics is used, the deep structure meaning of concepts and ideas is transformed to the surface structure where people express themselves. Furthermore, the spoken communications and actions at the surface structure in everyday life are not adequately probed to get at their deeper meaning and definition.

Methodologically the actors often fail to ask probing questions of one another. They either assume meanings or simply dismiss the concepts. Interview-type questions between actors are needed to explore the deep structure and intention of actor's actions. These probing questions must also be substantiated by observations and constant participation in the business situations. There is no better method for the actors to understand one another, than inquisitive questions linked with observational verification of actions in business events.

The ability to combine, plan, and execute productive and constructive surface structure business actions is universal. Human beings do this in their everyday lives within a wide range of cultural circles. Everyday people must orient and organize themselves in order to accomplish what actions that they seek to perform. As such, human interaction cuts across all cultural and national barriers.

While there may be differences and subtleties in approach, tenor, or tenure of inquiring questions, there can be no mistake that human nature is universal. From this universality can be derived some rules of business interaction. Here an attempt will not be made to definitively specify these rules here but instead consider this as an outline of some examples as they apply to the case study.

## Management and Organizational Interaction in New Ventures

Management and administration are good places to start since they are derived from conventional economic thinking yet can be framed within the interactionist perspective and Lifeworld tradition. Consider how the ZAFC case about a new environmental technology for power systems and zero-emission vehicles can yield a new approach to management in business economics. Romm (1994) argues that better management within companies can produce more environmentally sensitive, if not clean industrial operations. "Every company can increase its profits and productivity dramatically by reducing pollution" (1993: 3) which is most likely true and well-worth advocating as part of the industrial ecology approach to the global environment. Nonetheless, there are many other economic analysts that make the same point in reference to general business practices (Drucker 1993; Deming 1993).

Romm's basic point is nevertheless significant: changes in the management of companies can be both profitable and environmentally sound. This is a significant issue debated by most corporate board of directors. Yet management within industry does not appear to be enough to assure "responsible corporate" decision-making about the environment. As Porter and van der Linde (1995) argue from a case in Holland, in order to have environmentally responsible companies, there needs to be some form of governmental regulation or guidelines. In short, the "environmental invisible hand" from neo-classical economics if left to corporations is suspect and visible by its absence.

Allenby et al. place the economics of industrial ecology directly on the shoulders of businesses, "especially product and process design" (1996: 26). In other words, if companies consider what they produce, manufacture, and distribute, then they will make environmentally "friendly" goods and services. The decision to manufacture, sell, and distribute environmentally sound products rests in the hands of management. Again while this perspective is important, it does not cover the basic concern for how businesses introduce new technologies that are environmentally friendly and reverse international ecological problems such as global warming and climate change.

However, Allenby does note that in the past, academic, governmental, private sectors have created "fiefdoms" that narrowly viewed sustainable development, including the economics of industrial ecology, through their own special disciplines. In other words, industrial ecology is seen by business and economic experts as "an economic programs" (ibid., p. 26), the same as lawyers see it as "legal programs" and engineers as a "technical program." What is needed is a multidisciplinary approach to sustainability.

Clearly an interaction perspective to sustainability and industrial ecology can be derived. That has been done with the intent of presenting an economic model that is applied to the industrial ecology's point of view by creating a new economic model from the application of linguistic theory in a specific environmental technology, the ZAFC.

If management oversees company decisions, it is done through constant surface structure interaction between actors. The question often asked is: What kind of management organization exists that can facilitate the firm? A number of scholars have attempted to answer that question. However, the more basic issue is: Can organizations provide management that allows and encourages creativity and innovation of environmentally important technologies at the deep structure levels of a company as can be seen in the ZAFC case?

The answer to this issue rests not with conventional debates over organizational and management schemes. Instead the resolution of the problem is embedded in the everyday business situation of the interacting group. If the group can understand, explain, and analyze how it best makes decisions, then it can move rapidly ahead in whatever direction that it deems necessary.

How does an organization get to understand itself – that is, act as if it were reflecting upon itself, like Blumer's "generalized other"? The process, while difficult at first, is to derive its own set of transformational rules upon which group actions can be seen in the surface structure.

Clark (1996) outlined some of these ideas in a paper directed towards understanding how organizations transfer technology. Here, that argument is taken much further. The business group must first figure out how it acts and then it can better manage its business relations. Next is an attempt to do just that from the ZAFC case. The rulemaking is never complete and certainly subject to change. Nevertheless, it is an attempt to understand and explain business everyday surface structure actions so that the resultant rules can better manage itself for future activities.

## Intersubjectivity and Construction: Business Situations Rules[2]

### *Surface Structure Rules*

The constant interaction between the technical and business staff of the new Australian business venture, the bus manufacturers, fuel cell/battery makers, and the laboratory proved to be essential in building trust by establishing an iterative, intense, and constant dialogue. The surface structure result was the formation of an informal consortium with a broader and more dynamic set of rules for a new organization dedicated to creating zero-emission vehicles for mass transit initially but refocused upon power energy storage for the near term. The common long-term goal was to commercialize the ZAFC for the Australian Olympics for transportation. This goal was changed when the new venture was formed and the entrepreneurial company then saw the Australian power-utility company (as well as others) as customers.

---

[2] See also Clark and Bradshaw (2004, Clark 2017a, b) which is based upon Clark (1996) and discussed in the application of a case in Clark and Fast (2005).

Intersubjectivity and Construction: Business Situations Rules

The laboratory goal was to seek funding for final research, development, and design of its zinc-air technologies. The new venture and the laboratory formed a surface structure relationship (signed agreements and even a Public "Product Launch" in the fall of 1997) and then expanded it with desirable partnerships to accomplish their mutually compatible goals.

For an international interaction between a company and a research laboratory, the interactionism perspective and Lifeworld traditions specify a number of rules drawn from transformation grammar theory. At this point, the focus is only on the power-utility company and the laboratory business rules. However, generalizations or applications to the other potential consortia partners appear valid. There is a need for future research in this area for corroboration on the empirical data and rules.

While particularistic legal constraints and covenants apply to both organizations (due to government, foreign ownership, and nature of the respective business), they will not be distinguished separately here. Instead, these considerations are part of the overall surface structures that impact and govern the rules. Hence, the rules established from the interactionist perspective are applied to business situations.

Each rule is an example of the interaction theories from Blumer and Mead, whereby $A \leftrightarrow B \leftrightarrow C$. When A is an actor who interacts with actor B and then interacts back again to A after some thought, reflection, discussion with others, and further planning, throughout the entire process, A and B are interacting with one another as well as with others (C). The process involves intense discussion and definitions of what is being done or actions to take. Formalized into transformational grammar is the surface structure as seen (Chart 9.5):

Consider below an example of how the rules work as seen from the ZAFC case:

***Surface Structure Action***  New Green Technology – Environmental breakthrough

**Rule #1.** $\wedge$ Search for New Technology = Technology due diligence

$\quad |$ Exchange of Data $\leftarrow$ Staff interactions

$\quad |$ Interactions (discussions) $\rightarrow$ Networks (technical / business contact)

$\quad \vee$ Old Networks $\leftrightarrow$ New Networks

What can be noticed with this first example is that all the rules, while logically derived, are coupled nonlinearly. In short, the rules are not determined or conditioned upon prior external forces but upon the everyday situations requiring interaction among actors. The rules are dynamic and operate independently of the other. Rule #1 represents universal business behavior from the everyday life of the labora-

Surface Structure Action (series of situations and interactions among actors)
Rule #1 -----> = ----->
Rule #2 -----> = ----->
Rule #3 -----> = ----->

**Chart 9.5** Surface structure rule formation

tory and business venture actors as they initially began to become engaged in the commercialization of the ZAFC.

The partners need to find new levels of interacting, especially since they had not contacted or been associated with one another in the past. In order for the new business partners (initially the power-utility company and later the new business venture) to know about the new technology (ZAFC), they had to read about it or be told by some actor who was knowledgeable about it. The CBD did just that by igniting the interest among the technical and business people seeking new technological solutions to current transportation and energy problems within the constraints of environmental laws and regulations. The result was a new network.

Before other rules are explored, consider the content of the rules. The actors bring into the business situation their values and concerns (e.g., over the environment) which tend to influence the rulemaking. It is these embedded set of values or beliefs that allow us to see representations made of specific topics, ideas, or concepts under discussion by the actors. Furthermore, these embedded representations are constantly transformed from the deep structure depending and influencing the surface structure situations. Consideration of the deep structure rules will be explored later in this chapter.

Suffice it to say that the surface structure rules appear to be linear but are not. Part of the problem is the linear nature of the printed text. These rules are in fact very dynamic and clearly influenced by rapid and constant interaction between the actors, depending upon everyday business situations. For purposes of written expression, the rules are notational with one concept followed by another. Other empirical research will establish the universality of the rules in other everyday business situations.

Consider now a series of rules that are incomplete. From the ZAFC data, however, they begin to provide a moving picture of the development of a new technology into a business venture.

**Rule # 2.** $\wedge$ New Networks = Institutionalize interpersonal Relations

    | Nondisclosure agreement $\leftrightarrow$ Telephone / electronic contacts

    | Institutional linkages proven $\rightarrow$ Trust established

    $\vee$ New Networks created $\leftrightarrow$ Complimentary goals forms

**Rule # 3.** $\wedge$ Internal Plan Formation = Core Value Clarification

    | Goal and vision $\rightarrow$ Clarified within and between actors

    | Parameters for action $\leftrightarrow$ Resource allocation

    $\vee$ Proposals and Plans $\leftrightarrow$ Shared and used jointly

***Surface Structure Action*** New Business Created – One Partner replaced with Solid Partner

**Rule # 4.** ∧ Collaborative Strategies = Identify or Create Other Partners

    | Business team formed ← Technical staff collaborate

    | Financial needs delineated → Search for Funding

    ∨ Select basic funding sources ↔ Varied interest groups

*Surface Structure Action*  Expanded Network with Actors – Multi-partners

**Rule # 5.** ∧ Basic Organizational Composition = Industrial Ecological View

    | Agreement upon Core Values → Establish Public / Private Partners

    ∨ Expand Core Firms → International Partnership Consortia.

Each of these surface structure rules is incomplete yet provides an initial indication of how the business rules would be represented from the ZAFC case data. The entire process is qualitative, inductive, by beginning with observable empirical data that follows into the overall interactionism perspective, which examines the business situation for the commercialization of ZAFC.

The rules are written with an equal sign to indicate the relation between each concept. Embedded within each rule are the logically derived operations in the equation. Similar to the generative grammar theories, the rules are linked due to the interactive nature of the actions between actors (extended herein to organizations as well in which they act) and then transformed between surface and deep structures forming an economic situation that explains and even predicts business surface structure activities. Consider in detail one of the rules above:

**Rule # 3.** Internal Plan Formation = Core Value Clarification

Once the market or technology pull is established for ZAFC, the actors need to formulate their own internal plan. The interaction among the actors within any organizations establishes a core group of people who makes the decisions and in the process clarifies their personal and institutional goals. The actors generally seek to answer the basic question: Why is this being done?

Embedded within the rule are the logical mechanisms to get there. Through long and often difficult interactive processes, each actor must understand his/her own purposes and how they fit the overall organization. Take the laboratory situation; a team of six key people did just that over a 2-year period of time. For example, one person saw ZAFC as a new source of institutional financing; another as continued research funds; another as building an internal laboratory organization; another as a source of employment; and so on. Each actor reflected, modified, and changed behavior, always through interaction with other actors including some from outside the laboratory (e.g., spouses, friends, and family).

Once these motives and values were clarified, established, and communicated internally, specific parameters for action can be derived and implemented. More significantly, resources (financial, personnel, and logistical) can be identified and applied to commercialize the ZAFC. The same set of circumstances and perhaps even situations exist for the actors in the other partner organizations. For example, after considerable internal discussion within the Australian power-utility company, the key executive who left to form the new venture had a series of meetings that resulted in legal agreements allowing him to leave in order to pursue on his own, the ZAFC (and other technologies that he had originally identified but which were no interest to the new focus of the power company).

This same scenario with these sets of rules occurred with a potential partner for the new Australian venture. The Australian key executive furthermore reported numerous family discussions with his spouse about his decision to leave and start the new company. Even more significantly, he engaged in extensive discussions with new partners to form the company. This extensive dialogue continued especially when separated by time and space across the Pacific.

Organizations need to be seen as a collection of people. As such, they have values and needs that constitute their core. Collins and Porras (1994) provide an excellent historical analysis of "visionary corporations" (defined as companies that have thrived for at least 50 years) that make these points: need to establish core values within an organization.

With the internal personal and then organizational basics established, various proposals and plans can be advanced. These activities are usually outward (externally) directed and now represent a significant business interaction. The plans commit the actors to written and commonly understood goals. Furthermore, the plans are iterative with external organizations, leading to Rule #4: Collaborative Strategies = Identify Solid Partners.

While these rules (#3 and #4) are operating, they are also interacting with the deep structure rules identified here as #A, #B, etc. below. These constant vertical interactions are described below as transformational linkages between nodes. However, at this point, suffice it to note that transformations are continuous interactions between the surface and deep structures. In the ZAFC case, they define and refine terms, ideas, and concepts into focused everyday business reality at the surface structure.

## *Deep Structure Rules*

Beneath the surface structures with its set of rules are the deep structures with its own set of rules. Think of the deep structure as the level of interaction that defines business actions within specific situations. In short, deep structures provide the meaning behind the observable behavior seen at the surface structure. The linguistic concept of generative grammar is equivalent to the dictionary or lexicon of a language by providing definition in the deep structures. For the qualitative economic perspective, there is an extremely significant need to define ideas and concepts, especially since international business, even conducted in the same language (as in this case, English spoken by Australians, Americans, Danish, Germans, and Swedes), is subject to misunderstanding and therefore further interactions and erroneous decisions.

The outcome of defined concepts and even the meaning of specific English words (e.g., as in "commercially viable" used to define the agreement between the American and Australian understanding of when ZAFC leaves the laboratory for business use) are the set of rules in the deep structure. Due to the interaction within the deep structure and the transformations with the surface structure, these terms, concepts, and hence common goals become clearer. With common "lexical" definitions, the actors and their organizations can move rapidly forward in business activities.

A few rules are derived herein from the contextual case of the commercial development of the ZAFC. The deep structure rules are indicated with letters rather than numbers for two reasons: first to distinguish the two realms of rules (surface and deep) from each other and second to demonstrate that the deep structure rules can be applied repeatedly or more than once to surface structures. In other words, deep structure rule #B can be applied to surface structure rules #1, #3, and #4, respectively.

Chart 9.6 illustrates how deep structure rules transform into surface structure ones which can be seen in situations, events, and various phenomenon.

Deep structure rules represent numerous interactions that can be written from the ZAFC case materials as in the following examples.

**Deep structures**      **Surface structures**
**Rule #A** technical staff interact    Rule #1: Technical due diligence
     Technology detailed → Verifications made on assertions
**Rule #B** definition of concepts and terms    Rule #2: Legal documents
     Common lexicon established → Use of terms understood
**Rule #C** lines of communication    Rules #1–#3: Clarification into plans
     Specific dates/times set → Benchmarked/checked

Other deep structure rules are established beyond these. Further delineation of these rules is left for other researchers. For the purposes here, the basic notion of deep structure can be understood as the clarification of terms, concepts, and purposes within and across organizations. Interactions establish strong trust and create new networks for everyday business activities to occur.

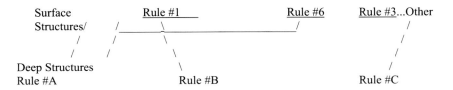

**Chart 9.6** Deep structure rules

In the ZAFC case, the senior laboratory staff had to convene a series of meetings in early January 1996 (over 2 years after the actual research project began) to define technical terms. The result was a "Glossary of Terms" that could be used in any interactions within the laboratory and worldwide with other partners (see Firth 1990 as an example from discourse analyses). These basic definitions of terms (Rule #B in the deep structures) allow accurate communication and understanding for surface structure interactions in everyday discussions among the various laboratory and international actors and organizations.

A more detailed discussion from data collected in the ZAFC case study demonstrates how Rule #B (definition of concepts and terms) is useful for understanding how the theory works. Two examples are worth elaboration. The first concerns the concept of the zinc-air fuel cell itself. As noted earlier, initial reports on the ZAFC called it a "zinc-air battery."

However, when the principal investigator and the program manager went to Europe to attend a conference on electric vehicles, they found that the concept of a fuel cell more accurately described the advanced technology, which went beyond that of a battery. Upon further discussion with the key staff in Australia as well as within the laboratory, the conclusion was certain. From early December 1995, the zinc-air battery would be known as a zinc-air fuel cell. The critical distinction was that a battery requires "recharging," whereas with the ZAFC, it needed to be "refueled."

While there was scientific and technical evidence to support the name change for the zinc-air technology, the international interaction was crucial. Clearly, the technology was more of a fuel cell that is requiring refueling, rather than recharging. Yet the concept of a fuel cell itself denoted even higher technical advancements than a battery and therefore had more perceived business appeal. The decision was made. A common definition was adopted and put into use worldwide.

The term "fuel cell" had been agreed upon at the deep structure level in order that it could be used precisely through transformation rules on the surface structure in everyday language usage. However, the American car manufacturers were locked into research and development for advanced batteries, through long-established lobbying groups for industry corporations. So when the laboratory researchers approach the American automakers and their US Battery consortia for funding, they were refused (Clark and Paolucci 1997a, b).

It took about 1 year of interaction between the federal government funding source and the laboratory staff before ZAFC would even be considered for minimal funding since "industry" did not demand the fuel cell technology but in fact preferred modification on established technologies like batteries and ICE.

The second example of a Rule #B application is the correct terminology for the other zinc-air technology: known as the zinc recovery unit (ZRU). Originally the principal investigator described the process for the zinc to be cycled through some sort of undefined unit that pushed spent zinc and electrolyte into an external hopper from the fuel cell. After many hours of intensive discussion among the lead scientists, two issues were clarified. The zinc itself was the issue and not the zinc in combination with the air. In other words, the external and separate unit needed to be concerned only with zinc processing.

The other definitional point of clarification concerned the concept of the zinc recovery unit itself. Again in checking earlier documents, the process unit was called a refueling unit" when in fact it was a "recovery unit." The difference is significant in the context of industrial ecology. Refueling implies that a raw material (zinc) has been mined and processed so that it is ready for refueling the fuel cell. In fact, the zinc is not refueled at all. The zinc is recovered because it is reformed after being used in the fuel cell. In other words, there is little loss of zinc (unlike gasoline, e.g., that is burned and needs to be refueled). The ZRU therefore is simply an external unit that takes out the zinc from the fuel cell, reconstitutes it, and pumps it back into the fuel cell after regular use.

The clarification of the recovery unit is an enormously significant deep structure issue. Aside from the understanding and communication of the meaning into surface structure situations, the clear definition allows the scientists to actually create the ZRU. In this case, the actual ZRU had not been created and designed. Now a clear technological path could be followed. The significance of the ZRU definition could lead to new research and development because the definition of a ZRU was clarified and the business partners knew of another zinc recovery process that could fit into the ZAFC technology to form an ecological sound energy system. Subsequently, the Australian company made a separate business deal to secure the ZRU technology. Rule #B in the deep structure predicted the activities from Rules #1–3 in the surface structure as events and situations from actors' interactions.

## Transformations

The relationship between the deep and surface structures occurs through transformations, which are vertical interactions between the sets of rules within each structure. In the ZAFC case, there are three "nodes" or key interactive points of contact for the rules: (1) personal or people interactions built into personal trust; (2) organizing relationships formed into networks; and (3) technological modes of interaction such as the telephone, fax, travel, the Internet, etc. Each node is referred to as a

| Surface Structures | | Phrase Markers or Nodes |
|---|---|---|
| Everyday Situations and Events | ^ | |
| Phenomenon of business activities | \| | |
| Set of Rules | \| | (1) Personal Trust |
| | \| | |
| **Deep Structures** | \| | (2) Organizing relationships |
| Debate, discussions and reflection | \| | |
| Definitions and clarifications | \| | (3) Technical modes to communicate |
| Set of Rules | v | |

**Chart 9.7**  Surface and deep structure nodes

"phrase marker" since it has definition and universal meaning. By way of example, consider the three nodes in the ZAFC case. Chart 9.7 demonstrates how the surface and deep structures nodes provide for interaction among actors.

## Personal Trust

As continual personal trust is being built through interaction within and between partnering organizations, personal nodes are triggered that move back and forth between deep and surface structures. For example, telephone conference calls (lasting hours) occur, but then a point is reached when some of the principals within the organizations need to meet face-to-face. In the ZAFC case, the personal node occurred twice within a 2-month period: once in Australia due to a Professional Academic Conference and once in Europe due to the International Electric Vehicle Conference. The transformational relations moved or transformed the common definition of terms and concepts to the surface structure following the set of rules outlined above. Other opportunities were deliberately created: one laboratory team member traveled to Europe on other business and visited the key consortia bus manufacturer. Various meetings were planned that would connect the key actors from each organization.

## Organizing Networks

Early on in a technological case such as the ZAFC, the establishment of a transformational node must occur in order to protect proprietary business relationships. In the ZAFC case, the node was the execution of a nondisclosure agreement. While not a final business deal, it marked or symbolically signaled the connection between a power-utility company in Australia and a national research laboratory in the USA. Furthermore, it memorialized the desire for both organizations to work closely together. Other MOUs were then signed with other organizations involved in the consortia.

Through a variety of interactions, as seen in the surface and deep structure rules, the power-utility company and the laboratory then established more organizational nodes in order to transform them into an internal network. Aside from the nondisclosure agreement, two other nodes resulted: (1) establishment of a consortia and (2) the actual funding mechanism for the ZAFC. The establishment of the interpersonal network allowed representatives within the separate organizations to trust one another in other to form a larger surface structure (consortia) with the combined capability to commercialize the ZAFC technology.

## *Technological Modes of Communication*

A separate node is the use of modern technologies (e.g., telephone, travel, the Internet, email, etc., including the establishment of regular international communication times and dates for communication. The technological modes of interaction are a significant node for transformations between surface and deep structures. A significant factor in an interactive relationship is the ability of people to establish means of communications and then set specific dates and times.

In the ZAFC case, one technology node is to set up telephone conference call times and dates between Australia and the USA. These conference calls are constant interactive dialogues between actors within each organization. They serve to further clarify and define common goals, as well as build trust. The transformations are continuous and follow the rules noted above in the surface and deep structures. When other members of the consortia are added in other parts of the world, the need for constant interaction among the actors becomes heightened and more complex.

Expansion and alteration of the surface and deep structure rules can occur. However, they establish the basic set. Upon further scrutiny and verification, the rules need to be applied to other cases. In a future series of articles, mathematical representations can be made of the rules for further elaboration to business situations. The rules provide an understanding of everyday business activities in the context of commercializing a new technology.

# Prediction in Subjectivist Paradigm

What is purposively missing at this point and from the earlier analyses and discussions are the "predictive rules" for economic and business analyses. In short, for the interactionist theories to be complete, they must be predictive. Most economic theorists purposely avoid such conclusions. If one believes the economics' professionals, then there is good reason. Few economists have ever been correct in their predictions.

The ability of the economics' field to theoretically predict economic events has been limited. Quantitative models and simulations have not been very successful. Even the current interest in" game theory" for economics, it too falls far short of providing predictability. The interactionist approach provides a qualitative perspective on the economics of business. As such and through its use of theories from symbolic interactionism in sociology and generative grammar in linguistics, the paradigm appears to be able to state predications.

What then, in summary, are some of the predictions from the ZAFC case study? Since this chapter is being prepared in advance of the year 2000 Olympics, the description and explanation of the commercialization of ZAFC are currently in progress. The final results (defined as the commercialization or mass manufacturing of ZAFC) of the case study have not been completed. However, the predictive capability of this approach can be demonstrated. Consider one set of surface and deep structure rules:

From the surface structure, some rules are:

**Rule # 3**) Internal Plan Formation = Core Value Clarification

Goal and vision → Clarified within and between actors

Parameters for action → Resource allocation

Proposals and Plans → Shared and used jointly

From the deep structure is Rule #B, which applies to all the surface rules, but notice it here as it transforms to Rule #3:

**Rule # B**) Definition of concepts and terms

Common lexicon established → Use of terms understood

Predictions can be made with a series of postulates. With the ZAFC case data and these rules, predictions are possible. For example, staff members within each organization must understand technological terms and concepts in the same way. Common understanding of technical terms is the key to building a "lexicon" or dictionary of shared terms. The laboratory staff did that and then, according to the rules, communicated that to their international partners.

## Prediction *#1: Build Shared Technological Terminology*

As any business opportunity develops, common understandings of words and terms add significantly to the overall trust and relationship building between partners, clients, and related organizations. Part of the purpose of defining terms and agreeing upon shared meanings and concepts leads directly to stating the scope of work and making proposals for the business activity. This process is constantly interactive and strengthens the partnership.

Defining terms for the researchers is one level of specificity within an organization. Another level is the common definition of terms and concepts across nations and organizations. Accomplishing this requires the usage of the transformational technological node described above, since the organizations involved will have to base their business decisions upon common understood concepts and terms. This lexicon will need to be technically based but must expand to business concepts as well. In other words, as part of this prediction from the rules, the key actors in each organization will have to develop a series of business terms and concepts mutually understood by all parties.

# Prediction #2: *Expansion of Overall Business Consortia Vision*

The initial market pull from ZAFC for the "Green Olympics" will significantly expand once common terms and concepts are understand and communicated. The internationalization collaborative effort directly leads to further global partners between the firms as well as in other technological areas. This expansion brings with it companies and organizations who have their own definitions of purpose, set of goals, and rules. They further define the overall vision of the consortia relationship between all parties such that every member will be able to enhance (break into new markets, make profits, or position their products) its own particular business activities.

The building and sharing of a common lexicon allows for the expansion of the business opportunity. The partners come to understand the technological advances as well as create trust among themselves. In the case of the ZAFC technology, other related technologies begin to enter into the overall goals of the consortium. Other cases can also be seen in both technology and economics. Consider the case of "green" technologies.

From early 2007 and through 2008, the use of the word "'green' became common due to the widespread global acceptance that mankind causes "global warming" and hence has changed the climate. Awareness of this issue, as it certainly had been discussed in the scientific literature since the UN Rio Summit in 1992 and four separate Intergovernmental Panels on Climate Change (IPCC) as well as the formation of the creation of a UN Framework Convention for Climate Change (FCCC) reports, was due in large part to former American Vice President Al Gore's film, "An Inconvenient Truth" that won Gore and his team in 2007 both an Academy Award for a "documentary" from the film industry and later that year a Nobel Peace Prize.

As acknowledged in the Nobel Peace Prize, the co-awardees were the UN IPCC with over 2000 scientists[3] (∗) who produced UN Three Reports. Clark has written articles on the topic of what is "green" since early 2000 (2002, 2007a, b) and teamed with Jeremy Rifkin (2006) for other papers. Basically "green" means renewable energy technologies and sources such as wind, solar, water, geothermal, and ocean power. Then in 2005, Clark and Fast (2005) gave a paper on the case of green in qualitative economics before the Western Economic Association Conference annual meeting. By 2008, the issues surrounding green technologies had produced dozens of new organizations, groups, and companies.

However, there are also warnings: Will green be the next "dot.com" that turns into a "dot.bomb"? There are some indicators such as definitions, meanings, and analyses of data that might be the same case for "green" based upon a qualitative

---

[3] Dr. Clark served on the IPCC Third Report as co-author on Chapter #2: "Finance and Economic Mechanisms" and as co-editor of Chapter #3: "Legal/Political Mechanisms" 1999–2000. He was also the Co-director with RaeKwon Chong of the first series of six reports by the UN FCCC: "Technology Transfer of Renewable Energy from Developed to Developing Countries." Public Funds for technology project. Framework Convention for Climate Change, United Nations, Nov 00. It was the first study of "green" energy technologies and their economics in six countries.

economic analysis. Some analysts are even beginning to refer to this new sector as potentially becoming a "green washing." Consider the origins and financial definitions and backers of "green technology." Most are located in Silicon Valley where the "dot.com" generation grew from the computer industry. The lasting results were companies like Google, Yahoo, and Apple Computers, among others, but there were also a long list of failures.

## Summary

As noted, qualitative economics is based on the formation of questions that result in definitions and meanings. Thus, the definition of the zinc-air technology as a fuel cell rather than a battery was a matter of constant interactionism between the surface structure organizations and individuals, which directly impact the lexical meaning of the technology itself in the deep structure.

Once these terms and their definitions were agreed to, the expansion into other related technologies to creating a zero-emission vehicle becomes clear and far less complex to implement. The interaction rules allowed the ZAFC to be commercialized since there was common definition, and hence agreement, on the need and application for the technology. Furthermore, a detailed generic proposal (with different modifications for various consortia members) was written with exact tasks, costs, and timelines outlined.

Thus the entire consortia could build around the core ZAFC technology into exploring other technologies for zero-emission vehicles and power-utility applications. Once the ZAFC was clearly defined, a technical gap existed that could be solved by another laboratory. While the solution was known to the laboratory staff, they did not pressure or pursue the technology. Instead, the consortia requested it. Again this is an example of the pull ↔ push dynamics of interactionism rules.

Similarly, the new Australian company initially came up with the creative notion of linking the energy needs for the actual Olympic Village with those of the people movers within the complex. When the ZAFC and ZRU are under one roof, they can conceivably service both the energy storage and mass transit needs of the Olympics. The concept was then taken elsewhere. More recently in Norway and Denmark, parallel investigations for dual use or hybrid systems from one technological source (ZAFC and ZRU) are seriously under active consideration. The interactionist perspective provided a prediction (#2) that related technologies and extended business considerations of new technologies would occur.

Prediction #2 (The Expansion of Overall Business Consortia Vision) is seen as a result of the interaction between the individuals and organizations. It was only a matter of time that the partners saw fruitful and extended business relations being built. There will be other consortia built as well (such as in other fuels, materials, and intelligent systems) from the new advanced technologies, as well as from other R&D facilities who offer solutions to current vehicle needs to meet or exceed regulatory requirements. While economist's debate "market demand" and "supply-side"

Summary

issues, technological innovation and commercialization are not adequately explained or understood with these conventional and neo-classical theories.

The process of business innovation through technological commercialization, using the transformational rules, is interactive. Business and economics occur as a result of considerable interactions at the surface and deep structure levels. The use of the Lifeworld philosophical tradition with the subjectivism paradigm and interactionism perspective provides a better understanding of everyday business phenomenon.

In the end, the use of transformational linguistics within interactionism perspective provides a formalism (as opposed to quantification, measurement, statistics, etc.) rarely seen in the field of economics. The results of this analysis from the Lifeworld philosophical tradition is a formal set of interactive rules that are situational yet dynamic in terms of covering universal basic economic concepts. By providing descriptive case understanding of real-world business situations, the subjectivist paradigm can provide explanatory and even predicative theories. The conventional functionalist and neo-classical paradigms, on the other hand, approach business economics typically as quantitative models that lack both substance or content and the scientific requirement for predictability.

What has been developed in this book are basic theories espoused and drawn from Blumer in sociology as well as American and European philosophers which are then expanded upon with Chomsky in linguistics. A similar scientific formalism for business economics can take these fields into areas of thinking and understanding of economics in everyday business life (Clark and Fast 2012). It is the desire of qualitative economics to see more work done in this area with the empirical results subject to the same scrutiny given the natural and physical sciences. For economics to be considered or called a "science," it must meet those standards and criteria associated with other scientific fields.

Qualitative economics is science and lends itself well to the analysis of economic issues and problems. The "green revolution" is a current example. There are others. The key is to understand the meaning and definitions of numbers, words, terms, and sentences. The statistics and data from gathering of historical numbers then make sense. They also can prove or disprove a theory and set of hypotheses. In short, economics needs to become a science.

# Chapter 10
# Everyday Economic Life

## Introduction[1]

In this chapter, some practical empirical cases are discussed that utilize the application of qualitative economics in an interactionist scientific perspective. For the purposes of the chapter and within the theoretical considerations already outlined, the cases are far from the typical analyses seen in conventional business economic publications. What is demonstrated here are qualitative economic studies utilizing interactionism and Lifeworld as "daily" interactive perspective. From these theoretical conceptions, empirical data provides clear examples of this perspective to understanding businesses activities, actions, events of people, and groups. Above all, the chapter provides the basic economic science paradigm cases noted in the previous chapters.

The updates in Chaps. 1, 2, 3, 4, 5 and also Chaps. 6, 7, 8 all reflect how neo-classical economics of Adam Smith never worked. And that the more modern theme that the world is "flat" is very wrong. Economics and its use in businesses have never been either "supply" or "demand" side real, proven, and accurate. Hence, economics has primarily been a quantitative "field of study" and never a science. Below are some of the earlier cases used in the first edition of QE updated, but also some new areas added in this second edition of QE.

Over the last decade since QE first was published, Clark has been very busy in this "field" with books that document and provide cases of smart green and healthy communities (Clark 2018, 2017a, b, 2014, 2013, 2012, 2010a, 2009; Clark and Cooke 2016, 2015, 2014, 2011) but also how economics and financing work in these cases. There is much more in the literature about behavioral economics which is different than neo-classical economics but is not a perfect fit into QE. For example, behavior refers mostly to individuals behaving on stimuli and not including the consciousness and acting upon what people see in their everyday of life. It rarely

---

[1] Gratitude to Drs. John Cooper and J. Ray Smith. Dr. Frank Tokarz, Mr. Anthony Chargin, Ms. Shelia Williams, and Ms. Erma Paddack assistance are all thankfully acknowledged.

© Springer Nature Switzerland AG 2019
W. W. Clark II, M. Fast, *Qualitative Economics*,
https://doi.org/10.1007/978-3-030-05937-8_10

included not only several people but teams of people from work, community, and even the family. That is what interactionism and Lifeworld are all about – people in groups and their daily life activities.

The main issue is that both behavioral and neo-classical economics site the "demand side" and the market are the places to go for understanding how economics and then finances work. This is not any good picture of what is "going on in economics and other social sciences" but misses the points of everyday interaction. Hence, what we do in this chapter and throughout the book is document and show how changes from social to political to technological and other forces are rarely useful if the demand and market are the key attributes for economics to perform and succeed.

Case in point from the first edition of QE is the commercialization of fuel cell technologies that would exceed the environmental and political demands. The technology was done in US national research laboratories during the 1990s and was commercialized into business applications in 2005 for stationary power applications (Clark et al. 2005a, b, 2006). Today commercialization for mobile purposes occurred next allowing vehicles to exceed legislative regulations for zero-emission regulations in California and other nation-states in the USA (Demirag et al. 2009). While we focus on this no-demand-side technology below in this chapter, a more up-to-date and accurate approach is to look at these technologies and their economics, applications, standards, and other environmental factors (Clark and Yago 2006). The key is to look closely at the meaning of words and ideas.

For example, historically and today, the word "clean" is attached to energy as a business, political, and governmental goal. Governor Brown has just signed into law legislation for California to be 100% on "clean energy" by 2045. He has promoted and pushed that term, "clean energy" at the State – UN summit held in San Francisco, CA (September 2018). The problem is that the word *clean* and *energy* are *not* defined.

Another case in point is that the US Department of Energy (USDoE) had programs for "clean coal" in the 1990s which it promoted and pushed around the world. The words "clean coal" are referred to by most people as an "oxymoron" which words are used that contradict one another. Today "clean" is now used with "natural gas" which is *not* clean or healthy for the environment. And even used to describe "nuclear power" energy, which has severe waste problems that are *not* clean either (Clark and Lund 2015).

So it is important to look into technologies that are needed in climate and environmental areas such as transportation to use non-fossil fuel vehicles which are electric powered, known as EVs. However, when the US car industry produced and distributed some to California, the fossil fuel industry stopped them. In the 1990s over 5000 EVs were destroyed by the Detroit, Michigan, BIG Three USA car manufacturers led by GM in California and shipped back to Michigan (Clark 2014).

Annual IDTechEx conference notice

Many saw this as the end of the EV business, until Elon Musk came forward with his Tesla cars in the first decade of the twentieth century. Meanwhile China had "leapfrogged" into the "Green Industrial Revolution" (Clark 2014; Clark and Isherwood 2007, 2010; Clark and Li 2012a, 2013; Clark and Cooke 2015) which China today notes as "Green Development" (Clark et al. 2014) and has gained international attention (Li and Clark 2009). Clark was interviewed on this topic by the China Energy review Press in September 2015.

*Who Killed the Electric Car?* (2006), a documentary and written film directed by Chris Paine and narrated by Martin Sheen, explores the creation, limited commercialization, and subsequent destruction of the battery electric vehicle in the USA, specifically the General Motors EV1 of the mid-1990s.

Then in 2011, Chris Paine produced a sequel, *Revenge of the Electric Car*, that follows four entrepreneurs from 2007 to 2010 as they fight to bring the EV back which Elon Musk tried to do with Tesla Motors in Northern California, near Silicon Valley, since the 2006 documentary, but had serious difficulties from the Detroit car companies. However, the new documentary was the "rebirth" of the EV cars including Tesla Roadster but also global companies such as Nissan Leaf and Chevrolet Volt (EV1).

However, that was not the only outcome. Just the opposite as a new all-electric car company has now started in China, titled NIO, and started trading on the NY Stock Exchange in September 2018 (as NYXE: NIO). "The company planned to use the funds to develop future electric cars for the U.S. and Chinese markets and to develop self-driving software."

Nio currently sells an electric SUV in China, the ES8, designed to compete with the Tesla Model X. The ES8 sells for $65,000 in China, about half what a Tesla Model X costs, and has 220 miles of range and 644 horsepower." from Green Carl: *Chinese electric-car startup Nio gets $1 billion in funding: report* Here below are the four all-electric NIO cars.

Four Mercedes-Benz electric cars (2018)

Recently Mercedes-Benz announced on September 5, 2018, that it will launch a fully electric car in 2019 (Mercedes, 2018). The company is investing more than £9 billion in the expansion of its electric range. By 2022, they will offer ten pure battery electric vehicles; this starts in 2019 with the launch of the EQC. Mercedes said: "To support the shift away from fossil fuel powered vehicles to more sustainable alternatives, our eMobility range is growing year on year with a range of choice in hybrid and plug-in hybrid vehicles."

Dieter Zetsche, chairman of Mercedes-Benz, revealed that by 2025, he expects electric car sales to occupy 15–20% of the company's sales.

Mercedes hydrogen fuel cell-powered car (2017)

This is dramatic and incredible. Yet where does the energy come from to recharge the car? An EV needs to be recharged. Where does the energy come from? In California over 65% of the states' energy comes now from national gas, which is a major problem for many reasons ranging from drilling and now fracking. While the state has closed all five of its nuclear power plants, the demand for energy continues to grow – now for Wi-Fi and other wireless systems. And batteries are NOT the solution.

Some of the research for technological solutions comes from medical and its applications to environmental and economic issues. Case in point is "Earth Accounting" Medical Doctor Bruce Hector (Hector et al. 2014) and "Re-Make 'Made in America'" (Greenfield and Clark 2013) which created app systems for buying goods and services that are useful, productive, and environmentally sound in terms of economics for "circular economics" (Clark and Bonato 2015) which was discussed earlier and featured as an Appendix to the book. The answer to that critical question is from all solar-powered cars (Hanergy 2017–2018), a Chinese company that has invented thin-film solar panels for its company buildings as noted below.

Introduction

The building here is the Hanergy Renewable Energy Exhibition Center in Beijing which is fully powered by solar – capacity is 270 Kw.

Hanergy Group Research Center – entire building powered by "thin-film" solar from Hanergy (2016)

See their website for more information and details at:
https://www.youtube.com/channel/UCySOrFh1DlORQ3cc10THk2A.

However, even more dramatic is that Hanergy has created an *all* solar-powered car – actually three (3) of them and a bus. Clark was interviewed after the launch of the cars in 2016 at the Hanergy Headquarters in Beijing, China.

http://v.qq.com/x/page/o0313vci9m6.html

All solar-powered car details from Hanergy Group Company: Released in July 2016

Another car – and there are more – including bus.

Such a dramatic change in curbing emissions from power and fuel generation reflects Schumpeter's theories and perspective of "creative destruction." Fuel cells provide that opportunity as compared to conventional battery technologies which have dominated energy storage with few significant advances or changes for over

150 years. Also fuel cells transportation could provide the commercial opportunities to mitigate environment and climate degradation.

As the car below demonstrates, there can be soon, even *no* demand, for all solar-powered cars.

One of four all solar-powered car – Hanergy Group Company: Released in July 2016

Well-documented evidence from a variety of economists indicate that research and development is the heart of the capitalist paradigm through, "organized inventive efforts undertaken by university-trained scientists and engineers, working in special facilities, tied to particular business firms, and focused on advancing their product and process technologies" (Nelson 1990: 199).

With a thorough examination not only of the creativity process and technological invention itself but also of the commercial and business applications, one can see how qualitative economics describes, understands, and explains business actions and events. One significant area in particular are island nations that are exposed to dramatic weather changes and especially the rise of ocean water. The Mauritius island nation between West India and East Africa has done a great deal enacting renewable (green) energy systems (Khoodaruth et al. 1 = 2017). Other island nations and those with coastal areas need to check what Mauritius has done so that they could follow and learn from them as Clark and Lund did (2008).

Perhaps the place to start with this analysis, is back to the very core of economic capitalism theory with Adam Smith. There is no need to repeat the earlier critique of his perspective of economics. Instead, Smith in *The Wealth of Nations* (1937 edition) did highlight one point of interest for an interactionism perspective within qualitative economics when he placed the act of exchange at the very center of economic life or as universal characteristic of human beings in that "a certain propensity in human nature…; the propensity to truck, barter, and exchange one thing for another" (Smith 1937: 13).

Introduction

The act of exchange between human beings is the central theme too in the Lifeworld traditions, when talking about interaction. Qualitative economics approaches the exchange act which is a core concept of neo-classical economics very differently. First is to define exchange from a qualitative economics perspective as the exchange interaction between two or more human beings. Following Blumer and Schutz among others, exchange is not just monetary but physical and symbolic through actions and gestures, as we discussed in relation to the concept of intentionality and action in Part I.

Given the discussion on exchange, the basic issue is about subsets of interactions. Exchange, as in the buying and selling of goods and services, is the foundation of modern and ancient economics, as it always been a part of peoples being. Yet exchange is a part of all human interactionism. When a person interacts with another for any reason, that person is part of an act, event, or series of activities to exchange something. Linguists have long seen this with their analyses of discourse and verbal communications. Again, such studies are components and parts of interactionism, which forms the core of qualitative economics.

Interactionism is more, however, than the exchange of business activities. Interaction, as have seen, is far more complex in that it presumes the ability of the actor's to think and reflect upon their actions. In Mead and Blumer, the interactionist perspective involves the actors literally talking to themselves. Or as Blumer calls it, the "generalized other" which provides the act of exchange with a far more comprehensive and significant definition. This very basic act is what distinguishes human beings from other forms of life. People interact and, as shown in Chap. 10, this is best understood through the science of linguists. Clark started this discussion at the turn of the twenty-first century as noted above but then applied it to environmental issues (Clark and Hall 2003) and technology solutions (Clark and Eisenberg 2008)

Anyone familiar with business activities, events, and buying and selling on whatever level knows, for example, that business is not done or consummated at one point in time. It develops over time and is the culmination of multiple business interactions among many actors after considerable reflection and thought. For some companies, and in more and more countries, business is also concluded after extensive legal scrutiny as well. Often these interactions (especially the financial and legal aspects) are due to the need for basic definition of words, concepts, and legal terms. Exchange from the interactionism perspective, therefore, is an engagement between actors over time, trying to create meaning of their situation. Two or more people have established relationships. They have engaged each other for some purpose.

It is this notion of engagement that underlies all business activities when understood as exchanges within the interaction perspective of qualitative economics. It is also the understanding of these engagements through *symbolic* and *nonsymbolic* activities that everyday business life is best understood. While some scholars might describe these interactions through quantitative numbers as case studies, a far more descriptive, accurate, and analytical understanding of business interactions are through the subtle and observable situations that surround these business actions with their meanings and interpretations explained. Therefore, the use of varied methodologies is the appropriate and best approach to describe and understand everyday business life and the phenomenon that influence it.

## Scientific Interactionism Process and Perspective

Three cases are presented below. There are many more including the EV transportation discussed above. However, the other cases which were in the first edition are primarily what are noted now. Clark and Fast have another book coming out soon (early 2019) on both Qualitative and Quantitative Economics (Q2E) from Palgrave which get into more current business, technologies, and economic cases.

The first case concerns the use of market economics in the manipulation of a specific infrastructure sector – the energy crisis in California from 2000 to 2003 which continues. Since one of the authors has had direct involvement, information, and knowledge in this sector during the energy crisis, the data and scientific case made from a scientific interactionism perspective are substantial and well documented.

In fact, in a related co-authored book titled "Agile Energy Systems (AES): global lessons learned from the California energy crisis" Clark co-authored with Professor Ted Bradshaw (Elsevier, 2004) that looked into public policy and governmental perspectives so that he (his co-author passed away at the young age of 61) updated the AES book in 2017 (Elsevier Press) to be global and not just focus on California. In both books a qualitative economic formalism and quantitative data set the basis for economics becoming a science as discussed in the next chapter which are global and international issues now.

The second case concerns the commercialization of a new emerging technology into the market. Fuel cells for transportation have become increasingly more commercial since the late 1990s. Government-funded research in the USA that led to "technology transfer" to companies and new business creation are criteria in economic development and job creation; the focus upon one particular fuel cell technology is described and analyzed. Again Clark has had direct and continuing involvement in fuel cell commercialization for over 15 years. Moreover, the current "clean air," energy crises, and environmental concerns make the fuel cell a very contemporary qualitative economic model to follow.

The third is the creation of a new business venture, which is critical for both individuals involved and society itself. Entrepreneurship, while dominant in America, has grown worldwide for many reasons. Capturing the essential elements of entrepreneurial firms is the key to understanding how markets and economies grow and expand. Again Clark as one of the authors, and entrepreneur himself, had been the Managing Director for an Entrepreneurial Center in California (Center for New Venture Alliance) at California State University Hayward (now East Bay) as CSUEB who also founded his first company, Wayne-Wood Nurseries, with his younger brother over 25 years ago in New England and then another company in mass media, Clark Communications (1980). He has taught the topic and created global programs for over 25 years.

Each of the cases concerns the application of qualitative economics and the related areas of corporate governance and accounting themselves. From the perspective of corporations, the cases show how numerous America companies went bankrupt during the early part of the twenty-first century. Corporate cases from the Internet "dot.com" era are *not* considered.

The "dot.bombs" presents another series of related discussions. Instead, the focus is upon the problems within corporate America that were dedicated and then adjudicated as a result of the Sarbanes-Oxley law. And the results impact government in terms of regulations, supervision, and legal actions.

Throughout this volume, a scientific formalist has been advocated for understanding the daily Lifeworld (or the subjectivist economic paradigm) in everyday business life through the use of "rules" derived from linguistic theory. The fundamental argument herein is that economics can be scientific when it acts like a science in terms of both theory(s) and method(s).

Economics should have the same aspirations, if it is to be scientific. Instead, as economists have only one definition. It is based in one "western European" tradition with theoretical biases and methodologies that lead to ethnocentric definitions, understandings, and results of businesses and their economic systems.

The best example can be seen in the neo-classical works based on Adam Smith. The basic arguments have been represented elsewhere. Now consider some discussion among economists. Thus when the *Economist* editorial declares that economics failed (Aug. 23, 1997b: 11), as noted earlier, it only means in not conveying strong enough that the market economy "is a marvel" (ibid., p. 11).

Citing the failure of command and control economics, the position is that the "market" should be the only consideration in any economic system. Thus, the biggest economic-policy mistake of the past 50 years, in rich and poor countries alike, has been and still is to expect too much of government (ibid., p. 11), Hence, the blame for this policy in large part is attributed to liberal economists like Paul Samuelson. Or in another issue, the *Economist* asks rhetorically, we are all capitalists now, are we not? These days the victory of market over state is quite taken for granted (Sept. 20, 1997c: 17). And again, what is surprising is the nearly unanimous support for the idea that government has in fact been in retreat (ibid., p. 17).

## Case #1: Market Forces Created and Manipulated the California Energy Crisis

### *Situational Analysis*

What becomes troubling in these analyses, aside from their influence on the policy makers and the general public, is that they reflect the objectivist philosophical tradition that promotes one paradigmatic view of the world. This particular viewpoint, while even internally contradictory and inconsistent (e.g., western economies such as France and Germany have a considerable amount of government involvement in their "markets"), relies upon statistical methods and probably theory to justify their philosophical (and politicized) position. It is exactly the distinction that Reinert was conveying in his analyses of Anglo-Saxon neo-classical versus German-American Renaissance historical roots in economics (Reinert 1996, 1997, 1998).

Quantitative models and simulations have not been very successful. Economics is a field dominated by statistical manipulation of numbers. It is not a field that uses mathematical models or more subjectivistic traditions. As McNeill and Freiberger (1993) note in economics, "the mathematical and linguistic realms stand quite apart" (ibid., p. 96). Since economics is seen as concerning money, and money is viewed as numerical, then mathematics is thought to bring powerful tools to the field of economics.

Yet the precision of math leads to overly crisp estimates and idealized models that seem to describe a society of robots. "Hence, economics also employs verbal concepts like recession. Language handles real-life questions better and treats details more subtly, but it also narrows the scope of models and shortens chains of reasoning" (ibid., p. 96). The analogy to language is a central theme of Clark and Fast (2002), which explores linguistic theories as applied to describing, understanding, and predicting business and economic everyday life.

Energy is a good example of how neo-classical economics works but does not apply or work in this sector and perhaps in others. The basic parameters are that economic theory presumes a balance or equilibrium between price and quantity. In energy, as the California energy crisis reached its peak, two American Nobel Launderettes along with ten well-known economists issued a Manifesto in the Spring of 2001. In general, the Manifesto argues and has been often repeated throughout 2001 that the energy sector, under deregulation, must be allowed to function on its own. That market power has its own natural way of correcting itself due to the demand and supply of energy. In other words, the argument goes that the market system will balance itself.

Not long after the Manifesto, several individual scholars modified their stance and noted that the California market was flawed and "dysfunctional" because it was not a true deregulated market. This in spite of several of them having helped craft it and vigorously supporting the California form of energy deregulated markets. Space does not allow a full review of the printed opinions in the press or professional journals from this group or others, but similar ongoing discussion around the same perspectives exists well into 2002.

A number of economists have argued (see various issues in the Economist in February–March, 2002a through 2018) that the collapse of Enron proves how neo-classic economics works. As the argument goes, a company cannot perform in the market and thus fails. Other companies come in and take its place. The free market economy moves on. The problem with that argument is that it ignores what Enron did in the first place – set up and influence the deregulation market, then manipulate it, and used or profited from investors so that in the end, the collapse of the company was based on the value of its shareholders and creditors who lost their investment.

The neo-classical approach to economics, which has become dominant today not just in the energy sector, rests entirely upon the basis of exchange of goods and services. Reinert in a series of articles dismantles the neo-classical (Anglo-Saxon) view of economics by contrasting it with the German tradition whereby manufacturing or the creating of products is the key to economic analyses and everyday life. We concur with that perspective and will present below the subjectivist paradigm, which provides an entirely different approach to economics through the use of interactionism in everyday life. Therefore, economics is *about* everyday life and is *in* everyday life.

## *The Enron Case: Private Instead of Public Monopolies*

The date is Fall 2002. All the facts in the Enron bankruptcy will not be known for many years. Due to extensive legal and accounting litigation, and if even then, a picture has unfolded about Enron that symbolizes the problems with deregulation and privatization. While the Economist (various articles in 2002a, b, c) and Fortune (January 16, 2002) focus only on the accounting errors of Andersen, the basic fact remains that Enron executives instructed and managed Andersen's activities. In other words, the collapse of Enron is not only an accounting firm gone wrong but also the core issue of unfettered free market economics in the energy sector.

To be perfectly clear, Enron is (was) a merchant energy company that represented the mythic of neo-classical economics at its best: a "market force (firm)" unencumbered in its business activities due to its political influence and strong impact in forming the deregulated market, manipulating the prices (due to supply), and finally directing the spurious accounting of its cash funds.

As a point of departure for the Enron case, consider an outline prepared by the staff for the Governor of California (Staff, 02) as they prepare to address the impact of the Enron bankruptcy on the state. For a good updated overview of the Enron case, consult McGraw Hill PowerWeb (2002). As the Economist noted a year into the energy crisis:

> The end was not unexpected, but it was still spectacular. On December 2nd Enron, once America's seventh-biggest company, filed for Chapter 11 bankruptcy. Only days earlier, its bonds had been downgraded to junk and Dynegy, a smaller energy-trading rival, had pulled out of a planned takeover. Enron is the largest company ever to go bankrupt. Disentangling the resultant mess (and lawsuits) will keep legions of lawyers employed for years to come. (Economist, Dec. 6, 2001)

The monetary impact in California in terms of long contracts was relatively low. For example, about $84 million in contracts was obligated by the University of California system alone. Nevertheless, the prices paid for the supply of energy to the state were controlled by "market" companies or "merchant firms" like Enron so that about $9 billion in additional costs for power were paid by the state to ensure power in the Winter of 2000–2001.

In 2000 and the first half of 2001, Enron, among other market force suppliers, reaped enormous profits from California's deregulated energy market. Governor Davis stated in a Letter to the FERC Chairman:

> Since the summer of 2000, I have on numerous occasions demanded that the FERC investigate allegations of market manipulation by power generators and marketers, including Enron. In my testimony before the FERC on November 9, 2000, I urged the FERC to investigate and remedy California's dysfunctional electricity market. Last June I called upon the

FERC to investigate and refund the detailed overpayment by California consumers and businesses. (Davis, Jan. 31, 2002)

As the charts in Appendix A of the Addendum indicate, the prices paid for power over this short period of time were by hundreds of percent higher than normal or historical prices during this period (Chart 10.1).

FERC did finally take action in the late Spring of 2001 as Governor Davis acknowledged in a Press Release and noted the actions taken by the State and its citizens to curb the immediate energy crisis:

> I appreciate the action taken by you and your fellow FERC commissioners to finally reinstate price caps last June. Your action, combined with California's successful conservation efforts, our construction of 11 new power plants, and long-term contracts, caused energy prices to decline. (Governor Davis Press Release Jan 31, 2002)

Subsequent reports and studies have verified the State of California's analysis of how a far more devastating energy crisis was averted over the summer of 2001 with these and other policies (California Energy Commission, February, 2002). While acknowledging the role of more rain in the winter of 01 (hence supplying more water for hydroelectric power), the fact was that the summer of 2001 was one of the 25 hottest in California history. The California government programs and citizens conserved over 12% throughout the summer of 2001. And the market suppliers were forced to keep prices reasonable through price caps at the State (Public Utility) and Federal (FERC) levels. Long-term contracts further assured a constant supply of power, rather than relying upon market manipulation in the spot market.

Yet public records confirm that on April 17, 2001, for example, then Enron-CEO Kenneth Lay made eight recommendations to Vice-President Cheney regarding federal energy policy. One of those recommendations was continued opposition to price caps. A memo containing those recommendations was released the week March 20, 2002. On April 18, 2001 – the very next day – Vice-President Cheney told the *Los Angeles Times* that the White House emphatically opposed price caps.

When the White House released the final report of its energy task force, seven of Enron's eight recommendations had been fully adopted by the report. But this was

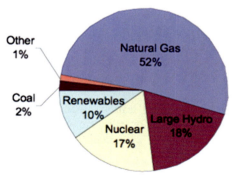

**Chart 10.1** Share of current in-state power generation fuel M. (Source: Rand Institute, February 2001)

# Case #1: Market Forces Created and Manipulated the California Energy Crisis 299

not unusual. Further documentation reveals that Enron staff and senior officers as well as members of its Board had tried to influence the White House during the Clinton administration and systematically pursued its self-interests in states like California who were considering deregulation. As Kuttner (March 25, 2002) notes, "Perhaps the most damaging effect of all is the eclipse of an opposition politics. Embrace of deregulation by 'pro-business' Democrats is more than a mistaken philosophical conversion."

The White House's energy policy, as enforced by the Federal Energy Regulatory Commission (FERC), particularly its opposition to price caps, helped to sustain the outrageous prices of the wholesale energy market. "This prolonged California's energy crisis and continued the massive transfer of wealth from our state to out-of-state energy companies such as Enron" (Staff 2002). It is still unclear how much direct influence Enron had over on the White House.

> What is clear, however, is that the White House's energy policy was nearly a mirror image of Enron's energy policy. It is also clear that that policy was detrimental to California and the wholesale energy market throughout the West. If Enron was able to use its market power and public influence to unfairly manipulate the California energy market, then FERC must take action. (Staff 2002)

Here is a checklist (Kuttner 2002) of the several icons that collapsed with the fall of Enron:

*A pension double standard* Enron's retirement plan was heavily invested in its own stock. Executives cashed out over a billion dollars, while ordinary employees were locked in. Janice Farmer, who retired with $700,000 in Enron, told a Senate hearing last week that she is left with a $63 monthly Social Security check.

*Bogus accounting* Since the Great Depression, the one form of regulation that even Wall Street has supported is the regulation of stock trades and corporate accounting… (when) once asked an ultra-Chicago economist if there was any regulatory agency that he endorsed. "The SEC," he said instantly, explaining that capitalism itself depends on honest information. Enron's entire game was to make its business plan so complex that neither investors nor regulators nor even its own auditors could penetrate it. While its core energy business made money (at the expense of consumers), it had speculative off-the-books subsidiaries. These borrowed heavily to make risky investments and eventually took the whole company down.

*The business press* Enron's breathless cheerleaders included not only its own insiders and stock touts but also a business press that pronounced it the epitome of the new economy. It surely was that – epitomizing all the smoke and mirrors. In the wake of its collapse, Enron's former sycophants have turned on it, with *Forbes* and *Fortune* running scathing denunciations. *BusinessWeek* asked giddy Enron boosters what they thought now. (Gary Hamel, chairman of Strategos, before the collapse: "Enron isn't in the business of eking the last penny out of a dying business but of continuously creating radical new business concepts with huge upside." After: "Do

I feel like an idiot? No, but if I misread this company in some way, I was one of a hell of a lot of people.") Well, yes. The one holdout among the business press is, of course, *The Wall Street Journal*, still trying to blame the debacle on regulators.

*Deregulation generally* Enron's collapse impeaches the conceit that a market economy can be efficiently self-policing. Enron fleeced consumers by manipulating prices of electricity and gas; it fleeced investors and its own employees. Tycoons do this because they can. Enron should signal a whole new era of re-regulation – of everything from electricity to pensions to accounting standards. And it is another warning that Social Security pensioners cannot trust Wall Street.

Nevertheless the Economist (Dec 6, 2001) and economists in general continue the same theme today is it did when the Enron bankruptcy began:

> The company's opaque accounting makes it hard even now to understand why it got into trouble, and whether the cause was bad luck or worse (see our special report, http://www. economist.com/printedition/displaystory.cfm?story_id=896844) The close links between Enron's chairman, Kenneth Lay, and George Bush will keep the affair in the political limelight. And Enron's staff, whose retirement fund was, at the company's urging, mostly invested in Enron shares that they, unlike e the company's bosses, were then unable to sell, deserve public sympathy. But if America's capital markets are to stay the cynosure of the world, some quick lessons need to be drawn. (Economist Dec 6, 2001)

The bottom line to the neo-classical economic community with unflagging support market power content is that "proper" deregulation or privatization will sort out the Enron's and other companies. Some will survive and others will disappear. Business as usual is the economic creed. Or as the Economist concludes one article "In the drama of capitalism, bankruptcy plays an essential part—until the next boom" (Economist, Dec. 6, 2001). However, in the Enron case, the culprit is the accounting firm that ventured from its traditional and honorable function in the audits to the consulting role now seen in all accountancy firms. As the Economist wrongly puts it:

> The most important concern auditing. Enron has restated its profits for the past five years, chopping $600m off its earlier numbers. The company's auditor was Andersen, now a target of many lawsuits. Last year Enron paid Andersen a fat audit fee of $25m; it also paid the firm $27m for consulting services. (Economist, Dec. 6, 2001)

The Economist goes on to cite other wrongdoings by Andersen. That was December 2001 just after the Enron bankruptcy. Since then, a number of firms have confessed to questionable accounting practices; and a number of accounting firms have owned up to their use of "liberal accounting methods." Certainly, the Economist is correct in saying that "After Enron, the SEC should do what its former chairman, Arthur Levitt, has long urged: ban accounting firms from doing consulting work for their audit clients. Accounting rules also need updating" (Economist, Dec 6, 2001). Nevertheless, what is lost in this spurious debate is the core issue of deregulation itself.

"Last are regulatory lessons" according to the Economist.

> There is a risk of turning any bankruptcy into an excuse for massive new regulation. Some have argued that energy is too important to be left to markets of the sort that Enron pioneered; or that, since it was engaged in financial speculation, Enron should have been regu-

lated like a bank. Neither conclusion is justified. Energy deregulation has brought huge benefits in lower prices and more secure supplies: energy trading will continue to grow regardless of Enron's collapse. Nor would it be wise to subject all companies with financial arms to stifling bank regulation. Enron's energy exchange was, however, explicitly exempted from oversight by financial regulators: that should be changed. (Economist, Dec 6, 2001)

There has yet to be any evidence supporting these claims from the Economist or economist proponents of deregulation anywhere in the world. In the end, the best lessons of all will come from the mere fact of Enron's bankruptcy. The Economist argues that:

The first is the regulation of auditors. For years the profession has insisted that self-regulation and peer review are the right way to maintain standards. Yet Enron has shown that this is no longer enough. Second is the urgent need to eliminate conflicts of interest in accounting firms. Andersen collected audit fees of $25m from Enron, its second-biggest client, last year, but it earned even more for consulting and other work. Lastly come America's accounting standards. GAAP standards used to be thought the most rigorous in the world. Yet under British standards (sic), Enron would not have been able to overstate its profits by so much. And, once again, although Enron may have been egregious, it is not a lone offender. The Enron scandal shows that America can no longer take the pre-eminence of its accounting for granted. That is a far bigger concern than any number of congressional investigations. (Economist, January 19, 2002c)

The Economist (January 19, 2002c), Fortune (January 16, 2002), other international business journals, and most economists worldwide come to the same conclusion: Enron was a case of bad accounting (or at least mixing accounting and consulting) rather than a mistake to deregulate public good markets like energy. The culprit here is the mythology of neo-classic economics that fosters and encourages market forces to manipulate.

## Case #2: The Economics and Commercialization of an Advanced Storage Technology – The Fuel Cell and Now All Solar-Powered Cars

This case was in the first edition of QE as it focuses upon the commercialization of a new advanced technology from a large research laboratory in the USA. The concern is with the fundamental business notion of how innovation is brought into the marketplace. Hence, the empirical study herein violates many of the commonly accepted economic perspectives in business economics.

The use of the interactionism perspective is far more significant for understanding economic phenomenon and is radically different than the subjectivism paradigm. And it meets a need for describing, understanding, explaining, and perhaps predicting events (Clark and Lund 2006).

As noted earlier, the electric vehicles (EV) and other modes of transportation have come back, especially due to the Tesla from Elon Musk who prior to Tesla was a key part of other "green companies" such as PayPal and SolarCity, which he had now taken back combined with Tesla. Musk has also started a big battery company in Nevada, but the question is, are these batteries for regular energy storage? Or are they for hydrogen fuel cell-powered transportation thus having hydrogen storage (Clark 2008)?

This section is not going to predict the future, but the combination of SolarCity now into Tesla could be so that the EV transportation is what Hanergy has already done in China. As also noted above, Hanergy has three cars and one bus all powered by solar panels (Clark draft paper and report, July 2018).

Now a new company called Sono in the EU is producing cars that are all solar powered. No need to recharge them, especially with fossil fuels such as natural gas, coal, diesel, or nuclear power. With the Sono all solar-powered vehicles this time means that the vision of "changing the world by green power" and the strategy of "mobile energy" of Hanergy have made a substantial breakthrough, which symbolizes that Hanergy has formally entered the new energy vehicle industry. The end of fossil fuels and even recharging with power generated from fossil fuels will end by 2020.

Hanergy has been leading the world in the field of thin-film solar technology for buildings. Now the four wholly solar-powered vehicles released this time are equipped with the technology of GaAs thin-film solar chips whose highest conversion rate reaches 31.6%, a world record holder recognized by the NREL. Besides, the electricity-generating modules of GaAs thin-film possess many advantages, such as flexibility, light quality, high conversion rate, good performance in the low-light environment, etc. It lays a solid technological foundation for Hanergy to carry out researches about wholly solar-powered vehicles. It is the core competitiveness held uniquely by Hanergy as well.

The modules of thin-film solar are perfectly integrated into the roof or body of the vehicles, providing clean energy for vehicles through the sunniness, which greatly enhances environment protection and driving comfort of vehicles.

Solar-powered car – from Sono Car Company (2018)

Finally, Hanergy's fully solar-powered vehicle depends on the world's leading GaAs solar power technology, entirely overturning the traditional charging model counting on fixed charging facilities. In theory, with sufficient sunlight, Hanergy's wholly solar-powered vehicle can drive 20,000 kilometers each year relying on the sun, which is able to meet daily traveling demand inside any city. Except for using solar power as the main driving power, Hanergy's wholly solar-powered vehicle can also use the traditional fixed charging facilities as a complementary charging method.

Internet intelligent technology opens up a new field for the development of vehicles, and Hanergy also applies these technologies to the design of wholly solar-powered vehicles. Users can select charging modes according to weather by apps on the phone, realizing interconnection between a car and mobiles and computers. At the same time, Hanergy's wholly solar-powered vehicle uses lightweight environmentally friendly material in a large scale and applies light and advanced appearance design to cater the development tendency of new energy vehicles.

Meanwhile the case for advanced innovative technology, such as zinc-air fuel cells (ZAFC) for the automotive industry in the long term, is now here but for stationary power (Clark and Cooke 2011) when Clark had authored the California Executive Order for the State to start a hydrogen highway in September 2003, but given in February 2004 (Clark et al. 2005a, b, 2006). In the energy and environmental industries, for a variety of reasons, the data was collected over a 2-year period of time. One of the authors (Cooper and Clark 1996) was a participant-observer with the commercialization of the ZAFC.

However, one other compelling reason also created the need for this case study. As Lowe puts it:

> The fixation on mobility – and the associated seemingly endless increase in kilometers of travel – also exacts a heavy toll. National economies stagger under the burden of acquiring oil to fuel their growing fleets of cars. Billions of hours are wasted each year in highway gridlock, and hundreds of thousands of lives are lost in road accidents.

And even more significantly, Lowe notes that "Environmental damage from driving plagues the farthest reaches of the globe – polluting the air in cities, squandering valuable land, and even altering the earth's climate" (ibid.). While advanced technology has been touted as the solution to this universal human characteristic of "mobility," there are a number of barriers to the commercialization (see Clark and Paulocci 1997a, b; as well as Nelson 1990; and Teece et al. 1994a, b, 1996 among others). The case goes even beyond the automotive industry because such new technologies today must also meet the environmental needs and demands of future generations.

For that reason alone, this case is significant since the ZAFC and other fuel cell technologies also have applications in the power/energy industries. Therefore, the commercialization of a new technology from the interactionist perspective provides insights into both the business and technological development of the ZAFC. As such, the case study will violate much, if not all, of the conventional business economic theories as well as challenge most of the current methodologies employed today.

The first violation of conventional business economics is the hypothesis or assumption that environmental regulations provide a positive, if not economic incentive to business development. Porter and van der Linde (1995) began to make this argument when they noted that environmental laws in Holland that encouraged the growth and reuse of waste for plants stimulated new business growth. Similarly, Clark and Paulocci (1997a, b) argue that new technologies for mass transit vehicles can be environmentally benign as well as commercially viable.

Another violation of the conventional business economic discussion and the functionalist paradigm is the use of multi-methods, as explained in more detail below. The conventional focus on unimethods violates the very nature of everyday business life, which is composed of multi, complex, and nonlinear activities of business interaction among actors. Therefore, the researcher must employ a variety of methods in order to understand the phenomena under study, in relation to the ontological and epistemological basis of the study as the understanding of business Lifeworld as a social construction of interaction.

Finally, a scientific explanation and even "prediction" of business activities related to the commercialization of the any innovation under study will challenge most attempts by economists to understand business itself. In short, a methodological interactionism perspective is to observe actors and participate in the everyday business events surrounding the ZAFC innovation in order to capture its application in everyday business usage. If scholars hope to contribute to business economics, they must be engaged by it. They too must be part of the activity under study.

The empirical results below about the ZAFC case study for QE which demonstrates how interactionism perspective works in everyday life. This chapter applies the interactionism perspective to the commercialization of a technological innovation. Understanding the phenomena of business development in terms of situations and events allows, perhaps, a clear concrete evidential path to be drawn for generalizable research, development, and technology commercialization. The study provides a road map in the form of a business economic model to which other technological innovations and programs can follow with impunity, success, and evaluative documentation. However, the challenge to other scholars is to select the interactionist perspective for the study of business economics.

## Fuel Cell Technology: US National Energy Research Laboratories

"Technology should be regarded a consisting of technique, organization and knowledge" (Hvelplund and Lund 1998). Consider now the knowledge basis for a new advanced technology. ZAFC is an interesting case study, developed at a national laboratory into an environmentally sound technology (EST) to be commercialized. Firms want to commercialize the technology in order to meet and even exceed the zero-emission requirements (ZEV) for vehicles in California, as well as other American states and a growing number of foreign countries.

Case #2: The Economics and Commercialization of an Advanced Storage Technology ...    305

The ZAFC is a fuel cell invented, patented, and now commercialized for mobile (e.g., vehicles) and stationary power sources (e.g., utilities). ZAFC and the zinc recovery unit (ZRU) are the case study material for this chapter. ZAFC technology is capable of powering a standard car for 250–300 miles between recovery stops, which take 10 min from the ZRU.

The laboratory solution to ZEV regulations was in energy storage devices, such as a flywheel or ZAFC. Therefore, a team created the ZAFC to make use of the high demonstrated energy density capability of zinc-air (>540 kJ/kg [>150 Wh/kg]) at up to 100 W/kg. The high energy density in part is due to the high operating voltage of the cell (1.2 V) and the use of atmospheric oxygen as a reactant. Not only is energy density insufficient, but the available batteries require long recharge times (4–8 h) in order to assure maximum life and acceptably low life cycle cost. While rapid battery recharge is possible, in most cases it is not desirable: to recharge a bus battery in 15 min requires design of the battery for rejection of waste heat associated with 0.5 MW.

The refuelable fuel cell has no expensive components other than the air electrode (quoted large volume cost, $120/m$^2$ [Alupower, Ltd.]). The high surface power (5 kW/m$^2$) gives the fuel cell a low producer's cost proportional to power, approximately $50/kW, half of which is attributable to the air electrode. Zinc recovery equipment is also inherently inexpensive. Zinc is electrodeposited on cathodic surfaces of a series of bipolar-connected stainless steel sheets, while the opposite surface of each sheet is catalyzed for oxygen evolution. Other components such as a 10 gpm slurry pump and metering devices are also low cost.

## *Technology as an Element in the Creation of New Business Venture*

Today, electric vehicle propulsion is severely limited by the low energy density of available batteries, of which lead/acid is the only mass-produced technology of acceptable cost. Battery exchange requires spare sets of batteries (which more than doubles battery investment), special vehicle designs, and expensive off-loading equipment. All-electric vehicles powered by secondary batteries cannot be simply restored to full energy.

Understanding the ZAFC as a "fuel cell" rather than a battery is an extremely important scientific and business conceptualization. The Economist (October 1997g) declared that the "fuel cell" had finally arrived ready for the marketplace. That article further linked both the vehicular and power-utility applications of fuel cells to energy generation and storage. Subsequent research indicates that communities can be powered from renewable systems when advanced storage devices are introduced as part of the energy grid (Isherwood et al. 1998). By the end of the 1990s, the US government began to seriously recognize the importance of new advanced technologies that were environmentally begun, completed foreign policy, and created new industries (Hydrogen and Fuel Cell Letter 1998).

For 3 years earlier within the laboratory and only after an intensive discussion, the laboratory staff concluded that they had a fuel cell instead of a battery. In fact, many of the publications about the technology initially labeled it as a battery. The basic distinction is that a fuel cell requires refueling (in this case of the zinc) of the cells in order that the chemical reaction (in this case with air) and another substance (electrolyte) will process a chemical reaction generating electricity.

With batteries, while the process is similar, the typical battery must be recharged, usually with some sort of external unit. The recharging, unlike the refueling process, which takes from 8 to 10 min, takes from 4 to 6 h depending upon the extent of the battery discharge.

After the very successful demonstration of ZAFC on a standard size bus from Santa Barbara, California, the commercial viability (defined as "successful laboratory and demonstration on vehicles of ZAFC for performance, reliability, safety and cost-benefit") of the ZAFC into a demonstrable prototype would require additional funding for 18–24 months. There were no US federal government resources. Only internal laboratory funds were used. Other economic models had to be found.

The issue of how to commercialize ZAFC for vehicles is an economic and business problem normally outside the realm of a research laboratory. Hence, the case is an example of an organization creating a new social construction or reality and operating within its perimeters. Therefore, a new business economic model had to be developed and demonstrated for the ZAFC technology within a national laboratory. The interactionism perspective is appropriate, since it agrees for a dynamic and creative approach to a business problem (technology commercialization). Nonetheless, by 2002, the company created in the USA with an Australian partner firm had collapsed into bankruptcy.

The individual actors would blame each other and even mention nation or cultural barriers to the new venture. But the reality was clearly something else. As discussed below, the interactionism perspective was able to provide a perspective and approach to understanding the problems for an advanced technology commercialization that provide concrete, positive, and productive direction for other such ventures.

Since the turn of this century, much has happened in the commercialization of fuel cells. Aside from national and state centers being formed to promote the research and development of fuel cells, new companies and established firms have been rapidly commercializing a variety of fuel cells. References and web sites are listed herein, but two points need to be made. First is that the commercialization of fuel cells like all other new technologies has historically involved and been promoted by the public sector.

The interaction among scientists and business people with the government as a source of grants, incentives, and tax credits has been critical. These relationships have even turned into formal organizations and associations for both networking and strategic planning. It is worth mentioning two in California that focus on the mobile or vehicle application of fuel cells (California Fuel Cell Partnership) and the power plant uses (California Stationary Fuel Cell Collaborative). Both organizations have been models for similar ones in other states, nations, and regions.

The second point is even more significant: the role of government in setting standards, protocols, or regulations that set public sector signals to the private sector that it must create new products that are environmentally friendly or at least non-polluting. New alliances and forms are created, known as "civic markets" (Clark and Lund 2001a, b; Clark and Bradshaw 2004), that bring together both the public and private sectors in order to address, define, and solve societal problems. The auto industry is certainly the largest and most impacted industrial sector. However so are other industries that pollute the environment such as energy, water, transportation in general, and waste sectors. The public message is that related health and societal impacts on communities and regions can be measured. These externalities must be reversed through government and business actions to commercialize new technologies.

## Case #3: Economics of Entrepreneurship, SMEs, and New Ventures

A variety of economic theories and models today identify the deployment of innovations in the firm. The conventional approach developed by Michael Porter at Harvard University uses a structural analysis of the firm in order to understand its competitive advantages and plot strategies against other firms (Porter 1980, 1990). In order to accomplish the analysis of the firm, Porter created what he calls the "five forces" framework: entry barriers, substitutes, buyers' and suppliers' bargaining power, and intraindustrial rivalry. Each force needs to be adequately understood in order that the firm becomes competitive.

The pro-government ideological perspective is reflected in the "push economic model" (Clark 1993, 1996) by the research and development (R&D) laboratories, centers, and incubators. "The Technology Pipeline" demonstrates how new ideas and research move from the concept stage logically into the marketplace as "stars" or successful industries of tomorrow. All the researcher or inventor needs to do is follow the logical process outlined by business schools: business plan, venture capital, and industrial alliances. Basically, this approach argues that R&D needs to be pushed out from universities and laboratories into the private sector (Crossley 1996: 3; Clark 1996).

In basic economic terms, the federal government approach is supply-side "technology push" which for business applications is unsatisfactory. Economists will talk about the demand-side "technology pull" approach, which is "market" dominated. This implies that the customer knows what it wants, better than the laboratory scientists. A new model of "technology interaction" whereby the research scientist within the laboratory must be in constant interaction with the private sector in order to create new technologies for a 3–5-year time frame.

On the other hand, the neo-classical economic model argues that the private sector itself (often described as the "market") must see the demand and therefore the needs for new technologies come first from the market or industry. In other words, the private sector must "pull" technologies that it defines and sees as important from university and laboratory R&D. The market or industry, therefore, so goes the argument, must define where public R&D funds should be expended. The market defines the most significant research areas for publicly funded R&D.

Both the liberal or neo-classical economic models ignore the give-and-take, the interactionism in conducting everyday business activities. In short, businesses are interactive, iterative, and not a static or even a linear process. As seen in the Appendix, studies of R&D characterize the demands of industry as being short term and often too narrow to satisfy markets and shareholder pressures. Whereas the universities are long-term oriented in their research programs, in part due to the time needed for graduate students to finish their dissertations (note the time frame is about 5–8 years, often the time needed for students to conduct research, write the thesis, and publish it).

Research laboratories have a 2–5-year time frame, which places them closer to the commercialization time frame of industry, which is within months of the funding, and certainly not more than a year or two, before R&D must see products in the marketplace. These time frames are important because industry or the market rarely funds R&D that takes over 2–3 years before it is commercialized. Competition and certainly shareholders demand a far quicker return on the R&D investment than the more long-term laboratory and university R&D cycle.

Entrepreneurs enter the R&D scenario as teams or groups who provide the funding for demonstration and final commercialization of a new technology. Schumpeter (1934) viewed the entrepreneur as an individual who is the creator of new business within a society.

While entrepreneurial ventures create new businesses within a community, the new venture or entrepreneurial enterprise is rarely an individual business activity (Clark and Sørensen 1994a, b), but much more of a team and collaborative effort. Much of the literature attempts to refine Schumpeter's individualistic definition (Freeman 1994; B. Berger 1991; Vesper 1990, among others).

Barth (1962) and Saxenian (1994) tend to see business development much more as community and regional phenomenon. As Barth puts it, "to see the rest of the community as composed of actors who also make choices and pursue strategies… (and) analyze routinized institutionalized community life in terms of the choices that are available and the values that are ascribed…" (1962: 7). It is the interactionism among the actors that is the concern of this study as in terms of how to analyze any emerging technology becoming a new venture.

In the 1990s to the present, portrays the need to analyze "clusters" of activities on a regional basis primarily in Northern California and Silicon Valley. Researchers at the Milken Institute in Los Angeles take a more Southern California regional perspective as well as state-by-state analyses also using a cluster theory approach. While these studies are useful in some ways for understanding the economic development and job creation potential for technologies, they often fail to account for the networks and interactions among the intellectual or knowledge leaders both in the region and globally.

The development of a new company requires many actors constantly communicating, exchanging knowledge, and debating issues as they start the new venture. This far more international and global form of interacting is due in part to the Internet but also primarily to longtime personal relationships from graduate school, international meetings, and conferences. Usually the new company will consist of a technical person, a marketing or businessperson, and a financial person or backer. As Freeman noted in 1989 and again in 1994, there is a distinction between the "business and technical innovator" and rarely should be the same person.

The "American entrepreneurial spirit" fosters innovation through research and development. The creation and growth of many new firms is directly linked to new discoveries that are financed when they are more "mature" by venture capitalists for entrepreneurs who attempt to commercialize the technologies into product(s) and must get over the "Valley of Death" (lack of funding and cash flow). The organizing and managing of the resulting new company(s) generally only benefit directly from either seed or venture capitalist forms of high-risk finance, experienced management, access to funds and markets, and a network of business contacts (Clark et al. 1998a, b, c).

The outcome is even more significant: new industries and new capital are recycled again into more companies. Rarely, however, are the funds placed into the second "D" (demonstration) and certainly not in the R&D itself. The role of government (and perhaps getting equity for the investment) must continue to interact with new applied technologies especially in the areas of energy and environmental concern (Clark et al. 1997).

## Methodological Considerations in Theory Building

The interactionism perspective in business economics is an excellent example of qualitative methods and action research. One of the authors (Clark) was a participant-observer in these cases studies. He was the manager of strategic planning at the national laboratory (fuel cells), the senior policy advisor to Governor Davis (California energy crisis), and both a founder of a new company and professor of Entrepreneurship. Hence, Clark was able to have access to key decision-makers, data, and technical staff for all the cases. The participant-observer role also allowed Clark to participate in meetings and interview key staff members. The results of this constant interaction were then implemented into action plans for the further business development.

Qualitative methods are common within anthropology, linguistics, and some areas of sociology, and participant observation is one of the preferred research methods along with interviews and action research as other primary modes of data gathering. Where necessary, we provide documents and reports such as emails, court records, and legal documents.

In anthropology, the product for most research is normally a written ethnography of a culture, group or class of people. Participant observation, interviews, and sometimes action research are the common research methods. In more recent years, many anthropologists employ local people, use survey techniques, and take videotape as part of their research. The qualitative methods of anthropologist are useful in understanding the dynamics of interaction within any human organization.

When applied to businesses, the outcomes can be dramatic, revealing and insightful. Suchman (1987) did just that with her groundbreaking work at Xerox when she applied qualitative methods to understand the interface (as business engineers would call it) between copy machines and humans. Since then, her anthropologically trained team has explored other avenues of research about machine and human interaction. Nardi (1996a) at Apple Computer has completed also an edited volume with articles on the human-computer interaction or interface through the use of qualitative methods while constructing new theoretical perspectives.

An anthropologist conducting qualitative research is directly relevant to this study. In the course of conducting research, everyday discussion and dialogue are often the prime sources for data. Linguistics, a related field to anthropology depends heavily upon qualitative methods since the researchers will solicit words and sentences from native speakers of the language. A native speaker would be asked for sentence examples and then for interpretations and meanings. Alternative sentences would be suggested and critiqued by other native speakers. Often such sessions are in groups or in a classroom setting whereby the participant can hear, ask, and diagnose the words and sentences.

In the case that follows, the exercise of clarifying words, phrases, and meanings was initiated by senior staff members, not for linguistic research reasons, but in order to understand the exact meanings of ideas among technical experts. In other words, while technical people all understood one another on one level, they did not share specific definitions and meaning on another level. Therefore, several work sessions were adjourned where intensive discussion over terms and meanings were clarified and sorted out. In other words, the scientists themselves participated in the research in order to assist their own technical needs.

Such meetings did serve to clarify ideas and terms and became a consistent and frequent interactive data collection method. In Blumer's terms, the scientists needed to make indications to themselves within the context of their social world so that they could communicate among themselves as well as to the outside world of other scientists and more particularly to the business community.

The need for common definitions and understandings allow for more complex levels of technical and business activities. In short, deriving common meanings and hence understandings creates the social context in which to conduct technical research and by extension commercial business.

The following pages present an empirical case where Clark was a participant-observer over a 2-year period of time (1995–1997). The research and hence the applied actions continue. By definition, interaction provides a dynamic and constantly changing framework which in this case leads to an entrepreneurial business development for an advanced technology from a large research laboratory in the USA.

The concern is to understand the application of the interactionist perspective to a new technology being commercialized into a business venture. The case documents

Practical Applications in Entrepreneurship and Business Development

one federally funded technology, the zinc-air fuel cell (ZAFC) along with the environmental concerns for its use and by-products from an industrial ecology framework (Cooper and Clark 1996). A significant part of action research methods within an interactionism perspective is to argue for a sustainable development or environmental considerations in the creation of any new technology and related business ventures.

Graedel and Allenby (1995) discuss industrial ecology as part of an overall sustainable development consideration. They note that "the evolution of technology and economic systems such that human economic activity mimics a mature biological system from the standpoint of being self-contained in it material and resource use" (ibid., p. 24). In other words, the global environment is interlinked with business and industrial activities. Everything that human beings do impacts the environment.

For Graedel and Allenby, the globe is a closed system operating under as if it is biological "life cycle." In short, human beings interact with themselves and their environment. When anyone develops a new business, they must take that perspective into account as well. The ZAFC does just that, since the use of zinc (once mined) is converted into electricity, becomes slurry in the fuel cell process and then is reconstituted into pellets to be fed back into the fuel cell (Cooper et al. 1995; Cooper and Clark 1996).

## Practical Applications in Entrepreneurship and Business Development

### *The Organizational Actions and the Actors*

The US government is the primary funding agency for the American laboratory in this case study, which has a contract with a major American university system for the operation of the laboratory. The US government funds over 735 R&D laboratories through various departments and agencies. NASA, for example, has 12 laboratories. The US Defense Department through its various military branches has over 20 laboratories. The US Department of Energy funds more than a dozen laboratories for over US $16 billion annually. Many of the federal laboratories are world renown in their fields.

The US federal government spends about US $43 billion in R&D annually and the private sector another $30 billion annually (Clark 1997a, b). The congressional and administration drive to balance the federal budget in the late 1990s meant, however, a decrease in R&D funding by about 3–7% annually over the next 5 years. It is this uncertainty in federal funding that is motivating the laboratory researchers and administration to seek "alternative" sources of R&D funding. Clearly one source is the commercialization process from the private sector.

By the end of the 1990s, however, a balanced US federal budget began to show surplus revenues from which both political parties decided to allocate more R&D

funds for basic scientific work. Therefore, while small increases in R&D began to appear across federal agencies and departments (from 3 to 6% with the National Science Foundation receiving the largest increase of 6%), they were targeted towards basic research rather than applied and typically had no increase and little impact on energy and environmental R&D budgets (Clark 1997a, b). During the 1990s, Clark saw, learned, and worked on these issues due to his role as the Manager for Technology Transfer at the Lawrence Livermore National Laboratory (LLNL). A "double gap" resulted: one gap between the need for increased funds for environmental and alternative energy research and the other gap between basic and applied research often inhibiting solid basic research from having demonstration funding for prototyping and field tests.

The LLNL laboratory has five "Supporting Academic Divisions" such as engineering, physics, chemistry, etc. and six cores "Program Divisions," of which environmental and energy are two. The laboratory is operated on a "matrix" model whereby specialists from different disciplines will work on projects within programs for a specific period of time and then move on to another project. For example, anyone research project may have a mixture of engineers, chemists, mathematicians, and physicists in it. The matrix structure is very unlike the typical university where people and research projects are organized by academic disciplines and rarely inter- or multidisciplinary.

There are almost 8300 employed at this laboratory (of whom 1200 are PhD-level scientists and another 2000 are engineers at the college and graduate levels) for an annual budget of over US $1 billion in FY98. The facilities cover one-square mile with over US $5 billion in equipment and buildings representing one of the world's most renown research and development organizations. The laboratory is among of the largest (in terms of annual revenues) research laboratories in the USA and probably the world.

In late 1995, two LLNL Divisions collaborated with others seeking research projects under the overall title of "industrial ecology." While the ZAFC technology (Clark et al. 1996; Cooper et al. 1995) had been created under the Chemistry and Materials Division, it clearly fits into a broader multidisciplinary effort within the laboratory for industrial ecology-oriented technologies. Fuel cell research and development are administratively within energy program division since it supplied the research funds to chemistry.

Almost all federal laboratory technologies available for commercial application have been historically taken "off-the-shelf" and "pushed" (some call it marketed) into applied research areas or commercial use. The current laboratory technologies are described in books, magazines, or newsletters, such as the biannual collection of technologies from laboratory. NASA, for example, publishes through a private contractor, "Tech Briefs," which is a monthly magazine featuring new NASA technologies. In most cases, a one-page description outlines each technology available for transfer to businesses, listing the laboratory contact person with telephone, fax, and email addresses.

The actors in the ZAFC case are five people within the laboratory: the lead scientist and inventor of the technology (electrochemist), leader of transportation pro-

Practical Applications in Entrepreneurship and Business Development 313

grams (civil engineer), his marketing assistant (social science undergraduate degree), the lead technology manager in related technologies (mechanical engineer), and the author as participant-observer (qualitative economist) who assists in business planning and strategic alliances.

The interaction within this group was frequent and sometimes intense. Several situations arouse in which the group had to or was forced to define some scientific concept terms, because of technical confusion among the various disciplines. Intense all-day meetings, briefing sessions, and casual meetings had to be held frequently as the research changed the definition of the ZAFC and the effort to seek commercialization funds changed business strategies. All were interactive processes demanding constant dialogue and discussion.

## *Organizations as Social Construction of Interactionism*

The purpose of this section is to describe the interactionism perspective as applied to fuel cell technology developed at the laboratory into a business reality.

The problem that confronted the laboratory was the need to obtain additional funding for the final research and development of fuel cells. This was a significant issue since as the team proceeded to "market" the technology; it became clear that fuel cells needed some more funding in order to be "commercially viable." After some internal discussion and debate, it was clear that these "demonstration" (e.g., prototyping, designing, and field-testing) funds would only come from sources outside the laboratory itself. The fuel cell technology was not funded initially through traditional laboratory sources from the US federal government and was ignored (if not outright dismissed) by the most obvious American industrial resources: the American Big Three automakers. The laboratory team was forced to find alternative funding routes to commercialization via demonstration of the technology first.

Not until a series of events occurred in late 1997 and throughout 1998 did Detroit announce over \$500 million in R&D for fuel cells: First an announcement by Mercedes-Benz from Germany that it formed a partnership with Ballard Corp., a new fuel cell company in Vancouver, Canada. Then came The Economist article of October 1997, touting fuel cells as a viable technology for vehicle and power storage. Toyota next demonstrated a fuel cell-powered vehicle at the December 1997 auto show. Soon thereafter, Mercedes announces that it will have 100,000 fuel cell-powered vehicles for sale in the year 2000. The Big Three American firms were losing ground and fast.

Putting the financial problem for demonstration of fuel cells into an interactionist perspective meant that new funding sources needed to be sought and the most likely sources would come from Europe or the Far East. Why? The American automakers' definition of economic and business reality is that of the status quo. Change in environmental laws, for example, that impact automobiles are viewed as an economic threat to Detroit. On the other hand, foreign automakers realized that environmental and safety laws in California and by extension the USA in general set a trend, which would foretell future American and international market demands.

Thus, the California laws would force new technologies into the marketplace. Mercedes-Benz established a 40-member engineering LLNL group (to track and work with the latest R&D) in Northern California in early 1997. Volkswagen followed with a smaller group in 1998. Ford Motor Company finally got the message and announced the relocation of it Lincoln-Mercury Headquarters from Detroit to Irvine, California, close to the University of California, Irvine campus, which has a major Fuel Center located on site. This is the first time a major US automaker has moved its Headquarters outside the immediate Detroit region.

There are a number of simple examples of how regulations have compelled companies to introduce new technologies into products. Porter and van der Linde (1995) examine how this government regulatory process worked successfully in Holland with environmental laws and new approaches to technologically improve products (tulips in this case) to be more globally competitive. Consider also the auto industry. The introduction of seat belts and air bags were all vigorously fought against by the American automakers as being impractical and too expensive. The car companies fought political and legal battles against these laws. They are doing so now with zero-emission vehicles (Shaynneran 1996).

In short, the American auto industry's view of reality is narrow and very conservative (in the sense of not wanting to change). Only in early 1998 did the American auto industry announce that it too would have electric vehicles by the year 2001 (Watson and Healey 1998). However, the Big Three automakers will not have zero-emission vehicles as required by California law and that of New York, Maine, Massachusetts, and Vermont or 10% of the US market. Instead, the new electric vehicles will emit 30% fewer lung disease causing hydrocarbons and 70% fewer smog emitting nitrogen oxides. As Hvelplund and Lund (1998: 17) note in energy and environmental industries, "public regulation analysis are often influenced by the interests and thinking of the established energy supply companies."

International automakers, on the other hand, have shown a considerable creative and innovative form of social construction when they examine the reality of future vehicles. By the end of 1998, with the Toyota all-electric vehicle and Mercedes-Benz announced sale of 100,000 all-electric vehicles in the year 2000, it was clear the American auto industry was losing technological ground and market share. While the foreign companies may not actually have developed and perfected the new advanced technologies, they are nonetheless very much in the forefront of implementing new approaches to solving or exceeding environmental and safety regulations.

Some non-American automakers, especially Volvo, for example, use safety as marketing tool in the USA with advertising not only about how well their car is built but also about side air bags that are installed for further safety. The strategy from Volvo's social reality works in the USA where they have solid sales because the consumers indeed embrace Volvo's definitions of automotive reality. In short, the American auto consumers have "bought" Volvo's definition of that reality, since Volvo clearly interacts and understands the needs of its customers.

Many foreign automakers take a global "long-term" interactive perspective where they examine government policies with industrial changes to "create," understand, and know what customers wants from their products. This proactive (having R&D offices located geographically close to where the new research is being conducted) means of conducting business is a social construction based on constant and intense interaction.

There are other examples of this within the auto industry and other industries. Suffice to say at this point that the commercialization of new technologies is more a matter of an organization creating its own social construction of reality and then being able to match that with other organizations. The key is to find those "other organizations." As discussed below, in a shrinking world or one that is being globalized rapidly, the task is not that difficult and appears to be of increasing necessity for companies to grow and prosper.

The interactionism perspective posits that if the fuel cell could not be pushed out of the laboratory. Other financial sources had to be found to "pull" it into final development for commercial applications through a variety of interactions among actors in a broad array of organizations. The interactionism perspective is the key approach in this case and probably can be applied in most other cases of technical commercialization and business development. Additional technological cases will further exemplify the model.

# Organizational Development as Uncertainty and Change

## *Operational Concepts*

Consider a theoretical refinement of the interactionist perspective drawn from transformational linguistics (Chomsky 1975, 1988), as presented in Chap. 4. At this point, the concern is with a few theoretical concepts to help order empirical results of the fuel cell case (Clark and Lund 2006; Lund 1996).

Gullestrup (1994) presents a multilevel construct, whereby social reality is viewed as having two levels. Hofstede (1980a, b, 1991) presents many levels of culture within any society. The difference with linguistics in terms of creating levels is that the linguistic theory argues for a surface and deep "structure" in language. Or as in this business case, an organization and its actors are attempting to bring a new technology to the marketplace and the interaction among the various actors' needs to be understood in terms of concepts, meaning, and actions.

Structures in language theory are not rigid, as in the conventional functionalist paradigm in social science. Instead the notion of structure in linguistics is fluid, flexible, and multilevel or nonlinear. Structures are not stagnant in either time or space, but dynamic. In language structures simply provide a set of universal rules (grammar) and database (lexicon) upon which to draw. Language skills and their application to everyday life must be flexible and fluid by definition. This dynamic and nonlinear nature of linguistic structures is exactly the opposite of the conventional functionalist paradigm.

For the interactionist application of linguistic transformational theory, a surface structure allows the action researcher to describe and understand organizations and the actors within them. A far more detailed discussion of deep and surface structures is given in a later chapter. Clark and Sorensen (2001) develop some of the ideas in relationship to entrepreneurship. Later, Clark and Bradshaw (2004) present some theoretical constructs in attempting to describe and analyze how the California energy crisis can be explained.

Consider surface structures as part of any research investigation, which continuously analyzes actors and groups within organizations of any size. The surface structures are seen publicly in terms of events and situations that occur within or between organization(s) among the actors. These events are seen in terms of business activities such as sales, promotions, manufacturing, distribution, etc. It is this continuous disharmonic dynamic through constant interaction of the actors that defines and redefines surface structures.

Deep structures are the basic building blocks of surface actions and interactions because they define and refine concepts, ideas, and symbolic objects in terms of their meaning. In other words, deep structures are the "meaning" attached to actions. Deep structures cannot be seen, as surface structures, because they are the mental representations or definitions of ideas that people bring to situations. It is the deep structural level in which people communicate (or do not communicate). Here people interact because they define and thus understand one another.

One other theoretical operation from linguistics is useful within the interactionism perspective: transformations. In the study of language, deep and surface structures are interactive in that one level influences the other. A linguist would create rules and representations to describe and understand everyday language usage. That is a major intent of this book with the advanced technology case of fuel cells. The notion of "representations" is very useful and appropriate for the case. Below, representations are discussed, and examples from the case are given.

Basically, a representation is similar to what Mead and Blumer call "notions" to oneself. In other words, when people interact, they are constantly creating, thinking, and reflecting on their actions as well as those of others. These notions are representations in that human beings will define and act upon how they think about their action or that of others. The ability of humans to make such representations allows them to change, adjust, and advance ideas. In short, for the case herein, representations provide agreement among the actors and therefore further collective group actions.

## *Surface Structure Representations*

For the fuel cell case and within the context of the surface structure analysis, two primary organizations are interacted in the initial stages: a large power energy company in Sydney, Australia, and a large American national laboratory. The laboratory is responsible for the technology development, while the power company needed a new technology to meet the legislative demands for zero-emission vehicles in Australia (similar to the earlier ZEV requirements in California) and as a major sponsor to create a "Green Olympics" in the year 2000.

Organizational Development as Uncertainty and Change

The laboratory provided the ZAFC technology by attempting to commercialize it. The role of the American government in supporting the initial research and development of the technologies while helpful was not enough to make the end product usable for commercial application on vehicles. As Clark and Paolucci (1997a, b) document, the automaker and battery consortia in the USA were admittedly opposed to fuel cell R&D from federal funding sources. Since these consortia either controlled or advised the federal funding sources, very few R&D funds were directed towards fuel cell R&D.

The constant interaction between the technical and business staff of both the power-utility company and the laboratory proved to be essential in building trust and establishing an iterative dialogue. In fact, the key power-utility executive saw the fuel cell as a large entrepreneurial venture. Thus, he left the power-utility company to form with partners, a new company to commercialize the fuel cell. The global surface structure event was the formation of a new consortium with the two initial partners (the power-utility and the laboratory) and, then when the new entrepreneurial company was formed, a broader and more dynamic new surface structure business network consisting of firms in the USA, Australia, and eventually Europe. The common goal by early 1997 was to commercialize and operate zero-emission vehicles for the Australian Olympics in the year 2000.

Within each organization, there are surface structures that provide both constraints and opportunities for the actors. In fact, because of the need to commercialize the fuel cell, but with limited financial resources, the actors with each larger organization had to reconstitute a group to work on the fuel cell. This group then had to endure extraordinary surface structure organizational changes in 1996, namely, the power-utility company was merged, a national Australian election totally changed the government, and privatization along with deregulation came into the marketplace.

For the laboratory, the conservative American Congress was continuing to cut R&D budgets. The laboratory itself had to become more oriented towards defense and nuclear weapon "stewardship" (e.g., dismantle and stockpile), which restricted all internal R&D funds. Overall the US government retreated from seeking industrial partnerships and commercialization of its technologies. Industrial ecology became, for example, an unacceptable mission for many government laboratories. Technology transfer was drastically cut and even eliminated in most US government agencies and departments. A pale was felt and dark cloud cast over applied and demonstration research such as a fuel cell.

The result was the group of actors at the laboratory focused their efforts on the commercialization of the fuel cell because of each individual's commitment to the concept and belief in fuel cell technology for a cleaner environment. The tasks required to do so, however, were not really part of neither the actor's job description nor their defined daily routine. Certainly one of the critical decision points for the Australian executive to leave the power-utility company there came as a consequence of the organizing turmoil both there and in the USA.

In the early days of establishing the collaboration between the laboratory and the power-utility company, however, the team coordinated and collaborated at new

318                                                                                           10  Everyday Economic Life

levels by achieving results internally and with the new global consortium. Only later when the new entrepreneurial firm was formed did the relationships develop in much deeper and broader areas, which included and then excluded some of the earlier actors in the commercialization process. For the international interaction between a large corporation and research laboratory to occur, the interactionism perspective specifies a number of representations had to be made between the actors and their respective organizations.

Particularistic legal constraints and covenants are defined as rules and apply to both organizations due to government regulations, foreign ownership rules, and the nature of business. They will not be considered here (see Clark 1996). The interactionism perspective provides a framework in which actors within groups and organizations can be described and understood in situations (e.g., meetings, discussions, or work sessions), activities (e.g., daily work as with computers, conference calls, telephone usage, and research), and events (e.g., conferences, travel, and larger level or management meetings). Each representation is an example of the discussion from Blumer and Mead, whereby A $\rightarrow$ B $\rightarrow$ A (A interacts with B) and then interacts back again to A after some thought and planning A $\leftarrow$ B $\leftarrow$ A.

## *Deep Structure Representations*

Beneath the surface structures with its set of rules are the deep structures with its own set of rules. Think of the deep structure as the level of interaction that defines business actions within situations. Everyday business life is an endless series of surface structure business situations, with shared concepts and meanings in order to conduct business formed in the deep structure interaction between actors. The derivation of these meanings comes from the often nonbusiness interactions in situational events that are part of everyday life.

In short, deep structures provide the meaning behind the observable business activities seen of actors and organizations at the surface structure. The linguistic theory of generative grammatical is equivalent to the dictionary or lexicon of a grammar for providing definition of ideas and concepts in the deep structures depending upon the everyday interactions. The interactionism perspective is particularly significant since there is an extreme need to define these ideas and concepts in the international business arena, even when business is conducted in the same language. As in the fuel cell case, English may be spoken by Australians, Americans, Danish, Germans, and Swedes, but it is subject of misunderstandings and therefore further need for constant interactions, actions to make decisions, and definitions.

The outcome of defined concepts and even the meaning of specific English words (e.g., in "commercially viable" had different meanings between the Americans and Australians leading to misunderstandings) are the representations in the deep structure. Due to the interaction within the deep structure and the interactive transformations with the surface structure, terms, concepts, and hence common goals become clearer. With common "lexical" definitions, the actors and their organizations can move forward into continuous business activities.

Organizational Development as Uncertainty and Change

For fuel cell technologies, the senior laboratory staff had to convene a one all-day meeting in early January 1996 (over 2 years after the project began) to define technical terms across the academic multidisciplines involved in the commercialization process. The result was a "Glossary of Terms" that could be used in any interactions within the laboratory and worldwide with other partners (see Firth 1990 as an example from discourse analyses). These basic deep structure definitions of terms allow accurate communication and understanding for surface structures interactions in everyday discussions among the various laboratory and international actors and other organizations. Understanding the business process for commercializing this technology is the basis for an interactionism perspective. When actors have defined representations of basic concepts and ideas, they can conduct business and create new mutually beneficial economic opportunities.

## *Organizations as Collectivity in Competency Building*

The interactionism perspective has a multidimensional theoretical range in that it describes and incorporates concepts from industrial ecology into everyday life. For example, industrial ecology is applied to specific products within a company. In the fuel cell case, that life cycle, recycling, and refueling component of the fuel cell is readily apparent.

With fuel cell vehicles are seen as part of the transportation system in a much larger industrial ecology context than the individual firm. In other words, the use of zinc as a fuel cell element eliminates the pollution of the environment by vehicles, but more importantly applies an environmentally friendly element to energy power and storage. By mining zinc and then recycling it through a recovery unit (making pellets) after use in the fuel cell on-board a vehicle, the environment can be protected at the source for the raw material mining as well as for the end user within the transportation system (no air pollution and 100% recycling of the zinc itself).

Consider another organizational surface structure level to which the fuel cell has significant implications to basic infrastructure environmental issues. Either as a hybrid electric vehicle or potentially as a self-sustaining electric vehicle, the fuel cell provides a significant impact on vehicular environmental performance and hence the transportation infrastructure. With other fuel cell-powered vehicles, the internal combustion engine (ICE) and fossil fuels are relics of the past, antiquated industrial technology from the twentieth century.

Imagine the new transportation infrastructures of the future. A world of silent vehicles, clearly a problem for pedestrians, runners and cyclists (especially with earpieces for listening devices), and blind and disabled, accustomed to hearing vehicles approaching. A number of new technologies will be required to assist the transportation infrastructure. Intelligent roadways will need to have sensors for traffic of all sorts. Gas stations become refueling stations. Traffic control uses other markers and signals. Endless new technologies and businesses would be needed, as the entire infrastructure would convert from the ICE to ZEV vehicles.

Now consider the key to the transportation revolution: it is the "battery" or as noted earlier, a "fuel cell" which in a larger context are both "energy storage devices" (Shaynneran 1996). When The Economist article (October 1997) proudly proclaimed that the fuel cell has finally arrived, it made another even more startling observation: energy storage was the natural technological link between two infrastructures: transportation and power-utility systems. In other words, through the mutual use of energy storage devices, power energy and transportation systems could be "mapped" upon each other. The fuel cell becomes the common link between significant needs in the two systems that could have an enormous positive impact on the environment.

This observation was made in 1996 or well over a year before The Economist article was published. It was confirmed by a major bus manufacturing company working with the fuel cell international consortium. More importantly, the mapping of energy and transportation infrastructures had become a strong interest within governmental policy and planning circles in Denmark among other countries. Studies began to confirm the viability, cost savings, and positive environmental impact of such a merger of infrastructures (Isherwood et al. 1998; Clark and Paolucci 1997, among others) through energy storage devices.

The interactionism perspective posits that if the fuel cell could not be "pushed" out from the laboratory, then financial sources must be found to "pull" it towards final commercial development. The only way to communicate that message effectively, without prejudice or bias to any one company or group, was through placing an announcement in the "Commerce Business Daily" (CBD). At that time (September 1995), the idea was to announce the laboratory plans for an "Industry Day" (October 1995) in which any company interested in the fuel cell could come to the laboratory for a briefing and business discussions.

The result of the CBD was overwhelming. Several hundred telephone calls were received, and each responded to with materials and details on the ZAFC technology. Soon, the laboratory staff discovered, however, that competing companies did not want to attend an Industry Day together. Instead, they requested that the laboratory staff visit them to explain the technological advance. Two months were spent doing so with the laboratory staff traveling across America in a series of meetings about the ZAFC. Still there were no takers – no company would come forward to fund the final stage of development to commercialization. There were a variety of reasons (lack of funds, downsizing, business slow, no market, etc.). All the companies acknowledged the laboratory breakthrough in exceeding ZEV regulations. Nevertheless, no company or even venture capital firm would provide the funding necessary.

In summary, three issues emerged from an interactionism perspective as being a problem with EV, ZAFC, and R&D:

1. A general collective resistant among American companies to change or venture into new technological areas
2. The lack of capital within small- or mid-sized firms for starting new internal ventures

Organizational Development as Uncertainty and Change

3. The collective belief that current infrastructure and vehicle configurations were established and enough to satisfy the customers

In other words, the collective and hence conventional wisdom within business and industry are resistant to change and innovation. For a new innovation, like the fuel cell, either a redefinition of the collective organizations had to be made or resources sought outside the collectivities. The latter appeared to be the only alternative.

Parallel to this period of time for fuel cell commercialization, the interactionist model worked on another level and signaled what appears to be the successful path. One basic and growing principle of American industry is that an increasing amount of business comes from international and global markets. In other words, while American creativity and innovation is world renowned, American industry is not.

Foreign or international industry (not necessarily multinationals) is often more innovative and willing to take risks that the American marketplace is unwilling to do. Some economists would agree that this is due to market size: the American market is simply too big to experiment with, while the German or French markets are smaller and therefore more likely to provide new product viability. In that context, the CBD attracted worldwide attention and therefore attracted firms outside the American collective organizational and traditional arenas. One source was the committee for the Australian Olympics for the year 2000. The lead organizing companies responsible the Olympics, are the power-utility company, which contacted the laboratory staff and an interactive dialogue, began. The power-utility company theme will be a "Green Olympics" and all the "people movers" which would need to be zero-emission vehicles or hybrids close thereto.

The power-utility company would order 1000 people movers (buses, vans, and other vehicles) that, once the games are completed, will be owned and operated by various cities throughout Australia. The estimated price paid per people mover is between US \$300 and 400,000. The total value of the contract for the vehicles is about US \$3–400 million.

In other words, the procedure for obtaining zero-emission vehicles for the Green Olympics is a major business transaction for one or many companies. When the power-utility company put out a request for proposals for the ZEV for the Olympics, however, only European bus manufacturers responded. No American company bid or offered to apply. In large part that lack of interest is due to the fact that no American company builds transit or people mover buses. Innovative business opportunities, pulled into the marketplace by the Australian Olympics' demand, were being met by European manufacturers. Once these companies produced and operated these vehicles, they would have a commanding lead in the marketplace. The key again is the "battery" or fuel cell. Fuel cells meet and exceed the ZEV requirements; hence in 1999, the creation by the California Air Resources Board in Sacramento, California, of the California Fuel Cell Partnership for vehicles and transportation.

While the commercial outcomes of the interaction have yet to be finalized, it appears that the fuel cell will be funded for its final development by an international multinational consortium. The European bus makers see the technology as a near-term (by the year 2000 through the EU Commission) commercialization of fuel cells for buses which will lead to worldwide markets for other cities and events. By 2004, 33 fuel cell-powered buses produced from Daimler were placed in 10 European cities under the CRITU program. Clearly the global strategy has yet to be grasped and appreciated by the American automakers.

## *Networks and Changes*

A significant concept of the interactionism perspective at the microeconomic level is the use of "networks" or relationship between people and organizations. These are personal connections, partnerships, and relationships between technical staff and separately between business executives are collaborations in which often intense exchanges of information are commonplace. Some networks (Håkansson 1994) form in many different ways, but primarily link businesses with compatible strengths (and in some cases weaknesses) to achieve common goals.

Other networks form between government and private industry (Sørensen and Nedergaard 1993). Networks can form on horizontal and vertical plains, depending on the nature of the interactions between the actors, organizations, and situations involved (Clark Jr. 1995, 1996). Jones et al. (1998) consider networks as being distinctively from "markets" or conventional approach to economic and business development.

With the interactionism view, the understanding of networks, as interpersonal and linkages between the interactions of people in that networks, takes on a new meaning and dimension. In short, networks cut across and even violate company or firm organizational structures.

While government and business networks are familiar in other industrialized countries, they are new concepts for American industry and government. Nevertheless, the interactive network between an American government laboratory and an Australian government public utility and a variety of international private sector corporations is a significant achievement. The basic explanation of why it is working can be seen in the interactionism perspective to networks.

The network approach as a theory often has its basic assumptions in the functionalistic paradigm and draws upon system theory and structural functionalism (especially upon Blau 1960; Pfeffer and Salancik 1978). For example, in an earlier article, Jones et al. (1998) saw networks as defined by the functional roles in an industry. Their approach changed significantly by 1997, when a general theory of network governance was proposed.

But the idea of networks is an important issue in the interactionism perspective because the result or manifestations of interactive representations are interpersonal relationships linked together into personal networks that are formed over periods of time. When one examines the relationships and representations formed by and between researchers, networks are very apparent.

One technological colleague calls another to verify engineering research data. A researcher finds a new piece of information and communicates with others about the findings. The same set of interpersonal networks exists in business. Further, interactive networks are being formed between the public and private sectors. New forms of partnerships between government and private industry are especially becoming more common in the American economic system.

Such concepts of networks and relationships are not new to other industrialized countries. Swedish scholars have researched networks for two decades (Håkansson 1994), which concern "core corporations" and their relationship to smaller (SMEs) companies. While the worldwide recession dramatically changed these networks (Håkansson and Snehota 1994), the basic form of the Swedish economy, the largest and most significant in Scandinavia, remains the same: close networks of partnerships between large corporations and private industry.

Denmark, on the other hand, developed an entirely different network economic structure (Sørensen 1993). Private industry and government have a strong and interrelated relationship. However, there are few large "core corporations" in Denmark. For the Danes a large corporation has between 1300 and 2000 employees. As in the USA, official statistics classify a firm as being large when it has 500 or more employees. There are only a few companies of that size in Denmark, while several have many times that number of employees outside the country. On the other hand, Sweden has many corporations who employ over 10,000 people each within the country.

In other words, the concept of networks in Denmark means the personal relationship between and among small- and medium-sized enterprises (SMEs), rather than large corporations and SMEs. The attempt to structure networks, as many do from within the functionalist paradigm, both misrepresents the phenomena of how networks themselves came into existence and grossly exaggerates the need of scholars to overly orchestrate or organize them.

In much of the literature, when they are defined, networks can be almost anything: associations of similar small companies who collectively have more purchasing power, regional groups of vertically organized companies, companies and local educational institutions, or even governmental units with common goals and purposes.

In point of fact, successful networks (those that accomplish something over a period of time) are formed in order to achieve the collective or common goals of the members. The successes of networks in Denmark over the last years have often been recognized as contributing to the country's economic success during the worldwide recession of the early 1990s, when this assertion was debatable.

Networks are centered on basic shared philosophical concepts. Networks must utilize or leverage resources within a triangular relationship between government, private industry, and support institutions like education, training, and technical assistance centers. While a network can certainly change and even disappear or purposely disband, the initial formation of a network needs facilitation and continued support from a dispassionate outside party.

The key to networks within the network theory is "trust." This can only be achieved after people work together on a common problem and find that others are able to keep secrets, share valuable information, and exchange new ideas. The interactionist perspective best describes, understands, and explains how networks are created and operate. In themselves, networks are neither theory nor scientific. Instead, the understanding of networks allows both the scholar and the businessperson to create meanings and pursue shared goals.

If networks are institutionalized as formal permanent structures, they will implode from their own administrative weight. The very notion or idea of a network is something that exists at moment or situation in time to accomplish some task(s). People know one another and form the network to solve the problem at hand.

The fuel cell case demonstrated a form of network building in three ways:

First the participant-observer (author Clark), as an action researcher, knew from past experience how international companies might act in best development. He had understood some surface and deep structure rules used in international business activities. Critical to any interaction with a company, and especially in Germany, France, Scandinavia, and most English-speaking countries, is to establish linkage, rapport, and trust. That was done in the fuel cell case by coordinating the interaction between the laboratory technical staff and the key international actors through conferences and meetings outside the USA. The international firms then sent staff to visit the laboratory.

Second, in order to protect priority information as well as further establish trust in a legal manner, nondisclosure agreements were executed and signed. While to some these legal agreements may appear to violate "trust" in the conventional personal usage of the term, for international business purposes, such agreements are (1) a signal of trust building, (2) satisfaction to company legal departments, and (3) necessary in order to have specific technological discussions.

Finally, constant communication via telephone calls, fax, and email are essential. When working in the international business world, such communications can be difficult due to different time zones, language problems, and costs. Today, email allows constant communication and overcomes these problems; nevertheless, it too has limitations. The best communication method is personal contact. This was purposefully done with visits between the various consortia companies.

The laboratory pursued the same interactive process with domestic USA companies who might be potential manufacturers of fuel cell and therefore consortia members. Tokarz would lead the effort either with Cooper, the lead technical researcher or some other member of the team. Follow-up information would be sent with periodic telephone calls and fax or email communication. However, the domestic market never materialized in large part due to the inherent resistance of American corporations to change.

## Qualitative Scientific Descriptive Analysis

Intense and constant interaction must take place between the members of the international consortium in order to commercialize the technology itself. This close collaboration supersedes industrial competitive issues and conflicts. For example, in the fuel cell case presented herein, several major bus and battery or control unit manufacturers are part of the international consortium.

The economic competition arises between companies in the marketing and distribution of the final zinc-air technologies on vehicles much the same way as oil, gas, and vehicles are competitive today. This is the interactionist perspective at the macroeconomic level and the subject of another book.

Applying the interactionism perspective on a microeconomic level, a number of specific interactions become apparent.

## *Interactionism for Surface and Deep Representations*

The first issue must clarify the surface and deep structure interactions within and between organizations forming the consortia. Using the interaction perspective outlined above, the following representation can be made of the basic organizational interactions.

The goal of the action researcher within an interactionism perspective is to establish the business opportunities. Sets of representations provide guidelines for business actions as well as a road map to future interactive decisions. The representations must be stated, subject to further scientific verification, and applied in other cases. Ultimately the representation could be reduced to mathematical relational symbols. Elsewhere are several sets of rules derived from the fuel cell case for over a decade from Clark (1996 to 2017).

A second interactionist result was the clarification of representations or meaning attached to words, ideas, and concepts. Considering the example of fuel cell case at the laboratory when the principal researcher and the program manager went to Europe to attend a conference on electric vehicles, they found that the definition of a "fuel cell" more accurately described the technology of zinc-air, rather as an "advanced battery." Upon further verification with the key staff in Australia as well as at the laboratory, the conclusion was certain.

From early December 1995, the zinc-air battery would be known as a fuel cell. While there was scientific and technical evidence to support the name change for the zinc-air technology, the international interaction was crucial. Clearly, the technology was more of a fuel cell (i.e., requiring refueling rather than recharging). Furthermore, the concept of a fuel cell itself denoted high-tech advancements and therefore had more business appeal. The decision was made. A common definition was adopted and put into use worldwide. The term "fuel cell" had been agreed upon at the deep structure level in order that it could be used precisely through transformation rules to the surface structure groups and organizations in everyday language usage.

A second example of creating clear and precise definitions can be seen in the creation of a new technology to parallel for refueling the fuel cells. Through numerous meetings both within the laboratory and with the international parts, the concept of a zinc recovery unit (ZRU) with its own representations was created.

Originally the principal research described the process for the zinc to be cycled through an undefined external stationary unit that pushed or spent zinc and electrolyte into an external hopper from the fuel cell. After many hours of intensive discussion among the leaders scientists (Cooper, Smith, and Tokarz particularly), two issues were clarified. The zinc was the issue and not the zinc in combination with the air. In other words, the external and separate unit needed to be concerned only with zinc processing.

The other point of clarification concerned the concept of this unit itself. Again in checking earlier documents, the process unit was called a "refueling unit" when in fact it was a "recovery unit." The difference is significant in the context of industrial ecology. Refueling implies that a raw material (zinc) has been mined and processed so that it is ready for refueling the fuel cell. In fact, the zinc is not refueled at all. The zinc is recovered because it is reformed after being used in the fuel cell. In other words, there is little loss of zinc (unlike gasoline, e.g., that is burned and needs to be refueled). The ZRU therefore is simply an external unit that takes out the zinc from the fuel cell, reconstitutes it, and pumps it back into the fuel cell after 250–300 miles of use.

The clarification of the recovery unit (rather a refueling unit) is an enormously significance deep structure issue. Aside from the understanding and communication of the meaning into surface structure situations, the clear definition allows the scientists to actual create the ZRU. In this case, the actual ZRU had not been created and designed. Now a clear technological path could be followed. The significance of the ZRU definition will lead to patentable intellectual property among other yet unknown scientific breakthroughs.

## *Transformations*

The relationship between the deep and surface structures occurs through transformations, which are vertical interactions between the sets of rules within each structure. In the fuel cell case, there are three "nodes" or key interactive points of contact for the rules: personal or people interactions, organizational relationships, and technology operations such as use of telephone, fax, travel, the Internet, etc. Each node is noted as a "phrase marker" since it has definition and universal meaning.

As continual personal trust is being built through constant interaction within and between partnering organizations, personal nodes are triggered that move back and forth between deep to surface structures. For example, telephone conference calls (lasting hours) occur, but then a point is reached when some of the principals within the organizations need to meet face-to-face. Above, one aspect of building personal trust was described as essential for establishing networks. Such trust could only be built through constant interaction among the actors.

In the fuel cell case, personal trust was firmly established within a 2-month period between the laboratory and the power-utility company: once in Australia due to a Professional Academic Conference and once in Europe due to an International

Conference. The transformational relations moved or transformed the common definition of terms and concepts to the surface structure following the set of rules outlined above. Other opportunities were deliberately created: the action researcher (Clark) as a participant-observer on the laboratory team traveled to Europe on two other businesses and visited the key consortia bus manufacturer. These two meetings established an already solid interpersonal relationship through a factory tour, confidential exchange of data and information, and joint collaborative research which leads to seek funding for fuel cells. Various meetings were planned in various parts of the world that would connect the key actors from each organization.

## Conclusion: Understanding Economic Theory Building to Be a Science

As noted, the definition of the zinc-air technology as a fuel cell rather than a battery was a matter of constant interaction between the representations made on the surface structure organizations and actors who must create a common set of definitions in the deep structure. Once these terms were agreed to, the expansion into other related technologies for a zero-emission vehicle becomes clear and far less complex to implement. The interaction rules allowed the fuel cell to be commercialized since there was common definition of ideas, concepts, and terms. Thereafter agreement, on the need and application for the technology, could be readily made and advanced through proposals, contracts, and seeking other consortia members.

The results of interaction between and among the actors and organizations over fuel cells lead directly to other cooperative technological commercialization. It is only a matter of time. There will be other technologies that the consortia will purse as well (such as in other fuels, materials, and intelligent systems). While economists' debate "market demand" and "market supply" issues, the facts are that technological innovation and commercialization are very much outside these simplistic theories. Business, in general, when seen as a dynamic and ever-changing collection of people (defined as a firm or company) will change due to the interaction of its actors. Change is the norm in business.

The process of business innovation through technological commercialization, using the transformations between surface and deep levels of representations, is interactive. It is not simply a pull or push economic approach. The use of interactionism perspective provides for a better understanding of everyday business phenomenon. Furthermore, much can be learned about conducting research and implementing business practices.

The discussion starts with how to understand the constitution of what can be called the "firm." A more detailed discussion of "interactionism" is provided in the development of a "new economics" later in this volume. A few issues are worth presenting in the context of the development of the energy "market" and restructuring or creating firms in that sector. One issue that the Enron case has clearly demonstrated is how important "knowing" people can be. That is, close friendships can be useful for political influence. In academic terms, this has been called "networks" (Håkansson and Johanson 1993, 1994).

In Chap. 7 and elsewhere (Fast et al. 2014), the firm is discussed and how it should be understood as the actions and knowledge of the individual actor and of the actors' collective actions over time. These actions and interactions have some consequences, i.e., the organizing of activities and knowledge. In this organizing or intersubjective moving pictures of what the firm and the environment are will be created among the actors.

The manipulation of markets by firms is rooted in the notion that the firm acts and behaves as seen above in the Enron case in its (the actors) own self-interests. In this case, the firm involved and subjected its accounting firm to do its bidding. Individuals communicating in an interactive or face-to-face manner, where the relations consist of concrete meetings between members in the firm, conduct all business.

When organizations are examined, especially the larger, older, famous ones, they seem solid, they seem permanent, and they seem orderly. This is, after all, what scholars and the public often call organizations. Images of organizations as solid, permanent, orderly entities run through many textbooks. But they only tell half the story. They obscure the other half: the chaos which looms behind the order, surfacing from time to time, such as when computer systems break down, when products are sent to the wrong destination or when bookings are made for the wrong dates. They also obscure the immense human efforts and energies, which go into keeping organizations solid and orderly.

The word "organization" is (only) a concept, which is used to describe a phenomenon. It is a conceptualization of what people believe and do and what they orient towards actions. In other words, an organization is a phenomenon that people experience when and where they see more than one person involved in activities over time. Thus, organization becomes a collective arrangement where people try to give the situation and the activities meanings. In line with Blumer (and in Clark and Fast 2002), organizations consist of the fitting together of lines of activity – the interlinking of lines of action. Actors mixing, sharing, competing, and cooperating are parts of the interactive process that define groups and organization. And that is why most organizations, by definition, change and move dynamically in space and time.

By fitting together the lines (what can be called the "rule") of action and interaction as logically prior in organization, actors are discouraged from mistakenly regarding organizations as "things" or simply "solid entities" such as a building or structure. Some scholars argue that organizations are "living things" akin to the biological sciences. And refer to organizations as "evolving" with "life cycle" attributes (Graedel and Allenby 1995).

An organization should be understood through the actors who by their actions and knowledge create the firm in their everyday pursuit of life. The focus and start of understanding organizations is the members or the actors within the organizational life. In this the relation between action and knowledge is the central issue of interaction.

Action expresses the behavior of people, expressed in advance by the actor whose behavior is then based upon an anticipated project. The expression "the act" expresses the result of the ongoing process or the fulfilled action. Action could be hidden or open intervening into the outer world. All projection consists of an anticipation of future behavior with help of "fantasy" (thinking-in-future) or, as Blumer puts it, acting in relation to "the generalized other." But it is not the ongoing action process, but the fantasized act, *as it* was fulfilled, that starts all the projection.

The collective actions constitute the firm, but it is understood in relation to interpretation and intersubjectivity. The constitution is formed by the actors, but at the same time, it is a restriction for the actors through the moving picture of reality that they have built and act in relation to. This is central, because the relation between the development of knowledge and the actions is the foundation for the process of interaction. All this is about how to understand everyday of life processes in the actors' construction of the firm.

People understand themselves retrospectively and act accordingly, but additionally they are thinking-in-future: What are the projects they are thinking upon? In which way do they try to realize them? How do the projects change through the process of action and interaction?

People construct their organizational reality through actions in everyday life, and they build paradigms in order to orient themselves to their own reality. Individual actors have to relate themselves to this discussion if it is the empirical reality and not the theoretical "reality" in which one is interested. In other words, understanding of the social construction of people's organizational life and activities is the context of their everyday business life within the firm.

The basic issue for most actors in firms is how to make the company survive and grow during any particular point in time. They must be free to move in the marketplace but also be secretive enough to protect its privacy. More importantly, firms must have concern for others and their environment. The public good must be protected because it is in the best interests of the firm to maximize its profits for shareholders and executives alike. The protection of the public good is essential in various infrastructures and sectors (Clark and Lund 2001a, b). In recent months, the protection of the transportation sector must be embedded in the government. The energy crisis in California has clearly shown that the energy sector is a public trust. The same could be argued for environment, water, and even telecommunications.

# Current (2018) EV Data and References

Large Opportunity for 48VMH Medium and Large Trucks?
14 Sep

Like the car equivalents, 48 V mild hybrid trucks do not start as electric vehicles (driving the wheels electrically some or all of the time) but they are headed that way.

Electric vehicles are the new material battleground
14 Sep

Electric vehicles are rapidly scaling up in production, but under the surface of this explosive growth there are significant competitions taking place across the supply chain.

How does the Vespa Elettrica stack up?
14 Sep | Worldwide

After surfacing its Vespa Elettrica concept at EICMA last year, a large motorcycle trade show known for these sort of announcements from manufacturers, Piaggio finally announced that it will go to production this September, and that it will take preorders in October with the first deliveries later that month.

Research helps make buses smarter
14 Sep | Switzerland

A rather unusual trolleybus has been navigating the streets of Zurich in recent months. With its large windscreen and covered wheels, it could easily be mistaken for a tram. It features a hybrid electric drive system that allows it to draw power from an on-board traction battery as well as overhead wires. But this bus is also "smart," boasting specially designed software that automatically gathers information on the route.

Massless Energy: Structure Becomes Lighter
13 Sep

This is a technological megatrend. Dumb load-bearing metal structures move to plastic and composite and incorporate energy harvesting and storage material – massless energy. Indeed you could call some of it negative mass energy. Goodbye components-in-a-box.

Theresa May will announce £106 million for R&D in green vehicles
13 Sep | United Kingdom

UK Prime Minister Theresa May will announce £106 million for R&D in green vehicles, new batteries and low carbon technology.

Walmart Canada 100 percent alternatively powered vehicles by 2028
12 Sep | Canada

Walmart Canada announced plans to power its fleet using 100 per cent alternative power by 2028. To meet that goal, the company has announced plans to acquire an additional 30 Tesla 18-wheeler semi-trucks, building on its original order of 10 trucks in November 2017.

Webinar Tuesday 25 September – Electric two-wheelers: the EV underdog?
12 Sep | Worldwide

IDTechEx will be hosting a free webinar on Tuesday 25 September titled Electric two-wheelers: the EV underdog?

Toyota plans to recall 1 million hybrid vehicles
11 Sep | United States

Toyota is conducting a safety recall involving certain 2016–2018 model year Toyota Prius vehicles. The subject vehicles have an engine wire harness which is connected to the hybrid vehicle Power Control Unit. A portion of the wire harness could contact the cover at this connection and wear over time, causing an electrical short circuit, which can generate heat. If sufficient heat is generated, there is an increased risk of a vehicle fire.

Volvo Cars' 360c autonomous concept: why fly when you can be driven?
10 Sep | United States

Volvo Cars reveals its new Volvo 360c concept, a holistic view of a future of travel that is autonomous, electric, connected and safe. It could open up new growth markets for Volvo Cars, for example in the multi-billion dollar domestic air travel industry.

Advancements in emerging conductive materials
10 Sep

In April 2018, IDTechEx gave a presentation at the world copper conference in Santiago Chile. This was part of work carried out for the International Copper Association to benchmark the commercial status of emerging conductive material. The presentation delivered can be seen below.

## *Company Press Releases*

Tritium receives DOE funding to develop high-powered charging for EVs
Press Release | 14 Sep | United States

Tritium is receiving a portion of $3.2 million in federal funding awarded to the Electric Power Research Institute for developing an extreme fast charging system that can connect to the grid.

# Chapter 11
# Summary and Conclusions

## Introduction

Volumes have been written about the future. And economics is frequency cited.

However, unlike the sciences, economists make predictions that have conflicts and often fail. For the most part, economists take the present and past data to reformulate it into predictions. While the future can be rooted in the past, the future will need to be based upon thinking "outside the box" as the Toffler calls it. From the work on the future ("Future Shock" and "The Third Wave" in particular), it nonetheless is admitted and advocated the need for "the intellectual framework that might unify management theory and economics is not yet in place. The task of creating that framework still lies ahead" (in "Forward" to Gibson 1997: x).

In 2005, Jeremy Rifkin published a book, *The European Dream*, whose subtitle states "How Europe's vision of the future is quietly eclipsing the American Dream" by moving into a "Third Industrial Revolution," that is, fossil fuel-free, localized renewable energy for travel and power through public and private partnerships. The key is in Rifkin's definition of the European Dream since it:

> Emphasizes community relationships over individual autonomy, cultural diversity over assimilation, quality of life over the accumulation of wealth, sustainable development over unlimited material growth, deep play over unrelenting toil, universal human rights and the rights of nature over property rights, and global cooperation over the unilateral exercise of power. (Rifkin 2005: 3)

Rifkin and others need economics in order to provide the data and understanding for the new European Dream let alone those new dreams coming in Asia, Africa, and the Americas. Many of the economic policies advocated in Rifkin's book are becoming a reality in the EU as the Parliament passed a three-tier program for implementing the "Third Industrial Revolution" (May 2007).

Meanwhile, America cannot resist its reliance on statistics, quantitative reports, and the "art" of economics. Economic data is historical by its very nature and definition, but is open for different interpretations and understandings.

© Springer Nature Switzerland AG 2019
W. W. Clark II, M. Fast, *Qualitative Economics*,
https://doi.org/10.1007/978-3-030-05937-8_11

For example, political leaders call for "clean" energy, but they often do not or cannot define what clean energy is.

Case in point was when Clark was working with one of the largest research laboratories in the world that got funding from the US Department of Energy (USDoE) in the 1990s. One of the contracts was for "clean coal" technologies to be installed in China. To call "coal" "clean" is legally what is known as an oxymoron (OX). In short two words that are in conflict with one another. Other clean energy OX are when natural gas is called a clean fuel. More recently is the 2015 case of Volkswagen (VW) and Audi in Germany with their claim that diesel fuel for their cars and especially buses is clean. The settlement to car owners is $10 billion done in 2018. The evidence that they had was investigated since the 1990s and only found a few years ago to be "fraud" and not true.

Statistics from a week or a month ago were gathered over weeks from data collected over more time in the past, and not all "data" are gathered as it is impossible. Data in itself is a construction and dependent on the way people are thinking. Future economic trends or predictions are impossible and baseless. If any established, new, or emerging nation is to advance, it must understand its past and present and strategically interact for its future based on the application of scientific know-how, ideas, and wants and thereby creating its future.

Indeed, economics has been toted as the science for explaining or even predicting the future. However, its analyses are all based on the numbers, as noted earlier in the case of Enron (Clark and Demirag 2002, 2005, 2006a, b). What this book has done is provide a scientific framework rooted in philosophy, theory, and empirical data to create a science of economics. Furthermore, the volume has applied qualitative economics to business and management through a Lifeworld perspective and the use of interactionism.

In our perspective there is as well a discussion of what have been growing in the field of economic – the matter of economic behavior.

This is a discussion that has been going on for the last 200 years. In Europe there is a distinction between act and behave – which can be seen in the distinction of understand (*Verstehen*) and explain (*Erklären*) (as discussed in Chaps. 3 and 4). This is a discussion between objectivism and subjectivism – the difference in ontology. Behave is a notion of what we can tell from observation, but it does not emphasize that people have a mind and are conscious defining situations and tries to create their reality.

Exactly therefore we talked about action, which indicates that the human being is both mind and body.

This discussion can also be seen in the USA whereby Mead wrote about being a social behaviorist, but what he actually meant was to formulate a critique of behaviorism and the whole model of stimuli-response thinking. It can be seen in his first part of this book that the discussion of meanings and interpretations with Blumer's concept of "indication" means pointing something out. People are constructing situations and things by being engaged in actions. Such interactionism is what communities and people do.

Behavior is only what we observe. Thus our perspective is that there is something behind individual behavior. We think in general that there is a problem, not only in the USA but also in Europe, Asia, and around the world, whereby people are not informed and conscious about philosophy, backgrounds, and history of science. Therefore, people use words and create theories that can contradict each other or be without content or meaning. There must also be a difference in everyday language and an attempt to philosophically investigate what business is in everyday life. It is the matter to develop a language that captures the meaning of human actions, interactions, and situations.

This volume presents not only a "think-outside-the-box" perspective on conventional and dominant functionalist economics paradigm but also a dynamic, interactive, and new perspective based in philosophy of science and an alternative tradition. Frankly, the book is "thinking inside the box" when the box is defined as science. Furthermore, Gibson and others in his volume (1997) argue that the world of the future is uncertain and even chaotic. It is a dramatic departure from the post-World War II world. New thinking in economics, and other fields, must be nonlinear and dynamic as circular economics presents and points out the near-term future need (Clark 2014, 2015) in order to account for a world in which the future is "terra incognita" as the Toffler puts it. The landscape of tomorrow is both unchartered and accelerated. Economist can think of it as a speeding uncontrollable automobile or as a challenge for making some sense from it.

Some economist have put forth a different approach to economics, such as Levitt and Dubner in "Freakonomics" (2005), in order to signal that there is something radically wrong with the conventional paradigm. What Levitt, a young and increasingly well-established economist, is described as being of interest is "the stuff and riddles of everyday life" (ibid., p. xi). As Levitt says later in the book:

> There is at least a common thread running through the everyday application of Freakonomics. It has to do with thinking sensibly about how people behave in the real world. (Levitt and Dubner 2005: 205)

However, the authors fail to probe into the depth of the interaction between people in situations and events. They do not "ask the second" or follow on question. But their book does raise questions about economics and provokes scholars to think outside the box.

Other economists argue that it is time to re-examine the accepted economic norms and popularization of globalism (Saul 2005). What is obvious about the future of economics is that, as Gibson notes (1997: 3), "economics will be based not on land, money, or raw materials but on intellectual capital." That is the reason that the fuel cell case in Chaps. 9 and 10 was chosen. When the case was first written in the late 1990s, fuel cells were not known to economists let alone the general public. Today, fuel cells and especially now EV cars are widely known, especially in Asia and the EU.

New innovations and commercialization into the marketplace are the economic drivers for future. However, the technological innovation case study exemplifies another significant issue: current economic theories and business management practices cannot describe or explain the commercialization phenomenon for business development.

Conventional economic development theories of today are inadequate by defining innovation commercialization as due to "externalities" of one sort or another. Or more insignificantly, new business products or services depend upon "market study" and demands. There are, for example, simply not "five forces" at work. And to attempt to explain the commercialization of the fuel cells in that manner is fallacious. Business economics is simply not a phenomenon that occurs in a "black box" subject to external influences.

Still other economic theorists have attempted to create new frameworks for understanding and explaining the commercialization and deployment of innovations into the business community. Yet these attempts are drawn from the same neoclassical functionalist paradigm and therefore suffer from the same problems. Resource-based theory is a good attempt in its investigation of those elements (both tangible and intangible) to which a firm may then turn into various business opportunities.

This approach clearly recognizes "intellectual" or knowledge capital, for example, as a valuable resource beyond the conventional economic definition of the firm. With its focus on capabilities as central to business development, there is a growing concern that any business or "firm" still remains a mystery. In other words, no economist knows how companies, businesses, or firms develop, grow, and sustain themselves. The basic problem remains, and forward-thinking economic theorists recognize it: what is the firm? and is there a theory of the firm?

Nonetheless, this volume argued that indeed there is a "theory of the firm" when the scholar uses as the starting point, looking inside the firm first. An understanding of the everyday business life of the firm (in our case, research that turns innovation into a new commercial venture) provides the opportunity for theory building, which has never before been considered in economics. In other words, when the economist starts from a Lifeworld perspective that is rooted inside the firm and builds from the ground up, then the results are likely to be more significant, accurate, and scientific as how a business operates, grows, and is managed.

Furthermore, through a growing body of literature, the firm, interactionism, and its linguistic framework for analysis provide hypotheses, description, explanation, and rules that become generalizable. In short, qualitative economics is science. However, for our purposes now, the consideration of the firm, and particularly the commercialization of an innovation, provides an understanding on the building of economic theory from the Lifeworld paradigm in everyday business life.

Interactionism is the cornerstone for moving from the microeconomics or case study perspective to the larger more "universal" macroeconomic one. In that context, research on more cases about innovation in light of business economics must be gathered and analyzed. Transformational linguistic theory provides the framework for scientific rulemaking. The definition of economics as exchanges and therefore as engagement allows for an understanding of economic phenomena, events, and situations when the data is drawn from a knowledge base in order to construct the economic reality of everyday life. Since action among actors is predicated upon their knowledge and understanding of others, consider the description of the cases presented earlier in such terms.

To summarize the research framework from Blumer for symbolic interactionism draws its roots from the subjectivists' philosophical tradition in European and American academic and research communities which is now conceptualization in the Lifeworld paradigm. When we look at symbolic interactionist theory and the interactionist perspective applied to business economics, cases can be described, understood, and explained for business activities in a scientific manner. When transformational linguistics is included, then there is a very powerful and robust theoretical model from which to formalize (not quantify) business economics into sets of rules, interactions, and predictive analyses.

## Phenomenology: The Tradition of the Lifeworld Perspective

Central in our discussion of a new perspective on economics is also phenomenology. The connection of individuals in interaction is one of the cornerstones to understand the development of the firm. The present and past actions and interactions of people within any situation define an organization. As Fast (1993) argues, the very definition of an organization or firm or company is the sum of all its *past, present, and future actions* interpreted by the actors and attached meanings. Consequently, understanding a company can be seen in the actor's actions and interactions among the people that comprise it. To understand how organizations operate in a region, nation, or international context, it is critical to analyze its *interactions* within itself and with other organizations.

Any organization must be understood through the actors who by their actions and knowledge create the everyday life of any firm. The actions and interactions exist in a context that is created by the actor through his actions. The action is related to the actors understanding of the situation and his context of meanings. Actors have motives and definitions of situations that make their social world into an inner logic. As we have showed in the cases, this is the start of any study of organizations and business.

The world constantly moves in which actors are confronted and composed of various experiences in which the process of consciousness develops or simplify shifts towards different paths (or structures), which can be transformed, into further actions. Knowledge is constructed by the actors in their "environmental" situations and events. Precisely because knowledge is a relation to and an orientation towards the "environment" through action, the environment itself can be defined as *the experiential space* and as *the interpretation space*. The experiential space is what is close and concrete, where, e.g., the actors travel and interact. This can be seen in the consciousness of human being in "the natural attitude" interested in that part of everyday life world that is in reach and that in time and space are centered around the person (Schutz 1973b: 73–).

Actors construct their own reality, individually and collectively, but they do not experience it in the same way. Moreover, actors see reality as if they live in an external world independent of themselves. Through their language, behavior as actors who often understand events, situations, and actions of others as being natural and that society is something "out there" that cannot change. They are wrong. The reason for this vies of stability is that from the actor's knowledge, human beings "know" the world and that other actions confirm that in their given understanding of the world. However, reality is not something that exists independent of the actors and through the action-knowledge process; actors create their view on reality.

The central point is not only the product, the marketing, or the economic development of the firms in which actors talk and act but also the way in which they talk or communicate about behaviors and the way in which this talking creates a situation and interactions and meanings. A moving picture of reality is created. The actors have to understand how they create their experiential space and in which way they can act sensibly in it. Actors who are conscious about their experiential space will be less oriented towards rigid views of what is true or false and more oriented towards what is flexible, creative, and sensible and a fluid depiction of everyday life. Therefore, no interaction represents truth or falsehood but only versions which are more or less sensible and explain everyday life.

## Symbolic Interactionism: In the Subjectivist Theoretical Paradigm

The primary mode for understanding organizational or collective interactions are through the *symbols* (or *meaning of*) involved in the situations and events. *Symbolic interactionism* is the study of collective action between groups and organizations from the actors' Lifeworld and daily perspective. The analysis of organizational actions must be seen within that context which helps define the interactions. However, each context has a history of events that frame it. And the interactions themselves redefine and create a new set of circumstances from which the organization operates.

Contextual analysis, therefore, can be limited and static since they reflect the status quo and on-dimensional perspective of the past. In order to understand the present actions of an organization, and even attempt to predict its future actions, specific situations must be studied. Therefore, transformational grammar provides the framework of scientific analyses and rulemaking. From human interactionism through language, scientific hypotheses can be created with explanations and predictive models.

George Herbert Mead (1962; originally 1932) at the turn of the twentieth century from the University of Chicago formulated the philosophical basis for the symbolic interactionist perspective upon which Herbert Blumer (1969) expounded. The symbolic interactionist perspective discusses how human beings act and interact in everyday life. Mead, with his student and subsequent chief proponent, Blumer, laid the groundwork for much of the theory behind "qualitative theory" today in sociology. Mead rejected the classical English and American traditions and drew instead upon philosophical elements in both continental European and Far Eastern philosophy to counteract the empiricist and positivist determinists who were beginning to dominate the development of the social sciences.

Mead and Blumer argued that individuals are actors who alone or in groups interact in a variety of daily situations, be they personal, business, social, or whatever. Since human beings are thinking and reflecting, these interactions and the study of them are the basis of all human behavior. Language is used between actors as they interact and communicate. The ability of humans to create symbols (language, gestures, etc.) distinguishes the human species from all others. Bugs, animals, and fish (even dolphins) do not communicate to understand, gain, and restore knowledge or act. Understanding and explaining everyday actions, however, is the extension and essence of human interactions.

Blumer refined Mead's theories into a practical and straightforward approach to understand how people act and interact in everyday life. Blumer assumes that since humans think, then they must reflect before they act. In short, humans create and take action in various situations through the thinking process based upon their reflective ideas and thoughts. In order to theorize as to how this is done, Blumer used Mead's concept of the "generalized other" or the fact that people think and reflect to themselves before they take action.

Human behavior is unpredictable, full of uncertainty, and therefore not rational. When scientists study and theorize about normative behavior, they have focused on some set of elements that compose human behavior. Because people are human beings, their everyday lives are made up of uncertainties and nonlinear actions. Human beings have an infinite set of behaviors and possible patterns to follow. Everyday life may be composed of sets and regular routines, but these are neither normal nor indicative of the creative potential of individual actors. They simply signify what people follow for convenience or expediency sake. They certainly are not the situations from which to draw significant conclusions about actors, situations, groups, or collective behavior.

In short, human interaction is by definition "abnormal." The essence of abnormal is that it constitutes its own processes and orderliness for individual actors and groups. The understanding of "abnormal" is really the knowledge of what is "normal" for actors and can best be seen in conflictual situations where actors will display underlying emotions, feelings, and thoughts. Thus everyday life in business is not predictable or even normal. It is more often than not, composed of change and irregularities. In short, the abnormal is normal from which rules can be constructed.

Key to collecting data on actors, situations, groups, and collective behavior are the methodologies employed. Here the qualitative methods[1] from anthropology and sociology play a significant role. For decades, anthropologists and sociologists have conducted research studies using qualitative methods. The results of these studies are often case studies that describe the "static state" of a culture or group of people. As described in this volume, one of the basic methods used in qualitative economics is "participant observation."

---

[1] That is, field work, participant observation, action research, interaction and dialogue analyses, etc.

Most qualitative studies require that the researcher live and work in a particular environment in order to understand the people in their everyday life activities. In addition to the traditional anthropological methods, other related qualitative methods are used. Collection of prior data is a method used by a qualitative researcher before going into the "field." In the context of business, this method would be called "market assessment," whereby the researcher/businessperson would want to know what information is already available about the culture.

However, the researcher needs to be "objective" about these materials since previous studies may be biased. As outlined, field or site visits are used to gather data, analyze it, and then draw conclusions. Today, the use of electronic data is more and more common. But in particular, legal data such as depositions, court testimony, and the like are a large part of qualitative data collection since it is legally factual and variable.

What remains critical in the qualitative economic perspective are the interactive methods utilized in the actual data collection process along with the interpretation itself. These methods are akin to the scientific methods used in physics, chemistry, biology, or engineering among the natural sciences. Actual verbal data from linguistic interactions are similar to the data collected in physics or chemistry.

The "site or field visit" through extensive interaction with the actors such as action research as participant observation and use of interviews is the single most important method in qualitative research. Here the researcher/businessperson must actually go and see what the culture looks like. The researcher/businessperson must live in another place and experience the culture and people. It is not enough to visit or tour. There are a number of subtle but often critical facts learned from such visits. Among others is the local infrastructure of a community or region such as transportation, communications, housing, and commerce, which may influence a business and economic development.

However, observation and recording data are not enough. And in many cases, observations can be wrong or misleading. In-depth interviews are necessary from a variety of people. Usually, anthropologists identify key individuals or "opinion leaders," that is, someone whose information is variable as consistently "correct" and "adequate." Such people are not always the leaders in the culture, but they have rare insights into how the culture operates. Opinion leaders can verify and correct observations. More importantly, through interactions with them, a deeper understanding of the everyday phenomenon, situation, event, and local markets can be made.

Sørensen and Nedergaard (1993) have described how "intuition" plays a role in business which can be seen as that of the visionary. In other words, the businessperson who uses their own sense of what product or market works may also be the same person with a vision. Often that concept (vision) is applied to businesspersons. These individuals have an idea and then pursue it. While others may have had the same idea or vision, it is the businessperson who actually does something about it.

Research results are analyses which check the results and provide verification in order to provide useful written descriptions. This entire process is what Blumer (1969) describes as the "symbolic interactionist perspective." The basic assumption for the symbolic interactionism is that actors interact with one another and form relationship with others. However, each actor also interacts with him-/herself. In short, the actor reflects and contemplates his/her actions. Blumer calls this thinking process, the "generalized other," because actors do this all the time: they think, reflect, think again, act, think, and continue to move ahead. In other words, Blumer provides a theoretical framework for understanding intuition when seen as part of an actor's interaction with others.

For the businessperson, the result of qualitative research can be a strategic plan of action. Even though the anthropologist rarely does any analyses or prediction with their data, the businessperson can. In particular, the anthropologists never forecast, predict, or explain situations and cultures. They try not to influence the local culture in any way. This nonaction model has come under considerable criticism, but is considered by anthropologists as following the natural scientific method: objectivity. A businessperson would develop an "action plan" and move on it immediately. The businessperson would want to see the needs of the culture and fulfill them. In many cases, the businessperson has the vision of a concept for the future economic development of the culture and will act upon it. Typically, the businessperson will "carry through" or "follow up" on their analysis of the culture because they see a business opportunity, can set goals, and create performance objectives.

## Transformational Linguistics: Economic Rules of Formalism in Economics and Business Practices

The entire qualitative approach is the process of symbolic interaction at work. It also sets the stage to understand how actors interact and create universal concepts which can be applied in a variety of situations. The underlying rules that explain the action of the actors can then follow the linguistic paradigm outlined by Chomsky (1980) so that the explanation of interaction is seen in the formation of rules.

Linguistics uses a qualitative methodology in order to identify sources of data such as native speakers/hearers of a language. Sentences are created and repeatedly tested against that of native speakers. Underlying the transformational grammar approach to linguistics is the assumption that languages have universal characteristics. The task of the linguistics is to identify and derive the grammar for a language. Data is collected and comparisons are made to other languages. However, linguistics (and now cognitive psychologists) has found that native speakers/hearers do know rules and representations of their own language. They know what sounds right and correct.

> Some evidence may bear on process models that incorporate a characterization of grammatical competence, while other evidence seems to bear on competence more directly, in abstraction from conditions of language use. (Chomsky 1980: 201)

In order words, qualitative methods for language usage are the basic data collection procedure for linguists. They use discovery and description of everyday language as the basic core for their analyses and theories. Within the last 20 years, we have refined qualitative economics in terms of theory and methodology. In particular, the direct application of the theories and methods in this volume to specific business cases has proven invaluable. Of particular interest for the business community has been the plethora of legal cases involving corporate governance, scandals, and bankruptcies in America. Qualitative economics is both useful and scientific in the analysis, understanding, and prediction of future corporate actions (Clark and Demirag 2005, 2006a).

## In Conclusion: On a Personal Note

Attempting to summarize over two decades of work (since the early 1990s) that is rooted in each of our over 30 years ago spent in graduate school, teaching, and practicing in business is a formidable task. Nevertheless, this volume has brought together significant historical and philosophical threads of thought in order to present a new perspective for economics. The application of symbolic interactionism and phenomenology to understanding everyday business activity provides economics with a different perspective. The bridge to formalism from linguistics is the last link in making economics a science. We discovered our similar interests and pathways while pursuing our PhDs separately on two continents. Then in 1994 while Clark as a Fulbright Fellow at Aalborg University, Fast and Clark discovered that they had much intellectual curiosity in common.

We are both anxious and excited about this volume. In particular, we are anxious for the reaction from our peers. It is just the beginning of a dialogue in which some of us from around the world have been engaged already. For many years now, across various disciplines, a growing number of scholars have considered many of the issues that we have posited here. What we have done is simply draw these perspectives together by following a common philosophical line of thinking. What we believe is that often the most creative and revolutionary thinking is just that: the simplest approach. We hope so.

What we plan to do next is gather examples of our perspective into a collection of work to be published soon for use by students, professors, and especially business managers in a book that is less academic and more practical, Qualitative and Quantitative Economics ($Q^2E$): Making Economics into a Science (Palgrave Press, 2019). To start, we thought that the best sources of such examples of our perspective are our own students.

Over the last 10 years or so, we have had over 150 graduate MBA and PhD student projects that reflect this paradigm. Some of them and now others from California have been interested in qualitative economics. In fact, Clark whose business cards note that he is a "Qualitative Economist" has been asked to do business studies in California and has been a consultant to private companies and public organizations in Los Angeles area using this approach. Now he is a Research Professor in Economics with a focus on qualitative economics for a globally respected business school in Southern California.

In Conclusion: On a Personal Note 343

Our thought was to publish this study and others with permission from people and business involved. Our vision is to create and be editors for a journal on $Q^2E$. Moreover, we have both noticed that qualitative economics is part of our daily lives. Clark, for example, had one consulting contact in which definition of numbers is critical in implementing the project. Literally millions of dollars in green building construction are involved and the need for definition, rules, and legal terms to form contracts that require qualitative economics.

We think that a publication effort in these areas would be useful for others and is illustrative of our concerns and perspectives. We also think that it is an acknowledgment for our students as they each go into the everyday business world creating and changing it forever. It is, after all, to our families and students that this volume is dedicated. They are the ones who will enter the new economic world and must understand as well as master it. To them, we are thankful; to them we give our best wishes.

# Appendix

## Circular Economy in the European Union: The Transition Towards a Better Future

The transition towards a circular economy could be the answer to some of the main challenges of our time. It can help preserve resources that are increasingly scarce and subject to greater than ever, environmental pressure. It can boost Europe's economy and competitiveness, by generating new business opportunities as well as innovative and more efficient ways of producing and consuming. It can bring local jobs and create opportunities for social integration and cohesion and even find an answer to the terror of the fanatics: provide desperate people with viable, safe, and strong future for their families and children.

The European Union Circular Economy is a long-awaited package that will play a key role in supporting this transition to the future, today, by providing a clear message to the industry and society on the pathway forwards. The package will have to drive investments and create a level playing field, removing obstacles stemming from European legislation, deepening the single market, and providing favorable conditions for innovation.

© Springer Nature Switzerland AG 2019
W. W. Clark II, M. Fast, *Qualitative Economics*,
https://doi.org/10.1007/978-3-030-05937-8

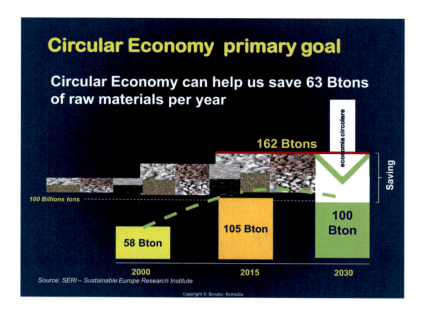

This chart shows how the circular economy works and has been working in different countries and communities already.

**Product and Process Design**

One of the main tasks of the circular economy package is the development of innovative product requirements under the ecodesign directive, such as durability and recyclability. In this respect, it is very likely that the Commission will adopt a proposal to differentiate fees paid by producers in extended producer responsibility schemes according to the real end-of-life costs and recyclability of their products (http://ec.europa.eu/growth/industry/sustainability/ecodesign/index_en.htm).

As part of the regular reviews of BAT (Best Available Techniques), the circular economy package should also include guidance on best waste management and resource efficiency practices for production processes in industrial sectors, improving the uptake of the European Eco-Management and Audit Scheme (EMAS) and the environmental technology verification system as well as methods to evaluate and make decisions on products (health, environment, nature ingredients, etc.) such as "earth accounting" that has started to do within the circular economy paradigm (http://wwwearthaccounting.com).

# Appendix

**Circular Economy and Waste Management Strategies**

The circular economy package will also address in a systematic way the challenge related to the management of end-of-life products. Each year in Europe, 2.7 billion tons of waste are generated, but only 40% – limited to a few streams – of this amount of waste is nonetheless collected and sent to reuse, recycling, energy recovery, or composting. Yet there is room for improvement, especially if we consider that in many European countries, landfilling is still the preferred option for waste management. Valuable but also hazardous waste streams are not properly tracked and managed along with illegally exported abroad. Even when recycled, the current processed are not designed to optimize the recovery of valuable raw materials.

Moreover, collection systems are still too expensive and inefficient which does not help industrial companies to abandon the traditional production systems based on the linear (flat economic) transformation of materials into products and their disposal once they are consumed. Therefore, the Commission is considering the possibility of introducing further simplifications to promote increased efficiency of collection systems through the circular economy paradigm. Hence by integrating these systems with the upstream industries that make use of recycled components and raw materials from products entering, the end of their life stage can be profitably met as well as protecting the environment (http://ec.europa.eu/environment/waste/legislation/).

Another issue on which Brussels wants to put some focus is the development of professional networks specialized in the uses of equipment reconditioning and reusing products of all kinds. Thus European nations can avoid the generation of waste and encouraging the development of new technical skills, and new jobs, especially for young people and their future tomorrow. The new package will in some respect develop pre-demolition guidelines to ensure adequate recovery of valuable resources and proper management of hazardous waste, as well as voluntary industry-wide recycling protocols, based on the highest common standards in each waste stream. For example, one of many issues is waste management choices for nations in the EU.

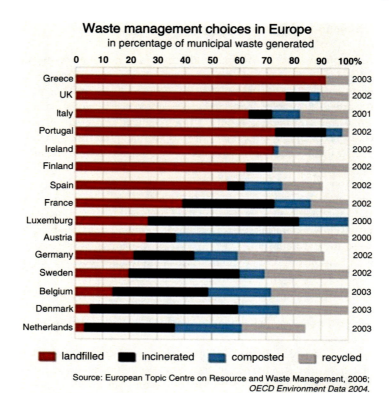

Variables and measurable policies are needed for waste management. Consider these.

**Standards for Secondary Raw Materials**

The Commission, through the circular economic package, will probably launch work (jobs, new businesses, and education) to develop quality standards for secondary raw materials where they are needed – in particular for plastics. The EU regulation on fertilizers will probably be revised in order to facilitate recognition of organic and waste-based fertilizers, hence supporting the role of bio-nutrients in the circular economy. A key priority of the circular economic package will be the sharing of good practices between member states and stakeholders on the cascading use of biomass and bio-based products.

Among the other key areas, the circular economy package will also develop analysis and policy options to facilitate shipment of secondary raw material across the EU (electronic data exchange and possible other measures) and improve data availability on raw materials. Such standards are measurable and thus able to be evaluated, if needed for changes, revisions, and improvements. The results are the then

Appendix 349

other areas in the circular economy can be developed and implemented based on these results. Thanks to these initiatives, experts expect that the circular economy package will enable more effective strategies to increase the demand for secondary raw material coming from reuse and recycling operations (http://www.rreuse.org).

The Commission seems to understand that the demand generation from European industrial value chains connected to the waste management sector could be a clever, innovative, and environmentally friendly way that is best to feed a virtuous product production, distribution, and reuse circle based on the circular economy concept. It is no coincidence that in Europe, over the last 24 months, there are now several new companies created and operating in the field of secondary raw materials brokerage services to efficiently connect supply- and demand-generating benefits for the market and significant profits for investors. In this perspective, the new circular economic package aims to encourage the creation of new industrial initiatives, based upon a greater integration between different companies and businesses along with governmental institutions. By deploying in a more effective environmental way, the most innovative information and communications technologies reduce information asymmetries that hinder trade but develop groundbreaking cooperative processes.

**European Funds for Innovation and Skills Development**

The European strategy for the circular economy will rely on Horizon 2020, the mainstream – 80 billion Euro innovation program activated by the EU Commission. Through Horizon 2020, several high-impact European business value chains will speed up their transition to the circular economy (http://ec.europa.eu/programmes/horizon2020/). Hence, it is worth emphasizing that Europe present several cultural and infrastructural strengths to be exploited, which could place the entire EU into the global leading position towards the circular economy. Europe can lead in sustainable mobility, remanufacturing, sustainable development of nature-based solutions, and implementation of new hydrometallurgical processes for the recovery of rare earths and precious metals.

Furthermore, it would be important to support industrial companies in developing a clear vision of their priorities, by choosing few selected high-impact projects to be targeted and thus funded. Value chain leaders are required, with the capability to aggregate different partners (including industry, research centers, academia, institutions, governments, etc.) and lead them towards the realization of a new industrial model based on the circular economy paradigm.

The circular economy paradigm certainly addresses the goal of developing a stronger innovation culture, by supporting greater action in education, both at academic and at industrial levels. As already mentioned, the EU Commission is aware that the lack of skills and professionalism in institutions and companies is one of the biggest obstacles in the adoption of a new industrial approach. The priority for education and jobs must begin immediately and build upon programs, publications, and people who are already involved in the circular economy.

## Simplify to Innovate

Needless to say, several European countries, such as Sweden, the UK, and France are already strongly involved with the circular economy to modernize and simplify the current legislative framework needed from the European Commission. In modern economies, the environment is an essential resource to be protected but today not only and so much through a formal, prescriptive approach. Rather, it should be possible to precisely measure the impact of environmental externalities ranging from environmental costs associated with the use of ecosystems by individuals and businesses (http://www.amazon.com/The-Next-Economics-Environment-Climate/dp/1461449715) that are penalizing those who do not change their bad habits and rewarding those who design the company business with the goal of mitigating their impact on the ecosystems (www.elsevierpress.com/Clark-Fast).Today very often these attempts are thwarted by rigid and outdated legislation, which sees waste solely as an environmental issue and not as an opportunity to create any economic and societal values. Yet as the graphic below illustrates, all of these issues and their solutions are integrated and need to be done.

**Copyright © D. Bonato 2015**

Appendix 351

## A Matter of Priorities

Waiting to see the transposition in each member states of the EU circular economy package is necessary to select high-impact sectors with high growth potential on which Europe should bet on its near and long-term future. As for such goods with very long life cycles (construction and infrastructure), high-potential long-term investment programs can be activated. Meanwhile in the short-term, specific actions can be developed on durable consumer goods, such as electrical and electronic equipment, furniture, and vehicles. The annual turnover attributable to this type of industry is around 2600 billion euros, reflecting the importance of the recovery of raw materials that form end-of-life products (http://www.digitaleurope.org/).

Assume that the cost of raw materials, on average, contributes for 25% of the total cost of these products and then it can be expected an economic value associated with their optimal recovery of at least 500 billion euro/year! Everyone benefits – and the roses will bloom forever. This goes beyond a *Third Industrial Revolution* to what is now called the *Green Industrial Revolution* (GIR) around the world noting many EU and Asian nations (in English):

http://www.amazon.com/The-Green-Industrial-Revolution-Engineering/dp/0128023147/ref=sr_1_3?ie=UTF8&qid=14

With an earlier version of the GIR book now in Mandarin (September 2015), China sees the circular economy as a viable way to control and stop their climate problems due to greenhouse gases and extensive pollution that impacts the entire nation – as well as the rest of the world.

http://www.sgcc.com.cn/ywlm/gsgk-e/gsgk-e/gsgk-e1.shtml

The key now with the UN Conference focused on the solutions to client change is for the global leaders as well as all other nations work together to see how they can manage the waste or recycling of products into viable and useful economic opportunities. The rapid transition in the USA, especially in California, for example, from fossil fuel-powered cars through their combustion engines to hybrid cars to all-electric cars. No longer are their combustion engines. Nor is there processing of fossil fuels for gasoline. Instead cars are using batteries and moving rapidly into fuel cells for the energy to move cars on electricity. The circular economy has a significant role in all of this as the use of reuse of combustion engines has demised, but the "smart" cars are now mostly electrically operated and functioning which means new circular economy needs for their systems.

Aside from the reduction of greenhouse gases and lowering pollution, despite a 5-year water drought, the rapid grow of all-electric cars has created over 300,000 new jobs in the USA, focused mostly on California (www.latimes.nov18,2015;p1). What that means a massive change in economics and industrial growth since the automotive business was the basic business that built many nations in the past and will do so in the future. China is embarking on that pathway now. In their case, they are seeing the future now and embarking on "leapfrogging" into it as "The Future Car" (www.economist.corporate.unit.beijing/future-car-breakfaatsymposium/November19-2015) from the film *Back to the Future* (1989) is here today.

# References

Aldrich H, Whetten DA. Organization-sets, action-sets, and networks: making the most of simplicity. In: Handbook of organizational design. Oxford: Oxford University Press; 1982.

Allaire Y, Firsirotu ME. Theories of organizational culture. Organ Stud, Issue 1. 1984;5(3):193–226.

Allenby BR, Gonzales MA, Raber E. Implementing industrial ecology and design for environmental practices: Lawrence Livermore National Laboratory. Total Qual Environ Manag. 1996;5(3):37–59.

Alter C, Hage J. Organizations working together. Newbury Park: SAGE; 1993.

Alvesson M. A critical framework for organisational analysis: Towards a critical organisation theory, Studies in the economics and organization of action, no. 19. Lund: University of Lund; 1983a.

Alvesson M. Organisations teori och teknokratiskt medvetande. Stockholm: Natur och Kultur; 1983b.

Alvesson M, Sköldberg K. Tolkning och reflektion – vetenskapsfilosofi och kvalitativ metod. Lund: Studenterlitteratur; 1994.

Andersen H, editor. Videnskabsteori og metodelære, Bind 1 and 2. Gylling: Samfundslitteratur; 1990a.

Andersen I, editor. Valg af organisations-sociologiske metoder – et Kombinationsperspektiv. København: Samfundslitteratur; 1990b.

Andersen I, et al. Om kunsten at bedrive feltstudier – en erfaringsbaseret forskningsmetodik. København: Samfundslitteratur; 1992.

Andersson S. Känslornas filosofi. Brutus Östlings Bokförlag Symposion, Stockholm; 1992.

Arbnor I, Bjerke B. Företagsekonomisk metodlära. Lund: Studentlitteratur; 1981.

Arbnor I, Bjerke B. Methodology for creating business knowledge. Thousand Oaks: SAGE; 1997.

Arbnor I, Rasmussen J. Erhvervsøkonomisk kultur – Historien om en samfundsmæssig kulturspreder. Viborg: AUC; 1979.

Argyris C. Reasoning, learning and action – individual and organizational. San Francisco: Jossey-Bass; 1982.

Arndt J. The political economy paradigm: foundation for theory building in marketing. J Mark. 1983;47:44–54.

Astley WG. Administrative science as socially constructed truth. Adm Sci Q. 1985;30:497–513.

Astley WG, Van de Ven AH. Central perspectives and debates in organization theory. Adm Sci Q. 1983;28:245–73.

Atwood T, Clark WW II. Bio mass and hydrogen production. ANPA report, Rome; 2004.

Baker TJ. Doing social research. Singapore: McGraw-Hill International Editions; 1988.

Baran P, Sweezy PM. Monopoly capital. New York: Monthly Review Press; 1966.

354 References

Bärmark J. Världbild och vetenskapsideal. Några ledande temata hos Abraham Maslow (rap. nr. 84). Göteborgs Universitet; 1976.

Barnes B, editor. Sociology of science. London: Penguin Books; 1972.

Barth F, editor. The role of the entrepreneur in social change in Northern Norway. "Preface" and "Introduction". Bergen: Universitetsforlaget; 1962.

Bartunek JM. Changing interpretive schemes and organizational restructuring: the example of a religious order. Adm Sci Q. 1984;29:355–72.

Bate P. The impact of organizational culture on approaches to organizational problem-solving. Organ Stud. 1984;5(1):43–66.

Bauman Z. Hermeneutics and social sciences – approaches to understanding. London: Hutchinson & Co; 1978.

Bengtsson J. Sammanflätningar – Husserls och Merleau-Pontys fenomenologi. Uddevalla: Daidalos; 1993.

Benson JK. Organizations: a dialectical view. Adm Sci Q. 1977a;22:1–21.

Benson JK. Innovation and crises in organizational analysis. In: Benson JK, editor. Organizational analysis – critique and innovation. London: SAGE; 1977b.

Benson JK. A dialectical method for the study of organizations. In: Morgan G, editor. Beyond method. Beverly Hills: SAGE; 1983.

Berger PL. Invitation til Sociologi – ett humanistisk perspektiv. Stockholm: Rabén & Sjögren; 1980.

Berger B, editor. The culture of entrepreneurship. San Francisco: Institute for Contemporary Study Press; 1991. – "Introduction," Berger B, p. 1–12. – "The culture of modern entrepreneurship," Berger B, p. 13–32.

Berger PL, Luckmann T. The social construction of reality – a treatise in the sociology of knowledge. New York: Doubleday & Company; 1966.

Bertalanffy von L. General system theory. London: Allen Lane, The Penguin Press; 1971.

Bjurwill C. Fenomenologi. Lund: Studenlitteratur; 1995.

Blau P. Structural effects. Am Sociol Rev. 1960;25(2):178–93.

Blomber J, Giacomi J, Mosher A, Swenton-Wall P. Ethnographic field methods and their relation to design. In: Schuler D, Namioka A, editors. Participary design: principles and practices. Hillsdale: Lawrence Erlbaum Associates; 1993.

Blumer H. Symbolic interaction – perspective and method. Englewood Cliffs: Prentice-Hall; 1969.

Blumer H. Qualitative methods: lectures. Berkeley: University of California/Institute for Qualitative Research; 1976a.

Blumer H. Social interaction: lectures. Berkeley: University of California/Institute for Qualitative Research; 1976b.

Blumer H. A critique of the conventional scientific paradigm: social action: lectures. Berkeley: University of California/Institute for Qualitative Research; 1976c.

Blumer H. The self and social action: lectures. Berkeley: University of California/Institute for Qualitative Research; 1976d.

Blumer H. Symbolic interaction – perspective and method. Englewood Cliffs: Prentice-Hall, 1969; 1986.

Boden D. The business of talk. Organizations in action. Cambridge, UK: Polity Press; 1994.

BostonBank. Study of MIT students and faculty. Boston; 1997.

Bradley MF. Nature and significance of international marketing: a review. J Bus Res. 1987;15:205–19.

Bravermann B. Arbejde og monopolkapital – om arbejdets fornedrelse under kapitalismen. København: Demos; 1978.

Broch T, et al., editors. Kvalitative metoder i dansk samfundsforskning. København: Nyt fra Samfundsvidenskaberne; 1987.

Brown RH. Bureaucracy as praxis: towards a political phenomenology of formal organizations. Adm Sci Q. 1978;23(3):365–82.

# References

Brunsson N. The irrationality of action and action rationality: decisions, ideologies and organizational actions. J Manag Stud. 1982;19(1):29–44.

Brunsson N. The irrational organization. Chichester: John Wiley & Sons; 1986.

Buchholz TG. New ideas from dead economists. New York: Penguin Press; 1989.

Burnham D, Fieser J. http://www.utm.edu/research/iep/d/descarte.htm (2001).

Burrell G, Morgan G. Sociological paradigms and organisational analysis. London: Heinemann; 1980.

Bushell D, Burgess R (eds) (1969): Behavioral Sociology, New York, Colombia University Press.

California Energy Commission. Report on Summer 01. Sacramento, February 2002.

Caporaso JA, Levine DP. Theories of political economy. Cambridge: Cambridge University Press; 1992.

Capra F. The Tao of physics. 1975 Korpen, Göteborg; 1981.

Castells M, Hall P. Technopoles of the world. London: Routledge; 1994.

Cavusgil ST. On the internationalisation process of firms. Eur Res. 1980;8:273–81. ESMAR, Amsterdam.

Cavusgil ST. Some observations on the relevance of critical variables for internationalization stages. In: Czinkota MR, Tesar G, editors. Export management: an international context. New York: Praeger; 1982.

Cavusgil ST. Organizational characteristics associated with export activity. J Manag Stud. 1984;21(1):3–22.

Cheng JLC. Organizational coordination, uncertainty, and performance: an integrative study. Hum Relat. 1984;37(10):829–51.

Child J. Organizational structure, environment and performance: the role of strategic choice. Sociology. 1972;6(1):1–22.

Chomsky N. Syntactic structures. The Hague: Mouton & Co.; 1957.

Chomsky N. Aspects of the theory of syntax. Boston: MIT Press; 1965.

Chomsky N. Cartesian linguistics. New York: Harper & Row; 1966.

Chomsky N. Language and mind. Berkeley: University of California Press; 1968.

Chomsky N. Reflections on language. New York: Pantheon Books; 1975.

Chomsky N. Rules and representations. New York: Columbia University Press; 1980.

Chomsky N. Language and problems of knowledge. Boston: MIT Press; 1988.

Christensen P, Lund H. Conflicting views of sustainability: the case of wind power and nature conservation in Denmark. Eur Environ. 1998;8:1–6.

Christensen S, Molin J. Organisationskulturer – Kultur og Myter, Deltagerstyring, ledelse og omstilling, Viden og erfaring, Design. København: Akademisk Forlag; 1983.

Circourel AV. Cognitive sociology – language and meaning in social interaction. New York: Free Press; (1964)1974/1984.

Clark C. The conditions of economic progress. London: Macmillan; 1940.

Clark WW II. Political structure of neighborhood Black gangs. Bloomington: Central States Anthropological Society; 1970.

Clark WW II. A grammar of conflict within an educational institution. New Orleans: American Anthropological Association; 1973.

Clark WW II. Educational decision-making process: a case study of community involvement: mimeo; 1974.

Clark WW II. On formalism, Section Five, Anthropology and education; 1977.

Clark WW II. Revitalization of Silicon Valley. Technol Transfer Mag. 1993;20–28. Washington, DC.

Clark WW II. Defense conversion: lessons from the American and European cases. J Bus Ind Mark. 1994a;9(4):54–68.

Clark WW II. Networks and international SMEs. Report in preparation on the Danish Technological Institute "Network Program.". England: MCB University Press; 1994b. p. 54–68.

Clark WW II. Sharing the American and European economic experiences in technology conversion. J Technol Transfer. 1995a;20(1): 9–14. US Department of Energy, Washington, DC.

356 References

Clark WW II. Defense conversion: the economic conversion of the American economy. Ind Mark Manag. 1995b;24(5):391–409.

Clark WW II. The conversion of a defense company: the case of Watkins/Johnson, Published in parts with news media. Palo Alto: Corporate Communications, Watkins/Johnson; 1995c.

Clark WW II. International technology transfer: lessons learned. Washington, DC: Technology Transfer Society; 1995d.

Clark WW II A technology commercialization model: the case of fuel cells for zero emission vehicles. J Technol Transf. 1996. Washington, DC.

Clark WW II. Transfer of publicly funded R&D programs in the field of climate change for Environmentally Sounds Technologies (ESTs): from developed to developing countries – a summary of six country studies. UN Framework Convention for Climate Change, Report. Frankfurt, 1997a.

Clark WW II Publicly-funded environmentally sound technologies: the case of the US. Report for United Nations (one of ten industrialized country studies). New York/Geneva; 1997b.

Clark WW II. Developing and diffusing clean technologies: experience and practical issues. OECD conference, Seoul, 2000a.

Clark WW II. Markets in transitional economics. J Mark. 2000b. Pecs.

Clark WW II. California energy challenge: from crisis to opportunity. American Western Economic conference, San Francisco, 2001.

Clark WW II. Entrepreneurship in the commercialization of environmentally sound technologies: the American experience in developing nations. In: Kuada J, editor. Culture and technological transformation in the South: transfer or local development. Copenhagen: Samfundslitteratur Press; 2002a.

Clark WW II. Innovation and capitalisation. Int J Technol Manag. 2002b;24(4):391–418.

Clark WW II. The California challenge: energy and environmental consequences for public utilities. Util Policy. 2002c. Elsevier.

Clark WW II. Greening technology. Int J Environ Innov Manag. 2002d. Inderscience, London.

Clark WW II. California energy challenge: solutions for the future. Energy pulse: insight, analysis and commentary on the global power industry, 2003a. http://www.energypulse.net

Clark WW II. Point and counter-point: de-regulation in America. Util Policy. 2003b. Elsevier.

Clark WW II. Hydrogen: the pathway to energy independence. Util Policy. 2004a. Elsevier.

Clark WW II. Innovation for a sustainable hydrogen economy, Boosting innovation from research to market. Brussels: European Union; 2004b. p. 65–67. www.partnersforinnovation.org

Clark WW II. The hydrogen freeway, Boosting innovation from research to market. Brussels: European Union; 2004c. p. 74. www.partnersforinnovation.org.

Clark WW II. Distributed generation: renewable energy in local communities. Energy Policy. 2004d. Elsevier, London.

Clark WW II. The green hydrogen paradigm shift. Cogeneration and Distributed Generation Journal. 2007a;22(2):6–38.

Clark WW II. Eco-efficient energy infrastructure initiative paradigm. Bangkok: UN Economic Social Council, Asia; 2007b.

Clark WW II. Sustainable communities. London: Springer Press; 2009, which includes chapters authored: Introduction, Cases and Conclusion

Clark WW II. Sustainable development design handbook. London: Elsevier; 2010a.

Clark WW II. Sustainable communities design handbook: Elsevier Press; 2010b, which includes chapters authored: Introduction, Cases and Conclusion.

Clark WW II. The next economics: global cases in energy, environment, and climate change. London: Springer Press; 2012.

Clark, WW II. The next economics. Springer Press; 2013 which includes chapters authored: Introduction, p. 1–20; Chapter 4: Fast M, Clark WW II, editors. Qualitative economics: the science needed in economics, p. 71–92; Chapter 7: Clark WW II, Xing LI, editors. Social capitalism: China's economic rise. Springer Press. p. 143–64 and Conclusion: The science of economics, p. 275–86.

# References

Clark WW II. Global sustainable communities design handbook. London: Elsevier Press; 2014, which includes chapters authored Overview, Introduction. p. 1–12, Chapter 2: Clark WW II, Cooke G, The green industrial revolution, p. 13–40 and Conclusion, p. 559–70.

Clark WW II. Circular economics in HuffPost, (2014 and 2015). http://www.huffingtonpost.com/woodrow-clark/.

Clark WW II. Agile energy systems: global green distributed on- site and central power grid. London: Elsevier Press; 2017a.

Clark WW II. Sustainable communities design handbook. 2nd ed. London: Elsevier Press; 2017b.

Clark WW II. Climate preservation. London: Elsevier Press; 2018.

Clark WW II, Bonato D. Circular economy and raw material strategy: a critical challenge for Europe and the rest of the World. HuffPost. 2015;

Clark WW II, Bradshaw T. Agile energy systems: global lessons from the California energy crisis. London: Elsevier Press, 2004 and updated Elsevier 2017.

Clark WW II, Cooke G. The Third Industrial Revolution, Chapter #2. In: Sustainable communities design handbook. New York: Elsevier Press; 2009. p. 9–22.

Clark WW II, Cooke G. Global energy innovations. Praeger Press, Santa Barbara, CA, USA; 2011.

Clark WW II, Cooke G. Green industrial revolution. New York: Elsevier Press; 2015.

Clark WW II, Cooke G. Smart green cities. Abingdon-on-Thames: Routledge Press; 2016.

Clark WW II, Dan Jensen J. Economic models: the role of government in business development for the reconversion of the American economy. J Technol Transfer. 1997.Washington, DC.

Clark WW II, Dan Jensen J. Capitalisation of environmental technologies in companies: economic schemes in a business perspective. Int J Energy Technol Policy. 2002;1(1/2). Inderscience, London.

Clark WW II, Dan Jenssen J. The role of government in privatization: an economic model for Denmark. Int J Technol Manag. 2001;21(5/6). Inderscience, London.

Clark WW II, Decker-Ward J. Encyclopeadia Britannica: case of successful technology transfer from National Science Foundation: science curriculum in the public schools. Technology Transfer Society, Annual conference and proceedings, Washington, DC. 1995.

Clark WW II, Demirag I. Investment and capitalization: American firms. Int J Technol Manag. 2001. Inderscience.

Clark WW II, Demirag I. Enron: the failure of corporate governance. J Corp Citizsh. 2002;8:105–22.

Clark WW II, Demirag I. Regulatory economic considerations of corporate governance. Special issue on Corporate governance, Int J Bank. 2005.

Clark WW II, Demirag I. US financial regulatory change: the case of California energy crisis. Special issue, J Bank Regul. 2006a;7(1/2):75–93.

Clark WW II, Demirag I. Regulatory considerations of corporate governance: the case of the California energy crisis. Special issue, Public Manag Rev. 2006b.

Clark WW II, Demirag I. Investment and capital in the USA. Unpublished manuscript.

Clark WW II, Fast M. Blumer Graduate School lectures: symbolic interactionism. Berkeley: University of California; 1978. (Edited and revised 1997) Unpublished.

Clark WW II, Fast M. Qualitative economics: toward a science of economics. Presented at the Western Economics Association conference, San Francisco, July 2005, published in 2006.

Clark WW II, Fast M. Economics as science: why we need both qualitative and quantitative economics ($Q^2E$). Oxford: Coxmoor Press; 2018.

Clark WW II, Isherwood W. Energy infrastructure for inner Mongolia autonomous region: five nation comparative case studies. Beijing: Asian Development Bank, Manila, PI and PRC National Government; 2007.

Clark WW II, Isherwood W, Creating an Energy Base for Inner Mongolia, China: 'the leapfrog into the climate neutral future. Util Policy J. 2009.

Clark WW II, Isherwood W. Leapfrogging energy infrastructure mistakes for inner Mongolia. Util Policies J, Special Issue. 2010.

Clark WW II, Jensch J. Turning swords into plowshares: Lawrence Livermore National Laboratory. Channels. 1995;8(6):14–15. SEMI Publication, Mountain View.

Clark WW II, Jensen JD. The IO Fund: international alliances for developing SMEs. Paper on the Danish Government Fund for business development in transitional economies; 1994.

Clark WW II, Jensen JD. Economic models: the role of government in business development. Paper in preparation on the Danish Government Fund for business development in transitional economies, Copenhagen. 1995.

Clark WW II, Kuhn L. Violence in schools, colleges, universities. Hauppauge: NOVA; 2017.

Clark WW II, Li X. The political-economics of the green industrial revolution: renewable energy as the key to National Sustainable Communities. Chapter #22. In: Clark WW II and Editor of The Next Economics. Chapter # 7: Social capitalism. Oxford, UK: Springer Press; 2013: p. 143–64.

Clark WW II, Lund H. Civic markets in the California energy crisis. Int J Global Energy Issues. 2001a;16(4):328–344. Inderscience, London.

Clark WW II, Lund H. Civic markets. Int J Global Energy Issues. 2001b;X(X):471–83.

Clark WW II, Lund H. Special issue on sustainable development: the economics of energy and environmental production. J Clean Prod. 2006;

Clark WW II, Morris G. Policy making and implementation process: the case of intermittent resources. J Int Energy Policy. 2002. Interscience.

Clark WW II, Paolucci E. Environmental regulation and product development: issues for a new model of innovation. J Int Prod Dev Manag. 1997a.

Clark WW II, Paolucci E. An international model for technology commercialization. J Technol Transfer. 1997b. Washington, DC.

Clark WW II, Paolucci E. Commercial development of environmental technologies for the automobile. Int J Technol Manag. 2000.

Clark WW II, Paulocci E. Commercial development of environmental technologies for the automotive industry: toward a new model of technology innovation. Int J Environ Technol Manag. 2001;1(4):363–83.

Clark WW II, Sørensen OJ. Toward a theory of entrepreneurship. Paper presented at the 39th World Congress of Small Business, Strasbourg. Aalborg: Aalborg University Press; 1994a.

Clark WW II, Sørensen OJ. Linguistics in constructing a theory of business/economics: some empirical applications. Paper in Preparation. Aalborg: Aalborg University; 1994b.

Clark WW II, Sorensen OJ. Entrepreneurship: theoretical considerations. Int J Technol Manag. 2001. Inderscience, London, UK.

Clark WW II, Yago G. Financing the hydrogen highway. Public Policy, Milken Institute, Santa Monica, 2005.

Clark WW II, Smother N, Singson R, Udell L. The pipeline model: from invention to product development. Washington, DC: Technology Transfer Business Magazine; 1993. p. 45.

Clark WW II, Tao W, Jensen D. Capitalization of environmental technologies in companies: economic schemes in a business perspective. Paper and seminar coordinator, Greening of industry international conference, Santa Barbara, 1997.

Clark WW II, Demirag I, Bline D. Financial markets, corporate governance and management of research and development: reflections on US managers' perspectives. In: Demirag I, editor. Corporate governance, accountability and pressures to perform: an international study. Oxford: Oxford University Press; 1998a.

Clark WW II, Isherwood W, Ray Smith J, Aceves S, Berry G, Johnson R, Das D, Goering D, Seifert R. Economic impact on remote village energy systems of advanced technologies. University of California, Lawrence Livermore National Laboratory, UCRL-ID-129289; January 1998b.

Clark WW II, Bline D, Demirag I. Financial markets, corporate governance and management of research and development: reflections on US managers' perceptions. In: Demirag I, editor. Comparative capital systems. London: Pinter; 1998c.

Clark WW II, Monroe G, Lipi S. Intrapreneurship in transitional economies. In: Varga A, editor. Entrepreneurship and innovation: the case of Hungary. Pecs: University of Pecs Press; 2000.

Clark WW II, Paulocci E, Cooper J. Commercial development of energy – environmentally sound technologies for the auto-industry: the case of fuel cells. Special issue, J Clean Prod. 2002.

# References

Clark WW II, Isherwood W, Smith JR, Aceves S, Berry G, Johnson R, Das D, Goering D, Seifert R. Remote power systems with advanced storage technologies for Alaskan villages. Energy Policy. 2003;25(10):1005–20.

Clark WW II, Isherwood W, Smith JR, Aceves S, Berry G. Distributed generation: public policy in local communities. Util Policy. 2004a. Elsevier.

Clark WW II, Isherwood W, Ray Smith J, Aceves S, Berry G. Distributed generation: remote power systems with advanced storage technologies. Energy Policy. 2004b;32(14):1573–1589. Elsevier Press.

Clark WW II, Rifkin J, et al. A green hydrogen economy. Special issue on Hydrogen. Energy Policy. 2005a. Elsevier.

Clark WW II, Rifkin J, et al. Hydrogen energy stations: along the roadside to an hydrogen economy. Util Policy. 2005b;13(1):41–50. Elsevier Press.

Clark WW II, Rifkin J, et al. A green hydrogen economy. Special issue on Hydrogen, Energy Policy. 2006;34:2630–2639. Elsevier.

Clark WW II, Cooke G, 伍德罗•克拉克,格兰特•with Anjun Jerry Jin, Ching-Fuh Lin 库克,金安君,林清富. Green development paradigm (Mandarin). Ashgate/China Electric Power Press; 2014.

Collins JC, Porras J. Built to last. Successful habits of visionary companies. New York: HarperBusiness; 1994.

Comte A. On the three stages of social evolution. In: Parsons T, et al., editors. Theories of society – foundation of modern sociological theory. New York: The Free Press; 1965.

Comte A. Om Positivismen (Discours préliminaire sur l'esprit positif, 1844). Göteborg: Korpen; 1991.

Cooper JF, Clark WW II. Zinc/air fuel cell: an alternative to clean fuels in fleet electric vehicle applications. Int J Environ Conscious Des Manuf. 1996;5(3–4):49–54.

Cooper JF, Fleming D, Hargrove D, Koopman R, Peterman K. A refuelable zinc/air battery for fleet electric vehicle propulsion, SAE paper 951948; 1995.

Council of Economic Advisors. Supporting research and development to promote economic growth: the federal government's role. Washington, DC; 1995.

Crossley N. Intersubjectivity – the fabric of social becoming. London: SAGE; 1996.

Cuff EC, Payne GCF. Samhällsvetenskapliga perspektiv. Uddevalla: Korpen; 1982.

Daft RL. Organization theory and design. St. Paul: West Publishing Company; 1989.

Dalton M. Conflict between staff and line managerial officers. Reprinted in Etzioni A, editor. A sociological reader on complex organizations; 1950.

Dalton DH, Serapio MG Jr. Globalizing industrial research and development. Washington, DC: Office of Technology Policy, US Department of Commerce; 1995.

Dalum B. Local and global linkages: the radiocommunications cluster in Northern Denmark. J Ind Stud. 1995;2(2).

Damanpour F, Evan WM. Organizational innovation and performance: the problem of "organizational lag". Adm Sci Q. 1984;29.

Danish Innovation Centre. Innovative entrepreneurs: experiences from the scholarship scheme. Taastrup: Danish Technological Institute; 1994.

Davis G, Governor. Letter to FERC Chairman Wood. 31 Jan 2002.

Deiaco E, Forsberg HG. Profit from innovation: a comparison of Swedish and Japanese intellectual property management. OECD workshop on innovation, patents and technological strategies. Paris: EC & Royal Swedish Academy of Engineering Science; 1994.

Delanty G. Social science. 2nd ed. Glasgow: Open University Press; 2005.

Delanty G, Strydom P. Philosophies of social science – the classical and contemporary readings. Open University Press; London, 2003.

Deming WE. The economics: for industry, government, education. Cambridge, MA: MIT Press; 1993.

Demirag I, Khadaroo MI, Clark WW II. The institutionalization of public-private partnerships in the UK and the nation-state of California. Int J Public Policy. 2009;4(3/4):190–213.

360 References

Deutch JM, Moniz EJ. The nuclear option. Role for fission, Special issue. Sci Am. 2006;295(3):76–83. http://www.sciam.com

Diamond MA. Psychoanalytical phenomenology and organizational analysis. Adm Sci Q. 1990.

DiStefano T. Interorganizational conflict: a review of an emerging field. Hum Relat. 1984;37(5).

Douglas J, editor. Understanding everyday life. Chicago: Aldine; 1970.

Drucker P. Post-capitalist society. Oxford: Butterworth-Heinemann, Ltd.; 1993.

Due J, Madsen JS. Slip Sociologien løs – en invitation til 80'ernes sociologi. København: Hans Reitzel; 1983.

Dunning JH. The eclectic paradigm of international production – an up-date and a reply to its critics. Discussion papers in international investment and business studies, no. 91. University of Reading; 1985.

Durkheim E. Organic solidarity and contract. In: Parsons T, et al., editors. Theories of society – foundation of modern sociological theory. New York: The Free Press; 1965.

Durkheim E. On mechanical and organic solidarity. In: Parsons T mf.l., editor. Theories of society – foundation of modern sociological theory. New York: The Free Press; 1965.

Durkheim E. Sociologins metodregler (Les règles de la méthode sociologique, 1895). Göteborg: Korpen; 1991.

Economist. Modern economic theory: where it went wrong – and how the crisis is changing it. Special issue with cover of Bible Melting, London, 18 Jul 2009.

Edström A, Högberg B, Norbäck LE. Alternative explanations of interorganizational cooperation: the case of joint programmes and joint ventures in Sweden. Organ Stud. 1984;5(1):147–68.

Eisenstadt SN, Curelaru M. The form of sociology – paradigms and crises. New York: John Wiley & Sons; 1976.

Elster J. Explaining technical change. Cambridge University Press; 1983.

Elster J. Vetenskapliga Förklaringar. Göteborg: Korpen; 1988.

Enderud H, editor. Hvad er organisations-sociologisk metode? Bind 1 & 2. Gylling: Samfundslitteratur; 1986.

Energy 21: the Danish government's action plan for energy 1996. Købenbavn: Ministeriet Miljø & Energi; 1997.

Eneroth B. Hur mäter man "vackert"? Stockholm: Akademi Litteratur; 1984.

Etzioni A, editor. A sociological reader on complex organizations. New York: Holt, Rinehart & Winston; 1964.

Etzkowitz H. The triple helix: a North American innovation environment. NAFTA conference, British Columbia; 1994.

Fast M. Internationaliseringens subjektivitet og intersubjektivitet – en udvikling af en hermeneutisk forståelse af virksomheders internationalisering som alternativ til mainstream teori. Aalborg Universitet, Institut for samfundsudvikling og planlœgning; 1992a.

Fast M. The internationalization subjectivity and intersubjectivity: a development of a hermeneutic understanding of companies internationalization as an alternative to mainstream theory. Institute of Development and Planning, International Business Studies, Aalborg University; 1992b.

Fast M. Internationalization as a social construction". In: Proceedings of the 9th IMP- conference, Bath; 1993.

Fast M. Videnskabsteori & Metodologi i studier af livsverden – En diskussion af en Livsverden tilgang indenfor samfundsvidenskaben, specielt virksomhedsøkonomi. Aalborg University, Department of Planning & Development. International Studies/International Business Economics. 1997.

Fast M, Clark WW II. Qualitative economics—a perspective on organization and economic science. Theor Econ Lett. 2012;2(2):162–74.

Fink A. Teori – Praksis. Positivistisk Hermeneutisk Kritisk – Videnskabsteori. Grenå: GMT; 1973.

Firth A. "Lingua franca" negotiations: towards an interactional approach. World Englishes. 1990;9(3):269–80.

Flato I. Historie – nyere og nyeste tid. – Videnskabernes historie i det 20. århundrede. Haslev: Gyldendal; 1985.

# References

Flor JR. Vor tids filosofi. København: Politikkens forlag; 1982.

Florida R, Smith DF. Agglomeration and industrial location: an econometric analysis of Japanese-affiliated manufacturing establishments in automotive-related industries. J Urban Econ. 1994;36(1):23–41.

Flyvbjerg B. Rationalitet og Magt – Det konkretes videnskab. Odense: Akademisk Forlag; 1991.

Fondas N, Wiersema M. Changing of the guard: the influence of CEO socialization on strategic change. J Manag Stud. 1997;34(4):561–84.

Ford D, Håkansson H, Johanson J. How do companies interact? Reprint series. Uppsala University; 1986/12.

Fortune. The letter to Ken Lay, 16 Jan 2002.

Freeman C. Japan: a new national system of innovation? In: Dosi G, Freeman C, Nelson R, Silverberg G, Soete L, editors. Technological change and economic theory. London: Pinters Publ; 1989. p. 330–48.

Freeman C. Lecture series: Interfirm cooperation and innovation; technical change and unemployment: the links between macro-economic policy and innovation policy; Schumpeterianism: between history and economic theory, 2–7 Mar 1994. University of Aalborg, Aalborg.

Freeman C, Hagedoorn J. Convergence and divergence in the interantonalization of technology. In: Hagedoorn J, editor. Technical change and the world economy: convergence and divergence in technology strategies. Aldershot: Edward Elgar; 1995.

Freeman C, Perez C. Structural crisis of adjustment, business cycles and investment behaviour. In: Dosi G, Freeman C, Nelson R, Silverberg G, Soete L, editors. Technological change and economic theory. London: Pinters Publ; 1989.

French WL, Bell CH. Organization development: behavioral science interventions for organization improvement. Englewood Cliffs: Prentice-Hall; 1984.

Gadamer H-G. Reason in the age of science. Cambridge, MA/London: The MIT Press; 1986.

Gadamer H-G. Truth and method. London: Sheed & Ward; 1993 (1975).

Garfinkel H. Studies in ethnomethodology. Englewood Cliffs: Prentice-Hall; 1967.

Geddes D. Economic development in the 1990s: toward a sustainable future. Econ Dev Rev. 1993:71–4.

Gelven M. A commentary on Heidegger's being and time. DeKalb: Northern Illinois University Press; 1989.

Gibbs WW. Plan B for energy, speculative technology. Special issue, Sci Am. 2006;295(3):102–114. http://www.sciam.com

Gibson R, editor. Rethinking the future: rethinking business, principles, competition, control and complexity, leadership, markets and the world. London: Nicholas Brealey; 1997.

Giddens A. Hermeneutics, ethnomethodology, and problems of interpretative analysis. In: Coser LA, Larsen ON, editors. The uses of controversy in sociology. New York: The Free Press; 1976a.

Giddens A. New rules of sociological method. London: Padstow Press; 1976b.

Giddens A. Central problems in social theory. Action, structure and contradiction in social analysis. London: The Macmillan Press Ltd; 1979.

Giddens A, Turner JH, editors. Social theory today. Padstow: Polity Press; 1990.

Giorgi A. Phenomenology and experimental psychology. In: Giorgi A, Fischer C, Von Echartsberg R, Murray E, editors. Duquesne studies in phenomenological psychology, vol. II. Pittsburgh: Duquesne University Press; 1971.

Giorgi A. An application of phenomenological method in psychology. In: Giorgi A, Fischer C, Murray E, editors. Duquesne studies in phenomenological psychology, vol. II. Pittsburgh: Duquesne University Press; 1975a.

Giorgi A. The phenomenological psychology of learning and the verbal learning tradition. Section II, phenomenological psychology. In: Giorgi A, Fischer C, Murray E, editors. Duquesne studies in phenomenological psychology, vol. II. Pittsburgh: Duquesne University Press; 1975b.

Giorgi A. Concerning the possibility of phenomenological research. J Phenomenol Psychol. 1983;14(2):129–70.

Giorgi A. Status of qualitative research in the human sciences: a limited interdisciplinary and international perspective. Methods. 1986;1:29–62.

Giorgi A. Validity and reliability – from a phenomenological perspective. In: Batsen WF, et al., editors. Recent trends in theoretical phenomenology. New York: Duquesne University Press; 1988.

Goffman E. The presentation of self in everyday life. New York: Doubleday; 1959.

Goffman E. Strategic interaction. Philadelphia: University of Pennsylvania Press; 1969.

Goffman E. Behaviour in public places. New York: Anchor; 1971.

Goodenough WH. Description and comparison in cultural anthropology. Chicago: Aldine; 1970.

Gore A. An inconvenient truth. Hollywood: Paramount Studios; 2007

Grabher G, editor. The embedded firm: on the socioeconomics of industrial networks. London: Routledge; 1993.

Graedel TE, Allenby BR. Industrial ecology. Englewood Cliffs: Prentice Hall; 1995.

Granovetter M. Problems of explanation in economic sociology. In: Nohria N, Eccles RG, editors. Networks and organizations: structure, form, and action. Boston: Harvard Business School Press; 1992. p. 25–56.

Granovetter M. Business groups. In: Smelser NJ, Swedberg R, editors. The handbook of economic sociology. Princeton: Princeton University Press; 1994. p. 453–75.

Griliches Z. Patent statistics as economic indicators. J Econ Lit. 1990;28:1661–707.

Grindley P, Mowery DC, Silverman B. SEMATECH and collaborative research: lessons in the design of high-tech consortia. J Policy Anal Manage. 1994;13(4).

Gulati R. Does familiarity breed trust? The implications of repeated ties for contractual choice in alliances. Acad Manag J. 1995a;38(1):85–112.

Gulati R. Social structure and alliance formation patterns: a longitudinal analysis. Adm Sci Q. 1995b;40:619–52.

Gullestrup H. Kultur, Kulturanalyse og Kulturetik – eller hvad adskiller og forener os? København: Akademisk Forlag; 1992.

Gullestrup H. Evaluating social consequences of social change in the third world countries. Development research series, working paper no. 30. Aalborg: Department of Development & Planning, Aalborg University; 1994.

Gullestrup H. Culture, cultural analysis and cultural ethics. (Extracted chapters 2 and 3). Aalborg: Aalborg University Press; 1997. p. 1–54.

Gurwitsch A. Husserl's theory of the intentionality of consciousness. In: Dreyfus HL, editor. Husserl intentionality and cognitive science. Cambridge, MA/London: The MIT Press; 1982.

Guthrie J, Deepak KD. Contextual influences on executive selection: firm characteristics and CEO experience. J Manag Stud. 1997;34(4):537–60.

Habermas J. Knowledge and human interests. London: Heinemann; 1972.

Habermas J. Knowledge and interest. In: Emmet D, Macintyre A, editors. Sociological theory and philosophical analysis. New York: The Macmillan Company; 1978.

Habermas J. The theory of communicative action, vol. 1 & 2. London: Heinemann; 1984.

Hagedoorn J. Understanding the rationale of strategic technology partnering: interorganizational modes of cooperation and sectoral difference. Strateg Manag J. 1993;14:371–85.

Hagedoorn J, Duysters G. The Cooperative Agreements and Technology Indicators (CATI) information system. Unpublished manuscript. Maastricht: MERIT; 1993.

Hagedoorn J, Schakenraad J. Inter-firm partnerships and co-operative strategies in core technologies. In: Freeman C, Soete L, editors. New explorations in the economics of technical change. London: Frances Printer; 1990.

Hagedoorn J, Schakenraad J. Leading companies and networks of strategic alliances in information technology. Res Policy. 1992;21

Håkansson H. The Swedish approach to Europe – introduction – international marketing strategies. In: Turnbull PW, Valla J-P, editors. Strategies for international industrial marketing. Kent: Kent Press; 1986.

Håkansson H. Lecture: Network theory. Aalborg: Aalborg University Center; 1994.

References 363

Håkansson H, Johansson J. Formal and cooperation strategies in international industrial networks. WP, Uppsala University; Copenhagan1987/1.

Håkansson H, Johanson J. The network as a governance structure: interfirm cooperation beyond markets and hierarchies. In: Grabher G, editor. The embedded firm: on the socioeconomics of industrial networks. London: Routledge; 1993. p. 35–51.

Håkansson H, Snehota I. Developing relationships in business networks. Uppsala: University of Uppsala; 1994.

Hall ET. The silent language. New York: Doubleday; 1959.

Hallén L, Sandström, M. Relationship atmosphere in international business. Reprint series, Uppsala University; 1991/6.

Hamilton P. Talcott Parsons. London: Tavistock Publications; 1983.

Harste G. Organisationskultur og Kulturel Livsverden – om institutioners kommunikative rationalisering. Copenhagan: AUC, Institut for Kommunikation; 1988.

Hawkins DG, Lashof DA, Williams R. What to do about coal. Carbob capture and storage, Special issue, Sci Am. 2006;295(3):68–75. http://www.sciam.com

Hayek FV. Scientism and the study of society. Economica. 1942–1943;8–11.

Heap JL, Roth PA. On phenomenological sociology. Am Sociol Rev. 1973;38:354–67.

Hedberg BLT. How organizations learn and unlearn. In: Nystrom PC, Starbuck WH, editors. Handbook of organizational design, vol. 1: Adapting organization to their environments. Oxford: Oxford University Press; 1981.

Hedberg BLT, Nystrom PC, Starbuck WH. Camping on seesaws: prescriptions for a self-designing organization. Adm Sci Q. 1976;21:41–65.

Hegland TJ. Aksjonsforskning – noen bakgrunnsforhold og randbemerkninger. In: Hegland TJ, editor. Aktionsforskning – erfaringer og refleksioner. København: Nyt fra Samfundsvidenskaberne; 1981.

Heidegger M. Being and time (1927). Oxford: Blackwell; 1992.

Heilbroner R. The making of economic society: revised for the 1990s. London: Prentice-Hall International; 1989.

Heilbroner R, Thurow L. Economics explained (rev). New York: Touchstone Press; 1994.

Held D. Introduction to critical theory – Horkheimer to Habermas. Oxford: Blackwell Publishers (University of California Press); 1980.

Hennestad BW. Organizations: frameworks or frame work? Scand J Manag Stud. 1986.

Henriksen LB. Etablering af virksomhedsnetvœrk. Licentiat afhandling, Aalborg University, Institut for Samfundsudvikling og planlægning; 1992.

Herva S. The genesis of Max Weber's Verstehen Soziologie. Acta Sociologica. 1988;31(2):143–56.

Heydebrand W. Organizational contradictions in public bureaucracies: towards a Marxian theory of organizations. In: Benson JK, editor. Organizational analysis – critique and innovation. Beverly Hills: SAGE; 1977.

Heydebrand W. Organization and praxis. In: Morgan G, editor. Beyond method – strategies for social research. London: SAGE; 1983.

Heyman K. Making connections, NewsFocus. Science. 2006;313:604–606. http://www.sciencemag.org

Heywood JB. Fueling our transportation future. Automotive answers, Special issue. Sci Am. 2006;295(3):60–63. http://www.sciam.com

Hinton D, et al. Civic entrepreneur. Cambridge, MA: MIT Press; 1997.

Hirschman EC, Holbrook MB. Postmodern consumer research: the study of consumption as text. New York: SAGE; 1992.

Hofstede G. Culture's consequences: international differences in work-related values. Beverly Hills: SAGE; 1980a.

Hofstede G. Motivation, leadership, and organization: do American theories apply abroad? Organ Dyn. 1980b;9:42–63.

Hofstede G. Cultures and organizations: software of the mind. Intercultural cooperation and its importance for survival. Berkshire: McGraw Hill; 1991.

Holland JH. Adaptation in natural and artificial systems. Cambridge, MA: MIT Press; 1992.

Holroyd S. Nya Perspektiv – en uppslagsbok. Göteborg: Korpen; 1991.

Hrebiniak LG, Joyce WF. Organizational adaptation: strategic choice and environmental determinism. Adm Sci Q. 1985;30:336–49.

Huff AS, editor. Mapping strategic thought. Chichester: John Wiley & Sons; 1990.

Hult M, Lennung S-Å. Towards a definition of action research: a note and bibliography. J Manag Stud. 1980;17:241–50.

Hummel RP. Applied phenomenology and organization. Adm Sci Q. 1990;14(1):9–17.

Husserl E. Ideas. New York: Macmillan; 1962.

Husserl E. Fenomenologins idé. Uddevalla: Daidalos; 1989.

Hvelplund F, Lund H. Feasibility studies and public regulation in a market economy. Aalborg: Aalborg University Press; 1998.

Hydrogen & Fuel Cell Letter. DoE selects three teams for developing remote H2/fuel cell utility systems, February 1998.

Imai K. In: Carlsson B, editor. Industrial dynamics: technological, organizational and structural changes in industries. London: Kluwer; 1989.

Imershein AW. Organizational change as a paradigm shift. In: Benson JK, editor. Organizational analysis – critique and innovation. London: SAGE; 1977.

Ingebrigtsen S, Pettersson M. Marketing – en videnskabsteoretisk analyse. Et humanistisk alternativ. København: Samfundslitteratur; 1979.

Inzerilli G. The organization-client relationship as an aspect of interorganizational analysis. Hum Relat. 1979;32(5):419–37.

Isherwood W, Ray Smith J, Aceves S, Berry G, Clark W, Johnson R, Das D, Goering D, Seifert R. Remote power systems with advanced storage technologies for Alaskan villages. University of California, Lawrence Livermore National Laboratory, UCRL-ID-129289; January 1998.

Isherwood W, Ray Smith J, Aceves S, Berry G, Clark WW II with Johnson R, Das D, Goering D, Seifert R. Economic impact on remote village energy systems of advanced technologies. University of California, Lawrence Livermore National Laboratory, UCRL-ID-129289, January 1998. Energy Policy; 2000.

Israel J. Om relationistisk socialpsykologi. Uddevalla: Korpen; 1981.

Jackson NV, Carter P. The attenuating function of myth in human understanding. Hum Relat. 1984;37(7):515–33.

Jehenson R. A phenomenological approach to the study of the formal organization. In: Psathas G, editor. Phenomenological sociology – issues and applications. New York: John Wiley & Sons; 1978.

Jencks C, et al. Inequality. New York: Basic Books; 1972.

Jenkins BM, Clark WW II, Isherwood W, England S, Yates J. Development of an operating plan for acquisition and management of the PVUSA/Davis facility by the University of California. Davis: University of California; 2000.

Jenkins BM, Clark WW II, Fung VA, Atwood T, Tiangco V, Julian R. Distributed power generation for agro-energy in sustainable development in the Philippines. Final report. Lexington: State Environmental Initiative, Council of State Governments; 2001.

Jensen TK. Statskundskab som viden for praksis. Grus 33, Aalborg; 1991.

Jochen E. An efficient solution. Energy efficiency, Special issue, Sci Am. 2006;295(3):64–67. http://www.sciam.com

Johansson T, Hägg I. Extrapreneurs – between markets and hierarchies. Copenhagan: WP, Uppsala University; 1987/8.

Johansson J, Mattsson L-G. Internationalisation in industrial systems – a network approach. Reprint series: Uppsala University; 1988/1.

Johansson J, Vahlne J-E. The mechanism of internationalization. Unpublished paper, Uppsala University; 1989.

Jones C. Careers in project networks: the case of the film industry. In: Arthur M, Rousseau D, editors. The boundaryless career. New York: Oxford University Press; 1996. p. 58–75.

# References

Jones C, Hesterly WS. Network organization: alternative governance form or glorified market? Presented at National Academy of Management, Atlanta, 1993, Unpublished paper; 1995.

Jones C, Hesterly WS, Borgatti SP. A general theory of network governance: exchange conditions and social mechanisms. Acad Manag Rev. 1997;22(4):911–45.

Jones C, Borgatti SP, Walsh K. Career competencies in a cultural industry: sources of individual advantage and industry influence. Special issue, Organ Sci. 1998.

Jordan B, Henderson A. Interaction analysis: foundations and practice. Palo Alto: Xerox Publications (SPL-94-059), Systems and Practices Laboratory; 1993.

Kahn J. One plus one makes what? Fortune. 7 Jan 2002.

Kallinikos J. Bureaucracy and organizational culture: a dialectical view. Olso: Uppsala University, Working paper; 1986/1.

Kallinikos J. Network as webs of signification. Olso: Uppsala University, Working paper; 1989/5.

Kammen DJ. The rise of renewable energy. Clean power, Special issue, Sci Am. 2006;295(3):84–93. http://www.sciam.com

Kant I. Critique of pure reason (*"Kritiken der reinen Vernunft" (1781/1787)*). Hong Kong: Macmillan; 1929.

Katz D, Kahn RL. The social psychology of organizations. New York; 1966.

Katz ME, Ordover JA. R&D cooperation and competition. Brook Pap Econ Act. 1990:137–203.

Kiesler S, Sproull L. Managerial response to changing environments: perspectives on problem sensing from social cognition. Adm Sci Q. 1982;27:548–70.

Kinch N. management – tro och vetande. Tro & Tanke, Svenska Kyrkans Forskningsråd; 1991, p. 3.

Kjørup S. Forskning og Samfund – en grundbog i videnskabsteori. Haslev: Gyldendal; 1987.

Knudsen C. Økonomisk metodologi – om videnskabsidealer, forklaringstyper og forskningtraditioner. Charlottenlund: Jurist- og Økonomiforbundets Forlag; 1991.

Kogut B, Shan W, Walker G. Knowledge in the network and the network as knowledge: the structuring of new industries. In: Grabher G, editor. The embedded firm: on the socioeconomics of industrial networks. London: Routledge; 1993. p. 67–94.

Kuada J. Managerial behaviour in Ghana and Kenya: a cultural perspective. Aalborg: Aalborg University Press; 1984.

Kuada J. Culture and international management: concepts and applications. Aalborg: University of Aalborg, International Business Economics. No. #1, working paper series; 1992.

Kuhn T. The structure of scientific revolution. Chicago: University of Chicago Press; 1970 (1962).

Kuttner R. The Enron economy. Am Prospect. 2001;13(1):2.

Kuttner R. The road to Enron. Am Prospect. 2002;13(6):2.

Kvale S. To validate is to question. In: Kvale S, editor. Issues of validity in qualitative research. Lund: Studentlitteratur; 1987.

Kvale S. Det kvalitative interview. In: Andersen I, editor. Valg af organisations-sociologiske metoder – et kombinationsperspektiv. København: Samfundslitteratur; 1990a.

Kvale S. Ten standard responses to qualitative research interviews. Aarhus: Aarhus University, Psykologisk Institut; 1990b.

Lakoff G. Linguistics and natural language. Synthese. 1970a;22:151–271.

Lakoff G. Global rules. Language. 1970b;46(3):626–39.

Lakoff G. Introduction to the version of linguistics and natural logic. In: Mehler J, editor. Handbook of cognitive psychology. Englewood Cliffs: Prentice-Hall; 1971.

Lamont A, Clark WW Jr. The LLNL China energy model. Paper presented at USDOE conference on energy models and systems, Washington, DC, August 1997.

Larsen B. Styringstœnkning – er ledelse mulig? København: Nyt Nordisk Forlag, Arnold Busck; 1981.

Lenneberg E. Biological foundations of language. The Hague: Mouton; 1970.

Levitt SD, Dubner SJ. Freakonomics: a rogue economist explores the hidden side of everything. New York: William Morrow; 2005.

Lewin K. Field theory in social science – selected theoretical papers. New York: Harper & Brothers Publishers; 1951.

Lincoln YS, editor. Organizational theory and inquiry. Beverly Hills: SAGE; 1985.

Lübcke P (red.). Politikens filosofi leksikon – Filosofi. Aalborg: Politikens Forlag; 1994a.

Lübcke P (red.). Vor tids filosofi – Engagement og Forståelse. Glostrup: Politikens Forlag; 1994b.

Lund H. Elements of a green energy plan which can create job opportunities. General Workers Union in Denmark. Copenhagen; 1996.

Lund H. Economic development and CO2 reduction policies. In: Proceedings of international conference on urban regional environmental planning in an era of transition, Athens; 1997. p. 570–9.

Lund H. Environmental accounts for households: a method for improving public awareness and participation. Local Environ. 1998;3(1):43–54.

Lund H, Hvelplund F. Does environmental impact assessment really support technological change? Analyzing alternative to coal-fired power stations in Denmark. Environ Impact Assess Rev. 1997;17(5):357–70.

Lundvall B-Å. Technical unemployment in a small open economy. In: Lund R, Pedersen PJ, Schmidt-Sorensen JB, editors. Studies in unemployment. Copenhagen: New Science Monographs; 1987.

Lundvall B-A. Explaining interfirm cooperation and innovation: limits of the transaction- cost approach. In: Grabher G, editor. The embedded firm: on the socioeconomics of industrial networks. London: Routledge; 1993. p. 52–64.

Machlup F. Methodology of economics and other social sciences. New York: Academic Press; 1978.

Mangham I. Interactions and interventions in organizations. New York: John Wiley & Sons; 1978.

Mansfield R. The international study of organizational structure. In: Mansfield R, Poole M, editors. International perspectives on management and organization. Hampshire: Gower; 1981.

March JG, Simon HA. Cognitive limits on rationality. In: March JG, Simon HA, editors. Managerial insights. Butor RH & Moses MH; 1966.

Masterman, M. (1970) The Nature of a Paradigm. In Lakatos, I. & Musgrave, A. (Eds.) *Criticism and the Growth of Knowledge*. London, Cambridge University Press.

Marx K. Bidrag til kritik af den politiske økonomi – Indledning fra Grundrids. København: Bibliotek Rhodos; 1974.

McGraw Hill, PowerWeb. Entrepreneurship. http://register.dushkin.com (2002).

McGuire JB. A dialectical analysis of interorganizational networks. J Manag. 1988;14(1):109–24.

McNeill D, Freiberger P. Fuzzy Logic: the discovery of a revolutionary computer technology- DOUBLEHYPHEN and how it is changing our world. New York: Simon & Schuster; 1993.

Mead GH. Mind, self, & society – from the standpoint of a social behaviorist. Chicago: University of Chicago Press; 1962 (1934).

Merleau-Ponty M. The phenomenology of perception. London: Routledge & Kegan Paul; 1994 (1962).

Meyerson D, Martin J. Cultural change: an integration of three different views. J Manag Stud. 1987;24(6):623–47.

Montgomery CA, Hariharan S. Diversified expansion by large established firms. J Econ Behav Organ. 1991;15:71–89.

Monthoux PG d. Handling och existens – anarkoexistensiell analys av projekt, företag och organisation. Uddevalla: Liber förlaget; 1978.

Morgan G. Paradigms, metaphors, and puzzle solving in organization theory. Adm Sci Q. 1980;25:605–22.

Morgan G, editor. Beyond method – strategies for Social Research. Beverly Hills: SAGE; 1983.

Morgan G. Images of organization. Beverly Hills: SAGE; 1986.

Morgan G, Ramirez R. Action learning: a holographic metaphor for guiding social change. Hum Relat. 1984;37(1):1–27.

Morgan G, Smircich L. The case for qualitative research. Acad Manag Rev. 1980;5(4):491–500.

Morrow PC. Explorations in macro communication behaviour: the effects of organizational feedback on organizational effectiveness. J Manag Stud. 1982;19(4):437–46.

# References

367

Moustakas C. Phenomenological research methods. Thousand Oaks: SAGE; 1994.

Mowery DC, editor. International collaborative ventures in U.S. manufacturing. Cambridge, MA: Ballinger Publishers; 1988.

Mowery DC. Collaborative ventures between US and foreign manufacturers. Res Policy. 1989;18:19–32.

Mowery DC. Public policy influences on the formation of international joint ventures. Int Trade J. 1991;VI(1):29–62.

Mowery DC, Oxley JE. Inward technology transfer and competitiveness: the role of national innovation systems. Camb J Econ. 1995;19(1):67–93.

Mowery DC, Oxley JE, Silverman BS. Technological overlap and interfirm cooperation: implications for the resource-based view of the firm. Res Policy. 1997;27:507–23.

Næss A. Filosofiens Historie, Bind 1. Viborg: Hans Reitzels forlag; 1991a.

Næss A. Filosofiens Historie, Bind 2. Viborg: Hans Reitzels forlag; 1991b.

Nardi B. A small matter of programming: perspectives on end user computing. Cambridge, MA: MIT Press; 1993.

Nardi B, editor. Context and consciousness: activity theory and human-computer interaction. Cambridge, MA: MIT Press; 1996a.

Nardi B. Studying context: a comparison of activity theory, situated action models and distributed cognition. In: Context and consciousness: activity theory and human computer interaction. Cambridge, MA: MIT Press; 1996b.

National Academy of Science. Recommendations for federal science and technological funding. Washington, DC; 29 Nov 1995.

Negandhi AR. International management. Boston: Alley & Bacon; 1987.

Neimark M, Tinker T. Identity and non-identity thinking: a dialectical critique of the transaction cost theory of the modern corporation. J Manag. 1987;13(4):661–73.

Nelson RR. Institutional supporting technical change in the United States. In: Dosi G, Freeman C, Nelson R, Silverberg G, Soete L, editors. Technological change and economic theory. London: Pinters Publ.; 1989.

Nelson RR. Capitalism as an engine of progress. Res Policy. 1990. Elsevier Science Publishers B.V., North Holland.

Nelson RR. Why do firms differ, and does it matter? In: Rumelt RP, Schendel DE, Teece DJ, editors. Fundamental issues in strategy. Boston: Harvard Business School Press; 1994.

Nelson RR, Winter SG. An evolutionary theory of economic change. Cambridge, MA: Harvard University Press; 1982.

Nerheim H, Rossvær V. Filosofiens historie – fra Sokrates til Wittgenstein. Viborg: Politikens Forlag; 1990.

Nielsen TSMT. Contrary market research: the Japanese way of conducting market research. Aalborg: University of Aalborg, International Business Economics. No. #2, Study Materials series; 1993.

Nietzsche F. Den glada vetenskapen. Göteborg: Bokförlaget Korpen; 1987.

Norman R. Skapande företagsledning. Lund: Aldus; 1976.

Nørreklit L. Positivisme og samfundsvidenskab. Aalborg: Aalborg University; 1984.

Nørreklit H. Konstruktion af aktørstilpassede økonomistyringssystemer. Ledelse & Erhvervsøkonomi. 1992;56(3):149–55.

O'Neill J. Can phenomenology be critical? In: Luckmann T, editor. Phenomenology and sociology. London: Penguin; 1978.

Ogden J. High hopes for hydrogen. Fuel cells and more, Special issue, Sci Am. 2006;295(3):94–101. http://www.sciam.com

Osborn RN, Hunt JG. Environment and organizational effectiveness. Adm Sci Q. 1974;19(2):231–46.

Østerberg D. Sociologins Nyckelbegrepp – och deres ursprung. Göteborg: Korpen; 1991.

Pareto V. Combinations and group persistence. In: Parsons T, et al., editors. Theories of society – foundation of modern sociological theory. New York: The Free Press; 1965a.

Pareto V. On logical and non-logical action. In: Parsons T, et al., editors. Theories of society – foundation of modern sociological theory. New York: The Free Press; 1965b.

368 References

Parkin F. Max Weber. Sussex: Ellis Horwood Limited; 1982.

Parsons T. The social system. Glencoe: The Free Press; 1951.

Parsons T. Economy and society. Glencoe: The Free Press; 1956.

Parsons T. The structure of social action. New York: The Free Press; 1968.

Parsons T, et al., editors. Theories of society – foundation of modern sociological theory. New York: The Free Press; 1965.

Pavitt K, Robson M, Townsend J. Technological accumulation, diversification and organization of U.K. companies 1945–1983. Manag Sci. 1989;35(1):81–99.

Perez C. The social and political challenge of the present paradigm shift. Workshop on evolutionary economics and spatial income inequality, Oslo; 15–16 May 1997, p. 1–16.

Perkins LJ. What is physics and why is it a "science"? Lecture presented at graduate physics seminar, University of California, Berkeley; 1996.

Pfeffer J. Organizations and organization theory. Stanford: Stanford University; 1982.

Pfeffer J, Salancik GR. The external control of organizations – resource dependence perspective. New York: Harper & Row; 1978.

Pisano GP. The R&D boundaries of the firm: an empirical analysis. Adm Sci Q. 1990;35(1):153–76.

Plaschke H. National economic cultures and economic integration, Reprinted. Aalborg: Aalborg University; 1991.

Polkinghorne D. Methodology for the human sciences – system of inquiry. Albany: State University of New York Press; 1983.

Popova J, Sørensen OJ. Marketing as social construction: alternative views on the interface between the enterprise and the environment. Unpublished, Aalborg: Aalborg University. Department of Development & Planning, International Business/Economics; 1996.

Porter ME. Competitive strategy: techniques for analyzing industries and competitors. New York: Free Press; 1980.

Porter ME. Competitive advantage. New York: Free Press; 1990.

Porter ME, van der Linde C. Green and competitive. Harv Bus Rev. 1995;September–October:120–34.

Radcliffe-Brown A. Structure and function in primitive society. London: Cohen & West; 1968 (1952).

Rand Report, Bernstein M. California energy market report, Winter 2000–2001. Unpublished paper presented to staff in California State Legislature, Sacramento. Santa Monica: Rand Corporation; January 2001.

Rask M, Skræm K. International Markedsføring på World Wide Web. Unpublished final thesis at master of Science in Economics and Business Administration, Aalborg; 1997.

Reed M. Redirections in organizational analysis. London: Tavistock; 1985.

Reed M, Hughes M, editors. Rethinking organization – new directions in organization theory and analysis. London: SAGE; 1992.

Reekie WD. Industrial economics: a critical introduction to corporate enterprise in Europe and America. Hants: Edward Elgar Press; 1989.

Rees M. The G8 on energy: too little. Science. 2006;313:591. http://www.sciencemag.org

Reich R. The work of nations. Preparing ourselves for 21st century capitalism. New York: Vintage Books; 1991.

Reinert E. Symptoms and causes of poverty: underdevelopment in a Schumpeterian system. Forum Dev Stud. 1994;21(1–2):73–109.

Reinert E. Competitiveness and its predecessors – a 500 year cross-national perspective. Struct Chang Econ Dyn. 1995;6:23–42.

Reinert E. Economics: 'the dismal science' or 'the never-ending frontier of knowledge'?: On technology, energy, and economic welfare. Nor Oil Rev. 1996;(7):18–31.

Reinert E. The role of the state in economic growth. Working paper #1997.5, University of Oslo, Centre for Development and the Environment; 1997, p. 1–58.

Reinert E. Raw materials in the history of economic policy. In: Cook G, editor. The economics and politics of international trade. London/New York: Routledge; 1998. p. 275–300.

Reinert E, Daastol AM. Exploring the genesis of economic innovations: the religious gestalt-switch and the duty to invent as preconditions for economic growth. Eur J Law Econ. 1997;4(3/4):1–58.

# References 369

Report: Industrial revival through technology. Organization for Economic Co-operation and Development, Paris; 1988.

Rifkin J. The European dream: how Europe's vision of the future is quietly eclipsing the American dream. New York: Penguin; 2005.

Ritzau T. Between two worlds: a survey among university scientists on industrial exploitation of research. Taastrup: DTI. Danish Innovation Centre; 1992.

Ritzer G. Fundamentale perspektiver i sociologien. Odense: Fremad; 1977.

Robinson D. The naked entrepreneur. London: Cogan Page; 1990.

Romm J. Lean and clean management: how to boost profits and productivity by reducing pollution. New York: Kodansha America; 1994.

Rose AM. A systematic summery of symbolic interaction theory. In: Rose A, editor. Human behavior and social processes – an interactionist approach. London: Routledge & Kegan Paul; 1962.

Rosen CM. Differing perceptions of the value of pollution abatement across time and place: balancing doctrine in pollution nuisance law, 1840–1906. Law Hist Rev. 1993;11(2):303–81.

Rosen CM. Noisome, noxious, and offensive vapors, fumes and stenches in American towns and cities: 1840–1865. Hist Geogr. 1997;25:49–82.

Rosen CM, Bercovitz J, Beckman S. Implementing environment programs across dispersed supply chains: a transaction costs analysis of exchange hazards in green supplier relations in the computer industry. 1998.

Rosenberg S. Competitive networks. New York: Free Press; 1991.

Sacramento Bee. Gorging profits. Sacramento: California Energy Commission; 2001.

Sarason S. Culture of the school and the problem of change. New York: Allyn; 1971.

Saul JR. The collapse of globalism: and the reinvention of the world. Toronto: Viking; 2005.

Saxenian A. Regional advantage: culture and competition in Silicon Valley and route 128. Cambridge, MA: Harvard University Press; 1994.

Schein EH. Organisations-kultur og ledelse – et dynamisk perspektiv. København: Valmuen; 1989.

Scherer F. International high-technology competition. Cambridge, MA: Harvard University Press; 1992.

Schmid H, editor. Aktionsforskning. Sociologisk Forskning, nr 2–3, årgang 19, Kristianstad, 1982.

Schumpeter J. The theory of economic development. Cambridge, MA: Harvard University Press; 1934.

Schumpeter J. Capitalism, socialism and democracy. New York: Harper & Brothers; 1942.

Schutz A. Reflections on the problem of relevance. New Haven/London: Yale University Press; 1970.

Schutz A. The phenomenology of the social world. London: Heinemann Educational Books; 1972.

Schutz A. Some leading concepts of phenomenology. In: Collected papers I: The problem of social reality. Haag: Matinus Nijhoff; 1973a.

Schutz A. Hverdagslivets sociologi. København: Hans Reitzel; 1973b.

Schutz A. Concepts and theory formation in the social sciences. In: Emmet D, Macintyre A, editors. Sociological theory and philosophical analysis. New York: The Macmillan Company; 1978a.

Schutz A. Phenomenology and the social sciences. In: Luckmann T, editor. Phenomenology and sociology. London: Penguin; 1978b.

Schutz A. The theory of social action. Bloomington/London: Indiana University Press; 1978c.

Schutz A. The problem of rationality in the social world. In: Emmet D, Macintyre A, editors. Sociological theory and philosophical analysis. New York: The Macmillan Company; 1978d.

Schutz A. Life forms and meaning structure. London: Routledge & Kegan Paul; 1982.

Schutz A. Collected papers I: the problem of social reality. Dordrecht: Kluwer Academic Publishers; 1990a.

Schutz A. Collected papers II: studies in social theory. Dordrecht: Kluwer Academic Publishers; 1990b.

Schutz A. Collected papers III: studies in phenomenological philosophy. Dordrecht: Kluwer Academic Publishers; 1990c.

Schutz A. Collected papers IV. Dordrecht: Kluwer Academic Publishers; 1990d.

370 References

Schutz A, Luckmann T. The structure of the life world. London: Heinemann; 1974.

Scott WR. Developments in organization theory 1960–1980. Trends in theoretical models. In: Short Jr JF, editor. The state of sociology – problems and prospects. London; 1981.

Scott WR. Organizations: rational, natural, and open systems. Englewood Cliffs: Prentice-Hall; 1987.

Shaynneran M. The car that could: the inside story of the GM impact. New York: Simon Schuster; 1996.

Shekerian D. Uncommon genius: how great ideas are born. Harmondsworth: Penguin Books; 1991.

Shrivastava P, Schneider S. Organizational frames of reference. Hum Relat. 1984;37(10):795–809.

Silverman D. The theory of organisations. London: Heinemann; 1983.

Silverman D. Six rules of qualitative research: a post-romantic argument. Symb Interact. 1989a;12(2):215–30.

Silverman D. Telling convincing stories: a plea for cautious positivism in case-studies. In: Glassner B, Moreno JD, editors. The qualitative – quantitative distinction in the social sciences. Dordrecht: Kluwer Academic Publishers; 1989b.

Silverman D. Interpreting qualitative data – methods for analysing talk, text and interaction. London: SAGE; 1993.

Silverman BS. Technical assets and the logic of corporate diversification. Haas School of Business, Unpublished doctoral dissertation, University of California, Berkeley; 1996.

Simmel G. The philosophy of money. 2nd ed. London: Routledge; 1990.

Simmel G. Hur är samhället möjligt? – och andra essäer. Göteborg: Korpen; 1995.

Simmel G, Levine DN, editors. On individuality and social forms. Chicago: The University of Chicago Press; 1971.

Sims D, Fineman S, Gabriel Y. Organizing "organisations". London: SAGE; 1993.

Singelmann P. Exchange as symbolic interaction: convergences between two theoretical perspectives. Am Sociol Rev. 1972;37(4):414–24.

Sköldberg K. Den motsatta kulturen. Organisationssymbolik och – kultur i ett dialektiskt perspektiv. Ledelse & Erhvervsøkonomi; 1987.

Skytte H. Qualitative methods: how to develop new concepts and hypotheses about interorganizational relations. The Nordic workshop on interorganizational research, Bergen; 1991.

Smith A. The wealth of nations. New York: Modern Library; 1937.

Smith JR, Aceves S, Clark WW Jr, Perkins LJ with Gehl S, Maulbetsch J, Vemuri VR, Nakata T. Optimization for power utility applications. University of California, Lawrence Livermore National Laboratory, internal R&D project proposal (unfunded); 1997.

Snow CP. The two cultures and the scientific revolution; 1959. unpublished paper.

Socolow R, Pacala S. A plan to keep carbon in check. Strategy, Special issue, Sci Am. 2006;295(3):50–59. http://www.sciam.com

Soderberg A-M. Do national cultures always make a difference? Theoretical considerations and empirical findings related to case studies of foreign acquisitions of Danish companies. Paper presented at intercultural communication and national identity conference, Aalborg University, Aalborg; 20–23 Nov 1996.

Sørensen TB. Fænomenologisk Mikrosociologi – interview- og samtaleanalyse 1. Randers: Forlaget Gestus; 1988a.

Sørensen TB. Taleture og hørerkommunikation – Interview- og samtaleanalyse 2. Randers: Forlaget Gestus; 1988b.

Sørensen TB. Talehandlinger – interview- og samtaleanalyse 3. Randers: Forlaget Gestus; 1989.

Sørensen OJ, Nedergaard A. Management decision making in an international context: the case for intuition and action learning. Aalborg: University of Aalborg, International Business Economics. No. #2 Reprint series; 1993.

Sorgen M, et al. State, school, and family. New York: Mathew Bender; 1974.

Spencer H. The factors of social phenomena. In: Parsons T, et al., editors. Theories of society – foundation of modern sociological theory. New York: The Free Press; 1965.

Staff, Governor Gray Davis. Talking points: Enron, Sacramento; 21 Mar 2002.

# References

State of California, Press Release. Governor Davis calls for federal investigation of Enron's role on California energy crisis; 31 Jan 2002.

Stix G. A climate repair manual. Introduction, Special issue, Sci Am. 2006;295(3):46–49. http://www.sciam.com

Stubbs M. Discourse analysis – the sociolingustic analysis of natural language. Oxford: Basil Blackwell Ltd; 1989.

Suchman L. Plans and situated actions: the problem of human/machine communication. London: Cambridge University Press; 1987.

Suchman L. Working relations of technology production and use. In: Computer supported cooperative work, vol. 2. Dordrecht: Kluwer Academic Publ; 1994.

Sun X, Li J, Wang Y, Clark WW. China's Sovereign Wealth Fund Investments in overseas energy: the energy security perspective. Energy Policy. 2013;

Susman GI, Evered RD. An assessment of the scientific merits of action research. Adm Sci Q. 1978;23:582–603.

Teece DJ. Towards an economic theory of the multiproduct firm. J Econ Behav Organ. 1982;3:39–63.

Teece DJ. Technological change and the nature of the firm. In: Dosi G, Freeman C, Nelson R, Silverberg G, Soete L, editors. Technical change and economic theory. London: Francs Pinter; 1988.

Teece DJ. Interfirm collaboration. Haas School of Business, working paper. Berkeley: University of California; 1989.

Teece DJ. Graduate seminar lectures on economic theory. Berkeley: Haas School of Business, University of California; 1996.

Teece DJ, Bercovitz JEL, De Figueiredo JM. Firm capabilities and managerial decision-making: a theory of innovation biases. Unpublished, Berkeley: Haas School of Business, University of California; 1994a.

Teece DJ, Pisano G, Shuen A. Dynamic capabilities and strategic management. Center for Research in Management, working paper. Berkeley: University of California; 1994b.

Teece DJ, Rumelt RP, Dosi G, Winter SF. Understanding corporate coherence: theory and evidence. J Econ Behav Organ. 1996;23(1):1–30.

The Economist: Examining the mystery; 4 Jan 1992, p. 17.

The Economist: The Economist review: Who dare call it the dismal science?; 19 Jul 1997a, p. 6.

The Economist: The puzzling failure of economics; 23 Aug 1997b, p. 11.

The Economist: The visible hand; 20 Sept 1997c, p. 17.

The Economist: Europe, "Remodelling Scandinavia"; 23 Aug 1997d, p. 37–39.

The Economist: Finance and economics: "Assembling the new economy"; 13 Sept 1997e, p. 71–73.

The Economist: The third age of fuel; 25 Oct 1997f, p. 16.

The Economist: Science and technology: "At last, the fuel cell"; 25 Oct 1997g, p. 89–92.

The Economist: The amazing disintegrating firm; 6 Dec 2001.

The Economist: RE: Enron; February–March, 2002a.

The Economist: Social science comes of age; 4 Mar 2002b, p. 42–43.

The Economist: The real scandal; 19 Jan 2002c.

Thompson JD. Hur organisationer fungerer (Organizations in actions, 1967). Stockholm: Prisma; 1971.

Thompson C, Delin B. How is public venture capital different from private? A comparative geographical study of two recipient firm samples. Final report to US Dept. of Commerce, EDA. 1993.

Thurow LC. The future of capitalism: how today's economic forces shape tomorrow's world. New York: William Morrow & Comp; 1996.

Toffler A, Toffler H. Future shock. New York: Bantam Books; 1970.

Toffler A, Toffler H. The third wave. New York: Bantam Books; 1980.

Tonboe J. Rummets sociologi – kritik af teoretiseringen af den materielle omverdens betydning i den sociologiske og den kulturgeografiske tradition. Copenhagen: Akademisk Forlag; 1993.

372 References

Tørnebohm H. Paradigm i vetenskapernas värld och i vetenskapsteorin. Göteborgs Universitet, Avdelning för vetenskapsteori, nr 59; 1974.

Tørnebohm H. Paradigms in Fields of Research. Göteborgs Universitet, Avdelning för vetenskapsteori (rapport. nr. 93); 1977.

Tyler S, editor. Cognitive anthropology. New York: Holt, Rinehart & Winston; 1969.

Van de Ven AH, Joyce WF. Overview of perspectives on organization design and behavior. In: Van de Ven AH, Joyce WF, editors. Perspectives on organization design and behavior. New York: John Wiley & Sons; 1981.

Vesper KH. New venture strategies. Rev. ed. Englewood Cliffs: Prentice Hall; 1990.

Vogel D. Trading up: consumer and environmental regulation in a global economy. Cambridge, MA: Harvard University Press; 1995.

Watson T, Healey JR. Big 3: expect cars emitting less pollution by 2001. USA Today; 2 Feb 1998.

Weber M. The methodology of the social sciences. New York: The Free Press; 1948.

Weber M. Social and economic organization. New York: The Free Press; 1964.

Weber M. Economy and society – an outline of interpretive sociology. New York: Bedminster Press; 1968.

Weber M. The interpretation of social reality. London: Thomas Nelson & Sons Ltd; 1972.

Weber M. Vetenskap och Politik. Göteborg: Korpen; 1977 & 1991.

Weick KE. Educational organizations as loosely coupled systems. Adm Sci Q. 1976;21:1–19.

Weick KE. Enactment processes in organizations. In: Staw B, Salancik GR, editors. New directions in organizational behavior. Chicago: St. Clair Press; 1977.

Weick KE. The social psychology of organizing. Reading: Addison-Wesley Inc.; 1979a (1969).

Weick KE. Cognitive processes in organizations. In: Research in organizational behavior, vol. 1. Greenwich: JAI Press; 1979b.

Weick KE. That's moving – theories that matter. J Manag Inq. 1999;8:134–42.

White JD. Phenomenology and organizational development. Adm Sci Q. 1990;28:331–496.

Whitley R. The fragment state of management studies: reason and consequences. J Manag Stud. 1984;21(3).

Williamson OE. Markets and hierarchies: analysis and anti-trust implications. New York: The Free Press; 1975.

Williamson OE. Transaction cost economics and organization theory. In: Smelser NJ, Swedberg R, editors. The handbook of economic sociology. Princeton: Princeton University Press; 1994. p. 77–107.

Williamson OE. Economic organization: the case of candor. Acad Manag Rev. 1996;21:48–57.

Wind HC. Filosofisk hermeneutik. København: Berlingske leksikon bibliotek; 1976.

Wind HC. Historie og forståelse – filosofisk hermeneutik. Aarhus: Aarhus Universitetsforlag; 1987.

Winter SG. The research program of the behavioral theory of the firm: orthodox critique and evolutionary perspective. In: Gilad B, editor. Handbook of behavioral economics, vol. 1, Micro. Greenwich: JAI Press; 1986.

Wittgenstein L. Filosofiska undersökningar. Stockholm: Thales; 1992.

Wittgenstein L. Tractatus Logico-Philosophicus. Haslev: Samlarens Bogklub; 1993.

von Wright GH. Vetenskap och förnuftet – ett försök till orientering. Stockholm: Månpocket; 1991.

von Wright GH. Myten om Fremskridtet. København: Muncksgaard-Rosinante; 1994.

Xing LI, Clark WW. Crises, Opportunities and alternatives globalization and the next economy: a theoretical and critical review, Chapter 4. In: Xing L, Winther G, editors. Globalization and transnational capitalism. Denmark: Aalborg University Press; 2009.

Yin KR. Case study research – design and methods. Newbury Park: SAGE; 1989.

Zadeh L. Fuzzy sets. Inf Control. 1965;8(3):338–53.

Zeitz G. Interorganizational dialectics. Adm Sci Q. 1980;25:72–88.

Zender TR, Hesterly WS. The disaggregation of corporations: selective intervention, high-powered incentives, and molecular units. Organ Sci. 1997;8(3):209–22.

Zobaa A. Different issues related to the operation of wind energy conversion systems. Special issue, Int J Energy Technol Policy. 2005;3(4). Interscience Press.

# Author Index

**A**

Adorno, T.W., 69, 180
Allaire, Y., 225
Allenby, B.R., 213, 252, 271, 311, 328
Althusser, L., 67
Alvesson, M., 41, 69
Andersen, H., 50, 54, 56, 58, 59, 96, 240, 247, 297, 300, 301
Andersen, I., 58, 96, 240, 247, 297, 300, 301
Andersson, S., 41
Arbnor, I., 33, 50, 53, 55, 80, 115, 219
Aristotle, 107, 234
Arndt, J., 65
Astley, W.G., 54

**B**

Bacon, F., 32
Baran, P., 67
Bärmark, J., 50
Barth, F., 24, 252, 253, 308
Bartunek, J.M., 68, 215, 221
Bate, P., 224
Bauman, Z., 106, 113, 121
Bell, C.H., 65
Bengtsson, J., 43, 88, 92, 94, 95, 114, 116, 117
Benson, J.K., 69, 209, 219, 220, 226, 234
Berger, B., 24, 180, 240, 308
Berger, P.L., 42, 102, 115, 203, 219, 238, 240
Bergson, H., 142, 182
Berkerly, G., 38–39
Bittner, E., 180
Bjerke, B., 33, 50, 53, 55, 80, 115, 219
Bjurwill, C., 79, 97
Blau, P., 64, 65, 322
Bline, D., 210, 309

Blumer, H., 3, 4, 9–11, 25, 26, 50, 132, 133, 141–182, 201, 213, 214, 216, 217, 231, 233, 235, 246, 249, 251, 253, 256, 272, 273, 285, 293, 310, 316, 318, 328, 329, 334, 337–340
Boden, D., 252
Bradley, M.F., 54
Bradshaw, T., 3, 272, 294, 307, 316
Brown, R.H., 25, 49, 68, 197, 213, 214, 221, 227, 288
Burnham, D., 38
Burrell, G., 20, 35, 45, 49, 54, 56, 58–60, 62, 63, 65, 66, 68–74, 77, 92, 95, 102, 103, 107

**C**

Capra, F., 21
Castells, M., 192
Cavusgil, S.T., 65
Cheng, J.L.C., 65
Child, J., 65
Chomsky, N., x, 3, 4, 23, 132–137, 139, 140, 195, 198, 201, 207, 229, 231, 234, 235, 249–251, 253, 256–261, 285, 315, 341
Circourel, A.V., 180, 238
Clark II, W.W. Jr., vii–x, 1–11, 19, 158, 185, 186, 188, 189, 192–195, 198, 201, 202, 233, 234, 244, 246, 249, 254, 256, 272, 278, 283, 285, 287–294, 296, 301, 303, 307–312, 315–318, 320, 322, 324, 325, 327–329, 334, 335, 342, 345–351
Clark, C., 196
Collins, J.C., 276

© Springer Nature Switzerland AG 2019
W. W. Clark II, M. Fast, *Qualitative Economics*,
https://doi.org/10.1007/978-3-030-05937-8

374 Author Index

Comte, A., 20, 33–36, 142
Cooper, J.F., 287, 303, 311, 312, 324, 326
Crossley, N., 149, 157
Cuff, E.C., 33, 35, 54, 149
Curelaru, M., 54

**D**
Daastol, A.M., 198, 202
Daft, R.L., 65
Dalum, B., 188
Das, D., 55, 70
Davis, G. (Governor), ix, 246, 297, 298, 309
Decker-Ward, J., 194
Delanty, G., 37, 56, 142
Deming, W.E., 271
Demirag, I., ix, 2, 210, 246, 288, 334, 342
Diamond, M.A., 225
Dilthey, W., 84–85, 102–105, 107, 108, 110,
    115, 157, 181, 234
Douglas, J.D., 180
Drucker, P., 16–20, 271
Dubner, 4, 335
Due, J., viii, 277, 297, 318
Dunning, J.H., 65
Durkheim, E., 20, 33–36, 64, 70, 73

**E**
Eisenstadt, S.N., 54
Evered, R.D., 22, 234, 235

**F**
Fast, M., vii–x, 1–11, 19, 25, 186, 249, 272,
    283, 285, 294, 296, 309, 328, 337,
    342
Fieser, J., 38
Fineman, S., 212, 219
Fink, A., 35
Firsirotu, M.E., 225
Firth, A., 244, 278, 319
Flato, I., 33, 103
Flor, J.R., 55
Florida, R., 19
Freeman, C., 198, 199, 308, 309
Freiberger, P., 18–20, 198, 208, 210, 296
French, W.L., 65

**G**
Gabriel, Y., 212, 219
Gadamer, H.-G., 2, 7, 42, 81, 84, 85, 88, 94,
    101, 102, 104, 107–112, 114, 115,
    179, 181, 182, 225, 238

Garfinkel, H., 42, 180, 217, 221, 224, 238
Gelven, M., 118, 119
Gibson, R., 333, 335
Giddens, A., 20, 108, 122, 125, 127, 142, 221
Giorgi, A., 211, 236
Goffman, E., 42, 224
Grabher, G., 204, 205
Graedel, T.E., 213, 252, 311, 328
Gullestrup, H., 24, 190, 224, 315
Gurwitsch, A., 91, 182, 216

**H**
Habermas, J., 54, 69, 84, 180
Hagedoorn, J., 201, 209
Håkansson, H., 188, 201, 205, 206, 322, 323,
    328
Hall, E.T., 23
Hall, P., 192
Harste, G., 69
Healey, J.R., 314
Heap, J.L., 94, 96
Hedberg, B.L.T., 68, 218
Heidegger, M., 2, 15, 42, 84, 91, 94, 95, 101,
    107, 114, 116–119, 179, 181
Heilbroner, R., 76, 198, 202, 248
Hennestad, B.W., 25, 68, 222
Herva, S., 84, 105
Heydebrand, W., 67, 69
Hinton, D., 188
Hirschman, E.C., 203
Hobbes, T., 38–39, 199
Hofstede, G., 24, 65, 190, 191, 265, 270, 315
Holbrook, M.B., 203
Holland, J.H., 250, 271, 304, 314
Hughes, M., 54
Hummel, R.P., 213, 220
Husserl, E., 2, 79, 82, 84, 87–88, 91–97, 101,
    112–114, 116, 118, 128, 142, 147,
    156, 180, 182, 222
Hvelplund, F., 304, 314

**I**
Imershein, A.W., 69, 221
Ingebrigtsen, S., 50, 54
Isherwood, W., 193, 289, 305, 320

**J**
Jehenson, R., 25, 214, 216, 220
Jensen, J.D., 96, 194, 202, 309
Jensen, T.K., 101, 102, 108
Johanson, J., 201, 205
Johansson, J., 65

# Author Index

Johnson, R., 205
Jones, C., 187, 188, 190, 322
Joyce, W.F., 54

**K**
Kahn, R L., 40
Kallinikos, J., 68, 69
Kant, I., 2, 21, 22, 44, 45, 47, 55, 80–85, 87, 92, 142, 148, 175, 179, 181, 222
Katz, D., 40
Kjørup, S., 29, 34
Knudsen, C., 54
Kuada, J., 24
Kuhn, T., 6, 8, 47–49, 52, 254
Kuttner, R., 299
Kvale, S., 247

**L**
Lakoff, G., 250
Levitt, S.D., 4, 300, 335
Lincoln, Y.S., 314
Lübcke, P., 36, 45, 83, 93, 94, 107, 108, 118, 181
Luckmann, T., 42, 203, 238
Lund, H., 288, 292, 301, 304, 307, 314, 315, 329
Lundvall, B.-A., 194, 199, 204

**M**
Mangham, I., 218
Martin, J., 224
Marx. K., 17, 49, 67, 69, 70, 74, 116, 179, 234
Mattsson, L.-G., 65
McGuire, J.B., 69
McNeill, D., 18–20, 198, 208, 210, 296
Mead, G.H., 3, 25, 26, 132, 133, 141–182, 214, 219, 253, 256, 273, 293, 316, 318, 334, 338, 339
Merleau-Ponty, M., 42, 43, 80, 91–94, 96, 97, 112, 114–117, 181, 182
Meyerson, D., 224
Morgan, G., 20, 35, 45, 49, 52–54, 56, 58, 60, 62, 63, 65, 66, 68–74, 77, 92, 95, 102, 103, 107, 217, 224, 232
Moustakas, C., 91, 93, 96, 232, 236
Mowery, D.C., 192, 209

**N**
Næss, A., 37
Nardi, B., 244, 246, 310
Nedergaard, A., 188, 322, 340

Nelson, R.R., 76, 248, 252, 292, 303
Nerheim, H., 37, 82
Neimark, M., 69
Nietzsche, F., 31

**O**
O'Neill, J., 107
Oxley, J.E., 209, 246, 295

**P**
Paolucci, E., 202, 278, 317, 320
Parkin, F., 86, 105, 106, 178
Parsons, T., 54, 141
Payne, G.C.F., 33, 35, 54, 149
Perez, C., 198, 199
Pettersson, M., 50, 54
Pfeffer, J., 54, 65, 322
Polkinghorne, D., 20, 34, 45, 47, 61, 85, 97, 103–105, 234
Popova, J., 204, 205
Porras, J., 276
Porter, M.E., 188, 200, 201, 204, 209, 271, 304, 307, 314

**R**
Radcliffe-Brown, A.R., 40
Ramirez, R., 217
Reich, R., 16–20, 252
Reinert, E., 5, 6, 198–202, 208, 228, 295, 296
Rifkin, J., 189, 283, 333
Ritzer, G., 47–49, 64, 65, 67, 69–71, 74, 75, 77, 80, 92, 120, 124, 142
Romm, J., 271
Rose, A.M., 160, 180, 217
Roth, P.A., 94, 96

**S**
Salancik, G.R., 65
Saul, J.R., 335
Saxenian, A., 188, 190, 308
Schakenraad, J., 201, 209
Schumpeter, J., 76, 198–201, 248, 251, 291, 308
Schutz, A., 2, 22, 23, 25, 42, 84, 88–91, 94, 97–101, 112–114, 119–132, 148, 149, 151, 176, 177, 179, 181, 182, 214, 216, 221, 224, 237, 238, 293, 337
Scott, W.R., 54, 65
Shaynneran, M., 314, 320
Silverman, B., 239

Silverman, B.S., 239
Silverman, D., 25, 54, 68, 115, 220, 222, 238, 239
Simmel, G., 142
Simon, H.A., 40
Sims, D., 212, 219
Singelmann, P., 144, 145, 159, 217, 219
Sköldberg, K., 41
Smircich, L., 20, 232
Smith, A., 3, 5, 17, 19, 187, 197, 199, 204, 207, 287, 292, 295
Smith, D.F., 19
Smith, J.R., 287
Snehota, I., 188, 201, 205, 322, 323
Snow, C.P., 6, 198
Soderberg, A.-M., 191, 266
Sørensen, O.J., 201, 204, 205, 256, 316, 322, 323
Spencer, H., 39
Strydom, P., 56, 142
Suchman, L., 216, 246, 252, 310
Susman, G.I., 22, 234, 235
Sweezy, P.M., 67

**T**
Tao, W., 202, 309
Teece, D.J., 194, 210, 211, 251, 252, 303
Thurow, L.C., 16, 18, 20, 251
Toffler, A., 333, 335
Toffler, H., 333, 335
Tonboe, J., 83, 142

**V**
van de Ven, A.H., 54
van der Linde, C., 188, 271, 304, 314
Vesper, K.H., 308
von Bertalanffy, L., 40
von Wright, G.H., 31, 32

**Y**
Yago, G., 288

**W**
Watson, T., 314
Weber, M., 67, 70, 84–87, 97, 105–108, 123–124, 126, 132, 142, 157, 177–179, 181, 182, 213, 224, 238, 247
Weick, K.E., 15, 68, 212, 215, 216, 222
White, J.D., 80, 96, 213
Williamson, O.E., 65, 204
Wind, H.C., 80, 81, 84, 85, 101, 103, 107, 108, 110, 116, 118, 181
Winter, S.G., 65
Wittgenstein, L., 31

**Z**
Zadeh, L., 20, 208, 210
Zeitz, G., 69

# Subject Index

**A**

Action(s), the
    research, 22, 23, 42, 60, 76, 230, 232, 233,
        240, 243, 309–311, 339, 340

Act, the
    of thinking, 90

Adjustment, 54, 145, 146, 150, 151, 153–155

*Aktuelles Verstehen*, 106

*Alter egos*, 119

Anomalies, 8, 48, 72, 167

Anti-positivism, 61

Atomistic, 32

**B**

Because motives, 126, 130

Becoming, 4, 93, 186, 202, 245, 284, 294,
    308, 323, 333

Behaviorism, 3, 21, 65, 73, 141–143, 252,
    258, 334

Being, 1, 17, 30, 79, 141, 187, 197, 232, 249,
    292, 334

Body, 25, 32, 36, 37, 43, 81, 94, 98, 99, 113,
    116, 117, 119, 136, 139, 148, 173,
    180, 216, 235, 255, 302, 334, 336

Brackets, puts in, 96, 98

**C**

Case studies, 8, 76, 185, 194, 207, 228, 230,
    243, 248, 249, 253, 268, 270, 278,
    281, 293, 303, 304, 311, 335, 336,
    339

Civic markets, 307

Classical positivism, 55

Clean technologies, 189, 190

Cluster theory, 308

Cognition, 29, 30, 35, 36, 39, 45–48, 52, 55,
    58, 60, 71, 72, 80–84, 91, 101, 102,
    109, 110, 112, 118, 130, 136, 176,
    179, 212, 240

Collective actions, 26, 171, 173, 212, 227,
    328, 329, 338

Collectivities, 171, 172, 233, 319–322

Common
    constructions, 22, 89
    meanings, 120, 151, 310
    sense
        knowledge, 67, 90, 113
        structures, 99, 130, 131
        thinking, 89, 98, 131, 176, 237
        world, 89, 113, 119, 240

Communication, 9, 23, 100, 115, 117, 121,
    129, 136, 140, 143, 145, 146, 152,
    153, 155, 157, 160, 165, 169, 204,
    214, 217, 224, 241, 244, 253, 255,
    258, 277–279, 281, 319, 324, 326

Competence, 69, 135, 211, 231, 250, 253, 260,
    341

Complex of meaning, 126

Consciousness, 7, 25, 36, 79, 142, 203, 237,
    258, 287, 337

Constructions, 3, 22, 25, 32, 61, 71, 73, 75, 79,
    80, 89, 111, 117, 132, 144, 175,
    178, 179, 195, 203, 204, 211, 212,
    229, 233, 237, 247, 256, 258,
    265–266, 272–279, 298, 304, 306,
    313–315, 329, 334, 343, 351

© Springer Nature Switzerland AG 2019
W. W. Clark II, M. Fast, *Qualitative Economics*,
https://doi.org/10.1007/978-3-030-05937-8

## Subject Index

**Context**
  interaction, of, 4, 25, 167
  meaning, of, 25, 100, 121, 125, 126, 129, 155, 162, 211, 214, 337
  traditions, of, 102
Conventional paradigm, 8, 18, 20, 251, 335
Critical theory, 3, 21, 55, 68, 69, 72, 180
**Cultural**
  definitions, 19
  sciences, 45, 79, 87, 177
  world, 23, 89, 119, 120
**Culture(s)**
  inherent, 190

### D

Das Ding an Sich, 55, 82, 92
Das Ding für Uns, 55, 82, 87, 92
Dasein, 42, 114, 116–119
**Deep**
  structural, 207
  structure(s)
    meanings, 137, 138, 261, 262, 270
    rules, 274, 276–282, 324
Definitions, 1, 18, 30, 90, 145, 186, 201, 230, 251, 293, 333
Dialectical, 108, 115, 159, 209, 212, 219, 234, 239
Dialogue, 45, 75, 76, 108, 110, 117, 136, 140, 149, 152, 154, 214, 229, 247, 248, 255, 264, 269, 272, 276, 281, 310, 313, 317, 321, 339, 342
Dilthey, W., 181
*Durée*, 100, 122, 131

### E

Empathy, 41, 101, 102, 105, 108
Empiricism, 8, 10, 16, 33, 36, 38–39, 55, 92, 186
Empirism, 40
Energy, 2, 186, 206, 235, 288, 333
Engagement, 41, 254, 293, 336
Enron, ix, 246, 296–301, 327, 328, 334
Entrepreneurial, 138, 139, 159, 189, 190, 192, 201, 253, 263, 264, 268, 272, 294, 308–310, 317, 318
Entrepreneurism, 201
Entrepreneurship, 24, 137–140, 198, 246, 251, 253–255, 264, 294, 307–309, 311–316
Epistemological, viii, 2, 6–8, 15, 19–21, 24, 39, 44–46, 53, 58, 69, 71, 74, 76, 79, 101, 104, 109, 113, 127, 142, 175, 176, 179, 180, 304

Epistemologies, 1, 7, 21, 29, 36, 41, 54, 55, 58, 61, 63, 64, 71, 75, 77, 91–114, 119, 175, 207, 209, 229
*Epoché*, 93, 95, 96, 98, 122
*Erklären*, 2, 46, 61, 102, 157, 334
*Erklärendes Verstehen*, 106
Essence(s), vii, 2, 17, 26, 29, 30, 51, 55, 58, 61, 65, 71, 88, 93–98, 109, 112, 123, 128, 141, 144, 146, 147, 151, 156, 163, 164, 181, 217, 221, 232, 236, 249, 252, 339
Essentia, 95, 97, 118
Ethnography, 8, 309
Ethnomethodology, 3, 21, 180, 250
Everyday life, vii, 1, 21, 29, 84, 143, 185, 202, 230, 250, 296, 335
**Exchange**
  act, 187, 293
  process, 187, 204
Exchanging, 202, 309
Existence, 3, 6, 35–38, 44, 48, 49, 60, 64, 68, 87, 88, 90, 94–98, 105, 109, 110, 112–118, 128, 133, 144, 146, 151, 152, 154, 155, 173, 179, 181, 213, 222, 323
Existensia, 118
Existentia, 95, 97
Existentialism, 21, 203, 235
Expectations, 73, 82, 85, 107, 109, 124, 127, 149, 152, 165, 208, 214, 220, 221, 224, 239
Experience(s), the, vii, 22, 31, 38, 44, 73, 81, 82, 88, 90–92, 95, 96, 102, 103, 105, 113, 115, 116, 119, 121, 130, 143, 148, 152, 157, 182, 206, 218, 226
Experiential space, 216–220, 222–223, 225, 226, 269–270, 337, 338
Explain, 1–3, 8, 9, 11, 20, 24, 32, 37, 55, 56, 60, 61, 72, 77, 82, 102, 104, 126, 132, 136, 140, 157, 177, 195, 199, 207, 231, 232, 237, 251, 252, 254, 256, 258, 260, 261, 272, 275, 292, 320, 324, 334, 335, 338, 341
Explanations, ix, 4, 8, 24, 31, 33, 34, 41, 48, 51, 53, 54, 56, 57, 61, 62, 84, 86, 106, 115, 137–139, 142, 173, 194, 195, 203, 205, 231, 232, 236, 238, 242, 254, 262, 264, 266, 281, 304, 322, 336, 338, 341

### F

Finite provinces of meaning, 121, 149
Fitting

Subject Index 379

lines of action, 160, 164, 171, 172, 213, 233, 328
lines, the, 160, 213, 328
together of lines of activity, 163, 213, 219, 328
Fore-conception of completeness, 109
Fore-understanding, 108
Function, 24, 35, 37, 45, 47, 49, 73, 86, 93, 94, 118, 120, 131, 135, 137, 151, 152, 157, 204, 208, 210, 258, 259, 261, 296, 300
Functionalism, 6, 21, 24, 32, 39, 55, 65, 70, 95, 141, 142, 252, 322
Functionalist paradigm, 24, 64–66, 70, 72–74, 114, 252, 304, 315, 323, 336
Fusions of horizon, 108, 111

**G**
Game theory, 208, 281
Generalized other, the, 26, 145, 150–158, 168, 182, 214, 231, 249, 251, 272, 293, 329, 339, 341
Generative grammar theory, 138, 264, 275
German
idealism, 45, 55, 74
Gesture(s), 26, 121, 143–146, 150–158, 165, 166, 293, 339
Grammar, 133–140, 249–251, 255–264, 273, 276, 281, 315, 318, 341
Green, 185, 186, 189, 190, 192, 273, 283, 285, 287, 289, 292, 301, 316, 321, 343, 351

**H**
Hand, an invisible, 19, 197, 271
Here, 25, 29, 30, 33, 36, 42, 52, 53, 68–70, 73, 76, 84, 91, 95, 97, 99, 100, 104, 105, 107, 112–115, 118, 119, 122, 127, 130, 132, 136, 140, 157, 161, 164, 166–168, 170, 173, 174, 179, 186, 189, 191, 194, 201, 202, 216, 230, 233, 242, 244–246, 254, 256, 261, 265, 269, 270, 272, 273, 276, 277, 282, 287, 289, 291, 299, 301, 303, 316, 318, 339, 340, 342, 351
Hermeneutic(s)
approach, 9
circle, 104, 107–108, 115, 234
reflection, 103, 107
Historical
consciousness, 7, 72, 84, 85, 111
experience, 42, 85, 114

tradition, 7, 107
understanding, 72, 74, 181
Historically effected
consciousness, 108, 110
History of effect, 108, 110
Holistic, 15, 32, 104, 234
Horizon, 101, 102, 108, 111, 112, 115, 229, 349
Humanistic sciences, 45
Human nature, 20, 58, 59, 187, 232, 270, 292

**I**
Idealism, 21, 45, 55, 74
Idealization of the reciprocity of the motives, 99, 130
Ideal type, 24, 71, 120, 177–179, 238, 240, 247
Idiographic, 61, 74, 142
Indicate, 48, 49, 52, 62, 127, 135, 146, 153, 154, 156, 162, 166, 167, 178, 179, 260, 275, 292, 298, 305, 334
Indicated, 117, 154, 156, 166, 167, 173, 177, 237, 242, 277
Indicating, 53, 154, 155, 160, 169
Indication(s), 3, 100, 116, 127, 128, 130, 153, 160, 162, 165–170, 172, 173, 194, 233, 275, 310, 334
Individual, the, 3, 34, 84, 143, 190, 199, 238, 253, 306
Innovation(s), 50, 76, 139, 190, 194, 195, 198, 209, 211, 220, 227–229, 233, 248, 251, 253, 268, 272, 285, 301, 304, 307, 309, 321, 327, 335, 336, 345, 349
In-order-to motives, 126, 130
Intentional
act, 95, 97, 100, 127
Intentionality, 18, 82, 88, 91–95, 144, 176, 203, 214, 293
Interact, 6, 20, 26, 75, 117, 122, 134, 142, 152, 159, 162, 166, 169, 191, 210, 215, 216, 223, 224, 231, 233, 239, 243, 246, 249, 251, 254, 259, 264, 273, 277, 293, 309, 311, 314, 316, 318, 337–339, 341
Interacting, 4, 144, 162–164, 166, 223, 245, 265, 272–274, 276, 309
Interaction, 1, 15, 30, 89, 142, 187, 203, 229, 249, 288, 335
Interactionism, 3, 21, 54, 141, 186, 201, 229, 249, 287
Interactive process, 139, 163, 213, 215, 264, 275, 313, 324, 328

Intercommunication, 23, 89
Interlinkage of action, 171–172
Interpret, 77, 89, 99, 100, 102, 108, 111, 113, 116, 120, 124, 127, 160, 165, 166, 168, 169, 173, 180, 214, 215, 223, 224, 226, 227, 233, 242, 247
Interpretation(s)
paradigm, 46, 49, 52, 53, 58, 67, 77, 220, 224, 225
space, 216, 222, 337
Interpretative process, 162, 173
Interpreted, 22, 25, 89, 90, 101, 103, 113, 118, 120, 121, 125, 129, 165, 247, 337
Interpreting, 49, 85, 90, 99, 101, 107, 160, 165, 172, 217, 224, 234, 240
Interpretive
paradigm, 9, 67–70, 73, 74, 77, 162, 172, 233
understanding, 107, 113, 128
Intersubjective, 21, 23, 43, 44, 67, 71, 73, 76, 82, 89, 117, 119, 120, 122, 128, 182, 211–213, 217–222, 226, 236, 328
Intersubjectively, 50, 119, 227
Intersubjectivity, 21, 44, 57, 74, 101, 112, 117, 119–120, 176, 218, 219, 223, 224, 226, 227, 233, 272–279, 329
Intuition, 81, 83, 231, 236, 340, 341
*Invisible* hand, an, 19, 32, 197, 271
I, the, 37, 85, 102, 148, 149, 152

## J
Joint
action(s), 165, 171, 172, 233

## K
Knowledge, 1, 16, 29, 79, 142, 191, 200, 229, 254, 294, 336

## L
Language(s), 16, 31, 80, 142, 200, 231, 249, 296, 335
Laws, ix, 10, 20, 31–36, 39, 45, 47, 56, 60, 61, 64, 74, 82, 86, 87, 104, 106, 109, 131, 173–175, 178, 201, 205–208, 246, 274, 288, 295, 304, 314
Leap of consciousness, 121
Learning, 20, 54, 147, 204, 232, 235, 264, 265
Lebenswelt, 2, 87–88
Lexical, 138, 262, 277, 284, 318
Lexicon, 138, 139, 262–264, 276, 277, 282, 283, 315, 318

Life, 1, 15, 29, 79, 141, 185, 229, 249, 287, 333
Lifeworld
ontology, 7
tradition, 3, 4, 8–10, 42, 46, 54, 67–69, 75, 77, 79–140, 143, 145, 175, 179, 194, 206, 211, 239, 247, 253–255, 261, 271, 273, 293
Linguistics, x, 3, 4, 8, 9, 19, 56, 75, 76, 132–140, 154, 159, 186, 194, 195, 198, 201, 203, 206–208, 228, 231, 234, 235, 243, 248–285, 295, 296, 309, 310, 315, 316, 318, 336, 337, 340–342
Lived
experiences, 85, 99, 101, 113, 119, 129, 176, 214, 227
through, 90, 113, 126
Living body, 116
Logical
empiricism, 55
positivism, 8, 39, 55

## M
Management, 15, 24, 96, 195, 200, 205, 209–211, 225, 266, 271–272, 309, 318, 333–335, 346–348
Market, 5, 16, 66, 178, 187, 204, 230, 252, 288, 336
Marxism, 21, 69
Meaning, 1, 15, 29, 79, 144, 187, 203, 229, 250, 288, 334
context, 100, 125, 127–130
defining, the, 25, 128, 270
Meaningful
action, 86, 124–127
Meristic, 32, 104
Me, the, 148, 149, 152
Methods, 3, 20, 32, 79, 144, 185, 202, 229, 249, 295, 339
Methodological
procedures, 98
Methodology, 6, 9, 24, 32, 41, 46, 49, 53, 54, 56–58, 60, 61, 77, 85, 94–98, 102, 132, 142, 157–158, 176, 177, 181, 207, 209, 224, 230–232, 234, 237, 240, 241, 244–246, 253, 293, 295, 303, 339, 341, 342
Mind, the, 21, 34, 46, 63, 71, 80, 85, 91, 92, 100, 128, 133, 134, 136, 140, 143–147, 155, 190, 198, 203, 209, 212, 249, 256, 258, 261

Subject Index

Motive(s), 25, 73, 86, 98, 99, 105, 106,
126–128, 130, 132, 141, 161, 168,
176, 213, 214, 224, 227, 237, 275,
337
Moving
picture, 220, 222–224, 274, 328
pictures of reality, 219–222, 224, 225, 329,
338
Multi-methods, 57, 240, 246, 304

**N**
Naive, 39, 88, 94
Natural
attitude, 23, 25, 42, 43, 52, 80, 88, 89, 96,
99, 101, 112, 114, 121, 122, 176,
181, 216, 337
laws, 31, 32, 35, 47, 101, 109
science(s), 30–35, 37, 42–47, 58, 61, 79,
84, 88, 92, 102, 113, 114, 132, 157,
167, 178, 198, 206, 238, 256, 258,
340
Neo-classical economics, 4–6, 199, 202, 207,
228, 252, 271, 287, 288, 293, 296,
297, 300, 307, 308
Neo-classic paradigm, 1, 5, 201
Neo-Kantianism, 55, 84, 142
Neopositivism, 55
Network(s), viii, 2, 52, 55, 64, 67, 82, 139,
188, 189, 201, 204–206, 269, 270,
274, 275, 277, 279, 280, 308, 309,
317, 322–324, 326, 328, 347
*Noema*, 92, 93, 97
Noemata, 92
Noematic, 93
*Noesis*, 92, 93, 97
Noetic, 93
Nominalist, 6, 60
Nomothetic, 61, 74
Non-symbolic, 164, 168, 293
Notions, 18, 20, 21, 23, 35, 47, 61, 62, 66,
68–70, 72, 73, 79, 86, 102, 106,
112, 116, 117, 121, 179, 181, 187,
188, 191, 195, 198, 206, 209, 210,
214, 243, 250, 251, 253, 277, 284,
293, 301, 315, 316, 324, 328, 334
Notions of objects, 18
Now
actual, 25

**O**
Object
of culture, 120

of thought, 90, 154
Objective
approach, 20, 22, 68, 232
Objectively, 74, 83, 113, 125, 128, 144, 146,
154, 155
Objectivism
paradigm, 10
Objectivist(s)
paradigm, 4–6, 9, 10, 186, 205
tradition, 8, 16, 35, 40, 181, 186, 190, 203,
295
Objectivistic, 35, 40, 43, 45, 54, 55, 74, 181,
186
Objectivity, 41, 55–58, 86, 88, 92, 94, 109,
128, 231, 341
Observation, 24, 34–36, 48, 51, 57, 61, 71, 74,
88, 99, 106, 113, 125, 158, 173,
178, 201, 206, 220, 230, 232, 235,
238, 243, 270, 309, 320, 334, 339,
340
Ongoing action, 126, 128, 160, 165, 214, 329
Ontological, viii, 2, 6–8, 15, 19–21, 34, 36, 46,
52, 58, 60, 63–69, 71, 74, 76, 79,
91, 101, 107, 121, 125, 142, 175,
179, 180, 182, 208, 211, 240, 304
Ontology, 1, 2, 20, 29, 36, 41, 44, 50, 54, 58,
63, 71, 75, 77, 80, 91–114, 175,
181, 207, 229, 232, 334
Openness, 6, 56, 95, 112, 33
Organizational
identity, 224, 226
knowledge, 218
paradigm, 219–221, 223, 225
Organizations, 1, 15, 49, 86, 156, 188, 209,
233, 251, 304, 337
Organizing, 6, 10, 22, 34, 44, 49, 51, 86, 104,
105, 149, 212, 213, 217, 219–220,
223, 225, 226, 268, 279, 280, 309,
317, 321, 328
Other, the, 15, 20, 24, 31, 36, 45, 52, 55,
57–59, 62, 65, 69, 71, 72, 81, 83,
85, 90, 99–102, 105, 109, 111, 113,
116–119, 121–123, 125, 126, 128,
130, 131, 140, 148–154, 156, 157,
163, 165, 168–170, 173, 175, 180,
191, 200, 205, 212, 217, 222, 226,
233, 241, 253, 273, 276, 278, 285,
294, 307, 312–314, 316, 323, 326,
328, 348

**P**
Paradigm(s), the, 1, 18, 46–54, 79, 185, 198,
241, 249, 287

Performance, 96, 102, 124, 133, 141, 177, 211, 250, 253, 257, 302, 306, 319, 341
Performing the phenomenological reduction, 112
Perspective of the other, 119
Phenomena, 5, 8, 10, 17, 20, 31, 35, 39, 41, 45, 47, 49, 52, 54, 55, 57, 62–64, 67, 76, 82–84, 86, 87, 93–97, 104, 108, 112, 125, 133, 143, 144, 148, 175, 178, 181, 195, 206, 211, 219, 227, 241, 247, 248, 253–257, 304, 323, 336
Phenomenological
method, 95, 97, 236
perspective, 22, 25, 137
research, 20, 232
Phenomenology, 2–4, 21, 42, 49, 54, 55, 68, 75, 79, 88–90, 94–98, 101, 107, 112, 115, 116, 132, 140, 144, 156, 175, 181, 186, 203, 229, 234, 236, 248, 250, 251, 337–338, 342
Philosophical hermeneutics, 9, 107, 112, 181
Philosophy
in science, 6, 142
of science, 2, 6, 8–10, 29–30, 79, 142, 144, 176, 185, 199–202, 240, 335
Positivism, 6, 8, 21, 33–36, 39, 41, 43, 45, 54, 55, 59, 61, 64–67, 114, 211
Positivist
science, 23
Positivistic, 33, 34, 41, 44, 45, 55, 58, 72, 74, 80, 91, 101, 175, 177, 181, 239
Praxis, 50, 179, 227, 234
Predict, vii, 1, 24, 26, 35, 55, 61, 132, 136, 195, 198, 206, 207, 211, 228, 243, 256, 260, 281, 302, 338, 341
Prediction(s), 1, 4, 10, 57, 188, 195, 203, 210, 243, 281–284, 304, 333, 334, 341, 342
Predictive rules, 194, 281
Prejudice, 96, 108–112, 216, 320
Puts in brackets, 98
Putting the world in
brackets, 95, 112

## Q

Qualitative
economics, vii, 1–11, 185–228, 287, 292–294, 334, 336, 339, 340, 342
methods, 4, 7, 10, 20, 22, 24, 46, 60, 76, 137, 205, 224, 229–234, 241, 244, 246–248, 309, 310, 339–341
perspective, 9, 230, 247, 281

principles, 237
research, 8, 132–139, 230, 231, 241, 244, 245, 254, 310, 340, 341

## R

Radical
humanist paradigm, 66, 68–70, 72–74
paradigm(s), 70, 73, 74
structuralist, 66, 70, 73, 74
Rationalism, 6, 10, 21, 33, 36–38, 43, 46, 54, 55, 64–67, 79, 109, 186, 211
Rationalist, 7, 9, 15, 209, 234
Rationalistic, 33, 36, 44, 55, 72, 74, 80, 175, 235
Rationality, 31, 32, 34, 35, 45, 68, 69, 204, 221, 234, 251
Realism, 21, 39–41, 60, 161
Reality, 1, 15, 30, 79, 141, 186, 203, 229, 251, 306, 333
Reciprocity of perspectives, 119
Reflecting, 16, 26, 41, 69, 77, 88, 236, 272, 316, 339, 351
Reflection(s), 7, 15, 46, 52, 71, 72, 80, 85, 88, 93, 95, 96, 103, 149, 150, 158, 176, 181, 214, 215, 236, 266, 270, 273, 293
Reflexive act, 150
Reflexivity, 90, 147
Relations, 8, 16, 29, 81, 142, 191, 204, 229, 259, 293, 337
Renewable energy, 186, 189, 283, 291, 333
Representation(s), 39, 71, 76, 81, 95, 113, 135, 138, 231, 248, 259, 262, 265–267, 274, 281, 316–319, 322, 325–327, 341
Retrospection, 25, 109, 214, 215, 217
Role-taking, 152, 156, 168, 169
Root images, 162
Rules, 3, 35, 89, 152, 194, 199, 231, 257, 295, 336

## S

Science(s) the, viii, x, 1–11, 21, 22, 30, 31, 34, 39, 41–46, 50, 57, 70, 74, 85, 101, 112, 132–139, 197–228, 246, 255–256, 293, 333, 334
Scientific
attitude, 35, 98, 99
experiences, 33, 35, 83, 177, 238
tradition, 41, 71
Second order
constructs, 22, 113

Subject Index

Seek understanding, 4, 101
Self, the, 92, 143, 144, 148–150, 156, 157, 160, 179, 225
  cognition, 112
  consciousness, 111, 146, 149, 153, 155
  understanding, 43, 102, 103, 125, 176
Sense-making, 219
Sign(s), 100, 128–130, 153, 275
Significant symbol, 145, 146, 150–156, 164
Situated, 2, 15, 116, 118, 269
Situation, the, 10, 25, 26, 59, 109–111, 123, 148, 156, 162, 163, 165, 169, 172, 193, 203, 209, 212–215, 217, 218, 222–227, 230, 233, 235, 238, 242, 243, 265, 266, 328, 337–339
Social
  action, 67, 85–87, 89, 90, 105, 106, 123–132, 171, 177, 178, 182, 204, 215
  act, the, 122, 142, 144, 145, 150, 151, 153–157
  construction, 3, 22, 71, 73, 195, 204, 205, 212, 215, 220, 221, 223, 227, 258, 304, 306, 313–315
  interaction, 15, 64, 130–132, 143–145, 152, 162, 164–166, 168, 206, 216
  process, 67, 68, 80, 143–148, 150–156, 162, 166, 167, 169, 204
  reality, vii, 3, 21, 23, 24, 34, 63, 66, 67, 75, 80, 85, 87, 89, 90, 98, 99, 113, 119, 122, 128, 141, 144, 176, 177, 182, 213, 214, 238, 314, 315
  science(s), vii, 2, 6–8, 10, 20, 21, 23, 26, 31, 33, 35, 36, 41–43, 45, 49, 54–70, 75, 79, 84–87, 89, 90, 98–102, 113, 123, 132, 141, 142, 158, 159, 161, 174, 175, 177, 179, 181, 182, 186, 195, 198, 234, 237, 238, 248, 249, 252, 254, 256, 288, 313, 315, 339
  world, 22, 25, 35, 57, 58, 60, 61, 66–68, 74, 88–90, 98, 99, 101, 112, 122, 123, 125, 130, 131, 145, 157, 172, 177, 178, 203, 214, 238, 310, 337
Sociality, 122
Society, the, 35, 62, 65–67, 72, 144, 146, 156–157, 214
Sociological
  phenomenological, 25
  phenomenology, 9, 25, 123, 124, 181, 236
  positivism, 55
Solipsism, 21

Space, 19, 25, 39, 48, 52, 81–83, 92, 94, 99, 116–118, 131, 143, 174, 175, 182, 189, 213, 216, 218–220, 222–226, 269–270, 276, 296, 315, 328, 337
Stock of knowledge, 120, 121, 130, 214, 239
Stream(s) of consciousness, 90, 92, 100, 101, 127
Structural
  functionalism, 6, 21, 39, 65, 252, 322
  functionalist paradigm, 24
  functional perspective, 20, 209
Structuralism, 8, 66, 159
Structure(s)
  functionalism, 32, 55, 65, 70, 141, 142
  in language, 315
Subjective
  approach, 20, 22, 232
  interpretation, 90, 113, 132, 177, 237
  meaning, 90, 105, 106, 112, 120, 123, 125, 128, 177, 178, 182, 213, 232, 237, 240
  objective, 72, 74
  purpose, 106
Subjectively, 74, 92, 106, 119, 120, 125, 144
Subjectivism
  paradigm, 8–11, 76, 77, 176, 181, 202, 241, 285, 301
Subjectivist
  paradigm, 8, 10, 187, 202, 205, 255, 281–285, 296
Subjectivistic
  approach, 43
  paradigm, 77
Subjectivity, 21, 55–58, 91, 98, 109, 115, 227, 233, 238
Surface
  rules, 282
  structure(s), x, 134–140, 255, 256, 259–264, 266, 267, 269, 270, 272–280, 282, 284, 315–319, 325–327
Symbolic
  discourse, 22, 229
  interaction, 50, 75, 144, 159, 164, 166, 168, 187, 191, 227, 231, 246, 341
  interactionism, 3, 4, 9–11, 21, 26, 27, 54, 55, 68, 76, 94, 132, 141, 143, 158–173, 180, 186, 194, 205, 234, 248, 281, 337–342
Symbols, 23, 26, 36, 120, 136, 138, 140, 144, 146, 150–153, 155, 156, 160, 163, 214, 217, 220, 225, 255, 260, 262, 264, 325, 338, 339

System
   of relevance, 98, 99
   theory, 6, 21, 32, 41, 55, 65, 70, 322

**T**

Taken for granted, 30, 43, 51, 89, 112, 119,
      121, 131, 161, 207, 213, 216, 221,
      239, 295
Temporal distance, 108, 110
The Economist, vii, 198, 206, 207, 300, 301,
      305, 313, 320
Theorizing, 4, 6, 16, 46, 47, 49, 51–54, 72,
      219, 220, 240
There, 25, 41, 76, 115, 144, 181, 194, 205,
      222, 248, 252, 338
Thinking, viii, 3, 6, 7, 22, 23, 31–34, 36, 37,
      39–41, 44, 46, 49, 54, 55, 68, 72,
      75, 79, 81, 89, 90, 92, 94, 98, 107,
      111, 131, 141–144, 146–148, 151,
      153, 160, 171, 175–177, 179–181,
      190, 203, 214, 215, 224, 227, 231,
      236, 242, 270, 271, 285, 314, 316,
      329, 333–336, 339, 341, 342
Think in the future, 126
Time, 6, 16, 30, 81, 143, 186, 231, 250, 275,
      293, 334
Transaction-costs, 187, 195, 204
Transformational
   grammar, 140, 231, 249, 251, 256, 273,
      338, 341
   rules, 137–139, 261–264, 272, 285
Transformation rules, 138, 263, 264, 278, 325
Transformations, 135, 137–139, 259, 261–263,
      276, 277, 279–281, 316, 318,
      326–327

Trust, 36, 253, 269, 270, 272, 277, 279–283,
      300, 317, 323, 324, 326, 329
Typification(s), 25, 89, 90, 120–123, 214, 216,
      220–222, 224

**U**

Understand, 1, 22, 30, 79, 141, 187, 249, 334
Understanding
   seek, 4, 101
Universal
   grammar, 134, 135, 137, 258, 260–262
   laws, 56, 60

**V**

Validity, 20–22, 42, 56, 82, 86, 88, 100, 106,
      114, 176, 178, 203, 206, 207, 237,
      241
*Verstehen*, 2, 46, 67, 85, 102–103, 105–106,
      113, 157, 182, 234, 238, 334

**W**

We
   relation, 131
   relationship, 121
World, 2, 16, 31, 79, 142, 186, 197, 233, 254,
      287, 334
Worldview, 21, 31, 37, 47, 50, 52, 86, 200, 214

**Z**

ZAFC
   technology, 266, 268, 279, 280, 283, 284,
      305, 306, 317, 320

Printed in the United States
By Bookmasters